Structuralist and Behavioral Macroeconomics

Mainstream macroeconomics is founded on the idea of perfectly rational representative agents. Yet there is a growing realization that economic theories based on such agents are inadequate guides to real-world decision-making. The behavioral evidence has had significant impacts on microeconomics, but the same cannot be said of macroeconomics. This book is part of the movement to do for macroeconomics what behavioral thinking has done for microeconomics. Using behavioral evidence and insights from Keynesian and institutionalist traditions, it presents an empirically grounded alternative to the paradigm that currently dominates macroeconomic theory. It highlights how dynamic interactions across markets can generate instability, endogenous cycles, and secular stagnation. It fully engages with macroeconomic theory, provides a multifaceted view that explains how and why it is time to rethink its foundations, and offers a path forward.

Peter Skott is Professor Emeritus at University of Massachusetts Amherst, USA, and Professor of Economics at Aalborg University, Denmark. He has published widely in mainstream and heterodox journals on growth and development, business cycles, income distribution, and financial instability. He is the author of the book *Conflict and Effective Demand in Economic Growth* (Cambridge University Press).

Structuralist and Behavioral Macroeconomics

PETER SKOTT

University of Massachusetts Amherst
Aalborg University

 CAMBRIDGE
UNIVERSITY PRESS

CAMBRIDGE
UNIVERSITY PRESS

Shaftesbury Road, Cambridge CB2 8EA, United Kingdom

One Liberty Plaza, 20th Floor, New York, NY 10006, USA

477 Williamstown Road, Port Melbourne, VIC 3207, Australia

314–321, 3rd Floor, Plot 3, Splendor Forum, Jasola District Centre, New Delhi – 110025, India

103 Penang Road, #05–06/07, Visioncrest Commercial, Singapore 238467

Cambridge University Press is part of Cambridge University Press & Assessment, a department of the University of Cambridge.

We share the University's mission to contribute to society through the pursuit of education, learning and research at the highest international levels of excellence.

www.cambridge.org
Information on this title: www.cambridge.org/9781009367325

DOI: 10.1017/9781009367349

First published 2023

A catalogue record for this publication is available from the British Library

Library of Congress Cataloging-in-Publication Data
Names: Skott, Peter, author.
Title: Structuralist and behavioral macroeconomics / Peter Skott,
University of Massachusetts, Amherst.
Description: Cambridge, United Kingdom ; New York, NY : Cambridge University Press, 2023. | Includes bibliographical references and index.
Identifiers: LCCN 2022062004 (print) | LCCN 2022062005 (ebook) | ISBN 9781009367325 (hardback) | ISBN 9781009367349 (ebook)
Subjects: LCSH: Macroeconomics.
Classification: LCC HB172.5 .S553 2023 (print) | LCC HB172.5 (ebook) | DDC 339–dc23/eng/20230113
LC record available at https://lccn.loc.gov/2022062004
LC ebook record available at https://lccn.loc.gov/2022062005

ISBN 978-1-009-36732-5 Hardback
ISBN 978-1-009-36730-1 Paperback

Contents

List of Figures   *page* ix
Preface and Acknowledgments   xi

1 Introduction: The State of Macroeconomics   1
   1.1   Aims and Themes   1
   1.2   Background   3
   1.3   Overview   8
         1.3.1   Behavior   8
         1.3.2   Structure   10
         1.3.3   Instability, Cycles, and Economic Growth   12
         1.3.4   Core Models   14
         1.3.5   Terminology and Notation   14

2 The Lucas Critique and Representative Agents   16
   2.1   Background   16
   2.2   The Lucas Critique and Contemporary Macroeconomics   17
   2.3   The Representative Agent   20
         2.3.1   The Sonnenschein–Debreu–Mantel Results   20
         2.3.2   A Pragmatic Defense?   23
   2.4   Welfare and Inequality   29
         2.4.1   The Representative-Agent Approach   29
         2.4.2   An Intrinsic Distributional Bias   30
         2.4.3   Discussion   33
   2.5   A Lucas Critique of the Lucas Solution   34
   2.6   Conclusion   35

3 Household Consumption and Saving   41
   3.1   Introduction   41
   3.2   Expectations, Present Bias, and Credit Constraints   42
         3.2.1   Expectations and Learning   42
         3.2.2   Present Bias, Credit Rationing, and Mental Accounts   46
   3.3   'Social Preferences'   49
         3.3.1   Welfare Analysis   50
         3.3.2   Differences in Average Saving Rates   53

3.4   Aggregate Consumption   57
        3.4.1   Income Distribution and Aggregate Consumption   57
        3.4.2   A Hybrid Aggregate Consumption Function   59
3.5   A More Radical Perspective   61
3.6   Conclusion   64

4   Saving in a Corporate Economy   70
4.1   Introduction   70
4.2   Saving and Portfolio Decisions   73
        4.2.1   Differential Saving Rates   73
        4.2.2   The Neo-Pasinetti Theorem   76
        4.2.3   An Aside: The Pasinetti Theorem and DSGE Models   81
4.3   Feedback Effects on Firms' Financial Decisions   82
4.4   Wealth and Portfolio Effects   87
4.5   Household Heterogeneity   91
4.6   Conclusion   95

5   Phillips Curves and the Natural Rate of Unemployment   102
5.1   Introduction   102
5.2   Phillips Curves   104
5.3   OECD Evidence   112
5.4   Theoretical Fragility: Unions and 'Inflation Bias'   116
        5.4.1   A Model with a Central Union   118
        5.4.2   Implications   121
        5.4.3   Phillips Curves   122
5.5   Conclusion   123

6   Fairness, Money Illusion, and Path Dependency   131
6.1   Introduction   131
6.2   Fairness and Unemployment   133
6.3   Money Illusion and Downward Rigidity of Nominal Wages   136
6.4   Endogenous Norms and Path Dependency   145
6.5   Inflation in a Developing Economy   155
        6.5.1   A Structuralist Model of 'Natural Underemployment'   157
        6.5.2   Endogenous Norms and Aspirations   161
6.6   Conclusion   165

7   Earnings Inequality, Power Bias, and Mismatch   173
7.1   Introduction   173
7.2   Coordination, Control, and the Power of Workers   178
        7.2.1   Technology, Coordination, and Institutions   178
        7.2.2   Agency and Power   181
7.3   A Model of Power-Biased Change   182
        7.3.1   Assumptions   182

| | 7.3.2 | Power-Biased Technological Change | 184 |

7.3.2   Power-Biased Technological Change   184
7.3.3   Power-Biased Institutional Change   186
7.4   Power, Skill, and Mismatch   188
7.5   CEO Pay   192
    7.5.1   Firm-Level Volatility   192
    7.5.2   Contingencies and Implications   194
    7.5.3   Fairness Norms, Reference Groups, and Ratchet Effects   196
7.6   Conclusion   198

8   Macroeconomic Adjustment and Keynes's Instability Argument   203
8.1   Introduction   203
8.2   IS–LM   207
8.3   Changes in Money Wages   214
8.4   Kalecki   219
8.5   Taylor Rules and the ZLB   220
8.6   Conclusion   225

9   Growth and Cycles   228
9.1   Introduction   228
9.2   Harrod's Problems and the Solow Solution   229
    9.2.1   A Harrodian Benchmark Model   229
    9.2.2   The Solow Solution   230
9.3   The Neoclassical Production Function   232
    9.3.1   The Choice of Technique and the Elasticity of Substitution   233
    9.3.2   Aggregation and the Cambridge Capital Controversy   235
    9.3.3   Pragmatic Defenses and Empirical Evidence   239
9.4   Reconciling Warranted and Natural Growth Rates without a Neoclassical Production Function   242
    9.4.1   A Kaldor–Solow Solution   244
    9.4.2   A Marx–Goodwin Solution   245
9.5   Endogenous and Exogenous Growth Cycles   249
9.6   Conclusion   252

10   Endogenous Growth Cycles with or without Price Flexibility   256
10.1   Introduction   256
10.2   Are Prices Flexible?   258
10.3   A Model with Sticky Output and Flexible Prices   262
    10.3.1   Output and Employment   262
    10.3.2   Investment   266
    10.3.3   Saving   268
    10.3.4   A Baseline Model   268
10.4   Analysis   269
10.5   Empirical Evidence and the Baseline Model   275

10.6 An Extended Model: Economic Policy, Investment Dynamics, Credit Constraints, and Okun's Law 279
10.7 A Model with Flexible Output 285
10.8 Conclusion 289

11 Secular Stagnation and Functional Finance 299
11.1 Introduction 299
11.2 Some Simple Algebra for a Mature Economy 301
11.3 Possible Answers 302
 11.3.1 Dynamic Stochastic General Equilibrium 302
 11.3.2 Finite Lives and Overlapping Generations 303
11.4 Functional Finance 305
11.5 Implications 309
 11.5.1 Public Debt and Economic Growth 309
 11.5.2 Secular Stagnation and 'Equilibrium Interest Rates' 312
 11.5.3 Austerity 315
 11.5.4 Income Distribution and Saving 316
 11.5.5 Negative Effects of Public Debt 317
 11.5.6 Empirical Relevance of Functional Finance 318
11.6 Functional Finance in Developing Economies 320
 11.6.1 A Two-Sector Model 321
 11.6.2 Discussion 325
 11.6.3 Japanese Growth and Stagnation 328
11.7 Conclusion 329

12 Concluding Comments: Evidence-Based Macroeconomics and Economic Theory 336

References 342
Author Index 375
Subject Index 381

Figures

2.1 Budget constraints and choices of the representative agent   *page* 23
4.1 Retention rate; US nonfinancial corporate business   72
4.2 Ratio of net equity issues to gross fixed investment; US nonfinancial
corporate business   72
4.3 Tobin's q for US nonfinancial corporate business, 1946–2020   86
5.1 Phillips curve; USA 1920–1940   104
5.2 Phillips curve; USA 1954–1992   106
5.3 Phillips curve; USA 1993–2021   111
5.4 US labor force participation rate for people aged 25–54 years, 2006–2021   112
5.5 Phillips curve; Germany 1962–1989   113
5.6 The central bank's optimal response   120
5.7 Combining the central bank response function (GG) with the union's
first-order condition   121
5.8 Equilibrium in the case with multiple unions   128
6.1 Wage and price setting in a model with money illusion   138
6.2 Long-run Phillips curve in the Rowthorn model   140
6.3 Short-run Phillips curves in the Rowthorn model   141
6.4 Phillips curve; UK 1911–1940   142
6.5 Short-run Phillips curve with homogeneity and full downward rigidity
of money wage   143
6.6 Long-run Phillips curve with homogeneity and full downward rigidity
of money wage   144
6.7 Long-run Phillips curve with heterogeneous labor and idiosyncratic shocks   144
6.8 Endogenous shifts in real-wage norms   147
6.9 Endogenous shifts in norms for real-wage growth   148
6.10 Smooth f-function depicting the salience of inflation   162
6.11 Phase diagram for a 2D system of relative wages and inflation
expectations in a dual economy   164
7.1 Income inequality, USA, 1920–2021   174
7.2 Profit; US nonfinancial corporations   174
7.3 Income inequality, France, 1920–2021   175
8.1 Unemployment, wage and price inflation; US 1929–1939   206
8.2 Unemployment, wage and price inflation, UK 1926–1939   206
8.3 Ultra-short run Keynes–Marshall equilibrium   208
8.4 AD–AS representation of Keynesian model   210

8.5   IS–LM representation of short-run equilibrium   211
8.6   Misleading IS–LM dynamics   213
8.7   Phase diagram for the 2D version of the Tobin model   218
8.8   Multiple stationary solutions in the Tobin model with a Taylor rule and
      a ZLB   223
8.9   Output and inflation dynamics in the Tobin model with a Taylor rule and
      a ZLB   225
9.1   Samuelson's champagne example   236
9.2   Capital output ratios in Samuelson's example   237
9.3   Phase diagram for the Goodwin model   248
9.4   Capacity utilization, US manufacturing (SIC)   249
10.1 Adjustment cost function for employment   264
10.2 Phase diagram for the baseline model   273
10.3 Baseline model   278
10.4 Baseline model with gradual adjustment of investment   280
10.5 Extended version with a public sector, economic policy, Okun's law, and
      investment dynamics   284
10.6 Flex-output model   288
11.1 Real interest rate on three-month treasury bills and debt–GDP ratio; US
      1948–2021   311

Preface and Acknowledgments

This book has had a long gestation period, with early drafts of three chapters dating back to 2004 when I was invited to give a series of lectures at Kobe University, Japan. Having put it aside again, I returned to the project around 2013 as part of the preparation of lecture notes for a graduate course I have been teaching regularly at the University of Massachusetts Amherst. Other commitments slowed down the process, however, and there were times when I doubted that the book would ever be completed.

The intention is for the book to present an alternative to the paradigm that has dominated macroeconomic theory since the 1980s. There have always been dissenters within the profession who have questioned this paradigm, and the structuralist elements of the analysis presented here resonate with existing literatures, including institutionalist, post-Keynesian and Marxian economics, as well as the structuralist tradition in development economics. There is no attempt to provide a survey of these nonmainstream approaches as they relate to macroeconomics. The book in this sense is idiosyncratic: It outlines my view on what a promising macroeconomic paradigm may look like. The behavioral aspects of the analysis are in line with established and empirically well-founded research from behavioral economics, and the presentation has been structured in a way that I hope – maybe naively – will facilitate dialogue with macroeconomists who work within a mainstream tradition.

Most of the chapters draw liberally on earlier work, including coauthored papers with Leila Davis (Chapter 2), Amitava Dutt (Chapter 8), Frederick Guy (Chapter 7), Hyeon-Kyeong Kim (Chapter 7), Guilherme Klein Martins (Chapter 6), Soon Ryoo (Chapters 4 and 11), Fabian Slonimczyk (Chapter 7), and Ben Zipperer (Chapter 10). Working with these coauthors has been enormously helpful as well as a great pleasure, and I thank them all.

I have incurred many other debts in the writing of this book. Paul Auerbach, first and foremost, has read several iterations of the entire manuscript, making numerous suggestions, large and small, with respect to the overall structure, emphases, and exposition. His comments have helped shape and substantially improve the final version. I have also received very helpful comments on multiple chapters from Alex Coram, Itai Sher, Daniele Girardi, Arslan Razmi, Daniele Tavani, Codrina Rada, Ian McDonald, Tom Michl, Juan Montecino, Finn Olesen, Adam Aboobaker, and Mohit Arora.

Valuable input has come from discussions with cohorts of graduate students at the University of Massachusetts Amherst who have suffered through early drafts of the manuscript. I am grateful for the insistence of at least some of these students that I must write this book – without that encouragement, the book probably would not have seen the light of day. Material from the book has also been used in lecture series and short courses at other universities and research institutes, including Aalborg University, Aarhus University, New School for Social Research, Kobe University, Hitotsubashi University, Universidad Javeriana, University of Sao Paulo, and Instituto de Pesquisa Econômica Aplicada (Brasilia). I have benefitted from feedback from participants at these lectures and courses, as well as from participants at conferences and workshops; discussions of key material from different chapters in the annual Analytical Political Economy Workshops have been particularly important. Reviewers for Cambridge University Press, finally, have added constructive comments that have also improved the final product.

1 Introduction: The State of Macroeconomics

1.1 Aims and Themes

Capitalist economies fluctuate and periodically experience large disruptions in economic activity. The peculiar nature of these fluctuations is that, unlike in earlier times, they typically fail to have straightforward natural causes such as harvest failures, with the pandemic of the 2020 and the ensuing recession as an exception in this respect. A central focus of economics has been on understanding the sources of these fluctuations and recommending policies that might mitigate their harmful consequences. This book is an attempt to contribute to these tasks but, along the way, much effort will be devoted to a critique of dominant contemporary macroeconomic theories, which – strikingly – denies even the possibility that fluctuations and crises may be generated endogenously.

With its emphasis on stable equilibria and the self-regulating potential of market mechanisms, the contemporary macroeconomic orthodoxy represents a reversion to pre-Keynesian positions. Unlike the empiricist defense of free markets associated with Milton Friedman, however, it has devolved into a scholastic emphasis on 'microeconomic foundations,' demanding that core macroeconomic relations be derived directly from intertemporal optimization by representative agents. These microeconomic foundations are far less secure than advertised. Furthermore, empirical failures (some of them revealed by the financial crisis of 2008 and associated with the inadequacy of a worldview of inherent stability) have led to a great deal of patching up; *ad hoc* modifications have increasingly complicated the models and undermined the coherence of the approach.

The orthodoxy still maintains great hold over the levers of power in both an academic and policy making context. After the financial crisis of 2008, however, there has been growing disillusionment. The theory is becoming widely perceived as irrelevant, at best, to real-world issues, spurring a move in the direction of purely data-driven approaches. And indeed, such approaches can bring real progress in the context of expansions of available data and advances in econometrics. This had been the case with the pioneering work by Ragnar Frisch, Jan Tinbergen, Lawrence Klein, and others in the mid-twentieth century, and we may be going through another period of rapid progress, driven by the emergence of 'big data' and ever-expanding computer power. Big data and sophisticated econometric techniques do not, however, obviate the need for a conceptual and theoretical framework to select and structure empirical studies and to interpret the statistical results that have been collected.

The alternative theoretical approach presented here departs from the dogmas of the prevailing orthodoxy in academic macroeconomics, drawing on recent developments in behavioral economics as well as older literatures from the Keynesian and Marxian traditions. The intention is to give readers a multifaceted view of contemporary macroeconomics as well as a path forward.

Macroeconomic models, first, tell stories about the interactions between myriad decision-makers operating within a particular structural setting. The microeconomic behavior of decision-makers is an essential part of these stories. The current orthodoxy, however, bypasses a series of aggregation problems and relies on assumptions about microeconomic behavior that are simplistic and misleading. The alternative approach in this book uses microeconomic assumptions that are informed by behavioral evidence, integrating these assumptions into a macroeconomic environment that has far more correspondence to present-day realities than can be found in orthodox models. There will be no infinite-horizon optimization by representative agents, but microeconomic behavior will be central to the analysis.

Macroeconomic theories, second, must be structuralist as well as behavioral: Economies in which households own the capital stock directly may perform differently in some respects than economies in which the capital stock is owned indirectly in the form of financial assets; increasing inequality cannot be understood without attention to institutional change; fiscal policy faces different challenges in advanced and developing economies. Focusing almost exclusively on technology and preferences as the basic parameters of an economy, the current orthodoxy is largely blind to these and other social, institutional, and structural contingencies.

Macroeconomics, third, is general as opposed to partial. As recognized by microeconomic theorists in the 1970s, there can be no presumption of stability in Walrasian models of general equilibrium. Using a different framework of analysis, Keynes had reached a similar conclusion years earlier: The *General Theory* does not deny the existence of a full-employment equilibrium, focusing instead on the stability properties of this equilibrium. The main message was that flexible prices and wages cannot be relied upon to eliminate involuntary unemployment. Taking into account interactions across markets, the full-employment equilibrium may not be stable. The current orthodoxy does not even consider these stability questions.

Going beyond the short run, fourth, the analysis challenges mainstream views of the growth process as involving stochastic fluctuations around a stable full-employment trajectory, with movements along a smooth neoclassical aggregate production function guiding the economy toward steady growth. The theoretical and empirical justifications for the aggregate neoclassical production function are flimsy, and this function is unnecessary to account for the empirical patterns. There are good reasons, furthermore, to think that steady growth paths will be locally unstable and that business cycles would exist in the absence of shocks. In this sense, the cycles become endogenous.

The analysis of complex, dynamic interactions between decision-makers and across markets, fifth, requires the use of formal mathematical models. The problem with the current orthodoxy is not so much that it uses excessive formalization but that it makes the wrong basic assumptions. The straightjacket of full intertemporal optimization misrepresents real-world decision-making, but also has another negative effect: It reduces the ability of the theory to incorporate important aspects of reality in a tractable manner, including mechanisms that can lead to local instability and endogenous fluctuations.

Unlike macroeconomic orthodoxy, finally, the analysis in this book is not justified on an *a priori* basis, following instead traditional approaches to scientific methodology, including requirements of logical coherence and consistency with empirical observations. Present-day economic orthodoxy is an outlier in this respect: The claim that macroeconomic theory must be founded on extreme versions of individual rationality and intertemporal optimization represents a peculiar scholastic admonition, unknown and without parallel in any other discipline.

1.2   Background

In the period after the Great Depression, and especially after the Second World War, a broad-based Keynesian consensus had emerged. The post-War boom had helped give credence to this consensus; the disruption of the boom in the 1970s set the stage for the breakup of the consensus.

By the early 1980s, challenges from traditional monetarist ideas had given way to Robert Lucas's more radical critique: The reduced-form relations in Keynesian macroeconomic models reflect economic behavior that will not, he argued, be invariant to changes in economic policy. Following this 'Lucas critique,' a methodological imperative gradually gained general acceptance: Macroeconomic theories, it was suggested, must be based explicitly on microeconomic optimization.

The Lucas critique was valid in principle and, potentially at least, had practical significance. But the doctrines that emerged in the wake of the critique presumed extravagant levels of intertemporal rationality on the part of the public, ignored aggregation problems, and reasserted pre-Keynesian beliefs that the capitalist macroeconomy was inherently self-equilibrating. The initial formulations of the new theories faced serious empirical problems, necessitating a range of modifications and extensions, and coalescing in the contemporary 'dynamic stochastic general equilibrium' (DSGE) models, the flagship macroeconomic theory of mainstream macroeconomics. Despite successive modifications, the DSGE orthodoxy retains central elements of the earlier models – including the presence of optimizing representative agents with infinite horizons and rational expectations, and the presumption of a stable equilibrium linked to a natural rate of unemployment.

By the beginning of the 2000s, a self-congratulatory consensus had taken hold among macroeconomists. The desirability of microeconomic foundations had become generally accepted, and the Lucas-inspired research program was dominant in academic macroeconomics. Undergraduate textbooks still discussed Keynesian models, but the takeover was complete at the graduate level, and policymakers increasingly relied on the new theory. Traditional Keynesian economics had been displaced, and Chari and Kehoe (2006, p. 4) could declare victory: "Macroeconomists now take policy analyses seriously only if they are based on quantitative general equilibrium models in which the parameters of preferences and technologies are reasonably argued to be invariant to policy."

Inadequate theoretical foundations and a reliance on ephemeral empirical correlation allegedly rendered Keynesian models unreliable and misleading. The new models, by contrast, were seen as firmly grounded in economic theory. Woodford (1999, p. 31) saw convergence, not just within macroeconomics but also in relation to the rest of economics: "Modern macroeconomic models are intertemporal general equilibrium models derived from the same foundations of optimizing behavior on the part of households and firms as are employed in other branches of economics." Blanchard (2000, p. 1375) suggested that "progress in macroeconomics may well be the success story of twentieth century economics," with Chari and Kehoe (2006, p. 26) claiming that the theoretical advances had great practical value: "Macroeconomic theory has had a profound and far-reaching effect on the institutions and practices governing monetary policy and is beginning to have a similar effect on fiscal policy. The marginal social product of macroeconomic science is surely large and growing rapidly."

The 'great moderation' and a dynamic American economy in the 1990s (along with the breakup of the Soviet Union) formed the background to this broadly shared sentiment. Business fluctuations had become milder after the mid 1980s, and Lucas pronounced the problem of depression prevention as "solved, for all practical purposes." He went on to argue that "the potential for welfare gains from better long-run, supply-side policies exceeds by far the potential from further improvements in short-run demand management" (Lucas 2003, p. 1).

Rapid US growth demonstrated the benefits of free markets and an economic policy focused on low inflation, economic incentives, and liberalization. At least that was the claim. Historically, the US performance after the 1970s was not, in fact, particularly successful. Average growth rates had been higher in 1950–1975, and the distribution of the gains became highly skewed after 1975. The rich (and especially the super rich) got richer; the rest experienced stagnating or falling real incomes. Women and minorities experienced some material improvements, but the median wage of a male worker was virtually unchanged between 1973 and 2020, and at the low end of the distribution, male workers have seen declining real wages. Macroeconomists, however, have traditionally given little weight to distributional issues; Lucas (2004, p. 14) famously commented that of "the tendencies that are harmful to sound economics, the most seductive, and in my opinion the most poisonous, is to focus on questions of distribution."

The financial crisis of 2008 took the profession by surprise. The timing of financial crises will always be difficult to predict, but the problem for economists ran deeper. The macroeconomic consensus had converged on a theoretical model in which finance played no significant role and in which a financial crises could not occur: Any meaningful treatment of finance and financial crises has, as a prerequisite, the existence of distinct agents with different financial positions; the standard model, by contrast, was built around a single, representative household.

Once the financial crisis did occur, the model also proved useless as a guide to economic policy. It had nothing to say about financial issues; it implied that although price stickiness could lead to temporary unemployment, these aggregate demand-related unemployment problems would be short-lived; it suggested that adjustments in household saving would largely offset fiscal policy, leaving fiscal policy with little or no effect on aggregate demand; it pointed to monetary policy as the preferred instrument for stabilization, but the traditional monetary instruments ceased to be available when interest rates hit the zero lower bound.

The poverty of the new models led to a resurgence of crude empiricism, a resurgence that is deeply ironic. A profession that had touted the Lucas critique and the necessity of economic theory and solid microeconomic foundations now extrapolated from past evidence to suggest that, for unspecified reasons, financial crises must lead to prolonged recessions. Meanwhile fiscal retrenchment was advocated on the basis of evidence suggesting a correlation between high levels of public debt and slow growth (Reinhart and Rogoff 2009, 2010).

The implications have been devastating. The American Recovery and Reinvestment Act of 2009 (a fiscal stimulus package) and aggressive quantitative easing attenuated the downturn in the US but were insufficient in scale to prevent a painful and prolonged recession. Matters have been worse on the other side of the Atlantic where policymakers, with a predominant influence of German ordoliberal ideas, pursued austerity policies that have been ripping Europe apart. Millions of citizens have suffered needless hardship as a result of soaring unemployment and cuts to pensions and social benefits. Political turmoil, social unrest, and the rise of extremist nationalist movements have followed, threatening the democratic fabric.

Not all of these ills can be attributed to poor economic policy, but it would be hard to deny the influence of worsening economic conditions on social and political events. And the economics profession and macroeconomic theory in particular must accept its share of responsibility for the policies that have been pursued. The insistence on markets as self-regulating and fiscal policy as ineffective or harmful provided theoretical justification for neoliberal policies before the crisis and for inadequate and misguided policies after the crisis.

Economic theory is not the only influence on policy. Opportunistic attempts to 'starve the beast' and cut back the welfare state have undoubtedly contributed to policy formation. But macroeconomic theory has acted to disguise the political nature of these attacks. It has also done little to confront and dispel misleading analogies between Swabian housewives and sound macroeconomic policy.[1] On the contrary,

---

[1] According to the *Economist* (2014, Feb. 1), the Swabian hausfrau as an archetype was invoked by Angela Merkel when she suggested failing banks "should have consulted a Swabian housewife because she could have told them how to deal with money." The same article quotes the prime minister of Baden–Württemberg as saying:

viewing the macroeconomy as essentially a single representative household plays into that same mindset.

Applied economists cannot afford to ignore empirical evidence, especially in a deep recession. Not surprisingly, therefore, a body of policy research has questioned the presumptions and implications of the current orthodoxy, sometimes explicitly and sometimes implicitly. The International Monetary Fund (IMF) and Organisation for Economic Co-operation and Development (OECD) studies, for instance, have debunked claims about 'expansionary austerity' and documented strong fiscal multipliers during recessions. More generally, a booming body of applied research has addressed a number of important issues; Nakamura and Steinsson (2018) discuss some of this recent work.

At a theoretical level, by contrast, the DSGE approach has met little resistance within the mainstream of the profession. The work by George Akerlof and several coauthors represents an exception, challenging both the behavioral assumptions and key notions such as the 'natural rate of unemployment.'[2] Another example could be the recent revival by Larry Summers of the notion of 'secular stagnation' and the closely related suggestions by Paul Krugman that liquidity traps may have become increasingly relevant. But neither Summers nor Krugman has proposed a full-fledged alternative to the DSGE consensus.

The failures of current versions of the DSGE models are hard to ignore, however, and their limitations have been widely and increasingly acknowledged, even if the methodology goes unquestioned by many of those who are critical. Blanchard (2018a), for instance, sees "current DSGE models as seriously flawed, but they are eminently improvable and central to the future of macroeconomics" (p. 44). Moreover, he argues, "starting from explicit microfoundations is clearly essential: where else to start from? Ad hoc equations will not do" (p. 47). Thus, he concludes, "DSGE models can fulfill an important need in macroeconomics, that of offering a core structure around which to build and organize discussions" (p. 48). Christiano et al. (2017) present a more extreme version of this position in their defense of DSGE models. Macroeconomists, they argue, cannot perform experiments on actual economies in order to learn the relative strengths of competing forces. Experiments are necessary, however, and "[t]he *only* place that we can do experiments is in dynamic stochastic general equilibrium (DSGE) models" (abstract; italics in original) – a claim that is both audacious and blatantly false: We need formal models, but not all logically consistent macroeconomic

---

"Yes, she's a cliché, but much more than a cliché," says Winfried Kretschmann with some pride, because "the Swabian housewife represents the starting point" in German thinking on the euro and fiscal management.

[2] Other behavioral macroeconomists have also chipped away at the standard DSGE models (e.g., De Grauwe 2012), and Robert Solow has been another consistent critic of the Lucas paradigm (e.g., Solow 1986, 2008). See also two special issues of *Oxford Review of Economic Policy* (2018, Vol. 34(1–2); 2020, Vol. 36(3)) on 'Rebuilding macroeconomic theory,' which contain a range of papers that discuss, defend, or critique the DSGE approach.

models with dynamic and stochastic elements follow the particular 'DSGE' approach to macroeconomic theory.[3]

Outside the mainstream, (post-)Keynesian, (neo-)Marxian, and institutionalist critics have always been scathing in their critique, even before the onset of the financial crisis.[4] As an example, Dutt and Skott (2006) argued that "what has happened in macroeconomics since the late 1960s has been a wasteful detour. A generation of macro-economists has grown up learning tools that may be sophisticated, but the usefulness of these tools is questionable. Moreover, a great deal of damage may be, and has been, done when the tools are applied to real-world situations."

After the crisis, similar conclusions have been voiced by a number of economists who were previously seen as part of the mainstream. Paul Krugman is quoted as saying that most of modern macroeconomics is "spectacularly useless at best, and positively harmful at worst" (*Economist*, July 16, 2009); Willem Buiter (2009) referred to the last 30 years of macroeconomics training at US and UK universities as a "costly waste of time," and Brad DeLong (2009) commented on the Chicago school's "intellectual collapse." More recently, Paul Romer (2016) has berated the DSGE models for their use of "incredible identifying assumptions to reach bewildering conclusions" (p. 1). Macroeconomics, he suggests, has been guided by deference to the leaders in the field and "progress in the field is judged by the purity of its mathematical theories, as determined by the authorities" (p. 16). Ferocious as these comments may be, it is often unclear what is being promoted by these critics as an alternative to the orthodoxy. And an alternative is needed.

Blanchard sees the DSGE model as providing a core structure for understanding capitalist economies. The flawed DSGE approach is a poor choice, but Blanchard is correct, in my view, that a core structure or theoretical vision is necessary, even if one's goal is 'merely' sound policymaking rather than grand system building for its own sake – as Keynes observed, "practical men who believe themselves to be quite exempt from any intellectual influence, are usually the slaves of some defunct economist"

---

[3] Some DSGE models incorporate traditional, pre-Lucas elements and insights. The large 'indirect effect' of monetary policy identified by Kaplan et al. (2018) and highlighted by Christiano et al. as an example of cutting-edge research basically identifies (as they acknowledge on p. 20) a standard Keynesian multiplier. The attempts to include deviations from rational expectations point in the same direction, and perhaps the term DSGE will lose its distinctive meaning sometime in the future. But as of today, DSGE is not a simple synonym for the macroeconomic model. The Euler equation for optimizing, representative agents with infinite horizons is at the center of analysis for DSGE models, which are guided by particular rules of the game and a particular underlying vision.

[4] The marginalization of these traditions within the profession will be seen by the mainstream as a reflection of their weaknesses, rather than as an indication of the close-mindedness of the mainstream itself. In the words of the *Economist* (July 16, 2009, "What went wrong with economics?"), "[t]oday's economists tend to be open-minded about content, but doctrinaire about form. They are more wedded to their techniques than to their theories. They will believe something when they can model it." There is some truth in this claim. But the distinction between content and the modeling technique breaks down in the case of contemporary macroeconomics. It is reasonable to demand that an argument be clearly articulated, logically coherent, and consistent with relevant empirical evidence, but the prevailing orthodoxy in macroeconomics has a particular methodology, demanding explicit intertemporal optimization as a central element of any acceptable macroeconomic model.

(*General Theory*, p. 383). But in order for it to be useful and relevant for real-world applications, we need a core structure that is quite different from what is being offered by the research program on DSGE models.

1.3   Overview

1.3.1   Behavior

Macroeconomic models incorporate pure accounting equations, but on their own these equations do not take us very far. Behavioral elements must be added, and the specification of these elements requires assumptions about microeconomic behavior. This recognition of the importance of microeconomic behavior does not imply that macroeconomic equations must be derived directly from the intertemporal utility maximization of a representative agent.

Chapter 2 examines the Lucas critique and the way it has been addressed through the introduction of an optimizing representative agent. The message of this chapter is simple: The Lucas *critique* is unexceptionable, but the Lucas *solution* developed by mainstream macroeconomics represents an abject failure. Heroic aggregation assumptions are embodied in the creation of a representative agent: Even if individual preferences could be taken as well defined, exogenous, and stable over time, the celebrated Sonnenschein–Debreu–Mantel results show that microeconomic rationality imposes only very weak constraints on the properties of aggregate excess demand functions.

Chapter 2 also questions the utility function of the representative agent as the basis for welfare analysis. This approach to welfare analysis has been hailed as a strong and distinctive advantage of the contemporary approach because, supposedly, it uses a 'correct' and 'objective' welfare criterion. This claim is false: Using a 'descriptive' representative agent's utility function imparts a systematic bias against the poor and in favor of the rich. The derivation of macroeconomic relations from the optimization of a representative household "is not simply an analytical convenience as often explained, but is both unjustified and leads to conclusions which are usually misleading and often wrong" (Kirman 1992, p. 117).

Even if we put aggregation issues to one side, the standard behavioral assumptions are questionable. Much of economic activity is goal oriented in a relatively clear way. This applies most obviously to capitalist firms. Given the complexity of the decision problem and the pervasive clouds of uncertainty in which these decisions must be made, firms cannot 'maximize profits' in a strict sense, but formal models embodying profit maximization can be useful for many purposes. The optimization approach is more questionable with respect to households, which are at the center of DSGE models. Indeed, in light of much behavioral evidence, the microeconomic assumptions of contemporary macroeconomics appear mechanical, primitive, and misleading. Behavioral economics has demonstrated systematic deviations from the simple assumptions of perfect instrumental rationality and rational expectations. These deviations from predicted behavior have important implications for key elements of macroeconomic theory, including wage formation and saving.

Chapter 3 considers households' saving decisions. Some deviations of actual behavior from that of an idealized 'homo oeconomicus' are quite trivial and irrelevant for macroeconomics: Households make mistakes in their daily activities and sometimes fail to choose consumption baskets that could have made them better off, but if the mistakes are random, the implications for macroeconomic theory are limited. Matters are different when the mistakes are systematic and occur in areas that affect aggregate economic outcomes.

The evidence shows that a large proportion of households have saved very little by the time they reach retirement. There may be several reasons for low saving, including impatience, lack of self-discipline, and peer effects on consumption. But pervasive uncertainty also poses questions for the general notion that long-term decisions like household retirement saving can be based on meaningful notions of optimization. Technical change can make skills obsolete and create new job opportunities, and alterations in economic policy can have major effects on household finances. Obvious examples include uncertainties concerning future social security, health benefits, and the cost of sending children to college. Even if it successfully identifies these contingencies, the household still faces the daunting task of incorporating them into optimal plans.

These complications and the systematic deviations of household behavior from the postulates of the model do not merely add random errors that cancel out on aggregation. And they affect the core of the DSGE model: It is precisely the intertemporal utility maximization under perfect foresight (or rational expectations) that supposedly establishes the superiority of the model. As noted by Blanchard (2016, p. 1), the derivation of consumption demand in DSGE models is "strongly at odds with the empirical evidence" with respect to both "the degree of foresight and the role of interest rates in twisting the path of consumption." One can try to patch up the model in various ways – by introducing a subset of 'hand-to-mouth' consumers or adding 'habit formation,' for instance – but these are "repairs, rather than convincing characterizations of consumers" (Blanchard 2016, p. 2). Thus, we have here a research program which, 40 years after its inception and after at least 20 years of near-total dominance, has to admit that its key innovation does not fit the facts (Chapter 3).

The treatment of wage formation and the labor market is another example of failure. The existence of a well-defined 'natural rate of unemployment' informs much of economic policy, but the evidence is weak: Strong prior beliefs are required to justify interpretations of the evidence as supportive of a natural rate of unemployment. Natural-rate theory, second, is fragile even on its own terms: Minor changes in the Barro–Gordon (1983) analysis of inflation bias can eliminate the natural rate of unemployment and generate policy conclusions that are radically different, even when assumptions of perfect foresight and well-defined preferences over inflation and output are retained (Chapter 5).

The behavioral assumptions underlying wage formation in the current orthodoxy also exclude forces that have a systematic influence on outcomes in the labor market.

Abundant evidence suggests that notions of fairness are important for wage setting and labor relations. These behavioral findings fit badly within the current orthodoxy. Norms of fairness, moreover, are likely to have strong historical and conventional elements: Reductions in wages relative to a previously established level are typically seen as unfair. These systematic, behavioral deviations from homo oeconomicus have macroeconomic significance. 'Fair wages' can be a source of unemployment, as suggested by Akerlof and Yellen (1990), and money illusion (Akerlof et al. 1996), while conventional elements in fairness can lead to path dependencies (hysteresis) in both the rate of unemployment and the structure of relative wages (Chapters 6 and 7).

The deviations from homo oeconomicus with respect to both consumption and wage setting do not deny the importance of microeconomic behavior for macroeconomics. On the contrary, DSGE models fail because they have been based on misleading assumptions about microeconomic behavior. Macroeconomic relations should indeed reflect microeconomic behavior, and macroeconomics must be 'behavioral.' But the core assumptions of the DSGE approach represent a poor approximation to real-world behavior.

1.3.2   Structure

Microeconomic behavior takes place within a macroeconomic environment, and macroeconomic theory should ignore neither the structures that define the environment nor the individual agency within these structures. All theories have, implicitly or explicitly, a structural setting that is macroeconomic in nature – even the Walrasian general equilibrium model with its simple set of abstract assumptions about property rights and markets. Thus, the critique of the current orthodoxy is not the absence of any structural assumptions, but the poor choice of assumptions actually made. The underlying position appears to be that preferences and technology dominate and that, otherwise, institutions are largely irrelevant or simply reflect preferences and technology.

Discussing the labor market and the time patterns of work, Lucas (1981) expresses this view explicitly. Social convention and institutional structures affect the time patterns, he argues, but

conventions and institutions do not simply come out of the blue, arbitrarily imposing themselves on individual agents. On the contrary, institutions and customs are designed precisely in order to aid in matching preferences and opportunities satisfactorily.

Theories that take into account the complicated institutional arrangements in actual labor and product markets

would have to explain why, given their opportunities, people *prefer* arrangements involving erratic employment patterns. Ignoring this simple point seems to me simply bad social science: an attempt to explain important aspects of human behavior without reference either to what people like or what they are capable of doing. (Lucas, 1981, p. 4; italics in original)

This reductionist argument is unconvincing. Institutions change over time, and the aggregate and cumulative effects of individual behavior undoubtedly play a part in the generation of such changes. But collective action problems and simple game theory make it abundantly clear that an institutional equilibrium need not reflect what "people prefer" (assuming that it is even possible to define an outcome that "people prefer"). Nash equilibria need not be Pareto optimal, and they rarely describe outcomes that are preferred by all players – the prisoners' dilemma shows that equilibria can even be strictly Pareto inferior to other possible outcomes. At a more general level, the Lucas argument seems to imply a notion that all of human history and its institutions can be reconstructed as an emanation from exogenous, human preferences. It is hard to take this notion seriously. As Karl Marx noted,

Men make their own history, but they do not make it just as they please; they do not make it under circumstances chosen by themselves, but under given circumstances directly encountered and inherited from the past. The tradition of all the generations of the dead weighs like a nightmare on the brain of the living. (Marx 1852 [1978], p. 9)

Economic history and institutional structures are better viewed as path dependent and as evolving to a large extent under the influence of the – often unintended – consequences of myriad microeconomic decisions. The institutions are given in the short run and influence the properties of an economy in important ways. The goals and preferences of individuals will themselves be molded in large part by the economic environment that the individuals have been born into: How else would one explain the cultural differences across societies? This influence implies that there can be no unidirectional causation between 'preferences' and 'institutions' institutions shape preferences and human actions and interactions generate institutional change (Hodgson 1988, p. 64–65). There can be no microeconomic *foundations* in a reductionist sense; the 'foundations' metaphor is misleading, and metaphors matter (King 2012).

Most economists, I expect, will accept the need to consider both the behavior of decision-makers at the micro level (agency) and the environment that constrains and molds their behavior (structure).[5] But by putting the infinitely lived representative agent at the center of the analysis, DSGE models *de facto* (and perhaps inadvertently) become reductionist. The setting does not allow for interactions between decision-makers with different beliefs, goals, and constraints, and there can be no fallacies of composition and unintended consequences. The analysis essentially treats the macroeconomy as a single optimizing agent with exogenously given preferences, thereby also eliding issues of social conflict and relative power.

An integration of macro and micro (rather than a unidirectional foundation of one for the other) was what Keynesians like James Tobin, Paul Samuelson, or Robert Solow were aiming for. Most post-Keynesian and neo-Marxian macroeconomists share this goal but give less weight to rational decision-making at the micro level and

---

[5] Hahn (1973) accepted the long-run endogeneity of preferences. Their exogeneity in general equilibrium models is justified, he argued, because for practical purposes they can be taken as given in the short run. Acemoglu's (2009) position seems more puzzling. It is not obvious how one can reconcile growth models based on representative agents and Ramsey optimization with an emphasis on institutions (and institutional change) as "a major – perhaps the most significant – fundamental cause of economic growth."

instead tend to emphasize the constraining and enabling influence of institutions.[6] The differences between old Keynesians, post-Keynesians, and neo-Marxists are important, but methodologically the aim is the same: To build an integrated micro–macro story of how capitalist economies work and evolve.

I will touch on issues relating to the change in institutions, most notably in Chapter 7 on changes in inequality. Many factors have contributed to the trends in inequality, and the chapter does not attempt to offer a complete explanation, focusing instead on a couple of elements that have received little attention. Power-biased technological and institutional changes, first, have weakened the position of some (mostly low paid) groups of workers and strengthened that of others (often high paid). Mismatches in the labor market, second, can give rise to paradoxical results: A rise in minimum wages, for instance, may *increase* the employment of low-skill workers.

Structural and institutional features also influence the way an economy works at the macroeconomic level, a simple fact that often goes unrecognized. The sources of inflation, for instance, may be quite different in mature economies with near full employment compared with dual economies with large amounts of disguised unemployment (Chapter 6). Advanced capitalist economies, as another example, are corporate economies. Households may be the ultimate owners of firms, but typically they do not own physical capital directly. The ownership is mediated through financial assets: Households own equity in firms, either directly or indirectly through financial institutions, including pension funds and insurance companies. This corporate structure has macroeconomic implications. Firms' financial decisions, for instance, will influence the aggregate saving rate, while the macroeconomic effects of a desire by households to build up their financial wealth depend critically on the type of assets in which households choose to hold their increased wealth (Chapter 4). Or consider the sustainability of public debt. Some countries have debt denominated in their own currency, while others have debt denominated in a currency they do not control. This structural difference makes a world of difference. Yet, a large literature on public debt makes no distinction between the two cases (Chapter 11).

1.3.3   Instability, Cycles, and Economic Growth

Macroeconomics is by definition 'general.' It is about the economic system as a whole and the interactions between markets rather than about the *ceteris-paribus* analysis of single markets. The realization that things can look very different from a systems

---

[6] Discussing John Cornwall's work, for instance, Setterfield and Thirlwall (2010) suggest:

> In an environment of uncertainty, institutions enable action, by prescribing behaviour when it is impossible to identify an optimal response to a situation. ... [I]nstitutions provide relatively enduring macrofoundations for economic behaviour: they act as a quasi-inert 'operating system' within which the income-generating process functions (p. 489).

> Cornwall related medium and long-term fluctuations in economic performance to an economy's 'institutional fitness'; in this sense, his work had a close affinity with the French 'regulation school' or its US counterpart on 'social structures of accumulation' (e.g., Boyer 1990, Kotz et al. 1994).

perspective than from the perspective of a single market gave birth to the Keynesian revolution and modern macroeconomics. Pre-Keynesian economists had erred, Keynes argued, precisely by trying to extend to the system as whole conclusions that had been obtained by looking at a single firm or industry. A fall in nominal wages would raise employment if the price of output could be taken as given, but this assumption of given prices cannot be sustained when the interactions across markets are considered: Changes in average wage rates affect aggregate nominal demand and thereby the nominal price level. These dynamic interactions lie behind the market failures that Keynes identified: Assuming that a well-defined position of full employment exists, market mechanisms cannot be relied upon to bring the economy from a depression back to full employment.[7] Keynes's analysis of aggregate demand problems and the (in-)stability of full employment is addressed in Chapter 8.

Contemporary macroeconomic theory has effectively abandoned the concerns that defined traditional macroeconomics. Price and wage stickiness may call for short-run stabilization in new Keynesian DSGE models, but if only prices and wages had been flexible, there would be no Keynesian problems of effective demand in these models; cyclical fluctuations are generated by introducing stochastic shocks into models otherwise possessing a stable equilibrium solution. The coordination and stability problems that were at the heart of Keynes's message have been forgotten.

Chapters 9–10 extend the analysis to the medium and long run. The neoclassical aggregate production is still ubiquitous in the macroeconomic literature, despite the theoretical weaknesses that were exposed by the Cambridge capital controversy. Chapter 9 presents an overview of this controversy and of subsequent attempts to provide an empirical justification for the aggregate production function. These attempts are unconvincing, and the function is not needed: Other mechanisms can reconcile the average long-run rate of growth with the growth rate of the labor force.

This reconciliation tells only part of the story. Capitalist economies contain both stabilizing and destabilizing forces. Depending on the balance of these forces, bounded fluctuations around a locally unstable steady growth path can emerge. This outcome is in line with empirical studies that find evidence of local instability (Beaudry et al. 2017). By contrast, in DSGE models, the steady growth path represents a saddle point, and it is assumed that forward-looking agents seek out the stable saddle path. There are no endogenous cycles.

Endogenous cycles are analyzed in Chapter 10. Goods prices, I shall argue, are more flexible and output less flexible than commonly assumed, and Keynesian theory does not need assumptions of price rigidity. Flexible prices combined with an explicit analysis of output adjustment and investment decisions governed by a stock adjustment principle can produce endogenous business cycles in benchmark models of a closed economy without a public sector. Surprisingly, essentially the same cyclical patterns for employment, capital utilization, and profit shares can be derived from

---

[7] This Keynesian argument, which did not make it into most textbooks, was widely accepted by old Keynesians (e.g., Hicks 1975, Solow 1998, Tobin 1975, 1993).

models with output flexibility and sticky prices, assumptions that may fit parts of the service sector. When the benchmark models of endogenous cycles are extended to include fiscal and monetary policy, simulations show a remarkable correspondence to observed cyclical patterns for the US.

The analysis in Chapter 10 also indicates that structural aggregate demand problems may jeopardize the existence of a steady growth path (and not just its local stability). Long-run aggregate demand problems of this kind cannot arise in DSGE models that – although they may include 'hand-to-mouth consumers' – are anchored by the intertemporal optimization of a representative agent. Outside the rarefied world of these models, however, mature capitalist economies can experience secular stagnation in the absence of sustained fiscal policy. Chapter 11 analyzes these issues in greater detail, showing that the need for long-term fiscal stimulus in some mature economies does not imply explosive public debt ratios. An important result, moreover, shows that the asymptotic debt ratio associated with full-employment growth depends *inversely* on both the rate of economic growth and the share of government consumption in income The chapter also argues that, in contrast to mature economies, developing economies do not face structural aggregate demand problems of this kind; their policy problems are quite different.

1.3.4   Core Models

Dynamic interactions across markets are hard to keep track of, and formal techniques are required to make any headway. The techniques can be analytical or numerical. Numerical techniques have been gaining influence and have obvious advantages: We can simulate systems that are far too complicated to allow analytical solution. The downside of numerical methods is equally obvious: It can be hard to know precisely what drives the outcome, which is a serious drawback for models that aim to provide, in Blanchard's words, "a core structure around which to build and organize discussion." Core models are needed as well in relation to empirical work, an issue discussed briefly in the concluding chapter.

In line with this need for core models, the emphasis in this book will be on small-scale analytical models. The ambition is not to provide a single 'theory of everything' but to set out a coherent approach that can serve as an alternative to the current orthodoxy in macroeconomic theory.

1.3.5   Terminology and Notation

Terminology

A quick note of terminology and notation may be useful before proceeding. 'Contemporary macroeconomic orthodoxy' in my use of the term refers to theories that impose rational expectations and insist on explicit optimization by representative agents as a core element of macroeconomic models. Orthodoxy in this sense includes DSGE models as well as most overlapping-generations (OLG) models. Within orthodoxy, New Keynesian DSGE models retain explicit optimization and rational expectations but, unlike real business cycle (RBC) theory, emphasize the presence of real and nominal rigidities, thereby allowing aggregate demand to play a role in the short run.

Old Keynesian macroeconomics follows a more eclectic methodology. Economic decision-makers are seen as goal oriented, with optimization sometimes used to model behavior at the microeconomic level. In general, however, decision-makers do not have rational expectations, and it is recognized that they may be boundedly rational. The transition from micro to macro, moreover, involves aggregation problems; the first-order conditions that characterize microeconomic optimization therefore do not carry over to macroeconomic relations.

Post-Keynesian theories differ from old Keynesian macroeconomics by emphasizing the role of aggregate demand in long-run economic growth, the importance of social conflict, economic institutions and conventions, the presence of pervasive uncertainty, and the tendencies of unregulated capitalist economies to experience market failures and recurrent economic crises.[8]

Notation

Many economic variables have standard notation; Y, C, I, and K for aggregate output, consumption, investment, and capital, respectively, are obvious examples. These standard notations will be followed whenever possible. Conflicts may arise, however, in cases when two different variables with the same standard notation appear in the same model; the notation π, for instance, is commonly used to denote both the profit share and the inflation rate. There is no conflict if the variables do not appear in the same model, but the reader should be aware that the same mathematical notation may denote different variables, depending on the model under consideration.

This problem becomes more acute with respect to parameters and functions: The sheer number of parameters and functions makes the use of model-specific notation almost inevitable; the function $f()$, for instance, will be used for the investment function in one model but the choice of technique in another, while, depending on the context, the parameter α may appear in utility functions, production functions, or behavioral equations. The alternative – a completely consistent, uniform notation for all variables, parameters, and functions – would require a cumbersome, nonstandard set of definitions. Thus, the mathematical notation in this book sacrifices consistency for simplicity and conformity with standard practice.

Some elements are consistent. Following general convention, 'dots' and 'hats' will be used throughout to represent time derivatives and proportional growth rates: For any variable x, the notations $\dot{x}$ and $\hat{x}$ are defined by $\dot{x} = dx/dt$ and $\hat{x} = \dot{x}/x = (dx/dt)/x$, respectively. The partial derivatives of a multivariate function are denoted by subscripts: The function $f(x, y)$ has the partial derivatives f_1 and f_2. With respect to variables, finally, the subscript i has been used to indicate agent-level variables, while the subscript t indicates the time period in discrete-time models.

---

[8] Hein (2014), Lavoie (2014), and Blecker and Setterfield (2019) provide surveys of post-Keynesian theory.

2 The Lucas Critique and Representative Agents

2.1 Background

Just as the Great Depression of the 1930s formed the backdrop to the Keynesian revolution, so too did the counter revolution of the 1970s have a historical context. Inflation had been increasing, and the 1960s had seen rising labor militancy, high levels of strike activity, youth revolts, massive mobilization against the Vietnam War, and falling profit shares. These trends continued into the 1970s when inflation was further exacerbated by oil price shocks and rising commodity prices.

Critics of the Keynesian consensus of the day saw the rising inflation as indicative of fundamental theoretical weaknesses in Keynesian thought. Keynesian economics, it was argued, lacked microeconomic foundations. While students of microeconomics examined the implications of utility and profit maximization for the determination of equilibrium prices, the Keynesian models were cast in terms of investment and consumption functions; prices and wages were either taken as exogenous, or a Phillips curve was added to explain the rate of inflation. Micro- and macroeconomic theorists seemed to inhabit different worlds, and the links between the different worlds were unclear.

A turning point in changing mainstream academic opinion came with Milton Friedman's presidential address to the American Economic Association in 1967, which articulated this argument in a striking way. Phillips's analysis, he argued "contains a basic defect – the failure to distinguish between nominal wages and real wages" (Friedman 1968, p. 8). Elaborating on this claim, Friedman argued that

At any moment of time, there is some level of unemployment which has the property that it is consistent with equilibrium in the structure of *real* wage rates. ... A lower level of unemployment is an indication that there is an excess demand for labor that will produce upward pressure on real wage rates. A higher level of unemployment is an indication that there is an excess supply of labor that will produce downward pressure on real wage rates. (p. 8; italics in original)

This view of a labor market in which the supply and demand curves determine a unique equilibrium solution for employment and the real wage leads to the definition of the "natural rate of unemployment" as

the level that would be ground out by the Walrasian system of general equilibrium equations, provided there is imbedded in them the actual structural characteristics of the labor and commodity markets, including market imperfections, stochastic variability in demands and supplies, the cost of gathering information about job vacancies and labor availabilities, the costs of mobility, and so on. (p. 8)

From this perspective the apparent trade-off between unemployment and inflation depicted by the traditional Phillips curve was symptomatic of a "basic defect": Macroeconomic models had failed to incorporate fundamental economic principles.

The demands for microeconomic foundations were hardened by the emergence of new classical theory. Early versions of the theory included informational imperfections that made it difficult for individual decision-makers to disentangle aggregate monetary shocks from shifts in relative demand (Lucas 1975). These versions subsequently gave way to RBC theories in which the cycles represented efficient responses to exogenous shocks (Kydland and Prescott 1982). The pure RBC story faced empirical difficulties, and the consensus around DSGE models that has emerged from this literature incorporates a range of frictions and imperfections. But methodologically, the key principle remains unchanged: There is general agreement that macroeconomics must be built on firm microeconomic foundations.[1]

The central methodological principle behind the consensus view has been subjected to forceful critiques from, among others, Kirman (1989, 1992), Hoover (1988, 2001), and a host of heterodox economists.[2] Yet, it seems that many macroeconomists are unfamiliar with these critiques or have chosen to ignore them. Certainly, I am not aware of satisfactory responses from proponents of the current consensus.

This chapter presents internal critiques of the 'Lucas solution' which posits explicit optimization by representative agents as a methodological imperative for macroeconomic theory. The critique is internal because it accepts the presumptions about the preferences and perfect rationality of individual households. The chapter serves as a prelude to external, behavioral, and structuralist critiques and the presentation of an alternative approach to macroeconomic modeling in subsequent chapters.

Section 2.2 discusses the Lucas critique. The critique of the Lucas solution has three distinct parts: The nonexistence of a representative agent with the stipulated characteristics (Section 2.3), the misuse of descriptive representative agents for welfare analysis (Section 2.4), and the vulnerability of the purported Lucas solution to a Lucas critique (Section 2.5). Section 2.6 offers a few concluding comments.

2.2 The Lucas Critique and Contemporary Macroeconomics

The need for microeconomic foundations was illustrated by Lucas (1976) using three examples. The first one pointed out that the effect on consumption of a change in

---

[1] This principle appears to take precedence over all other criteria, including descriptive realism. Thus, the element of continuity between Friedman and Lucas should not obscure a sharp discontinuity between Friedman's empiricist methodology and a much more formalist methodological justification of optimizing representative agents as a foundation of macroeconomic models in new classical economics and the current consensus.

[2] Textbooks by Hein (2014) and Lavoie (2014) devote considerable space to these issues; King (2012) discusses the 'microfoundations delusion' in detail.

income depends on whether the change is expected to be temporary or permanent. The second, analogously, discussed how the effect of a tax credit on investment depends on whether the credit is temporary or permanent, while the third example focused on the Phillips curve, noting how changes in expected inflation affect the relation between output and actual inflation, and how expected inflation in turn depends on the policy regime.

The substance of these examples was well known at the time, but Lucas drew a general lesson: Existing econometric models, he argued, were deeply flawed. Summarizing the analysis, he concluded that (p. 41)

given that the structure of an econometric model consists of optimal decision rules of economic agents, and that optimal decision rules vary systematically with changes in the structure of series relevant to the decision maker, it follows that any changes in policy will systematically alter the structure of econometric models.

This Lucas critique essentially has three elements:

- Microeconomic behavior is goal oriented, has an intertemporal dimension, and is influenced by expectations.
- Reduced-form macroeconomic equations that link current decisions to observable variables will reflect these expectations.
- Shifts in expectations – for instance, as a result of changes in policy rules – can affect these reduced-form equations and render them unstable.

All three elements are unexceptionable. One can debate the size and significance of the shifts in particular equations following particular shocks, but the general argument clearly is correct. Indeed, how could any economist, especially a Keynesian one, not agree that economic behavior is goal oriented, that it has an intertemporal dimension, and that it is influenced by expectations? The role of expectations was at the center of Keynes's analysis. Does anyone disagree that reduced-form equations will reflect these expectations? Does it not follow that shifts in expectations can affect the reduced-form equations and render them unstable?

Keynesians and others had made similar points long before Lucas. Lerner (1943, p. 48), for instance, had argued that the introduction of Keynesian policy rules will affect expectations and change private sector behavior:

Since one of the greatest deterrents to private investment is the fear that the depression will come before the investment has paid for itself, the guarantee of permanent full employment will make private investment much more attractive, once investors have got over their suspicions of the new procedure. The greater private investment will diminish the need for deficit spending.

Whether or not one agrees with the specifics of Lerner's argument, it clearly reflects a Lucas critique: Firms' expectations and investment behavior will shift if governments start following a Keynesian policy regime.

'Goodhart's law' – developed in response to the emerging monetarist emphasis on the targeting of monetary aggregates – is another prescient example. A brief general statement of the law says, "Any observed statistical regularity will tend to collapse once pressure is placed upon it for control purposes" (Goodhart 1975; reprinted in Goodhart 1981, p. 116).

Specifically, Goodhart argued that although the demand for money may have been relatively stable historically, this statistical regularity would collapse in a monetarist policy regime, a prediction that was proved right by subsequent experience. Outside economics, 'Campbell's law' expresses similar concerns: "The more any quantitative social indicator is used for social decision-making, the more subject it will be to corruption pressures and the more apt it will be to distort and corrupt the social processes it is intended to monitor" (Campbell 1976, p. 34).

These prior expressions of a Lucas critique do not invalidate Lucas's point. His article expressed the argument forcefully and with great precision, and it has justifiably become a classic. One can quibble with his wording: Are real-world decisions rules really optimal in the way he implies? The main problems, however, with Lucas's argument and the emerging research program that gradually took over economics stem not from the diagnosis but from the treatment.

The new research program identified preferences and technology as uniquely invariant to shifts in economic policy and other shocks to the environment in which agents operate. Hence, the problems associated with the Lucas critique could only be overcome by developing macroeconomic models that derived macroeconomic outcomes directly from explicit microeconomic optimization. Consumption and labor supply could and should be derived explicitly within the macroeconomic model as the outcome of intertemporal household optimization subject to budget constraints, with production decisions following from profit maximization subject to a production function. In this way, the response to changes in policy rules could be predicted accurately.

One caveat was added to this optimistic assessment: To make the prediction possible, it had to be assumed that agents have rational expectations: "Agents responses become predictable to outside observers only when there can be some confidence that agents and observers share a common view of the nature of the shocks which must be forecast by both" (Lucas 1976, p. 41). This is an extraordinary, categorical claim for the necessity of rational expectations. No rules of logic or principles of scientific methodology dictate that for an expert theorist to be able to predict the behavior of an agent, both must share identical information and expertise, resulting in the same view of world. The expert may need to know how the agent views the world, but there is no logical foundation for Lucas's claim that they must share the same view. And if the claim is not logically based, where is the supporting empirical evidence? Marketing firms, political consultants, and illusionists make a living precisely by exploiting their ability to predict and manipulate the behavior of people who have limited information and (in many cases) mistaken beliefs.

I shall return to questions of expectations in Chapter 3. For now, it is sufficient to note simply that assumptions about well-defined preferences and optimization are conceptually distinct from the rational expectations hypothesis. Informational limitations and mistaken beliefs by economic actors about the forces that determine future outcomes do not preclude well-defined preferences or a decision-making process that is consistent with these preferences and the decision-maker's beliefs.

Even if we disregard questions surrounding expectation formation, however, the microeconomic optimization approach faces an obvious obstacle. In practice, a macroeconomic model cannot include the explicit intertemporal optimization by myriad different individuals with different preferences and constraints. A model of this kind would become far too unwieldy. Without restrictions on the structure of preferences, endowments, and technologies, furthermore, a general model of this kind would also be virtually devoid of implications.

The solution, by necessity, has been to introduce a representative household. This intertemporally optimizing representative agent supposedly provides the robust, microeconomic foundation for the analysis. It is claimed, moreover, that the microfounded approach has an additional advantage: The utility function of the representative agent can serve as a solid basis for welfare analysis. Neither of these claims is sustainable. The Lucas critique is correct, but the contemporary approach to macroeconomics that has emerged along with it fails to solve the problem; the Lucas solution is deeply flawed.

2.3   The Representative Agent

2.3.1   The Sonnenschein–Debreu–Mantel Results

The representative agent's choices are meant to encapsulate the behavior of a large number of microeconomic decision-makers. The agent, therefore, must provide a meaningful representation of these decision-makers and their preferences; the construction of the agent, by necessity, involves aggregation. In the absence of strong arguments to show the possibility of such an aggregation, the assumed existence of a representative agent would be just that "an assumption." It would be an assumption, moreover, about the determinants of *aggregate* outcomes.

In fact, matters are worse: The implications of optimizing behavior at the microeconomic level *have* been examined extensively, and the results are unambiguous. Unless highly restrictive assumptions are imposed, well-behaved preferences at the microeconomic level do not produce aggregate outcomes that can be characterized as if they were the result of optimization by a single representative agent:

There is no plausible formal justification for the assumption that the aggregate of individuals, even maximizers, acts itself like an individual maximizer. Individual maximization does not engender collective rationality, nor does the fact that the collectivity exhibits a certain rationality necessarily imply that individuals act rationally. There is simply no direct relation between individual and collective behavior. (Kirman 1992, p. 118)

These results have been known since the work of Sonnenschein (1972), Debreu (1974), and Mantel (1976); the aggregation conditions are discussed in standard microeconomic textbooks like Mas-Colell et al. (1995).

An Example

The impossibility of describing aggregate outcomes as the result of optimization by a representative agent can be illustrated by a simple example. Consider an exchange economy with two types of agent, A and B; and two goods, q_1 and q_2. There is a large number (the same number, n) of each type of agent, and all agents are price takers. Both types of agents have preferences that can be described by a Stone–Geary utility function, with both types having the same minimum consumption needs, q_1^{min} and q_2^{min}, of the two goods.[3] The two types differ, however, with respect to initial endowments and the parameters in the utility function. Agents of type A have initial endowments $\bar{q}_1$ of good 1 and no initial endowment of good 2; in terms of preferences, they value good 1 more highly than good 2, once the minimum consumption needs have been met. Analogously, agents of type B have initial endowments $\bar{q}_2$ of good 2 and value good 2 more highly than good 1, once their minimum consumption needs for the two goods have been met. Formally, the utility functions for agents of type i ($i = A, B$) are given by

$$U^i(q_1, q_2) = \begin{cases} (q_1 - q_1^{min})^{\alpha_i}(q_2 - q_2^{min})^{1-\alpha_i} & \text{if } q_1 \geq q_1^{min}, q_2 \geq q_2^{min} \\ 0 & \text{otherwise} \end{cases}, \qquad (2.1)$$

with $\alpha_A > 0.5 > \alpha_B$.

The assumptions imply that after meeting their minimum consumption needs, type-A agents will spend most of their resources on good, 1 while type-B agents will spend most of their resources on good 2. The analysis becomes particularly simple if $\alpha_A = 1$ and $\alpha_B = 0$. In this limiting case, the utility functions simplify to

$$U^A(q_1, q_2) = \begin{cases} q_1 - q_1^{min} & \text{if } q_1 \geq q_1^{min}, q_2 \geq q_2^{min} \\ 0 & \text{otherwise} \end{cases} \qquad (2.2)$$

$$U^B(q_1, q_2) = \begin{cases} q_2 - q_2^{min} & \text{if } q_1 \geq q_1^{min}, q_2 \geq q_2^{min} \\ 0 & \text{otherwise} \end{cases}. \qquad (2.3)$$

Agents of type A spend all their remaining resources on good 1 after meeting their minimum consumption of good 2 (q_2^{min}). The value of their initial endowment is $p_1\bar{q}_1$, and the cost of covering the minimum consumption of good 2 is given by $p_2 q_2^{min}$. This leaves $p_1\bar{q}_1 - p_2 q_2^{min}$ to be spent on good 1. Thus, agent A has demands for goods 1 and 2 that are given by $q_1^A = \bar{q}_1 - \frac{p_2}{p_1}q_2^{min}$ and $q_2^A = q_2^{min}$. Analogously, agent B has demand functions that are given by $q_1^B = q_1^{min}$ and $q_2^B = \bar{q}_2 - \frac{p_1}{p_2}q_1^{min}$.

---

[3] The Stone–Geary utility function modifies the Cobb–Douglas version by introducing minimum levels of consumption that must met. Formally, a general version the Stone–Geary function can be written as

$$U = \prod_{i=1}^{n}(q_i - q_i^{min})^{\alpha_i}; \qquad q_i^{min} \geq 0, \alpha_i \geq 0.$$

Combining these results and noting that there are n agents of each type, the aggregate demand functions for goods 1 and 2 can be written as[4]

$$q_1^D(p_1,p_2) \;=\; n\left(\bar{q}_1 - \frac{q_2^{min}p_2}{p_1} + q_1^{min}\right) \tag{2.4}$$

$$q_2^D(p_1,p_2) \;=\; n\left(\bar{q}_2 - \frac{q_1^{min}p_1}{p_2} + q_2^{min}\right). \tag{2.5}$$

These aggregate demand functions have the property that

$$\frac{\partial q_1^D}{\partial(p_1/p_2)} \;>\; 0$$

$$\frac{\partial q_2^D}{\partial(p_2/p_1)} \;>\; 0.$$

Thus, an increase in the relative price of good i raises the demand for good i.

The aggregate demand structure in Equations (2.4)–(2.5) *cannot* be derived as the outcome of optimization by a representative agent: It violates the weak axiom of revealed preference. To see this, note that:

- The endowment of the representative agent is $(n\bar{q}_1, n\bar{q}_2)$.
- The representative agent faces a budget constraint that rotates around this endowment point as relative prices change. Let $\left(\frac{p_1}{p_2}\right)^*$ represent the market-clearing relative price (i.e. the value of $\frac{p_1}{p_2}$ for which $q_1^D = n\bar{q}_1$ and $q_2^D = n\bar{q}_2$, where q_1^D and q_2^D are given by (2.4) and (2.5), respectively).
- The representative agent chooses a consumption bundle on the budget constraint. Since $\frac{\partial q_1^D}{\partial(p_1/p_2)} > 0$, this bundle satisfies $q_1^D < n\bar{q}_1$ when $\frac{p_1}{p_2} < \left(\frac{p_1}{p_2}\right)^*$ and $q_1^D > n\bar{q}_1$ when $\frac{p_1}{p_2} > \left(\frac{p_1}{p_2}\right)^*$.

The outcome is illustrated in Figure 2.1. At the market clearing price ratio $\left(\frac{p_1}{p_2}\right)^*$, the composition of demand corresponds to the initial endowment at E^*. The bundle E_1 with $q_1^D < n\bar{q}_1$ is chosen when $\left(\frac{p_1}{p_2}\right) < \left(\frac{p_1}{p_2}\right)^*$, and the bundle E_2 with $q_1^D > n\bar{q}_1$ is chosen when $\left(\frac{p_1}{p_2}\right) > \left(\frac{p_1}{p_2}\right)^*$. Now observe that the point E_2 lies in the interior of the budget set when $\frac{p_1}{p_2} < \left(\frac{p_1}{p_2}\right)^*$. Thus, by revealed preference, E_1 is strictly preferred to E_2. The consumption bundle E_2, however, is chosen when $\frac{p_1}{p_2} > \left(\frac{p_1}{p_2}\right)^*$, that is, in a situation when E_1 is attainable. Hence, E_2 is preferred to E_1. In other words, the aggregate excess demand functions cannot be described by a representative agent with well-behaved preferences.

The nonexistence of a representative agent derives from the fact that changes in relative prices have both substitution and income effects: An increase in the relative

---

[4] The expressions in (2.4) and (2.5) assume that prices are such that $\bar{q}_1 - \frac{p_2}{p_1}q_2^{min} \geq q_1^{min}$ and $\bar{q}_2 - \frac{p_2}{p_1}q_1^{min} \geq q_2^{min}$. If these conditions fail to hold, then type-A or type-B agents will be unable to satisfy their minimum consumption needs.

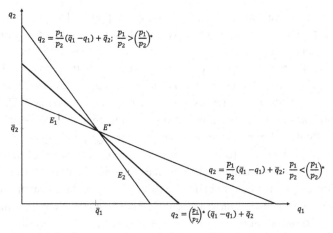

Figure 2.1 Budget constraints and choices of the representative agent.

price of good 1 raises the real income of agent A but reduces the income of agent B. The presence of income effects jeopardizes the existence of a representative agent. In the example, the 'benign' substitution effects are eliminated by having each agent value only one of the goods. This assumption implies that the income effects must dominate and, by giving the agent who values good i an endowment that contains only good i, a rise in the relative price of good i must increase the demand for this good. These stylized features are what make the example so simple. But income effects of changes in relative price are ubiquitous – bakers benefit if the price of bread goes up, while debtors lose from rising interest rates. The qualitative conclusion, therefore, is quite robust: As shown by Debreu, Sonnenschein, and Mantel, highly restrictive assumptions are needed to ensure the existence of a representative agent. In short, it is impossible to defend the representative-agent approach on methodological grounds as the uniquely sound approach to macroeconomic modeling.

2.3.2 A Pragmatic Defense?

The restrictiveness of the assumptions behind the representative agent is typically glossed over or completely ignored in the macroeconomic literature. Acemoglu (2009) is an exception. He considers the aggregation issue explicitly, acknowledges the Sonnenschein–Debreu–Mantel results, and stresses the need for restrictive assumptions to allow aggregation. But having stated the general results from the microeconomic literature, he goes on to suggest that the situation may not be as hopeless as these results suggest because "approximately realistic preference functions, as well as restrictions on the distribution of income across households, enable us to rule out arbitrary aggregate excess demand functions (p. 151)."

Acemoglu's claim is potentially very powerful. All theories simplify, and models built around an optimizing representative agent could be justified if a case can be made for the approximate realism of the underlying assumptions. The ensuing argument, however, fails to deliver. Acemoglu merely describes the 'Gorman aggregation theorem' and then shows that some commonly used specifications in the macroeconomic literature satisfy the required conditions: Utility functions with a constant elasticity of substitution (CES) satisfy the Gorman conditions, and aggregation becomes possible if *all* agents have *identical* preferences, and these preferences take the *CES form.*

Aggregation into a single consumption good is common in macroeconomic models, whether of a DSGE or Keynesian variety. The crucial aggregation question, therefore, concerns the preferences with respect to the intertemporal allocation of spending: The representative agent in the DSGE setting makes a choice over the trajectory of consumption. Consumption goods are identified by the timing of the consumption, and the constant elasticity of substitution in the static case becomes the constant intertemporal elasticity of substitution (CIES) in this dynamic setting. Analogously to the static case, a representative household exists if the dynamic model has a constant number of households and these households have identical preferences of the CIES type.[5]

Formally, assume that individual households maximize a time-additive intertemporal utility function

$$U^i = \sum_{0}^{T_i} (1 + \rho)^{-t} u(c_{it}),$$ (2.6)

where c_{it} and T_i are the household's consumption in period t and the household's horizon, respectively.[6] All households have the same discount rate ρ and per-period utility function $u(.)$, and the per-period utility function takes the CIES form, $u(c_{it}) = (c_{it}^{1-\theta} - 1)/(1 - \theta); \theta \geq 0$. Capital markets are perfect, and the household can borrow and lend at the interest rate r. Under these conditions, the household's optimal consumption path satisfies the Euler condition

$$\frac{c_{it+1}}{c_{it}} = \left(\frac{1 + r}{1 + \rho}\right)^{1/\theta}.$$ (2.7)

It follows that the household's consumption will be increasing (constant, decreasing) if $r > \rho$ $(r = \rho, r < \rho)$.

In this example with identical, homothetic utility functions, the growth rate of aggregate consumption will satisfy the same Euler condition if the time horizon is infinite and there is a constant number of households (Appendix A outlines the basic analysis using a continuous-time setting). Economists often assume that these conditions are met, and that each household can be viewed as an infinitely lived, altruistic dynasty (or more commonly, it is simply assumed that aggregate behavior can be described by an infinitely lived representative consumer with CIES preferences). But the widespread acceptance of these assumptions establishes neither their realism

---

[5] The two goods in the example in Section 2.3.1 can be interpreted as describing consumption in two different periods.

[6] For simplicity, all households have the same size, the size remains constant over time, and household consumption is proportional to consumption per household member,

nor the robustness of conclusions derived from models that impose the assumptions. *A priori* there are reasons to be skeptical, and it will be worthwhile to review the assumptions underlying such claims.

Finite Lives

If the infinite horizon is abandoned, the close link between micro and macro is severed: The profile of aggregate consumption can be quite different from the consumption profiles of individual households.

The OLG model in Diamond (1965) incorporates a special case of Equations (2.6) and (2.7) in which all households live for two periods. Each household is endowed with one unit of labor. The household works in the first period, lives off its savings in the second period, and has a consumption profile that satisfies the Euler condition (2.7). Assuming, that the total population, N, is constant, $N/2$ agents die and $N/2$ new agents take their place in each period. The growth rate of aggregate consumption, therefore, does not follow the Euler equation. By assumption, the demographic composition of the population is constant; there is always exactly $N/2$ agents in a cohort, and (in the absence of productivity growth) aggregate consumption will be constant in steady growth. *The profiles of aggregate and individual consumption are determined by different mechanisms and will not respond in the same way to shocks.* A tax on capital, for instance, will reduce the after-tax rate of return, with effects on the consumption profiles of individual households and aggregate consumption that can be qualitatively different, both in the short and the long run (see Appendix B for details).

These implications of OLG models can be contrasted with those for a Ramsey model where households have infinite horizons.[7] Like in the OLG model, the Ramsey model without population growth implies that in steady-growth aggregate consumption must grow at the rate of labor saving technical change. Unlike in the OLG model, however, the aggregate consumption profile coincides with the consumption profile of the representative household; the steady-growth solution for the after-tax rate of return is equal to the discount rate and completely independent of the tax rate in the Ramsey model.

The Diamond model illustrates that even if all households are perfectly rational and have identical preferences, the time profiles of individual consumption bear no necessary relation to the profile of aggregate consumption. This qualitative result from the model applies more generally when lives are finite and perfect intergenerational altruism is absent.[8] Finite lives represent a basic human condition and although altruism exists, most households enter retirement with limited resources. Those that leave significant bequests may do so for 'strategic' reasons or because of 'warm glow'

---

[7] Ramsey (1928) analyzed optimization over an infinite horizon. Unlike in contemporary 'Ramsey models,' however, he viewed the analysis as purely normative and rejected discounting as ethically indefensible.

[8] It is possible to preserve a simple Euler condition for aggregate consumption in 'perpetual youth' versions of OLG models without bequests (Blanchard 1985). But logical possibility does not imply real-world relevance.

effects, rather than because of the kind of infinite-horizon optimization that characterizes the representative agent (e.g., Andreoni 1989, Bernheim et al. 1985, Wilhelm 1996).

Infinite Horizons but Different Utility Functions

Preferences differ, and not all households have the same utility function. Some households may be more patient than others and have a lower discount rate. The consumption profiles, therefore, will be different, and aggregate consumption increases, at least in the short run, if resources are transferred from patient to impatient households. In long-run steady growth, however, the share of capital owned by the most patient household (and hence also the most patient household's share of total saving) converges to one.[9] Thus, it would appear that the profile of aggregate consumption in steady growth will follow the Euler equation of the most patient household.[10]

Two-agent new Keynesian (TANK) models have this property. Some household dynasties are optimizers, while others (hand-to-mouth households) spend all their current income on consumption. In these models, the optimizers satisfy an Euler equation, and the same Euler equation describes the dynamics of aggregate consumption in steady growth.

Perhaps surprisingly, this setup has a close similarity with Marxian two-class models in which workers spend all income on consumption, while capitalists save and invest. Most mainstream economists would, I suspect, question this division of households into two distinct classes, capitalists, and workers. But why then accept this same permanent division of households, just because the labels have changed? Is it reasonable to divide households into distinct dynasties with permanently different utility functions and discount rates?

Contemporary macroeconomic models have added bells and whistles in the form of explicit optimization but operates with the same division of households into permanent groups with different saving behavior. If this fiction is rejected, the shares of capital owned by different households will not be constant, and the Euler equation of the most patient households no longer describes the dynamics of aggregate consumption in the long run: Ultra–long-run steady-growth paths in which the most patient dynasties own all wealth become irrelevant. I shall return to these issues in Section 4.1.

Infinite Horizons with Life-Cycle Patterns

Even if households behave as infinitely lived dynasties and even if they are identical, each generation of a household dynasty presumably goes through a life cycle.

---

[9] If impatient households are allowed to borrow on a perfect capital market, their shares of consumption and income will also go to zero as they become increasingly indebted to patient households.

[10] The output capital ratio and the share of consumption in income are constant, and the growth rate of capital equals the growth rate of saving in steady growth. Thus, if the share of household i in total saving converges to one, we have

$$\hat{C} = \hat{Y} = \hat{K} = \hat{S} = \hat{S}_i = \hat{C}_i.$$

As emphasized by the life-cycle hypothesis, this affects the optimal consumption trajectory: The utility associated with a particular amount of consumption – and the elasticity of the utility with respect to changes in consumption – is likely to depend on the composition of the household, which will vary over the life cycle. These differences in household composition compromise the aggregation of household behavior.

As a simple example, assume that an individual goes through three stages: Childhood, youth, and old age. Generations overlap, and children are born at the end of the period in which the parents are young. Thus, each dynasty alternates between periods in which the household consists of one child and one old person, (state A) and periods in which the household consists of one youth (state B). The per-period utility function may have the constant elasticity form in any given period, but the value of the parameter is likely to be different, depending on the composition of the household.

For simplicity, let

$$u(c) = \begin{cases} \frac{c^{1-\theta_1}-1}{1-\theta_1}, & \text{with } \theta_1 \text{ being 'small' in state A} \\ \frac{c^{1-\theta_2}-1}{1-\theta_2}, & \text{with } \theta_2 \text{ being 'very large' in state B.} \end{cases}$$

In the extreme case in which $\theta_2 \to \infty$, an increase in the wealth of the household will be used entirely to raise the household's consumption when it is in state A.[11] Assume that in any given period, half of the dynasties in the economy are in state A, and the other half are in state B; thus, the aggregate population and the composition of the population are constant. Now consider a transfer of wealth from the group of dynasties that are currently in state B to those that are currently in state A.[12] If real rates of interest (the relative prices of consumption in different periods) are constant, the dynasties that are currently in state A will want to increase their current consumption (but leave the consumption unchanged, in those future periods in which they will be in state B); the state B dynasties, on the other hand, will not want to change their current consumption (but will reduce their consumption in those future periods in which they are in state A). Aggregate wealth is unchanged, but the redistribution affects the trajectory of aggregate consumption (for any given trajectory of interest rates). In other words, aggregate consumption cannot be described as the outcome of optimization by a representative agent whose budget constraint is defined by prices and aggregate wealth.

---

[11] In the limiting case when $\theta_2 \to \infty$, the utility function $u(c) = (c^{1-\theta_2} - 1)/(1 - \theta_2)$ converges to

$$u(c) = \begin{cases} 0, & \text{for } c \geq 1 \\ -\infty, & \text{for } c < 1. \end{cases}$$

[12] Households in different states will typically have different levels of wealth and different portfolio compositions. The capitalized effects of unanticipated changes in tax structures, for instance, could produce relative wealth effects of this kind.

This last example may seem contrived. But although less important than the issues surrounding finite horizons and heterogeneity, it illustrates a general point: A household dynasty is unlikely to have the same instantaneous utility function in all periods unless the composition of the dynasty remains constant over time. For that to be the case, the dynasty – the decision-making unit – not only has to have an infinite horizon, it also must be very large because otherwise the demographic composition of the dynasty will undergo fluctuations. The demographic household composition must mirror the aggregate composition.

Empirical Evidence

Acemoglu fails to provide evidence of any kind that specifications satisfying the Gorman conditions are "approximately realistic" or, alternatively, to show that aggregate models in the representative-agent tradition perform well empirically. This failure does not in itself prove that he is wrong. It is logically possible that, in practice, models based on infinitely lived, optimizing representative households could perform well and produce a better, more robust understanding of aggregate consumption than any existing alternatives. But direct appeals to the approximate realism of the assumptions underlying the representative agent look heroic: The aggregation conditions discussed above are very restrictive, and the microeconomic evidence shows significant departures from optimizing behavior (see Chapter 3).

Purely instrumentalist claims that – despite its unrealistic assumptions – the model has successfully accounted for aggregate consumption also lack support: The Euler equations do not perform well empirically. A large body of literature has shown that predictable changes in income produce predictable changes in consumption. Campbell and Mankiw (1989) is among the papers that document this 'excess sensitivity' of consumption to predictable changes in income using aggregate data; Shea (1995) and Parker et al. (2013) reach similar conclusions using household data. These empirical findings are at odds with the behavior prescribed by the Euler equation.

Canzoneri et al. (2007) approach the issue slightly differently. The observed time path of consumption can be used to derive a path of 'Euler interest rates,' that is, a path of interest rates that would satisfy the Euler equation, given the observed trajectory of consumption. These Euler rates, it turns out, are negatively correlated with actual money market interest rate. Monetary contractions and a rise in money market interest rates typically produce a reduction in the growth rate of consumption for several quarters, an outcome that is inconsistent with the Euler equation: An increase in the interest rate should raise the growth rate of consumption.

If the empirical evidence fails, one may try to fall back on a methodological defense. In the words of Blanchard (2018a, p. 45), the Euler equation gives a "badly flawed" description of reality, and its implications "are strongly at odds with the empirical evidence." Having effectively rejected the pragmatic, empiricist defense, however, Blanchard goes on to claim a superiority for DSGE models on the basis that, starting from explicit microfoundations, these models "make the right basic strategic choices."

The methodological defense brings us full circle: Having failed empirically, the models are defended by a scholastic demand that any proper macroeconomic model must be supported by microeconomic foundations rooted in a peculiar and strict form of rationality and highly restrictive aggregation conditions.

Clearly, macroeconomic equations should not be specified without serious consideration of the microeconomic behavior that is reflected in the equations. Blanchard's statement, however, appears to conflate this reasonable requirement with the specific DSGE approach. Paradoxically, aggregate-level Euler equations, which cannot be justified by micro-level optimization, are considered microfounded, while old-Keynesian consumption functions, including versions based on the life-cycle hypothesis and explicit aggregation, are faulted for their lack of microeconomic foundations.

2.4   Welfare and Inequality

2.4.1   The Representative-Agent Approach

Economic policy generally benefits some people, while others are hurt. Pareto rankings of the outcomes become impossible when this is the case. Instead, policy decisions have to be based on social welfare evaluations that make (implicit or explicit) interpersonal comparisons, weighing up costs and benefits so as to arrive at a net result.[13]

The utility function of the representative agent, it has been argued, can be used as a social welfare function. Indeed, this possibility has been seen as a distinctive advantage of the representative-agent approach. Woodford (2003, p. 12; emphasis added) suggests that the utility function of the representative agent "provides a *natural objective* in terms of which alternative policies should be evaluated," while, according to Blanchard (2008, p. 9, emphasis added), contemporary macro models with formal optimization enable one "to derive optimal policy based on the *correct* (within the model) welfare criterion." Most tellingly, perhaps, the welfare evaluations based on the stipulated utility function of the representative agent are usually presented without any argument or caveat.

The literature on climate change represents an exception in this respect. The representative agent is at the heart of the integrated assessment models (IAMs) pioneered by Nordhaus (1994). The Stern Review (Stern 2006) also included a representative agent but, departing from the standard practice, Stern adopted a prescriptive approach, arguing that on ethical grounds the pure discount rate in the welfare function should be close to zero.[14] Nordhaus (2008) challenged this argument and – in line with most other studies – advocated a 'descriptive' approach in which the welfare function of the representative agent has to be calibrated to fit empirical observations. This

---

[13] Even when applicable, the Pareto criterion is extremely weak. Allocating all resources to one agent may be Pareto efficient, but would anyone consider this distributional change irrelevant for an evalution of social welfare?

[14] This approach is in line with Ramsey's (1928) analysis.

approach, Nordhaus argues, "does not make a case for the social desirability of the distribution of incomes over space or time under existing conditions." Instead, using the descriptive approach, "Calculations of changes in world welfare arising from efficient climate-change policies examine potential improvements within the context of the existing distribution of income and investments across space and time" (Nordhaus 2008, pp. 174–175).

Assuming that aggregate outcomes can be described consistently by a representative agent, the use of this agent's preferences to measure social welfare has the appearance of neutrality and objectivity. The analyst does not impose her own preferences but merely takes as given the revealed preferences of the population as a whole. Martin Weitzman makes this argument explicitly. Like Nordhaus, he rejects the prescriptive approach of the Stern Review, arguing that

economists understand the difference between their own personal preferences for apples over oranges and the preferences of others for apples over oranges. Inferring society's revealed preference ... is not an easy task in any event ... but at least a good-faith effort at such an inference might have gone some way towards convincing the public that the economists doing the studies are not drawing conclusions primarily from imposing their own value judgments on the rest of the world. (Weitzman 2007, p. 712)

According to Weitzman, Nordhaus's "careful pragmatic modeling throughout his DICE series of IAMs has long set the standard in this area" (p. 713).[15,16]

2.4.2 An Intrinsic Distributional Bias

These claims for the representative agent are puzzling. Although widespread and well-established in the profession, there is nothing objective about the representative-agent approach to welfare analysis. On the contrary, there is no justification for the implicit claim that the same function which describes the representative agent can do double duty as a measure of social welfare. This again, should be well known. As pointed out by Mas-Colell et al. (1995, pp. 121–122), "the existence of preferences that explain behavior is not enough to attach to them any welfare significance. For the latter, it is also necessary that these preferences exist for the right reasons."

For reasons that are both simple and intuitive, the descriptive representative agent has a built-in distributional bias: The representative agent is designed to explain average behavior and, loosely speaking, in order to fit market outcomes, this average must be determined using the economic resources of individual agents as weights. Because a rich agent influences aggregate consumption patterns more strongly than a poor agent, *the preferences of the rich agent will inevitably be given greater weight in the*

---

[15] Despite his endorsement of Nordhaus's descriptive approach, Weitzman's conclusions are similar to those of Stern: His analysis of risk and the possibility of catastrophic change generates conclusions that are in line with those in the Stern report. In Weitzman's words, the Stern report may have been "right for the wrong reasons" (2007, p. 724).

[16] Broome (2012) presents an interesting analysis of ethical issues relating to discounting and climate change.

construction of the representative agent. It follows that the rich will also be given greater weight in the evaluation of social welfare if the utility function of the representative agent is used as the welfare criterion. This conclusion applies to the climate literature (where the biases can affect the abatement recommendations) as well as to other macroeconomic policy analysis.

An Example

As shown in Section 2.3, well-behaved preferences at the micro level do not imply that aggregate outcomes must behave as if they were generated by an optimizing representative agent. One can, however, create special cases in which the outcomes can be generated in this way; these are clearly the cases that are most favorable to the representative-agent approach to welfare analysis.

Consider an economy with two goods and two types of agents: Type-A agents who value only good 1 and type-B agents who value only good 2. Formally, the preferences of the two types can be represented by the utility functions $U^A = u(q_1^A)$ and $U^B = u(q_2^B)$, where $u' > 0$. These preferences imply that type-A agents will spend all their resources on good 1 and type-B agents will spend all their resources on good 2. Thus, the aggregate nominal demand for goods 1 and 2 ($p_1 q_1^D$ and $p_2 q_2^D$) will be equal to the aggregate nominal income of the A agents, Y^A, and the nominal income of the B-types, Y^B, respectively. There are n agents of each type and the aggregate endowments of the two goods are $n\bar{q}_1$ and $n\bar{q}_2$. Type-A agents are richer than type-B agents, but, unlike in Section 2.3, all agents in this example have the same endowment compositions; the endowments of the type-A agents are larger, however, with respect to both goods 1 and 2. Formally, $(\bar{q}_1^A, \bar{q}_2^A) = \lambda(\bar{q}_1^B, \bar{q}_2^B)$, with $\lambda > 1$. Because the composition of the endowment is the same, changes in relative prices have no distributional effects (which allows the construction of a representative agent): For all values of the prices p_1 and p_2, we have

$$Y^A = n\left(p_1\bar{q}_1^A + p_2\bar{q}_2^A\right) = \lambda n\left(p_1\bar{q}_1^B + p_2\bar{q}_2^B\right) = \lambda Y^B$$

or

$$Y^A = \alpha Y,$$

where $Y = Y^A + Y^B$ is the aggregate income and $\alpha = \lambda/(1 + \lambda) > 0.5$ is the share of A agents in total income.

The assumptions about preferences and endowments imply that the share of good 1 in total expenditure is equal to A agents' share of total income (= their share in endowments). Thus, the pattern of aggregate demands can be derived from the maximization of a Cobb–Douglas utility function

$$U = q_1^\alpha q_2^{1-\alpha} \tag{2.8}$$

subject to the aggregate budget constraint $p_1 q_1 + p_2 q_2 = p_1\bar{q}_1 + p_2\bar{q}_2$. It follows that Equation (2.8) can be used to describe the preferences of a representative agent for this economy.

Assume that initially $\bar{q}_1 = \bar{q}_2 = \bar{q}$ and that a choice now has to be made. There are two options: The original endowment bundle $(\bar{q},\bar{q})$ can be increased to either $(\bar{q}+\Delta,\bar{q})$ or $(\bar{q},\bar{q} + \Delta)$. Which option should we choose? Using the utility function (2.8) as the yardstick, the change in welfare from the first option is given by

$$dU = \alpha \left(\frac{\bar{q}_2}{\bar{q}_1} \right)^{1-\alpha} \Delta = \alpha\Delta. \tag{2.9}$$

The second option gives the welfare gain

$$dU = (1 - \alpha) \left(\frac{\bar{q}_1}{\bar{q}_2} \right)^{\alpha} \Delta = (1 - \alpha)\Delta. \tag{2.10}$$

Hence, the analyst must conclude in favor of the first option if, as assumed, A agents are richer than B agents. The resulting increase in the aggregate endowment of good 1 will have no effect on the welfare of the poor B agents; all benefits will go to the rich A-types. The composition of the endowments is still the same for the two types, the distribution of income will be unchanged, and both types seemingly benefit from a rise in their endowment. But the rich A-types experience a decline in the relative price of their consumption good, which enables them to buy the entire increase Δ and reap the full benefit. Putting it differently, representative-agent evaluations will give different conclusions if we apply them to two economies in which A agents are richer than B agents in one economy, while type-B agents are richer than type-A agents in the other economy. The analyst will recommend the policy that favors type-A agents in the economy with rich type-A agents but reject the policy when type-A agents are poor.[17]

Acemoglu's (2009) analysis of the 'normative representative agent' glosses over these issues. His theorem 5.3 on the existence of a normative representative agent states that – assuming Gorman preferences and the existence of a descriptive representative agent – "any feasible allocation that maximizes the utility of the representative household ... is Pareto optimal" (p. 154). This is correct. The outcome in the above example does not violate Pareto optimality. But maximizing the utility of the representative agent has selected a Pareto optimal allocation that benefits those with large initial endowments. And had the two policy options been to increase q_1 by one unit at the cost of reducing q_2 by one unit or, alternatively, to increase q_2 at the cost of reducing q_1, the representative agent would still have chosen the option that favors the rich. The allocation after the implementation would be Pareto optimal, but the change would not have been Pareto improving in this case.

The example was deliberately kept extremely simple. Empirically, the consumption sets of the rich and the poor are not completely disjoint; some goods are valued by all agents. As shown in Appendix C, adding a third good that is valued by all agents does

---

[17] The example is related to Proposition 4.D.1 in Mas-Colell et al. (1995), which states that if wealth is allocated appropriately, a utilitarian social optimum may be achieved by maximizing the utility of the representative consumer. If wealth is not allocated in this way, the preferences of the representative consumer carry no necessary implications for social welfare.

not materially affect the conclusion. The representative agent must – to be descriptively successful – give extra weight to the preferences of the rich. But the introduction of a third good circumvents an odd aspect of the two-good example in which the welfare of the two types of agent depends only on the composition of the endowment bundles; the initial distribution of the bundles is irrelevant. In the three-good case, the distribution of the bundles affects the welfare of the agents.

The absence of intertemporal aspects may seem to limit the relevance of the example. But the representative agent's per-period utility function involves static aggregation of individual households' preferences over multiple goods into a simple representative utility function defined over a single composite good. Furthermore, if the discount rate of the representative agent reflects the preferences of the most patient household dynasty (cf. p. 28), then by construction no other households influence this key element of a welfare criterion that was supposedly neutral and objective. Or consider the case when current households do not behave as altruistic dynasties with infinite horizons. An intertemporally optimizing representative agent calibrated to match observed outcomes now gives no voice to future generations.

2.4.3 Discussion

There are no objective, value-free answers to normative questions, including those that involve distributional conflicts. Any attempt to derive an 'optimal' outcome is contingent on some underlying – implicit or explicit – value judgment. The descriptive representative-agent approach tries to avoid judgments of this kind. But not wanting to take sides leads to a *de facto* siding with the rich. Under the guise of neutrality and objectivity, the representative-agent approach provides policy recommendations that favor the rich.

Evaluating policy based on the preferences of the representative agent is closely related to evaluations based on prices and GDP.[18] Take a simple example, and imagine that R&D funds can be directed to one of two projects: One that treats a disease that typically affects the poor (at a world level, many infectious and parasitic diseases fall into this category) and the other a disease that predominantly affects the rich (cancer, for instance).[19] The poor cannot pay for a treatment, and profitability criteria will tend to favor the project that benefit the rich. This bias of market-based allocation is well known. But a welfare function based on a descriptive representative agent would reach the same conclusion. As another example, take a country like Bolivia: Based on a GDP criterion and given the inequality that prevailed in 2000, a policy that raised the income of the top 10 percent by 0.5 percent would have seemed preferable to one

---

[18] Prices reflect purchasing power, and the biases associated with the representative agent are similar to those that arise in cost-benefit analysis. See Ackerman and Heinzerling (2005), Baum (2009), Sen (2000), Stanton (2010), and Stern (2006) for recent discussions with reference to climate change.

[19] Stevens (2004) provides data on the prevalence of different diseases across income levels.

that doubled the incomes of the bottom 10 percent.[20] In terms of the formal analysis in Subsection 2.4.2, an increase in the income of the rich maps into an increase in the supply and consumption of luxury goods and an increase in the income of the poor into an increase in basic goods. Choosing appropriate units, the increases in the quantities of luxury and basic goods may be the same, but the rich are able and willing to pay much more for one unit of the luxury good than the poor can pay for an extra unit of the basic good.

Our current measure of GDP has many weaknesses, but the weaknesses are not primarily related to welfare: GDP was not designed as a measure of welfare and should not be used as such. As a simple analogy, doctors may want to know your temperature and blood pressure but don't aim to maximize either. Policymakers and economists likewise need information to conduct macroeconomic policy, and GDP is one of many useful – even if imperfect – diagnostic tools. It becomes a serious problem, however, if policymakers and others start believing that GDP is a good measure of welfare. Other simple performance indicators like the Human Development Index, the multidimensional indicators considered by the Sarkozy commission (www.stiglitz-sen-fitoussi.fr/en/index.htm), or the measure presented in Jones and Klenow (2016) may be interesting. But the limitations of GDP as a measure of economic performance do not imply that measures of GDP should be discarded. The usefulness of the representative agent, by contrast, is highly questionable.

2.5   A Lucas Critique of the Lucas Solution

The intuition behind the results in Section 2.4 is simple: If we want a representative agent to describe the average outcome in the economy, this agent must weigh the preferences of the rich more heavily than the preferences of the poor. It is the rich who have the ability to influence market outcomes.

Disregarding the implications for welfare analysis, this conclusion has an important corollary: The definition of the representative agent will be contingent on the distribution of income. In order to describe aggregate outcomes, shifts in income distribution may require a respecification of the preferences of the representative agent. This implication is deeply ironic. The microeconomic foundations for macroeconomics were needed, Lucas argued, because the preferences of individual agents could be taken as invariant to changes in economic policy. This claim is questionable with respect to the micro-level preferences but, even if it were true at the microeconomic level, the invariance property would not carry over to the representative agent. Real-world policies invariably have distributional consequences, and it follows that contemporary macroeconomics is itself subject to a Lucas critique: The preferences of the representative agent are not structurally invariant.

---

[20] The income share of the top 10 percent was 49 percent and the income share of the bottom 10 percent was only 0.13 percent, according to data from the World Bank, Development Research Group (http://data.worldbank.org/country/bolivia).

Is this point empirically significant for most macroeconomic issues? As with the original Lucas critique of traditional Keynesian models, the answer will depend on the details of the policy change and the issues that are being examined. But the effects on the representative agent can be important: Changes in income distribution can affect aggregate consumption, even if aggregate disposable income and the interest rate are unchanged. Income inequality has increased dramatically over the last 40 years in many economies, including the United States, and *a priori* there is no reason to dismiss the significance of distributional changes and the macroeconomic effects of these changes.

The exceptionally large distributional shifts that have taken place in the United States have emerged in the context of economic policies and institutional changes, including falling minimum wages, declining unionization, financial deregulation, and tax reforms (see Chapter 7). For many purposes, however, it is not critical whether the distributional changes have occurred for reasons that can be related to specific institutions and policies. Even if rising inequality could be explained entirely by technological forces or by the 'great doubling' of the world labor market (Freeman 2007), it would still require a recalibration of the representative agent. Income distribution, moreover, is not the only factor that can influence the representative agent. Demographic changes or generational differences in behavioral norms and attitudes also affect aggregate consumption.[21] Some of these changes may be relatively slow, but that does not make them irrelevant for a literature that has championed the Ramsey model with its representative household as the core of economic growth theory and views the economy as fluctuating around a long-run steady-growth path defined by the representative agent's utility function.

2.6 Conclusion

Pragmatic claims for the empirical superiority of the DSGE approach must show that the restrictive assumptions that could justify the approach happen to be met – at least approximately – in real-world capitalist economies. Alternatively, adopting an instrumentalist perspective, it must be shown that aggregate variables happen to behave 'as if' they were generated by a maximizing representative agent. There is no reason to believe, however, that the problems of aggregation are negligible and that in practice the Euler equation provides a good description of aggregate consumption behavior. And, in fact, the empirical performance of the Euler equation has been poor; *ad hoc* adjustments and exogenous shocks have been introduced in DSGE models to improve the fit.

Given these empirical weaknesses, the defense of microeconomic foundations and the general DSGE approach typically relies on theoretical claims. Wren-Lewis (2007, pp. 47–48), for instance, explicitly suggests that "econometric consistency is not essential (and can be 'handled' via ad hoc, non-core relationships)," but that "internal

---

[21] The sociological literature points to significant generational differences (e.g., Twenge et al. 2010, Twenge et al. 2012).

consistency is vital because only then can we be sure that relationships are consistent with the axioms of microeconomic theory." A more strident defense has been offered by Chari (2010) who comments "that any interesting model must be a dynamic stochastic general equilibrium model. From this perspective, there is no other game in town."

Christiano et al. (2017) echoed this TINA defense ("there is no alternative," as Margaret Thatcher used to say). Formal models are needed to evaluate different policies, and this need for formal theory has implications, they suggest[22]:

People who don't like dynamic stochastic general equilibrium (DSGE) models are dilettantes. By this we mean they aren't serious about policy analysis. ... Dilettantes who only point to the existence of competing forces at work – and informally judge their relative importance via implicit thought experiments – can never give serious policy advice.

This kind of intellectual bullying is laughable. Yes, formal models are immensely useful. But how does that establish the DSGE approach as the only option? The claim that macroeconomic models *must* follow this approach is plainly absurd.

A defense of the contemporary DSGE approach on purely methodological grounds is unsustainable. The Lucas *critique* is valid, but the suggested *solution* is unconvincing. Representative agents are not microeconomic decision-makers, and there is no justification for the belief that aggregate outcomes can be described as if they were generated by the maximizing behavior of a representative agent. Even in cases where a descriptive representative agent can be defined, the preferences of this representative agent are contingent on the distribution of income and therefore subject to a Lucas critique. Moreover, the preferences of the representative agent cannot be taken as a neutral social welfare criterion: To be descriptive of actual market outcomes, a representative agent has to give the highest weight to those who spend the most.

Appendix A: A Baseline Ramsey Model of Infinite-Horizon Optimization in Continuous Time

Consider an economy with production function $Y = F(K, AL)$. There are constant returns to scale, and the technology can be represented in intensive form:

$$y = f(k); \qquad f' > 0,$$

where $y = Y/AL$ and $k = K/AL$ denote the output and capital per unit of effective labor, respectively. The rate of labor augmenting technical change is constant, $\hat{A} = a$.

The economy is populated by a constant number of household dynasties, with the size of each dynasty growing at a constant rate n. There is full employment, and labor is supplied inelastically. The dynasties optimize over an infinite horizon; all have the same discount rate ρ and the same per-period CIES utility function: Household utility

---

[22] The final version of the paper Christiano et al. (2018) omits this paragraph. The substance of their TINA claim is unchanged, however, as is the presumptive disrespect for any alternative view.

at time t is

$$u(t) = \frac{[e^{at} c(t)]^{1-\theta}}{1 - \theta} e^{nt}; \qquad \theta \geq 0,$$

where $c(t)$ is consumption per effective unit of labor.[23] Household wealth per effective unit of labor (Ω) follows the dynamic equation

$$\dot{\Omega} = w + r\Omega - c - (n + a)\Omega,$$

where w and r are the wage per effective unit of labor and the rate of return on wealth, respectively.

With these assumptions, each household solves the following optimization problem:

$$\max_c \int e^{-\rho t} \frac{[e^{at} c]^{1-\theta}}{1-\theta} e^{nt} \, dt$$

$$st. \dot{\Omega} = w + r\Omega - c - (n + a)\Omega.$$

The first-order conditions for a maximum require that the following Euler equation be met:

$$\hat{c} = \frac{1}{\theta}(r - \rho) - a.$$

All households satisfy this same condition. Thus, the trajectory of aggregate consumption $- C = ce^{(n+a)t} -$ grows at the rate

$$\hat{C} = \hat{c} + n + a = n + \frac{1}{\theta}(r - \rho).$$

Like household consumption, aggregate consumption can be described by a simple Euler equation: Its growth rate depends on the difference between the rate of return (r) and the discount rate (ρ). In equilibrium, moreover, aggregate wealth is equal to the aggregate capital stock, while the rate of return is equal to the marginal product of capital net of depreciation: $\Omega = k, r = f'(k) - \delta$.

Appendix B: Individual and Aggregate Consumption in an OLG Model

Consider a Diamond OLG model with a constant population N. Assume that wealth is taxed at the rate τ and that the tax revenue is distributed as lump-sum payments (s) to the young generation. The utility function is logarithmic, and the production function is Cobb–Douglas with exogenous technical progress at the rate α.

A young household maximizes

$$U = \log c_1 + \frac{1}{1 + \rho} \log c_2,$$

subject to the budget constraint

$$c_2 = (1 - \tau)(1 + r)(w + s - c_1). \tag{2.11}$$

---

[23] The variables y, k, and c all vary over time. In subsequent expressions the explicit indication of this dependence on time will be omitted for reasons of notational simplicity.

The first-order conditions for his maximization problem imply that

$$\frac{c_2}{c_1} = \frac{(1-\tau)(1+r)}{1+\rho} \tag{2.12}$$

$$c_1 = \frac{1+\rho}{2+\rho}(w+s). \tag{2.13}$$

Combining Equations (2.11) and (2.13), the household's consumption in the first period is given by

$$c_1 = \frac{1+\rho}{2+\rho}(w+s). \tag{2.14}$$

Hence,

$$w + s - c_1 = \frac{1}{2+\rho}(w+s).$$

Assuming a Cobb–Douglas production function, $Y = K^\alpha L^{1-\alpha}$, and perfect competition, the wage is equal to

$$w = (1-\alpha)k^\alpha,$$

where k is the capital labor ratio ($k = K/L$). If the labor force (population) is constant, the lump-sum payment to a young household in period t is simply $s = \tau k$, and the movements in k are described by a first-order difference equation:

$$k_{t+1} = (w_t + s_t - c_{1t})$$
$$\frac{1}{2+\rho}[(1-\alpha)k_t^\alpha + \tau k]. \tag{2.15}$$

From Equation (2.15), it follows that an increase in the tax rate τ raises the growth rate of the aggregate capital stock. Total consumption is proportional to $(1-\alpha)k_t^\alpha + \tau k t$; to see this, use Equations (2.12)–(2.14) – and the growth rate of aggregate consumption also increases along the trajectory toward a new stationary solution in which both aggregate consumption and aggregate capital are constant. But the profile of individual household's consumption changes in the opposite direction: An increase in the tax rate on wealth reduces the growth rate of an individual household's consumption (use Equation (2.12) and the fact that r depends inversely on k).

As a limiting case of the Cobb–Douglas production function, let $Y = AK$ (corresponding to $Y = K^\alpha(AL)^{1-\alpha}$, with $\alpha = 1$). With this technology, both the OLG version and a Ramsey version produce endogenous growth, but the comparative statics are completely different: An increase in the tax rate τ raises the long-run growth rate in the OLG case but reduces growth in the Ramsey case.

Appendix C: Welfare Analysis in a Three-Good Example

As in the two-good example, there are two types of agent, A and B, and all agents have the same endowment composition. The new element is the introduction of a third good that is valued and consumed by both types of agents. The preferences of the agents are given by Cobb–Douglas utility functions

$$U^A = q_{1A}^\beta q_{3A}^{1-\beta} \tag{2.16}$$

$$U^B = q_{2B}^\beta q_{3B}^{1-\beta}, \tag{2.17}$$

where q_{ij} is the consumption of good i by agent j. As described in Section 2.1, let α denote the A agent's share of total income ($Y_A = \alpha Y$ and $Y_B = (1 - \alpha)Y$).

With this combination of preferences and endowments, the consumption patterns of the two agents satisfy

$$p_1 q_{1A} = \beta Y_A, \quad p_2 q_{2A} = 0, \quad p_3 q_{3A} = (1 - \beta)Y_A \tag{2.18}$$

$$p_1 q_{1B} = 0, \quad p_2 q_{2B} = \beta Y_B, \quad p_3 q_{3B} = (1 - \beta)Y_B. \tag{2.19}$$

Thus, the aggregate demands ($q_1 = q_{1A} + q_{1B}, q_2 = q_{2A} + q_{2B}$, and $q_3 = q_{3A} + q_{3B}$) for the three goods are given by the following equations:

$$p_1 q_1 = \alpha \beta Y \tag{2.20}$$

$$p_2 q_2 = (1 - \alpha)\beta Y \tag{2.21}$$

$$p_3 q_3 = (1 - \beta)Y. \tag{2.22}$$

The demand structure in Equations (2.20)–(2.22) can be derived from the optimizing behavior of a single representative agent with utility function

$$U = q_1^{\alpha\beta} q_2^{(1-\alpha)\beta} q_3^{1-\beta}, \tag{2.23}$$

and budget constraint $p_1 q_1 + p_2 q_2 + p_3 q_3 = p_1 \bar{q}_1 + p_2 \bar{q}_2 + p_3 \bar{q}_3 = Y$.

Consider a policy question that is similar to the one in Section 2.1. Should we increase the supply of good 1 at the expense of a reduction in the supply of good 2? With a one-for-one trade-off and supplies of the two goods that are equal initially, a marginal change of this kind would have a welfare effect given by

$$dU = \beta \left(\frac{\bar{q}_3}{\bar{q}}\right)^{1-\beta} [2\alpha - 1], \tag{2.24}$$

where $\bar{q} = \bar{q}_1 = \bar{q}_2$ is the initial supply of the goods 1 and 2. The conclusion is similar to the earlier example: Implement the policy if $\alpha > 0.5$. The policy, in other words, is implemented if it benefits the rich.

Unlike the two-good example, the policy decision here does not directly prejudice the distributional outcome. A agents are the direct beneficiaries of the policy, but the B agents could be compensated by raising their share of the consumption of good 3. Having the third good means that Pareto improvements become possible.

There are two extreme cases of Pareto improvements: One in which all the improvements go to A agents and another in which only B agents benefit. Keeping U^B unchanged following a marginal increase in q_1 (and an equal marginal decrease in q_2) requires

$$0 = dU^B = \beta\frac{U^B}{q_{2B}}dq_{2B} + (1 - \beta)\frac{U^B}{q_{3B}}dq_{3B} \tag{2.25}$$

or

$$\frac{dq_{3B}}{d\bar{q}_1} = \frac{\beta}{1-\beta} \frac{q_{3B}}{q_{2B}} = \frac{\beta}{1-\beta} \frac{(1-\alpha)\bar{q}_3}{\bar{q}_1}, \tag{2.26}$$

where I have used $d\bar{q}_2 = -d\bar{q}_1$ (by assumption, this is the trade-off) and $q_{3B} = (1 - \alpha)\bar{q}_3$, $q_{2B} = \bar{q}_2 = \bar{q}_1$ at the initial position (these equilibrium conditions follow from (2.18) and (2.19)). Since $dq_{3B} = -dq_{3A}$, we can now derive the gain to the A agents in the case where $dU^B = 0$:

$$dU^A = \alpha^{-\beta}\beta\left(\frac{\bar{q}_3}{\bar{q}_1}\right)^{1-\beta}[2\alpha - 1]d\bar{q}_1. \tag{2.27}$$

Analogously, setting $dU^A = 0$, the increase in q_{3B} and the marginal increase in the utility of B agents can be found:

$$\frac{dq_{3B}}{d\bar{q}_1} = \frac{\beta}{1-\beta}\frac{q_{3A}}{q_{1A}} = \frac{\beta}{1-\beta}\frac{\alpha\bar{q}_3}{\bar{q}_1} \tag{2.28}$$

$$dU^B = (1-\alpha)^{-\beta}\beta\left(\frac{\bar{q}_3}{\bar{q}_1}\right)^{1-\beta}[2\alpha - 1]d\bar{q}_1. \tag{2.29}$$

The largest improvement in aggregate utility, $U^A + U^B$, comes when all the net gains are given to the poor B agents: The symmetric specifications of the utility functions in Equations (2.16) and (2.17) imply that poor agents have a higher marginal utility of q_3. If one rejects the cardinality of the utility function, however, no significance attaches to the magnitudes of the expressions in Equations (2.27) and (2.29), and interpersonal comparisons of utility gains become meaningless. But the expressions in (2.26) and (2.28) still hold without cardinality, and the policy generates a Pareto improvement if the compensating change $dq_{3B}/d\bar{q}_1$ falls in the interval between the expressions on the right-hand sides of (2.26) and (2.28).

To implement the Pareto improvement, the change in the endowment composition can be combined with a transfer of income from A to B agents. It should be noted, however, that if we change the distribution of income in order to compensate the poor B agents for a decline in their consumption of good 2, the appropriate definition of the representative agent is affected: The income share of A agents (α) is a parameter in the representative agent's utility function, Equation (2.23).

3 Household Consumption and Saving

3.1 Introduction

Even if we were to disregard the aggregation issues in Chapter 2, the behavioral assumptions that are at the core of the dominant contemporary approach to macroeconomic theory can and should be questioned. Assumptions of perfect intertemporal optimization provide a poor approximation to real-world decision making. Household preferences, moreover, may not take the form typically assumed.

In defense of DSGE-type modeling, it could be argued that although cognitive limitations and biases lead to deviations of actual behavior from that of a traditional 'homo oeconomicus,' these complications need not be of great significance. Random mistakes in decision-making do not matter much when the stakes are small, and in many cases they are self-correcting, as decision-makers learn from past mistakes. Macroeconomic theory, moreover, typically focuses on average behavior, and random errors at the micro level may cancel out in variables that are of interest to macroeconomists. Well-documented deviations from traditional specifications in which utility depends only on own consumption could also, in principle, be insignificant for the analysis of macroeconomic issues.

According to Laibson and List (2015), "behavioral economists embrace the core principles of modern economics – *optimization* and *equilibrium* – and wish to develop and refine those ideas to make them more *empirically* accurate" (p. 389; italics in original). This refinement, they argue, will give greater precision to the theory and its predictions, but the scale of the contribution (the significance of the inaccuracies of the traditional models) is indicated by a simple metaphor:

If you want to get from Chicago to the bleachers of Fenway Park to watch the Boston Red Sox, standard economics will get you to Cambridge, or even Boston University (which is adjacent to Fenway), but you may need behavioral economics to take the final steps and find your seat in the bleachers. (Laibson and List 2015, p. 385)

From this perspective, behavioral economics, it would seem, has relatively minor implications for traditional economic theory. A similar assessment of behavioral economics has been voiced by some critics of orthodox economic theory; Dutt (2003) and Lavoie (2014), for instance, have been quite dismissive of behavioral economics and its contributions. I disagree with this assessment. Some of the deviations from homo oeconomicus have far-reaching implications for macroeconomics. This chapter discusses examples that are related to consumption.

Section 3.1 considers expectations and reviews some of the behavioral evidence that may explain why most American households appear to save too little. Section 3.2 turns to 'social preferences' and the influence of social norms and reference groups on consumption. Section 3.3 discusses implications for aggregate consumption. Section 3.4 briefly comments on more radical perspectives that question the usefulness of utility maximization as the central tool for understanding consumption behavior. Section 3.5 offers a few concluding comments.

3.2   Expectations, Present Bias, and Credit Constraints

3.2.1   Expectations and Learning

The absence of systematic deviations of outcomes from expectations is a key element in rational expectations. Rational expectations in this sense had been used before Muth (1961) coined the term.

Harrod's 'warranted growth path,' for instance, requires that firms' demand expectations be met (on average), an assumption that may be justified in the analysis of hypothetical steady growth paths. Demand expectations influence production and investment decisions, and presumably firms would revise their expectations and change their production and investment decisions if they encountered significant and systematic differences between expectations and outcomes. These changes, in turn, imply that steady growth becomes inconsistent with demand expectations that are systematically wrong. This observation does not, however, justify the universal application of rational expectations: The process of revision need not produce convergence to a state where expectations are met – the steady growth path may be unstable, as Harrod suggested.

The general notion that decision-makers must gradually gain a complete understanding of how outcomes are determined has neither theoretical foundation nor behavioral and empirical support. Well-defined preferences and goal-oriented behavior do not imply that decision-makers also have the information and skills to form expectations that are consistent with the predictions of the 'correct model' of the economy.

Presentations of rational expectations sometimes stress their 'forward-looking' nature, in contrast to the 'backward-looking' nature of other forms of expectations, in particular adaptive expectations. This distinction makes little sense. All expectations are both forward-and backward-looking. They are forward-looking, by definition, in that expectations concern something that lies in the future, but backward-looking in that the information upon which the expectations are built must come from the observations of past and present events. Expectations hypotheses differ in the assumptions they make about what information is being used to form expectations and about how the information is being used, not by being backward-or forward-looking.

A decision-maker forming expectations about a particular variable may base the expectation on a 'model' that is simple or sophisticated. The choice of model is likely to depend on the general circumstances and the importance that the decision-maker attaches to the variable, the model may or may not include only past and present values of the variable itself, different decision-makers may or may not use the same model, and the expectations may or may not be consistent with the predictions of some particular economic model of how the variable is determined. A rejection of rational expectations does not commit one to a belief in the universal applicability of adaptive expectations, while a rejection of the universal applicability of adaptive expectations or any other simple expectation hypothesis, likewise, does not imply an endorsement of rational expectations. A restriction to these alternatives has no basis in human psychology or observed behavior.

Rational Inattention

Most decision-makers face specific problems and uncertainties whose effects on the outcome of their decisions dominate the effects of movements in economy-wide, aggregate variables. Thus, the incentives to try to uncover and take into account aggregate regularities may be small; individual decision-makers with limited informational and cognitive resources may focus on the idiosyncratic elements that influence their particular situation.[1]

As a simple example, assume that a firm's profits depend on the accuracy of its forecast of demand for its product. The position of the firm's demand curve is influenced by shifting consumption patterns as well as by product innovations, the actions of competitors, and other forces that impact the firm's particular situation. Economy-wide aggregate demand shocks and macroeconomic policy also affect the firm, but these are likely to be less important. Now suppose that the firm can employ its limited resources to analyze and understand the idiosyncratic elements or the general, macroeconomic shock, but not both. Facing this choice, it may be sensible for the firm to focus on the idiosyncratic elements.

Fleshing out the example, assume that firm i faces the following conjectured demand curve:

$$q_{it}^D = B_{it}\phi(p_{it}).$$

For simplicity, shifts in the demand curve affect only the multiplicative constant B_{it}. Formally, it is assumed that the change in $\log B$ is the sum of idiosyncratic elements (d_{it}) and an economy-wide term (x_t):

$$\log B_{it+1} = \log B_{it} + d_{it} + x_t.$$

Focusing their attention on the idiosyncratic elements, firms treat x_t as constant, $x_t = a$. Assuming that there are a large number of equal-sized firms (n) and that the errors (ε_{it}) in their estimates of d_{it} are unbiased and uncorrelated, the average forecast is given by

---

[1] A growing literature with early contributions from Sims (2003) and Reis (2006) discusses 'rational inattention.' Attempts to derive the *optimal* degree of inattention seem misguided, however. If decision-makers had the knowledge, sophistication, and computational capacity to derive the optimal degree of inattention, then almost by definition they would not need to be inattentive to anything.

$$\frac{1}{n} \sum_i (\log B_{it+1})^e = \frac{1}{n} \sum_i \log B_{it} + a + \frac{1}{n} \sum_i (d_{it} + \varepsilon_{it})$$

$$\log B_t + a + \frac{1}{n} \sum_i d_{it}.$$

Thus, the error in the average forecast is given by $x_t - a$. Firms disregard – rationally, given their limited resources – the economy-wide term x_t and its determinants.

Macroeconomists and policymakers, by contrast, will focus on the aggregate term, and insofar as macroeconomic theory can yield insights about the dynamics of aggregate demand and the determination of x_t, there will be predictable differences between actual outcomes and the outcomes expected by firms (the decision-makers described by the model), as well as between the outcomes predicted by the macroeconomic model and those expected (on average) by the decision-makers described by the model.

Using New Zealand survey data on inflation expectations, Coibion et al. (2018) find support for this perspective:

Many firms view inflation as relatively unimportant to their business decisions and choose not to track its recent values, leading to large misperceptions about recent inflation dynamics and forecasts that are far out of line with historical values, even though they display significant knowledge about industry-specific price changes. (p. 2711)

Consequently, there are significant differences between firms' average beliefs and those of professional forecasters.

Other recent studies also find systematic deviations from rational expectations. Jonsson and Osterholm (2012) examine inflation expectations in Sweden. The Swedish central bank adopted inflation targeting in 1992, and the policy has been judged a success. The bank uses survey measures of inflation expectations as one input to its policy decisions. The surveys show that expectations are neither unbiased (the forecasts have systematic errors) nor efficient (readily available macroeconomic data could improve the forecasts).[2]

This and other evidence led Mankiw and Reis (2018, p. 85) to suggest that "Friedman's assumption that expectations are sluggish rather than rational seems prescient." Friedman, one may add, was not the only economist who rejected the folly of rational expectations, but on this issue, at least, he was correct.

Limitations of Learning

Persistent differences between average outcomes and average expectations can induce changes in behavior as decision-makers learn from experience and revise the way they form expectations. Learning, however, does not justify the rational expectations hypothesis.

---

[2] The evidence against the rational expectations hypothesis is not new. In his monograph on rational expectations, Sheffrin (1983) considered a number of empirical studies before proceeding to discuss the theoretical implications of the rational expectations hypothesis. Most of these empirical studies rejected the hypothesis. Undeterred, Sheffrin dismissed the studies, suggesting that "people may not do what they say" and that "an examination of the rational expectations hypothesis must go beyond these tests" (pp. 22–23).

It is difficult to get convergence to rational expectations, even in simple models of rational learning (e.g., Frydman and Phelps 1983), and real-world learning takes place within a much more complex environment than that postulated by the learning models. It is not merely a matter of learning the values of parameters in a known model, but of trying to understand a world that is constantly undergoing change, for which the appropriate model is unknown, and in which 'animal spirits' can be a critical determinant of many decisions – a traditional Keynesian view that has regained attention in recent years (e.g., Akerlof and Shiller 2009).

Institutional or structural changes complicate any learning process. Actors who ignore the possibility of structural change may discover that they have adapted to an environment that no longer exists. Actors who recognize the possibility of change face a different problem. Real or imagined structural changes are often invoked to justify expectations that would otherwise seem unreasonable; examples include the appeal to a 'new economy' during the stock market boom of the 1990s and the faith in financial engineering in the early 2000s. There is always some reason to think that 'this time is different.' Far from leading to rational expectations and stable outcomes, shifts in expectations are often a source of instability.

Learning can be successful, of course. The convergence of actual outcomes toward those predicted by traditional models of constrained optimization is plausible in relation to repeated, small-scale decisions – what ice cream to buy or whether it is faster to commute by car or public transport. But small-scale decisions in this category typically are of limited macroeconomic interest.

A range of other decisions do not fall into the convergence category. Obvious examples include educational choices, whether to have children, and how much to save for retirement – decisions that *are* central to macroeconomics. Educational choices and decisions to have children are difficult or impossible to undo later in light of experience. The same applies to long-term saving decisions. The provision for old age is critical, both for the individual and for the properties of the economy as a whole. The learning argument, however, is largely irrelevant in this context. Retirement-age households may realize that they should have saved more for retirement. But there is no repetition; the learning comes too late.

Learning could come indirectly from observing older generations and their situation, with the failure of parents to save enough providing a lesson for children to act differently. Intergenerational learning of this kind may take place, but its extent is questionable, and there are limitations to what can be learned in this way. Modern societies have undergone constant change, and children typically confront an environment that is quite different from the one their parents faced. Earning profiles, life expectancies, healthcare costs, the extent of employer-provided pensions, and the level of publicly provided social security are among the factors that can change – and have changed – significantly from one generation to the next. Following a rule of thumb that would have worked well for older generations can be a recipe for disaster in a new and radically different environment. Long-term planning is notoriously difficult in a world of change and uncertainty, and extrapolation from current conditions can be treacherous. After the British had bombarded Copenhagen in 1807 and seized the Danish fleet, one response by the Danish crown was the planting of new oak forests. Oak was essential for shipbuilding, but about 150 years would be needed before the new forests could provide timber of sufficient quality. Still, this farsighted policy ensured that by the middle of the twentieth century Denmark would have the oak that was necessary for rebuilding the fleet (Toksvig 2007).

Active decision-making based on reasoning and a good understanding of current options are needed to ensure (near-)optimal retirement saving if conventions and adaptive learning cannot be relied upon to do the job. Unfortunately,

most Americans do not understand financial concepts such as interest, inflation, expense ratios or diversification, and are unaware of the terms that govern their borrowing or the incentives facing those who provide them with products and services. (Bhargava and Loewenstein 2015)

These empirical observations on cognitive limitations and the difficulties of learning are at odds with assumptions of intertemporal optimization and rational expectations. But the precise implications of the observations for consumption are unclear. Poor financial skills and the absence of repetition do not necessarily imply that saving will be too low. In principle, bad decisions could produce saving rates that, in hindsight, would seem too high. Something else is needed to explain widespread observations of undersaving.[3]

3.2.2   Present Bias, Credit Rationing, and Mental Accounts

The standard discounted utility model assumes that individuals maximize an intertemporal utility function given by

$$U = \sum_{0}^{T} D(t)u_t = \sum_{0}^{T} \delta^t u_t, \tag{3.1}$$

where $t = 0$ represents the current period, u_t is utility in period t, δ is the discount factor between periods, and the factor $D(t) = \delta^t$ is applied in order to obtain the present value of u_t.

This specification with exponential discounting does not fit the behavioral evidence (e.g., Frederick et al. 2002, O'Donoghue and Rabin 2015). Many people appear to use a higher discount factor when discounting between periods in the near future than when discounting between periods in a more remote future. This 'present bias' can be captured by a variety of functional forms. One possibility is 'hyperbolic discounting'[4]; another, even simpler version of present bias specifies the discount factors in the following way:

---

[3] The most recent 'National Retirement Index' from Center for Retirement Research at Boston College (https://crr.bc.edu/briefs/the-national-retirement-risk-index-an-update-from-the-2019-scf/) indicates that more than half of today's workers in the United States are financially unprepared for retirement (Munnell et al. 2021).

[4] Formally, hyperbolic discounting assumes that

$$D(t) = \frac{1}{1 + \delta t}.$$

$$D(t) = \begin{cases} 1 & \text{if } t = 0 \\ \beta\delta^t & \text{if } t > 0 \end{cases} \quad \text{with} \quad \beta < 1, \delta \leq 1. \tag{3.2}$$

This '$\beta - \delta$' formulation implies relatively steep discounting between the current period and the next period: Utility in period 1 is discounted by the factor $\beta\delta$ relative to utility in period 0, while utility in period $t + 1$ is discounted by the factor δ relative to utility in period t for any $t \geq 1$.

Present bias generates time inconsistency and procrastination. As a simple example (Akerlof 1991, O'Donoghue and Rabin 1999) consider a decision-maker who has the discount structure in Equation (3.2), with $\beta = 0.5$ and $\delta = 1$. The decision-maker needs to decide whether to carry out some unpleasant task with future benefits; specifically, the utility cost of undertaking the task is six, while the utility gain in the next period is eight. With these numbers, the decision-maker will decide against doing the task today: The gain in the next period will be discounted by the factor 0.5, and the net utility would be $-6 + 0.5 \times 8 = -2$. It would seem attractive, however, to do the task tomorrow: The present value of the net gain would be $0.5 \times (-6 + 8) = 1$. Thus, the decision-maker will plan to carry out the task tomorrow. When tomorrow comes around, however, it will have become the new today; the calculations will, once again, show that it is better to postpone the task. The plan to carry out the task tomorrow is time inconsistent, and a naive decision-maker with this preference structure will never perform the task.[5]

Present bias may explain undersaving – 'I want to save for my retirement, but this year we really need a nice family vacation (a new car, a 4K ultra HD tv,...), and I will start paying into the retirement account next year.' Perceived current needs dominate decision-making and planned future saving never takes place.

Impatient households with high discount rates would want to go into debt if credit markets were perfect. But, of course, credit markets are not perfect. Liquidity constraints are well documented. Even students with high expected future income will find it near impossible to borrow in the absence of loan guarantees, and even when there are loan guarantees, students typically see a significant rise in their standard of living when they graduate.[6] The increase in household indebtedness in the United States in the early 2000s, likewise, was not due to a spontaneous desire of households to borrow but to a relaxation of credit constraints and increases in households' collateral from rising house prices (Mian and Sufi 2009, Muellbauer 2010).[7]

But something other than credit rationing is at play as well. Take the case of credit card debt. Analyzing the effects of provider-initiated changes in credit limits on credit

---

[5] Read et al. (1999) provide experimental evidence for the postponement of 'unpleasant tasks.'

[6] Liquidity constraints may not be the only factor. Akerlof (2007) argues that norms play a role:

People's expenditures are supposed to reflect their stations in life, and those stations usually reflect their earnings. Thus, for example, college students with little earnings are supposed to live that way–like college students. Their current spending is supposed to reflect their current earnings, not what they will be earning in the future.

[7] Other studies of credit constraints include Zeldes (1989), Johnson et al. (2006), and Parker et al. (2013).

cards, Gross and Souleles (2002) find that "increases in credit limits generate an immediate and significant rise in debt" with changes that are larger for people who are closer
to their credit limit, a result indicating the presence of credit constraints. But Gross and
Souleles also find that many credit card borrowers simultaneously hold low-yielding
assets. As they point out, this finding is not easily explained by conventional models of
credit constraints. It is consistent, however, with Shefrin and Thaler's (1988) 'behavioral life cycle model' self-control is difficult, and most households use rules of thumb
in combination with 'a system of mental accounts' as a way to improve self-discipline
and prevent over-spending. Thus, the model predicts portfolio decisions that can seem
irrational; low-yielding saving accounts and high-interest credit card debt belong to
different mental accounts.

The behavioral deviations from homo oeconomicus also suggest that "the saving
rate can be affected by the way in which increments to wealth are 'framed'" (Shefrin
and Thaler 1988, p. 610). This implication is confirmed by Thaler and Benartzi (2004),
who report findings from a program that enabled people to commit in advance to allocating a portion of their future increases in salary to retirement saving. Seventy-eight
percent of those offered the plan decided to participate, and the average saving rates
for program participants increased from 3.5 percent to 13.6 percent over the course
of forty months. A study by Somville and Vandewalle (2018) finds similar effects in
India. Randomly assigned villagers received identical weekly payments either as bank
deposits or in cash. The assignment to payment method was random, but the recipients reacted quite differently: Being paid into a bank account more than doubled the
saving.

Differences in retirement saving for people with and without mandatory saving
plans point in the same direction. According to Gustman and Steinmeier (2002, p. 8),

When we hold constant the effects of a large number of variables that theory suggests influence
desired saving, pensions add to total wealth by at least half the value of the pension and, in
most specifications, by a good deal more. Those with higher pensions do not correspondingly
reduce their holdings of other wealth.

Studies by Chetty et al. (2014) and Lachowska and Mych (2018) reach similar conclusions using high-quality data for Denmark and Poland, respectively. Chetty et al.
find that a mandatory savings plan that required a contribution of 1 percent of earnings
to a retirement savings account "raised total saving by nearly 1 percent of earnings
on average even for individuals who were previously saving more than 1 percent of
their earnings in voluntary retirement savings accounts" (p. 1143). Examining the
effects of pension reforms that reduced public pensions, Lachowska and Mych find
that increases in household saving make up only 30 percent of the reduction. These
recent studies take advantage of large datasets that were not available in the past. The
recognition that pension plans influence aggregate saving is not new, however (e.g.,
Green 1981, 1991).

The split of current income between consumption and saving is not the only
decision with an intertemporal dimension. The variability of hours in response to fluctuations in wages is a key element in models of real business cycles: The supply of

labor falls in these models when negative productivity shocks have reduced the real wage. Like consumption, the labor supply should follow an Euler condition.

Many workers are institutionally constrained from varying their hours of work. Some professions, however, do allow variations. A well-known study by Camerer et al. (1997) examines data for taxi drivers in New York City. The drivers rent the taxis and pay a fixed fee for a twelve hour window. Within this window, they are free to choose how much to drive. The fares are fixed, but demand for taxi services fluctuates significantly from day to day, creating day-to-day variations in the effective hourly wage that the driver can earn. These hourly wages are highly correlated within days but not across days. The intertemporal optimization story, therefore, has a clear implication: Drivers should work long hours on days with strong demand and increase leisure on days with weak demand. The evidence, by contrast, shows negative wage elasticities: Taxi drivers tended to work long hours when the effective hourly wage was low.[8]

Negative elasticities can be explained by daily income targeting. As pointed out by Camerer et al., daily income targeting is consistent with the general finding from psychology and behavioral economics that "people are 'loss averse'– they dislike achieving outcomes below a reference point about twice as much as they like exceeding the reference point by the same absolute amount" (Camerer et al. pp. 410–411).[9] A daily income target has the advantage that it is simple (a relevant quality for agents that do not have unlimited cognitive abilities) and that it may alleviate problems of self-control (present bias may give a strong temptation to stop early 'today' with the intention of making up for it 'later').[10]

Overall, there is strong evidence that models of perfect intertemporal optimization misrepresent microeconomic behavior and paint a misleading picture of the determination of variables that are central to macroeconomic models.

3.3   'Social Preferences'

As argued in Chapter 2, the representative-agent approach to welfare analysis favors the rich. This section considers another questionable aspect of the representative-agent approach.

---

[8] Martinez et al. (2021) reach similar conclusions. Examining the effects of staggered Swiss tax holidays, they find very low labor supply responses and suggest that some of the responses were driven by tax avoidance rather than real labor supply. Insignificant or negative wage elasticities have also been found in other studies (e.g., Browning et al. 1985, Mankiw et al. 1985). The interpretation can be difficult, however, if wage shocks are persistent. The cases of taxi drivers and Swiss tax holidays offer a cleaner test.

[9] Tversky and Kahneman (1992). Rabin (1998) provides a survey of 'psychology and economics.'

[10] Several studies discuss the robustness and interpretation of the findings by Camerer et al. Drawing on empirical work by Farber (2005, 2008) and theoretical models by Koszegi and Rabin (2006), Crawford and Meng (2011, p. 1932) maintain that "reference dependence is an important part of the labor-supply story."

Using Amartya Sen's terminology, *relative* income and consumption may determine a person's *absolute* capabilities, an argument that (as pointed out by Sen 1983, p. 159), was foreshadowed by Adam Smith (1776, pp. 351–352):

By necessaries I understand not only the commodities which are indispensably necessary for the support of life, but what ever the custom of the country renders it indecent for creditable people, even the lowest order, to be without . . . Custom . . . has rendered leather shoes a necessary of life in England. The poorest creditable person of either sex would be ashamed to appear in public without them.

The notion of capabilities emphasizes that how much you *need* to spend to reproduce your life depends on the social context, including sociological aspects (the ability to appear in public without shame) and 'hard' constraints like the need to own personal transport to get to work when there is no public transport. In this section, however, I shall follow a standard approach and leave out capabilities from the formal analysis. The drawback is obvious: The omission of capabilities and the link between relative income and absolute capabilities can obscure the social components of individual behavior and make the whole question of relative income seem less significant. But elements of Adam Smith's observation can be captured by models in which objective societal dimensions appear only indirectly by assuming that people may derive utility not just from their own absolute consumption but also from their consumption relative to other people. 'Social preferences' of this kind imply that relative income can influence consumption behavior and general economic welfare.[11]

3.3.1   Welfare Analysis

The correlation between average income and average reported well-being is weak, at best (Easterlin 2001). By contrast, the influence of relative income and consumption on well-being has empirical support: Relative income and reported well-being show a strong positive correlation; Blanchflower and Oswald (2004) examine data for the United States and United Kingdom, Luttmer (2005) uses data for the United States, and Fafchamps and Shilpi (2008) use data for Nepal.[12]

The identification in these studies of reported 'well-being' or 'happiness' with utility raises many issues. Even language is a problem. The intensity of the feelings associated with 'happiness' can vary across languages as well as over time within a given language. Hirschman (1970, p. 113) tells a revealing anecdote about two German immigrants who meet in New York after many years: "One of them asks the other: 'Are you happy here?' Reply: 'I'm happy, *aber glücklich bin ich nicht*'." This reply in translation says "I am happy, but I am not happy." The German word glücklich may translate as happy, but it is not quite the same. Happiness studies are not the only source of empirical evidence, however. The experimental and behavioral

---

[11] A substantial literature has emphasized this point, including Veblen (1899), Duesenberry (1949), Hirsch (1977), Easterlin (1974, 2001), Sen (1983, 1992) and Frank (1985a, 2005); Dutt (2009) provides a typology of different explanations for the effects of relative consumption.

[12] Frey and Stutzer (2002) survey the behavioral literature on 'happiness.'

literature also suggests that social preferences influence most people's behavior (Fehr and Schmidt 2003), while Johansson-Stenman et al. (2002) analyze experimental choices between hypothetical societies, finding a strong concern for relative income.

Social preferences are not directly observable, and descriptive representative agents are constructed to generate the patterns of aggregate consumption. The result can be substantial errors in the analysis of social welfare if the representative agent's utility function is used as the welfare criterion. Consider an example in which, following Frank (1985b), households have identical utility functions and in which, more specifically, the utility of each household depends positively on the household's own consumption of goods and the household's own leisure, but negatively on the average level of consumption. As a stylized description, this treatment of consumption goods as 'positional' – having utility depend on average consumption – and leisure as 'nonpositional' would seem to fit contemporary economies.

Formally, let

$$U^i(c_i, l_i, c) = \alpha \log c_i - \beta \log c + \gamma \log l_i, \tag{3.3}$$

where U^i, c_i, and l_i denote the utility, consumption, and leisure of household i, respectively, and c is the average level of consumption. The parameters α and β are both positive, with $1 > \alpha > \beta$. Each household maximizes its own utility subject to a budget constraint given by

$$c_i = (1 - t)(1 - l_i) + s. \tag{3.4}$$

The household receives after-tax wage income $((1-t)(1-l_i))$ and a lump-sum transfer s; t is the tax rate and $1 - l_i$ is the supply of labor; for simplicity, the pretax real wage is set equal to 1.

Standard calculations imply that a utility maximizing household chooses the following levels of consumption and leisure[13]:

$$c_i = \frac{\alpha}{\alpha + \gamma}(1 - t + s) \tag{3.5}$$

$$l_i = \frac{\gamma}{\alpha + \gamma}\left(1 + \frac{s}{1 - t}\right). \tag{3.6}$$

All households have the same preferences, and average consumption and leisure (l and c) satisfy the analogous equations, that is, $l_i = l, c_i = c$.

---

[13] The household maximizes (3.3) subject to the constraint (3.4). The Lagrangian for this problem is given by $\mathcal{L} = \alpha \log c_i - \beta \log c + \gamma \log l_i + \lambda((1 - t)(1 - l_i) + s - c_i)$, where λ is the Lagrange multiplier. The first-order conditions are

$$\frac{\partial \mathcal{L}}{\partial c_i} = \frac{\alpha}{c_i} - \lambda = 0$$

$$\frac{\partial \mathcal{L}}{\partial l_i} = \frac{\gamma}{l_i} - \lambda(1 - t) = 0$$

$$\frac{\partial \mathcal{L}}{\partial \lambda} = (1 - t)(1 - l_i) + s - c_i = 0.$$

These conditions can be used to solve for c_i and l_i.

A descriptive representative agent needs to match these outcomes. This can be achieved if the utility function is defined as

$$V = \alpha \log c + \gamma \log l. \tag{3.7}$$

The representative agent takes s and t as exogenously given, and the consumption and leisure in Equations (3.5) and (3.6) can be generated by maximizing the utility function (3.7) subject to the constraint[14]

$$c = (1 - t)(1 - l) + s. \tag{3.8}$$

The utility function V successfully describes the aggregate outcome, but that does not make it a good measure of social welfare. Households are identical, there are no distributional complications of the kind discussed in Section 2.4, and all households achieve the same level of utility:

$$
\begin{aligned}
W = U(c,l) &= \alpha \log c - \beta \log c + \gamma \log l \\
&= (\alpha - \beta) \log c + \gamma \log l. \tag{3.9}
\end{aligned}
$$

Suppose that the lump-sum transfer is financed by taxes

$$s = t(1 - l). \tag{3.10}$$

Combining the symmetry conditions $c_i = c$ and $l_i = l$ with Equations (3.5), (3.6), and (3.10), the outcome generated by decentralized decisions is given by

$$c = \frac{(1 - t)\alpha}{\alpha(1 - t) + \gamma} \tag{3.11}$$

$$l = \frac{\gamma}{\alpha(1 - t) + \gamma}. \tag{3.12}$$

A utilitarian social planner should maximize (3.9) subject to (3.11) and (3.12), yielding an optimal tax rate of $t = \beta/\alpha$. A social planner using V as the objective function, by contrast, will choose the tax rate t to maximize (3.7) subject to (3.11) and (3.12), implying that $s = t = 0$.

Individual households ignore the negative consumption externalities, and in a decentralized economy, the utility function U^i in (3.3) is observationally equivalent to one without the negative consumption externality i.e., with $\beta = 0$. The social planner should not, however, ignore the externalities. A reduction of the tax rate from $t = \beta/\alpha$ to $t = 0$ increases the utility of the representative agent but reduces the welfare of all households. Thus, the example illustrates Kirman's (1992, p. 118) statement that

The "representative individual" whose choices coincide with the aggregate choices of the individuals in the economy is a utility maximizer. However it may well be the case that in two situations of which the representative prefers the first to the second, every individual prefers the second to the first.

---

[14] The normalization of the real wage at the aggregate level implicitly presumes constant returns to labor.

The utility function *V*, which in this example captures the behavior of a representative consumer, provides a misleading welfare criterion, even if agents are identical and there are no distributional conflicts.[15]

The example shows how a belief in the representative agent as the 'correct' or 'natural' welfare criterion becomes particularly problematic when combined with the widespread predilection to play down externalities and use Walrasian assumptions as the benchmark. Yet, most New Keynesians seem to endorse this approach.[16] Commenting on the modeling choices made by DSGE models, Blanchard (2018a, p. 47) argues, "Thinking in terms of a set of distortions to a competitive economy implies a long slog from the competitive economy to a reasonably plausible description of the economy. But again, it is hard to see where else to start from."

As indicated by the example, a failure to complete the 'long slog' can seriously distort the analysis. The representative agent attaches too much weight to consumption and income. In this sense, the representative-agent approach mirrors the focus on aggregate income and economic growth in most policy debates. In the presence of strong consumption externalities, however, economic growth may have limited effects on welfare, even disregarding distributional issues and negative environmental externalities.[17]

Recent empirical studies strengthen the case for strong social effects on consumption. De Giorgi et al. (2020) examine peer effects on consumption, where peers are defined as coworkers at the same workplace and with similar occupation and education. Using a large administrative dataset for Denmark, they find an elasticity of own consumption with respect to peers' consumption of about 0.3. Agarwal et al. (2021) identify social effects on consumption among residents living in the same building by looking at the effects of personal bankruptcies. A bankruptcy reduces the consumption of the bankrupt resident, but this direct consumption effect, they find, is amplified by the social effects: The total consumption impact of the bankruptcy on the consumption by peers is 2.8 times the effect of the bankruptcy on the bankrupt resident's own consumption.

3.3.2   Differences in Average Saving Rates

James Duesenberry's relative income hypothesis emphasized how household saving could be influenced by the household's income relative to other households and

---

[15] Libertarians may argue that positional externalities are different from other externalities and should be treated differently; Frank (2008) discusses these issues.

[16] DSGE models often introduce consumption habits, but the motivation is largely *ad hoc*: Habit formation is used to improve the empirical fit of the model by generating the smoothness and humpshaped response of consumption to shocks that can be found in the data. The consumption habit can be internal (e.g., Christiano et al. 2005) or external (e.g., Smets and Wouters 2007). External habits imply consumption externalities, but the use of external as opposed to internal habits sometimes appears to be motivated primarily by tractability: It simplifies the optimization if the individual household can treat the evolution of habits as exogenous.

[17] Hoel and Sterner (2007) and Skott and Davis (2013) discuss implications for the evaluation of climate change.

relative to its own past income. As a simple formalization, assume that these relativities are captured by a 'consumption norm' and that the consumption decision of
household i is given by

$$c_{it} = \beta y_{it} + \mu \bar{c}_t, \tag{3.13}$$

where $\bar{c}_t$ captures the prevailing consumption norm and y_{it} is income. Equation
(3.13) implies that rich households have a higher average saving rate than poor
households.

This prediction is consistent with evidence showing strong cross-section correlations between income and the saving rate. These correlations could potentially be
explained by the life-cycle hypothesis, the permanent income hypothesis, or, more
generally, by intertemporal optimization and consumption smoothing. But evidence
also shows that saving rates out of permanent income depend on relative income;
Dynan et al. (2004) "find a strong positive relationship between saving rates and
lifetime income" (p. 397). The relative income hypothesis would seem to offer a
promising explanation for this finding. The hypothesis, however, is often ignored in
the literature, and when it is discussed, the attitude is largely dismissive.

David Romer's (2018) textbook devotes two paragraphs to a discussion of some
statements that are "common" but "incorrect" (p. 368). It is incorrect, Romer argues,
to believe that the poor save a smaller proportion of their income because their incomes
are little above the level needed to provide a minimal standard of living. This claim,
he argues,

overlooks the fact that individuals who have trouble obtaining even a low standard of income
today may also have trouble obtaining that standard in the future. Thus, their saving is likely to
be determined by the time pattern of their income, just as it is for the wealthy. (p. 371)

Similarly, the relative income hypothesis reflects a misunderstanding of the nature of
the saving decision. The common assertion that

individuals' concern about their consumption relative to others' tends to raise their
consumption as they try to 'keep up with Joneses'... fails to recognize what saving is: since
saving represents future consumption, saving less implies consuming less in the future, and
thus falling further behind the Joneses. One can just as well argue that concern about relative
consumption causes individuals to try to catch up with the Joneses in the future, and thus
lowers rather than raises current consumption. (p. 371)

As indicated by the static example in Section 3.3.1, a concern for relative consumption can increase consumption and reduce leisure, even in the context of behavior that
is perfectly rational from an individual perspective: If an increase in average consumption raises the marginal utility of the household's own consumption, the response is to
reduce leisure and raise consumption. This result, however, does not directly affect the
division of income between consumption and saving that is at the center of Romer's
analysis: "as long as the individual does not value saving in itself, the decision about
the division of income between consumption and saving is driven by preferences
between present and future consumption and information about future consumption
prospects" (p. 371). Essentially the relative income hypothesis is rejected here on the

scholastic grounds that it violates *a priori* presumptions in the orthodox canon. Even on its own terms, however, the argument is unconvincing.[18]

If relative consumption affects utility, intertemporal optimization requires knowledge about other people's saving and future resources, as well as about the household's own future circumstances. Other people's saving and future financial resources typically will not be known, however; a household may observe the neighbor's car or a colleague's suit, but not their bank balance. A household may not even know the composition of its own future reference group. This composition will not remain unchanged: In retirement, there will be no work colleagues to keep up with, and when the children have left home, there will be no peer pressures associated with children and their demands for the 'right' shoes and clothes, cell phones, sports equipment, and participation in costly social activities. In short, it may be unclear who the future Joneses will be. To some extent, the future reference group even becomes a matter of choice: In retirement, the household may choose to move to a smaller house in a different geographical location.

If we disregard both these uncertainties and the endogeneity of the future reference groups, there is an additional problem: Behavioral economics questions the standard concave utility function. The relative income hypothesis specifically points to the potential importance of reference points, and evidence suggests that the value function is convex over losses (Tversky and Kahneman 1992). This convexity implies that households may prefer to keep up with their neighbors for some period of time – even if it means falling behind (or finding new, poorer neighbors) later in life – rather than to fall behind by a smaller amount all the time.

But one does not need to appeal to loss aversion or to uncertainty about the characteristics of the future Joneses. Romer's logical argument against the possible influence of peer effects on saving also fails in a standard setting embodying a traditional, concave utility function. Consider a household whose utility function includes the negative external effect associated with relative position. Let[19]

$$U = \alpha \log(c_1 - \eta_1 \bar{c}_1) + \gamma \log l + \frac{1}{1 + \rho} \alpha \log(c_2 - \eta_2 \bar{c}_2).$$

The household works in the first period and the average consumption $\bar{c}_i$ exert a negative effect on utility; l is leisure, and the total available time in period 1 is normalized to 1. The intertemporal budget constraint is given by

---

[18] From a broader perspective, the widespread reluctance by economists to admit social pressures on current consumption is surprising. Would one also deny the influence of peer pressure on, say, substance abuse? Do teenagers who follow current peer pressure fully anticipate the potential effects of their current behavior on their standing in relation to future peers as well as the composition of the future peers (the future reference group)?

[19] The earlier specification in Equation (3.3) assumes that the marginal utility of own consumption is independent of the level of average consumption, which implies that the household's saving rate will be unaffected by changes in average consumption. With a general utility function ($U = U(c, \bar{c}, l)$), the level of $\bar{c}$ will typically affect the marginal utility of own consumption (the partial derivative U_1).

$$c_1 + \frac{1}{1+r}c_2 = w(1-l) = y, \tag{3.14}$$

where w is the real wage and y is the household income.

Utility maximization implies that (see Appendix A for details)

$$\frac{c_2 - \eta_2 \bar{c}_2}{c_1 - \eta_1 \bar{c}_1} = \frac{1+r}{1+\rho}. \tag{3.15}$$

If we combine this Euler equation with the budget constraint (Equation (3.14)), consumption in period 1 can be written as

$$c_1 = \frac{1+\rho}{2+\rho}y + \frac{1+\rho}{2+\rho}\left[\frac{1}{1+\rho}\eta_1\bar{c}_1 - \frac{1}{1+r}\eta_2\bar{c}_2\right]. \tag{3.16}$$

Intuitively, after covering the cost of the basic needs ($\eta_1\bar{c}_1 + \frac{1}{1+r}\eta_2\bar{c}_2$), the preferences over additional consumption are Cobb–Douglas. Thus, when households split their remaining income between the two periods, the fraction $(1+\rho)/(2+\rho)$ goes to period 1.

The consumption function for the young (Equation (3.16)) takes the same form as the simple specification of the relative income hypothesis in Equation (3.13). More importantly, if wage rates differ across households, the equation implies that poor households have a relatively high consumption rate – as predicted by the relative income hypothesis – if the constant term on the right-hand side is positive, that is, if

$$\frac{1}{1+\rho}\eta_1\bar{c}_1 - \frac{1}{1+r}\eta_2\bar{c}_2 > 0.$$

This inequality condition is satisfied as long as households with children and active labor market participation have higher consumption needs and consumption standards than older households.

Changes in inequality can have interesting implications, too. Households that fall behind as a result of an increase in average consumption will reduce their saving rate if they do not adjust the anticipated average consumption of the (unknown) future reference group: A rise in $\bar{c}_1$ raises the households' consumption in period 1 if $\bar{c}_2$, the expected norm in period 2, is unchanged. A failure to make adjustments in $\bar{c}_2$ could be seen as violating standard notions of intertemporal optimization and rational expectations. That, however, may represent a problem for the standard theory, not the relative income hypothesis.

Arguably, an even stronger case in favor of the relative income hypothesis comes from a simple reinterpretation of the model: Consumption in the second period can be interpreted as bequests (or, alternatively, the model can be extended by adding a third period representing bequests). Using this interpretation, the argument now proceeds by noting that bequests are less likely to be positional, which will make η_2 equal to zero (or small, relative to η_1).[20] It follows that poor households save less; they sacrifice

---

[20] This interpretation implies that it would also be reasonable to include bequests received by the household in the budget constraint. This modification leads to minor changes in the detailed expressions but does not affect the qualitative conclusions. If a young household receives bequests b, its consumption will still

nonpositional bequests in order to keep up with the Joneses. Alvarez-Cuadrado and Long (2011) develop a model along these lines. Including bequests explicitly, they find that poor households work longer hours and save a smaller proportion of their lifetime income. It should be noted, however, that financial bequests, which are the focus of this literature, constitute only a small part of what parents pass on to their children – some broader implications of this observation for our understanding of consumption will be discussed briefly in Section 3.4.

'Sociological' and intertemporal influences on consumption are not mutually exclusive (and, in fact, the example in this subsection includes both types of influences). Duesenberry himself argued as much. Writing in 1949, he commented that "no one will deny that a very large part of saving is done either for retirement or protection of dependents" (p. 41). He also anticipated many of the results derived by the life-cycle hypothesis and the permanent income hypothesis. Thus, he argued:

> To the extent that saving for retirement is important, the age distribution of the population and the rate of growth of income will be important in the determination of the rate of saving. These variables are important because they determine the size of negative saving by retired persons relative to the size of positive savings by persons preparing for retirement. Indeed if all saving was done for retirement, a community with stable population and income would have a zero aggregate saving.... A growing society with stable income per capita will have positive saving even if every individual liquidates all his savings before he dies. (Duesenberry 1949, p. 42)

The relative income hypothesis adds to these insights. The importance of 'social preferences' is well documented, and the hypothesis helps explain why high-income groups typically have a lower propensity to consume than low-income groups, even when adjustments have been made for transitory income and life-cycle effects.

3.4 Aggregate Consumption

3.4.1 Income Distribution and Aggregate Consumption

Equation (3.13) implies that the average saving rate of the rich will tend to be higher than the saving rate of the poor. By assumption, however, in this example the marginal propensity to consume was identical across households; redistribution of income, therefore, has no effects on aggregate consumption as long as the reference levels of consumption are independent of the distribution of income. The same result applies to redistribution among young households in the case with explicit optimization (Equation (3.16)).

As a simple example, assume that the value of $\bar{c}_t$ is equal to average consumption in the previous period,

$$\bar{c}_t = \frac{1}{n} \sum c_{jt-1}.$$

be governed by Equation (3.16). The only difference is that now the expression for lifetime resources in Equation (3.14) will include the bequest: $y = b + (1 - l)w$.

Summing Equation (3.13) over i now gives the aggregate consumption function

$$C_t = \beta Y_t + \mu C_{t-1}, \tag{3.17}$$

where

$$C_t = \sum c_{jt}; \qquad Y_t = \sum y_{jt}.$$

Equation (3.17), which is similar to the aggregate consumption function under the permanent income hypothesis, excludes distributional effects on aggregate consumption.[21]

Distributional effects on consumption arise – quite intuitively – if the marginal propensity to consume depends on income: Aggregate consumption falls if income is shifted from a poor household with a high marginal propensity to consume to a rich household with a low propensity. If desired, such differences can be derived from utility maximization; Corneo (2018), for instance, derives the result by introducing time constraints and assuming that consumption takes time.

There are other potential sources of distributional effects on aggregate consumption. If a household's reference level of consumption is defined asymmetrically by the consumption of those that are richer than the household, a rise in inequality may increase consumption (Bowles and Park 2005, Frank 2005). This negative effect of inequality on the saving rate of households with a given income runs counter to the compositional effect of inequality associated with increasing marginal saving rates (a strictly concave relation between income and consumption). The net effect, in principle, can go either way. If the reference effect dominates, average saving rates decline as rising inequality and social pressures to 'keep up with the Joneses' force low-and middle-income groups to go into debt in order to maintain their position (e.g., Carr and Jayadev 2015, Cynamon and Fazzari 2008, Ryoo and Kim 2014). This explanation of falling US saving rates between the mid-1970s and the financial crisis in 2008 faces challenges, however. Most debt is owed by households near the top of the income distribution, and consumption inequality has largely followed income inequality. Middle-income debt ratios, moreover, did not start rising until 2001, while income inequality has been increasing since the early 1980s. The rising debt levels for middle-income households after 2001, in turn, may be better explained by a relaxation of credit constraints than by increasing inequality (Mason 2018).

---

[21] According to the permanent income hypothesis,

$$C_t = k Y_t^P.$$

If expectations of permanent income are formed adaptively, as assumed by Friedman (1957), we have

$$Y_t^P = Y_{t-1}^P + \lambda (Y_t - Y_{t-1}^P)$$

and

$$C_t = k Y_t^P = k(1-\lambda)Y_{t-1}^P + k\lambda Y_t = k\lambda Y_t + (1-\lambda)C_{t-1}. \tag{3.18}$$

Comparing Equations (3.17) and (3.18), the permanent and relative income hypotheses may, thus, be observationally equivalent with respect to their implications for the aggregate consumption function.

Whatever the relation between inequality and households' desired consumption, credit constraints are ubiquitous, and importantly, they change over time.[22] Regulatory changes and financial innovation can provide sudden shifts in the extent and severity of constraints, and gradual changes in financial practices can affect the constraints even when no obvious structural change occurs. Financial change of this kind was at the center of Hyman Minsky's 'financial instability hypothesis':

> Acceptable financing techniques are not technologically constrained; they depend upon the subjective preferences and views of bankers and businessmen about prospects. . . . success breeds a disregard of the possibility of failure . . . As a previous financial crisis recedes in time, it is quite natural for central bankers, government officials, businessmen, and even economists to believe that a new era has arrived. (Minsky 1986, p. 213)

Endogenous and exogenous shifts in the severity of credit constraints as well as in households' own perceptions of the riskiness of their financial positions can be a critical source of variations in the aggregate saving rate. Muellbauer (2010) describes an example. Between 1984 and 1988, the ratio of consumption-to-nonproperty income rose by six percent in the United Kingdom. These movements cannot, Muellbauer argues, be explained as the result of intertemporal optimization by a representative agent with perfect foresight or rational expectations: The assumption of perfect foresight or rational expectations can be used to construct measures of the movement in permanent income, and it turns out that during 1984–1988, the ratio of permanent-to-actual income declined. This observation poses a problem for the theory: Representative-agent optimization implies that a rising consumption ratio will be associated with an increasing ratio of permanent-to-actual income, the opposite of what happened. The inability of the theory to account for movements in the consumption ratio is particularly striking for 1984–1988, but, Muellbauer argues, the "dissonance is a problem not just for the second half of the 1980s, but holds over the last 40 years of data" (p. 7).

3.4.2 A Hybrid Aggregate Consumption Function

Traditional Keynesian theory combined the analysis of microeconomic behavior with explicit attention to the problems of aggregation; there was no illusion that the dynamics of aggregate consumption could be described by a simple Euler equation.

Consider Ando and Modigliani's (1963) derivation of the aggregate implications of the life-cycle hypothesis. Starting from micro-level optimization and assuming a perfect capital market, they derived the following consumption function:

$$C_t = cy_t + v\Omega_t, \tag{3.19}$$

---

[22] The absence of a perfect capital market has been central to non-mainstream macroeconomics; e.g., Kalecki (1937) and Minsky (1986). A large literature explains credit constraints on the basis of asymmetric information (Stiglitz and Weiss (1981) is a classic reference). In his critique of the DSGE approach, Stiglitz (2018) emphasizes the importance of these asymmetries for macroeconomic questions. DSGE models have failed, he argues, and "at the heart of the failure were the wrong microfoundations" (p. 70).

where y and Ω denote current labor income and the stock of (nonlabor) assets. The derivation – and in particular the constancy of the parameters c and v – depended on aggregation conditions. The parameters are constant if (a) all agents have the same desired consumption profile, (b) the asset and income shares of the different age groups remain constant over time, and (c) for each cohort, the present value of expected future labor income is proportional to current labor income (see Appendix B for details). These conditions are highly restrictive. But by making the aggregation conditions explicit, it becomes possible to examine the validity of the conditions in particular applications and analyze the implications of violations of one or more of the conditions. Saving and portfolio behavior, for instance, is influenced by demographic variables, and changes in the demographic composition of households, therefore, affect both aggregate household saving rates and aggregate portfolio and debt compositions (Hendry and Muellbauer 2018).

Large-scale pre-DSGE models like the Federal Reserve's FRB/US model and the Bank of England's Medium-Term Macro Model typically included consumption functions that build on Equation (3.19). The specifications have weaknesses, but the DSGE-based models developed by the Bank of England over the last fifteen years have performed worse than the earlier models they replaced. The DSGE-based model that was introduced in 2004 represented "a lurch further away from data coherence" and the newer model from 2011 "could be regarded as another milestone on this road" (Hendry and Muellbauer 2018, p. 305).

Methodologically, optimization (as a stylized version of goal-oriented behavior) has been used in old Keynesian models to identify variables that will influence consumption and indicate their likely effects at the household level. But acknowledging aggregation issues, first-order conditions of optimality are not imposed on the macro equation. Whatever one may think of the detailed specifications of particular Keynesian consumption functions, this general approach can make for greater transparency and facilitate the incorporation of the effects of structural changes, including the relaxation of credit constraints (which, as discussed in Section 3.4.1, may have been particularly important in the early 2000s) and demographic or distributional shifts. Other extensions may also be important in applied work; liquid assets, illiquid financial assets and housing wealth, for instance, may impact consumption differently (Muellbauer 2020).

In short, the lack of rigor in the old Keynesian derivation of aggregate consumption functions is not a weakness: It would be a mistake to impose exact first-order conditions that may hold for a single homo oeconomicus with perfect foresight in a rarefied world of perfect capital markets. These first-order conditions have no place in a relation that attempts to describe aggregate consumption in the real world. They have no theoretical justification, and consumption functions that build on (3.19) perform better empirically than specifications based on the Euler equation for a representative agent.

Ando and Modigliani derived Equation (3.19) from orthodox assumptions of intertemporal optimization and selfish preferences. The dependence of consumption on wealth and income is consistent, however, with social preferences and present bias. Adding these elements points to aspects that need to be taken into account, including institutional features like mandatory pension savings plans (which gain particular importance if there is a present bias) or changes in the distribution of income (which affects peer effects on consumption). But current wealth and income will still exert a powerful influence on consumption, even if the parameters of the aggregate consumption function may now depend on a wider range of institutional and distributional forces.

It should be noted that the equation can also be given a very different, two-class interpretation. Karl Marx, along with other classical economists, assumed that workers spend all their income on consumption, while capitalists, forced by competition, save and invest. In a contemporary version of this approach, Foley et al. (2019) assume that capitalists optimize intertemporally with an infinite horizon, while workers engage in life-cycle saving, leaving no bequests. Their specification implies that aggregate consumption is determined by aggregate wage income, aggregate wealth, and the share of wealth owned by capitalists a specification that reduces to (3.19) if capitalists' share of total wealth is constant.

Its empirical support and compatibility with a range of different interpretations and assumptions about microeconomic behavior make the aggregate consumption function (3.19) useful as a benchmark specification for the macroeconomic analysis in Chapters 8–11.

3.5   A More Radical Perspective

Some of what passes for consumption in the national income accounts represents investment or intermediate inputs. Commuting to work is an intermediate input that may require a car, if no public transport is available; a cell phone may be essential for workers whose employers demand flexible scheduling of hours; households may need refrigerators and freezers if neighborhood shops disappear. But the problems run deeper:

> For the well-off most of the consumption registered as such in GDP accounts are just what it appears to be – goods electively consumed to satisfy desire. For the poor, by contrast, much of the expenditure registered in GDP accounts as consumption is ... what Marx called the 'reproduction of labour power.' The resources devoted by a poor person to basic foodstuffs, or to the heating of her dwelling, or to the health and education of her children, contribute to the maintenance of the human assets of her and her family. (Auerbach 2016, p. 303)

Frank (2012) expresses a similar human-asset perspective when he describes a choice faced by many Americans: Should they save for a comfortable retirement if it means having to send their children to a poor school in a relatively inexpensive neighborhood or, alternatively, be financially irresponsible by moving to a more expensive school district?

As these observations suggest, much consumption has an investment character that goes beyond standard distinctions between consumption services (which matter for utility) and current spending on durable consumption goods (which represents household investment and matters for aggregate demand). Traditional measures of bequests become misleading in this context. For children in low-or middle-income families, a financial bequest would be a poor substitute for growing up in a safe neighborhood or attending a good school. There are similarities here with the discussion of public debt. The Popular notion that public debt 'robs our grandchildren' focuses on the wrong issues. Our grandchildren do not benefit from public saving if it means destroying the environment, reducing spending on infrastructure and education, or increasing unemployment and social conflict.[23]

Learning and the development of skills take place in the workplace and in households, as well as in formal education. In fact, a predominant part of the crucial inputs that shape the next generation are provided by households. These inputs (or investments) are affected when unemployment forces families to relocate in search of a job or to find cheaper accommodation; they are affected when parents have to work flexible hours or take multiple jobs to make ends meet, or when medical bills force parents to pull kids out of after-school programs. Low income and pervasive uncertainty, more generally, affect the ability of families to make long-term plans.[24] But while the need for a stable business climate is recognized as important for business investment, there is little recognition that inequality and a precariously unstable environment can inhibit household planning and the creation of human assets. On the contrary, working people "are called upon, in the name of flexibility, to abandon accumulated skills and life plans in response to transitory economic conditions, or accommodate themselves to unemployment in their sector of work in the name of creative destruction" (Auerbach 2016, p. 224). The consequences can be devastating for families, and the microlevel instability also has macro implications. Strong human assets and a well-educated population bring benefits for society, including high labor productivity and other, less tangible but perhaps more important benefits; informed citizens, for instance, are a precondition for a functioning democracy.[25]

The social and economic context of the reproduction of labor power also accentuates issues that have received little attention. If 'nudging' of the kind analyzed by Thaler and Benartzi (2004) and Somville and Vandewalle (2018) can produce large effects on household saving, it would seem plausible that household consumption can be manipulated in other ways, too. And there is a large industry devoted to doing just that.

Suggestions that advertising and marketing in a broad sense may influence total consumption (as opposed to the composition of spending) are often disputed. It is hard to see, however, how a constant bombardment of households with sophisticated attempts to link consumption with success, happiness, and status can fail to have an

---

[23] There are also crucial differences between household and government debt, however: The treasury bonds that make up the public debt will also be owned by our grandchildren. Public debt issues will be discussed in detail in Chapter 11.

[24] Research at the Shift Project has documented how unstable and unpredictable work schedules give rise to household economic insecurity and hardships. Moreover, by creating instability in children's routines and care arrangements, children manifest heightened anxiety and acting out (Schneider and Harknett 2019).

[25] Auerbach and Skott (2021) discuss implications of these observations for policies that aim to promote human development and democracy.

impact – attempts that have been enhanced in recent years by the formidable information about individual consumers compiled by Facebook, Google, and Amazon.[26] Sales promotion interacts with the desire to keep up with the Joneses by extending reference groups to include rich celebrities, as suggested by Dutt (2009, p. 144). Advertisers, Dutt argues,[27]

work on consumers in complicated ways which exploit their propensity to emulate and seek status, by suggesting – in subtle and sometimes not so subtle ways – why this or that product will increase their status or make them more like people who are rich and beautiful.
(Dutt 2009, p. 144)

Consumption norms are part of the social and economic context within which labor power is reproduced. Adam Smith's account of the need for leather shoes to avoid shame is an example and, drawing on a sociological literature, Akerlof (2007) extends the argument. Norms regarding "what people should consume" exert, he argues, a strong influence on consumption. Wall Street bankers, for instance, "do not live like mothers on welfare. They do not want to. But, even if they did, it would occasion gossip. It is not what they should do (p. 16)."

Akerlof emphasizes the dependence of consumption norms on the individual's particular situation, including current income. Hoff and Stiglitz (2016), along similar lines, describe 'encultured actors' whose preferences, perception, and cognition are influenced by 'social contexts' and 'cultural mental models.' The endogeneity of preferences, more generally, has been discussed extensively by Bowles and Gintis (1986) and Bowles (1998).

The social context of consumption points to a significant difference between households and firms. Unlike households, firms have relatively well-defined goals that are also relatively easy to measure. Profit is a dominant objective, and as a first approximation, it seems reasonable to assume that profit maximization guides the firm's production, investment, and financial decisions, even if uncertainty makes maximization impossible in any strict sense. 'Utility' and 'preferences,' by contrast, are more nebulous constructs, and the appeal of individual utility maximization as a central organizing principle may derive partly from a simple tautology: In some limited sense, people always do what they want to do, given the real and perceived constraints that they face. But if household behavior is shaped by the exigencies of the reproduction of labor, changing social norms, and the constant bombardment from powerful commercial interests, the focus on individual optimization can distract attention from what really matters. Insistence that consumption and saving be derived from well-defined utility functions and explicit optimization easily evolves into vacuous mathematical exercises and increasingly complicated models, as more

---

[26] Advertising aimed at young children is particularly noxious.
[27] Marglin (1984, pp. 361–362) makes a similar point:

The cultural pressure to spend stems from the fact that in our society, consumption is a sovereign remedy for the problems of life. Whether what ails one is a physical, emotional, spiritual, or even a sexual lack, some commodity or other will cure the problem.

and more modifications and extensions are included to make the model consistent with observations.[28]

From this perspective, a particular approach – constrained optimization – that is useful in some contexts as a representation of goal-oriented behavior has become hegemonic and is applied to situations where it adds little and generates needless complications. To be clear, there is no blanket rejection here of goal orientation at the household level, nor is there a claim that constrained optimization can never be useful in the analysis of household behavior. The argument concerns the limitations of these tools, their excessive use in contemporary economics, and the neglect of other, more important forces that influence consumption behavior.

3.6   Conclusion

Recognition of the intertemporal aspects of consumption and saving decisions is universal. Keynes's (1936) discussion of consumption in the *General Theory* is sometimes presented as advocating a simple 'absolute income hypothesis' without any recognition that current consumption may be influenced by other factors than current income. This is a travesty. Keynes's analysis explicitly notes the potential influence of, *inter alia*, changes in interest rates (p. 93), changes in the relation between present and expected future income (p. 95), the need to "build up a reserve against unforeseen contingencies" (p. 107), and anticipated changes in future needs "in relation to old age, family education, or the maintenance of dependents" (p. 107). He concludes the analysis by arguing that movements in current income are likely to have a large impact on consumption. But this is an empirical judgment – one that happens to have strong empirical support. In fact, current descriptions of household behavior in terms of 'buffer stock saving' have reached essentially the same conclusion, while DSGE models routinely include hand-to-mouth consumers in an attempt to improve empirical performance.

The relevance for current consumption of expected future income and expected future needs did not originate with Friedman and Ando/Modigliani. The real story is different: As the profession embraced and developed the formalization of intertemporal optimization, there was a progressive neglect of all *other* factors that may influence the consumption decision, as well as an increasing disregard of deviations of actual behavior from perfect intertemporal optimization. With respect to welfare assessments, the reasonable position that consumption affects welfare morphed into formalizations in which *only* consumption affects welfare, while implicit denials of the endogenous formation of preferences blocked the insidious effects of consumerism from view.

The emergence and increasing popularity of behavioral economics may help reverse the trend. So far, however, the influence on macroeconomics has been limited. Even

---

[28] A large and growing literature attempts to extend models of formal optimization to make them consistent with some set of stylized facts; Fershtman and Segal (2018) represent a recent example.

macroeconomists who concede the empirical superiority of specifications that are more loosely related to economic theory than the Euler-based aggregate consumption models often see this empirical superiority as a reflection of temporary shortcomings of the theory.[29] The perspective here is different. Households – a multifarious group – do not maximize a well-defined, stable utility function, and 'theory' – in the restrictive sense in which the term is typically used in contemporary macroeconomics – will never provide an accurate description of aggregate consumption.

Could it not be argued that DSGE models have made significant progress and that promising ongoing research aims at further improvement? The recent 'heterogeneous agent New Keynesian' (HANK) models, for instance, are lauded by Christiano et al. (2018): This research "typifies the cutting edge of DSGE models" (p. 132). According to Kaplan et al. (2018), their HANK model adds to the literature by providing "an empirically realistic model of the consumption side of the economy." To achieve this, they introduce a continuum of households, each subject to idiosyncratic income shocks and each potentially facing borrowing constraints. Constrained households do not satisfy the standard Euler condition but respond strongly to any change in their income – a mechanism that essentially corresponds to "the Keynesian multiplier in undergraduate textbooks," as Christiano et al. (2017, p. 20) note in the working paper version of their 2018 article. The explicit optimization, however, gives rise to computational complexities which, Kaplan and Violante (2018, p. 170) suggest, helps explain why heterogeneous agent models have not until recently "been used much to study business cycles." Elaborating on these complexities, they explain that (p. 170)

households require a lot of information in order to solve their dynamic optimization problems: each household must not only know its own place in the cross-sectional distribution of income and wealth, but must also understand the equilibrium law of motion for the entire wealth distribution. Under rational expectations, this law of motion is an endogenous equilibrium object, and solving for it is a computationally intensive process.

The complexities arise despite the assumption that all households have identical, constant elasticity utility functions, despite a focus on steady states and stationary distributions of assets and labor income, and despite a range of *ad hoc* assumptions to make the model tractable. There is an underlying presumption that real-world households solve the more complicated real-world optimization problems and that the model – despite its *ad hoc* simplifications and focus on steady states – will give a good account of the resulting aggregate dynamics.

The model is clever, and solving it clearly requires a lot of skill and technical expertise. But the complexities of the model magnify the strain on the assumptions of full dynamic optimization with rational expectations: The chasm between the DSGE assumptions and the behavioral evidence for the real world is wider than ever. If the HANK model represents the cutting edge in DSGE research and an attempt to provide a "realistic treatment of the consumption side of the economy," then we would seem to have *prima facie* evidence of a degenerating research program.

---

[29] Some of the contributors to a special issue of the *Oxford Review of Economic Policy* (issue 1–2, 2018) on 'Rebuilding macroeconomic theory' adopt positions along these lines.

Empirically, the introduction of households that face or act as if they face bind-ing credit constraint has been used to improve the fit of DSGE models. The earlier "TANK" models, however, assumed that the proportion of hand-to-mouth households remains constant and that a household's current decisions do not influence the likeli-hood that the household will become credit constrained in the future. This approach allows for cognitive limitations and deviations from full optimization. But TANK models face other problems. If these nonoptimizing hand-to-mouth households are 'microfounded,' the general case for Euler equations as the *sine qua non* of micro-foundations goes by the wayside. Why retain the Euler equation? Granted, there are people with substantial wealth, people who are not liquidity constrained and who pass on large fortunes to their heirs. But this observation does not prove that the rich act in accordance with the theory. If deviations from homo oeconomicus are widespread, why assume that these deviations apply only to people with limited wealth? Luxury goods are among the most cyclically sensitive components of demand, which would seem to be at odds with the consumption smoothing implied by the Euler equation.[30] There may be clever ways of reconciling the cyclicality of luxury consumption with optimization by the rich, but – absent compelling theoretical and empirical arguments in its favor – it would seem more promising to abandon the notion that Euler equations must be at the core of the specification of aggregate consumption.

A messy process of combining goal orientation – who would deny that saving is influenced by perceived future needs? – with cognitive limitations, evolving norms and social pressures, class divisions, and changing structural constraints (like credit rationing) is needed to account for behavior at the household level. Moreover, the step from household behavior to aggregate consumption involves tricky aggregation, inter-action effects, and unintended consequences. This messiness is not just a reflection of temporary shortcomings that we may have to live with while awaiting improved and fully microfounded theories. It reflects the nature of real-world consumption deci-sions and is intrinsic to any macroeconomic theory that takes microeconomic behavior seriously.[31]

Wren-Lewis (2018) and Blanchard (2018a) contrast 'theory models' with 'applied models.' I am not sure this dichotomy is helpful. Relevant theory must be informed by empirical observation, just as applied models must be informed, explicitly or implic-itly, by theory. Clearly models serve different purposes and therefore make different

---

[30] *The Economist*, October 21, 2010, likened the instability of the luxury industry to a bungee jumper:

Luxury has always been a cyclical industry, but in the past decade it has soared and plunged like a well-dressed bungee-jumper. The early 2000s were grim: terrorist attacks in America, a global outbreak of SARS and the war in Iraq all tempered people's appetites for international travel and frivolous purchases. From 2004 to 2007, however, luxury shoppers worked themselves into a frenzy of indulgence. Then, as the financial crisis bit, they stopped. Last year the global luxury market shrank by 8%. But the luxury recovery that began towards the end of 2009 has now gathered momentum. Bain predicts 10% growth for this year.

[31] Agent-based models may – as argued by, among others, Haldane and Turrell (2018) and Holt et al. (2010) – contribute to our understanding of some of these messy processes. I expect, however, that simulation techniques will be a complement to more traditional models, rather than a substitute.

assumptions. Simple models that make stark and seemingly unrealistic assumptions can be useful to explore the logical implications of particular mechanisms – I make use of many such models in this book. These models are heuristic (using the terminology in Musgrave (1981)).[32] But models that take the Euler equation as an essential, theory-based determinant of the dynamics of aggregate consumption impose a purely scholastic criterion on a scientific, empirical set of problems. The Euler equation has no theoretical justification as a description of aggregate consumption, it lacks empirical support, it diverts attention from factors that are much more important, and it complicates the analysis.

This chapter has focused on household saving and consumption. Importantly, however, household saving does not tell the full story of private saving, and it tells us nothing about the desirable aggregate level of saving. Aggregate saving rates are influenced by corporate saving (Chapter 4), and while many individual households may find that they have saved too little, high aggregate saving rates can generate aggregate demand problems that call for expansionary policy intervention to avoid secular stagnation (Chapter 11).

Appendix A: Consumption Externalities and Saving

Consider the two-period maximization problem

$$\max \left[\alpha \log(c_1 - \eta_1 \bar{c}_1) + \gamma \log l + \frac{1}{1+\rho} \alpha \log(c_2 - \eta_2 \bar{c}_2) \right]$$

$$s.t. \quad c_1 + \frac{1}{1+r} c_2 = w(1-l) = y.$$

The Lagrangian is given by

$$L = \alpha \log(c_1 - \eta_1 \bar{c}_1) + \gamma \log l + \frac{\alpha}{1+\rho} \log(c_2 - \eta_2 \bar{c}_2) + \lambda \left(w - wl - c_1 - \frac{1}{1+r} c_2 \right),$$

with first-order conditions

$$\frac{\alpha}{c_1 - \eta_1 \bar{c}_1} - \lambda = 0 \tag{3.20}$$

$$\frac{\frac{\alpha}{1+\rho}}{c_2 - \eta_2 \bar{c}_2} - \frac{\lambda}{1+r} = 0 \tag{3.21}$$

$$\frac{\gamma}{l} - \lambda w = 0$$

$$w - wl - c_1 - \frac{1}{1+r} c_2 = 0.$$

---

[32] Musgrave distinguishes between three types of assumptions: Heuristic, domain, and negligibility. Negligibility assumptions serve to exclude factors that can be legitimately ignored because they have no significant effects; domain assumptions specify conditions that have to be met for a theory to be applicable; heuristic assumptions purposefully exclude factors that are believed to be important in order to analyze more clearly a particular mechanism that is of interest. Heuristic assumptions and heuristic models represent steps in the process of developing theories that can help us understand complex real-world phenomena.

The first-order conditions can be solved for $c_1, c_2, l,$ *and* λ:

$$\lambda = \frac{\alpha + \frac{\alpha}{1+\rho} + \gamma}{w - \eta_1 \bar{c}_1 - \frac{1}{1+r}\eta_2 \bar{c}_2}$$

$$l = \frac{\gamma}{w}\frac{1}{\lambda} = \frac{\gamma}{w}\frac{w - \eta_1 \bar{c}_1 - \frac{1}{1+r}\eta_2 \bar{c}_2}{\alpha + \frac{\alpha}{1+\rho} + \gamma}$$

$$c_1 = \alpha\frac{1}{\lambda} + \eta_1 \bar{c}_1 = \alpha\frac{w - \eta_1 \bar{c}_1 - \frac{1}{1+r}\eta_2 \bar{c}_2}{\alpha + \frac{\alpha}{1+\rho} + \gamma} + \eta_1 \bar{c}_1$$

$$c_2 = \frac{\alpha(1+r)}{1+\rho}\frac{1}{\lambda} + \eta_2 \bar{c}_2 = \frac{\alpha(1+r)}{1+\rho}\frac{w - \eta_1 \bar{c}_1 - \frac{1}{1+r}\eta_2 \bar{c}_2}{\alpha + \frac{\alpha}{1+\rho} + \gamma} + \eta_2 \bar{c}_2.$$

The solution for leisure can be used to derive the level of income

$$y = w(1 - l) = w - \frac{\gamma}{\lambda} = \frac{\alpha + \frac{\alpha}{1+\rho}}{\alpha + \frac{\alpha}{1+\rho} + \gamma}w + \frac{\gamma}{\alpha + \frac{\alpha}{1+\rho} + \gamma}\left(\eta_1 \bar{c}_1 + \frac{1}{1+r}\eta_2 \bar{c}_2\right).$$

The first-order conditions (3.20) and (3.21) imply that

$$\frac{c_2 - \eta_2 \bar{c}_2}{c_1 - \eta_1 \bar{c}_1} = \frac{1+r}{1+\rho}$$

or

$$c_2 = \frac{1+r}{1+\rho}(c_1 - \eta_1 \bar{c}_1) + \eta_2 \bar{c}_2.$$

Combining this expression for c_2 with the budget constraint, we obtain the reduced-form relation (3.16) between income and consumption in period 1:

$$c_1 = \frac{1+\rho}{2+\rho}y + \frac{1+\rho}{2+\rho}\left[\frac{1}{1+\rho}\eta_1 \bar{c}_1 - \frac{1}{1+r}\eta_2 \bar{c}_2\right].$$

The utility function is of the Stone–Geary type. After covering the cost of the basic needs ($\eta_1 \bar{c}_1 + \frac{1}{1+r}\eta_2 \bar{c}_2$), households split their remaining income between the two periods, the fraction $(1 + \rho)/(2 + \rho)$ going to period 1.

Appendix B: Aggregate Consumption and the Life-Cycle Hypothesis

Following Ando and Modigliani (1963), assume that all agents live for T periods and consider an agent born in period j. Intertemporal optimization typically gives a relation that links current consumption to the present value of the total resources available to the agent (V_{ijt}):

$$c_{ijt} = \gamma_{ijt} V_{ijt},$$

where the subscript ij denotes an agent i born in period j, and t is the current period. The proportionality factors γ_{ijt}, which reflect the desired consumption profile, may depend on the rates of return on assets as well as on the agent's age and the specific form of the agent's utility function.

The agent's total resources are given by

$$
\begin{aligned}
V_{ijt} &= \Omega_{ijt} + y_{ijt} + \sum_{\tau=t+1}^{j+T} y_{ij\tau}(1+r)^{-(\tau-t)} \\
&= \Omega_{ijt} + y_{ijt} + y_{ijt}^e,
\end{aligned}
$$

where Ω_{ijt} represents the agent's nonlabor assets, y_{ijt} is current labor income, and y_{ijt}^e is the present value of the agent's expected future labor income.

Now assume that (a) all agents have the same desired consumption profile, that is, that the proportionality factor γ_{ijt} linking current consumption and total resources is fully determined by the age of the agent ($c_{ijt} = \gamma_{t-j} V_{ijt}$),[33] (b) the asset and income shares of the different age groups remain constant over time (the income and asset shares in period t of the agents that are m years old in period t are the same as the income and asset shares in period t' of the agents that are m years old in period t'), and (c) for each cohort, the present value of expected future income is proportional to current income, $y_{jt}^e = \delta_{t-j} y_{jt}$, where the proportionality factor depends only on the current age of the cohort. With these assumptions, we obtain

$$
\begin{aligned}
C_t &= \sum_j \gamma_{t-j}(\Omega_{jt} + y_{jt} + \delta_{t-j} y_{jt}) \\
&= \left(\sum \gamma_{t-j}\frac{\Omega_{jt}}{\Omega_t}\right)\Omega_t + \left(\sum \gamma_{t-j}(1+\delta_{t-j})\frac{y_{jt}}{y_t}\right) y_t \\
&= c y_t + v \Omega_t,
\end{aligned}
$$

where $\Omega_{jt} = \sum_i \Omega_{ijt}$ and $y_{jt} = \sum_i y_{ijt}$. Ω_{jt}/Ω_t is the cohort's share of aggregate wealth and y_{jt}/y_t is the share in current wage income. The parameters c and v are given by

$$
c = \sum \gamma_{t-j}(1+\delta_{t-j})\frac{y_{jt}}{y_t}
$$

$$
v = \sum \gamma_{t-j}\frac{\Omega_{jt}}{\Omega_t}.
$$

The three aggregation conditions ensure that c and v are constant over time.

---

[33] The proportionality factor is independent of the rate of return if the utility function is Cobb–Douglas.

4   Saving in a Corporate Economy

4.1   Introduction

Corporate business dominates economic activity in most rich countries, with gross value added of the corporate sector typically exceeding 50 percent of GDP. Households may be the ultimate owners of these businesses, but the ownership is mediated by financial assets. Yet, DSGE models largely ignored financial issues and the interaction between goods and financial markets until the financial crisis in 2008. Gali's (2016) 'basic New Keynesian model' has no capital and no investment; there are financial assets, but all households are identical, there is no trade in financial assets, and the net financial position is zero for all households. More elaborate DSGE models include investment. But in the Smets–Wouters (2003, 2007) model, which is still being held up as "a standard reference" (Blanchard 2018a, p. 44), investment is carried out by households who rent capital services to firms.

The role of financial assets and financial mechanisms has been hard to ignore following the financial crisis, but much of the recent work in this area is only loosely, if at all, related to the DSGE approach. There is no attempt, for instance, in the highly cited studies by Mian and Sufi (2009, 2011, 2018) to integrate the analysis of the 'credit-driven household demand' into a complete macroeconomic model, and the key mechanisms – belief heterogeneity, behavioral biases, and endogenous changes in credit supply – have a strong Minskian flavor.

The formal DSGE models have been modified after the crisis, of course. The HANK models discussed at the end of Chapter 3 include two financial assets and emphasize the possibility that households may face borrowing constraints. Other contributions have set out with the explicit aim of explaining the slow recovery after the financial crisis. Recognizing that the Smets–Wouters 2007 model "needs a cocktail of extremely unlikely shocks" (p. 1) to account for the depth of the recession, Linde et al. (2016) discuss some of the challenges and propose three extensions: The explicit introduction of a zero lower bound on the nominal interest rate, allowance for time-variation in the volatility of the exogenous shocks that drive the dynamics around the steady growth path, and, as a third element, the introduction of 'entrepreneurs' and financial intermediation.

The producers of final goods still rent capital services in the Linde et al. model, but households save in the form of bank deposits, with final-good producers buying the capital services from entrepreneurs. Investment is undertaken by the entrepreneurs and financed in part by external finance. Asymmetric information implies that external finance is subject to a risk premium, with the size of the premium depending on the entrepreneur's net worth. The model now adds stochastic shocks to net worth, which translate into shocks to the 'corporate finance premium.' With these extensions – adding entrepreneurs and their net worth as a new state variable along with a new set of stochastic shocks to net worth – the model generates a financial accelerator along the lines of Bernanke et al. (1999). The endogenous dynamics of net worth (as generated by other shocks in the model) produce only minor fluctuations in the finance premium, however, leaving the new exogenous shocks to net worth as the main driver of the fluctuations.[1] The fit of the model is also greatly improved by allowing the volatility of the shock (like that of the other shocks) to vary over time.[2] These improvements in fit may sound like progress, but as noted by Romer (2016) in his scathing indictment of DSGE models, pretty much anything can be explained by the creative use of "imaginary forcing variables."

Linde et al. acknowledge that the extended model has limitations, and many of their objectives for further development may seem eminently reasonable. It is striking, however, how little has been achieved by the DSGE literature since the financial crisis. Even more striking, perhaps, the analysis appears oblivious to the drastic changes with respect to both financial institutions and the behavior of the nonfinancial sector that began long before the financial crisis. Linde et al., for example, emphasize shocks to net worth. But if cyclical fluctuations in net worth over the business cycle are deemed worthy of explicit analysis because of their effect on the risk premium, then changes in financial behavior that affect firms' net worth would seem to demand careful attention. Corporate retention rates have declined since the 1970s (Figure 4.1), share buybacks have soared (Figure 4.2), and the balance sheets of nonfinancial corporations have seen large increases in both financial assets and financial liabilities (Davis 2018, Rabinovich 2019). Yet, these changes in financial behavior find no place in the analysis. Instead, the model relies on exogenous shocks to net worth, introducing a number of assumptions to ensure tractability and to prevent entrepreneurs from gradually accumulating sufficient wealth to become fully self-financed.

This chapter will focus on the implications of financial decisions for the average saving rate, treating the level of investment as exogenous; the determination of aggregate investment is addressed in Chapter 10. Financial stocks and flows are introduced explicitly, with firms making financing decisions and households making

---

[1] Linde et al. (2016, p. 50) note that

most of the fluctuations in the external finance premium are generated by the new exogenous shock that is assumed to hit directly at the net worth of the entrepreneurs. This highly volatile shock explains up to 70 percent of the variance in the spread and one-third of the variance in investment.

[2] As they note, a linear Gaussian DSGE model

considers the strong economic downturns that we typically observe during recession periods as extremely unlikely tail events. (Linde et al. 2016, p. 29)

A time-varying volatility structure alleviates this problem: It "drastically improves the log marginal likelihood of our models" (p. 47).

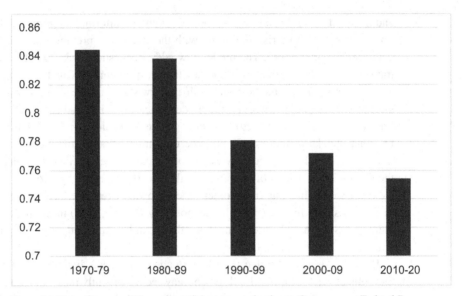

Figure 4.1 Retention rate; US nonfinancial corporate business. Data source: Federal Reserve Statistical Release Z1, 2022.

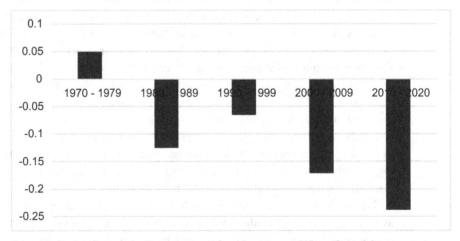

Figure 4.2 Ratio of net equity issues to gross fixed investment; US nonfinancial corporate business. Data source: Federal Reserve Statistical Release Z1, 2022.

saving and portfolio choices.[3] Three main results emerge. Changes in firms' financial behavior, first, affect the average saving rate. Changes in households' portfolio behavior, second, influence the saving rate and can have large and drawn-out effects on aggregate demand. Shifts in income distribution, third, influence aggregate demand partly through financial channels and can be a source of financial instability.

---

[3] 'Stock-flow consistent models' with explicit attention to the accounting relations between stocks and flows have gained increased attention. Godley and Lavoie (2007) have been influential in post-Keynesian macroeconomics. But the ideas have a longer history, including Tobin (1969, 1980). The analysis in this chapter draws mainly on Skott (1981, 1988, 1989b) and Skott and Ryoo (2008).

Section 4.2 presents a version of Kaldor's 'neo-Pasinetti theorem.' This 'theorem' challenges the presumption that households successfully pierce the corporate veil and that firms' financial behavior has no influence on the determination of aggregate saving: Arguments for the independence of the average saving rate from firms' financial decisions are based on a fallacy of composition and/or unrealistic assumptions about household behavior. Section 4.3 discusses interactions between households' portfolio behavior and firms' financial decisions. In principle, these interactions could produce an equilibrium in which households call the tune. In practice, coordination problems and destabilizing feedback effects make this outcome implausible. Sections 4.4. and 4.5 examine some implications of the analysis. Section 4.4 looks at the effects of changes in portfolio compositions on saving and aggregate demand. Section 4.5 introduces heterogeneity among households and examines the effects of increasing inequality. Section 4.6 concludes.

4.2   Saving and Portfolio Decisions

4.2.1   Differential Saving Rates

The classical economists took it for granted that saving rates were higher for profits than for wages, an assumption that is also employed routinely in post-Keynesian and neo-Marxian models.

Differential saving rates can arise because of the heterogeneity of households. The main recipients of profit income ('capitalists' and 'rentiers') tend to be rich, and rich households may save a larger proportion of their income than poor households (Chapter 3). Following Kaldor (1966), however, this section considers a structural mechanism that does not depend on household heterogeneity. Differential saving rates, Kaldor argued, are rooted in the structure of a corporate economy: The saving rate out of profits is high because firms retain a fraction of their profits. This argument does not exclude other mechanisms, including the possibility that rich (profit receiving) households may have a high saving rate.[4] The argument does not depend on heterogeneity, however, and it becomes more transparent in a setting with homogeneous households. Household heterogeneity is considered in Section 4.5.

It may appear that Kaldor's argument can be made quite simply. In a closed economy without public sector, households' flow of disposable income (Y^D) is given by

$$Y^D = Y - R,$$

where R is retained earnings. If retained earnings are proportional to profits and households save a constant fraction s of their disposable income, aggregate saving – the sum of household and corporate saving $(S^H$ and $S^F)$ – is given by

---

[4] Heterogeneity can also take the form of some households – small business owners – investing directly in productive capital. On the asset side, the analysis could be extended to include housing (as in Ryoo 2016). These possible extensions do not nullify the corporate-economy mechanism identified by Kaldor.

$$S = S^H + S^F = sY^D + R$$
$$= [s + s_f(1-s)\pi]Y,$$

where π is the profit share and s_f denotes the share of retentions in profits. Thus, if the retention rate is given, it would seem that an increase in the profit share must raise the average saving rate. The simple proportionality between household saving and household disposable income may be hard to justify, however. It could be argued, in particular, that households adjust their own saving out of disposable income so as to offset changes in corporate saving.

Retained earnings can be used by the firm to finance investment, pay off debt or buy back shares. These possible uses of retained earnings all raise future profits per share (net of interest payments) relative to what profits would have been without the retentions; moreover, greater reliance on internal finance reduces the riskiness of the firm's shares. The increase in future profits per share and the reduced risk will tend to raise the value of the firm's shares. A household that wants to maintain its consumption despite higher retentions and an unexpected reduction in dividends now has two options.

One option is for the household to take out loans or reduce its holdings of liquid assets by an amount corresponding to the reduction in its dividends. This option, following Modigliani and Miller (1958) and Miller and Modigliani (1961), will neutralize the effects of the firm's retention policy: Households offset the fall in firms' leverage by increasing their own leverage. The option, however, may be barred by credit constraints. Unlike the firm, the household may not be able to obtain loans, at least not on the same terms as the firm, even if the value of its shares has increased.[5]

There are other reasons to disregard this option. Sophisticated real-world households diversify their portfolios and adjust the compositions in response to changes in their own circumstances, shifting toward less risky assets as they approach retirement age, for instance. They may also change their portfolios in response to major – real or imagined – shifts in the riskiness and returns of different types of assets. But as argued in Chapter 3, one would expect households – even sophisticated ones – to focus on the factors that seem most important, and the influence of firms' average retention rate on the optimal portfolio composition is likely to be far down on this list, if it makes an appearance at all. Assessments of the riskiness of and likely returns on tech shares will have to take into account, *inter alia*, the regulatory zeal of the EU, Chinese industrial policy, and the effects of pandemics on the demand for tech services; likewise, climate change and its effects on government interventions and policies are crucial to the prospects of not just the energy sectors but a whole slew of industries, from airlines to real estate in Florida.[6]

---

[5] It is generally recognized that credit constraints – as well as tax distortions and the possibility of costly bankruptcies – constrain the validity of the Modigliani–Miller result (e.g., Stiglitz 1969).

[6] Matters are complicated, as indicated by Keynes's observations on the nature of uncertainty: Probability theory cannot reduce "uncertainty to the same calculable status as that of certainty itself" (Keynes 1937b, p. 213). He went on to explain that by 'uncertain knowledge' he did not

The case against fluctuations in average retention rates as a significant influence on portfolio choice is reinforced by the fact that uncertainty surrounds not just the future performance of different financial assets but also the household's own situation, which will be affected by idiosyncratic shocks (illness, unemployment, a leaking roof, etc.). The knowledge that shocks of this kind are likely to occur will influence portfolio decisions: The proportion of wealth in low-yielding liquid assets may be determined primarily by the household's assessment of its idiosyncratic risk, making the portfolio allocation relatively insensitive to changes in the riskiness and returns of different types of assets. Just like a household may engage in buffer stock saving, it may want a certain amount of liquid assets, putting the rest of its wealth into illiquid high-yield assets. The household's use of different mental accounts (cf. Chapter 3) may reinforce the insensitivity of the portfolio composition to changes in asset risks and relative returns.

Empirical evidence supports the insensitivity. The Swedish government introduced a defined contribution component to its social security system in 2000. Each retirement saver could select among hundreds of mutual funds, allocating her retirement savings among up to five funds. Analyzing detailed data on the choices made by the entire population of 7,315,209 retirement savers in Sweden during the period 2000–2016, Cronqvist et al. (2018) show that "nudging" had strong effects on the choices and that the effects of nudging were highly persistent: "the participants seem to have a 'set it and forget it' mindset" (p. 154). Following a change in regulation in 2010, the default fund, which had attracted a large proportion of savers and which had been entirely in equity, switched to having 50 percent leverage. Despite this large, sudden increase in the riskiness of the fund almost no one switched away from the default fund. Cronqvist et al. conclude that (p. 157) "[i]n outer space, an object that has been nudged will keep going in that direction until it is nudged again. Retirement savers appear to resemble such objects."[7]

Overall, the behavioral evidence makes it implausible to assume that households respond to an increase in the average retention rate by taking out loans and/or reducing their holdings of bonds and bank deposits. But even if this mechanism is rejected, households are have a second option: They may respond to a rise in share prices by selling a fraction of their shares. Thus, if an increase in retained profits causes the share valuation of a company to go up by the same amount, a household owning shares in the company can maintain exactly the same consumption and wealth as if it had

---

mean merely to distinguish what is known for certain from what is only probable. The game of roulette is not subject, in this sense, to uncertainty; nor is the prospect of a Victory bond being drawn. Or, again, the expectation of life is only slightly uncertain. Even the weather is only moderately uncertain. The sense in which I am using the term is that in which the prospect of a European war is uncertain, or the price of copper and the rate of interest twenty years hence, or the obsolescence of a new invention, or the position of private wealth-owners in the social system in 1970. About these matters there is no scientific basis on which to form any calculable probability whatever. We simply do not know. (pp. 213–214)

[7] The results in Cronqvist et al. are consistent with many other studies. See Gomes et al. (2021, Section 2.5.4) for a recent survey.

received the dividends (rather than the capital gain): The household can 'declare its own dividends,' not by adjusting its own borrowing but by selling shares. This is the argument addressed by Kaldor's 'neo-Pasinetti theorem.'

4.2.2   The Neo-Pasinetti Theorem

The intuition behind Kaldor's counterargument is simple. The suggestion that share prices will appreciate automatically in line with retained earnings involves a fallacy of composition, Kaldor argued. It may be correct that the share price of a single firm (relative to the general level of share prices) responds positively to an increase in the firm's retained earnings. It is also correct that an individual shareholder can declare her own dividends by selling some of her shares. But households as a group cannot finance consumption by selling shares: There is no one to buy. Households' attempt to compensate for compressed dividends by selling off equity will lead to capital losses as equity prices fall, with these capital losses reducing wealth and tempering the desire to consume. Thus, the average saving rate out of income increases as a result of the rise in corporate retentions.[8]

A Simple Formalization: The 'Neo-Pasinetti Theorem'
Contrary to the assumptions in much of the macroeconomic literature, households in a corporate economy do not save in the form of physical capital. Disregarding housing and other, less important real assets, household wealth is financial wealth. Households may be the ultimate owners of the capital stock, but the ownership of productive capital takes the form of equity.

Equity is not the only financial asset, and even as a first approximation it is essential to include at least two types of financial assets: An asset with a contractual rate of return and an asset, equity, that gives ownership rights to firms but promises no contractual rate of return. Thus, following Skott (1981, 1989b) and Skott and Ryoo (2008), assume that household wealth consists of equity and bank deposits.[9]

Firms finance investment, dividends, and interest payments on external debt by a combination of profits, share issues, and new bank loans. The financial constraint is given by

$$I + D + iL = \Pi + p_N \dot{N} + \dot{L},$$

where N and L are the number of shares and the external debt (bank loans); a dot is used to indicate a time derivative ($\dot{N} = dN/dt$ and $\dot{L} = dL/dt$ denote the rate of new issues and the rate of increase in bank loans); $p_N, i, I, D,$ and Π are the price of

---

[8] The replacement cost of fixed capital is predetermined in the short run, and the ratio of financial valuation to the replacement cost of fixed capital (the valuation ratio, in Kaldor's terminology) changes as a result of movements in equity prices. The valuation ratio subsequently has become known as Tobin's q.

[9] Little would be added, for present purposes, by the introduction of bonds as a second contractual-return asset.

shares, the interest rate, investment, dividends, and profits. To simplify the exposition, the price of output is taken to be constant and normalized to one.

If s_f is the retention rate, the financial constraint can be rewritten

$$I = \Pi - D - iL + p_N \dot{N} + \dot{L} = s_f \Pi - iL + p_N \dot{N} + \dot{L}.$$

For given profits and a given level of investment, firms choose two of the three financial variables. If they set the retention rate s_f ($= 1 - D/\Pi$) and the rate of new issues $\dot{N}$, the financial constraint pins down the required change in bank loans (external finance). Formally, firms could also choose the rate of increase of external debt (the value of $\dot{L}$) and let either the retention rate or the rate of new issues do the adjusting. Retentions and new issues, however, are less flexible in the short run, and I shall take external finance to be the accommodating variable: It is assumed that firms have a margin of available external finance (which allows external finance to do the adjusting) and, for simplicity, that external finance is available at a constant rate of interest, i.

In analogy with firms' financial constraint, households have a budget constraint. They receive wage income $(1 - \pi)Y$ and interest income $(i^M M)$ on their bank deposits (M), and their holdings of equity yield a flow of dividends (D). By assumption, firms retain a fraction s_f of their gross profits Π, and the dividends are given by $D = (1 - s_f)\Pi$. Neither firms nor households hold cash (by assumption there are only two assets, equity and bank deposits), and the flow of household income is either added to bank deposits or spent on consumption and the purchase of new shares. Thus, we can write households' budget constraint as

$$(1 - \pi)Y + (1 - s_f)\Pi + i^M M = C + \dot{M} + p_N \dot{N}^H. \tag{4.1}$$

If, for simplicity, it is assumed that banks hold no reserves and have neither costs nor profits, we have $i = i^M$ and $L = M$.[10] The number of shares owned by households must also be equal to the number of shares issued by firms ($N^H = N$), with the price of shares adjusting to ensure that this equilibrium condition will be satisfied. Thus, the budget constraint simplifies to

$$(1 - \pi)Y + (1 - s_f)\Pi + iM = C + \dot{M} + p_N \dot{N}. \tag{4.2}$$

Using a consumption function with non-property income and wealth as the determinants of household consumption (cf. the discussion in Section 3.3), let

$$C = c(1 - \pi)Y + \nu\Omega, \tag{4.3}$$

where π is the profit share and $\Omega = M + p_N N$ denotes household wealth (which in this model equals the financial valuation of firms; the economy is closed and without a public sector). Empirical specifications of this consumption function – including the FRB-US model – typically assume that actual consumption adjusts gradually toward an equilibrium defined by (a more general version of) Equation (4.3). An extension

---

[10] The analysis is substantively unchanged if banks make profits $\left(i^D < i^L\right)$ and pay out these profits as dividends.

of this kind increases the dimensionality of the dynamic system. Appendix A outlines the stability conditions for two- and three-dimensional systems of differential equations; Appendix B analyzes a 2D model with gradual adjustments of consumption. The qualitative results are similar to those for the 1D system below.

The specification (4.3) implies that consumption will be independent of firms' financial decisions if the Modigliani–Miller theorem holds and households' financial wealth Ω is independent of firms' decisions; if financial wealth depends on profits, consumption could also become independent of the distribution of income. As argued in Section 4.2.1, however, the behavioral assumptions that would make consumption independent of financial behavior and the share of profits are highly implausible.

In the simple benchmark model in this section, households maintain a constant portfolio composition. If α_M denotes the share of deposits in household wealth, we have

$$M = \alpha_M \Omega; \qquad p_N N = (1 - \alpha_M)\Omega. \tag{4.4}$$

Using Equation (4.4) and dividing by Y, the consumption rate can now be written as

$$\frac{C}{Y} = c(1 - \pi) + v(1 + \alpha)\frac{M}{Y}, \tag{4.5}$$

where $\alpha = (1 - \alpha_M)/\alpha_M = \frac{p_N N}{M}$. The stock of deposits is predetermined, while the endogenous determination of the share price makes it possible to adjust the value of shareholdings instantaneously: The equilibrium share price is given by

$$p_N = \alpha \frac{M}{N}.$$

The short-run consumption rate in Equation (4.5) depends inversely on the profit share and positively on the ratio of equity to deposits (the portfolio parameter α) and the deposit–income ratio. Changes in the portfolio shares (in α) will be considered in Sections 4.4 and 4.5. For the moment, however, suppose that α is constant and that output and the number of shares grow at constant rates.

The evolution of the deposit–income ratio can be found from the budget constraint (4.2):

$$\dot{M} = (1 - s_f \pi)Y + iM - p_N \dot{N} - C$$

or[11]

$$\left(\frac{\dot{M}}{Y}\right) = (1 - s_f \pi) - c(1 - \pi) - [\alpha \hat{N} + \hat{Y} + v(1 + \alpha) - i]\frac{M}{Y}, \tag{4.6}$$

---

[11] We have

$$\left(\frac{\dot{M}}{Y}\right) = \frac{M}{Y}\left(\frac{\widehat{M}}{Y}\right)$$

$$= \frac{M}{Y}\left[(1 - s_f \pi)\frac{Y}{M} + i - \alpha \hat{N} - \frac{C}{M} - \hat{Y}\right]$$

$$= (1 - s_f \pi) - (\alpha \hat{N} + \hat{Y} - i)\frac{M}{Y} - \frac{C}{Y}.$$

Using the consumption function to substitute for C/Y, Equation (4.6) now follows.

where 'hats' over a variable denote proportional growth rates, for example, $\hat{N} = \frac{\dot{N}}{N}$. Assuming that $\alpha\hat{N} + \hat{Y} + v(1 + \alpha) - i > 0$,[12] this differential equation is stable, and the deposit–income ratio converges to a stationary solution,

$$\frac{M}{Y} \to \frac{(1 - s_f\pi) - c(1 - \pi)}{\alpha\hat{N} + \hat{Y} + v(1 + \alpha) - i}. \tag{4.7}$$

A positive value of the stationary solution is ensured if $c \le 1$ and $s_f \le 1$. Combining Equations (4.5) and (4.7), we get

$$\frac{C}{Y} \to c(1 - \pi) + v(1 + \alpha)\frac{(1 - s_f\pi) - c(1 - \pi)}{\alpha\hat{N} + \hat{Y} + v(1 + \alpha) - i}. \tag{4.8}$$

Equation (4.8) implies that under weak conditions, the inverse relation between the consumption rate and the profit share carries over to the long run. Using the benchmark numbers in footnote 12, we have

$$\frac{\partial\frac{C}{Y}}{\partial\pi} = -c - v(1 + \alpha)\frac{(s_f - c)}{\alpha\hat{N} + \hat{Y} + v(1 + \alpha) - i}$$

$$\approx -\frac{3}{2}s_f + \frac{1}{2}c$$

$$< 0 \text{ for } s_f > \frac{c}{3}.$$

Thus, the very weak condition $s_f > c/3$ is sufficient for $\partial\frac{C}{Y}/\partial\pi < 0$.

Equation (4.8) also implies that firms' financial behavior (the values of s_f and $\hat{N}$) influence consumption: The consumption output ratio is decreasing in s_f and $\hat{N}$. The empirical literature on the aggregate saving effects of corporate retentions is sparse but supports this implication. Poterba (1987, p. 503) finds that

the most conservative estimates suggest that a one dollar shift in corporate saving induces a 23 cent shift in private saving. For the longer sample period, the implied effects are much larger.

In a more recent study, Bebczuk and Cavallo (2016) conclude that "a $1 increase in business saving raises private saving by approximately $0.59" (p. 2281).

The effects of changes in household behavior are more complex. The consumption ratio, first, is decreasing (increasing) in α if $\hat{N} > \hat{Y} - i$ (if $\hat{N} < \hat{Y} - i$). Intuitively, in steady growth households save out of disposable income in order to maintain the

---

[12] The rate of new issues has been negative in the United States since 1980s, but the condition is satisfied for plausible values of the variables and parameters. Empirically, the ratio of buybacks to gross investment has been of the order of 0.1–0.25 during this period, and with gross investment at about 15–20 percent of GDP, we have $p_N\dot{N} \approx -0.03Y$. A real interest rate on deposits that does not exceed the growth rate, a wealth–GDP ratio above 3, and a consumption rate out of wealth of more than 3 percent now imply that

$$\alpha\hat{N} + \hat{Y} + v(1 + \alpha) - i \quad = \alpha M\frac{p_N\dot{N}}{p_N N}\frac{1}{\Omega}\frac{\Omega}{M} + \hat{Y} + v\frac{\Omega}{M} - i$$

$$\approx -0.03\frac{Y}{\Omega}\frac{\Omega}{M} + \hat{Y} + v\frac{\Omega}{M} - i$$

$$> 0.02\frac{\Omega}{M}.$$

ratios of financial assets to income. As a group, however, they can only spend disposable income on shares to the extent that firms issue new shares. Thus, the fraction of disposable household income that goes into purchasing shares depends on both the rate at which firms expand the number of shares and on the valuation of the shares. If there are no new issues ($\hat{N} = 0$), attempts by households to buy shares merely lead to prices being bid up, and the long-run saving rate will only be positive if households want to increase their deposits (i.e., if the growth rate of output is positive). The extent of the required saving depends on the growth rate and the steady-growth value of the deposit–income ratio; the latter is inversely related to α if $\hat{N} = 0$ and $\hat{Y} - i > 0$ (Equation (4.7)). This result generalizes to cases where $\hat{N} \neq 0$: The net effect of an increase in α depends on the relative values of $\hat{Y} - i$ and $\hat{N}$.

Second, induced capital gains imply, paradoxically, that the long-run consumption rate can be *decreasing* in the consumption parameters c and v. An increase in the propensities to consume reduces the long-run wealth–income ratio, and if this reduction is sufficiently large, the net effect of a rise in a consumption parameter can be negative. The extent to which the wealth–income ratio is reduced depends on firms' new issue policies. Consider, again, the simple case when the number of shares is kept constant ($\hat{N} = 0$). Households as a group cannot buy shares, and no saving out of current income is needed to maintain a constant ratio of equity wealth to income: Equity wealth will grow in line with total wealth as a result of induced capital gains. The impact of reduced saving therefore falls entirely on bank deposits: Compared to a situation with $\hat{N} > 0$, any given reduction in saving will have a larger negative effect on the long-run ratio of deposits to income. Since share prices adjust endogenously to make the wealth–income ratio equal to the deposit–income ratio, it follows that the higher the rate of new issues, the smaller will be the effect on the wealth–income ratio. If $\alpha \hat{N} + \hat{Y} - i < 0$, the long-run wealth effect dominates: An increase in the consumption parameters c or v reduces the long-run wealth ratio to such an extent that $\frac{C}{Y} = c(1 - \pi) + v\frac{\Omega}{Y}$ falls.[13]

Equation (4.8) also embodies a standard result from the life-cycle hypothesis: If α is finite, the consumption rate is a decreasing in $\hat{Y}$ (since $1 - s_f\pi > c(1 - \pi)$). Intuitively, the wealth–income ratio is constant in steady growth, and if income is growing, some fraction of disposable income must go into saving in order to maintain a constant deposit–income ratio. This requirement applies even if there are no new issues of equity ($\hat{N} = 0$).

---

[13] The specification of household behavior in Equations (4.2)–(4.4) endogenizes movements in the wealth ratio Ω/Y. Changes in households' portfolio preferences, for instance, affect the value of Ω/Y, both in the short and in the long run; this wealth effect lies behind the dependence of the consumption ratio on α. As an alternative, households could adjust saving and portfolio decisions to achieve target wealth–income or wealth–consumption ratios. Specifications along these lines have been used by Skott (1981, 1989b), Skott and Ryoo (2008), and Ryoo and Skott (2017). The qualitative implications for the effects of changes in profits, firms' financial behavior, and household portfolio preferences are similar to those based on the consumption function in Equation (4.8).

4.2.3   An Aside: The Pasinetti Theorem and DSGE Models

Kaldor's (1966) analysis of the effect of corporate saving (and thereby the profit share and the retention rate) on the aggregate saving rate supported the position held by Luigi Pasinetti in a debate with Paul Samuelson and Franco Modigliani in the same issue of *Review of Economic Studies*, and Kaldor referred to the result as a 'neo-Pasinetti' theorem. The name is misleading, however. Pasinetti (1962) – the article that provoked the subsequent debate – was premised on the assumption that if workers save, they will receive profit income, and a distinction must be made between the profits going to capitalists (who have a high saving rate) and the profits going to workers (who have a low saving rate). His analysis showed that as long as capitalists own a positive share of the aggregate capital stock, a long-run equilibrium will satisfy the 'Cambridge equation' which links the profit rate to the growth rate and capitalists' saving propensity:

$$\frac{\Pi}{K} = \frac{1}{s_c} \frac{I}{K},$$

where Π is profits and s_c denotes capitalists' saving rate. Surprising as it may seem, this 'Pasinetti theorem' is quite intuitive. If capitalists own a constant share of the total capital stock, the growth rate of their capital K^c must equal the growth rate of the aggregate stock. The conclusion now follows from the assumption that capitalists save a fraction s_c of their profits, that is, $I/K = I^c/K^c = s_c(\Pi^c/K^c) = s_c(\Pi/K)$.

In their comments on Pasinetti's analysis, Samuelson and Modigliani (1966, p. 297) questioned "the existence of identifiable classes of capitalists and workers with 'permanent membership' – even as rough first approximation" (p. 271), especially because "since people do not live forever, one would have to extend the assumption to one's heirs, and their heirs, and so on, until Kingdom-come – both before golden ages are reached and forever afterwards" (p. 297).

This critique was relevant with respect to Pasinetti (1962). Workers were poor and undertook little or no saving in nineteenth century capitalism, and Marx could argue that capitalists, who owned and controlled the means of production, save and invest because competition compels them to behave in this way. In a corporate economy, however, ownership has been separated from the running of firms, and competition does not enforce a uniform saving behavior across owners of equity and other financial assets. Some capitalist households – Jeff Bezos, Elon Musk, and Mark Zuckerberg clearly belong to this group of capitalist households – may have high saving rates. But did their parents and will their children and grandchildren have the same saving behavior, as required by the assumption of permanent membership? Other members of the top 0.01 percent, including rock stars, baseball players and surgeons, may leave large bequests but their source of income is not primarily profits.

It may seem churlish to ask concrete questions like this of a model that is designed to analyze properties of capitalist economies at a high level of abstraction. But the model defines two groups of households, and it should be possible to outline general criteria for the delineation of the groups. Moreover, in Pasinetti's long-run analysis, it is assumed that the economy has converged to a stationary wealth distribution determined by the share of profits in income and the saving behavior of the two distinct groups. The convergence is slow, however, and a case must be made for why the saving behavior of the different groups remains unchanged from one generation to the next.

Samuelson and Modigliani's critique does not apply to Kaldor's analysis. For Kaldor the high saving propensity out of profits was "something which attaches to the nature of business income and not the wealth (or other peculiarities) of the individuals who own property" (Kaldor 1966, p. 310). His analysis also provided an answer to Pasinetti, who had motivated his original analysis by a 'logical slip' in Kaldor's earlier models: If workers save, they will receive profit income, Pasinetti had argued, and it would be inconsistent to assume that workers and capitalists apply the same saving rate to capital income. Kaldor's neo-Pasinetti theorem – which does not rely on distinctions between worker households and capitalist households – rebutted this criticism: There was no logical slip in assuming that saving rates are higher out of profits than out of wage income.

This old debate has contemporary relevance. Samuelson and Modigliani's concerns about assuming permanent classes of capitalists with a high saving rate and workers with a low saving rate can be raised equally well against two-agent New Keynesian (TANK) versions of the DSGE model, which make similar assumptions. In this case, the classes are represented by hand-to-mouth consumers and dynasties of intertemporal optimizers, and the analysis, as in Pasinetti (1962), focuses on (fluctuations around) long-run growth paths in which a group of dynasties with the same utility functions own all wealth. The HANK model does not distinguish between classes but, again like Pasinetti, it focuses on steady growth paths in which the joint distribution of assets and incomes across household is stationary. And, of course, infinitely lived intertemporally optimizing households represent permanent dynasties with constant consumption-saving preferences.

4.3   Feedback Effects on Firms' Financial Decisions

The neo-Pasinetti theorem has not attracted much attention outside the post-Keynesian literature. Bliss (1975), who devoted a chapter to the 'Cambridge Model,' is an exception. On the Kaldorian saving hypothesis he remarked (p. 135):

in the semi-stationary state, it is households that 'call the tune' when it comes to saving, not because only households can save, but because when firms save (retain earnings for investment) the ownership rights in those firms appreciate in value along with the new investment and so increase the net worth of households that share in the ownership of firms, and hence increases their ability to consume if they so wish.

The analysis leading to Equation (4.8) focused on households' consumption and saving decisions. It said nothing about the determination of output, employment, investment, and firms' financial behavior. Bliss, by contrast, refers to the properties of a full intertemporal general equilibrium in a model with perfect foresight and forward trading in all markets. He considers not the saving function, but the determinants of equilibrium saving. Equilibrium saving is equal to equilibrium investment, and if households call the tune with respect to saving, they also call the tune when it comes to investment. Although he presents his comments as a criticism of Kaldor's saving hypothesis, his argument in fact concerns the determination of firms' investment and financial behavior.

Households would only be calling the tune with respect to the average saving rate as well as the amount of saving if firms always made investment and financial decisions that fully reflected households' preferences, information, and expectations; investment would then match the amount of desired household saving at full employment. These heroic assumptions eliminate the coordination problems that are – or should be – at the center of macroeconomics.

Undoubtedly, firms react to signals from financial markets as well as from goods and labor markets, but dynamic feedback effects between consumption, investment, and financial decisions do not automatically solve the coordination problems between households and firms. Indeed, the feedback effects need not even produce adjustments in the right direction.

Consider a simple scenario in which the share of investment that is financed by retained earnings is subject to a financial norm – an element of what Minsky (1986, p. 213) referred to as "acceptable financing techniques." Specifically, let the ratio of financial valuation to the replacement cost of a firm's capital stock (the firm-level value of Tobin's q) depend on deviations of the firm's behavior from the norm and on the average value of Tobin's q; firms that deviate from the norm receive a lower valuation than other comparable firms.

Formally, for firm i,

$$q_i = f\left(\frac{s_{fi}\pi_i p_i Y_i}{p_{Ki} I_i} - \mu(z_i), \bar{q}, z_i\right)$$

and

$$f_1\left(\frac{s_{fi}\pi_i p_i Y_i}{p_{Ki} I_i} - \mu(z_i), \bar{q}, z_i\right) \gtreqless 0 \text{ for } \frac{s_{fi}\pi_i p_i Y_i}{p_{Ki} I_i} - \mu(z_i) \lesseqgtr 0.$$

Subscripts i indicate firm-level variables and μ denotes the financial norm for the share of internal financing. The average value of Tobin's q is denoted by $\bar{q}$; q_i is the firm-level value of q; z_i represents a vector of firm-level characteristics (size, industry, current profitability, future prospects, etc.) that affect the valuation directly and, if the financial norm is contingent on the firm's characteristics, indirectly. Path-dependent Minskian views on prudent behavior influence the norm, but legal and institutional factors – the structure of taxation, for instance, or whether share buybacks are permitted – will also play a role.[14] The prices of the firm's own output (p_i) and of the capital goods that it uses (p_{Ki}) may deviate from the average price level (which has been normalized to one).

---

[14] Seen as a form of stock market manipulation, share buybacks were effectively illegal in the United States for most of the twentieth century. A rule change in 1982 made them legal.

The firm can control its own retention rate, and in the absence of credit constraints, s_{fi} will be chosen to meet the financial norm, that is,

$$s_{fi} = \mu(z_i) \frac{p_{Ki} I_i}{\pi_i p_i Y_i}.$$

Now consider the effects of a change in financial norms. Specifically, suppose that for some reason there has been a rise in the average value of μ. In response to this change, firms raise their retention rates, the average saving rate increases, and aggregate demand declines. On average, consequently, firms experience a fall in their output Y_i or price p_i. If investment is kept unchanged, firms have an incentive to raise their retention rates further in order to satisfy the norm, but as they do so, the fall in aggregate demand is reinforced. Moreover, the aggregate demand problem is exacerbated if the fall in aggregate demand leads to a decline in investment. In short, the feedback effects may not be stabilizing.

Bliss's argument – like the implicit assumption in many macroeconomic models about the transparency of the 'corporate veil' and the irrelevance of corporate saving – essentially boils down to a belief that market signals solve these coordination problems between firms and households.[15]

As an illustration of this implicit belief, consider Romer's (2018) discussion of investment. In the chapter on investment, he presents a standard model with convex adjustment costs and intertemporal profit maximization. Formally, the representative firm's maximization problem takes the form

$$\max \int_{t=0}^{\infty} e^{-rt}[\pi(K(t))\kappa(t) - I(t) - C(I(t))dt$$
$$\text{st} \quad \dot{\kappa}(t) = I.$$

Using Romer's notation, I and κ denote the firm's investment and capital stock, K is the aggregate capital stock, and $C(.)$ is the convex adjustment cost function $(C(0) = C'(0) = 0, C''(.) > 0)$. The firm's gross profits are proportional to the firm's own capital stock (there is perfect competition and the firm operates under constant returns to scale) but depend inversely on aggregate capital $(\pi'(K) < 0)$. The real rate of interest r is constant.

The first-order conditions from the Hamiltonian produce an equation linking the firm's investment to the value of the costate variable:

$$1 + C'(I) = q, \tag{4.9}$$

where q is the costate variable for the maximization problem. Commenting on this result, Romer notes that in order to make its investment decision, 'the firm does not

---

[15] The steady growth path in DSGE models deviates from the semi-stationary state in Bliss's Walrasian intertemporal general equilibrium model: Monopolistic competition and other 'imperfections' and distortions reduce employment below the Walrasian level. But like Bliss, DSGE models ignore crucial coordination problems between distinct decision-makers. These coordination problems invalidate general claims that households call the tune.

need to know anything about the future other than the information that is summarized in q' (p. 429). This comment is correct but misleading. One might as well argue that 'to find the value of the costate variable q, all the firm needs to know is the optimal value of current investment.' The value of the costate variable is itself an output from the optimization: It is determined alongside the optimal level of investment, and the determination draws on all information about future demand and cost conditions.

The sufficiency of q for the determination of investment, however, leads Romer to the argue that

A unit increase in the firm's capital stock increases the present value of the firm's profits by q, and thus raises the value of the firm by q. Thus, q is the market value of a unit of capital. If there is a market for shares in firms, for example, the total value of a firm with one more unit of capital than another firm exceeds the value of the other by q. ... Thus [the first order condition, Equation (4.9); PS] states that a firm increases its capital stock if the market value of capital exceeds the cost of acquiring it. (p. 430)

Imperceptibly the argument has moved from the properties of costate variables in optimal control theory to strong claims about the market valuation of shares and the efficiency of the stock market. This critically important step is made by sleight of hand without any supporting argument. Coordination problems have disappeared from sight. The implicit assumption seems to be that the firm and all potential financial investors solve the same optimization problem, reaching the same conclusions about the optimal trajectory of investment and the associated costate variable. Alternatively, it could be assumed that only financial investors solve the optimization problem, that their financial decisions (the demand for the firm's equity) generate a q value that is equal to the costate variable from the optimization problem, and that the CEO can now determine investment simply by equating the marginal adjustment cost to $q - 1$. Or financial investors could act on the assumption that the firm has chosen investment optimally; assuming that the adjustment cost function is known, arbitrage may now bring the stock price into line with the implied value of the costate variable. The presumption in all cases is that the coordination problems have been solved.

Interactions across markets and between decision-makers should be at the center of macroeconomics. Decision-makers have diverse information sets, expectations, and incentives. CEOs will know more than shareholders about the options and prospects of the firm – the likelihood that current R&D projects will be successful, for instance. But compensation schemes also provide them with incentives to make decisions that are not always in the best interest of households as the ultimate owners. Individual firms, furthermore, may have incentives to follow financial strategies that reduce aggregate demand, thereby imposing negative externalities on other firms and affecting the dynamics of the system as a whole, as in the example discussed earlier in this Section. Households, likewise, choose portfolio compositions in their role as financial investors without considering external effects. The analysis of these information, incentive, and coordination problems is short-circuited by simply assuming that the stock market valuation represents the value of the costate

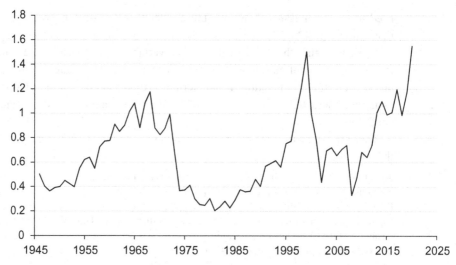

Figure 4.3 Tobin's q for US nonfinancial corporate business, 1946–2020. Data source: Federal Reserve Statistical Release Z1, 2022 (financial valuation) and Bureau of Economic Analysis, Fixed Assets Accounts Tables (current-cost stock of fixed assets).

variable in the optimal solution to the representative firm's intertemporal optimization problem.[16]

From this perspective, it is not surprising that the q theory of investment has had limited success in econometric studies (e.g., Blanchard et al. 1993) and that Tobin's q does not hover around one (or some other constant) as one would expect if the distinction between financial wealth and physical capital were irrelevant; see Figure 4.3. One may also note that the analysis in Sections 4.1 and 4.2 is consistent with trend movements in Tobin's q. Using Equation (4.7), the long-run value of Tobin's q is

$$
\begin{aligned}
q &= \frac{\Omega}{K} = \frac{\Omega}{Y}\frac{Y}{K} \\
&= (1+\alpha)\frac{1 - s_f\pi - c(1-\pi)}{\alpha\hat{N} + \hat{Y} + v(1+\alpha) - i}\frac{Y}{K}.
\end{aligned}
$$

Thus, falling retention rates and increasing share buybacks may have contributed to the trend increase in q since the 1980s. A trend increase in the share of equity in household wealth works in the same direction, while the effect of increases in the profit share is positive if $c > s_f$.

---

[16] Differences between marginal and average q-values also complicate the relation between the financial valuation and the incentive to invest, as is well known.

4.4   Wealth and Portfolio Effects

A single household treats its current wealth as exogenously given when making portfolio decisions, and in the simple two-asset setting, the household's portfolio preferences can be described by the desired equity–deposit ratio, alpha. In the aggregate, however, financial wealth does not remain constant if households change their portfolio behavior.

It may be useful to consider three stylized scenarios. The first scenario takes movements in α as exogenous, that is, the desired portfolio composition evolves without feedback effects from changes in the level of wealth or in rates of return. The second scenario assumes that households adjust their portfolio and consumption decisions so as to achieve an exogenously determined trajectory of the level of liquid assets (of M). Like the second scenario, the third also endogenizes the path of α, but the focus is on feedback effects from relative returns to the desired portfolio composition.

First Scenario: Exogenous Movements in α

The share price is a jump variable, and the average portfolio composition (the value of α) could, in principle, exhibit discontinuous jumps. Jumps, however, can be approximated by high rates of change of α, and for present purposes, it is convenient to treat α as moving smoothly over time. With this assumption (and keeping constant the consumption parameters and the share of profits), it follows from Equation (4.5) that[17]

$$\left(\frac{\dot{C}}{Y}\right) = v\frac{M}{Y}\dot{\alpha} + v(1+\alpha)\left(\frac{\dot{M}}{Y}\right).$$

Making use of Equation (4.6), this equation can be rewritten as

$$\left(\frac{\dot{C}}{Y}\right) = v\frac{M}{Y}\dot{\alpha} + v(1+\alpha)\left\{(1-s_f\pi) - c(1-\pi) - [\alpha\hat{N} + \hat{Y} + v(1+\alpha) - i]\frac{M}{Y}\right\}.$$

Starting from a long-run equilibrium (a stationary M/Y), the term in curly brackets is equal to zero initially, and the rate of change in the consumption rate is equal to $v(M/Y)\dot{\alpha}$. Assume for concreteness that $\dot{\alpha} > 0$, that is, households want to switch their portfolios toward equity and gradually raise α toward a new target level. As they try to buy shares, the price of the shares and their total wealth start rising, and the increase in Ω raises $\dot{C}$. This immediate impact is supplemented by additional effects as time passes: A positive $\dot{\alpha}$ gradually raises the level of α which in turn makes the term in curly brackets become negative (positive) if $\hat{N} + v > 0$ (if $\hat{N} + v < 0$). Moreover, the increase in $\dot{C}$ gradually raises the level of consumption which may boost aggregate demand – $\hat{Y}$ may increase. Even if the growth rate of output is unchanged, increased consumption slows the growth rate in households' deposits, which affects the movements in the deposit–income ratio M/Y.

The dynamics are complex, but if α converges to a new target level and $\hat{Y}$ is constant, the consumption rate converges to a constant long-run value: As shown

---

[17] Gradual adjustments in consumption toward a target level would preserve continuity in the movements of C/Y even if α were allowed to jump.

in Section 4.2, an increase in α will raise (reduce) the long-run consumption rate if $\hat{N} < \hat{Y} - i$ (if $\hat{N} > \hat{Y} - i$).

Second Scenario: Exogenous Movements in M

The parameter α describes the desired composition of financial wealth. But households may aim to increase the amount of liquid assets (the amount of deposits M), quite independently of total wealth. This scenario could reflect autonomous household decisions, or an increase in liquid assets (a decline in household debt) could be forced upon households by a tightening of credit constraints.[18]

Using the budget constraint (4.2) and assuming for simplicity that $\dot{N} = i = 0$, we have

$$C = (1 - s_f \pi)Y - \dot{M}.$$

Now suppose that the ratio of liquid assets M to base-year income (Y_{t_0}) must increase by 0.05 relative to what it would have been without a credit squeeze, and that this increase takes place over a five-year period from t_0 to $t_0 + 5$. Thus, on average, $\dot{M}$ must increase by $0.01Y_{t_0}$ every year during the transition period, and the required change in consumption is given by

$$\Delta C = (1 - s_f \pi)\Delta Y - \Delta \dot{M} = (1 - s_f \pi)\Delta Y - 0.01Y_{t_0}.$$

The direct impact of the credit squeeze is for consumption to fall by one percent of Y_0. Unless offset by policy intervention, the fall will be amplified by derived effects on aggregate demand and household income.

This implication of changes in $\dot{M}$ has been derived using only the budget constraint. Consistency with the consumption function is made possible by endogenous shifts in share valuation. Households that want to increase their liquid assets may expect to achieve this goal simply by reallocating their portfolio; initially, they may have no intentions of curtailing consumption. A generalized attempt by households to sell shares, however, causes a decline in share prices, and the associated fall in wealth produces a decline in consumption. Putting it differently, if households want to raise the deposit–income ratio, the portfolio parameter α becomes endogenous.[19] Algebraically, consistency between the budget constraint and the consumption function (4.3) requires that

$$(1 - s_f \pi)Y - \dot{M} = c(1 - \pi)Y + v(1 + \alpha)M.$$

---

[18] Mian and Sufi (2011) show that during the housing boom, the effects of house prices on borrowing were concentrated largely among house owners with low credit scores, a finding that could be explained by a relaxation of credit constraints (p. 2155). Similarly, the tightening of credit constraints after the crisis was asymmetric. Thus, a forced increase in the deposit–income ratio could be a derived effect of a prior collapse in the value of households' collateral.

[19] Many households own no equity. Household heterogeneity of this kind could be captured by a reformulation of the consumption function that explicitly distinguishes between credit constrained households without equity and non-credit constrained households with equity holdings. The behavior of the former group could be described by the budget constraint and exogenously imposed changes in $\dot{M}$. The latter group would see consumption determined by the consumption function, with the budget constraint determining the dynamics of M.

Hence, if $\dot{M}$ is exogenous, the solution for $(1 + \alpha)$ is given by

$$1 + \alpha = \frac{1}{vM}[(1 - s_f\pi - c(1 - \pi))Y - \dot{M}]. \tag{4.10}$$

The distinction between autonomous shifts in α (with $\dot{M}$ determined by Equation (4.10)) and autonomous shifts in the desired deposit–income ratio (with α determined by Equation (4.10)) is useful analytically, but in practice the shifts are likely to interact. A fall in household confidence, for instance, can induce an initial shift in the desired portfolio composition: α falls. The decline in α entails a fall in share prices, and as household wealth suffers, adverse effects on their credit worthiness may lead to a tightening of credit conditions and force households to increase the ratio of liquid assets to income.

The analysis suggests that high values of α are likely to be associated with financial fragility: They reduce the deposit–income ratio as long as $v + \hat{N} > 0$ (Equation (4.7)), and attempts to raise the ratio – the rebuilding of balance sheets following a shift toward safe assets – requires a protracted period of high saving. In the absence of compensating policy intervention, financial crises may cast a long shadow of recession, an implication that is in line with the evidence in Reinhart and Rogoff (2009). Compensating policy interventions, however, typically involve rising public debt, an outcome that Reinhart and Rogoff (2010) warned against; fiscal policy and public debt form the topics of Chapter 11.

Third Scenario: Endogenous Dynamics in α and M: Financial Instability

Portfolio compositions may be insensitive to variations in average retention rates or in the rate of new equity issues. They are likely, however, to respond to large, highly visible changes in rates of return. Stock market booms represent one such visible change: Stock markets receive a lot of attention, and a rising market tends to attract new investors. Thus, assume that the change in α is determined by

$$\dot{\alpha} = \lambda_\alpha(\alpha^* - \alpha); \quad \lambda_\alpha > 0; \quad \alpha^* = f(r^e); \quad f' > 0 \tag{4.11}$$
$$\dot{r}^e = \lambda_r(r - r^e), \tag{4.12}$$

where α^* is the target share of equity, r^e the expected rate of return on equity, and r the current rate of return.[20] The return on deposits – the other asset – is taken to be constant and, for simplicity, equal to zero.[21]

The specification in Equations (4.11) and (4.12) combines gradual adjustment in α (Equation (4.11)) with adaptive expectations (Equation (4.12)); if returns have been high for a while, there is a tendency to think that this will continue. This specification may be at odds with a rational expectations hypothesis, but rational expectations fare poorly in the context of asset market bubbles. In a discussion of credit supply expansions, Mian and Sufi (2018, p. 49) argue that "the rational expectations model with common beliefs is unlikely to explain the predictable boom-bust cycles

---

[20] The analysis in this section draws on Skott (2013).

[21] A more sophisticated specification would allow for heterogeneity among investors (e.g., Sethi 1996, Brock and Hommes 1998).

we witness in the data," while Muellbauer and Murphy (1997, p. 1721) find "strong evidence that both house prices and relative rates of return in housing are forecastable," suggesting that "housing markets are far from efficient." Gradual adjustment also has support. Giglio et al. (2021) find that the sensitivity of financial investors' equity share to changes in their beliefs is much lower than predicted by benchmark models, that trading is infrequent, that changes in investors' beliefs have little effect on the timing of trading and that there is large and persistent heterogeneity in beliefs about expected outcomes. Peer effects – portfolio shifts in response to outcomes experienced by friends, neighbors, or colleagues – may contribute to the lagged response; Gomes et al. (2021, Section 4) discuss peer effects on asset and debt behavior.

The current rate of return on equity is given by the sum of the dividend ratio $((1 - s_f)\pi Y/(p_N N))$ and the growth rate of the share price $(\dot{p}_N)$,

$$r = \frac{(1 - s_f)\pi Y}{p_N N} + \hat{p}_N = \frac{(1 - s_f)\pi Y}{\alpha M} + \hat{p}_N.$$

If $\dot{N} = 0$, we have $\hat{p}_N = \hat{\alpha} + \hat{M}$, and the dynamic equation for expected returns can be written as

$$\dot{r}^e = \lambda_r \left(\frac{(1 - s_f)\pi Y}{\alpha M} + \hat{p}_N - r^e \right) = \lambda_r \left(\frac{(1 - s_f)\pi Y}{\alpha M} + \hat{\alpha} + \hat{M} - r^e \right). \quad (4.13)$$

An equation for the change in deposits can be found by combining the budget constraint and the consumption function. Substituting Equation (4.3) into (4.2), we get

$$\dot{M} = (1 - s_f \pi)Y - c(1 - \pi)Y - v(1 + \alpha)M. \quad (4.14)$$

If, for illustrative purposes, it is assumed that policy intervention keeps output constant and that the profit share and retention rate are also constant, then Equations (4.11), (4.13), and (4.14) constitute a three-dimensional system of differential equations in M, α, r^e. The system has a unique stationary solution with $\alpha > 0$, and the Routh–Hurwitz conditions for local stability are satisfied if the portfolios respond slowly to changes in current returns. This response is determined by $\lambda_r, \lambda_\alpha$, and f'; local stability can be achieved by reducing these parameters sufficiently (see Appendix C). From the Routh–Hurwitz conditions, it can also be seen, however, that stability will be lost for high values of $\lambda_r, \lambda_\alpha$, or f'.

These results correspond to intuitive notions of how such a system might evolve. If $\lambda_r = 0$ and expected returns are constant, for instance, the target share of equity in the portfolio will also be constant, eliminating the destabilizing feedback effects from changes in the current demand for equity (the value of α) to the target share α^*. Formally, the system becomes two-dimensional when $\lambda_r = 0$, and this new 2D system is recursive: For a given r^e, Equation (4.11) is a stable one-dimensional equation in α, and for a given α, Equation (4.2) is a stable equation in M.

The example is stylized, and the aim is not to provide an accurate account of any particular episode of financial instability. It is, more modestly, an illustration that feedback effects can generate financial instability even in a setting in which output is assumed to grow at an exogenous rate – an assumption that neutralizes potentially important, destabilizing interactions with the real side of the economy.[22]

4.5   Household Heterogeneity

Rich and poor households differ in their consumption and portfolio decisions. Low and middle income groups in the United States have few financial assets, their wealth–income ratio is lower than that of the rich, and the composition of their portfolio is different: Their holdings of financial assets are skewed toward fixed income assets. The rich, by contrast, hold a large proportion of their wealth in stocks. In 2019, more than 90 percent of US families in the top 10 percent of the income distribution owned stock directly or indirectly (with a median value of $485K). The corresponding numbers for families in the bottom half of the income distribution were 31 percent of stockholders, with median holdings of less than $10K (Bhutta et al. 2020). In 2001, stockholding households had average financial wealth that was three to four times higher than that of non-stockholding households, and the mean and median shares of stocks in financial assets were 9.2 and 0.0, respectively, for households with a head of household aged between 55 and 64 and net worth between $10,000 and $100,000, but 31.5 and 30.5 percent for households with net worth above $1 million (Curcuru et al. 2005, Tables 4 and 6).

This section considers some implications of these stylized facts for the effects of changes in income distribution. The motivation for considering this change in distribution should be obvious: The United States and many other countries have seen a dramatic increase in earnings inequality over the last forty years. The distributional shift is taken as exogenous in this section; Chapter 7 considers possible reasons for the rise in inequality.

Inequality Effects on the Average Saving Rate

Consider an example with two types of households, poor and rich, and assume for simplicity that both the rate of new equity issues and the rate of interest on deposits are zero; $\hat{N} = i = 0$. The poor have a relatively high consumption rate out of non-property income and hold their wealth entirely in the form of bank deposits (money). The rich have a relatively low consumption rate out of non-property income and hold their wealth in equity and money.

Formally, the behavior of the poor is described by

$$C^P = cY^P + v\Omega^P$$
$$\Omega^P = M^P$$

---

[22] Ryoo (2016) develops a model of housing bubbles along similar lines; in an earlier paper, Ryoo (2010) analyzes Minskian long waves in a setting with endogenous fluctuations in aggregate demand and economic growth.

with

$$\dot{M}^P = Y^P - cY^P - vM^P,$$

where superscripts P denote 'poor.' Y^P represents the wage income of the poor which – since by assumption $i = 0$ – equals their total income.

The behavior of the rich, analogously, is determined by

$$
\begin{aligned}
C^R &= c\gamma Y^R + v\Omega^R; \quad \gamma < 1 \\
\Omega^R &= p_N N + M^R \\
p_N N &= \alpha M^R.
\end{aligned}
$$

Superscripts R denote 'rich.' Y^R represents the wage income of the rich, whose total disposable income is given by the sum of their wage income and distributed profits, that is, $Y^R + (1 - s_f)\pi Y$, where Y represents aggregate income ($Y = Y^P + Y^R + \pi Y$). Using the budget constraint of the rich, the evolution of M^R can be written as

$$\dot{M}^R = Y^R + (1 - s_f)\pi Y - \gamma c Y^R - v(1 + \alpha)M^R. \tag{4.15}$$

Aggregate consumption is given by

$$C = C^R + C^P = c\gamma Y^R + v(1 + \alpha)M^R + cY^P + vM^P.$$

In the short run, the wealth variables M^R and M^P and the portfolio composition α are predetermined, and a redistribution toward the rich reduces consumption. The wealth variables evolve over time, however.

In steady growth, all income and wealth variables grow at the same rate. If $g > 0$ is the growth rate, the two budget constraints can be used to derive wealth–income ratios. Equation (4.15) implies that

$$gM^R = \dot{M}^R = Y^R + (1 - s_f)\pi Y - \gamma c Y^R - v(1 + \alpha)M^R$$

or

$$\frac{M^R}{Y} = \frac{1 - \gamma c}{g + (1 + \alpha)v}\frac{Y^R}{Y} + \frac{(1 - s_f)\pi}{g + (1 + \alpha)v}.$$

Analogously,

$$\frac{M^P}{Y} = \frac{1 - c}{g + v}\frac{Y^P}{Y}.$$

If η denotes the share of non-property income going to the rich ($Y^R = \eta(1 - \pi)Y$), the steady growth value of the average consumption rate can be written as

$$\frac{C}{Y} = c\gamma\eta(1 - \pi) + v(1 + \alpha)\left[\frac{1 - \gamma c}{g + (1 + \alpha)v}\eta(1 - \pi) + \frac{(1 - s_f)\pi}{g + (1 + \alpha)v}\right]$$
$$+ c(1 - \eta)(1 - \pi) + v\frac{1 - c}{g + v}(1 - \eta)(1 - \pi).$$

It follows that[23]

$$\frac{\partial}{\partial \eta}\left(\frac{C}{Y}\right) = (1-\pi)\frac{\frac{g}{1+\alpha}}{\frac{g}{1+\alpha}+v}\left\{-c(1-\gamma)+(1-c)\frac{\alpha v}{g+v}\right\}. \tag{4.16}$$

The first term inside the curly brackets $(-c(1-\gamma))$ is negative while the second term $((1-c)\frac{\alpha v}{g+v})$ may be positive. The outcome is ambiguous. A decline in the average consumption rate may be more likely, but the net effect of an increase in inequality can be positive when the rich and poor have different portfolio compositions.[24]

Intuitively, the rich may have relatively high consumption rates because of their high wealth–income ratio. The aggregate wealth–income ratio is given by $\Omega/Y = \Omega^R/Y + \Omega^P/Y$, and we have

$$\frac{\Omega^R}{Y} = \frac{1-\gamma c}{\frac{g}{1+\alpha}+v}\frac{Y^R}{Y} + \frac{(1-s_f)\pi}{\frac{g}{1+\alpha}+v}$$

$$\frac{\Omega^P}{Y} = \frac{1-c}{g+v}\frac{Y^P}{Y}$$

$$\frac{\partial\frac{\Omega^R}{Y}}{\partial\frac{Y^R}{Y}} = \frac{1-\gamma c}{\frac{g}{1+\alpha}+v} > \frac{1-c}{g+v} = \frac{\partial\frac{\Omega^P}{Y}}{\partial\frac{Y^P}{Y}}.$$

The long-run effect of a rise in Y^R/Y on Ω^R/Y exceeds the long-run effect of a rise in Y^P/Y on Ω^P/Y for two separate reasons. The consumption parameter out of non-property income, first, is lower for the rich ($\gamma < 1$), which increases the numerator; the rich, second, hold part of their wealth in equity ($\alpha > 0$), which reduces the denominator.

The first effect is straightforward but cannot, on its own, produce paradoxical results: In the absence of the second effect, an increase in inequality must reduce the average consumption rate. To see this, set $\alpha = 0$ to eliminate the portfolio differences; as shown by Equation (4.16), the effect of increases in inequality now becomes unambiguously negative.

The second effect also has an intuitive explanation. Rising incomes and a constant portfolio composition mean that the rich want to increase the value of both deposits

[23] We have

$$\frac{\partial}{\partial \eta}\left(\frac{C}{Y}\right) = (1-\pi)\left\{-c(1-\gamma)+v\left[\frac{1-\gamma c}{\frac{g}{1+\alpha}+v}-\frac{1-c}{g+v}\right]\right\}$$

$$= (1-\pi)\left\{-c(1-\gamma)+v\left[\frac{c-\gamma c}{\frac{g}{1+\alpha}+v}+\frac{1-c}{\frac{g}{1+\alpha}+v}-\frac{1-c}{g+v}\right]\right\}$$

$$= (1-\pi)\left\{-c(1-\gamma)\left(1-\frac{v}{\frac{g}{1+\alpha}+v}\right)+(1-c)v\left[\frac{1}{\frac{g}{1+\alpha}+v}-\frac{1}{g+v}\right]\right\}$$

$$= (1-\pi)\frac{\frac{g}{1+\alpha}}{\frac{g}{1+\alpha}+v}\left\{-c(1-\gamma)+(1-c)\frac{\alpha v}{g+v}\right\}.$$

[24] If, for instance, $c = 0.7$, $v = 0.05$, $g = 0.03$, and $\alpha = 2$, an increase in inequality will raise the consumption rate $(\partial(C/Y)/\partial\eta > 0)$ if $\gamma > 26/56$.

and equity holdings. The increase in deposits requires saving out of current income. By contrast, if the number of shares is given, the rich as a group cannot buy additional shares. Instead, the desired increase in equity wealth is achieved through capital gains. These induced capital gains reduce the saving rate that is required for wealth to grow at the rate g.

Inequality and Bubbles

If an increase in inequality reduces the consumption rate, the resulting negative aggregate-demand effect can be alleviated by asset market bubbles, and weak aggregate demand gives central banks little incentive to burst any such bubbles. In this sense, increasing inequality may be said to permit the development of bubbles. Moreover, a rise in inequality can contribute to the initial creation of a bubble: If policy-makers reduce interest rates in response to a weakening of aggregate demand, financial investors may react by shifting their portfolios toward equity.

Important as policy-related connections may be, this subsection explores whether an increase in inequality can also directly produce a bubble. Intuitively, differences in portfolio behavior imply that an increase in inequality tends to raise the demand for stocks, thus setting the stage for dynamic repercussions along the lines of the third scenario in Section 4.4.

Equation (4.15) describes the dynamics of M^R. Retain the dynamic Equation (4.11) for α (as well as the assumption of constant output, profit share, retention rate, and number of shares), and replace M by M^R in the dynamic Equation (4.13) for r^e. Formally, we now have

$$\dot{M}^R = Y^R + (1 - s_f)\pi Y - \gamma c Y^R - v(1 + \alpha)M^R$$

$$\dot{\alpha} = \lambda_\alpha(\alpha^* - \alpha); \quad \alpha^* = f(r^e); \quad f' > 0; \quad ...\lambda_\alpha > 0$$

$$\dot{r}^e = \lambda_r\left(\frac{(1 - s_f)\pi Y}{\alpha M^R} + \hat{p}_N - r^e\right) = \lambda_r\left(\frac{(1 - s_f)\pi Y}{\alpha M^R} + \hat{\alpha} + \hat{M}^R - r^e\right).$$

This three-dimensional system in (M^R, α, r^e) is almost identical to the system in Section 4.4 and, as in Section 4.4, there is a unique stationary state which may or may not be stable.[25]

Now consider a permanent, upward shift in the income of the rich and assume, as in Section 4.3, that aggregate output is constant. The comparative statics become particularly simple if all profits are retained, that is, if $s_f = 1$. With these assumptions, the system simplifies to

$$\dot{M}^R = (1 - \gamma c)Y^R - v(1 + \alpha)M^R$$

$$\dot{\alpha} = \lambda_\alpha(\alpha^* - \alpha); \quad \alpha^* = f(r^e); \quad f' > 0; \quad ...\lambda_\alpha > 0$$

$$\dot{r}^e = \lambda_r(\hat{\alpha} + \hat{M}^R - r^e).$$

---

[25] It reduces to the system in Section 4.3 if $Y^R = Y$.

At the stationary point, we have $\hat{\alpha} = \hat{M}^R = 0$ and the dynamic equation for r^e implies that the stationary solution for r^e is zero. The dynamic equation for α now determines the stationary solution for α ($\alpha = f(r^e) = f(0)$), and the solution for M^R can be found by plugging the stationary values of r^e and α into the dynamic equation for M^R. Thus, the unique stationary state satisfies the following equations:

$$M^R = \frac{(1 - \gamma c)Y^R}{v(1 + \alpha)}$$
$$\alpha = f(0)$$
$$r^e = 0.$$

A rise in the income of the rich, Y^R generates an upward shift in the expression for $\dot{M}^R$, thereby increasing the stationary solution for M^R. The stationary solutions for α and r^e, however, are unaffected if $s_f = 1$. Appendix D considers the more complex case in which the retention rate is below one.

Irrespective of whether the stationary solution is stable or unstable, the dynamic trajectory following an increase in Y^R will be associated with an initial stock market boom. The value of M^R is predetermined in the short run and, starting from the old stationary point, the shift in Y^R leaves the initial value of M^R below the new stationary solution. The rise in saving produces gradual increases in M^R, but the equity market is affected as well. The increased demand for equity from the rich generates a rising stock market and – boosted by capital gains – the rate of return on equity increases, which shifts the desired portfolio compositions toward equity and reinforces the stock market boom.[26]

Empirically, this particular mechanism – the effects of increased inequality on the demand for equity – may not have been a major force behind the stock market boom of the 1990s. But the analysis illustrates a general point: Changes in the distribution of income – whatever their source – have repercussions for asset demands and financial markets (as well as for aggregate demand and the goods market).

4.6   Conclusion

Modeling choices reflect visions of how economies work. If firms' investment decisions are considered important for the dynamics of a capitalist economy, they should not be absent from the benchmark model. If interactions between households and firms are considered important, one should not leave out financial assets and assume that fixed capital is owned directly by households. If the evidence shows systematic deviations from the predictions of models with full information and perfect intertemporal optimization, one should not assume full information and perfect optimization.

---

[26] If the retention rate is below one, the new stationary point will have lower values of the rate of return and the share of equity in the portfolio of the rich. Convergence to the new stationary solution still involves a stock market boom, however – see Appendix C.

This chapter has addressed issues that are commonly ignored in macroeconomics. In a corporate economy, households do not own productive capital directly, and this institutional fact has important implications. Households – or a subset of rich households – may be the ultimate owners, but the ownership is mediated by financial markets. The separation of investment and saving decisions is at the heart of Keynesian economics, and the corporate character of the economy also influences the determination of saving. In the words of Marglin (1984, p. 432), orthodox theories of saving are "relevant at best to a comparatively small subset of households" and, moreover, "household saving is at best a small part of the story of accumulation in the capitalist sector of the economy."

The financial decisions of the corporate sector affect the average saving rate. Average saving rates depend positively on the profit share, the retention rate, and the rate of new issues of equity. Saving rates also respond, not surprisingly, to changes in the parameters of the consumption function (the consumption propensities out of income and wealth), but portfolio decisions play a role as well: They influence asset prices and household wealth, which feeds into consumption and saving.

Portfolio effects imply that attempts by households to increase the deposit–income ratio by shifting wealth from equity to deposits lead to capital losses and, possibly, prolonged weaknesses of aggregate demand. Conversely, relaxations of credit constraints (and/or a desire to shift wealth toward equity and reduce the deposit–income ratio) boost aggregate demand. These results reflect an asymmetry between equity and deposits: If output prices are stable and households want to increase the real value of their deposits, they must save some of their disposable income. By contrast, if households as a group want to raise the value of their equity holdings, it can be achieved without any squeeze on consumption: With an inelastic supply of shares, an increase in aggregate household demand for shares produces capital gains without any net increases in spending on the purchase of shares. Thus, changes in the desired deposit–income ratio have consumption and aggregate demand effects, while desired changes in the equity–income ratio have no such direct effects.

These distinctive features of the corporate structure of the economy do not depend on household heterogeneity. To highlight this fact, most of the analysis in this chapter has assumed homogeneous households. But households differ with respect to both portfolio and consumption decisions, and these differences can produce additional surprising results: Because of portfolio effects, an increase in inequality may (but need not) reduce the average saving rate in the long run. This outcome is possible even if the rich have a higher saving rate out of non-property income. Differences in portfolio behavior, moreover, imply that an increase in inequality may spark a stock market bubble.[27]

---

[27] The formal analysis in this chapter has been cast in terms of equity and deposits. Housing, like equity, is in inelastic supply in the short run, and an increase in the demand for housing is met by price increases that may develop into a housing bubble (e.g., Ryoo 2016, Gao et al. 2020).

Appendix A: Local Stability of Two- and Three-Dimensional Systems of Non-linear Differential Equations

Local Stability in 2D Systems

Consider the dynamic system

$$\dot{x} = f(x,y)$$
$$\dot{y} = g(x,y)$$

and let (x^*, y^*) denote a stationary solution,

$$f(x^*, y^*) = 0$$
$$g(x^*, y^*) = 0.$$

The first-order Taylor approximation for $(\dot{x}, \dot{y})$ in the neighborhood of (x^*, y^*) is given by

$$\begin{pmatrix} \dot{x} \\ \dot{y} \end{pmatrix} = \begin{pmatrix} f_1(x^*, y^*) & f_2(x^*, y^*) \\ g_1(x^*, y^*) & g_2(x^*, y^*) \end{pmatrix} \begin{pmatrix} x - x^* \\ y - y^* \end{pmatrix} = A \begin{pmatrix} x - x^* \\ y - y^* \end{pmatrix},$$

where A is the Jacobian matrix.

The local stability properties of the stationary solution (x^*, y^*) are determined by the real part of the eigenvalues of A. The eigenvalues in turn are calculated as the roots of the characteristic polynomial

$$\lambda^2 - tr\lambda + \det = 0,$$

where

- the trace tr is the sum of the diagonal elements of the Jacobian matrix (evaluated at the stationary solution) and
- det is the determinant of the Jacobian matrix (evaluated at the stationary solution).

The roots may be complex, but local stability is ensured if the real part of both roots are negative. This condition is satisfied if and only if

- $\det > 0$;
- $tr < 0$.

The stationary solution represents a saddle point if the determinant is negative; it is an unstable node or focus if both the determinant and the trace are positive. The first-order Taylor approximation leaves the local stability properties of a nonlinear system indeterminate if the trace or determinant is zero.

Local Stability in 3D Systems

The local properties of a higher-dimensional system can also be examined by analyzing the Jacobian of the system (evaluated at a stationary point). The following Routh–Hurwitz conditions are sufficient for local stability of a 3D system:

$$tr(J) < 0$$

$$\det(J) < 0$$

$$\det(J_1) + \det(J_2) + \det(J_3) > 0$$

$$-tr(J)[\det(J_1) + \det(J_2) + \det(J_3)] + \det(J) > 0,$$

where J_i is the 2 x 2 matrix derived from the Jacobian matrix by deleting row i and column i.

Appendix B: Gradual Adjustment of Consumption

Let

$$C^* = c(1 - \pi)Y + v\Omega \qquad (4.17)$$

$$\Omega = p_N N + M \qquad (4.18)$$

$$p_N N = \alpha M \qquad (4.19)$$

$$\dot{M} = (1 - s_f \pi)Y + iM - p_N \dot{N} - C. \qquad (4.20)$$

Introducing gradual adjustments in consumption, actual consumption follows the dynamic equation

$$\dot{C} = \lambda_c (C^* - C). \qquad (4.21)$$

Combining Equations (4.17)–(4.21), we get a two-dimensional system of differential equations:

$$\left(\frac{\dot{C}}{Y}\right) = \frac{C}{Y}\left(\frac{\widehat{C}}{Y}\right) = \lambda_c c(1 - \pi) + \lambda_c v(1 + \alpha)\frac{M}{Y} - [\lambda_c + \hat{Y}]\frac{C}{Y} \qquad (4.22)$$

$$\left(\frac{\dot{M}}{Y}\right) = \frac{M}{Y}\left(\frac{\widehat{M}}{Y}\right) = (1 - s_f \pi) - [\alpha\hat{N} + \hat{Y} - i]\frac{M}{Y} - \frac{C}{Y}. \qquad (4.23)$$

This system has a unique stationary solution,

$$\left(\frac{C}{Y}\right)^* = \frac{\lambda_c v(1 + \alpha)}{\lambda_c v(1 + \alpha) + (\lambda_c + \hat{Y})(\alpha\hat{N} + \hat{Y} - i)}(1 - s_f \pi)$$

$$+ \frac{\lambda_c (\alpha\hat{N} + \hat{Y} - i)}{\lambda_c v(1 + \alpha) + (\lambda_c + \hat{Y})(\alpha\hat{N} + \hat{Y} - i)}c(1 - \pi)$$

$$\left(\frac{M}{Y}\right)^* = \frac{(\lambda_c + \hat{Y})(1 - s_f \pi) - \lambda_c c(1 - \pi)}{\lambda_c v(1 + \alpha) + (\lambda_c + \hat{Y})(\alpha\hat{N} + \hat{Y} - i)}.$$

The Jacobian matrix for this system is given by

$$J\left(\frac{C}{Y}, \frac{M}{Y}\right) = \begin{pmatrix} -(\lambda_c + \hat{Y}) & \lambda_c v(1 + \alpha) \\ -1 & -(\alpha\hat{N} + \hat{Y} - i) \end{pmatrix}.$$

The trace and determinant are $tr = -(\lambda_c + \hat{Y}) - (\alpha\hat{N} + \hat{Y} - i)$ and det $= (\lambda_c + \hat{Y})$ $(\alpha\hat{N} + \hat{Y} - i) + \lambda_c v(1 + \alpha)$. The trace is negative and the determinant is positive for plausible parameter values. Thus, the stationary solution is stable, and the stationary solution for C/Y coincides with the solution in the case with fast adjustment (with $\lambda_c \to \infty$, corresponding to $C = C^*$ at all times).

Appendix C: 3D System of Financial (In-)Stability

Consider the dynamic system

$$\dot{M} = (1 - s_f\pi)Y - c(1 - \pi)Y - v(1 + \alpha)M$$
$$\dot{\alpha} = \lambda_\alpha(\alpha^* - \alpha); \quad \alpha^* = f(r^e); \quad f' > 0; \quad \lambda_\alpha > 0$$
$$\dot{r}^e = \lambda_r\left(\frac{(1 - s_f)\pi Y}{p_N N} + \hat{p}_N - r^e\right) = \lambda_r\left(\frac{(1 - s_f)\pi Y}{\alpha M} + \hat{\alpha} + \hat{M} - r^e\right).$$

Existence of a Unique Stationary Solution
A stationary solution requires that

$$M = \frac{(1 - s_f\pi)Y - c(1 - \pi)Y}{v(1 + \alpha)} \tag{4.24}$$

$$r^e = f^{-1}(\alpha) \tag{4.25}$$

$$r^e\alpha M = (1 - s_f)\pi Y. \tag{4.26}$$

Substituting the expressions for M and r^e into Equation (4.26), a solution for α must satisfy the condition

$$f^{-1}(\alpha)\frac{\alpha}{1 + \alpha} = v\frac{(1 - s_f)\pi}{(1 - s_f\pi) - c(1 - \pi)} = v\frac{(1 - s_f)\pi}{(1 - s_f)\pi + (1 - c)(1 - \pi)}. \tag{4.27}$$

The left-hand side of Equation (4.27) is strictly increasing in α. Thus, there is at most one solution. The existence of a solution is ensured if the required return on equity exceeds v as $\alpha \to \infty$. A violation of this condition would be economically implausible.

Having found a unique solution for α, solutions for M and r^e can be found using Equations (4.24) and (4.25).

Local Stability Properties
The local stability properties of the stationary solution are determined by the Jacobian which, evaluated at the stationary solution, takes the form

$$J(M,\alpha,r^e) = \begin{pmatrix} -v(1 + \alpha) & -vM & 0 \\ 0 & -\lambda_\alpha & \lambda_\alpha f' \\ -\lambda_r\frac{Y}{M^2}[(1 - s_f\pi)\frac{1+\alpha}{\alpha} - (1 - \pi)(\frac{1}{\alpha} + c)] & -\lambda_r[\frac{(1-s_f)\pi Y}{\alpha^2 M} + \frac{\lambda_\alpha}{\alpha} + v] & -\lambda_r[1 - \frac{\lambda_\alpha}{\alpha}f'] \end{pmatrix}.$$

The necessary and sufficient Routh–Hurwitz conditions for local stability are that

1. $tr(J) = -v(1 + \alpha) - \lambda_\alpha - \lambda_r[1 - \frac{\lambda_\alpha}{\alpha} f'] < 0,$
2. $\det(J_1) + \det(J_2) + \det(J_3) = v(1 + \alpha)[\lambda_\alpha + \lambda_r(1 - \frac{\lambda_\alpha}{\alpha} f')] + \lambda_\alpha \lambda_r[1 - \frac{\lambda_\alpha}{\alpha} f']$
   $+ \lambda_r \left[\frac{(1-s_f)\pi Y}{\alpha^2 M} + \frac{\lambda_\alpha}{\alpha} + v\right] \lambda_\alpha f' > 0,$
3. $\det(J) = -v(1 + \alpha)\lambda_r \lambda_\alpha \left\{1 + f'v + f'\frac{y}{\alpha^2 M}(1 - \alpha)\right\} =$
   $-v(1 + \alpha)\lambda_r \lambda_\alpha \left\{1 + f'v\frac{(1-s_f)\pi}{\alpha^2[1-s_f\pi-c(1-\pi)]}\right\} < 0,$ and
4. $-tr(J)[\det(J_1) + \det(J_2) + \det(J_3)] + \det(J) > 0.$

At the stationary solution, we have $Y/M = v(1 + \alpha)/[(1 - s_f\pi) - c(1 - \pi)]$, and tedious calculations show that the determinant can be reduced to the expression in condition 3; this condition is always satisfied. Conditions 1, 2, and 4, however, need not hold. The adjustment speeds $\lambda_r, \lambda_\alpha$ and the sensitivity of the portfolio composition to changes in expected returns (f' evaluated at the stationary solution) are critical. For any given, finite values of two out these three parameters, stability is ensured if the third parameter is sufficiently small (the conditions 1, 2, and 4 hold if the third parameter goes to zero). Conversely, the stability conditions will be violated if $\lambda_r, \lambda_\alpha$, and f' are large. The trace condition, for instance, will be violated if $f' \to \infty$, if $\{\lambda_\alpha \to \infty$ and $\lambda_r f' > \alpha\}$, or if $\{\lambda_r \to \infty$ and $\lambda_\alpha f' > \alpha\}$. Putting it differently, if the stationary solution is locally stable for $(f'(r^{e*}), \lambda_\alpha, \lambda_r) = (a_1, a_2, a_3)$, then there is some finite number m such that it becomes unstable when $(f'(r^{e*}), \lambda_\alpha, \lambda_r) > (ma_1, ma_2, ma_3)$.

Appendix D: Inequality and Bubbles When $s_f < 1$

The dynamic system is given by

$$\dot{M}^R = Y^R + (1 - s_f)\pi Y - \gamma cY^R - v(1 + \alpha)M^R$$
$$\dot{\alpha} = \lambda_\alpha(f(r^e) - \alpha); \quad f' > 0$$
$$\dot{r}^e = \lambda_r\left(\frac{(1 - s_f)\pi Y}{p_N N} + \hat{p}_N - r^e\right) = \lambda_r\left(\frac{(1 - s_f)\pi Y}{\alpha M^R} + \hat{\alpha} + \hat{M}^R - r^e\right).$$

A stationary solution satisfies the equations

$$M^R = \frac{(1 - \gamma c)Y^R + (1 - s_f)\pi Y}{v(1 + \alpha)} \tag{4.28}$$

$$\alpha = f(r^e) \tag{4.29}$$

$$r^e = \frac{(1 - s_f)\pi Y}{\alpha M^R}. \tag{4.30}$$

Substituting the expression for M^R into the equation for r^e, we get

$$r^e = \frac{v(1 - \alpha)}{\alpha} \frac{(1 - s_f)\pi Y}{(1 - \gamma c)Y^R + (1 - s_f)\pi Y}. \tag{4.31}$$

Equations (4.29) and (4.31) determine the stationary solutions for α and r^e. Equation (4.29) describes a positive relation between the two variables, and Equation (4.31) an inverse relation. It follows that there is (at most) one stationary solution for (α, r^e) and therefore – using Equation (4.28) – at most one solution for M^R.

An increase in Y^R produces a downward shift in Equation (4.31) but leaves Equation (4.29) unaffected. Thus, an increase in inequality must reduce the stationary solutions for both α and r^e. Intuitively, there are no capital gains in a stationary state – both α and M^R are constant – and the rate of return on equity must be equal to the ratio of dividends to equity. Dividends, by assumption, are constant in this example, with the total share valuation increasing when income shifts from the poor, who hold no equity, to the rich.

5   Phillips Curves and the Natural Rate of Unemployment

5.1   Introduction

Most economists view aggregate demand as an important determinant of economic activity in the short run. Matters are different with respect to the medium and long run. Even among Keynesian economists, a majority would likely endorse the existence of a stable natural rate of unemployment and see the trend in output and employment as being determined by supply-side factors.

Keynes himself assumed a well-defined level of 'full employment.' Full employment, in his sense, includes not only frictional unemployment but also unemployment that is

due to the refusal or inability of a unit of labour, as a result of legislation or social practices or of a combination for collective bargaining or of slow response to change or of mere human obstinacy, to accept a reward corresponding to the value of the product attributable to its marginal productivity. (Keynes 1936, p. 6)

Like Friedman (1968), quoted in Chapter 2, Keynes emphasizes the potential importance of specific labor market structures for the determination of what constitutes full employment, and substantively his definition corresponds to Friedman's notion of a natural rate of employment. Where Keynes differs is in his insistence that the achievement of full employment may require policy intervention: The natural rate may not be stable (an issue addressed in Chapter 8).

Arguably, Keynes chose to fight the most important battle of the day, the presence of mass unemployment, leaving other issues to one side. This kind of tactical decision influenced other choices in the *General Theory*. Thus, his assumptions of competitive product markets and diminishing returns to labor appear to be motivated in part by a desire to stay as close as possible to the received wisdom (Keynes 1939). His acceptance that a full-employment level of output can be defined independently of aggregate demand may have the same motivation. Whatever the reasons, there are clear similarities between Keynes and Friedman with respect to the definition of full employment. These similarities, however, do not prove that they are right and that the level of full employment can be defined independently of aggregate demand.

The issues have enormous real-world significance. Was high European unemployment and low growth after the breakdown of the 'golden age' in the 1970s the result of shifts in the natural rate, or was it due to misguided aggregate demand policy?

Is it sensible for monetary policy to focus narrowly on price stability? Can austerity policy do lasting damage? Are supply-side reforms the solution to Japanese stagnation? The broad consensus within the profession has been that European unemployment was due to generous unemployment benefits, strong labor unions, and inflexible labor markets; that central banks should engage in inflation targeting; that structural reforms are key to a revival of the Japanese economy, and (until recently, at least) that fiscal policy is quite ineffective, with long-term effects that derive primarily from the negative supply-side influence of distortionary taxes.

These positions are closely related to a belief in the existence of a natural rate of unemployment and in the tendency of the economy to gravitate toward this rate. With a well-defined natural rate of unemployment, any attempt to push unemployment below this rate through demand policy would lead to explosive inflation in the medium and long run. A downward-sloping long-run Phillips curve, by contrast, allows demand policy to play a role in the determination of employment in the long run. And if, for some reason, there is no well-defined long-run Phillips curve – vertical or non-vertical – the scope for demand policy could be enhanced even further.

The analysis of labor market issues is divided into three chapters. This chapter presents an internal critique of the natural rate hypothesis: The empirical evidence is weak, at best, and the theoretical case quite fragile, even if one accepts standard assumptions of optimization and rational expectations. This internal critique is followed in Chapter 6 by an analysis of norms of fairness and their implications for wage formation. The analysis of the distribution of wages in Chapter 7 represents a slight detour from traditional macroeconomic topics. The increase in wage inequality has been dramatic in many countries, however, and the analysis builds on and extends some of the main themes of this book, including the importance of institutional structures and behavioral deviations from orthodox notions of individualistic optimization.

The internal critique in this chapter first considers the empirical case for the natural rate hypothesis. Section 5.2 provides a brief discussion of the history of the Phillips curve, its different incarnations, and the US evidence. Section 5.3 extends the analysis to broader OECD evidence, which shows substantial cross-country differences as well as movements over time in unemployment. A large literature claims that these patterns can be explained by differences and changes in structural characteristics of the labor market. The empirical evidence in favor of this claim is weak, however. Section 5.4 turns to theoretical weaknesses of the hypothesis. Using a modified Barro–Gordon model of inflation bias under monetary discretion, it is shown that, in an otherwise identical economy, the introduction of labor unions changes the results fundamentally: Monetary policy now affects output and employment, and it becomes optimal to have central banks put zero weight on inflation and focus exclusively on the level of output. Moreover, there is no stable Phillips curve: Shifts in the parameters of the central bank's objective function affect both output and inflation but, depending on the precise shifts, the correlations between output and inflation can be positive or negative.

5.2   Phillips Curves

Phillips (1958) presented a relation between (wage) inflation and unemployment in the UK over a hundred-year period and, following Samuelson and Solow (1960), the relation has come to be known as the Phillips curve. The evidence for the United States showed some deviations from the pattern uncovered by Phillips – the 1930s when "money wages rose or failed to fall in the face of massive unemployment" (Samuelson and Solow 1960, p. 188), for instance, did not fit well with the overall Phillips curve (Figure 5.1). But the Phillips curve had an intuitive appeal and came to dominate much of the policy discussion in the 1960s.[1] In their Figure 2, Samuelson and Solow presented the curve as a "menu of choice between different degrees of unemployment and price stability" (p. 192) but went on to warn that

It would be wrong, though, to think that our Figure 2 menu that relates obtainable price and unemployment behavior will maintain its same shape in the longer run. What we do in a policy way during the next few years might cause it to shift in a definite way. (p. 193)

The precise nature of the shifts was seen as ambiguous, however, and Samuelson and Solow also left open the

important question of what feasible institutional reforms might be introduced to lessen the degree of disharmony between full employment and price stability. These could of course involve such wide-ranging issues as direct price and wage controls, antiunion and antitrust

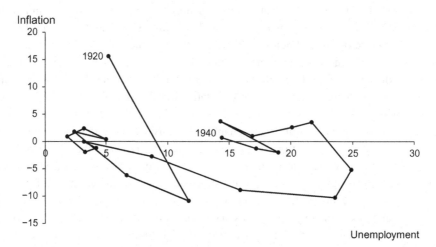

Figure 5.1 Phillips curve; USA 1920–1940. Data source: Lebergott, 1964 (unemployment); www.minneapolisfed.org/about-us/monetary-policy/inflation-calculator/consumer-price-index-1913-(inflation).

---

[1] See Akerlof (2019) for a discussion of the views on the Phillips curve held by Samuelson and other MIT economists in the early 1960s.

legislation, and a host of other measures hopefully designed to move the American Phillips' curves downward and to the left. (p. 194)

The Expectations Augmented Phillips Curve

The downward-sloping Phillips curve came under heavy attack in the late 1960s and early 1970s as the trade-off gave way to stagflation. The stylized picture suggested upward shifts in the Phillips curve, with Friedman (1968) and Phelps (1967) providing a theoretical argument for why this was happening.[2] In its simplest form, their analysis pointed to the dependence of the supply and demand curves for labor on the real wage rather than on purely nominal variables. The intersection of the two curves, they argued, determines a unique equilibrium solution for employment and the real wage, with deviations from this equilibrium implying that workers must be off their supply curve or firms off their demand curve, a state of affairs that would not persist in the long run. This basic argument extends to non-Walrasian conceptualizations in which price and wage setting curves take the place of traditional demand and supply curves for labor.

Following Blanchard's (2021) textbook, a simple derivation of the 'expectations augmented Phillips curve' may assume constant returns to labor, imperfect competition, and the determination of prices as a constant markup on unit labor cost. If labor productivity is normalized to one, the price setting equation (corresponding to the labor demand curve) is given by

$$p_t = (1 + m)w_t,$$

where p and w are the price and nominal wage, and $(1 + m)$ is the markup factor. Wage setting (corresponding to labor supply) is influenced by the expected price level and the state of the labor market as measured by the unemployment rate. Formally,

$$w_{t+1} = F(u_t, z_t)p_{t+1}^e.$$

The superscript e is used to denote expectation, u is the rate of unemployment, and z is a vector of structural variables that influence workers' bargaining position – the strength of unions, for instance, or the level and duration of unemployment benefits.

The price and wage setting equations can be combined to express price as a function of the unemployment rate, the expected price and the structural variables (z, m):

$$p_{t+1} = (1 + m)F(u_t, z_t)p_{t+1}^e.$$

Dividing by the current price level and taking logs, we get an expectations augmented Phillips curve:

$$\pi_t = f(u_t, z_t, m) + \pi_t^e; \quad f' < 0, \tag{5.1}$$

where $\pi_t = \log(p_{t+1}/p)$ is the inflation rate, $\pi_t^e = \log p_{t+1}^e/p_t$ the expected inflation rate, and $f(u_t, z_t, m) = \log(1 + m) + \log(F(u_t, z_t))$. The natural rate of unemployment

---

[2] Oil price and other supply side shocks clearly accounted for some of these shifts in the Phillips curve (Gordon 1997).

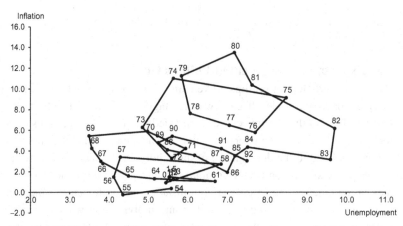

Figure 5.2 Phillips curve; USA 1954–1992. Data source: Bureau of Labor Statistics.

u^* is defined by the condition that expectations must be met and, imposing $\pi = \pi^e$, Equation (5.1) determines u^* as an implicit function of z and m.

Expectations

Equation (5.1) implies that the formation of expectations becomes critical for the trajectory of actual inflation. There had been no clear trend in prices in the UK during the period from 1861 to 1957, which had formed the basis for Phillips' original study. It therefore seems reasonable to suppose that expected inflation had been zero (i.e., there had been static expectations with respect to the *level of prices*). With this assumption, the original Phillips curve emerges as a special case of Equation (5.1).i

In the postwar period, by contrast, a clear upward trend emerged; prices rose every year, and inflation came to be expected. Assuming static (or more generally, adaptive) expectations with respect to the *rate of inflation*, the expectations augmented Phillips curve becomes 'accelerationist': Inflation tends to increase when unemployment is below the natural rate and decrease when unemployment is above the natural rate.[3] As shown in Figure 5.2, this predicted pattern is largely consistent with US data for the period between the early 1950s and the mid-1990s, the natural rate being somewhere around 6 percent.[4] Thus, both the original study by Phillips and the postwar US data could be interpreted within this framework.

---

[3] This property led to the common relabeling of the natural rate of unemployment as the Non-Accelerating Inflation Rate of Unemployment, or NAIRU. If inflation expectations are adaptive, it is actually prices, rather than the inflation rate, that are accelerating if unemployment is below the natural rate. But of course decision-makers may respond to persistent deviations from that natural rate – associated with changes in the inflation rate from one period to the next – by starting to form adaptive expectations with respect to the change in inflation. If that were to happen, the natural rate would become a NAIRU.

[4] Formal estimates of 'the time varying NAIRU' suggest that for the period between 1955 and 1995 the NAIRU varied within a range from 5 to 7 percent in the United States (Gordon 1997, Staiger et al. 1997).

The explicit introduction of inflation expectations radically changed the policy implications. The original Phillips curve had given the impression of a trade-off: A permanent increase in employment could be obtained, it seemed, at the cost of a permanently higher (but constant) level of inflation. The expectations augmented version, by contrast, implied that a permanently lower unemployment rate would lead to an explosive rise in inflation. The equation also implies that – disregarding stochastic shocks – disinflation requires high unemployment if expectations are adaptive.

Adaptive expectations fell out of favor with the Lucas revolution. The New Classical Phillips Curve retains Equation (5.1) and the natural rate is still characterized by the condition that inflation expectations be met. But rational expectations imply that there is no inertia in expectations: Inflation can jump in response to new information. A credible commitment by policy-makers to reduce inflation will have an immediate effect on expected inflation, and disinflation can be accomplished without any increase in unemployment.

The possibility of costless disinflation figured prominently in UK policy debates in the late 1970s. To combat inflation, the Thatcher government launched a four-year plan – the 'medium term financial strategy' – in 1980. In the words of Patrick Minford, a prominent supporter of the government:

on the assumption that policies are properly understood when they are announced and implemented, the disturbance to output and employment from reduction in the money supply and in the PSBR [the public sector borrowing requirement, PS] would be minimal. (Minford 1980, p. 142; quoted from Buiter and Miller 1983, p. 340)

Despite its pre-announced monetary targets and the government's firm commitment to reducing inflation, the disinflation that followed was far from costless: Unemployment rose from less than 4 percent in 1979 to over 10 percent in 1983, remaining above 10 percent until 1987. To explain this outcome, one would need to argue that the 'Iron Lady' had not been credible or that her policy had not been "properly understood."

The UK experience in the early 1980s is striking, but the episode is not unique. There is strong evidence of inflation inertia, and disinflation almost invariably is associated with high unemployment. Ball (1996) examined twenty-eight episodes where inflation decreased significantly; in twenty-seven of these episodes, output was below the normal level.

These findings could be rationalized by abandoning rational expectations, but this option meets resistance. According to Romer (2018, p. 261), for instance, "if one assumes that workers and firms do not form their expectations rationally, one is resting the theory on irrationality." Instead, the favored reconciliation of the evidence is based on modifying the New Classical Phillips Curve: Hybrid formulations of the curve achieve inertia by including a weighted average of past inflation and (rationally) expected inflation. The merits of this resolution are questionable. As noted in Chapter 3, rejection of a rational expectations approach does not presume the adoption of one based on 'irrationality,' as suggested by Romer. It is unclear, moreover, why it would be preferable – and more rational – to rest inflation inertia uniquely upon the unexplained influence of past inflation as a determinant of current inflation.

The New Keynesian Phillips Curve

Prices are flexible in the simple Blanchard derivation of the expectations augmented Phillips curve, with firms always achieving the markup that they consider optimal. The assumption of price flexibility is in line with Keynes's own analysis in the *General Theory* as well as with Hicks's original formulation of the IS-LM model (Hicks 1937). New Keynesian models, by contrast, emphasize price stickiness. It is a common perception that, empirically, prices are adjusted quite infrequently (e.g., Blinder 1991, Eichenbaum et al. 2011, Nakamura and Steinsson 2013). This perception, I shall argue, may be largely false (see Chapter 10), and the theoretical case also seems questionable. Price stickiness has been favored because some kind of nominal stickiness is seen as essential for Keynesian theory and because of a belief that theories based on wage (as opposed to price) stickiness would predict countercyclical real wages, a phenomenon that appears to be inconsistent with the data (e.g., Mankiw 2001). This belief is peculiar: The simple formalization above has a constant real wage, and a small dose of increasing returns or a countercyclical markup would produce a procyclical real wage. Chapters 8 and 10 consider price flexibility and its implications in greater detail.

Price stickiness is given a microeconomic foundation in the New Keynesian theory by assuming that menu costs prevent prices from being adjusted continuously. Instead, the New Keynesian Phillips curve takes the adjustments to be time-dependent and staggered: In each period, a subset of firms has the option of changing prices. The benchmark Calvo version of the model assumes that the proportion of price-changing firms is the same in every period, that the timing of price changes for individual firms is stochastic, and that the probability of a firm being able to change its price in a given period is independent of when the firm last changed its price (Calvo 1983). These seemingly complicated assumptions are analytically convenient and lead to a simple relation between current inflation, expected future inflation, and real marginal cost. Formally, the resulting New Keynesian Phillips curve can be written as

$$\pi_t = \beta E \pi_{t+1} + \mu c_t; \quad \beta \leq 1, \mu > 0, \tag{5.2}$$

where c_t is the proportional deviation of real marginal cost from its value under perfect price flexibility. Intuitively, a firm that has to maintain the same price for a number of periods will set the price as a weighted average of the current and future prices that would be optimal under full flexibility. The deviation of current price from the current optimum is captured by c_t, while the optimal future changes in the firm's price will depend on movements in other firms' prices, that is, on future inflation. The influence of future periods, however, will be discounted; the parameter $\beta < 1$ represents the discount factor.

The aggregation of the pricing decisions by individual units is explicitly considered in the derivation of the New Keynesian Phillips curve. But the timing of price adjustments lacks microeconomic justification, and the specific Calvo assumptions are picked for analytical convenience. The qualitative results may be fairly robust to deviations from the Calvo scheme as long as price adjustment is 'time-dependent.'

But why would the timing of a firm's price adjustments be given exogenously? Time-dependency of the adjustment implies that the distance between a firm's actual price and the price it considers optimal is irrelevant for whether the firm chooses to change its price. This assumption is difficult to defend. Surely, a profit maximizing firm can and will choose when to change its price, that is, the adjustment will be state dependent. A firm will change its price when it believes that its current price deviates so much from what it considers optimal that it becomes worthwhile to incur the menu cost.

The distinction between time-dependent and state-dependent adjustment is crucial: The macroeconomic implications of state-dependent pricing can be very different from those of time-dependent pricing. In the simple Caplin–Spulber (1987) model with state-dependent price adjustment, nominal shocks have no real macroeconomic effects, despite microeconomic stickiness. This result disqualifies the claim to solid microeconomic foundations for the New Keynesian Phillips curve: The curve is derived from *ad hoc* assumptions about time-dependent price adjustment that have no choice-theoretical rationale. As noted by Romer (2018, p. 349), the Lucas critique also rears its head: Firm-level pricing behavior "could change in response to policy changes, and this in turn could alter the effects of the policy changes." In other words, the 'micro founded' Phillips curve becomes subject to a Lucas critique.

Leaving aside these theoretical issues, the New Keynesian Phillips curve has several striking implications. First, if marginal cost is linked to the output gap – high output being associated with high marginal costs – the appearance of the discount factor $\beta < 1$ implies a long-run trade-off between inflation and unemployment. In other words, there is no natural rate of unemployment. The trade-off may disappear for practical purposes if the value of β is close to one (as suggested by King 2000), but it is not obvious that this condition will be satisfied (Karanassou et al. 2005).

A second implication is seen most easily if there are no shocks and $\beta = 1$. In this case, $E\pi_{t+1} = \pi_{t+1}$ and we have

$$\pi_{t+1} - \pi_t = -\mu c_t.$$

Disinflation, in other words, is associated with high real marginal cost, that is, high levels of output. This implication does not fit the evidence: Empirically, there is significant inflation inertia, and disinflation is associated with high unemployment and low output.[5] Other evidence against the New Keynesian Phillips curve comes from the predicted time patterns of output and inflation following a nominal shock: The

---

[5] Gali and Gertler (1999) suggest that the problem lies with the identification of high marginal cost with low unemployment, rather than with Equation (5.2). Using the labor share as an indicator of real marginal cost, they claim support for the New Keynesian Phillips curve. This alternative indicator has been questioned by Rudd and Whelan (2005). The wage share is largely countercyclical (rather than procyclical – hence the consistency of the Gali–Gertler specification with the evidence). But the labor share, Rudd and Whelan argue, is a poor proxy for real marginal cost. Moreover, "the labor's share version of the new-Keynesian model actually provides a very poor description of observed inflation behavior" (Rudd and Whelan, p. 2).

main effects of monetary shocks on inflation appear to come later than the effects of the shock on output, a pattern that is inconsistent with the New Keynesian Phillips curve (Woodford 2003, Chapter 3).

As in the case with the New Classical Phillips curve, the introduction of suitable extensions, a judicious choice of variables and estimation methods, and a little hard work can produce New Keynesian Phillips curves that appear to be consistent with the US evidence. To generate inflation inertia, for instance, a fraction of firms can be taken to be 'backward-looking' and to follow a rule of thumb. Alternatively, all firms may be 'forward-looking,' but those firms that do not get to reset their prices optimally in any given period adjust their prices mechanically in proportion to actual inflation in the previous period.

These extensions have a strong *ad hoc* flavor. Moreover, even sympathetic observers find the econometric evidence less than compelling. The New Keynesian Phillips curve, Mavroeidis et al. (2014) suggest, "gained its popularity from its appealing theoretical microfoundations and what appeared to be early empirical success" (p. 125). However, they find a "high degree of sensitivity in this literature to minor econometric changes" (p. 126), and there are "doubts about robustness to data choices and estimation methods" (p. 127). In fact,[6]

almost any parameter combination that is even remotely close to the range considered in the literature can be generated by some a priori unobjectionable specification. (p. 127)

Mankiw (2001, p. C52) puts it more forcefully:

Although the new Keynesian Phillips curve has many virtues, it also has one striking vice: It is completely at odds with the facts. In particular, it cannot come even close to explaining the dynamic effects of monetary policy on inflation and unemployment.

The Post-2008 Period

Recent experience has posed more specific questions, with disinflation after the financial crisis of 2008 much weaker than one might have expected (Figure 5.3).[7] Coibion and Gorodnichenko (2015, p. 208) comment that

to account for the missing disinflation, the natural rate of unemployment would have needed to track actual unemployment very closely over the entire period of the Great Recession, implying that essentially all of the unemployment dynamics during the Great Recession must have been structural.

Movements of such speed and magnitude in the natural rate would make a mockery of the very concept, and much work has been done to try to avoid this conclusion. The

---

[6] Checking specification sensitivity, Mavroeidis et al. (2014, pp. 153–158) examine the effects of different plausible choices in various dimensions – including data series, estimation samples, and instruments – for a 'hybrid specification' used by Gali and Gertler (1999):

$$\pi_t = \beta_f E_t \pi_{t+1} + \beta_b \pi_{t-1} + \mu c_t.$$

They find that only about half of the estimates give positive values for both β_f and μ.

[7] The Gali–Gertler specification of the New Keynesian Phillips curve with the labor share as a proxy for real marginal cost also fares badly in the period after 2000 (Ball and Mazumbar 2011, Section 5).

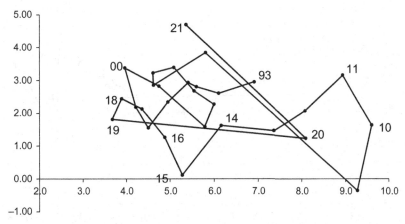

Figure 5.3 Phillips curve; USA 1993–2021. Data source: Bureau of Labor Statistics.

establishment by central banks of credible inflation targets and the resulting anchoring of inflation expectations provide a possible resolution (Bernanke 2010, Ball and Mazumbar 2011, 2015, Blanchard 2016b). Coibion and Gorodnichenko (2015), however, suggest that, on the contrary, expectations may have been quite volatile and unduly influenced by rising oil prices. In any case, in a world of rational expectations, it would seem slightly surprising if anchoring effects and the credibility of central banks did not suffer when nominal interest rates hit the zero lower bound, with central banks running out of their traditional ammunition against disinflation.

After the missing disinflation in the first few years after the recession, the issue turned to the missing inflation in the period 2015–2020. With unemployment rates in the United States below 5 percent from the beginning of 2016 and below 4 percent from early 2018, one would have expected inflation to pick up. There was no sign of any such pickup, with part of the explanation perhaps coming from a persistent underestimate of the slack in the labor market after the withdrawal of discouraged workers from the (measured) labor force during the Great Recession. This explanation, however, amplifies the puzzle of the missing disinflation during and in the years immediately after the Great Recession when the participation rate fell dramatically and the official unemployment rate was, presumably, even more misleading as a measure of labor market conditions (Figure 5.4).

The supply shocks associated with COVID-19 in combination with fiscal stimulus have added new twists. Inflation has risen in the United States and many other countries since the second quarter of 2021, with the policy debates focusing on the dangers that inflation may become 'deanchored.' With sufficient ingenuity and adjustments of parameters, these developments – however they play out – can undoubtedly also be made to fit some Phillips curve.

Despite all puzzles and anomalies, Blanchard (2016b) declares the Phillips curve "alive and well" (p. 31). He estimates a two-equation system:

Figure 5.4 US labor force participation rate for people aged 25–54 years, 2006–2021. Data source: Bureau of Labor Statistics.

$$\pi_t = \theta_t(u_t^* - u_t) + \lambda_t \pi_t^e + (1 - \lambda_t)\pi_{t-1}^* + \mu_t \pi_{mt} + \varepsilon_t$$
$$\pi_t^e = \alpha_t + \beta_t \pi_{t-1}^* + \eta_t.$$

Using Blanchard's notation, π_{t-1}^* is the average of the inflation rates in the previous four quarters, π_{mt} is import inflation relative to headline inflation, u_t^* is the natural rate of unemployment, and the parameters $\theta, \lambda, \mu, \alpha, \beta$, as well as the natural rate u^* are allowed to follow constrained random walks. The estimated parameter changes are significant. Inflation expectations "have become steadily more anchored": The effect of recent inflation on inflationary expectations (β) has dropped from about 0.2 in 1980 to less than 0.05 after the late 1990s, and the weight on long-run expected inflation (λ) has increased steadily from about 0.3 in the mid-1970s to about 0.8. The slope of the Phillips curve (θ) has changed as well, falling from about 0.7 in the mid-1970s to less than 0.2.

It is difficult to know what to make of this defense of the Phillips curve. Do these results demonstrate a Phillips curve that is alive and well? The parameter changes are dramatic and, even allowing for these changes, "the fit of the relation remains fairly poor" (p. 33). Furthermore, the relation has abandoned a rational-expectations justification, following instead a traditional accelerationist specification. Thus, it becomes hard to see how the results can be regarded as a vindication of the New Keynesian research program.

5.3 OECD Evidence

US experience in the interwar period and post-1995 does not represent the only puzzle for the natural rate hypothesis. The data for other OECD countries show large differences in unemployment across countries and large movements in unemployment within countries. Figure 5.5, for instance, depicts German data for the pre-unification period. Consistency with a natural rate hypothesis would require a substantial rise in

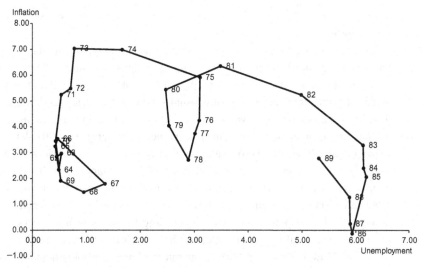

Figure 5.5 Phillips curve; Germany 1962–1989. Data sources: World Bank, World Development Indicators (inflation), and OECD, Main Economic Indicators (unemployment).

the natural rate of unemployment between the 1960s and the 1980s. In the absence of compelling explanations for such a shift, the German evidence for the second half of the twentieth century would seem inconsistent with the existence of a well-defined natural rate of unemployment.

Time-varying parameters in the Phillips curve as well as cross-country differences in unemployment could reflect institutional and historical contingencies in wage formation. The structure of the labor market has not remained constant, and the derivation of Equation (5.1) implies that shifts in the natural rate can occur as a result of changes in variables like unemployment benefits, labor union coverage, and the degree of competition in product markets. Cross-country differences and within-country changes in these structural determinants of the natural rate can account for the evidence, according to proponents of the natural rate hypothesis, an interpretation of the evidence that has informed a large literature as well as economic policy.

An influential study by the OECD (1994) epitomizes the policy recommendations: This "Jobs Study" concluded that most European countries needed a range of structural reforms in order to improve labor market flexibility and reduce the natural rate of unemployment.[8] One of the main planks of the argument was the suggestion that skill-biased technological change had weakened the demand for low-skill workers, with unemployment as the inevitable consequence unless relative wages were allowed to adjust. A comparison between the United States (which had accepted increasing inequality) and Europe (which had not) provided the prime exhibit. The real-world influence of these arguments was felt in countless labor market reforms aimed at

---

[8] The academic literature included prominent contributions by Layard et al. (1991), Nickell (1997, 1998), and Krugman (1994).

weakening union power, reducing job security and increasing workers' incentives to search for jobs.

The claims of empirical support for the natural rate hypothesis did not go unchallenged. Gregg and Manning (1997) found the empirical evidence "much less persuasive than is commonly believed" (p. 395). They noted, in particular, how regressions explaining the time series evidence usually "contain a time trend, suitably chosen dummy variables or some variable that behaves something like them (but is itself implausible as an explanation of the rise in unemployment)" (p. 400). A later study by Howell et al. (2007) points to a range of weaknesses in the empirical literature. Even basic data that are central to any evaluation of labor markets can be of questionable quality. The Netherlands, for instance, saw a fall in the unemployment rate between 1982 and 2003 of 4 percentage points according to one OECD series and a much more dramatic fall of 9 percentage points according to another OECD series. The measurement issues multiply with respect to the various indicators that involve subjective judgment. How, for instance, should one rate the level of employment protection in the different countries on a numerical scale? Seemingly simple measures like replacement rates for those losing their jobs can be misleading as well. Based on OECD measures, Nickell (1998) uses a high level of 90 percent as the replacement rate for Denmark. The 90 percent rate, however, applied only to workers with incomes below a certain threshold; the majority of workers experienced significantly lower rates.

The broad institutional patterns, second, do not look promising for the standard attempts to explain cross-country differences in unemployment. Howell et al. summarize some important institutional indicators in their Table 2. Eighteen OECD countries are divided into three groups: 'six liberal economies' (in the European sense of liberal), six European economies with high unemployment, and six European economies with low unemployment.[9] The 'liberal economies' and the 'low unemployment European economies' had similar unemployment rates in the early 2000s but differed widely along institutional dimensions. The liberal countries had labor union membership, collective bargaining coverage, and net replacement rates for unemployment benefits that were about half the levels in the low unemployment European countries, while tax revenues were about 32 percent of GDP in the liberal countries as against 43 percent in the low unemployment countries; wage inequality also differed significantly with ratios of median to 10th decile wages of 1.9 and 1.5, respectively. The 'high unemployment European countries' represent intermediate cases for most of the institutional variables, suggesting that based on an institutional explanation of unemployment, these countries should show similar unemployment rates. Yet, their unemployment rate was almost twice as high.

The results of econometric studies, third, have been fragile, with explanations of the unemployment pattern depending on contentious econometric specifications. A large

[9] The countries are Australia, Canada, Ireland, New Zealand, UK, and the United States (liberal); Belgium, Finland, France, Germany, Italy, and Spain (European high unemployment); Austria, Denmark, Netherlands, Norway, Switzerland, and Sweden (European low unemployment). The unemployment data are from 2004.

number of regressions have been run, and the magnitude and signs of the effects of the explanatory variables are sensitive to the precise specification. This fragility in the econometric results must be seen in conjunction with the data issues: Poor data and a range of possible explanatory variables increase the dangers of data mining, confirmatory biases, and 'Darwinian effects.' As noted by Blanchard and Wolfers (2000, p. c22) in comments on Nickell (1997) one must worry that

these results are in part the result of research Darwinism. The measures used by Nickell have all been constructed ex-post facto, by researchers who were not unaware of unemployment developments.

The step from correlation to causation, four, raises another set of issues If unemployment appears to be positively correlated with some feature of the labor market, it is tempting to interpret the correlation as evidence of a causal link from this feature to unemployment. The United States, however, extended the duration of unemployment benefits when long-term unemployment increased after the financial crisis, providing a clear case of reverse causation. This is not an isolated incidence. An econometric analysis of Granger causality between the unemployment rate and the gross replacement rate of unemployment benefits shows many more cases of changes in unemployment preceding changes in benefits than cases where benefits preceded changes in unemployment (Howell et al., 2007, Table 6).

Disaggregated data, five, fail to offer compelling support for the natural rate hypothesis. Youth unemployment, for instance, has been particularly high in many countries, and one would have expected institutionally determined incentive effects to show up clearly in this area. This is not the case: France and Italy, with youth employment rates of 26.5 and 31.1 in 1999, gave no financial support to an unemployed 20-year-old single person; the UK, Denmark, and Sweden with youth unemployment rates of 12.3, 10.0, and 14.2, by contrast, had net replacement rates between 44 and 89 percent (Howell et al., 2007, Table 5).

The notion, more generally, that high tax rates and generous welfare state provisions have important disincentive effects on the labor supply seems questionable. As pointed out by Kleven (2014), Scandinavian employment rates are among the highest in the OECD, despite the disincentives of high marginal tax rates and strong welfare provisions. In the Danish case, Pedersen and Smith (2002) calculate the proportion of workers who would be better off financially if they did not work. If financial incentives were important, this calculation should give very different results for employed and unemployed workers: One would expect the proportion to be close to zero for employed workers, while a non-negligible proportion of unemployed workers might be in this "unemployment trap." In fact, the proportions turn out to be virtually identical for the two groups: In 1996 (the latest year in the sample), the proportion was 10 percent for employed workers and 11 percent for unemployed workers, and in 1993, the proportion was *higher* for employed men than for unemployed men.[10]

[10] Rather than emphasizing this puzzling result, Pedersen and Smith search for evidence that financial incentives can play some role. In support of this notion, they highlight an indication in the data that women with a negative net replacement rate may retire relatively early.

Atkinson (1999) discusses the evidence on disincentive effects more broadly, concluding that although often statistically significant, the effects tend to be small.

Howell et al. (2007, p. 59) conclude that

a striking feature of this literature [on labor market institutions and unemployment; PS] is the contrast between the fragility of the findings (both within and across studies) and the confidence with which it is often concluded from them that labor market rigidities are indeed at the root of poor employment performance.... orthodox theoretical priors overly determine the variable construction, empirical testing and interpretation of the results. A healthier dose of skepticism is required to give the data a chance to challenge orthodox views. This is particularly important for this area of study – employment performance – since policy recommendations grounded in empirical research have had (and should have) a powerful influence on policy making.

In his comment on Howell et al., Heckman (2007) concurs that the evidence is fragile, and that current data and models are insufficient to decide whether particular labor market institutions cause the pattern of European unemployment.

Overall, the empirical evidence in favor of a natural rate of unemployment is weak, at best. This conclusion does not imply that the structural characteristics of an economy, including both the labor market and other markets, are of no importance and that wage formation is unaffected by changes in the structure of labor markets. Undoubtedly, changes in unionization, minimum wages, or unemployment benefits can have substantial effects, not least on the distribution of income, an issue I shall return to in Chapter 7. But the mechanisms can be complex, and a neoliberal perspective – an unqualified belief that labor unions and labor market regulation hurt employment – finds little support.

5.4   Theoretical Fragility: Unions and 'Inflation Bias'

The absence of money illusion is at the core of the argument against a traditional downward-sloping Phillips curve. By assumption, rational agents are not concerned with the absolute price level but with relative prices and real incomes. This indifference with respect to the absolute level of money wages and prices is not, however, extended to an indifference with respect to the rate of inflation: A large literature on the inflationary bias of discretionary monetary policy assumes that people dislike inflation. This assumption has been incorporated into the formal analysis by specifying a social welfare function that includes both output and inflation.[11]

A standard monetary policy game can be built around the following two equations:

$$V^b(y,\pi) \;=\; -\alpha\pi^2 - \beta(y - y^{**})^2 \tag{5.3}$$

$$y \;=\; y^* + \lambda(\pi - \pi^e), \tag{5.4}$$

---

[11] The initial analysis of inflationary bias and the dynamic inconsistency of optimal policies was due to Kydland and Prescott (1977); later work includes Barro and Gordon (1983), Rogoff (1985), and Persson and Tabellini (1990). Extended versions of the analysis allow for repetitions of the policy game and introduce reputational complications (e.g., Backus and Driffill 1985).

where π and π^e denote actual and expected inflation, V^b is the central bank's payoff function, y is the logarithm of output, y^{**} the logarithm of the central bank's desired level of output, and y^* the logarithm of the level of output corresponding to the 'natural rate of unemployment.' By assumption, distortions of various kinds – including labor market regulation, labor unions, imperfect competition in the goods market, and distortionary taxes – imply that the socially optimal level of output exceeds the level associated with the natural rate. Thus, if the central bank maximizes the social welfare function (i.e., if V^b represents the social welfare function), we have $y^{**} > y^*$.

The private sector forms expectations about the inflation rate, while the central bank chooses the actual inflation rate by maximizing (5.3) subject to the constraint (5.4). The first-order conditions for this maximization problem require that

$$-2\alpha\pi - 2\beta(y - y^{**})\frac{\partial y}{\partial \pi} = 0$$

or

$$\pi = \frac{\beta\lambda}{\alpha}(y^{**} - y). \tag{5.5}$$

Under rational expectations (perfect foresight in this setting without stochastic shocks), the private sector correctly foresees the actual inflation rate. Combining this condition – $\pi = \pi^e$ – with Equations (5.4) and (5.5), yields the following solutions for output and inflation:

$$y = y^* \text{ and } \pi = (\beta\lambda/\alpha)(y^{**} - y^*). \tag{5.6}$$

Thus, independently of central bank preferences, the actual level of output will be equal to the 'natural' level. Inflation, by contrast, is an increasing function of the sensitivity of output to changes in unanticipated inflation (λ), the relative weight of output in the central bank's payoff function (β/α), and the difference between desired output and the 'natural' level ($y^{**} - y^*$). Hence, in the absence of precommitment, the more conservative the central bank – the greater the relative weight attached to inflation – the better the outcome.[12]

This result is fragile. Labor unions play a significant role in wage formation in many countries, and if the labor market is unionized, it is misleading to assume that the private sector consists of atomistic agents whose role is limited to forming inflation expectations: When unions are large, their wage demands influence the inflation rate.[13]

The analysis in this section accepts the basic premises of fully rational agents with given preferences and perfect foresight, but extends the model by introducing labor unions explicitly. Consistent with most models of union behavior, it is assumed that unions maximize the utility of their members. Inflation enters the social welfare function because, by assumption, the population cares about inflation, and internal

[12] Allowing for stochastic shocks can modify this conclusion (Rogoff 1985).
[13] In many countries, union influence on overall wage formation greatly exceeds the union membership. France is a prominent example.

consistency suggests that union members – a large part of the population in many societies – are also concerned with inflation. Inflation, in other words, should enter the unions' objective functions.[14]

With these assumptions, the argument for a natural rate of unemployment collapses. An individual worker has no influence on aggregate inflation, and it may be plausible to treat expected inflation as independent of the worker's wage demand. But a rational labor union representing a large number of workers cannot ignore the effects of its wage demands on aggregate inflation. Thus, in a unionized economy, inflation and unemployment will be determined as the outcome of a game between agents – unions and monetary authorities – all of whom care about both the rate of inflation and the rate of unemployment, and all of whom recognize that through their choices of strategy they will affect the outcomes for both inflation and unemployment. In a setup like this, there can be no presumption that unemployment will be unaffected by changes in the behavior of the monetary authorities.[15]

5.4.1   A Model with a Central Union

For simplicity, consider a one-shot game between a single, central monopoly union and the central bank. The members of the union may prefer to keep wages high, even if it creates unemployment, but like the population at large, they also care about inflation. Thus, we may assume that the union's objective function includes three variables: The real wage, output (employment), and inflation. Employment decisions are made by firms, and if there is diminishing returns to labor, the real wage becomes a decreasing function of the level of output. These functional relations between employment, output, and real wages – which the rational labor union and its members recognize – make it possible to express union preferences in terms of two variables: Output and inflation. Formally, using a quadratic specification, let the payoff function of the union be given by

$$V^w(\pi_t, y_t) = -a\pi_t^2 - b(y_t - y^*)^2. \tag{5.7}$$

By assumption, firms are always on their supply curves, and price inflation in excess of wage growth corresponds to a reduction in the real wage, leading to an increase in output. Thus, we may suppose that the change in output is determined by the change in the real wage,

$$y_t = y_{t-1} + \lambda(\pi_t - \omega_t), \tag{5.8}$$

---

[14] Assumptions of inflation-averse unions are common in the literature on corporatism (e.g., Calmfors and Driffill 1988).

[15] The analysis in this section follows Skott (1997). Similar results have been obtained by, among others, Cukierman and Lippi (1999) and Lawler (2001). Cubitt (1992) focused on a related issue, comparing three different structures of the policy game: The Nash equilibrium under simultaneous play and the two Stackelberg equilibria with either the union or the central bank as the leader. He shows that when the union is inflation averse, monetary authorities may benefit from being in the position of a Stackelberg follower. In other words, policy precommitment can be harmful.

where ω denotes the growth rate of money wages. Equation (5.8) expresses firms' supply decisions. The union controls wage inflation, but has no direct control over prices and the change in the real wage.[16] Equation (5.8) is equivalent to Equation (5.4) if $y_{t-1} = y^*$ and $\omega_t = \pi^e$, but these restrictions should not be imposed *a priori:* The union may not want to raise wages in line with expected inflation, and one would want to examine the policy game for arbitrary starting positions, not just when the initial level of output is equal to y^*.

Empirically, wage contracts are negotiated at discrete intervals, while the short-term flexibility of monetary policy allows central banks to adjust policy in response to the union's wage demands. Thus, it is reasonable to assume that the game is sequential with the union as the first mover (the Stackelberg leader). This sequential structure implies that the central bank, as the second mover, knows the rate of wage inflation before setting policy. Formally, it is assumed that the central bank can control the growth rate of nominal demand $(y_t - y_{t-1} + \pi_t)$ and that this growth rate is chosen to maximize the payoff function (5.3) subject to the constraint (5.8) and the observed value of ω_t. The solution to this decision problem is given by (see Appendix A):

$$\pi_t = \frac{\beta\lambda(y^{**} - y_{t-1} + \lambda\omega_t)}{\alpha + \beta\lambda^2} \tag{5.9}$$

$$y_t = y_{t-1} + \frac{\beta\lambda^2}{\alpha + \beta\lambda^2}(y^{**} - y_{t-1}) - \frac{\alpha\lambda}{\alpha + \beta\lambda^2}\omega_t. \tag{5.10}$$

Anticipating the response of the central bank, the union decides the growth rate of money wages ω_t by maximizing its payoff function (5.7) subject to the central bank's response functions (5.9) and (5.10). The first-order condition for this maximization problem implies that

$$\pi_t = \frac{\alpha}{\beta}\frac{b}{a}\frac{1}{\lambda}(y_t - y^*). \tag{5.11}$$

Equations (5.9)–(5.11) can be solved for the three unknowns, π_t, y_t, and ω_t. Equations (5.9) and (5.10) imply that

$$y_t + \frac{\alpha}{\beta\lambda}\pi_t = y^{**} \tag{5.12}$$

and, using Equations (5.10) and (5.11), we get

$$y_t = Ay^{**} + (1 - A)y^* \tag{5.13}$$

$$\pi_t = B(y^{**} - y^*), \tag{5.14}$$

---

[16] The log-linear form of the relation in Equation (5.8) corresponds to a static supply curve given by

$$y = \gamma + \lambda(p - w)$$

or, equivalently,

$$Y = (\exp\gamma)\left(\frac{P}{W}\right)^\lambda,$$

where Y, P, W, and y, p, w are the levels and logarithms, respectively, of output, the price of output, and the nominal wage; $Y = \exp y$, $P = \exp p$, and $W = \exp w$.

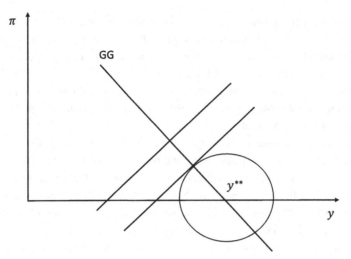

Figure 5.6 The central bank's optimal response.

where $A = [\lambda\beta/\alpha]/[\lambda\beta/\alpha + \alpha b/\beta a\lambda]$ and $B = \lambda\beta/\alpha(1 - A) = (b/a)/[\lambda\beta/\alpha + \alpha b/\beta a\lambda]$. Equations (5.13) and (5.14) imply that y_t and π_t are independent of y_{t-1}. Wage inflation is the accommodating variable that makes this possible. Using Equations (5.8), (5.13), and (5.14), ω_t is given by

$$\omega_t = \pi_t - \frac{1}{\lambda}(y_t - y_{t-1}) = \left(B - \frac{A}{\lambda}\right)(y^{**} - y^*) + \frac{1}{\lambda}(y_{t-1} - y^*). \tag{5.15}$$

The analysis can be illustrated graphically. Equation (5.12), which was derived from the central bank's optimization problem, describes the line GG in Figure 5.6. Independently of ω_t, the central bank always faces the same marginal trade-off between inflation and output: A unit increase in output can be obtained at the cost of an increase of λ in the rate of inflation. Variations in ω_t and/or in the initial output level y_{t-1} shifts the position of the constraint (5.8) but leaves the slope unaffected. The GG line represents the points of tangency between the indifference curves (ellipses around the central bank's bliss point $(y^{**},0)$) and the positively sloped constraint lines as ω_t (and/or y_{t-1}) varies.

Figure 5.7 superimposes the union's first-order condition (5.11) on the GG curve. The GG line represents the constraint on the union's optimization: The union chooses the point where GG is tangent to one of its indifference curves (ellipses around the union's bliss point $(y^*,0)$). Given the slope of GG, the line WW in Figure 5.7, depicting Equation (5.11), represents these points of tangency for different hypothetical positions of the GG line, keeping the slope of the GG line constant (for different values of y^{**}). The equilibrium solution is found at the intersection of the two lines. The GG line passes through the central bank's bliss-point at $(y^{**},0)$ and has a slope of $-\lambda\beta/\alpha$; the WW line passes through the union's bliss-point $(y^*,0)$ and has a slope of $(\alpha/\beta)(b/a)(1/\lambda)$.

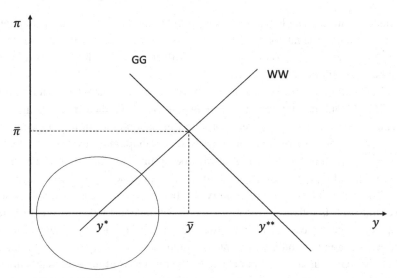

Figure 5.7 Combining the central bank response function (GG) with the union's first-order condition.

5.4.2   Implications

The monetary policy regime is defined by the parameters of the central bank's objective function, that is, by the weights α and β, the output target y^{**}, and the inflation target, which was set equal to zero. Changes in these parameters lead to shifts in the GG curve and, if $a > 0$, there will be derived effects on the slope of the WW curve and the level of output. If $a = 0$, the WW curve becomes vertical for all values of α, β, and y^{**}.[17] Putting it differently, changes in monetary policy have real effects on output and employment as long as the union is inflation averse.

In the general case with a, b, α, β all positive and $y^{**} > y^*$, the model produces a solution with $\pi > 0$ and $y^* < y < y^{**}$. As in the standard Barro–Gordon model, one may want to examine the desirability of giving the central bank an objective function that deviates from the true social welfare function.

Consider first the case where $\alpha \rightarrow 0$. This scenario implies that the central bank will attach no weight to inflation. In the Barro–Gordon version of the model without unions, the rate of inflation would go to infinity as α goes to zero while output would remain at the natural rate y^* (as long as α is positive; in the limiting case of $\alpha = 0$, the model without unions has no solution). The outcome in the case with unions is quite different. As long as the union cares about inflation (as long as $a > 0$), a first best solution is achieved by an inflation-indifferent central bank that pursues discretionary policies: A central bank that is totally indifferent to inflation ($\alpha = 0$) produces an outcome with zero inflation and output at the optimal level, $y = y^{**}$. Thus, it would be optimal to choose a constitutional setup in which an independent central bank is

---

[17] When $a \rightarrow 0$, the constant A in Equation (5.13) goes to zero while the constant B in Equation (5.14) goes to infininity for all finite values of $\alpha, \beta,$ and b.

charged with the single task of ensuring the target level of output, paying absolutely no attention to the rate of inflation. 'Prudent' central banks with a dislike for inflation produce stagflationary outcomes with $\pi > 0$ and $y < y^{**}$; they do worse with respect to both inflation and real output.

The traditional policy recommendation has been to target inflation and give low weight to output. It is readily seen that if $\beta \to 0$, then $\pi \to 0$ and $y \to y^*$. The inflation target is achieved, but output is suboptimal. In fact, precommitment to any particular level of inflation must lead to suboptimal outcomes: With a credible inflation-precommitment it will always be optimal for the union to choose $y = y^*$. Consequently, $(y, \pi) = (y^*, 0)$ is the best that can be achieved in this way.

These results may seem paradoxical, but the intuition is straightforward. If the central bank is inflation averse, the union can take advantage of this aversion: High money-wage increases will buy lower output (and higher real wages). Whether and to what extent the union will want to exploit this possibility depends on the terms on which it can 'purchase' output changes (the ratio α / β of the parameters in the central bank's objective function or, in the precommitment case, the nature of the precommitment) as well as on its own relative preferences with respect to inflation and output (the ratio a/b of the parameters in the union's objective function). At one extreme, we have the inflation targeting, output-indifferent central bank which makes it costless for the union to reduce output: The union reaches its bliss-point y^*. At the other extreme, an inflation-indifferent central bank ($\alpha = 0$) makes it infinitely expensive for the union to reduce output below y^{**}. The union, as a Stackelberg leader, has to set nominal wages first; the inflation-indifferent central bank observes the wage and, since it cares only about employment and output, sets nominal demand so as to achieve its desired level of output. A rational union anticipates this outcome and therefore abstains from any attempt to raise real wages and reduce employment below the full employment level: It chooses nominal wages so as to achieve its preferred rate of inflation. In between the two extremes are outcomes with $\pi > 0$ and $y^{**} > y > y^*$.

5.4.3   Phillips Curves

Using Equations (5.13) and (5.14), it is readily seen that the observed values of (y, π) will trace out an old-fashioned Phillips curve with $dy/d\pi = A/B > 0$, if variations in the central bank's output target y^{**} produce the fluctuations. Thus, an increase in output and employment can be attained (and maintained permanently) at the cost of an increase in inflation. This Phillips curve does not hinge on 'naive' expectations, money illusion, or irrational behavior. Even when inflation is perfectly foreseen, the union may choose not to raise money wages in line with prices, accepting a permanent reduction in the real wage as the best that can be achieved.

With a different source of disturbances other outcomes emerge. Variations in y^*, for instance, produce a Phillips curve with the 'wrong' slope: We have $dy/d\pi = -(1 - A)/B$, implying that high levels of output will be associated with low inflation. Oil price shocks raised both inflation and unemployment and exacerbated stagflation in the 1970s, and the mere presence of differences between the effects of demand

and supply shocks (shifts in y^{**} and y^*) in the present framework therefore may not seem surprising (even if the analysis describes long-run relations between inflation and unemployment). It may be more surprising that the implications of pure demand side shocks can be ambiguous. The ratio α/β represents the relative weights of inflation and output in the central bank's payoff function, and variations in this ratio influence monetary policy and aggregate demand. The resulting reduced-form correlation between output and inflation is ambiguous, however: An increase in α/β leads to a reduction in output and a rise (decline) in inflation if $(b/a) - \lambda(\beta/\alpha)^2$ is negative (positive).

In general, in the absence of restrictive and implausible assumptions, it is impossible to construct a well-defined long-run Phillips curve, traditional, vertical, or otherwise. Shifts in monetary policy affect both output and inflation, and the reduced-form correlation between unemployment and inflation depends on the underlying shocks.

5.5   Conclusion

The picture that emerges from the empirical evidence is much less favorable to the natural rate hypothesis than commonly suggested. The US evidence for the period from the early 1950s to the mid-1990s fits the hypothesis quite well. But in the case of Europe, one would need a compelling explanation for the shifts in the natural rate. The Japanese post-1990 experience also cries out for explanation and, as in the case of Europe, structural problems have been blamed for Japanese slow growth and rises in unemployment.[18] In the United States, the post-1995 evidence looks more problematic for the theory than the earlier period, as does the evidence from the interwar period.[19]

With weak and questionable empirical evidence, the theoretical case for the natural rate hypothesis would need to be strong in order to justify its prominence. But the theoretical case is fragile as well, even if one accepts the standard rules of the game, including rational expectations. Modifying a Barro–Gordon model of a game between a central bank and the private sector, this chapter has focused on the case in which a central labor union acts as first mover. The analysis can be extended to multiple unions (see Appendix B), however, and Markov-perfect equilibria in a repeated version of the game are considered in Skott (1997). The Nash case in which the union and the central bank choose their strategies simultaneously is considered in Appendix C.

---

[18] One may speculate that the popularity of the natural rate hypothesis can be partly explained by the dominance of US-based or trained economists within the profession.

[19] Robert Gordon (1997, p. 28) commented that

Within the postwar experience of the United States, the modest fluctuations in the NAIRU seem plausible in magnitude and timing. When applied to Europe or to the United States in the Great Depression, however, fluctuations in the NAIRU seem too large to be plausible and seem mainly to mimic movements in the actual unemployment rate.

The models in Section 5.4 and Appendix B have shown the following:

- If one allows for non-atomistic unions, there is no natural rate of unemployment.
- Expansionary demand policy (expansionary shifts in the central bank's payoff function) can generate a permanent increase in real output and employment without ever-increasing rates of inflation.
- There is no well-defined long-run Phillips curve: The correlation between unemployment and inflation associated with shifts in the central bank's payoff function is contingent on the specific parameters that are being changed.
- In the special case with a single centralized union, one gets a complete reversal of the standard policy advice: A first best outcome – zero inflation and full employment – can be achieved if the monetary authorities pursue the full employment target with a total disregard for any inflationary consequences.
- Even with decentralized unions, a first best outcome is attainable if the central bank's output target is allowed to depend positively on the rate of inflation (Appendix B).

These results depend on two assumptions. Nominal wages, first, are decided by unions and – reflecting the preferences of the membership – unions care about inflation as well as about output and real wages. The motivation for this assumption is simple. It is implausible that union members should be completely indifferent to inflation, and rejections of this assumption therefore seem to require a failure of the unions to reflect the preferences of their membership. Introducing rationality selectively, one might argue that union members fail to recognize the influence of their own wage settlements on inflation and that union officials are judged exclusively on outcomes for employment and real wages, while the central bank is held responsible for inflation. This behavioral explanation introduces non-rationality at a critical point, and it would be incumbent for anyone taking this route to consider whether other deviations from homo oeconomicus could be important for wage formation (Chapter 6). It has been assumed, second, that individual unions are large enough that their wage demands exert some influence on the average rate of inflation. The link between wage demands and average inflation will be weak if unions are highly decentralized, but this weakness does not undermine the second assumption except in the limiting case of atomistic unions, a case that is not relevant to most European countries.

It should be emphasized that the purpose of the model in this chapter is limited: It illustrates the fragility of the natural rate hypothesis on its own terms. As argued in Chapter 6, the assumptions of the model – and of the standard Barro–Gordon model – fail to capture important elements of wage formation.

Appendix A: A Central Union – Analysis

The central bank does not set the inflation rate directly. Through its control of interest rates, however, it may determine the growth rate of nominal aggregate demand. Thus, taking the rate of wage inflation ω_t as given, the bank solves the maximization problem

$$\max_{m_t} -\alpha\pi_t^2 - \beta(y_t - y^{**})^2$$

$$s.t.$$

$$y_t = y_{t-1} + \lambda(\pi_t - \omega_t) \tag{5.16}$$

$$m_t = y_t - y_{t-1} + \pi_t, \tag{5.17}$$

where m_t is the growth rate of nominal demand. The first-order condition of this problem can be written as

$$-2\alpha\pi\frac{\partial\pi_t}{\partial m_t} - 2\beta(y_t - y^{**})\frac{\partial y_t}{\partial m_t} = 0.$$

Combining Equations (5.16) and (5.17), we get $\partial\pi_t/\partial m_t = 1/(1 + \lambda)$ and $\partial y_t/\partial m_t = \lambda/(1 + \lambda)$. Hence, the first-order condition becomes

$$\pi_t = \frac{\beta\lambda}{\alpha}(y^{**} - y_t). \tag{5.18}$$

Equations (5.16) and (5.18) can be solved for the equilibrium values of π_t and y_t in terms of ω_t:

$$\pi_t = \frac{\beta\lambda(y^{**} - y_{t-1} + \lambda\omega_t)}{\alpha + \beta\lambda^2} \tag{5.19}$$

$$y_t = y_{t-1} + \frac{\beta\lambda^2}{\alpha + \beta\lambda^2}(y^{**} - y_{t-1}) - \frac{\alpha\lambda}{\alpha + \beta\lambda^2}\omega_t. \tag{5.20}$$

Anticipating the central bank's response, the union chooses the rate of wage inflation ω_t to maximize its objective function, $V^w = -\alpha\pi_t^2 - b(y_i - y^{**})^2$, subject to Equations (5.19) and (5.20).

Appendix B: Decentralized Unions

This appendix considers a case with multiple unions. In the limiting case with atomistic unions, it may be reasonable to assume that unions ignore the inflation effect of their particular wage demands. But for the empirically relevant, non-atomistic case, the inflation effect cannot be ignored without compromising the rationality assumptions.

Assume that the payoff function of the ih union is given by

$$V^i(\pi, y_i) = -a\pi^2 - b(y_i - y_i^*)^2, \tag{5.21}$$

where y_i is the (logarithm of) the level of employment of the union's members and $y_i^* = y_i^*$ the desired employment level. Each union sets the growth rate ω_i of money wages for its own members so as to maximize the payoff function in Equation (5.21) taking into account the (conjectured) effects of ω_i on inflation, π, and employment, y_i. These effects depend on the links between ω_i and the average rate of wage inflation ω, and between relative wages and the share of the union in total employment. Assuming symmetry across unions, the following specification is used:

$$\frac{\partial \omega}{\partial \omega_i} = \delta \tag{5.22}$$

$$y_{it} - y_t = y_{it-1} - y_{t-1} - \varepsilon(\omega_i - \omega) \tag{5.23}$$

$$y_t = y_{t-1} + \lambda(\pi_t - \omega_t), \tag{5.24}$$

where $y = \frac{1}{n}\sum_{j=1}^{n} y_j$, $\omega = \frac{1}{n}\sum_{j=1}^{n} \omega_j$. Equation (5.22), which captures the influence of union i on average wage inflation, includes a simple Nash specification as a special case.[20] Complete decentralization with atomistic unions appears as a special case with $\delta = 0$ while, at the other extreme, a single monopoly union implies $\delta = 1$ and $y_i = y$. Equations (5.23) and (5.24) express firms' employment decision. Equation (5.23) says that the change in the share of union i in total employment is inversely related to the change in its relative wage. Equation (5.24) describes the change in aggregate output. It restates Equation (5.8) from the case with a single monopoly union.

The central bank's maximization problem is unchanged, and Equations (5.9) and (5.10) still hold. Thus, the unions maximize the function in Equation (5.21) subject to Equations (5.9) and (5.10) and (5.22) and (5.23). The maximization yields the following first-order condition:

$$-2a\pi\frac{\partial \pi}{\partial \omega_i} - 2b(y_i - y_i^*)\frac{\partial y_i}{\partial \omega_i} = 0. \tag{5.25}$$

We have

$$\frac{\partial \pi}{\partial \omega_i} = \frac{\beta\lambda^2}{\alpha + \beta\lambda^2}\delta \tag{5.26}$$

$$\frac{\partial y_i}{\partial \omega_i} = -\frac{\alpha\lambda}{\alpha + \beta\lambda^2}\delta - \varepsilon(1 - \delta). \tag{5.27}$$

Hence, using (5.25)–(5.27),

$$\pi = (y_i - y_i^*)\frac{b\alpha + \varepsilon b(1 - \delta)(\alpha + \beta\lambda^2)/(\delta\lambda)}{a\beta\lambda}. \tag{5.28}$$

By assumption, there is symmetry across unions, and aggregating Equation (5.28) we get

$$\pi = C(y - y^*), \tag{5.29}$$

where $C = [b\alpha + \varepsilon b(1 - \delta)(\alpha + \beta\lambda^2)/(\delta\lambda)]/[a\beta\lambda]$. Equation (5.29) replaces the first-order condition for the central union, Equation (5.11). The equation generalizes

---

[20] By definition, the average rate of growth of wages is given by

$$\omega = \sum_{i=1}^{n} \frac{w_i L_i}{\sum_{j=1}^{n} w_j L_j}\omega_i = \frac{1}{n}\sum_{i=1}^{n}\omega_i,$$

where the last equality makes use of the symmetry assumption. Hence, assuming $\frac{\partial \omega_j}{\partial \omega_i} = 0$ for $j \neq i$,

$$\frac{\partial \omega_j}{\partial \omega_i} = \frac{w_i L_i}{\sum_{j=1}^{n} w_j L_j} = \frac{1}{n}.$$

Equation (5.11): For a central union, one would have $\delta = 1$ and Equation (5.29) reduces to Equation (5.11); the atomistic case with $\delta \to 0$ implies $C \to \infty$.

The value of C depends on the structure of unions, greater decentralization tending to increase C. In terms of the representation in Figures 5.6 and 5.7, the effect of decentralization is to rotate the WW line counterclockwise. As long as C is finite, however, central bank policy will affect real output; a finite C is ensured if the union has any monopoly power (i.e., if ε is finite) and its wage demand has any effect on aggregate inflation (δ is positive). Using Equations (5.28) and (5.12), we get

$$y_{t+1} = \bar{A}y^{**} + (1 - \bar{A})y^* \tag{5.30}$$
$$\pi_{t+1} = \bar{B}(y^{**} - y^*), \tag{5.31}$$

where $\bar{A} = [\lambda\beta/\alpha]/[\lambda\beta/\alpha + (\alpha/\beta)(b/a)(1/\lambda) + \varepsilon b(1-\delta)(\alpha + \beta\lambda^2)/(\delta a\beta\lambda^2)]$ and $\bar{B} = (1 - \bar{A})\lambda\beta/\alpha$.

For the general case with α, β, a, b all positive, we have $0 < \bar{A} < 1$ and $0 < \bar{B}$. Thus, Equations (5.30) and (5.31) give a solution with $\pi > 0$ and $y^* < y < y^{**}$. As in the case with a single monopoly union, variations in y^{**} will lead to (π, y) solutions that trace out a downward-sloping Phillips curve in unemployment-inflation space, that is, a positive relation between y and π: Equations (5.30) and (5.31) imply that $dy = \bar{A}dy^{**}$ and $d\pi = \bar{B}dy$, and variations in y^{**} give rise to the reduced-form relation $dy = \bar{A}/\bar{B}d\pi$.

For the limiting cases in which one of the parameters $\alpha, \beta, a, b, \delta$ goes to 0, Equations (5.30) and (5.31) imply that

1. if $\alpha \to 0$ then $\pi \to (y^{**} - y^*)\varepsilon\frac{b}{a}\frac{1-\delta}{\delta}$ and $y \to y^{**}$;
2. if $\beta \to 0$ then $\pi \to 0$ and $y \to y^*$;
3. if $a \to 0$ then $\pi \to (y^{**} - y^*)\lambda\beta/\alpha$ and $y \to y^*$;
4. if $b \to 0$ then $\pi \to 0$ and $y \to y^{**}$; and
5. if $\delta \to 0$ then $\pi \to (y^{**} - y^*)\lambda\beta/\alpha$ and $y \to y^*$

Cases 3 and 5, in which unions pay no attention to inflation or each union has a negligible influence on average inflation, reproduce the standard result from the Barro–Gordon model: Output is always at the 'natural rate' y^* and central-bank attempts to raise output ($\beta > 0$) lead to inflation. These policy conclusions no longer apply if unions are non-atomistic ($\delta > 0$) and care about inflation ($a > 0$). In these cases, an inflation-indifferent central bank secures output at the desired level, $y = y^{**}$, but unlike the case of a single monopoly union, there is now a cost in terms of inflation. Decentralization implies that even with an inflation-indifferent central bank, an individual union can affect the relative wage structure and thereby the employment and real wage of its members. Inflation in the $\alpha = 0$ case is the result of this interunion game over relative wages.

Despite this difference compared with the monopoly-union case, it will be optimal to have an inflation-indifferent central bank. To see this, let the true welfare function be

$$V = V(y, \pi); \quad V_y > 0 \text{ for } y < y^{***} \text{ with } y^* < y^{***}, V_\pi < 0 \text{ for } \pi > 0. \tag{5.32}$$

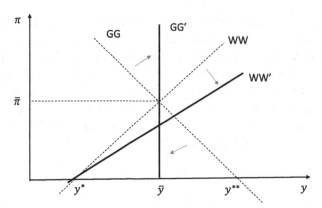

Figure 5.8 Equilibrium in the case with multiple unions.

Assume that the specification of central-bank objectives is restricted to quadratic pay-off functions as in Equation (5.3) and that the three parameters y^{**}, α, and β can be chosen freely. The implications of this setup can be illustrated graphically.

Equation (5.11), which was derived from the central bank's optimization problem, describes the GG line, which always passes through the central bank's bliss-point at $(y^{**}, 0)$ and has a slope of $-\lambda\beta/\alpha$ (Figure 5.8). The GG line is a constraint facing unions, and the implications of their constrained optimization are summarized by Equation (5.29). In Figure 5.8, this equation is depicted by the WW line, which passes through the unions' bliss-point $(y^*, 0)$ and has a slope C. The equilibrium solution is found at the intersection of the GG and WW lines. The GG curve can be defined quite independently of the unions' preferences (and hence independently of the WW curve), while the WW curve is constructed on the basis of a given slope of the GG curve. An increase in α, say, implies that both lines rotate counterclockwise, while increased decentralization leaves GG unchanged but increases C and rotates the WW line counterclockwise.

Let $(\tilde{y}, \tilde{\pi})$ be the outcome associated with $(\tilde{\alpha}, \tilde{\beta}, \tilde{y}^{**})$ where $y^* < \tilde{y}^{**}$ and $0 < \tilde{\pi}$. If $\tilde{\alpha} > 0$, then this cannot be optimal (with reference to the welfare function V in Equation (5.32)) since by choosing an alternative objective function with $\alpha = 0, \beta > 0$, and $y^{**} = \tilde{y}$, it would be possible to achieve the same output and lower inflation. Graphically, this alternative specification implies a vertical GG curve through $y = \tilde{y}$ and a flatter WW curve as indicated in Figure 5.8. It follows that given the general welfare function (5.32) and given the restriction to objective functions of the form (5.3), the objective function of the central bank should depend exclusively on output, $V^b = -(y - y^{**})^2$ with $y^* \le y^{**} \le y^{***}$. The central bank, in other words, should be inflation indifferent. The basic intuition behind the result is the same as in the case with a single monopoly union. If a central bank cares about inflation, rational unions will try to exploit this inflation aversion in order to reduce employment and increase real wages. It is therefore less costly in terms of inflation if any given level of output is reached through an inflation-indifferent central bank rather than through a central bank with a higher output target and some attention to inflation.

If a more flexible form of the objective function is permitted, it may be possible to reach the bliss point ($\pi = 0, y = y^{***}$). One way to do this would be to let y^{**}, the bank's output target, depend positively on the rate of inflation. Thus, let the central bank be inflation indifferent, but assume that its output target is defined by

$$y^{**} = y^{***} + \gamma\pi. \tag{5.33}$$

In order to achieve this output target, the central bank will choose (use Equation (5.33) in combination with Equation (5.24))

$$\pi_t = \frac{\lambda}{\lambda - \gamma}\omega + \frac{1}{\lambda - \gamma}(y^{***} - y_{t-1}).$$

Labor unions, anticipating this response, choose ω_i to maximize Equation (5.21) subject to Equations (5.22)–(5.24) and (5.33). The first-order condition from this maximization problem implies that

$$a\pi\frac{\lambda}{\lambda - \gamma} + b(y_i - y^*)\left[\frac{\lambda\delta\gamma}{\lambda - \gamma} - \varepsilon(1 - \delta)\right] = 0.$$

If γ is set such that $\left[\frac{\lambda\delta\gamma}{\lambda-\gamma} - \varepsilon(1 - \delta)\right] = 0$, the result is $\pi = 0$. Substituting $\pi = 0$ into Equation (5.33), we then have $y = y^{**} = y^{***}$, and the bliss point has been reached.

Appendix C: The Nash Case

The strong optimality result for an inflation-indifferent central bank depends on the Stackelberg structure with the union as the Stackelberg leader. But the nonexistence of a natural rate of unemployment – a weaker result – applies equally to the Nash case.

Consider the case with a centralized union and let the union's payoff be given by Equation (5.7). The union chooses the rate of wage inflation ω, while the central bank controls the rate of growth of nominal demand m which, by definition, can be written as

$$m = \pi + (y - y_{-1}). \tag{5.34}$$

Since the change in output is given by $y - y_{-1} = \lambda(\pi - \omega)$, we have $m = (1 + \lambda)\pi - \lambda\omega$. Thus, when the central bank acted as a Stackelberg follower, the ability to control m was equivalent to an ability to control π, and the inflation rate π could be taken as the choice variable: To attain any given value of π, the central bank simply responds to a rise in ω by reducing m. In the Nash case, however, the central bank's choice of m cannot be conditional on ω.

Retaining the determination of output by profit maximizing firms, Equation (5.8), the union's best response function is found by choosing the value of ω that maximizes the payoff function in Equation (5.7) subject to Equations (5.8) and (5.34) and a given value of m. Straightforward calculations yield

$$\omega = A_0(y_{-1} - y^*) + A_1 m, \tag{5.35}$$

where $A_0 = \frac{b}{b+a}\frac{1+\lambda}{\lambda}$ and $A_1 = \frac{b}{a+b} - \frac{a}{\lambda(a+b)} < 1$. Using the response function (5.35) in combination with Equations (5.8) and (5.34), we get a first-order difference equation for output y,

$$y = B_0 y^* + B_1 m + B_2 y_{-1}, \tag{5.36}$$

where $B_0 = \frac{b}{a+b}$ and $B_1 = B_2 = \frac{a}{a+b}$. Since $0 < B_2 < 1$, it follows (assuming m constant) that output will converge monotonically toward $\tilde{y}$ given by

$$\tilde{y} = \frac{B_0}{1 - B_2} y^* + \frac{B_1}{1 - B_2} m = y^* + Cm, \tag{5.37}$$

where $C = \frac{a}{b} > 0$. A constant level of output implies that $m = \pi = \omega$ (use the supply function (5.8) and the definition of the growth in nominal income (5.34)). Equation (5.37) therefore describes a permanent trade-off between inflation and unemployment: Real output converges to a new higher level if the central bank increases the growth rate of nominal demand.

6 Fairness, Money Illusion, and Path Dependency

6.1   Introduction

In his AEA presidential address, Akerlof (2007) focused on the 'missing motivation' in economic theory: Theories often fail to incorporate the influence of social norms on economic behavior. Nowhere, arguably, is the role of social norms more important than in relation to wage setting and the labor market.

Orthodox economic theory assumes that a worker's utility depends only on the worker's own consumption and leisure (and therefore indirectly on the worker's own wage) and that work, unambiguously, is a source of disutility. These assumptions are misleading. The psychological literature has found strong evidence that the consequences of unemployment cannot be understood in purely economic terms: Unemployment has a negative causal effect on psychological health (Wood and Burchell 2018, p. 235). In the economic literature, Oswald (1997, p. 1828) reaches a similar conclusion,

A consistent theme through the paper's different forms of evidence has been the vulnerability of human beings to joblessness. Unemployment appears to be the primary economic source of unhappiness.

Most workers care about their job and take pride in doing it well, but work can also be a source of stress and unhappiness, especially for workers who believe they are being treated unfairly by their employer.

Employment contracts are almost invariably incomplete, and the ability of firms to monitor the behavior of their workers is limited – how limited depends on the nature of the job and the available technology (a major theme of Chapter 7). Incomplete contracts and imperfect monitoring imply that labor productivity and profits can be influenced significantly by workers' attitudes and morale: Workers may reciprocate, providing high levels of effort in firms that treat them well and punishing firms for unfair treatment, even if it comes at a cost to themselves. The labor market, in Solow's (1990, p. 3) words, "cannot be understood without taking account of the fact that participants, on both sides, have well-developed notions of what is fair and what is not."

The wage is a central element in the relation between workers and firms, with norms of fairness playing an important role in wage formation. Akerlof and Yellen (1990) provide a range of evidence in support for this claim, including textbooks on personnel management that describe the need for equity as "perhaps the most important factor in determining pay rates" both "to attract and retain qualified employees" and so that internally in the firm "each employee should view his or her pay as equitable given other employees' pay rates in the organization" (Dessler [1984, p. 2231; quoted from Akerlof and Yellen 1990, p. 263).

Bewley's (1998, 1999) studies document the importance of equity concerns for wage setting. The reluctance of managers to cut pay, even when unemployment is high, is due to "the belief that doing so hurts morale and increases labor turnover." Morale, which he defines as "acceptance of and willingness to contribute to organizational objectives," is important "because people tend to benefit those who help them and to hurt those who harm them" (Bewley 1998, pp. 475–476).

Other evidence comes from experimental studies. When subjects are assigned roles as employers and employees, experimental evidence from one-shot interactions shows only modest productivity effects if employers raise the wage. But the relation between firms and workers is not confined to a single interaction, and experiments also show that if subjects "are allowed to enter finitely repeated interactions, a large effort increase occurs" (Fehr et al. 2009, p. 357).

Laboratory experiments face questions of external validity: The behavior observed in the lab may not carry over to real-world interactions. Field experiments, however, show a similar picture. In a study by Breza et al. (2018) that highlights the importance of relative pay, the authors randomized the pay structure of groups of Indian manufacturing workers. Some workers received the same flat daily wage as their coworkers within a well-defined group; workers in other groups were paid differential wages based on a baseline test of individual productivities. The design allowed comparisons between workers who received the same absolute wage but worked in groups with different pay structures. They show that "relative pay comparisons can substantially affect output and labor supply, with workers giving up earnings to avoid a workplace with ("unjustified") pay disparity" and that there can be "deleterious impacts on group cohesion and cooperation" (p. 617). Their findings, they conclude, "indicate that relative-pay concerns and their perceived justification could have potentially large implications for worker behavior." (p. 660). Econometric studies of quitting tell a similar story. Dube et al. (2019) exploit discontinuities in wage raises in a large US retailer, finding "strong evidence that peer comparisons matter" and that "changes in peer wages can have large, causal effects on job separations and quits in particular" (p. 621).

This chapter explores some implications of a behavioral perspective on wage setting. Section 6.2 outlines two streamlined versions of the models in Akerlof and Yellen (1990). The first version has homogenous labor with fairness defined in terms of real wages; the second includes two types of labor and fairness norms with respect to relative wages. The analysis is modified in Sections 6.3 and 6.4. Section 6.3 introduces money illusion, while Section 6.4 analyzes the implications of endogenous changes in the norms of fairness for the Phillips curve and the natural rate hypothesis. Both of these sections consider a mature economy without large amounts of underemployment in informal sectors. Section 6.5 analyzes some possible implications of endogenous norms of fairness in developing economies with relatively small modern sectors and high levels of underemployment. Section 6.6 offers a few concluding remarks.

6.2   Fairness and Unemployment

Homogeneous Labor

Consider a case with homogeneous labor and assume that workers shirk if the wage falls below a well-defined 'fair wage.' Formally, let

$$\varepsilon = \begin{cases} 1 & \text{if } w \geq w^f \\ 0 & \text{if } w < w^f, \end{cases} \tag{6.1}$$

where ε, w, and w^f denote effort, the nominal wage, and the fair nominal wage.[1]. Shirking is typically given a narrow individualistic interpretation, but norms of fairness also influence wage setting in unionized labor markets. Wage demands may be driven by the norms that prevail among union members, with shirking representing a collective response in the form of strikes, for instance, or organized work-to-rule campaigns.

The fair nominal wage is proportional to the general price level ($\bar{p}$) if workers focus on the real wage. But fairness also depends on conditions in the labor market: Outcomes and behaviors that are considered unfair in some circumstances may be deemed fair when circumstances are different. Thus, using employment as an indicator of labor market conditions, it is assumed that the fair wage is proportional to $\bar{p}$ and increases as a function of the employment rate, e,

$$w^f = \bar{p}\phi(e); \quad \phi' > 0. \tag{6.2}$$

Keeping the technology simple, assume that labor is the only input and that the production function is given by

$$Q = \varepsilon L,$$

where Q and L denote output and employment. The shirking specification implies that profit maximizing firms never set the wage below the fair wage; we always have $\varepsilon = 1$. The wage will be equal to the fair wage if the firm can attract workers by paying this wage; in an equilibrium with full employment, however, the wage may exceed the fair wage.

For simplicity, assume that firms set prices as a markup on unit labor cost, that is,

$$p = (1 + m)w. \tag{6.3}$$

Assuming symmetry across firms, the price levels set by firms must be equal, in equilibrium, to the general price level, and we have

$$p = \bar{p}. \tag{6.4}$$

---

[1] It simplifies the analysis if firms never pay less than the 'fair wage' and workers (who receive at least this fair wage) always provide the same effort. This outcome, which is ensured by the shirking formulation in Equation (6.1), also holds if the effort function is strictly increasing as long as the function has a sufficiently sharp kink at a particular 'fair wage.' The presence of a kink would be in line with behavioral evidence that losses relative to the reference point are weighted more heavily than gains (Kahneman et al. 1991).

There are three cases to consider. If $\phi(1) > 1/(1 + m) > \phi(0)$, the wage Equation (6.2), the price Equation (6.3), and the equilibrium condition (6.4) yield an interior solution for the employment rate: There is unemployment, and the actual wage will be equal to the fair wage. Formally, in this case, we have

$$e = \phi^{-1}\left(\frac{1}{1 + m}\right); \quad 0 < e < 1$$

$$\frac{w}{p} = \frac{1}{1 + m} = \frac{w^f}{p}.$$

If $\phi(1) \le 1/(1 + m)$, the equilibrium will be characterized by full employment, and the wage will exceed the fair wage if the inequality is strict:

$$e = 1$$

$$\frac{w}{p} = \frac{1}{1 + m} \ge \phi(1) = \frac{w^f}{p}.$$

In the third case, we have $\phi(0) \ge 1/(1 + m)$. The fair wage is so high that there can be no equilibrium with positive levels of employment and output, that is,

$$e = 0.$$

This (slightly modified) version of Akerlof and Yellen's model with homogeneous labor demonstrates how the dependence of effort on the fairness of the real wage rate can generate unemployment.[2] Indeed, the above determination of equilibrium unemployment is mathematically indistinguishable from Blanchard's textbook determination of the natural rate of unemployment described in Chapter 5. The detailed reasoning behind the dependence of real wages on employment is different, but the introduction of fairness considerations does not change the analysis substantively.

Heterogeneous Labor and Relative Wages

Akerlof and Yellen used the model with homogeneous labor as a stepping stone to a more interesting story with heterogenous labor and a focus on fairness with respect to relative wages. An extended version of their model therefore introduced two types of workers. As in the case with homogeneous labor, the precise specification in this chapter differs from the one used by Akerlof and Yellen.[3]

Suppose that all firms are identical and have the production function

$$Q = F(\varepsilon_1 L_1, \varepsilon_2 L_2),$$

---

[2] The version here differs from the Akerlof and Yellen specification in two respects. It assumes that any shortfall of the real wage below the fair wage leads to shirking and, more importantly, that the fair wage depends on the rate of unemployment.

[3] The main differences are that Akerlof and Yellen (i) assume a quadratic production function, (ii) specify the fair wage w_i for workers of type i as a weighted average of w_j and the wage that – given w_j – would lead to full employment for type-i workers, and (iii) define fairness with reference to within-firm wage relativities, with some firms potentially choosing to employ only one type of workers.

where ε_i and L_i denote the effort and employment of workers of type i. Retaining the shirking specification, effort levels are either 1 or 0, depending on whether the wage is deemed fair, and profit maximizing firms never offer a wage below the fair wage. Hence,

$$w_1 \geq w_1^f \tag{6.5}$$

$$w_2 \geq w_2^f \tag{6.6}$$

$$\varepsilon_1 = \varepsilon_2 = 1. \tag{6.7}$$

As in the homogeneous-labor case, the fair wages are affected by conditions in the labor market: The fair wage of type i depends positively on both the employment rate for group i and the wage rate for group j. For simplicity, assume that the aggregate labor supply is the same for the two types ($N_1 = N_2 = N$) and that fairness norms are symmetric. Formally, let

$$w_1^f = w_2\phi(e_1); \quad \phi' > 0, \quad 0 < \phi(0) < 1 < \phi(1) \tag{6.8}$$

$$w_2^f = w_1\phi(e_2); \quad \phi' > 0, \quad 0 < \phi(0) < 1 < \phi(1), \tag{6.9}$$

where $e_1 = L_1/N$ and $e_2 = L_2/N$ are the employment rates for the two groups of workers.

Turning to firms' pricing decisions, imperfect competition in the goods market and a constant markup on marginal cost imply that wage rates satisfy the conditions

$$w_1 = \frac{p}{1 + m} F_1(L_1, L_2) \tag{6.10}$$

$$w_2 = \frac{p}{1 + m} F_2(L_1, L_2). \tag{6.11}$$

The model in Equations (6.5)–(6.11) reproduces several stylized facts about the patterns of unemployment and wages. It implies that:

- There may be full employment for one type of worker, but at least one of the groups will experience unemployment. To see this, note that using inequalities (6.5) and (6.6) and Equations (6.8) and (6.9), full employment for both groups would require that $w_1 \geq w_1^f = w_2\phi(1) > w_2 \geq w_1\phi(1) > w_1$.
- If workers of type i experience unemployment, then $w_i = w_i^f$. This result is an immediate implication of the fact that no firm will want to pay more than the fair wage if it is able to attract workers by paying this wage.
- There is a link between relative wages and relative employment: We have $e_1 > e_2$ if and only if $w_1 > w_2$; see Appendix A for details.
- If workers of group j experience full employment, then, generically, $w_j > w_j^f$. This result follows by observing that wages must also be proportional to the marginal products of labor; see Appendix A for details.

The role of fairness considerations in wage setting has strong support, but the focus on fairness added little to an understanding of unemployment in the Akerlof–Yellen model with homogeneous labor. The version with heterogeneous labor is more interesting, with key results of this model, including the concentration of unemployment among low-wage workers, deriving from the fairness argument. Fairness norms provide the motivation for the influence of the relative wage on effort, an influence that would be absent in extensions of the Shapiro–Stiglitz (1984) model (or other efficiency wage models based on traditional specifications of workers' preferences) to a setting containing heterogeneous labor.

These strengths notwithstanding, two presumptions underlying the specification of the fairness norms in the Akerlof and Yellen models seem questionable. The fair wage, first, is defined in real terms in the version of the model with homogeneous labor. This definition ignores behavioral evidence which strongly suggests that purely nominal changes in wages matter for perceptions of fairness (Section 6.3). The Akerlof and Yellen definition of fair wages, second, implies that the actual wage can exceed the fair wage permanently. This implausible implication contradicts a basic feature of social norms: They have a large conventional element. Norms of fairness tend to erode or adjust gradually if there are sustained discrepancies between actual and fair outcomes (Section 6.4).

6.3   Money Illusion and Downward Rigidity of Nominal Wages

A substantial amount of evidence suggests that "utility is assigned to gains or losses relative to a reference point which is often status quo" (Kahneman, 1994, p. 22). Thus, people often consider it unfair to reduce the wage of an existing employee when labor market conditions change (Kahneman et al. 1986). In a similar vein, Rabin (1998, p. 20; italics in original) concludes that "people seem to implicitly (but pervasively) consider equitable sharing over *changes* in total endowments, not total endowments themselves." These behavioral findings suggest that in evaluating the fairness of a wage offer, workers may focus on *changes* in their own wage (as well as on relativities vis-a-vis other groups).

Wage changes can be real or nominal, and it appears that both real and nominal changes matter for the fairness assessment. Reductions in nominal wages may be deemed unfair, while an equivalent fall in real wages brought about by a combination of price inflation and small nominal wage increases may be acceptable (Kahneman et al. 1986). The sources and implications of 'money illusion' of this kind are explored by Shafir et al. (1997) and Akerlof et al. (1996).

Citing evidence from cognitive psychology, Shafir et al. argue that "different representations of the same situation can lead to systematically different responses" (p. 345) and that "people can entertain multiple representations contemporaneously" (p. 346). When this happens, the outcome depends on the mixture of representations and their relative weighting. These general findings, they argue, can account for money illusion. People are generally aware of the distinction between real and nominal measures, but the nominal representation of economic variables is "simpler, more salient, and often suffices for the short run" (p. 347). The nominal representation therefore influences behavior, but the extent to which this happens is context dependent. The relative salience of nominal and real representations depends on the overall circumstances.

Shafir et al. illustrate the relevance of money illusion by the responses in a number of small surveys. One survey found that a 7 percent reduction in nominal wages in an economy without inflation was considered much more 'unfair' by respondents than a 5 percent increase in an economy with 12 percent inflation. The outcomes for the real wage are virtually identical in the two economies, but the respondents viewed them quite differently. Another survey asked respondents to evaluate two different scenarios. In the first scenario, an employee took a job after graduation and was paid an annual salary of $30,000. There was no inflation and the employee received a 2 percent rise in salary after the first year. In the second scenario, the employee also took a job immediately after graduation and at the same salary, $30,000. But in this scenario, there was 4 percent inflation during the first year, at the end of which the employee received a 5 percent pay rise. A large majority of respondents thought that the employee in the first scenario did better in economic terms. But a large majority also thought that the employee in the second scenario would be happier and less likely to leave the job. These examples – and other experimental and real-world pieces of evidence – suggest that purely nominal changes in prices and wages can have a significant influence on behavior.

Shafir et al. use an extension of a standard efficiency wage model to highlight potential macroeconomic implications of money illusion. Firms set wages, and workers, they assume, reciprocate by adjusting their effort in response to their perceptions of how the firm treats them. These perceptions are influenced by nominal wage increases as well as by the (consumption) real wage, and – unlike Shafir et al. – I include the state of the labor market (the employment rate) as an additional influence on effort in this modified version of their model.

Formally, the effort function is specified as

$$\varepsilon = \psi\left(\frac{w}{p}, \frac{w}{w_{-1}}, e\right); \quad \psi_1 > 0, \psi_2 > 0, \psi_3 < 0. \tag{6.12}$$

The wage w_{-1} in the previous period is predetermined, and individual firms take the general price level p and the aggregate employment rate e as exogenously given when they set the current money wage.

Now consider two scenarios characterized by differences in the rate of wage inflation (differences in w/w_{-1}). If the real wage and aggregate employment were to be the same in the two scenarios, then effort – which by assumption is increasing in w/w_{-1} – would be higher in the scenario with high inflation. Thus, Equation (6.12) has an immediate consequence: Differences in wage inflation must be associated with differences in one or more of the real variables $\varepsilon, w/p, e$.

The precise effects of changes in inflation on real outcomes depends, not surprisingly, on the production function and the demand conditions in the goods market as well as on the effort function. Consider a shirking version of the model in which the function $G\left(\frac{w}{p}, \frac{w}{w_{-1}}, e\right)$ describes the degree of fairness and workers provide effort if $G\left(\frac{w}{p}, \frac{w}{w_{-1}}, e\right) \geq 0$ and shirk if $G\left(\frac{w}{p}, \frac{w}{w_{-1}}, e\right) < 0$ ($G_1 > 0, G_2 > 0, G_3 < 0$).[4] Using the

---

[4] This version represents a limiting case of the formulation in Equation (6.12).

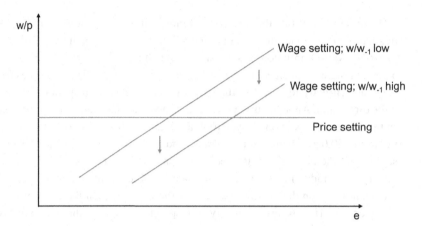

Figure 6.1 Wage and price setting in a model with money illusion.

implicit function theorem, the no-shirking condition $\left(G\left(\frac{w}{p},\frac{w}{w_{-1}},e\right) \geq 0\right)$ implies that w/p must be at or above a threshold value determined by w/w_{-1} and e:

$$\frac{w}{p} \geq f\left(\frac{w}{w_{-1}},e\right); \quad f_1 < 0, f_2 > 0. \tag{6.13}$$

Thus, assuming constant returns to labor in effective units and choosing appropriate units, we have

$$Q = \begin{cases} L & \text{if} \quad \frac{w}{p} \geq f\left(\frac{w}{w_{-1}},e\right) \\ 0 & \text{if} \quad \frac{w}{p} < f\left(\frac{w}{w_{-1}},e\right). \end{cases}$$

With imperfect competition and a constant markup, the product real wage becomes $1/(1 + m)$ – the limiting case of perfect competition corresponding to $m = 0$. If there is symmetry across firms, the firm's price is equal to the general price level p, and the consumption real wage that enters the no-shirking condition is determined by the markup,

$$\frac{w}{p} = \frac{1}{1 + m}. \tag{6.14}$$

Figure 6.1 illustrates the outcome. Equation (6.14) produces a horizontal 'price setting curve' in $(e, w/p)$-space. The wage setting curve follows from Equation (6.13). Conditional on a given rate of wage inflation w/w_{-1}, the no-shirking condition is depicted as an upward-sloping wage setting curve in $(e, w/p)$-space: Workers shirk if the real wage falls below this curve. The equilibrium is determined by the intersection between the two curves, assuming they intersect with $0 < e < 1$.[5] An increase in

---

[5] If the curves do not intersect in the interval with $0 < e$, then there is no equilibrium in which price expectations are being met and in which inflation takes the value associated with this position of the wage curve. If the curves intersect at $e > 1$, there will be full employment ($e = 1$) and the real wage will exceed the fair, no-shirking wage ($w/p > f(w/w_{-1}, 1)$).

the inflation rate generates a downward shift in the wage curve, and the equilibrium employment rate increases. Intuitively, an increase in inflation implies that if employment were to be unchanged, the real wage could be reduced without violating the no-shirking condition. The real wage, however, is determined by the markup, and the no-shirking condition is reestablished with equality by a rise in employment.

The analysis can be extended to cases with continuous effort. An increase in inflation reduces real unit labor costs ($\frac{w/p}{\varepsilon}$) if employment is unchanged. Thus, a firm can reduce its wage and still obtain the same effort from its workers or, alternatively, pay the same wage and obtain higher effort. Either way, there is a fall in unit costs and firms will expand output.

First Modification: Endogenous Salience

The dependence of real outcomes on inflation may be robust, but as Shafir et al. point out, the weight on nominal representations is context dependent. The salience of purely nominal representations increases when inflation is low and simple nominal evaluations yield results that are similar to more complicated real-wage calculations. When inflation is high, conversely, the weight shifts toward real representations. Endogenous shifts of this kind imply that effort need not be monotonically increasing in inflation.[6]

His terminology was different, but Rowthorn (1977) presented a model along these lines. Even if workers expect prices to rise, their wage demands may not always take the expected changes in prices into account; if this happens, inflation is expected but not anticipated, in Rowthorn's terminology. The divorce between expectation and anticipation, Rowthorn argued, is most likely to occur when inflation is low: With low inflation, the nominal representation (in the Shafir et al. terminology) becomes salient and dominates behavior. When inflation is high, by contrast, the nominal representation loses its salience and expected inflation will be fully incorporated into wage demands.[7] The transition between the two kinds of behavior is, Rowthorn suggested, likely to be quite abrupt. As a stylized description, there may be a threshold value of the inflation rate at which workers switch from ignoring price inflation (relying on nominal representation) to incorporating it fully (using a real representation).

Formally, let

$$\pi^a = \begin{cases} 0 & \text{if} \quad \pi^e < \pi^t \\ \pi^e & \text{if} \quad \pi^e \geq \pi^t, \end{cases} \tag{6.15}$$

---

[6] While noting the contingency of the weight of nominal representations in decision-making, Shafir et al. (1997) do not discuss the implications.

[7] Akerlof et al. (2000, p. 39) offers a similar argument, suggesting that

when inflation is low it is not especially salient, and wage and price setting will respond less than proportionally to expected inflation. At sufficiently high rates of inflation, by contrast, anticipating inflation becomes important, and wage and price setting responds fully to expected inflation.

They also point to evidence showing that cost-of-living adjustments of wages tend to be granted by employers when inflation is high but denied at low levels of inflation. "Blanchard (2018b) also discusses a 'Rowthorn formulation' with threshold values below which inflation ceases to be salient."

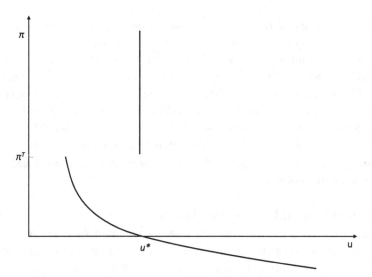

Figure 6.2 Long-run Phillips curve in the Rowthorn model.

where π^a, π^e, and π^t denote anticipated, expected, and threshold price inflation. Retaining a simple markup assumption, an anticipation-augmented Phillips curve can be written as

$$\pi = \hat{w} = f(u) + \pi^a, \tag{6.16}$$

where u is the unemployment rate.

The specification in Equations (6.15) and (6.16) implies that the long-run Phillips curve – imposing $\pi = \pi^a$ – takes an unusual form (see Figure 6.2). Corresponding to the threshold value of inflation, there is a threshold for unemployment:

$$u^t = f^{-1}(\pi^t).$$

As long as the inflation rate is kept below the threshold value, the long-run Phillips curve is downward sloping and exhibits a trade-off between inflation and unemployment. Policy-makers can push the unemployment rate below the rate that is consistent with zero inflation ($u^* = f^{-1}(0)$) without provoking ever-increasing inflation. But there is a discontinuity in the curve. Workers will switch behavior if the policy becomes overambitious and unemployment is pushed below the threshold value u^t. When expected inflation reaches the threshold π^t, the short-run Phillips curve (6.16) shifts upward. Workers now anticipate inflation when forming their nominal wage demands, and the intersection between the new short-run curve and the vertical line through the u^* jumps from $\pi = 0$ to $\pi = \pi^e$ (Figure 6.3). The long-run trade-off no longer exists, and inflation increases without bound if unemployment is kept below the 'natural rate' u^*. Importantly, inflation cannot be brought under control simply by raising unemployment to just above u^t: It now has to be raised above u^* in order to bring down inflation, assuming adaptive expectations.

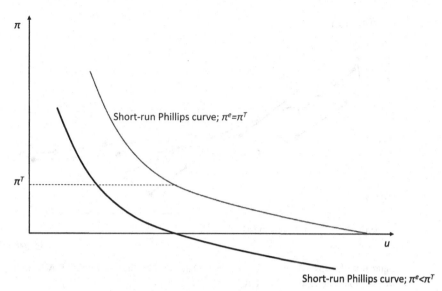

Figure 6.3 Short-run Phillips curves in the Rowthorn model.

A shift from unanticipated (non-salient) to anticipated (salient) inflation could help explain, Rowthorn argued, what happened in the advanced capitalist economies in the 1960s and 1970s. Inflation rose gradually and at some point[8]

countries were pushed over the expectations threshold and inflationary expectations were built into the whole system of decision making. Eventually, there was an economic crisis characterised by a combination of high unemployment and fast inflation (p. 229).

Second Modification: Downward Rigidity

The analysis of money illusion in Shafir et al. did not attach any particular significance to zero inflation rates. By contrast, an abundance of evidence shows that there is something special about the zero threshold and that an absolute decline in nominal wages meets with strong resistance.

At the macroeconomic level, the prolonged period of high unemployment after the financial crisis in 2008 failed to produce a large decline in inflation, and the picture from post-1990 Japanese stagnation has been similar. The Great Depression of the 1930s saw some decline in nominal wages during the early years, but that decline then came to a halt, despite continued high unemployment; see Figure 5.1 for the United States and Figure 6.4 for the UK.

The interwar observations formed the background to Keynes's analysis, which highlighted the downward stickiness of money wages, an empirical fact that he thought should be welcomed, since downward flexibility of money wages would have been likely to generate violent instability and exacerbate the unemployment problems (Chapter 8). Keynes's explanation in the *General Theory* for the stickiness focused

---

[8] There are parallels here to current debates (spring 2022) on the risks that inflation expectations may be become deanchored.

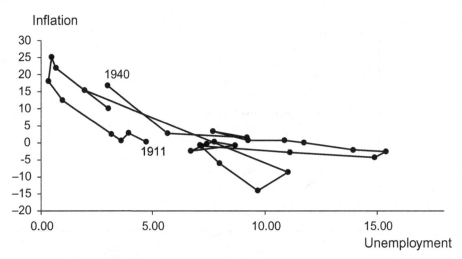

Figure 6.4 Phillips curve; UK 1911–1940. Data source: Bank of England, A Millennium of Macroeconomic Data for the UK.

on relative wages. It was, he argued, perfectly reasonable for workers to resist a fall in their money wage, even if they might be willing to work for a lower real wage:

> any individual or group of individuals, who consent to a reduction of money-wages relatively to others, will suffer a *relative* reduction in real wages, which is a sufficient justification for them to resist it. On the other hand it would be impracticable for them to resist every reduction of real wages, due to a change in the purchasing-power of money which affects all workers alike (p. 14; emphasis in original)

Bewley's (1998, 1999) studies of the reasons for downward wage rigidity strongly support the central importance of fairness and worker morale but indicate that although "concern about worker reaction and morale curbed pay cutting, the reaction was to reduction in pay relative to its former level" (Bewley 1998, p. 485). It is, he argues, primarily the change in wages that matters: "pay cuts hurt morale, but the pay level by itself has little impact on it" (p. 487). These findings, as Bewley points out, are consistent with other surveys, including Campbell and Kamlani (1997) and Agell and Lundborg (1995). Additional evidence of downward wage rigidity comes from microeconomic data on changes in nominal wages. Declines in money wages are rare, there is a pronounced spike at zero, and small positive changes are much more common than small negative changes (Kahn 1997, Daly et al. 2012).

Akerlof et al. (1996) outline the empirical evidence and proceed to derive the implications of this evidence for the Phillips curve. The basic ingredients are simple and intuitive. Disregarding all heterogeneity, consider a simple case in which all wages move together, and assume that prices are set as a fixed markup on wages, that changes in nominal wages are constrained to be nonnegative, and that wage inflation is determined by a standard expectations augmented Phillips relation when this nonnegativity constraint does not bind.

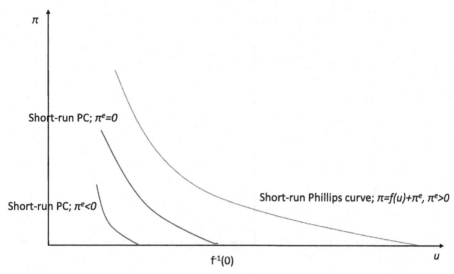

Figure 6.5 Short-run Phillips curve with homogeneity and full downward rigidity of money wage.

Formally, let

$$\pi = \hat{w} = \begin{cases} f(u) + \pi^e & \text{if} \quad f(u) + \pi^e \geq 0 \\ 0 & \text{if} \quad f(u) + \pi^e < 0. \end{cases}$$

Graphically, the short-run Phillips curves are downward sloping above the horizontal axis but become flat as they reach the horizontal axis and then follow the axis (Figure 6.5). The expected inflation rate associated with one of these short-run curves is positive if the curve hits the horizontal axis to the right of $u^* = f^{-1}(0)$ and negative if the curve hits the axis to the left of u^*. Adaptive expectations imply that the short-run curves shift up to the left of u^*, while to the right of u^*, they will converge down toward the horizontal axis. Thus, the long-run Phillips curve is kinked, consisting of the vertical half-line through u^* above the axis (the points with $u = u^*$ and $\pi \geq 0$) and the half-line along the horizontal axis (the points with $u \geq u^*$ and $\pi = 0$); see Figure 6.6.

This highly stylized picture provides a poor description of the data. But now introduce heterogeneity across firms, idiosyncratic shocks to wage setting and firm-level demand, and a (behaviorally well-motivated) assumption that nominal wages may fall in firms that have been hit by large negative shocks. The technical details become complicated, but the implications of these modifications for the long-run Phillips curve are what one would expect: The curve loses its kink, becomes strictly convex, and produces negative inflation rates for high rates of unemployment (Figure 6.7).[9]

Having derived the Phillips curve, Akerlof et al. estimate the relation on US data. The econometric results, they argue, show that unlike the standard model,

---

[9] This argument for a downward sloping long-run Phillips curve has strong similarities with that in Tobin (1972).

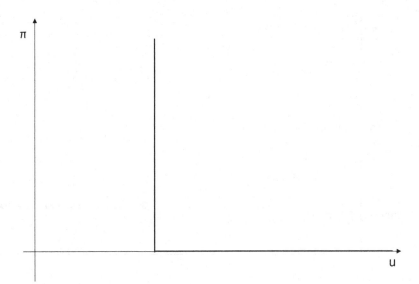

Figure 6.6 Long-run Phillips curve with homogeneity and full downward rigidity of money wage.

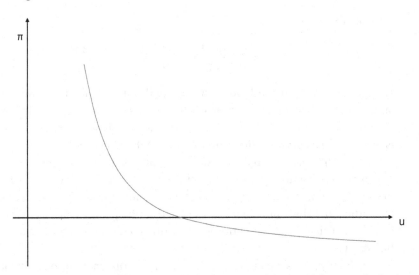

Figure 6.7 Long-run Phillips curve with heterogeneous labor and idiosyncratic shocks.

their formulation can provide a unified explanation of US experience in both the interwar and postwar periods. While discussants at the Brookings meeting where they presented their paper voice reservations,[10] the US evidence from the interwar period as well as evidence from Europe and Japan present formidable difficulties for the natural rate hypothesis, with the missing disinflation after the financial crisis in

---

[10] In their comments on Akerlof et al., Robert Gordon and Greg Mankiw both suggest that the downward stickiness will be less pronounced in periods with low inflation. The missing disinflation casts doubt on this suggestion and, interestingly, Rowthorn's (1977) argument implies that nominal wage rates become highly salient at low inflation.

2008 adding to these difficulties. In fact, just looking at the empirical patterns, it is not surprising that nominal wage rigidities improve the fit. And importantly, nominal wage rigidities are not *ad hoc* additions: They have independent behavioral support at the microeconomic level.

6.4 Endogenous Norms and Path Dependency

The heterogeneous-labor version of the Akerlof–Yellen model in Section 6.2 implies that the highly paid workers may receive a wage that exceeds their fair wage.[11] This implication of the model is inconsistent with a distinctive feature of norms: Norms only persist and retain their power if they are affirmed by actual behavior; family norms about having dinner together break down if the family stops having dinner together for a prolonged period. The models in Sections 6.2 and 6.3 do not capture this conventional aspect of norms.

Both the importance of norms of fairness and the conventional aspects of norms have been recognized by economists. Keynes (1930a), for instance, expressed his sympathy with the view that

there is a large arbitrary element in the relative rates of remuneration, and the factors of production get what they do, not because in any strict sense they precisely earn it, but because past events have led to these rates being customary and usual. (quoted from Keynes 1981, p. 7)

Marshall (1887) noted that fairness must be defined "with reference to the methods of industry, the habits of life and the character of the people" (p. 212). Fairness, he argues, requires that a worker[12]

ought to be paid for his work at the usual rate for his trade and neighbourhood; so that he may live in that way to which he and his neighbours in his rank of life have been accustomed. (p. 213)

Similar views have been advocated more recently by Solow (1990), while Hicks (1975) pointed out that it can be difficult to achieve a general consensus on what is fair and what is not. No system of wages, Hicks argues, "when it is called into question, will ever be found to be fair." Hence,

the system of wages should be well established, so that it has the sanction of custom. It then becomes what is expected; and (admittedly on a low level of fairness) what is expected is fair. (p. 65)

These quotes describe the influence of past wage patterns on the prevailing relative-wage norms. A similar argument applies to norms for wage increases. If wages have increased by 3 percent a year for a long time, anything less than an expected 3 percent increase will be considered unfair, assuming that the unemployment rate and the general conditions in the labor market are unchanged. If actual real wage growth drops

---

[11] This result always holds for the integrated equilibrium in Akerlof and Yellen's own version of the model in which there cannot be unemployment for the more highly paid group of workers. These workers will be paid a market clearing wage that exceeds the fair wage.

[12] I became aware of Marshall's argument from reading Solow (1990) who provides a more extensive quote on pp. 16–17.

permanently to 2 percent, however, aspirations will eventually converge to this new reality, still assuming an unchanged unemployment rate. The qualifier – assuming an unchanged unemployment rate – is important. The fairness doctrine, in Marshall's (1887) words, "is modified by the admission that changes in circumstances may require changes in wages in one direction or another" (p. 213). This conditionality, which was incorporated into the streamlined Akerlof and Yellen model mentioned previously, is in line with both experimental and survey evidence.

Clearly, the fact that Marshall or Keynes may have said something makes it neither right nor wrong. The quotes are not intended as 'proof' that norms are important but more as an indication of the extent of regression in macroeconomics over the last 40 years. Marshall, Keynes, Hicks, and Solow are not peripheral figures, but the Lucas paradigm and its emphasis on specific and very narrow types of microeconomic foundations forced out insights that once had broad acceptance. The insights are getting renewed attention in behavioral economics, but there is still a lot of 'undoing' to be done in macroeconomics, to quote the title of Michael Lewis's (2017) account of the Kahneman–Tversky project.

The premise of this section – gradual adjustments of notions of fairness to fit actual outcomes – is supported by psychological studies of adaptation. Thus, according to Kahneman et al. (1986, pp. 730–731)[13]

the reference transaction provides a basis for fairness judgments because it is normal, not because it is just. Psychological studies of adaptation suggest that any stable state of affairs tends to become accepted eventually, at least in the sense that alternatives to it no longer readily come to mind. Terms of exchange that are initially seen as unfair may in time acquire the status of reference transaction. Thus, the gap between the behaviour that people consider fair and the behavior that they expect in the market-place tends to be rather small.

To simplify the analysis, the formalization of these findings in this section assumes that all workers are identical and receive the same wage.[14] Relative wage norms therefore play no role. The analysis also abstracts from money illusion, assuming that fairness is defined with respect to the (expected) change in the real wage. Money illusion could be included, but the effects that are highlighted in this section are distinct from those arising from money illusion, and for analytical purposes, it seems preferable to keep the issues separate.

Several conclusions emerge:

- The conventional aspect of the wage norms implies that employment exhibits path dependency (hysteresis).
- In specifications with adaptive expectations, systematic aggregate demand policy can influence long-run employment and, depending on functional forms, policy-makers may or may not face a stable Phillips-curve trade-off.

---

[13] A related argument is developed by Sugden (1986) who suggests that conventions that evolve spontaneously acquire moral status. See Bowles (1998) for a broader survey of endogenous preferences and Hargreaves-Heap and Varoufakis (2002) for experimental evidence on the evolution of perceptions of fairness.

[14] Skott (2005) includes fairness norms with respect to both relative wages and the growth rate of own wages in a model with two groups of workers. Relative wage norms are considered in the discussion of CEO pay in Chapter 7.

- Changes in the rate of productivity growth and autonomous shocks to norms affect long-run employment.

Intuition

Consider the streamlined Akerlof–Yellen model with homogeneous labor and explicit attention to price expectation. Price setting is described by a constant markup on unit wage cost, there is no technical change, and unit wage cost is constant below full capacity. These assumptions imply that price setting can be described by a horizontal curve in a figure with employment on the horizontal axis and real wages on the vertical axis. Wage setting – the fairness norm – specifies expected real wages as an increasing function of employment, and the intersection of the two curves defines a unique equilibrium with $p = p^e$. Short-run deviations from this equilibrium can occur if prices diverge from the levels that were expected when nominal wages were set.

So far, the analysis is completely standard, and we get the natural rate result: If employment is kept above the equilibrium level, actual inflation will exceed expected inflation, the short-run Phillips curve will shift upward if expectations are adaptive, and the scene is set for ever-increasing rates of inflation. But if the position of the wage setting curve depends on norms of fairness that are shaped by past experience, the deviations from the equilibrium will set in motion a process of adjustments in wage norms: The wage setting curve will also be shifting.

If policy-makers keep employment at a constant level above the initial equilibrium, actual real wages – as determined by the markup – will be below the fair real wage that workers had expected to achieve. The fair wage reacts to this discrepancy, adjusting gradually toward the actual real wage: The curve describing wage setting shifts down, and the equilibrium rate of employment increases (Figure 6.8). The adjustment process is accompanied by increases in inflation, but the increases will not be unbounded. Instead, the equilibrium rate of employment converges to the actual rate: There is no natural rate of unemployment. Aggregate demand can have permanent effects on employment and output.

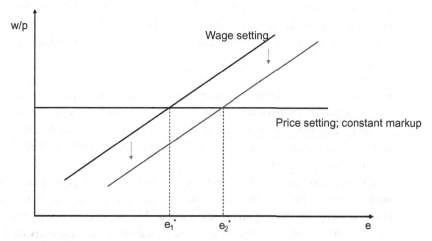

Figure 6.8 Endogenous shifts in real-wage norms.

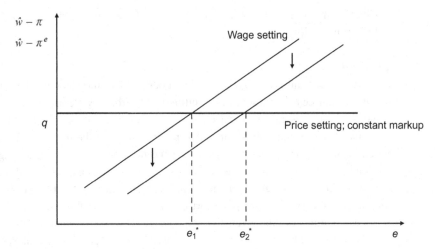

Figure 6.9 Endogenous shifts in norms for real-wage growth.

The argument carries over to the case where the norms of fairness relate to the change rather than the level of real wages. Wage setting can now be described by an upward-sloping relation between employment and the growth rate of the real wage. If labor productivity grows at the rate q, price setting – a constant markup on unit labor cost – implies that real wages grow at this rate as well (Figure 6.9). Expansionary policy that keeps employment above the initial equilibrium rate at e_1^* again leads to downward shifts in the wage curve. The fair growth rate of real wages and the equilibrium unemployment rate both fall.

A Formal Model
Using a continuous-time framework, the nominal wage rate w is taken to be a state variable, with wage formation determining the growth rate of wages. Fairness, analogously, is defined with respect to changes in wages, a specification that is in line with the discussion in Section 6.3 and that has additional appeal because of the conventional element of norms: If wages tend to rise over time, norms about the growth rate of wages – rather than about the absolute level of wages – are more likely to take root.

Formally, it is assumed that the fair growth rate of nominal wages is given by

$$\hat{w}^f = a(t) + be + \pi^e, \tag{6.17}$$

where e is the employment rate and π the rate of inflation; hats and dots denote growth rates and time derivatives (e.g., $\hat{w} = \frac{\dot{w}}{w} = \frac{dw}{dt}/w$), and superscripts f and e indicate fair and expected values of a variable. A shirking setup simplifies the analysis, and it is assumed that workers provide high effort ($\varepsilon = 1$) if they are treated fairly and $\hat{w} \geq \hat{w}^f$, but low effort ($\varepsilon = 0$) if $\hat{w} < \hat{w}^f$.

The slope coefficient b is taken to be constant, with endogenous shifts in fairness norms captured by the time-dependent term $a(t)$. Wages are set in nominal terms, but by assumption there is no money illusion: The fair growth rate of nominal wages depends one-for-one on expected inflation. It is assumed that the individual employer will not be held responsible for unanticipated movements in the general price level. Shortfalls of actual real wage growth below the fair rate therefore do not lead to shirking if they are due to unanticipated inflation.

The conventional aspect of the norms is captured by a simple adaptive specification for the change in a:

$$\dot{a} = \lambda_a \left[(\hat{w} - \pi) - (\hat{w}^f - \pi^e) \right]. \tag{6.18}$$

This equation makes the adjustment of the real-wage norm proportional to the difference between the actual *ex post* rate of growth of real wages and the fair *ex ante* growth rate of the real wage. The shirking assumption implies that the *ex ante* nominal wage increases will be fair, that is,

$$\hat{w} = \hat{w}^f = a(t) + be + \pi^e. \tag{6.19}$$

Hence, Equation (6.18) simplifies to

$$\dot{a} = \lambda_a \left(\pi^e - \pi \right). \tag{6.20}$$

Price setting is kept simple. As in the streamlined Akerlof–Yellen model, firms set price as a constant markup on unit labor cost and labor productivity grows at a constant rate q. With these assumptions, the rate of price inflation is determined by wage inflation and productivity growth,

$$\pi = \hat{w} - q. \tag{6.21}$$

Implications for Employment and Inflation

The parameters a and b are constant if the adjustment parameter λ_a in Equation (6.20) is set equal to zero. In this case, the specification in Equation (6.19) yields a standard, expectations-augmented Phillips curve. Using Equations (6.19) and (6.21) in combination with the equilibrium condition $\pi^e = \pi$, we get

$$e^* = \frac{q - a}{b}.$$

The case with $\lambda_a = 0$ and constant norms can be seen as a modified version of the first of the streamlined Akerlof–Yellen models in Section 6.2. The only difference is that norms attach to the growth rates of the real wage rather than to levels of the real wage.

The implications are quite different when $\lambda_a > 0$. In this case, the dynamics of the model depend on how expectations are formed. Under rational expectations, shocks to aggregate demand have permanent effects – there is path dependency in employment – but systematic demand policy has no real effects. The case with rational expectations is analyzed in Appendix B.

Suppose, more realistically, that expectations are not rational and, for simplicity, consider a case with adaptive expectations. Specifically, let

$$\dot{\pi}^e = \lambda_\pi (\pi - \pi^e). \tag{6.22}$$

If policy-makers were to manipulate aggregate demand so as to maintain actual employment at the level $\bar{e}$, then, substituting Equations (6.19) and (6.21) into Equation (6.20), we would get

$$\dot{a} = \lambda_a \left[q - a - b\bar{e} \right]. \tag{6.23}$$

This first-order differential equation has a globally stable solution

$$\bar{a} = q - b\bar{e}. \tag{6.24}$$

At $a = \bar{a}$, we have $\dot{a} = 0$ and hence, using Equation (6.20), $\pi = \pi^e$. The expected inflation rate is constant when $\pi = \pi^e$ (Equation (6.22)), and it follows that actual inflation will also be constant. Thus, the endogenous adjustment in wage norms implies that the 'natural rate of unemployment' converges to the actual rate of unemployment.[15]

The inflationary costs of raising the rate of employment depend on the adjustment speeds. To see this, note that – from Equations (6.20) and (6.22) – we have

$$\Delta a = \int_{t_0}^{t_1} \lambda_a (\pi^e - \pi) dt$$

$$= -\frac{\lambda_a}{\lambda_\pi} \int_{t_0}^{t_1} \lambda_\pi (\pi - \pi^e) dt = -\frac{\lambda_a}{\lambda_\pi} \Delta \pi^e.$$

This equation holds for any values of t_0 and t_1 and any trajectory of $(\pi - \pi^e)$. Furthermore, if the economy was at a stationary point with $\pi = \pi^e$ before the policy intervention and converges to a new stationary solution, then $\Delta \pi^e = \Delta \pi$. Using Equation (6.24), the long-run change in a associated with a change in e is given by $\Delta a = -b\Delta e$. It follows that $\Delta \pi = \frac{b\lambda_\pi}{\lambda_a} \Delta e$: A permanent increase in employment can be obtained at the cost of a permanent, but finite increase in inflation. The long-run Phillips curve is not vertical but downward sloping, the slope being determined by the ratio of the adjustment speeds for expected inflation and norms $(\lambda_\pi / \lambda_a)$ and the slope of the short-run Phillips curve $(-b)$.

The exogenous determination of employment at some rate $\bar{e}$ is a poor representation of actual policy formation. Suppose instead, in line with simple Taylor rules for monetary policy, that policy-makers have a target rate of inflation, $\bar{\pi}$, and that they respond to deviations of actual inflation from this target. Specifically, suppose that policy-makers control the growth of aggregate nominal demand: They allow aggregate nominal demand to grow at the rate that is consistent with a constant employment rate when inflation equals the target rate but set the growth rate of nominal demand so as to reduce (raise) the employment rate when inflation exceeds (is below) the target rate.

Formally, assume that because of this policy rule, employment growth can be specified as

$$\hat{e} = \lambda_e (\bar{\pi} - \pi); \quad \lambda_e > 0. \tag{6.25}$$

Using Equations (6.19) and (6.21), actual inflation is given by

$$\pi = a + be + \pi^e - q. \tag{6.26}$$

---

[15] Policy can have permanent real effects when expectations are adaptive, even without stochastic elements. For simplicity, stochastic shocks have therefore been omitted.

Substitution of Equation (6.26) into Equations (6.20), (6.22), and (6.25) yields a three-dimensional system of differential equations:

$$\dot{a} = \lambda_a(q - a - be) \tag{6.27}$$

$$\dot{\pi}^e = \lambda_\pi(a + be - q) \tag{6.28}$$

$$\hat{e} = \lambda_e(\bar{\pi} + q - a - be - \pi^e). \tag{6.29}$$

The linear dependence between $\dot{a}$ and $\dot{\pi}^e$ implies that the system can be reduced to a two-dimensional system: Using Equations (6.27) and (6.28), we have

$$\dot{a} = -\frac{\lambda_a}{\lambda_\pi}\dot{\pi}^e$$

and hence

$$a(t) = a(t_0) + \int_{t_0}^{t} \dot{a}\, dt = a(t_0) - \frac{\lambda_a}{\lambda_\pi}\int_{t_0}^{t} \dot{\pi}^e\, dt$$

$$= a(t_0) + \frac{\lambda_a}{\lambda_\pi}\pi(t_0) - \frac{\lambda_a}{\lambda_\pi}\pi^e(t) = c - \frac{\lambda_a}{\lambda_\pi}\pi^e(t), \tag{6.30}$$

where $c = a(t_0) + \frac{\lambda_a}{\lambda_\pi}\pi^e(t_0)$ is determined by the initial conditions.

Substituting Equation (6.30) into Equations (6.28) and (6.29), we get

$$\dot{\pi}^e = \lambda_\pi\left[-\frac{\lambda_a}{\lambda_\pi}\pi^e + c + be - q\right] \tag{6.31}$$

$$\dot{e} = \lambda_e e\left[\bar{\pi} + q + \left(\frac{\lambda_a}{\lambda_\pi} - 1\right)\pi^e - c - be\right]. \tag{6.32}$$

Assuming that $q + \frac{\lambda_a}{\lambda_\pi}\bar{\pi} - c > 0$, the system has a nontrivial stationary solution given by[16]

$$e^* = \frac{q + \frac{\lambda_a}{\lambda_\pi}\bar{\pi} - c}{b} \tag{6.33}$$

$$\pi^{e*} = \bar{\pi}. \tag{6.34}$$

The stationary solution for the inflation rate is determined by the target rate of inflation. This intuitive result follows directly from the dynamic equation for employment, Equation (6.25). The stationary solution for the employment rate, however, depends on the rate of productivity growth (q), the target rate of inflation ($\bar{\pi}$), and the constant of integration (c).

The Jacobian of the system (6.31) and (6.32)) is given by

$$J(\pi^e, e) = \begin{pmatrix} -\lambda_a & \lambda_\pi b \\ \lambda_e e^*\left(\frac{\lambda_a}{\lambda_\pi} - 1\right) & -\lambda_e e^* b \end{pmatrix}$$

---

[16] A trivial stationary solution with $e = 0$, $\pi^e = \frac{\lambda_\pi}{\lambda_a}(c - q)$ always exists; it becomes the only solution with $e \geq 0$ if $q + \frac{\lambda_a}{\lambda_\pi}\bar{\pi} - c < 0$.

with

$$tr = -\lambda_a - \lambda_e e^* b < 0$$

$$\det = \lambda_e \lambda_\pi e^* b > 0.$$

Thus, the stability conditions are satisfied, and the stationary solution is stable.[17]

Discussion

For present purposes, the most important property of Equation (6.33) is the long-run effect of target inflation on employment. Unlike the case of rational expectations in Appendix B, systematic expansionary policy influences employment. In this example with adaptive inflation expectations, demand policy is represented by the choice of an inflation target and, using Equation (6.33), we have $\partial e^*/\partial \bar{\pi} > 0$. As in the above mentioned example with a constant, demand-determined value of $\bar{e}$, variations in aggregate demand policy – now defined by the target rate of inflation – generate a non-vertical long-run Phillips curve.

The path dependency of the employment rate has other important policy implications. It follows from Equations (6.19), (6.21), and (6.22) that inflation tends to be increasing whenever actual unemployment is below the level that is consistent with expectations being met. The endogeneity of the wage norm, however, implies that the fair wage tends to decrease whenever inflation is increasing. Downward shifts in the fair-wage curve in turn are associated with a decline in the equilibrium rate of unemployment. Thus, it is not low unemployment as such that raises inflation; it is the transitional process of decreasing the equilibrium rate of unemployment. This distinction is essential. As pointed out by Solow (1990, pp. 74–75), a temporary incomes policy, rather than a permanent policy, is sufficient to allow a permanent non-inflationary reduction in unemployment in a model with employment hysteresis.

The effects on e^* of shocks to productivity growth or to initial conditions (the constant of integration) also have economic interest. The rise in unemployment in the 1970s was preceded by a drop in the growth rates of labor productivity and real wages: The trend increase in real wages was significantly higher in 1945–1970 than in 1970–1995 in most OECD countries. This drop in real-wage growth reduces employment: A one-percentage point drop in real-wage growth is associated with a decline of $1/b$ in the stationary solution for the employment rate.[18]

---

[17] Global asymptotic stability can be established by transforming the system. If $x = \log e$, Equations (6.31) and (6.32) can be restated as

$$\dot{\pi}^e = v \left[-\frac{\mu}{v} \pi^e + c + b \exp x - q \right] \tag{6.35}$$

$$\dot{x} = \lambda \left[\bar{\pi} + q + \left(\frac{\mu}{v} - 1 \right) \pi^e - c - b \exp x \right]. \tag{6.36}$$

This transformed system satisfies the conditions of the Olech theorem for global stability of the stationary solution: $(\pi^e, x) \rightarrow (\pi^{e*}, x^*) = (\pi^{e*}, \log e^*)$. It follows that (π^e, e) will converge to (π^{e*}, e^*) for any initial values $(\pi^e, e) \in (\mathbb{R}, \mathbb{R}_+)$.

[18] The analysis in this section has drawn on Skott (1991, 1999, 2005). A related argument about the effects of changes in productivity growth was presented by Stiglitz (1997) and developed more fully by Ball

Other shocks may have affected the real-wage norm directly. Associated in part with the escalation of the war in South East Asia and the anti-war movement, social and political radicalizations from the late 1960s spilled over into greater worker aggressiveness in the labor market and increasing strike activity: There may have been an autonomous increase in wage aspirations.[19] Any such shift in aspirations (in fair wages) corresponds to a positive shock to the arbitrary constant c in Equation (6.33) and reduces long-run employment. Ascendant neoliberal ideology from the late 1970s onward arguably reversed the earlier positive shock to fair wages, with a fall in c now raising the equilibrium employment rate.

Institutional changes and labor market policies reinforced these trends in aspirations and norms. Any given package of wage and work conditions will be seen as generous and fair in some circumstances (when alternatives to the job are poor) but as unfair in other circumstances (if the alternatives improve). A $15 wage offer may look generous if the minimum wage is $8 but unfair if the minimum wage stands at $14. Thus, neoliberal labor market reforms may have gradually forced down the fair wage (shifted down Equation (6.19)). The policies have had serious social and distributional consequences, however, and the justification for the policies therefore often takes the form that "there is no alternative."

This Thatcherite TINA argument breaks down if the conventional element in wage norms generates path dependency in the equilibrium rate of unemployment, in which case there are alternatives. In principle, it is possible for well-designed aggregate

---

and Moffitt (2002). They modeled the way aspirations are adjusted differently, however, which led to conclusions that are qualitatively different from those in this chapter.

In Ball and Moffitt's specification (as in Stiglitz 1997), the adjustment of wage norms takes no account of the effect of current market conditions on the fair rate of growth of wages. As a result, demand policy can have no lasting effects on employment, and changes in productivity growth rates lead to temporary rather than permanent shifts in the Phillips curve. Using the notation in this chapter and a continuous-time framework, a slightly streamlined version of the Ball and Moffitt specification implies that

$$\hat{w} = a + be + \pi^e \tag{6.37}$$

$$\dot{a} = \lambda_a[\hat{w} - (a + \pi)]. \tag{6.38}$$

Ball and Moffitt also allow for a direct influence of productivity growth on wage inflation. This additional influence is irrelevant for the qualitative results; it is also implausible, I think: Economists themselves have a hard time measuring productivity growth, and it seems unlikely that workers should have a clear idea of the current value of this variable.

Equation (6.37) is identical to Equation (6.19), and the critical difference between the two models relates to adjustment of wage norms. Ball and Moffitt assume that the fair wage depends on the rate of employment (Equation (6.37)) but do not take this dependence into account in their specification of adjustments in the wage norm: Equation (6.38) implies that adjustments in norms take place even if the actual and fair growth rates of wages coincide and, furthermore, that the evolution of a can be derived completely independently of what happens to employment (using $\pi = \hat{w} - q$ and Equation (6.38), we have $\dot{a} = \lambda_a(q - a)$). Equation (6.20), by contrast, implies that adjustments in norms take place if and only if the actual wage increase deviates from what is considered fair.

[19] Newell and Symons (1987) include a dummy variable for 1969–1976 in their wage equations to account for "the world-wide increased militancy over this period" (p. 581). Grubb (1986, p. 69) also suggests that "changes in union 'militancy' were involved in the 'wage explosion'"; he includes strike variables and dummies in his wage equations to capture these changes.

demand policies to exploit differences in functional forms and raise employment without long-run effects on inflation (see the analysis in the following subsection on "A Shifting Phillips Curve"). But the alternatives to neoliberal reforms also include combinations of aggregate demand policy with formal or informal, temporary incomes policies. Such combinations will be easier to implement in economies with highly centralized labor unions, which may help explain the relatively strong performance of the group of 'low unemployment Euro countries' (cf. the discussion in Chapter 5 of Howell et al. 2007). These potential benefits of centralized unions also exemplify the presence of complementaries between institutions – in this case unionization, income policies, and aggregate demand policy. Institutional effects are complicated, and labor markets do not and cannot function like a textbook version of perfect competition

A Shifting Phillips Curve

The specifications of $\dot{a}$ and $\dot{\pi}^e$ in Equations (6.20) and (6.22) imply a fixed proportionality between changes in the expected inflation rate and changes in the fairness norm. Because of this proportionality, we have $\Delta\pi^e = -\frac{\lambda_\pi}{\lambda_a}\Delta a$, and it becomes possible to derive the long-run effects of changes in employment on inflation without knowing the precise movements of the employment rate during the transition period: A well-defined, downward-sloping long-run Phillips curve links inflation to employment. This invariance result is contingent on functional forms; without proportionality, the precise trajectory affects the long-run outcome.

As an example, consider the implications of retaining the linear specification for the adjustment of fairness norms but using a cubic adjustment in inflationary expectations:

$$\dot{\pi}^e = \lambda_\pi(\pi - \pi^e)^3. \tag{6.39}$$

The cubic adjustment function for inflation expectations implies that small inflation surprises will have a disproportionate influence on the real-wage norm, while large surprises exert a disproportionate effect on inflationary expectations. As a consequence of this asymmetry, long-run employment can be raised without any inflationary costs if a sharp negative shock to employment is followed by a slow expansion. The sharp negative shock to employment pushes actual inflation far below the expected inflation. This large discrepancy generates a disproportionate effect on inflation expectations relative to its effect on the wage norm, which follows a linear specification. The ensuing period of mildly expansionary policy, by contrast, affects the wage norm more strongly than it affects inflation expectations. Thus, as inflation expectations slowly return to their old equilibrium level, the real-wage norm falls below its previous equilibrium level (see Appendix C).

The qualitative differences in this example with respect to functional forms have intuitive plausibility. The formation of inflationary expectations is a conscious mental activity, and small non-salient changes in the average price level may be ignored.[20] Changes in norms, by contrast, reflect a nonconscious adaptation. The way people

---

[20] Although different, this nonlinearity in the specification of adjustments in expectation has affinities with Rowthorn's treatment of anticipated inflation as a nonlinear function of expected inflation as well as

adjust to changes in real wages may be more akin to the apocryphal behavior of frogs getting boiled alive in slowly heating water: The adaptation to small changes may be facilitated precisely because the changes may not be consciously recognized. This is in line with Bewley's (1998) finding that although nominal wages were downwardly rigid, "gradual reductions in real wages were feasible, for the slow decline in living standards caused by pay freezes was less noticeable and more tolerable than abrupt nominal pay cut" (p. 477). The example is also consistent with Ball's (1997) study of disinflation. The study finds strong evidence of hysteresis: Disinflation is associated with long-run increases in unemployment.[21] But it matters how the disinflation is carried out. Unemployment rises less if disinflation is quick: "if policy makers choose to disinflate they should do so aggressively" (p. 184).

For present purposes, however, the main point is different and independent of the particular assumptions used in the example: The stable Phillips curve breaks down as soon as the adjustment equations for norms and expected inflation take different functional forms (and/or include different variables). Since there is no particular reason to expect that they will take the same, linear form, the stable trade-off between unemployment and inflation represents a fragile special case. Any differences in the functional form that break the proportional effects of unanticipated inflation on $\dot{a}$ and $\dot{\pi}^e$ imply the possibility of permanent non-inflationary increases in employment (and, analogously, the risk of permanent reductions in employment without reductions in inflation if the time patterns are wrong).

Appendix C outlines an example of well-designed policy, but the significance of this possibility clearly should not be exaggerated. In the absence of reliable information about the precise functional forms, it is not very helpful to be told that, in principle, 'clever policy' could reduce unemployment without any inflationary effects. This caveat about policy implications does not affect the crucial theoretical point: With different functional forms, there is no stable long-run Phillips curve.

6.5 Inflation in a Developing Economy

Whatever one may think of the Phillips curve for rich economies, notions of a natural rates of unemployment beg additional questions in relation to developing economies.[22]

According to the World Bank, the unemployment rate for India fluctuated between 4.8 percent and 6.2 percent between 1991 and 2019, while Mexico routinely has unemployment rates that are among the lowest in the OECD. These official numbers say

---

with the notion that expectations may remain anchored to the central bank's target rate despite minor deviations of actual inflation from this target.

[21] The prolonged recession after the financial crisis has led to renewed interest in hysteresis (e.g., Ball 2014, Ball et al. 2014, DeLong and Summers 2012, Yagan 2018).

[22] Partly because of data limitations, the empirical literature on Phillips curves in developing countries is relatively sparse. But the results are not encouraging. Bleaney and Francisco (2018) find that for low- and middle-income countries, the coefficient on the output gap is statistically insignificant in most of their Phillips-curve regressions. Maka and Barbosa (2013) discuss the case of Brazil in greater detail.

very little about the extent of underemployment. Most developing economies are dual economies in the sense of Lewis (1954): Modern sectors coexist with traditional and informal sectors that have low incomes and significant hidden unemployment. The growth of the modern sectors in India and Mexico is not hampered by a shortage of workers. There may be temporary shortages of particular skills, but the evidence suggests that large numbers of underemployed workers in the informal sectors have skills that are comparable to those of formal-sector workers and that formal-sector jobs pay better and are seen as highly attractive (La Porta and Shleifer 2014).[23]

These empirical observations create a puzzle: Despite large amounts of underemployment, many developing economies have experienced high rates of inflation. This is the case not least in Latin America, where structuralist explanations have focused on the interaction between bottlenecks that create price increases in particular sectors and propagation mechanisms that spread the price increases and lead to general inflation (Noyola 1956, Sunkel 1958, Seers 1962); Ros (2013, Chapter 12) presents a useful formalization.

With an inelastic supply of agricultural goods, an expansion of the modern sector and the associated increase in the demand for agricultural output leads to increases in the price of food and squeezes the consumption real wage. Workers try to defend their living standards and react by demanding increases in the money wages. As money wages rise, monopolistic firms raise the prices of modern sector goods, and the increase in prices and wages in the modern sector now feeds back into higher nominal demand for agricultural output. Agricultural prices rise further, leading to a new round of wage and price increases: The combination of bottlenecks (an inelastic supply of agricultural output) and propagation mechanisms (distributional conflict) has set the stage for explosive inflation.[24]

This structuralist story – rightly, in my view – emphasizes distributional conflict and interactions between sectors. But most basic agricultural goods are tradable, and in many countries, it seems implausible to designate inelastic agricultural supply as

---

[23] La Porta and Shleifer summarize their findings in five facts:

we establish five critical facts about the informal economy. First, it is huge, especially in developing countries. Second, it has extremely low productivity compared to the formal economy .... Third, ... the productivity of informal firms is too low for them to thrive in the formal sector.... Fourth, ... [i]nformal firms rarely transition to formality, and continue their existence, often for years or even decades, without much growth or improvement. Fifth, as countries grow and develop, the informal economy eventually shrinks, and the formal economy comes to dominate economic life (La Porta and Shleifer 2014, p. 110).

They also note that "at least on many observable characteristics the workers are rather similar in informal and formal firms" (p. 125) and that with incomes that are only a fraction of formal sector wages many "informal entrepreneurs would gladly close their businesses to work as employees in the formal sector if offered the chance" (p. 112).

[24] Although inelastic supplies of wage goods, especially agricultural output, were identified as an important source of inflation, other bottlenecks could play the same role. A high income elasticity of imports, for instance, could necessitate a depreciation of the currency to avoid balance of payments problems if domestic demand increases; a depreciated currency reduces domestic real wages, and distributional conflict now generates inflationary pressures and the need for further depreciation to restore international competitiveness (see Ros 2013, Section 12.3).

an important bottleneck. Particularly for middle-income countries like Mexico and Brazil, second, underemployment is increasingly to be found in informal urban sectors, rather than in agriculture. The specification of wage formation in the modern sector, third, may not be fully convincing, and this specification is central to the results. The models in this section modify the structuralist analysis to address these issues.

6.5.1 A Structuralist Model of 'Natural Underemployment'

Assumptions

A modern, formal sector produces an output M using a Leontief technology,

$$M = \min\{AL_M, \sigma^{\max}K\} = AL_M. \tag{6.40}$$

L_M and K denote modern-sector employment and capital. There is excess capital capacity, and labor productivity A grows at a constant rate. A constant markup $(1 + m)$ implies that the profit share, π, is constant, and if w_M and p_M are the wages and prices in the sector, we have

$$p_M = (1 + m)\frac{w_M}{A} \tag{6.41}$$

$$w_M L_M = (1 - \pi)p_M M. \tag{6.42}$$

The informal sector has labor as its only input. Workers in this sector sell goods and services as day laborers, street vendors, domestic workers, or employees in small corner shops and construction activities. As the residual 'employer,' this R-sector represents the fallback for workers who fail to get a job in the modern sector:

$$L_R = N - L_M, \tag{6.43}$$

where N is the total labor force. The informal sector may contain small-scale businesses that make a profit but, for simplicity, it is assumed that all incomes in the informal sector go to workers. Thus, if p_R and w_R are the price of output (R) and average incomes in this sector (the wage rate, for short), we have

$$p_R R = w_R L_R. \tag{6.44}$$

To simplify, workers in both sectors spend their income on consumption while all profits are saved. Thus, aggregate nominal consumption (pC) is given by

$$pC = p_M C_M + p_R C_R = w_R L_R + w_M L_M, \tag{6.45}$$

where C_R and C_M denote real consumption of goods from the two sectors. Nominal consumption is split between formal and informal goods, the proportion α of consumption expenditure going to the formal sector:

$$p_M C_M = \alpha pC \tag{6.46}$$

$$p_R C_R = (1 - \alpha)pC. \tag{6.47}$$

The informal sector produces a pure consumption good, and the equilibrium condition requires that

$$R = C_R. \tag{6.48}$$

Formal-sector goods can be used for investment or consumption, and the equilibrium condition is given by

$$M = I(M,K,r) + C_M. \tag{6.49}$$

Investment demand depends on the real rate of interest (r), the level of formal-sector output, and the predetermined capital stock; this specification includes investment functions that relate the accumulation rate to the utilization rate of capital as a special case.

Wage formation in the formal sector is shaped by wage norms but unlike in the one-sector model of Section 6.4, the norms may primarily concern the relation between formal-sector wages and the average income in the informal sector. Formal-sector workers cannot directly observe incomes in the informal sector but receive imperfect signals from a variety of sources, including news stories and social media; direct conversations with family, friends, and neighbors; and observable consumption behavior – the purchase of a new TV or dress by an acquaintance, for instance, or the ordering of more extravagant snacks by regulars in a neighborhood bar. The reference group may not encompass all groups of informal-sector workers. The incomes of, for instance, street peddlers will have little or no direct influence on the wage aspirations of high-skill, relatively well-paid metal workers in the formal sector; if they influence the aspirations and wages of low-skill retail workers in the formal sector, however, there will be a cascade of derived effects for other formal-sector workers.

As a simple two-sector approximation of these ripple effects of changes in the conditions of workers in the informal sector, it is assumed that workers' wage aspirations, w_M^T, are proportional to the average income in the informal sector,

$$w_M^T = \mu w_R; \quad \mu > 1, \tag{6.50}$$

where $\mu > 1$ represents the target wage premium in the formal sector.[25] For simplicity, the wage aspirations in Equation (6.50) have been related exclusively to informal-sector incomes. The specification could be extended to include a dependence on formal-sector prices and profitability. With a constant markup, however, this extension would not change much.

Nominal wage inflation reacts to deviations of actual wages from the target and (analogously to the expectations augmented Phillips curve) may incorporate the expected increase in average nominal incomes in the informal sector:

$$\hat{w}_M = \lambda_w \left(\frac{w_M^T}{w_M} - 1 \right) + x. \tag{6.51}$$

The variable x denotes the expected growth rate of average incomes in the informal sector and λ_w is the speed of adjustment in response to gaps between target and actual

---

[25] The informal sector provides a fallback option for workers in the formal sector. By assumption there is no open unemployment, but a large proportion of the workers that have been pushed into the informal sector may be underemployed. The average income in the sector can be seen as an indicator of the expected income for a worker that loses her formal-sector job.

wages in the formal sector. Expectations are assumed to follow a simple adaptive process,

$$\dot{x} = \lambda_\pi(\hat{w}_R - x). \tag{6.52}$$

Now suppose that general price inflation is related to the rate of price inflation in the modern sector. Formally, let

$$\hat{p} = \phi(\hat{p}_M); \quad \phi' > 0, \tag{6.53}$$

where p is the general price level. By assumption, the markup in the formal sector is constant, and if labor productivity in the formal sector grows at the rate q, Equation (6.41) implies that

$$\hat{p} = \phi(\hat{w}_M - q). \tag{6.54}$$

Implications

Total informal-sector income can be found by combining the consumption equations with the equilibrium condition for the informal sector (Equations (6.44)–(6.48)):

$$w_R L_R = p_R R = \frac{1-\alpha}{\alpha} w_M L_M. \tag{6.55}$$

Thus, the 'wage ratio' w_R/w_M is given by

$$\frac{w_R}{w_M} = \frac{L_M}{N - L_M} \frac{1-\alpha}{\alpha} = \Theta \frac{1-\alpha}{\alpha}, \tag{6.56}$$

where $\Theta = L_M/(N - L_M)$ is the ratio of formal-sector employment to the labor force in the informal sector.[26]

An inflation-targeting central bank sets an inflation target, which translates into a target for wage inflation in the formal sector (Equation (6.54)). A constant value of $\hat{w}_M$ in turn pins down the sectoral composition of workers – the value of Θ – that is consistent with income expectations being met. To see this, note that if expectations are met, then $x = \hat{w}_R$ and both x and $\hat{w}_R$ will be constant (Equation (6.52)). Using Equation (6.51), it now follows that

$$\hat{w}_M - \hat{w}_R = \lambda_w \left(\frac{\mu w_R}{w_M} - 1 \right). \tag{6.57}$$

Both $\hat{w}_M$ and $\hat{w}_R$ (and therefore also the left-hand side of Equation (6.57)) are constant. The right-hand side can only be constant if $\hat{w}_M = \hat{w}_R$, which in turn implies

---

[26] Aggregate income in the informal sector is demand determined, but Equation (6.55) says nothing about whether this income is achieved through low prices, high real output, and low degrees of underemployment or through high prices, low output, and high degrees of underemployment. No assumptions about the technology in the informal sector were needed, moreover, to derive Equations (6.55) and (6.56). The average income in the informal sector and the employment share of the modern sector can be determined without any reference to production functions and prices in the informal sector. This property of the model follows from the assumption that a constant share of consumption expenditure goes to the informal sector. This assumption simplifies the analysis but could be relaxed (see Martins and Skott 2021).

(using Equations (6.56) and (6.57)) that[27]

$$\left(\frac{w_R}{w_M}\right)^* = \frac{1}{\mu} \tag{6.58}$$

$$\Theta^* = \frac{\alpha}{1-\alpha}\frac{1}{\mu}. \tag{6.59}$$

Persistent deviations of the share of formal-sector employment from Θ^* would generate growth rates of average informal-sector incomes that deviate from the expected rate. If, say, $\Theta = \bar{\Theta} > \Theta^*$, we have

$$\left(\frac{w_R}{w_M}\right) = \bar{\Theta}\frac{1-\alpha}{\alpha} > \Theta^*\frac{1-\alpha}{\alpha} = \frac{1}{\mu}.$$

and (using Equations (6.50)–(6.52) and (6.56))

$$\dot{x} = \lambda_x(\hat{w}_R - x) = \lambda_x(\hat{\Theta} + \hat{w}_M - x) = \lambda_x(\hat{w}_M - x)$$

$$= \lambda_x\lambda_w\left(\frac{\mu w_R}{w_M} - 1\right) > 0. \tag{6.60}$$

Using Equation (6.51) it follows that wage inflation in the formal sector would increase steadily and without limit.

Equations (6.58) and (6.59) express necessary conditions for successful inflation targeting. The required value of M (M^*) can be found by combining Equations (6.40) and (6.59) to get

$$M = M^* = \frac{A}{1 + \mu^{\frac{1-\alpha}{\alpha}}}N. \tag{6.61}$$

The implications of this requirement for the interest rate can be seen by noting – using Equations (6.42), (6.46) and (6.48) – that

$$C_M = \frac{w_M}{p_M}L_M = (1-\pi)M.$$

With M determined by Equation (6.61), the equilibrium condition for the formal sector – Equation (6.49) – implies that

$$I(M^*,K,r) = \pi M^* = \pi\frac{A}{1 + \mu^{\frac{1-\alpha}{\alpha}}}N. \tag{6.62}$$

N, K, and A are predetermined and to maintain a constant target rate of inflation, central banks must adjust the (real) interest rate r to satisfy Equation (6.62).

---

[27] Formally, if $\hat{w}_M$ is kept constant, Equations (6.50)–(6.52), (6.53) and (6.56) can be used to derive a 2D system of differential Equations in x and Θ. The system has a unique, stable stationary solution at $x = \hat{w}_M$ (which translates into $w_R/w_M = 1/\mu$) and $\Theta = (\alpha/(1-\alpha))(1/\mu)$.

6.5.2   Endogenous Norms and Aspirations

Conflicting income claims – wage setting in the modern sector interacting with demand-determined incomes in the informal sector – pin down the share of modern-sector employment, as shown by Equation (6.59). A large wage premium in the formal sector (a high relative-wage demand μ) requires a small modern sector and a large informal sector. Structural transformation is blocked – or more accurately, the expansion of the modern sector will create explosive inflation in the absence of institutional changes or policy interventions that reduce the relative wage aspirations in the formal sector. In this respect, the model in Section 6.5.1 depicts a dual economy that is quite similar to the economies described by standard models of natural unemployment: Labor market reforms that reduce the power and wage aspirations of formal-sector workers would seem to be needed for non-inflationary expansion of the modern sector.

In mature economies, the path dependency of wage aspirations and fairness norms creates employment hysteresis, thereby undermining the notion of a natural rate of unemployment, as discussed in Section 6.4. By definition, mature economies are close to full employment, and the potential effects of hysteresis on the level of employment are relatively minor in these economies. Dual economies, by contrast, are far from any meaningful notion of full employment, and the effects of path dependency can be more radical: Distributional conflict need not prevent sustained increases in economic growth and the expansion of the modern sector if wage aspirations are endogenous. To see this, suppose that the fair wage ratio changes over time in response to differences between actual and fair relative wages; that is, μ changes in response to differences between w_M/w_R and μ:

$$\dot{\mu} = \lambda_\mu \left(\frac{w_M}{w_R} - \mu \right), \tag{6.63}$$

where λ_μ is the adjustment speed for the target relative wage. The specification in Equation (6.63) – like the specification in Equation (6.20) – is quite mechanical and leaves out many factors that may influence workers' aspirations and their willingness and ability to fight for wage increases. With these caveats, however, the equation may capture one, potentially important mechanism in the formation of wage aspirations.[28]

As in Section 6.4, the endogenous adjustment of norms generates employment hysteresis,[29] a result that is amplified by a 'Rowthorn extension': Adapting and

---

[28] Similar specifications have been used by Skott (2005) and Martins and Skott (2021). The symmetric specification in Equation (6.63) has the virtue of simplicity but misses an important aspect of norm adjustment: Fairness norms are likely to adjust quickly in an upward direction (we quickly feel that pay increases are 'fair') but more slowly in a downward direction (it is hard to accept that we may deserve less than what we used to get). This asymmetry in the adjustment of norms in combination with downward stickiness in nominal wages can make for inflationary pressures, even if average relative wages are trendless; volatility tends to raise the inflation rate.

[29] Consider an initial stationary solution with $\Theta = \Theta^*$, $w_M/w_R = \mu^* = \alpha/[(1-\alpha)\Theta^*]$, and $\hat{w}_M = \hat{w}_R = x = \hat{w}_M^*$. Now assume that the employment share of the modern sector starts to increase, perhaps as a result of expansionary policy. The relative wage w_R/w_M is proportional to Θ (Equation (6.56)) and with $\hat{\Theta} > 0$, the wage premium in the modern sector will be declining; faster growth in informal-sector incomes also generates upward adjustments in expected informal-sector incomes. Wage inflation in the modern sector will start to increase (Equation (6.51)), and price inflation increases with

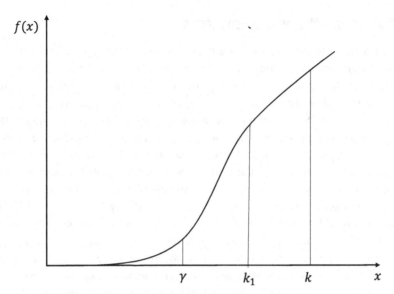

Figure 6.10 Smooth f-function depicting the salience of inflation.

generalizing Rowthorn's (1977) analysis, assume that wage inflation in the modern sector is determined by a modified version of Equation (6.51):

$$\hat{w}_M = \lambda_w \left(\frac{w_M^T}{w_M} - 1 \right) + f(x). \tag{6.64}$$

Formal-sector workers still have a target for relative wages, but low expected growth rates of informal-sector incomes tend to be ignored. This behavioral effect is captured by the f-function which is taken to be smooth (twice differentiable) and to satisfy the conditions

$$f(x) = 0 \text{ for } x \le 0 \tag{6.65}$$

$$f(x) = x \text{ for } x \ge k \tag{6.66}$$

$$f' \ge 0, f'(0) = 0, \quad f'(k) = 1 \tag{6.67}$$

$$f''(x) > 0 \text{ for } 0 < x < k_1 < k \tag{6.68}$$

$$f''(x) < 0 \text{ for } k_1 < x < k. \tag{6.69}$$

This sigmoid-shaped f-function includes Rowthorn's threshold specification as a limiting case in which $f(x) = 0$ for $x < k$ and $f(x) = x$ for $x \ge k$ (see Figure 6.10).

Consider first the implications of successful inflation targeting; that is, assume that policy is adjusted to keep inflation at a target level. It can be shown that for intermediate values of the target, the employment share of the formal sector (Θ) will be increasing steadily and the wage premium in the modern sector will be decreasing. Formally, if $\hat{p}^*$ is the inflation target, the associated rate of wage inflation in the modern

it (Equation (6.54)). But the wage norm also adjusts: If, after a while, the increase in Θ is brought to a halt at $\Theta^{**} > \Theta^*$, the fair wage ratio will converge to a lower level $\mu^{**} = \alpha/[(1-\alpha)\Theta^{**}]$ while the rate of wage inflation converges to $\hat{w}_M^{**} = \hat{w}_R^{**} = x^{**} > \hat{w}_M^*$.

sector is $\hat{w}_M^* = \phi^{-1}(\hat{p}^*) + q$, and we have (see Appendix D)

$$\hat{\Theta} < 0 \text{ for } \hat{w}_M^* < 0$$
$$\hat{\Theta} = 0 \text{ for } \hat{w}_M^* = 0 \text{ or } \hat{w}_M^* > k$$
$$\hat{\Theta} > 0 \text{ for } 0 < \hat{w}_M^* < k.$$

The speed of transformation ($\hat{\Theta}$), moreover, has a unique local (and global) maximum for some value γ in the interval $(0, k)$; the speed is increasing in the inflation target for $0 < \hat{w}_M^* < \gamma$ and decreasing for $\gamma < \hat{w}_M^* < k$.

This analysis suggests that modest rates of (constant) inflation can facilitate economic development[30]; low or very high rates, on the other hand, hurt growth and development. But if the model is correct, any development process that reduces underemployment will tend to generate wage inflation. This implication of the analysis does not imply that the observed correlation between growth and inflation must be positive for low rates of inflation: Inflation can also be – and often is – generated by policy regimes (or adverse circumstances like civil war or natural disasters) that are not conducive to economic growth. It is not surprising, however, to find countries with high, sustained growth as well as high inflation rates – the average annual inflation rate in South Korea, for instance, was above 10 percent during 30 years of miracle growth from 1960 to 1990, with several spikes above 25 percent. Nor is it surprising that econometric studies have found nonlinear relations between inflation and economic growth, with no statistical correlation for inflation levels below 8 percent (Sarel 1996) or 15 percent (Barro 1995). An influential paper by Bruno and Easterly (1998) even reports the absence of any evidence of a negative relationship for inflation levels below 40 percent, and the correlation becomes *positive* from 1961 to 1973. This result is corroborated by Pollin and Zhu (2006): Extending the period to 1961–2000, they find a positive relationship between growth and inflation for low-income countries with inflation rates below 15 percent.

As another experiment, suppose that relative informal-sector incomes are subjected to a large positive shock. In this simple model, the relative wage is determined by Equation (6.56), and the shock can come from a shift in the share of consumption going to the informal sector. In a more general open-economy setting with a public sector, the shock could be caused by shifts in fiscal policy or by a commodity boom in a resource-rich economy (see Martins and Skott 2021, Skott 2021). Whatever the source of the shock, inflation will increase if the trajectory of $\hat{\Theta}$ is kept unchanged despite the shock to relative incomes.

As shown in Appendix E, if $\hat{\Theta} = \delta > 0$ is constant, we have a 2D system of differential equations in x and $(\mu w_R / w_M)$:

---

[30] The falling wage premium and rising share of the formal sector must come to halt when the wage premium hits zero (or some lower bound) and the labor supply to formal sector ceases to be elastic. In developing economies with large amounts of underemployment, however, the process can proceed for a long time before hitting the lower bound, and to simplify the exposition the bound was not included explicitly in Equation (6.63).

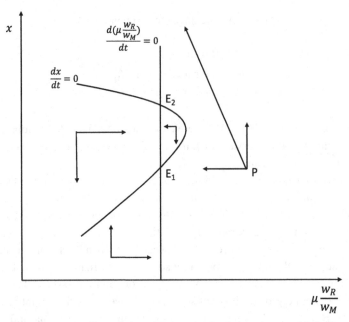

Figure 6.11 Phase diagram for a 2D system of relative wages and inflation expectations in a dual economy.

$$\dot{x} = \lambda_x \left[\delta + \lambda_w \left(\frac{\mu w_R}{w_M} - 1 \right) + f(x) - x \right] \tag{6.70}$$

$$\widetilde{\frac{\mu w_R}{w_M}} = \lambda_\mu \left(\frac{w_M}{\mu w_R} - 1 \right) + \delta. \tag{6.71}$$

The 2D system (6.70) and (6.71)) may have two, one, or no stationary points. Figure 6.11 depicts a phase diagram for the case with two solutions; one of them (E_1) is locally stable, and the other (E_2) is a saddle point.

Suppose that initially the economy is at the locally stable stationary point E_1 with $x = x^*, \left(\frac{\mu w_R}{w_M} \right) = \left(\frac{\mu w_R}{w_M} \right)^*, \hat{\Theta} = \delta > 0$ and that, starting from this position, at time t_0, there is a positive shock to the relative wage of workers in the informal sector. The fair wage ratio μ is predetermined, and the shock to the relative wage translates into a positive shock to the 'aspiration gap' $\mu w_R / w_M$. If, as seems likely, the adjustment of aspirations is slow (a low value of λ_μ), a large shock to relative wages takes the economy on a path of explosive inflation with $x \to \infty$, as in Figure 6.11: The shock at time t_0 has displaced the economy from E_1 to P, and with a slow adjustment speed λ_μ, the system now follows a steep, divergent trajectory. As x diverges, we have $f(x) \to \infty, \hat{w}_M \to \infty$, and $\hat{p} \to \infty$.

The dynamics of x and ($\mu w_R / w_M$) also imply that once expected inflation has risen above the threshold k, an absolute decline in Θ is needed to reduce inflation expectations. Above the threshold, we have (Equation (6.70))

$$\dot{x} = \lambda_x (\hat{w}_R - x) = \lambda_x \left[\hat{\Theta} + \lambda_w \left(\frac{\mu w_R}{w_M} - 1 \right) \right].$$

Setting $\hat{\Theta} = 0$ implies that $\frac{\mu w_R}{w_M}$ will converge to 1 from above (Equation (6.71)) and $\dot{x}$ will converge to 0 from above. Thus, to combat inflation and achieve a decline in x, a reduction in the employment share of the modern sector is needed. A shock to relative wages and the ensuing inflation may have led to a process of deindustrialization.

6.6 Conclusion

Microeconomic models based on homo oeconomicus give a distorted view of real-world behavior. These distortions, which are particularly important with respect to the labor market and wage formation, have significant macroeconomic implications.

Productivity typically suffers if workers are unhappy with their jobs, and paying wages that are perceived as unfair is a sure way to create unhappiness. Workers may accept a low-paying job but reciprocate by working carelessly or providing low effort. Low wages also have adverse effects on labor turnover and the quality of the firm's pool of job candidates. These microeconomic findings have support from the psychological and sociological literature. They also find confirmation in surveys of managers, consultants, and other people involved in wage setting as well as in laboratory and field experiments, and in econometric studies. The behavioral evidence, moreover, shows that money illusion is prevalent: Workers care about purely nominal changes in wages and there is strong resistance to cuts in the nominal wage. The evidence, finally, shows that norms of fairness are path dependent: The fair wage to a large extent is determined by what has been customary.

These behavioral findings invalidate the notion of a micro-founded 'natural rate of unemployment.' The microeconomic assumptions behind the derivation of the natural rate are at odds with the microeconomic evidence and the reality that pay norms emerge in a social context. But a rejection of the natural rate hypothesis does not necessarily imply a stable downward-sloping long-run Phillips curve. Some models with money illusion may have this implication, but others do not produce a stable trade-off. The path dependency in norms of fairness can generate path dependency (hysteresis) in employment, with implications that depend on the nature of expectations. Under rational expectations, systematic policy has no real effects, but unanticipated demand shocks produce permanent shifts in the equilibrium rate of employment. Adaptive expectations – as a simple example of expectations that are not rational – imply that systematic expansionary policies can raise employment permanently without ever-increasing inflation, but again there may be no fixed trade-off: The inflationary implications of an increase in employment may depend on the precise trajectory of employment.

I have focused on path-dependent fairness norms as a source of employment hysteresis. As is well known, other mechanisms can also create employment hysteresis. Insider-outsider effects (e.g., Blanchard and Summers 1987, Lindbeck and Snower 1987), duration effects (e.g., Hargreaves-Heap 1980), or capital capacity effects (e.g., Rowthorn 1995) may be as significant as fairness-based explanations. The different mechanisms are not mutually exclusive. The reason for emphasizing the potential effects of endogenously changing norms in this chapter is threefold: This mechanism is less widely recognized, it emerges in a straightforward manner from behavioral evidence, and the same mechanism – path dependency in norms – can be significant for movements in inequality (Chapter 7).

Some of the detailed results in this chapter are contingent on assumptions about matters where we have very little evidence – an obvious example is the specific functional forms for the adjustment of inflationary expectations and fairness norms that were used to illustrate the possibility of raising employment without increasing inflation. But the main conclusions (including the absence of a structurally determined natural rate of unemployment) are, I believe, quite robust, and there is considerable microeconomic evidence in favor of the central behavioral mechanisms. The very notion of a natural rate of unemployment and even the weaker notion of a stable, time-invariant long-run Phillips curve may represent a will-o'-the-wisp. If the data had come out strongly in support of a stable, vertical long-run Phillips curve, one could justifiably dismiss the complexities introduced in the theoretical scenarios and mechanisms in this and the previous chapter as empirically irrelevant. But the evidence does not support the existence of a vertical long-run Phillips curve.

The issues are fundamental for policy-making. Economic policies and reforms guided by the natural-rate paradigm have caused an explosion of inequality in the United States and significant increases of inequality in many other countries; as argued in Chapter 5, there is little evidence of compensating employment effects from these increases in inequality.[31] In developing economies, adherence to natural-rate orthodoxy may stand in the way of the structural transformations that are needed to raise incomes and reduce underemployment.

The welfare consequences of policies based on faulty theories can be devastating, and the natural-rate hypothesis should be rejected. But it is important to explore the reasons for its failures. The policy implications of a well-defined, downward-sloping long-run Phillips curve are quite different from the implications of a non-monotonic long-run Phillips curve (as in Rowthorn 1977) or from those that follow from employment hysteresis. Unfortunately, our knowledge of wage formation and inflation remains far less solid than one would have wished. Much more work – both theoretical and empirical – is needed, but tentative theories and a recognition of our ignorance are preferable to policy-making that is founded on a dogmatic, *a priori* belief in a structurally determined natural rate of unemployment.

Our ignorance is even more pronounced with respect to inflation in developing economies. The formal models in this chapter represent an attempt to explain the potential for strong inflationary pressures, even in economies with large amounts of open and/or hidden unemployment. Although simple and mechanical, the mechanisms that the models formalize are backed by insights from behavioral studies on the role

---

[31] In comments on an early draft of this chapter, Paul Auerbach pointed out that even if there were positive employment effects and even if these employment effects could not be achieved in any other way within the current economic system, the appropriate response might well be to seek more fundamental changes in the way the economy is organized.

of fairness norms in wage formation. Insofar as the models capture significant aspects of the inflationary process in developing economies, they carry important lessons for economic policy. As indicated by the first experiment in Section 6.5.2, ambitious low-inflation targets can choke economic development, while modest inflation rates help facilitate the structural transformation that characterizes the development process. Beyond a certain level, however, inflation ceases to be helpful and instead stands in the way of a successful development strategy. This last finding delivers an important warning, outlined in more detail by the second experiment: Large shocks to relative wages may send an inflation-targeting developing economy into premature deindustrialization.

Appendix A: The Modified Akerlof and Yellen Model with Heterogeneous Labor

Proof that $e_1 > e_2$ if and only if $w_1 > w_2$

To show that high relative employment is associated with a high relative wage, assume that $e_1 > e_2$. With unemployment among type 2 workers, we must have

$$w_2 = w_2^f = w_1 \phi(e_2).$$

Combining this equation with the general requirement that

$$w_1 \geq w_1^f = w_2 \phi(e_1),$$

we get

$$\frac{w_1}{w_2} \geq \frac{w_2}{w_1} \frac{\phi(e_1)}{\phi(e_2)}$$

or

$$\left(\frac{w_1}{w_2}\right)^2 \geq \frac{\phi(e_1)}{\phi(e_2)} > 1.$$

Thus, if $e_1 > e_2$, we have $w_1 > w_2$.

High relative wages also imply high relative employment. Assume that $w_1 > w_2$. If $e_1 = 1$, the result follows immediately from the impossibility of having full employment for both types. Thus, let $e_1 < 1$ and thereby $w_1 = w_1^f = w_2 \phi(e_1)$. We always have $w_2 \geq w_2^f = w_1 \phi(e_2)$. Combining the two equations, it now follows that

$$\frac{w_1}{w_2} \leq \frac{w_2}{w_1} \frac{\phi(e_1)}{\phi(e_2)}.$$

By assumption, $w_1 > w_2$ and $\phi' > 0$. Thus, we must have $e_1 > e_2$.

Proof that if workers of group j experience full employment. then, generically, $w_j > w_j^f$.

Let $e_1 = 1, e_2 < 1$, and assume that $w_1 = w_1^f$. Then

$$w_1 = w_2 \phi(1)$$

and

$$\frac{w_1}{w_2} = \phi(1).$$

We also have (since by assumption $e_2 < 1$ and $w_2 = w_2^f$)

$$w_2 = w_1 \phi(e_2) = w_2 \phi(1) \phi(e_2).$$

Hence,

$$e_2 = \phi^{-1}\left(\frac{1}{\phi(1)}\right).$$

This equation defines a unique value of e_2. The determination of e_2 is independent of the production function, but wages must also satisfy firms' first-order conditions which imply that

$$\frac{w_1}{w_2} = \frac{F_1(N, L_2)}{F_2(N, L_2)}.$$

This condition will only be satisfied by a fluke if w_1/w_2 and $L_2 = e_2 N$ are determined by the fair wage conditions.

Appendix B: Movements in Employment under Rational Expectations

The case with rational expectations can be analyzed more easily using discrete time. The dynamic Equation (6.20) then becomes

$$a_t = a_{t-1} + \lambda_a(\pi_t^e - \pi_t), \tag{6.72}$$

where $\pi_t = (p_{t+1} - p_t)/p_t$ and $\pi_t^e = (p_{t+1}^e - p_t)/p_t$. Now assume rational expectations and, for concreteness, suppose that random shocks to productivity growth are the source of deviations of actual from expected inflation. Thus, let

$$q_t = q + \eta_t \tag{6.73}$$
$$\pi_t = \hat{w}_t - q_t = \hat{w}_t - q - \eta_t \tag{6.74}$$
$$\pi_t^e = E(\pi_t) = \hat{w}_t - q = \pi_t + \eta_t, \tag{6.75}$$

where $\hat{w}_t = (w_{t+1} - w_t)/w_t$ and $\eta_t \sim NID$.

Combining Equations (6.72)–(6.75), we get

$$a_t = a_{t-1} + \lambda_a \eta_t.$$

The parameter a_t follows a random walk, and the implications for employment can be found by using Equations (6.19), (6.21), and (6.75):

$$\pi_t = \hat{w}_t - q_t = a_t + be_t + \pi_t^e - q_t$$

or

$$e_t = \frac{q - a_t}{b}.$$

Since a_t follows a random walk, the same applies to e_t.

Appendix C: Non-Inflationary Expansion

Using Equations (6.13) and (6.16), it follows that

$$\pi - \pi^e = a + be - q. \tag{6.76}$$

The changes in a and π^e are given by Equations (6.20) and (6.39), reproduced here for convenience,

$$\dot{a} = \lambda_a(\pi^e - \pi) \tag{6.77}$$

$$\dot{\pi}^e = \lambda_\pi(\pi - \pi^e)^3. \tag{6.78}$$

Assume that a stationary state with $\pi = \pi^e = \bar{\pi}$ and $e = \bar{e}$ has been reached at t_0 and consider a policy that yields the following path for employment,

$$e = \begin{cases} \frac{q-a(t)-2m}{b} & \text{for } t_0 < t < t_0 + 1 \\ \frac{q-a(t)+m}{b} & \text{for } t_0 + 1 < t < t_0 + 9 = t_1 \\ \frac{q-a(t)}{b} & \text{for } t_1 < t \end{cases} . \tag{6.79}$$

Using Equations (6.76)–(6.79), we get

$$\Delta\pi^e = \int_{t_0}^{t_1} \lambda_\pi(\pi - \pi^e)^3 dt$$

$$= \int_{t_0}^{t_0+1} \lambda_\pi(-2m)^3 dt + \int_{t_0+1}^{t_0+9} \lambda_\pi(m)^3 dt = \lambda_\pi(-8m^3 + 8m^3) = 0$$

$$\Delta a = \int_{t_0}^{t_1} \lambda_a(\pi^e - \pi) dt$$

$$= \int_{t_0}^{t_0+1} \lambda_a 2m dt + \int_{t_0+1}^{t_0+9} \lambda_a(-m) dt = \lambda_a(2m - 8m) = -6\lambda_a m.$$

The policy is inflation-neutral in the sense that expected and actual inflation at $t = t_1 = t_0 + 9$ are the same as they were at $t = t_0$: $\pi_{t_1} = \pi^e_{t_1} = \bar{\pi}_0$. But the economy has reached a new stationary solution with a lower rate of unemployment. For $t > t_1$, the employment rate is set such that $a + be - q = 0$, and both π^e and a will remain constant for $t > t_1$. With a constant, the employment rate $e = (q - a)/b$ will also be constant, and – since $a_{t_1} < a_{t_0}$ – this employment rate exceeds $\bar{e}$:

$$\Delta e = e_1 - \bar{e} = \frac{6\lambda_a m}{b}.$$

The policy has succeeded in raising the equilibrium solution for employment without any inflationary costs.

Appendix D: Inflation Targets and the Pace of Structural Transformation

Successful inflation targeting requires that $\hat{p} = \hat{p}^*$ where $\hat{p}^*$ is the target. Using Equation (6.53), this condition translates into targets for $\hat{p}_M$ and $\hat{w}_M$:

$$\hat{w}_M^* = \phi^{-1}(\hat{p}^*) + q,$$

where q is the rate of growth of labor productivity in the formal sector. Thus, using Equations (6.64) and (6.56), we must have

$$\hat{w}^*_M = \hat{w}_M = \lambda_w \left(\frac{\mu w_R}{w_M} - 1 \right) + f(x) = \lambda_w \left(\mu \Theta \frac{1-\alpha}{\alpha} - 1 \right) + f(x).$$

Solving for the employment composition Θ,

$$\Theta = \frac{\alpha}{1-\alpha} \frac{1}{\mu} \left(\frac{\hat{w}^*_M - f(x)}{\lambda_w} + 1 \right). \tag{6.80}$$

From Equation (6.80), it follows that

$$\hat{\Theta} = -\hat{\mu} - \frac{\lambda_w f'(x)\dot{x}}{\hat{w}^*_M - f(x) + \lambda_w} = -\hat{\mu} - \frac{f'(x)\dot{x}}{\lambda_w \mu \Theta \frac{1-\alpha}{\alpha}}. \tag{6.81}$$

Combining Equations (6.52), (6.56), and (6.81), the dynamic equation for x can now be written as

$$\dot{x} = \lambda_x(\hat{w}_R - x) = \lambda_x(\hat{\Theta} + \hat{w}_M - x)$$

$$= \lambda_x \left(-\hat{\mu} - \frac{f'(x)\dot{x}}{\lambda_w \mu \Theta \frac{1-\alpha}{\alpha}} + \hat{w}^*_M - x \right)$$

or

$$\left(1 + \frac{f'(x)}{\lambda_w \mu \Theta \frac{1-\alpha}{\alpha}} \right) \dot{x} = \lambda_x(-\hat{\mu} + \hat{w}^*_M - x).$$

Using the equations for $\hat{w}_M$ and $\dot{\mu}$, this equation can be rewritten as

$$\left(1 + \frac{f'(x)}{\lambda_w \mu \Theta \frac{1-\alpha}{\alpha}} \right) \dot{x} = \lambda_x(-\hat{\mu} + \hat{w}^*_M - x)$$

$$= \lambda_x[-\lambda_\mu \left(\frac{w_M}{\mu w_R} - 1 \right) + \hat{w}^*_M - x]$$

$$= \lambda_x[\lambda_\mu \frac{\hat{w}^*_M - f(x)}{\hat{w}^*_M - f(x) + \lambda_w} + \hat{w}^*_M - x]. \tag{6.82}$$

The coefficient on $\dot{x}$ on the left-hand side of Equation (6.82) is greater than 1 and the right-hand side is increasing in $\hat{w}^*_M$ and decreasing in x. It follows that x will converge to a stationary solution x^* with

$$x^* = x(\hat{w}^*_M); \quad x' > 0.$$

Moreover, we have (from Equation (6.64))

$$\frac{\mu w_R}{w_M} = \frac{\hat{w}^*_M - f(x)}{\lambda_w} + 1$$

and $\mu w_R / w_M$ will converge to

$$\left(\frac{\mu w_R}{w_M} \right)^* = \frac{\hat{w}^*_M - f(x^*)}{\lambda_w} + 1. \tag{6.83}$$

The shape of the f-function (see Equations (6.65)–(6.69)) implies that if $\hat{w}_M^* = 0$ or $\hat{w}_M^* \geq k$, the stationarity condition for x requires that

$$x^* = f(x^*) = \hat{w}_M^*$$

$$\left(\frac{\mu w_R}{w_M}\right)^* = 1.$$

But for intermediate values of the target – if $0 < \hat{w}_M^* < k$ – we have

$$x^* > \hat{w}_M^* > f(x^*)$$

$$\left(\frac{\mu w_R}{w_M}\right)^* > 1.$$

For negative values of $\hat{w}_M^*$, finally, the inequalities are reversed and

$$x^* < \hat{w}_M^* < f(x^*)$$

$$\left(\frac{\mu w_R}{w_M}\right)^* < 1.$$

The long-run rate of growth of Θ can now be found. Using Equations (6.56), (6.83), and (6.63), we have

$$\hat{\Theta} = \frac{\widehat{w_R}}{w_M} = -\hat{\mu} = -\lambda_\mu \left(\frac{w_M}{\mu w_R} - 1\right) = \lambda_\mu \left[1 - \frac{1}{\left(\frac{\mu w_R}{w_M}\right)^*}\right] = \lambda_\mu \left[1 - \frac{\lambda_w}{\hat{w}_M^* - f(x^*) + \lambda_w}\right].$$
(6.84)

It follows from Equation (6.84) that the speed of transformation (the growth in the share of formal-sector employment) is an increasing function of $(\hat{w}_M^* - f(x^*))$ Thus,

$$\hat{\Theta} < 0 \text{ for } \hat{w}_M^* < 0$$

$$\hat{\Theta} = 0 \text{ for } \hat{w}_M^* = 0 \text{ or } \hat{w}_M^* > k$$

$$\hat{\Theta} > 0 \text{ for } 0 < \hat{w}_M^* < k.$$

The sigmoid shape of the f-function also implies that $\hat{w}_M^* - f(x^*)$ will have a unique local (and global) maximum for some value γ in this interval. Thus, the speed of transformation is increasing in the inflation target for $0 < \hat{w}_M^* < \gamma$ and decreasing for $\gamma < \hat{w}_M^* < k$.

Appendix E: Dynamic System for the Aspiration Gap and Expected Growth of Informal-Sector Income

If policy-makers maintain a constant pace of development – keep $\hat{\Theta} = \delta \geq 0$ – the dynamics of $(\mu w_R/w_M)$ and x can be written (using Equations (6.56), (6.64), and (6.63))

$$\dot{x} = \lambda_x(\hat{w}_R - x) = \lambda_x(\hat{\Theta} + \hat{w}_M - x)$$

$$= \lambda_x[\delta + \lambda_w \left(\frac{\mu w_R}{w_M} - 1\right) + f(x) - x] \tag{6.85}$$

$$\frac{\widetilde{\mu w_R}}{w_M} = \hat{\mu} + \hat{w}_R - \hat{w}_M = \hat{\mu} + \hat{\Theta} = \lambda_\mu \left(\frac{w_M}{\mu w_R} - 1 \right) + \delta. \tag{6.86}$$

Equation (6.86) is a self-contained differential equation and – assuming that $\delta < \lambda_\mu$ – it has a unique, stable stationary point at $\frac{\mu w_R}{w_M} = \left(\frac{\mu w_R}{w_M} \right)^* = \frac{\lambda_\mu}{\lambda_\mu - \delta}$ (if $\delta > \lambda_\mu$, the equation implies that $\frac{\mu w_R}{w_M} \to \infty$ for any positive initial value of $\frac{\mu w_R}{w_M}$). Substituting $\frac{\mu w_R}{w_M} = \left(\frac{\mu w_R}{w_M} \right)^*$ into the stationarity condition for x, we get

$$x - f(x) = \delta + \lambda_w \left(\left(\frac{\mu w_R}{w_M} \right)^* - 1 \right). \tag{6.87}$$

The expression on the right-hand side of Equation (6.87) is unambiguously positive, and the conditions (6.65)–(6.69) imply that the function $x - f(x)$ on the left-hand side of the equation attains a positive maximum at some $x = \tilde{x}$ with $0 < \tilde{x} < k$ and that $x - f(x) = 0$ for $x \leq 0$ or $x \geq k$. Thus, the equation has two solutions if $\tilde{x} - f(\tilde{x}) > \delta + \lambda_w \left(\left(\frac{\mu w_R}{w_M} \right)^* - 1 \right)$, one solution if $\tilde{x} - f(\tilde{x}) = \delta + \lambda_w \left(\left(\frac{\mu w_R}{w_M} \right)^* - 1 \right)$, and no solutions if $\tilde{x} - f(\tilde{x}) < \delta + \lambda_w \left(\left(\frac{\mu w_R}{w_M} \right)^* - 1 \right)$. Figure 6.11 depicts the phase diagram for the 2D system (6.85) and (6.86)) for the case with two stationary solutions; one of them (E_1) is locally stable, while the other (E_2) is a saddle point.

7 Earnings Inequality, Power Bias, and Mismatch

7.1 Introduction

Income inequality in the United States fell dramatically in the 1940s, stayed relatively flat from the early 1950s to the late 1970s, and then started to rise rapidly (Figure 7.1). The functional distribution of income has also shifted toward profit income since the late 1980s, although the movement has been more modest: By the early 2000s, the profit share was roughly where it had been in the 1950s and 1960s (Figure 7.2).[1] What the high-income households lost in the 1940s was largely property income, while most of what they gained from the late 1980s onward has been wage and entrepreneurial income – the shares of wage and entrepreneurial income of the top 0.01 percent increased from 16.3 and 8.1 percent, respectively, in 1939 to 44.8 percent and 33.3 percent in 1998 (Piketty and Saez (2003, table III).

Evidence from a variety of sources suggests that a similar 'great compression' of the distribution of income took place in other capitalist economies in the 1940s, as did the subsequent replacement of property with wage and entrepreneurial income (Moriguchi and Saez 2007, Piketty et al. 2006, The World Inequality Database (https://wid.world/)). In some countries, however, the compression has not been reversed or was reversed later and to a lesser extent than in the United States (Figure 7.3).

One class of explanations attributes the compression in the 1940s in the United States to institutional changes that occurred before, during or just after the Second World War as part of the New Deal, including changes in tax rates, the creation of a national system of retirement pensions and unemployment insurance, minimum wage legislation, and a legal framework of industrial relations with the right to collective bargaining. The decompression, likewise, can be linked to the Reagan and Thatcher revolutions (and similar waves of liberalization in other, mainly Anglophone countries) that marked the beginning of sharp reversals of some of the equalizing institutional changes.

---

[1] Some of the pay going to top management should rightly be included with profit. This adjustment would amplify the shift in the functional distribution. Using a compensation series derived from the Bureau of Labor Statistics Employment Cost Index (ECI), Krueger (1998) finds that the increase in the profit share over 1988–1995 is somewhere between 1.9 and 4.6 percentage points rather than 0.6 percentage points before the modification. And CEO pay has increased significantly since 1995.

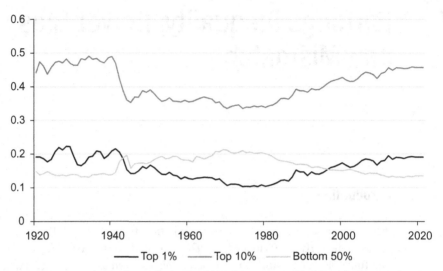

Figure 7.1 Income inequality, USA, 1920–2021. Data source: World Inequality Database; pretax shares of national income; adults; equal split; https://wid.world/wid-world/.

Figure 7.2 Profit; US nonfinancial corporations. Data: NIPA Table 1.14; net operating surplus / (net operating surplus + compensation of employees).

The contribution of institutional changes to the fall and rise of inequality may seem undeniable, while the equalizing institutional changes, in turn, would seem closely related to the experience from the Great Depression and the Second World War. But this explanation also raises many questions. Wartime mobilization may have been a spur to egalitarianism, but even in the United States where the compression was relatively short-lived, inequality continued to fall or stayed constant for several decades

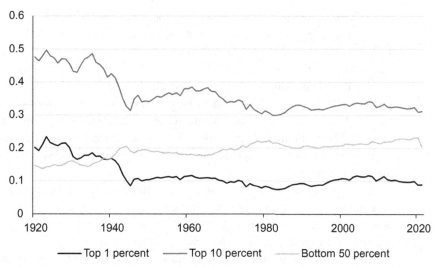

Figure 7.3 Income inequality, France, 1920–2021. Data source: World Inequality Database; pretax shares of national income; adults; equal split; https://wid.world/wid-world/).

after the war, with prewar levels of inequality not reached again until the late 1990s. Why did the leveling institutions last as long as they did, and why did the 1940s also see a reduction in inequality in neutral countries, such as Spain (Alvaredo and Saez 2006) and Sweden (Roine and Waldenstrom 2006)?

The argument for the predominance of institutional determinants of the observed movements in inequality also faces theoretical challenges. It is easy to see how the decline in unions and the fall in minimum wages since the late 1970s may have put downward pressure on low-skill wages. But a decrease in the relative wage of low-skill workers leads to a rise in the demand for low-skill workers in a standard model of the labor market. Contrary to this prediction, low-skill workers lost ground in terms of both wages and employment after the 1970s.

The movements of relative wages and relative employment in the same direction – movements that would seem to be at odds with purely institutional accounts – could be explained by shifts in the demand for skills. Firms may have chosen to employ an increasing proportion of those workers who have become relatively expensive because technical change produced upward shifts in the marginal products of high-skill workers and downward shifts in the marginal products of low-skill workers (e.g., Acemoglu 2002, Autor et al. 2008). This explanation based on skill-biased technological change (SBTC) has been highly influential. International trade and outsourcing offer another explanation. As with the SBTC story, the mechanism works through changes in the relative supply of and demand for skills, in this case with a focus on the downward pressures on the domestic demand for low-skill workers coming from the integration into the world economy of large numbers of low-wage workers in China and other emerging economies (e.g., Wood 1994, Feenstra and Hanson 1996).

Institutional changes cannot be blamed for increasing inequality, according to this line of reasoning: Attempts to prevent the increase in inequality – by maintaining or raising the real value of the minimum wage, for instance – would have resulted in unemployment for low-skill workers. Thus, the decline in minimum wages (the failure to raise the nominal minimum wage in line with inflation) should not be seen as causal but as a policy response to the underlying forces of skill-biased change (e.g., Autor et al. 2008).[2] In a similar vein, Acemoglu et al. (2001) explain deunionization as a result of SBTC. From this perspective 'there is no alternative' (as Margaret Thatcher used to tell her critics) to explanations based on shifts in the domestic demand for and supply of skills.

The TINA argument, I shall argue, is false. Technological and institutional changes can influence relative earnings through their effects on the balance of power between workers and employers. Like SBTC, such shifts in power relations can generate the observed patterns of relative employment and relative wages.

The influence of relative power on income distribution has been gaining increasing attention. Autor et al. (2020) find that profit margins increased as goods markets became increasingly concentrated between 1982 and 2012 and that the importance of increasing concentration has risen over time. Labor markets have also seen increased concentration. Benmelech et al. (2022) examine census data for 1978–2016, while Azar et al. (2022) explore a new data source with wider coverage but a much shorter time period. Both Benmelech et al. and Azar et al. find that high employer concentration – high monopsony power – is associated with low wages.

These studies of concentration in goods and labor markets are interesting and important. As pointed out by Bivens et al. (2018), however, they say little or nothing about *wage* inequality, and they employ a notion of power that is quite limited. Power relations involve much more than market concentration. There is a fundamental asymmetry in power between a single worker – who typically suffers a significant personal cost if laid off – and a firm with many employees. This asymmetry exists even when employer concentration is low in both goods and labor markets. Employment contracts, moreover, are incomplete, and there is – as Karl Marx suggested – a constant struggle over the length and intensity of the working day. In the United States, salaried workers with annual salaries as low as $23,660 in 2019 could be forced to work long hours without overtime pay, and employers' attempts to cut costs create constant pressures on all workers for the intensification of work, including increased 'flexibility' with respect to work schedules.

Market concentration in the labor market is likely to influence the balance of power with respect to workplace struggles, reducing workers' fallback position and making them accept working conditions that otherwise would have been rejected. But power relations can shift, even if market concentration is unchanged. This chapter focuses

---

[2] The SBTC argument also appeared in debates over the high unemployment in Europe in the 1980s and 1990s: The unwillingness of the Europeans to allow inequality to rise was commonly seen as the main cause of high unemployment (cf. Chapter 5).

on *power-biased technological and institutional changes* that may have this effect.[3] In short, technological and institutional changes may have been important for the movements in inequality, not because of skill bias but because of *power bias*: The changes have affected the ability of different groups to extract rents.

While the power bias of reductions in minimum wages or anti-union legislation is fairly obvious, the bias of technological changes may seem less clear, which motivates greater attention to these changes in the formal analysis in this chapter. The discussion of technological aspects is important for another reason. Production functions are often treated as simply representing technical constraints on the transformation of inputs into outputs. This approach overlooks both the direct power biases of different technologies and the way new technologies may facilitate institutional change. These indirect effects are not mechanical but, in a context of conflict and negotiation, technological change can contribute to a realignment of power relations between social groups and undermine the coalitions behind existing institutions.

Models embodying technological power biases do not depend on departures from orthodox assumptions of optimization and, highlighting this independence, much of the formal analysis in this chapter will use efficiency wage models that are quite standard in this respect. The agency problems underlying these models involve elements of power: The worker can influence outcomes that the firm's owners and managers care about, but by paying a wage premium the firm ensures that agents who lose their job will suffer a loss. Crucially, the parameters of this agency problem can be affected by technological change, both directly and indirectly. The direct effects include shifts in firms' ability to monitor workers' 'effort' on the job as well as the conditions (the 'state of nature') in which workers act. The indirect effects come via institutional changes. I shall argue in favor of these indirect effects, but the main conclusions do not depend on them. Some institutional changes clearly are unrelated to technological forces, and the presence of institutional power biases does not depend on whether or to what extent the observed institutional changes have been facilitated by technological developments. The key point is simply that power-biased technological and institutional changes have played a significant part in widening inequality.

Workplace power derives from the characteristics of the job, rather than from the skills of the worker. Jobs with high power may often require certain skills, but the distinction between jobs and workers is important. Workers sometimes work in jobs that do not require their skills – there are retail workers, taxi drivers and bartenders with college degrees – and this mismatch between job requirements and workers' skills has an endogenous component. In a depressed job market more high-skill workers will accept jobs for which they are overqualified, and these induced changes in the degree of mismatch invalidate standard comparative static results, with implications for the effects of institutional change and economic policy. An increase in the minimum wage,

---

[3] It should be noted, perhaps, that while broadening the discussion beyond market power, the analysis of power in this chapter remains quite limited. It leaves out, for instance, how ideological and cultural hegemony can make values and policies that promote the interests of particular groups seem like common sense.

for instance, may benefit low-paid workers both in terms of wages and employment (Skott 2006, Slonimczyk and Skott 2012).

Section 7.2 considers the role of power-biased technological and institutional change in the compression of the mid-twentieth century as well as in the inversion of this power bias beginning in the late twentieth century. Section 7.3 uses an efficiency wage model to analyze the effects of changes in firms' ability to monitor their workers on relative wages and employment. Section 7.4 considers the relation between power and skill before examining some implications of induced changes in the prevalence of mismatch between the skills of the worker and the skill requirements of the job. Section 7.5 discusses the dramatic rise in the pay of top managers and extends the analysis to include norms of fairness. Policy implications are addressed briefly in the concluding Section 7.6.

7.2   Coordination, Control, and the Power of Workers

7.2.1   Technology, Coordination, and Institutions

Some of the increasingly elaborate economy-wide division of labor is carried out in a deliberately coordinated way within large companies, as highlighted in Chandler's (1977) description of the growing importance of the visible hand during the Second Industrial Revolution.[4] The coordination poses problems, and companies are constrained by their technologies of coordination and control, with Beniger (1986) describing what he called a "crisis of control" in the mid-nineteenth century. Information and communications technologies (ICTs) and their applications have progressed enormously since then, but the division of labor has become more elaborate as well, escalating the demands for coordination. Effective coordination and control is a moving target.

Consider the pioneering of modern management by early railroads: Trains were unable to communicate with one another, so that collisions were only prevented by the adoption of roles and rules. In the 1850s, a train on the Boston and Worcester Railway could not move without the authorization of the conductor. The conductor was, in turn, bound by a strict set of rules: A westbound train was to stop in the station at Framingham, and could not proceed until an eastbound train had arrived on the opposite track (Chandler, 1977, p. 96). Doubtless such a system caused many inefficiencies, as a delay to one train meant a delay to the other, but the predictability created by the rules had clear benefits: rule-based predictability – and inflexibility – substituted for communication.[5]

---

[4] This section, adapted from Guy and Skott (2008), relies on insights and ideas developed by my coauthor Frederick Guy.

[5] There is a parallel here with the routines emphasized by Simon (1957) in his discussion of bounded rationality. These routines are usually explained with reference to the cognitive limits of individuals, but routine- or rule-based behavior in organizations can also reflect technological limits to communication and computation.

Going beyond the railway example, consider the development of other large businesses. Geographically dispersed activities were coordinated with the aid first of the telegraph and later with voice telephony. Both are high-speed communications technologies, but they suffer from very low bandwidths and no direct connection with any information storage or processing system. For the telegraph to be of use in discussing the purchase of some materials or merchandise, any relevant technical specifications had to be already known by the parties. This constraint was relaxed somewhat with the telephone - a fact often credited with furthering the spatial separation of operations within companies in the early twentieth century - but when compared with the torrent of technical specifications and market information that can pour down a strand of cable today, the world of the telephone looks much like that of the telegraph; a heavy reliance on preprocessing remained necessary.

The rigid bureaucratic structures for which the mid twentieth century was known were a reflection of both the capabilities and the limitations of the ICTs of the day. Economies of scale, scope, and speed offered substantial productivity benefits to large managerial firms, but realization of these productivity gains was contingent on solving problems of coordination and control, with the limitations of the information systems necessitating a relatively rigid, single-path flow of materials and information. As a result, in 1937 workers at General Motors were able to bring a large part of the operations of the company and many of its suppliers to a halt by sitting down in a few factories. Similarly, with telephone networks, the limited number of paths empowered operators – who instead of sitting down went on strike by standing up, at the same time, across the country. In this setting of organizational rigidity, labor unions and government regulation could play a significant role in promoting orderly industrial relations and preventing costly strikes. Thus, the limitations of ICT reduced the resistance of big business to the institutional changes that contributed to the great compression.

The employer's imprecise knowledge of the state of nature also created a functional role for labor unions. Bureaucratic organizations can be brought to a standstill by their employees 'working to rule,' since inflexible and rule-bound firms often require low-level employees to go beyond what their instructions specify. But if doing a good job means working beyond – and perhaps even in violation of – the rules, or suggesting changes to the rules, employees may expose themselves to arbitrary retaliation from supervisors simply by doing a good job. Part of the voice function of the union is to ensure fair treatment in such circumstances. Freeman and Medoff (1984) gave this as a reason why unionized companies in the United States enjoy higher productivity than nonunionized ones. In a similar vein, Fairris (1997) argues that it was the productivity benefits of voice that led to an organized movement among American employers during the first World War to establish company-sponsored employee associations; many of these associations were later supplanted by unions, which took over the voice function and combined it with such functions as wage bargaining. More recent evidence comes from Black and Lynch (2001), who study the effects of high-performance work practices on productivity in American manufacturing. High-performance work practices involve problem-solving and decision-making by individual workers and by teams, at some cost to central control. Black and Lynch's finding is that such practices bring productivity benefits only when unions are present; they attribute this to union voice.

The last third of the twentieth century saw a shift in the race between ICTs and the demands of coordination. Jonscher (1994) provides evidence of a breakthrough in coordination and control in the 1970s and 1980s, as the microprocessor and related technologies made it possible to integrate information systems with systems of production and of service delivery. The next subsection describes how direct effects of technology have led to a loss of power for, and more successful monitoring of, many groups of workers. As with the compression in the 1940s, however, the technological developments may also have facilitated broader institutional change. New technologies enabled the modularization and outsourcing of production. Single-flow, vertically integrated production systems gave way to flexible production with multiple suppliers, and coordination increasingly has been achieved through flexible arm's length relations. One implication of this development is that large companies have become much less vulnerable to industrial action among small groups of workers and therefore no longer have the same need for unions and regulated labor markets.

The technological element in institutional change should not be pushed too far. The compression in the 1940s was so close together in time across countries that it is not really plausible to see it as a result of independent national responses to technological changes, even if such responses were entirely mechanistic (which they are not). The Second World War undoubtedly played a role in the timing of the compression, and the influence of the Cold War and the perception that the Soviet Union could present a viable alternative economic system may have contributed to the durability of the compression.

Analogously, the institutional changes after the late 1970s have components that are non-technological. Social movements, increasing strike activity and working class militancy, rising inflation, and a declining profit share contributed to a major reorientation of macroeconomic policy as well as to attacks on institutions that helped empower workers. Coming after a prolonged period of near-full employment, the patterns display a remarkable conformity with Michal Kalecki's observation that

under a regime of permanent full employment, 'the sack' would cease to play its role as a disciplinary measure. The social position of the boss would be undermined and the self assurance and class consciousness of the working class would grow. (Kalecki 1943 [1971, pp. 140–141])

In this situation

a powerful block is likely to be formed between big business and the rentier interests, and they would probably find more than one economist to declare that the situation was manifestly unsound (p. 144).

The diversity of international experience since the 1980s also illustrates the limits of technological determinism. As noted above, increases in inequality and executive pay are widespread but vary considerably in magnitude between countries. Studies of 'comparative capitalisms' distinguish between 'liberal market economies' and other, more or less 'coordinated market economies' and offer an explanation of how coordinated economies came to have institutions of redistribution which have, so far, proved robust in the face of changes in technology and business organization (Estevez-Abe et al. 2001, Hall and Soskice 2001). Whether this robustness will persist remains to be seen.

7.2.2   Agency and Power

Leaving aside institutional changes, ICTs can affect power relations by influencing managers' ability to monitor the actions of workers and by shaping the amount and accuracy of the information that managers have about the state of nature in which the workers act.

Consider the case of truck drivers. 'Black boxes' enable truck companies to monitor driver performance in real time, including second-by-second information about vehicle speed, G-Force, throttle position and interior sound level. This technology marks a shift in the relationship between truck drivers and owners. Before the new technology, the owner was unable to monitor what happened *en route*; a late arrival at the destination could be blamed on mechanical problems, bad weather or heavy traffic. The information problem also meant that if the truck were to break down, it was difficult for the owner to tell whether the breakdown had been caused by driver negligence. With the new technology, this has all changed. A testimonial on the website of one of the producers of the device puts it like this (www.blackboxgps.com/):

We use the BlackBoxGPS to track our delivery drivers. I noticed soon after we installed them that our drivers were coming back earlier than usual. I like to be able to monitor their speeds, idle times and recommend the product.

The drivers do not come back earlier because of technical improvements in the performance of the truck or changes in the skills required by the driver. But technological change has affected the balance of power between the drivers and their employers, leading to an intensification of work.

Similar examples can be found in financial services with the movement of customer services from local branches to call centers. Or consider the case of retail clerks. The simple cash register – which in its control function ensured that the clerk could not pocket some of money paid by customers – has become part of a sophisticated system, including bar codes and networked computers, that allows managers to monitor employees as well as the state of nature in which they are acting.

New and even more intrusive cases of power-biased technological change are documented almost daily in the business press. The Economist (March 1, 2018) notes that Amazon has received patents for a wristband that could collect detailed information about each warehouse worker's movements and shepherd them through their jobs with maximum efficiency. Kevin Roose describes in the *New York Times* (June 24, 2019) how the insurance company Metlife uses artificial intelligence to monitor customer service representatives, including their speed of talking and their show of empathy, spewing out, at the end of each call, notifications and summaries that can be viewed by supervisors and managers. As Kevin Roose comments, "it's fairly clear why executives would want A.I. that can track their workers, it's less clear why workers would." Katie Johnston in the Boston Globe (July 16, 2019) explains how neuroscientists at a

Boston-based company have developed algorithms that record stress and fatigue and that could be used by employers to test the mental state of their employees. She goes on to note that "there is the possibility that employers could misuse the data to try to wring more work out of people."

The examples point to an important implication of power-biased technological change. Skill-biased changes may produce both winners and losers, but there is a presumption of net gains in the sense that, under SBTC, the gains of the winners would be sufficient, in principle, to compensate the losers. There is no basis for this presumption in the case of power bias. New techniques like black boxes and high tech wrist bands that reduce workers' power can be profitable and may be adopted even if technically they are less efficient (require additional monitoring equipment as well as more inputs in the form of worker effort) than existing techniques (Green 1988, Bowles 1989, Skott and Guy 2008).

7.3   A Model of Power-Biased Change

7.3.1   Assumptions

One direct manifestation of power-biased technological change – changes in firms' ability to monitor their workers – can be formalized in an efficiency wage model. The argument does not depend on fairness norms or other deviations from homo oeconomicus, and I shall use a standard framework.

Consider an economy with three inputs, capital (K) and two types of labor (L_L and L_H), and let the production of the representative firm be given by

$$Q = F(\varepsilon_L L_L, \varepsilon_H L_H, K),$$

where ε_i denotes the effort of workers of type i. Using standard assumptions, type-i workers decide their effort by maximizing an objective function

$$V^i = p^i(\varepsilon_i)[w_i - v(\varepsilon_i) - h^i(\bar{w}_i, b, u_i)],$$

$w_i, \bar{w}_i, u_i$, and b denote the worker's real wage, the average real wage, the unemployment rate for workers of type i, and the rate of unemployment benefits, respectively. A simple intertemporal optimization model reduces to a special case of this maximization problem (Appendix A).

The disutility associated with effort is described by the function $v(\varepsilon_i)$. In order to focus more clearly on the effects of changes in relative power, it is assumed that there is symmetry between the two groups of workers with respect to the v-function. The following specification is used[6]:

$$v(\varepsilon_i) = \varepsilon_i^{\gamma}; \qquad \gamma > 1. \tag{7.1}$$

---

[6] The parameter restriction $\gamma > 1$ is needed since otherwise the firm's unit cost would decrease monotonically as wages increase.

The function $p^i(\varepsilon_i)$ captures the effect of effort on the expected remaining duration of the job, with an increase in effort reducing the risk of being fired (i.e., $p^{i\prime} > 0$). Using a constant-elasticity specification, it is assumed that[7]

$$\frac{p^{i\prime}\varepsilon_i}{p^i} = \eta_i. \tag{7.2}$$

The parameter η_i is an inverse indicator of workers' power. A high value of η_i implies that workers are closely monitored, that the firing risk is very sensitive to variations in effort, and that workers have little power; small values of η_i indicate that variations in their effort are likely to go undetected.

The function $h^i(\bar{w}_i, b, u_i)$, finally, represents the worker's expected utility in the case of job loss; the partial derivatives satisfy $h^i_{\bar{w}} > 0, h^i_b > 0$ and $h^i_u < 0$. Using the specification associated with the intertemporal interpretation of the worker's maximization problem in Appendix A, h^i is given by

$$h^i = \frac{(r + \delta)u_i}{ru_i + \delta}b + \frac{\delta(1 - u_i)}{ru_i + \delta}(\bar{w}_i - v(\bar{\varepsilon}_i)), \tag{7.3}$$

where $\bar{\varepsilon}_i$ is the optimal effort associated with the wage $\bar{w}_i$. The parameters r and δ are the discount rate and the rate of job separations, respectively; assuming symmetry in all respects other than power, both types of workers have the same discount rate and the same average rate of separations.[8] Intuitively, the fallback position is a weighted average of the worker's utility when unemployed (b) and the utility when having another job ($\bar{w}_i - v(\bar{\varepsilon}_i)$). The weights depend on the unemployment rate u_i, which determines the proportion of time a worker can expect to be unemployed in a steady state. If there is no discounting ($r = 0$) the weights are simply u_i and $1 - u_i$; when $r > 0$, unemployment is weighted more heavily because workers who lose their job will be unemployed initially.

The first-order condition for the worker's maximization problem can be written

$$-p^i v' + (w_i - v - h^i)p^{i\prime} = 0.$$

Using the functional forms for v and p in Equations (7.1) and (7.2), this condition implies that

$$\varepsilon_i = \left[\frac{\eta_i}{\eta_i + \gamma}(w_i - h_i)\right]^{1/\gamma}. \tag{7.4}$$

Wages and employment are set by the firm, and the first-order conditions for profit maximization imply that the Solow condition must hold (i.e., the elasticity of effort

---

[7] The specification can be seen as a log-linear approximation of the p^i-function around the equilibrium solution for ε_i.

[8] Differences in the elasticities of the p-function – the values of μ_i – do not imply that the two groups cannot have the same average separation rates (see Appendix A for details).

with respect to the wage must be equal to 1)[9]:

$$\frac{\varepsilon_{iw} w_i}{\varepsilon_i} = 1. \tag{7.5}$$

Using (7.4) and (7.5), wages and effort are determined by the value of h_i:

$$w_i = \frac{\gamma}{\gamma - 1} h_i \tag{7.6}$$

$$\varepsilon_i = \left[\frac{\eta_i}{\eta_i + \gamma} \frac{1}{\gamma - 1} h_i \right]^{1/\gamma}. \tag{7.7}$$

For simplicity, output is determined by a nested CES production function,

$$Q = A\{\frac{2}{3}([\frac{1}{2}(\varepsilon_L L_L)^{-\rho_1} + \frac{1}{2}(\varepsilon_H L_H)^{-\rho_1}]^{-1/\rho_1})^{-\rho_2} + \frac{1}{3} K^{-\rho_2}\}^{-1/\rho_2}. \tag{7.8}$$

Under perfect competition, the demand for labor can be found from the first-order conditions

$$w_i = F_{L_i}(\varepsilon_L L_L, \varepsilon_H L_H, K)$$

$$= \frac{A}{3} \varepsilon_i^{-\rho_1} L_i^{-\rho_1 - 1} \left[\frac{1}{2}(\varepsilon_L L_L)^{-\rho_1} + \frac{1}{2}(\varepsilon_H L_H)^{-\rho_1} \right]^{(\rho_2 - \rho_1)/\rho_2}$$

$$\left\{ \frac{2}{3} \left(\left[\frac{1}{2}(\varepsilon_L L_L)^{-\rho_1} + \frac{1}{2}(\varepsilon_H L_H)^{-\rho_1} \right]^{-1/\rho_1} \right)^{-\rho_2} + \frac{1}{3} K^{-\rho_2} \right\}^{-(1+\rho_2)/\rho_2}. \tag{7.9}$$

To close the model, the equilibrium condition that $w_i = \bar{w}_i$ is imposed, and it is assumed that labor supplies are symmetric and inelastic. Normalizing these supplies at unity, we have

$$u_i = 1 - L_i. \tag{7.10}$$

The solutions for wage rates, unemployment rates, work intensities (effort levels), and profitability can be derived using (7.3) and (7.6)–(7.10). The effects of changes in the parameters η_L and/or η_H can now be examined.

7.3.2   Power-Biased Technological Change

Nonlinearities make it difficult to obtain analytical solutions, but Table 7.1 presents three numerical examples. All three examples use a discount rate of $r = 0.05$ and a separation rate of $\delta = 0.2$. This value of δ implies that a little less than 20 percent of workers will lose, or choose to leave, their jobs within a year (the unit period).

---

[9] The firm chooses L_i and w_i to maximize profits, $\Pi = F(\varepsilon_1 L_1, \varepsilon_2 L_2, K) - w_L L_L - w_H L_H$. The first-order conditions require that

$$\frac{\partial \Pi}{\partial L_i} = \varepsilon_i F_i - w_i = 0$$

$$\frac{\partial \Pi}{\partial w_i} = L_i F_i \varepsilon_{iw} - L_i = 0.$$

The first of these conditions implies that $F_i = w_i / \varepsilon_i$. The Solow condition follows from substituting this expression for F_i into the second condition.

Table 7.1 Effects of a decline in the power of L-workers on effort, wage, unemployment, and profits

1a: Benchmark case, $\sigma_1 = \sigma_2 = 0.5$

η_L	ε_L	w_L	u_L	ε_H	w_H	u_H	Π
0.1	0.156	23.4	0.255	0.156	23.4	0.255	20.2
0.4	0.200	21.7	0.256	0.159	26.2	0.241	24.0
0.8	0.224	20.6	0.251	0.161	27.5	0.236	25.9

1b: Strong labor–labor complementarity, $\sigma_1 = 0.2, \sigma_2 = 0.5$

η_L	ε_L	w_L	u_L	ε_H	w_H	u_H	Π
0.1	0.156	23.4	0.255	0.156	23.4	0.255	20.2
0.4	0.195	19.1	0.280	0.162	28.8	0.231	23.6
0.8	0.216	17.0	0.294	0.165	31.2	0.224	24.9

1c: Strong labor–labor substitutability, $\sigma_1 = 1.5, \sigma_2 = 0.5$

η_L	ε_L	w_L	u_L	ε_H	w_H	u_H	Π
0.1	0.156	23.4	0.255	0.156	23.4	0.255	20.2
0.4	0.206	24.9	0.237	0.155	23.1	0.257	24.4
0.8	0.234	25.3	0.222	0.555	22.8	0.259	26.7

The parameter γ in the utility function must be greater than 1 (cf. footnote 7), with the qualitative results appearing to be insensitive to the precise value; the table uses $\gamma = 5$. The rate of unemployment benefits ($b = 0.008$), the capital stock ($K = 0.1$), and the productivity parameter ($A = 0.5$) have been chosen to get employment rates of about 0.75, a replacement rate of about $1/3$, and a capital-output ratio of about 2.

With respect to the production function, it is widely accepted that the elasticity of substitution between capital and labor is well below unity (e.g., Klump et al. 2007), and the numerical example uses $\sigma_2 = 0.5$. To my knowledge, there have been no attempts to examine the elasticity of substitution between workers with different levels of workplace power. Three different values of the labor–labor elasticity σ_1 are considered: a benchmark value of $\sigma_1 = 0.5$, a high substitutability case with $\sigma_1 = 1.5$, and a low substitutability case with $\sigma_1 = 0.2$. The appropriate calibrations for the elasticities η_L and η_H are harder to pin down, but the variations in Table 7.1 are within a plausible range.[10] If we include top management with profit recipients, the stylized picture suggested by the argument in Section 2 is one in which large groups of workers have seen a significant decline in power (a rise in η_L) over the last 40 years, while others have experienced more modest changes or rough constancy of η_H. Thus, η_H is kept constant, while η_L varies between 0.1 and 0.8. The case of top managers, who have benefited from increased power, is considered in Section 7.4.

When there is labor–labor complementarity (the benchmark case with $\sigma_1 = 0.5$ and the strong-complementarity case with $\sigma_1 = 0.2$), workers with low power will

---

[10] The intertemporal interpretation of the worker's maximization problem implies that $p = 1/(r + \delta)$ and hence that $p'\varepsilon/p = -\frac{\varepsilon}{r+\delta}\frac{d\delta}{d\varepsilon} = -\frac{\delta}{r+\delta}\frac{d\log\delta}{d\log\varepsilon}$ where δ is the rate of job separations. Job separations happen for many reasons (including voluntary quits and plant closures), and it seems unlikely that $-\frac{d\log\delta}{d\log\varepsilon}$ should exceed unity (this statement is meaningful since the chosen scale for effort implies that the elasticity of output with respect to ε is the same as the elasticity with respect to L). It follows that μ will be less than 1.

be relatively low paid. An increase in η_L from 0.4 to 0.8 generates a decline in the absolute and relative wages of L-workers, and their work intensity increases, both absolutely and relative to that of H-workers; their relative employment declines, and absolute employment declines as well if there is strong complementarity. Thus, the simultaneous increase in the relative wage and the relative employment of high-skill workers does not require an explanation in terms of SBTC. Table 1 demonstrates that changes in power relationships – power-biased technological change – can explain these observations. The increase in work intensity, moreover, is in line with evidence for the United Kingdom and other industrial economies during the 1980s and 1990s (Green 2004); the standard SBTC approach sheds little light on this increase. Total profits (Π) and the profit share ($\Pi/(\Pi + (1 - u_L)w_L + (1 - u_H)w_H)$) increase as well; in the benchmark case, the proportional increase is higher for profits than for w_H.

Power-biased technological change also produces an increase in wage inequality and increased profits when we have good labor–labor substitutability ($\sigma_1 = 1.5$). In this case, however, low-power workers are relatively well paid, and to explain the observed increase in inequality over the last 40 years, one would need to argue, implausibly, that new ICTs have reduced the relative power of highly paid workers. The empirical relevance of the model, therefore, hinges on the assumption of complementarity between high- and low-power jobs.

Intuitively, 'black boxes' may reduce the power and wages of truck drivers, eliminate slack in their schedule and force them to work harder, but these changes are unlikely to raise the ratio of drivers to warehouse, office and managerial staff in trucking companies. Needless to say, these anecdotal observations do not settle the issue. However, I know of no direct empirical evidence on the substitutability between high-and low-power jobs; problems involved in using skill as a proxy for power are discussed in Section 7.4.

7.3.3   Power-Biased Institutional Change

The sensitivity of the risk of dismissal to changes in effort does not depend only on technology. Governmental regulation can put restrictions on the kind of information that employers are permitted to collect; the collection and/or use of biometric data can be restricted, for instance. The worker's risk of dismissal can also be influenced by legal and institutional constraints on the firm's ability to act on the information that may be available.

Consider the case of Korea, which has seen a substantial rise in inequality since the mid-1990s (An and Bosworth 2013). Institutional constraints on hiring and firing have taken a variety of forms in Korea. Some restrictions on the ability of firms to dismiss permanent workers affect the average termination rate (but not the determination of who gets dismissed); others restrict the ability of the firm to single out low-performance workers. Restrictions also apply to the employment of temporary workers, and there are legal limits on the roll-over of temporary contracts.

Labor market reforms have relaxed these constraints. In the late 1990s, Korean policymakers became increasingly influenced by the 'Washington Consensus.' The dominant view suggested that in an era of increasing globalization, Korea's competitiveness suffered from problems of high costs and low efficiency. These problems, it was argued, could be addressed by the deregulation of the Korean labor market, which would reduce labor costs and allow quick adjustments to changes in economic conditions. The relaxation of employment protection was accelerated after the East Asian financial crisis, when a bailout by the IMF in December 1997 was made conditional on the deregulation of dismissal law (Cho and Lee 2007).

Labor market reforms in 1998 loosened the strict employment protection for workers with regular employment contracts (Yoo and Kang 2012). Employment flexibility was further enhanced – also in 1998 – by a decision to allow temporary work agencies to hire out workers to firms for up to two years in 26 occupations that require special expertise and experience (OECD 2000). These reforms shifted the balance of power between workers and firms in ways that are similar to power-biased technological change: It matters little whether the changes in the risk of dismissal derive from changes in legal constraints on firing or from changes in the ability of the firm to monitor workers' effort.[11]

US examples of how the balance of power between workers and firms can be affected by institutional changes also abound. Unions, which can serve as a countervailing power, have been undermined, and unionization has declined despite a rise in the proportion of workers who want a union (Freeman 2007). Employers have fought aggressively to prevent union representation, and a flawed regulatory regime has failed to protect workers' rights (Bronfenbrenner 2009), while the so-called right-to-work laws that prohibit contracts in which employers collect membership dues or fees from all workers who benefit from a union-negotiated contract have played a role too; without this kind of 'union security agreement,' individual workers have a financial incentive to free ride (McNicholas et al. 2018).

Monopsony power has been enhanced by non-compete clauses in employment contracts as well as by employers' no-poaching agreements; these non-compete clauses and non-poaching agreements could have been outlawed or greatly restricted (Starr 2019). Or consider the 'gig economy.' Regulation could prevent companies from circumventing the protections and benefits of employees by recategorizing the employees as contractors. Josh Eidelson (Bloomberg Businessweek, July 22, 2019) describes the case of the full-service shopping company Instacart Inc. whose relation with its 'contractors' looks more like a *de facto* employment relationship: The contractors are hounded and punished for rejecting undesirable tasks. Franchising has similar aspects in that its contracts may serve to insulate the franchisor from regulatory requirements as well as to disempower both franchisees and workers (Callaci 2019).[12]

---

[11] Kim and Skott (2016) analyze the Korean reforms using a framework that is closely related to the model in Section 7.3.
[12] EPI's (2018) "policy agenda" presents a set of possible interventions to reshape the playing field and increase workers' relative power.

7.4   Power, Skill, and Mismatch

Power and skill may be correlated – other things equal, when the employer has a choice, more consequential discretion will typically be given to employees who know well what they are doing than to those who do not. But power, unlike skill, is a job attribute. Factors other than skill are involved in the determination of power.

Power is associated with the characteristics of the job: High educational attainments do not make a truck driver more powerful vis-à-vis the trucking company. Likewise, an investment banker who gambles with millions of dollars on behalf of the bank can inflict great damage on the bank and has great power; if this same worker moved to a job in a fast-food restaurant, the potential damage may be limited to burning a batch of burgers, and the worker would have minimal power. Even if, for the sake of argument, we assume that all high-power jobs require high skills, these simple examples point to potential differences between the skill set of the worker and the skill requirements of the job, differences that have implications for the analysis of earnings inequality.

A mismatch between workers' skills – often measured by educational attainments – and the skill requirements of their jobs is common, and the prevalence of mismatch is influenced by labor market conditions: If high-skill workers are unable to find jobs that matches their skills, they may broaden their search, rather than go unemployed. The recession after the financial crisis produced

a new cadre of underemployed workers dotting American companies, occupying slots several rungs below where they are accustomed to working. These are not the more drastic examples of former professionals toiling away at "survival jobs" at Home Depot or Starbucks. They are the former chief financial officer working as comptroller, the onetime marketing director who is back to being an analyst, the former manager who is once again an "individual contributor." (Luo 2010)

The measurement of mismatch is notoriously difficult, but the anecdotal evidence is supported by more comprehensive studies suggesting that 'overeducation' is widespread in all OECD countries. Estimates of the proportion of overeducated workers – those with qualifications that exceed the job requirements – range between 10 percent and 40 percent (Groot and Maassen van den Brink 2000). Moreover, the proportion of overeducated workers changes over time. Combining data from the Dictionary of Occupational Titles and the Current Population Survey, Slonimczyk and Skott (2012) found a substantial rise in the share of high-skill workers whose jobs have requirements below their skill level. In 1973, 15 percent of workers were in this category; by 2002, the percentage of overeducated workers had increased to about 25 percent.[13, 14]

---

[13] Educational attainment can be a poor measure of skill if there have been significant changes in the quality of education. Some SAT scores show slightly declining trends, but these trends have a downward bias because of the significant increase in the participation rate in these tests (Grissmer 2000). The more representative National Assessment of Educational Progress scores show minor fluctuations but no sustained decline since the 1970s in the performance of high-school students (Stedman 2009). Handel (2003) relates the evidence to the debate on skill requirements and mismatch.

[14] Other studies paint a similar picture. Fogg and Harrington (2011) find that the proportion of employed college-educated workers in jobs that do not require a college degree increased from 25 percent in 2000 to

The existence and persistence of significant mismatch in the form of overeducation may be surprising from a traditional Walrasian perspective. It is perfectly consistent, however, with assignment or matching models (e.g., Albrecht and Vroman 2002, Sattinger 2006) as well as with efficiency wage models that distinguish between the skill requirements of the job and the skills of the worker.

Consider a shirking model and assume that there are only two job categories (high tech and low tech) and two types of workers (high skill and low skill). Now, introduce an asymmetry between the options of high- and low-skill workers. A high-skill worker who is unable to get a high-tech job may accept a low-tech wage in a low-tech job for which she is 'overeducated.' Assuming that low-skill workers do not have the analogous option of getting high-tech jobs, there will be three no-shirking conditions: For high-skill workers in high-tech jobs, for high-skill workers in low-tech jobs, and for low-skill workers in low-tech jobs. No-shirking among workers in high-tech jobs is enforced by a combination of unemployment and employment in low-paying low-tech jobs; unemployment is the only discipline device for low-tech jobs.

Mismatch emerges from this analysis in a straightforward way: Some high-skill workers are lucky (or benefit from gender or racial discrimination) and get well-paid jobs that utilize their skills, while others are unemployed or get low-tech jobs with lower pay, that is, they are overeducated. The asymmetry in the fortunes of otherwise identical workers is similar to the asymmetries in other versions of efficiency wage models. A standard one-sector efficiency wage model with homogeneous workers explains why, in equilibrium, identical workers may have different employment status and different levels of income and utility; multisectoral versions of the model allow for the possibility that identical workers in different sectors may have different wages and utility levels (e.g., Bulow and Summers 1986). Analogously, in this extension with two types of workers, identical high-skill workers may be employed in different jobs with different skill requirements and different wages. The model determines equilibrium unemployment rates for both high- and low-skill workers as well as a rate of underemployment (the proportion of workers with jobs for which they are overeducated).[15] As long as some matches of high-skill workers and low-tech jobs are

---

28 percent in 2010. Using Bureau of Labor Statistics (BLS) data, Vedder et al. (2013) suggest that about 37 percent of employed US college graduates are in jobs that require no more than a high-school diploma. They also find that the proportion of overeducated workers has grown substantially, citing taxi drivers as a particular example: The proportion of taxi drivers with a college degree has increased from 1 percent in 1970 to more than 15 percent in 2012. Calculating 'underemployment' (their term for 'overeducation') using survey evidence from the Department of Labor's O*NET database, Abel and Deitz (2016) from the Federal Reserve Bank of New York show very high levels of mismatch as well as significant fluctuations over time in the degree of underemployment. The fluctuations mirror movements in the employment rate: Rates of underemployment – especially among recent college graduates – decline when aggregate employment rates are high. According to an interactive database at the New York Fed, underemployment among recent graduates rose from about 40 percent before the financial crisis in 2008 to above 47 percent in 2013 but then declined steadily to under 40 percent in early 2020, as the employment rate increased (www.newyorkfed.org/research/college-labor-market/index.html#/underemployment).

[15] Endogenous movements in the relative supply of high-skill workers will not eliminate overeducation. If the supply of high-skill workers responds over time to the average wage premium, the model determines a long-run equilibrium with overeducation.

sustained in equilibrium, changes in exogenous variables will affect not only wages and employment rates but also the degree of mismatch. These induced changes in the degree of mismatch have a number of implications with respect to the comparative statics.

Minimum Wages

Consider the case of minimum wages, and suppose that the minimum wage is binding in low-tech but not in high-tech jobs. When the minimum wage is binding, then, by definition, firms are forced to pay more than would be required to fill the low-tech jobs with no-shirking workers, and the no-shirking condition cannot be binding for both high- and low-skill workers in low-tech jobs. There is an extra degree of freedom in the determination of who gets the low-tech jobs, and additional assumptions are needed to determine whether the no-shirking condition will be binding for low- or high-skill workers, or perhaps for neither group.

Bewley's (1999) study shows that overqualified job applicants are common but that many employers are reluctant to hire them. Indeed, this "shunning of overqualified job applicants" is highlighted as one of two novel findings of the study (p. 18). Attitudes to overqualified applicants differed somewhat between primary and secondary sector jobs, where secondary sector jobs are defined as short-term positions that are often part time. Both sectors received applications from overqualified workers, but for primary sector jobs, 70 percent of firms expressed a "total unwillingness," to hire them, 10 percent were "partially unwilling" and only 19 percent were "ready to hire" overqualified applicants (pp. 282–283). Secondary sector employers had fewer reservations, but only a minority (47 percent) "were ready to hire them," with 30 percent being "totally unwilling" and 23 percent "partially unwilling" (p. 324). These findings suggest that (on average) firms have a preference for employing low-skill workers in low-tech jobs, as long as the no-shirking condition is satisfied. This preference can be incorporated into the formal model by assuming that when a minimum wage is imposed, the no-shirking condition will be binding for low-skill workers but not for high-skill workers in low-skill jobs.

The implications are striking: An increase in the minimum wage unambiguously raises the employment of low-skill workers and reduces the rate of underemployment of high-skill workers; it may also – but need not – generate a reduction in average unemployment (Skott and Slonimczyk 2012). What happens is that low-skill workers get pulled into low-tech jobs when a rise in the minimum wage forces a relaxation of the no-shirking constraint. Consequently, some high-skill workers lose their low-skill jobs and become unemployed. The fallback position of high-skill workers in high-tech jobs now deteriorates, which relaxes the no-shirking condition in high-tech jobs, and high-tech employment is stimulated as the high-tech wage falls. The positive effects of a rise in minimum wages on employment emerge as a result of these spillover effects from induced changes in the degree of mismatch.[16]

---

[16] A large empirical literature has shown small (and in some cases positive) effects of a rise in minimum wages on employment. Most of the literature on these monopsony effects has focused on specific groups

Other shocks can also have surprising consequences. A negative shock to aggregate employment may generate a decrease in both the relative wage and the relative employment of low-skill workers. Even more paradoxically, if there are decreasing returns to the two types of labor, an increase in the relative supply of high-skill workers may raise unemployment and reduce the relative wage for low-skill workers. These extreme effects of an increase in the supply of skills are empirically unlikely but indicative of a more general result: The relative wage can be quite insensitive to changes in relative labor supplies (Skott 2006).

Biases in the Estimation of Substitution Elasticities

Insofar as the power and skill-requirements associated with different jobs are correlated, the elasticity of substitution between high and low skill workers could be seen as an indicator of the substitutability between high-and low-power jobs. This elasticity is often taken to be above unity, which is what is required by models of SBTC in order to explain the simultaneous fall in low skill wages and employment. The model in Section 7.3, by contrast, required an elasticity of substitution between high- and low-tech jobs of less than one.[17] Although they are likely to be correlated, the correlation between power and skills is far from perfect and, in principle, both of these elasticity requirements could be met.

The econometric evidence for a high elasticity of substitution between high- and low-skill workers is weak, however,[18] and the presence of mismatch adds another complication: Induced mismatch affects the empirical correlation between the relative wages and relative employment of workers with different skills. As a simple example, suppose the production function is of the Leontief type with strict complementarity between high and low tech jobs, and suppose that high-tech jobs require high skills

---

of workers or industries that are likely to be strongly affected by the minimum wage, such as teenagers or restaurants (e.g., Card and Krueger 1995, Dube et al. 2010); see Manning (2003) for an analysis of monopsony effects in a range of labor markets with some kind of friction. The efficiency wage argument, by contrast, concerns macroeconomic effects on the entire labor market, and clean identification is hard to achieve. The predictions of the model, however, are consistent with panel regressions using state level data for the United States (Slonimczyk and Skott 2012). The effects of a rise in minimum wages on low-skill unemployment and the degree of mismatch are negative and statistically significant at the 1 percent level. The regressions also give the expected negative effect of the minimum wage on the wage premium in high-tech jobs. Cengiz et al. (2019) find a positive but statistically insignificant overall effect of a rise in the minimum wage on the total number of jobs in the wage range that may have been affected by the increase in the minimum wage.

[17] The elasticity of substitution is important in both the power-bias and the skill-bias models for basically the same reason. The workers whose productivity has increased benefit in terms of employment and wages in the skill-biased story (where the productivity of high skill workers increases because of factor-augmenting technical change) but suffer in the power-biased version (where the productivity of low-power workers increase because of a rise in the intensity of work).

[18] Katz and Murphy (1992) estimate an elasticity of 1.41 between high- and low-skill workers (college and above versus high-school or less) but also acknowledge that there are reasons to be "somewhat skeptical of estimates of σ recovered from 25 nonindependent time series observations"; in fact, a range of elasticities – including an estimate of 0.5 – is consistent with the data in their study. Another study, Card et al. (1999), obtains very low estimates (all at or below 0.5), and the survey of earlier work in Hamermesh (1993) does not present a clear picture.

while low-tech jobs can be filled by either high- or low-skill workers. Formally, let

$$Q = \min\{\theta H, L\}$$
$$H = L_{HH}$$
$$L = L_{HL} + L_{LL},$$

where H and L are the numbers of high- and low-tech jobs that are filled; L_{HH} and L_{HL} are high-skill workers in high- and low-tech jobs, respectively, and L_{LL} is low-skill workers in low-tech jobs.

Profit maximizing firms do not employ idle workers, and it follows that $Y = \theta L_{HH} = L_{HL} + L_{LL}$. Hence,

$$(\theta + 1)L_{HH} = L_{HH} + L_{HL} + L_{LL}$$

and

$$Q = \theta L_{HH} = \frac{\theta}{\theta + 1}(L_{HH} + L_{HL} + L_{LL})$$
$$= \frac{\theta}{\theta + 1}(L_H + L_L),$$

where L_H and L_L denote the employment of high and low skill workers, respectively. The production function, by assumption, is Leontief in this example, but mismatch implies that workers with high and low skill are perfect substitutes (within a certain range).

Consider an increase in the relative supply of high-skill workers and assume that initially both types of workers experience full employment. If there were no mismatch, the result would be unemployment for high-skill workers, and the ratio of high-skill to low skill employment would be unchanged, even if high-skill wages were to plummet. In a model with induced mismatch, by contrast, an increase in the supply of high-skill workers spills over into greater mismatch: The ratio of high-skill to low-skill employment increases, while the decline in the relative wage of high-skill workers may be quite modest. Econometric studies of correlations between relative wages and employment will suggest a production function with a high elasticity of substitution if the results are interpreted within a framework that excludes mismatch. By assumption, however, the production function is Leontief: It is the presence of induced changes in the degree of mismatch that permits the apparent substitution between high and low skill workers.

7.5   CEO Pay

7.5.1   Firm-Level Volatility

The ratio of CEO pay to average pay in the largest 350 US companies ranked by sales has gone from about 20 in 1965 to over 350 in 2020 (Mishel and Kandra 2021). Skyrocketing CEO pay is important in its own right as well as for explaining the general rise in inequality at the upper end of the distribution: Executives, managers, supervisors, and financial professionals account for about 60 percent of the top 0.1 percent income earners (Bakija et al. 2012).

Undoubtedly, many factors contributed to the explosion in CEO pay. Pay could have increased simply because profits have become increasingly sensitive to variations in the quality of the managerial input. This skill-based explanation is favored by a large literature (e.g., Murphy and Zábojník 2004, Garicano and Rossi-Hansberg 2006, Gabaix and Landier 2008). An older and even larger literature going back to Jensen and Meckling (1976) has stressed the importance of agency problems for the pay of top executives. Oddly, however, when the relationship between executive pay and technological and institutional change is discussed, the analysis tends to ignore the potential influence of technological and institutional change on the severity of the agency problems. The claim in this section is that increased firm-level volatility aggravated the agency problem for top executives, and that these effects were amplified by shifts in social norms.

Prior to the financial crisis in 2007–2008, macroeconomists were fond of referring to the 'great moderation' to describe the fall in the volatility of GDP and unemployment that had occurred from some time in the 1980s in many advanced economies. This reduction in the amplitude of fluctuations at the aggregate level did not, however, carry over to reduced volatility at the firm level. On the contrary, firm level volatility of key variables, including operating income per employee, had been growing throughout this period (Comin and Mulani 2006, Chun et al. 2011, Pastor and Veronesi 2009). Both technological and institutional factors contributed to the growth in firm-level volatility.

On the technological side, new information technologies have involved increasing 'codification': Tacit knowledge has been put in standard form that can be re-used and communicated. The initial codification can be extremely costly but reduces the marginal cost of production. These developments are obvious in extreme cases like software and genetically modified organisms, but also affect many other businesses. From recorded music to grocery distribution and aircraft manufacturing, increasing shares of the value of goods and services are stored in replicable code – recordings, designs, management systems, automated equipment – which underpin increasing returns and a tendency for market concentration.

It should be noted, however, that some of the same forces can work the other way. Once expensive forms of sophisticated, specialized software can now be purchased at low cost by small firms and startups, while the internet has lowered the costs of monitoring market activities. In fact, the acquisition by large IT companies of smaller startups can be seen in many cases as defensive reactions to what might otherwise be tendencies in the direction of deconcentration. Thus, the net effect of codification on market concentration may be unclear. Network effects, on the other hand, provide a powerful source of concentration. The internet has provided a meta-platform for a profusion of network products provided by Amazon, Apple, Facebook, Google, and a host of smaller companies. The network benefits of document file formats (Word, Excel, and Powerpoint) and PC-server connections (Windows) are exploited spectacularly by

Microsoft, for instance, while smaller versions of these business models – monopolies in niches of the web – include companies like Elsevier and AirBnB.[19]

Overall, there appears to have been a change from stable oligopoly markets to fluctuating winner-take-all markets.[20] Product life cycles shortened and markets became less stable in the late twentieth century (von Braun 1990, Kurzweil 1992): Nokia dominated the cell phone market (and Blackberry the market for smartphones); Apple meanwhile seemed a lost cause in the mid 1990s, while Microsoft appeared to have gone astray in the early 2000s.

New information technology (including transport technology) has also made it possible for outsourcing to explode. Here again codification plays a key role, enabling the necessary communication of technological and contractual information to allow arm's length coordination (Sturgeon 2002). Production can be modularized, and firms can focus resources on their 'core competencies.' Outsourcing and modularity, in turn, are associated with the development of markets for 'corporate parts.' General Electric alone made more than 100 acquisitions over a five-year period in the mid-1990s (Ashkenas et al. 1998), while Google has made more than 250 acquisitions (and more than one per week on average in 2010 and 2011). Mergers and acquisitions can be successful and highly profitable; until the early 2000s, GE was often seen as an example. But things can also go wrong; HP acquired the British company Autonomy paying more than $11 billion in 2011, only to write down the value of the acquisition by 79 percent in 2012 (*New York Times*, 11/30/2012 November 30, 2012).

7.5.2   Contingencies and Implications

Unstable winner-take-all markets and outsourcing have a technological side, but there are crucial institutional contingencies. Scale and network economies were not invented in 1980. Whether, when, and where scale and network economies provide the basis for monopoly depends on the institutional response. The oligopolies of mid-twentieth century America were to a large extent the product of antitrust policies that broke up monopolies but tolerated oligopolies. Where increasing returns were extreme – in 'natural monopoly' industries such as roads, the postal service, electric power, telecommunications, and railroads – the state imposed either regulation or public ownership.

After 1980, the use of all of these tools – antitrust policies, regulation, and public ownership – was severely curtailed, as the economic and legal theories emanating from Chicago gained influence and then congealed into neoliberal policies.[21] The same neoliberal push to extend market relations wherever feasible made more things

---

[19] Rising market concentration has been documented by Autor et al. (2020), De Loecker and Eeckhout (2020), and Eggertsson et al. (2021).

[20] Some of the disruptive effects have come from new international players, including Korea and China.

[21] Arguably, this shift in policies should also be seen as a defensive response to rising competitive challenges from Japan in the 1970s and continuing with Korea and China. Strict antitrust policies implicitly gave way to a perception that 'national champions' were needed in a competitive world.

patentable (genetic code, software, algorithms, business methods), extended the life of copyrights, and incentivized universities to collaborate with corporations in converting their research outputs into monopoly products (Freeman 1995, Sell and May 2001, Guy 2007, Boldrin and Levine 2008). Microsoft's position, for instance, depends on intellectual property rights, including control of certain application program interfaces (APIs), such as document formats. If these interfaces were public property, software markets would have very low entry barriers, and could function largely as markets for customization and service (Stallman 1985, Raymond 1998). Industry regulation provides other examples. The UK forces cell phone providers to lease their networks to competitors; the United States does not, and US cell phone users pay the price. In short, at the same time that new waves of technological advance were producing a host of new opportunities for monopoly, the institutions and policies that had kept monopoly at bay were being dismantled.

The institutional contingencies extend beyond intellectual property rights and industrial regulation. The effects of modularity depend on trade policy and the deregulation of capital flows; without free trade and capital mobility the outsourcing of production to China and other emerging economies would be unattractive or impossible. Deregulation of labor markets and weak protections for employment and workers' rights also play a role by making it easier for executives to exploit modularity to cut costs.

If the new monopolies had been of the Hicksian quiet-life sort,[22] we would have expected an effect on CEO pay similar to that of regulations restricting market entry or pricing, which Hubbard and Palia (1995) find reduces CEO pay. Even Google and Microsoft, however, must innovate steadily to shore up their positions of power; a pharma or biotech company must develop new products to replace those whose patent protection expires; Walmart must understand the effects Amazon has on its business model.

Shareholders inevitably lack some of the CEO's information about the firm's future options, as well as about exogenous conditions which may have improved or hurt the firm's recent performance. Increased firm level volatility exacerbates this information asymmetry between the CEO and the shareholders. Under stable conditions, shareholders can rely on comparisons of the firm's recent performance with its own past performance. Where there are competitors offering close substitutes, shareholders can compare performance with that of peers; peer comparisons also work for regulated monopolies serving limited, sub-national, territories, as with most American public utilities. When the environment is unstable, however, and there is winner-take-all competition for control of a unique market niche, shareholders have less information about the CEO's effort and performance. In hindsight, it may be obvious that HP should not have paid $11 billion to acquire Autonomy or that JP Morgan should have put in place mechanisms that could have prevented a $6 billion loss from the 'London Whale' trading. It may also seem obvious that Apple made a correct decision when it

---

[22] Hicks (1935, p. 8) commented that "the best of all monopoly profits is a quiet life."

introduced the iPhone, but at the time this was not so obvious.[23] The indivisibility of the portfolio decisions, the high stakes, and the impossibility of monitoring the CEO and evaluating the decisions in advance aggravate the agency problems.

These changes in the principal-agent relation have increased the power of the CEO, but the trend need not continue. Over time, the advantage may shift decisively to ever larger incumbent monopolists – seemingly unbudgeable companies like Google and Microsoft. If this happens, monopoly rents may remain high, but CEO pay could come under pressure if the agency problem is alleviated; large firms in the United States and the United Kingdom enjoyed high market power and profitability in the early post WW2 years, yet relative CEO pay was low, at least compared to what we see today.

7.5.3   Fairness Norms, Reference Groups, and Ratchet Effects

Efficiency-wage arguments can be cast in different ways. Using a version that is standard in the literature, the model in Section 7.3 depicted an adversarial relation between optimizing agents with traditional selfish preferences. Formulations that emphasize social norms and reciprocity, however, may have greater support, as noted in Chapter 6.

The fair wage may adjust endogenously toward the current wage, but fairness norms can also shift as the result of broader movements in ideology and attitudes. A greater focus on how women's wages compare to those of men and a growing rejection of gender wage gaps as socially acceptable, for instance, have played a role in reducing gender wage gaps. Analogously, changes in norms may have contributed to the explosion in the pay to top managers.

A fairness perspective is implicit in Elson and Ferrere's (2012) account of boards' and compensation committees' focus on median pay as a minimum compensation target:

> If a board were to award lower than expected pay by compensating below median (market), it is understandable that there may be psychological consequences as a result of perceived inequitable treatment . . . Theories of pay equity suggest that when paid less than one's peers, a person may seek redress through the withdrawal of effort. (pp. 38–39)

---

[23] Vogelstein (2013) describes some of the issues.

It's hard to overstate the gamble Jobs took when he decided to unveil the iPhone back in January 2007. Not only was he introducing a new kind of phone – something Apple had never made before – he was doing so with a prototype that barely worked. Even though the iPhone wouldn't go on sale for another six months, he wanted the world to want one right then. In truth, the list of things that still needed to be done was enormous. . . .

No one had ever put a multitouch screen in a mainstream consumer product before, either. Capacitive touch technology – a "touch" by either a finger or other conductive object completes a circuit – had been around since the 1960s. Capacitive multitouch, in which two or more fingers can be used and independently recognized, was vastly more complicated. . . . Even if multitouch iPhone screens had been easy to make, it wasn't at all clear to Apple's executive team that the features they enabled, like on-screen keyboards and "tap to zoom," were enhancements that consumers wanted.

Social norms also figure prominently in the 'managerial power approach.' Bebchuk et al. (2002, p. 756) suggest that

whether a compensation arrangement that is favorable to executives but suboptimal for shareholders is adopted will depend on how the arrangement is perceived by outsiders and, in particular, on how much outrage (if any) it is expected to produce.

They go on to argue that "for outrage to impose significant costs it must be sufficiently widespread among the relevant groups of people" (p. 756). In order words, the compensation arrangement should not egregiously violate commonly accepted standards. These standards affect both what managers themselves believe to be a fair pay and the threshold levels that may produce outrage among relevant groups, including shareholders and the media.[24]

Consider a simple shirking example. Managers either shirk or provide effort. There is a fixed number of top managerial positions (a fixed multiple of the number of firms) and a given pool of potential top managers. All members of this pool of potential managers are identical; members who fail to obtain a top managerial position have some other, less attractive position with a lower, exogenously given wage. In this setting it becomes reasonable to specify the prevailing norms for fair managerial pay as a multiple of a reference wage, with this reference wage determined as a weighted average of the pay of top managers in other firms ($\bar{w}$) and the average (firm-level or economy-wide) wage (z):

$$w \geq \mu[\alpha\bar{w} + (1 - \alpha)z],$$

where μ represents the relative wage norm.

According to Elson and Ferrere (2012), the composition of the reference group has changed over the last 40 years: Compensation committees have attached an increasing – and increasingly formalized – weight to the pay of CEOs of comparable companies. This shift may be explained partially by the increasing mobility of executives and by changes in the structure of the compensation. Greater mobility reduces the attachment of the executives to employees, while paying CEOs as if they were capitalists helps increase social separation between them and their subordinates, while increasing identification (as well as incentive alignment) with their principals.[25] Other developments may also have contributed to upward shifts in the reference point: The Thatcher–Reagan years heralded a change in the ideological and political atmosphere as it related to inequality and to the socially acceptable limits on greed and self-promotion, external or self-imposed, within elite circles.

Whatever the sources of the shift, an increase in α raises the value of the reference point, making it necessary to increase managerial pay to satisfy the no-shirking

---

[24] Outside compensation consultants and the construction of 'peer groups' to get a benchmark for compensation can be used to mollify outsiders by making pay increases seem justified (Wade et al. 1997).

[25] Tirole (1986) analyzes effects of managerial pay structures on the incentives for collusion between managers and workers. Acemoglu et al. (2022) show that the appointment of managers with business degrees leads to significant reductions in the wages of employees, arguing that the evidence reflects causal effects of practices and values that the managers have acquired in business education.

condition. If top managers feel badly treated at pay rates below $10 million, firms may have to pay $10 million to prevent shirking; if the pay norm increases to $15 million, the required pay also increases to $15 million.

Importantly, social norms magnify the effects of market-induced changes in agency pay. If an increase in the severity of the agency problem raises the pay for managers in particular sectors, social norms and comparisons can produce ratchet effects across other sectors. A similar ratchet effect can arise if (perceived or real) differences in managerial skill make some firms raise managerial pay in response to changes in the competitive environment.

Not everyone may share managers' views on what constitutes the relevant reference group and the fair wage. The population at large as well as the media and perhaps also shareholders would certainly have been outraged, had the ratio of managerial pay to average wages jumped from 20 to 350 within a very short time period. But the path dependency of social norms gradually reduce the outrage associated with high compensation. Chapter 6 discussed the implications of path dependent norms for employment hysteresis if past wages represent a reference point. Norms for relative pay and inequality also change endogenously: Levels of pay that would have would have been deemed obscene not so long ago have now become socially acceptable.[26]

7.6   Conclusion

The account of rising inequality in this chapter differs from theories that emphasize SBTC or the effects of globalization. These theories typically suggest that shifts in the relative demand for skills are necessary to explain the observed patterns of wages and employment. This claim is unconvincing: Simple formal models show that power biases can produce these patterns. Moreover, there is substantial evidence pointing to power biases in technological and institutional change as well as in changing social norms.

The analysis has also addressed broader issues concerning the relation between technological and institutional change. The compression of incomes in the 1940s may have been in part a response to problems created by the expansion of managerial business in the preceding decades. The substantial productivity benefits of a planned division of labor – benefits derived from economies of scale, scope, and speed – brought the rapid emergence of managerial firms in the early twentieth century. The productivity gains were contingent, however, on solving problems of coordination

---

[26] Efficiency wage models are not the only way to introduce power as a determinant of income distribution. Matching models with match-specific rents and Nash bargaining also assign a key role to power as a determninant of pay. The efficiency wage version has the advantage that it highlights the agency problem and directs attention to factors that determine relative power; increasing uncertainty and firm-level volatility, for instance. The agency setting also provides a clear story of norm-based effects: A change in pay norms has a direct effect on pay because it influences the willingness of the CEOs to hurt owners by providing less effort.

and control within these new, large enterprises, and the limitations of the available information and communication technologies created significant agency problems.

On balance, these agency problems strengthened the bargaining power of lower-ranking and less-skilled workers. At the same time, the organizational inflexibility inherent in coordinating extensive divisions of labor with crude ICT reduced top managers' scope for action, thus limiting their agency rents. The extent and timing of the compression cannot be explained without including the effects of institutional changes, but these changes may have been facilitated by technological forces. The productivity gains promised by managerial enterprise could easily dissipate as a result of industrial conflict, which in some cases might even threaten the larger social order. Under these circumstances, institutions which aided peaceful resolution of workers' claims were widely recognized as socially functional. Conversely, improvements in ICTs since the 1980s may have played a part in the weakening of many of the institutions that had strengthened labor in the 1940s and early post-second-world-war period.

Theories of SBTC view the links between technology and institutions quite differently. According to Acemoglu et al. (2001), unionization declined because SBTC improved the outside option for high-skill workers and undermined the coalition between high-and low-skill workers. But high-skill workers have not disproportionately left unions as income inequality has increased, which is what the theory would predict (Farber et al. 2021). Moreover, by emphasizing the internal disintegration as a result of divergent interests among different groups of workers, the theory plays down – and fails to explain – the sustained attacks by business interests on unions and on the ability of workers to organize, as well as the ways in which these attacks have affected government policies and led to legislative changes.

An SBTC perspective also discounts the role of minimum wages. Numerous studies have found strong statistical correlations between minimum wages and inequality. It has been suggested, however, that the correlations may be spurious and that shifts in the demand for skills, rather than autonomous changes in nonmarket factors, have been central to the movements in relative wages and employment. Acemoglu (2002) argues that minimum wages cannot explain inequality at the top of the income distribution and that "whatever factors were causing increased wage dispersion at the top of the distribution are likely to have been the major cause of the increase in wage dispersion throughout the distribution" (p. 50). Autor et al. (2008), echo this argument, pointing to the existence of a time series correlation not just between the minimum wage and lower tail inequality (the 50/10 ratio) but also between the minimum wage and upper tail inequality (90/50). Because of this correlation, they suggest, the causal influence of minimum wages in both regressions must be discounted.[27]

---

[27] Autor et al. (2016) also play down the role of the minimum wage. They find only modest effects of an increase in the minimum wage on inequality at the lower end of the income distribution, suggest that measurement error may account for the appearance of ripple effects in the data, and conclude that "[w]hile the minimum wage was certainly a contributing factor to widening lower tail inequality—particularly for females—it was not the primary one." (p. 89).

Of course, one would expect changes in the minimum wage to influence the lower tail more strongly than the upper tail of the distribution – an expectation that is actually in line with the results reported by Autor et al. (2008) – but ripple effects could affect workers with wages above the minimum. More importantly, a piecemeal dismissal of institutional effects of this kind is unconvincing. If the role of minimum wages is dismissed because it cannot explain inequality at the top end, then presumably changes in the tax rates for high income earners or regulatory changes that influence corporate buybacks can be dismissed as well (they cannot directly explain what happens at the low end of the distribution), as can any other institutional change, when looked at in isolation. But these institutional changes did not happen in isolation: They were part of the same neoliberal agenda. Movements in the minimum wage are related to political pressures and general ideological trends, which themselves have generated a range of nonmarket changes, from labor market legislation and declining unionization to changes in fairness norms and the deregulation of the financial industry. The correlation between the minimum wage and distributional changes at the top end of the income distribution may reflect the influence of these other nonmarket factors, rather than skill biases and market fundamentals.

The identification of the sources of increasing inequality is important. If income inequality were mainly the result of SBTC, the solution would be increased education to improve students' skills, as argued by Goldin and Katz (2008). This long-term remedy could be supplemented with employment subsidies or changes in tax structures (earned income credits, for instance). But the SBTC perspective implies that attempts to improve wages at the lower end of the distribution by raising the minimum wage or strengthening labor unions would have significant, adverse effects for employment. If, on the other hand, power biases are one of the main sources of increasing inequality, education on its own will do little to reverse the trend.[28]

The argument against education as the solution is strengthened if overeducation is widespread and a significant proportion of college educated workers have jobs that do not require their skills; education may simply increase the mismatch between job requirements and worker skills. There are indications that mismatch of this kind is prevalent and that the degree of mismatch changes endogenously in response to shifts in labor market conditions. If this is the case, the comparative statics also becomes complicated: Skill-neutral shocks to technology can lead to seemingly paradoxical outcomes in models with induced mismatch.

The emphasis in this chapter on power biases and mismatch is not meant to exclude the possibility that skill biases and, especially, the expansion of international trade may have played a role in increasing inequality. Indeed, it would be surprising if the expansion of international trade and outsourcing had not significantly affected relative

---

[28] Although it may not be the solution to rising inequality, the upgrading and reorientation of education is likely to be an essential component of a move toward a more humane and egalitarian society. It must be part of a multifaceted agenda, however, and the education system would not be aimed primarily toward enhancing students' marketable skills (Auerbach and Skott 2021; see also EPI 2018 and Piketty 2020).

wages.[29] But there are large cross-country variations in the rise of inequality, making it unlikely that the great U-turn in income distribution in the United States and other liberal market economies between 1930 and 2022 can be explained without including power-biased institutional changes.

Appendix A: Intertemporal Optimization and h^i

Consider an infinitely lived agent with instantaneous utility function

$$u(c,\varepsilon) = c - v(\varepsilon).$$

Assume that the interest rate r is equal to the discount rate. The time profile of consumption is then a matter of indifference to the agent, and we may assume that consumption matches current income. If U denotes the value function of an unemployed worker, a worker who is currently employed at a wage w faces an optimization problem that can be written

$$\max E[\int_0^T (w - v(\varepsilon)) \exp(-rt) \, dt + \exp(-rT) \, U],$$

where the stochastic variable T denotes the time that the worker loses the job. Assuming a constant hazard rate, T is exponentially distributed. In a steady state the objective function can be rewritten

$$E[\int_0^T (w - v(\varepsilon)) \exp(-rt) \, dt + \exp(-rT) \, U] = E \int_0^T (w - v(\varepsilon) - h) \exp(-rt) \, dt + U$$

$$= E(\frac{w - v(\varepsilon) - h}{r}(1 - \exp(-rT)) + U$$

$$= (w - v(\varepsilon) - h)p + U,$$

where $h = rU$ and $p = E(1 - \exp(-rT))/r = (1 - \frac{\delta}{r+\delta})/r = \frac{1}{r+\delta}$ is a decreasing function of the worker's hazard rate δ.

Effort affects the firing probability and thus the hazard rate. Thus, the worker's first order condition can be written

$$-v'(\varepsilon)p(\varepsilon) + (w - v(\varepsilon) - h)p'(\varepsilon) = 0.$$

The value function of an unemployed worker (U) and thereby the value of h will depend on the average level of wages, the rate of unemployment benefits and the hiring rate. With a constant rate of unemployment, the hiring rate q is proportional to the average rate of separations

---

[29] As Paul Auerbach noted in comments on an earlier draft, an obvious counterexample to explanations like the SBTC hypothesis comes from managerial pay: The gigantic increase in the remuneration of top executives is coincident with a vast increase in the supply of managers emerging from newly created or expanded business schools.

$$q = \bar{\delta}\frac{L}{N-L} = \bar{\delta}\frac{1-u}{u},$$

where u is the unemployment rate and $\bar{\delta}$ is the average rate of separations.

The risk of job loss gives an incentive for workers to provide effort. But an increased average firing rate does not help the firm unless it raises effort (on the contrary, high labor turnover is usually costly). Since effort is determined by the elasticity $p'\varepsilon/p$ (see the first order condition), it follows that the average firing rate in the economy need not be related to the average level of effort and, second, that an improved ability to detect individual effort - a rise in $p'\varepsilon/p$ - may change average effort but need not be associated with any changes in the firing rate for workers that conform to this new average level of effort. Thus, it is reasonable to assume that $\bar{\delta}$ is constant and that

$$h = h(\bar{w}, b, u).$$

In equilibrium, $w = \bar{w}$ and in order to find the value of h we note that

$$V - U = (w - h - v(\varepsilon))p \tag{7.11}$$

$$U - V = (b - rV)s = \left\{b - r[(w - h - v(\varepsilon))p + \frac{h}{r}]\right\}s, \tag{7.12}$$

where $s = E\left(\frac{1-\exp(-rT_u)}{r}\right)$ and the stochastic variable T_u denotes the remaining length of the spell of unemployment of a currently unemployed worker. With a constant rate of separations, random hiring and constant unemployment, the stochastic variable T_u follows an exponential distribution with expected value $ET_u = \frac{u}{1-u}ET$ where $ET = 1/\bar{\delta}$ is the average expected remaining duration of employment for an employed worker. Using (7.11) and (7.12) and the expressions for p and s ($p = 1/(r + \delta)$; $s = 1/(r + \delta(1 - u)/u))$), it follows that

$$h = (w - v(\varepsilon))\frac{p - rps}{p + s - rps} + b\frac{s}{p + s - rps}$$

$$= (w - v(\varepsilon))\frac{\delta(1 - u)}{ru + \delta} + b\frac{(r + \delta)u}{ru + \delta}.$$

Thus, the fallback position is a weighted average of the utility flows while employed and unemployed with the weights depending on the rate of unemployment.

8 Macroeconomic Adjustment and Keynes's Instability Argument

8.1   Introduction

The British economy had been doing badly throughout the 1920s, never fully recovering from the recession after World War I and a revaluation of the pound sterling in 1925. The Great Depression worsened the situation; catastrophic rates of unemployment in Britain and across most of the capitalist world were impossible to miss, but a theoretical understanding of their causes was lacking. Keynes laid out a theoretical framework in the *General Theory of Employment, Interest and Money* in 1936, arguing that market failures can lead to persistent problems of involuntary unemployment.

The notion of involuntary unemployment is often misunderstood. Any worker who loses her job may be involuntarily unemployed in the sense that she would have preferred to keep the job. Keynes's definition, however, is not based on this kind of individual-choice perspective. His definition of involuntary unemployment excludes both frictional unemployment and unemployment that is due to workers' inability (because of legal constraints, for instance) or refusal to "accept a reward corresponding to the value of the product attributable to its marginal productivity" (p. 6)

Involuntary unemployment describes a market failure. There are situations, Keynes argued, in which workers may not accept a cut in money wages but would be willing to work for the prevailing money wage even if the price level were to increase, and in which firms would be willing to increase employment if prices were higher and the money wage did not change. When these conditions are met, neither workers nor firms would prevent employment from rising if nominal aggregate demand were to increase.

The dual test of both workers and firms was embedded in the definition of involuntary unemployment, which required that[1]

> in the event of a small rise in the price of wage-goods relatively to the money-wage, both the aggregate supply of labour willing to work for the current money-wage and the aggregate demand for it at that wage would be greater than the existing volume of employment (GT, p. 15)

An increase in aggregate nominal demand merely raises prices and wages, leaving real output and employment unchanged in economies that are at full employment. When

---

[1] Keynes's definition is phrased with reference to economies with perfectly competitive goods markets ("in the event of a small rise in the price ...") but readily generalizes to cases of imperfect competition: The thought experiment concerns the effect of a rise in nominal demand on real output and employment.

workers are involuntarily unemployed, however, an increase in aggregate nominal demand boosts employment.

Market mechanisms – the response of wages and prices to disequilibrium – do not automatically eliminate involuntary unemployment, Keynes argued. The problem was not a lack of price and wage flexibility. He viewed prices as flexible, and while money wages were sticky, the stickiness was beneficial: An increase in the flexibility of nominal wages would not, he suggested, bring the economy to full employment.

To make his case, Keynes first rejected traditional, partial-equilibrium arguments. If a single firm or small industry experiences a decline in the nominal wages of its workers – all other wages remaining unchanged – it is reasonable to assume that the demand curve for the firm or industry's output will remain unaffected. In this situation profit maximizing firms will increase their supply for any given price. The supply curve shifts out, and output and employment in this firm or industry unambiguously benefit from a reduction in its wages.

This partial analysis does not carry over to the system as a whole: The general price level and the positions of the firm- and industry-level demand curves will be affected by an economy-wide reduction in nominal wages. The inapplicability of the partial method of analysis meant that a new approach was needed, and the contemporary orthodoxy and his Cambridge colleague A.C Pigou, in particular, were taken to task for having no theoretical method with which to analyze the macroeconomic problems of the day:

if the classical theory is not allowed to extend by analogy its conclusions in respect of a particular industry to industry as a whole, it is wholly unable to answer the question what effect on employment a reduction in money wages will have. For it has no method wherewith to tackle the problem (GT, p. 260)

The preface to the French edition of the *General Theory* linked the 'general' nature of his own theory explicitly to this distinction between partial and system-wide (i.e., general or macroeconomic) analysis:

I have called my book a *general* theory. I mean by this that I am chiefly concerned with the behaviour of the economic system as a whole, – with aggregate incomes, aggregate profits, aggregate output, aggregate employment, aggregate investment, aggregate saving, rather than with the incomes, profits, output, employment, investment and saving of particular industries, firms or individuals. And I argue that important mistakes have been made through extending to the system as a whole conclusions which have been correctly arrived at in respect of a part of it taken in isolation. (GT, p. xxxii; emphasis in original)

This argument for a general theory to understand macroeconomic phenomena does not challenge the necessity of analyzing micro-level decision making. Indeed, large parts of the *General Theory* are devoted to an analysis of the microeconomic behavior of firms and households under conditions of uncertainty and what we would now call bounded rationality. But the argument cautions against the application of micro-level analysis (partial theories) directly to the system as a whole.[2]

---

[2] One may note that, *a fortiori*, the argument questions any notion that the economic system can be analyzed as if it were a single representative household optimizing over an infinite horizon.

To replace existing partial theories, Keynes devoted the first eighteen chapters of the *General Theory* to an analysis of the determination of an economy-wide fix-wage general equilibrium. This analysis represented an enormous achievement. Walras's work was largely unknown in Cambridge at the time, and the work on general equilibrium by Hicks, Debreu, Arrow, and others was yet to come. Not only did Keynes describe and analyze interactions across markets, he did so in the context of a monetary economy with a fixed money wage.

Pathbreaking as it was, the key conclusion from the analysis in Chapters 1–18 was not really surprising: If some prices are fixed arbitrarily (in this case the money wage in an economy with fixed stocks of some nominal assets), one would not expect all markets to clear. As Davidson (2008, p. 550) put it:

If Keynes's theory is that unemployment is the result of price and wage rigidities, then Keynes was nothing new or revolutionary. For even in the 19th century classical economists had argued that the lack of flexible wages and prices (supply side imperfections) is the cause of unemployment.

Chapters 1–18, however, formed a necessary prelude to the revolutionary claim: They laid the foundation for an examination of the effects on the economy as a whole of a fall in money wages. Having derived the fix-wage general equilibrium, Keynes could turn – in Chapter 19 – to the key issue: The effects on this equilibrium of changes in the nominal wage. Wage flexibility, he argued, was likely to lead to violent instability rather than convergence to full employment.

The rejection of increased wage and price flexibility as a solution to unemployment represented the revolutionary part of the argument, but the observed – desirable – stickiness in money wages also needed an explanation; non-clearing markets prompt economists to ask why prices do not react to disequilibrium by changing in these markets. Keynes's theoretical argument for stickiness invoked the influence of concerns over relative wages on wage formation. With imperfect labor mobility and decentralized wage setting, the struggle over money wages determines relative wages. Fearing the effects on their relative wage, workers strongly resist reductions in money wages (Keynes 1936, p. 14). As argued in Chapter 6, this relative wage argument is closely related to broader notions of fairness.

Whatever the merits of Keynes's theoretical argument, he had a strong empirical case. In an economy with unemployment, money wages should fall, and indeed, wages and prices did fall during the depression. In the US consumer prices fell by 25–30 percent between 1929 and 1933; the decline in wages was much smaller, and both prices and wages then rose between 1933 and 1939 despite continuing high unemployment (Figure 8.1). Price movements were more modest in the UK (where unemployment did not rise as much either) and, as in the US, nominal wages fell much less than prices (Figure 8.2).[3] Thus, considering the scale of unemployment, the speed of adjustment was quite slow; unemployment affected wage inflation but there was clearly considerable downward stickiness.

---

[3] The relative 'success' of the UK in the 1930s must be seen in light of the deflationary effects of the revaluation in 1925, which were then alleviated with the floating of the pound in 1931.

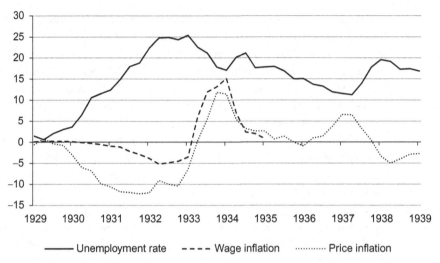

Figure 8.1 Unemployment, wage and price inflation; US 1929–1939. Data source: NBER Macrohistory Database.

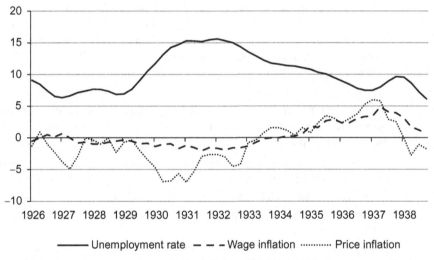

Figure 8.2 Unemployment, wage and price inflation, UK 1926–1939. Data sources: Bank of England (A Millenium of Macroeconomic Data) and NBER Macrohistory Database).

The rest of this chapter is structured as follows. Section 8.2 outlines a Marshallian version of the IS–LM model and discusses its usefulness as a representation of the basic argument in Chapters 1–18. Section 8.3 turns to changes in money wages and Keynes's discussion of their effects in Chapter 19 of the *General Theory*. The section presents a simple formalization of one of the destabilizing mechanisms. Coming from a very different tradition, the Polish economist Michal Kalecki developed theories that were quite similar to those of Keynes with respect to the role of aggregate demand and the effects of changes in money wages. Kalecki's version of the theory is discussed briefly in Section 8.4. Section 8.5 modifies the analysis by having monetary policy be described by a Taylor rule, rather than by an exogenous money supply. Section 8.6 offers a few concluding remarks.

8.2   IS–LM

Keynes's analysis in the *General Theory* was largely verbal, and it was left to Hicks (1937) to present a skeleton framework of the main interactions. This framework was the IS–LM model (or IS–LL, using Hicks's own labels).

It may be helpful to outline a version of the model explicitly. The equilibrium condition for the goods market in a closed economy is given by

$$Y = C + I + G, \tag{8.1}$$

where, in standard notation, Y is real output; C, I, and G denote real consumption, investment and government spending on goods and services.[4] Private consumption and investment are determined by behavioral equations while, for present purposes, we may take both government spending and taxes, T, as exogenous:

$$C = C(Y - T; \; Z_C); \quad 0 < C_1 < 1 \tag{8.2}$$

$$I = I(Y, i; \; Z_I); \quad 0 \le I_Y < 1 - C_1, \; I_2 < 0 \tag{8.3}$$

$$G = \bar{G}, \quad T = \bar{T}, \tag{8.4}$$

Z_C and Z_I represent vectors of variables that are taken to be exogenous in the short run. Z_C may include household wealth and variables that affect the relation between current and expected future income; Z_I, analogously, may include the capital stock, 'animal spirits' and expected inflation.

There are two financial assets, money and bonds, and the equilibrium condition for the money market ensures that both markets will clear: If households have allocated the desired share of their wealth to money, then by definition they must also have the desired share in bonds. The nominal demand for money, M^d, is determined by a behavioral equation

$$M^d = M^d(pY, i); \quad M_1^d > 0, M_2^d < 0, \tag{8.5}$$

where p is the price level and pY aggregate nominal income. The nominal money supply, M, is exogenous in this version of the model, and equilibrium requires that[5]

$$M = M^d. \tag{8.6}$$

---

[4] In Hicks's a original formulation, the model is disaggregated to allow for separate prices, production functions and equilibrium conditions for consumption and investment goods.

[5] Post-Keynesian critics have taken issue with the exogeneity of the money supply since the 1960s (e.g., Davidson 1968, Robinson 1970, Kaldor 1980, Moore 1988), and following the unhappy monetarist experiments of the late 1970s and 1980s, a 'Taylor rule' has now replaced the exogenous money supply in most macroeconomic models; Section 8.5 considers the implications of this change in policy regime.

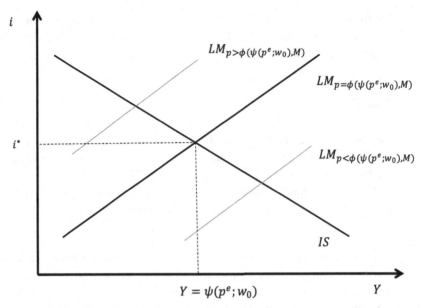

Figure 8.3 Ultra-short run Keynes–Marshall equilibrium.

A production function describes the supply side:

$$Y = F(L); \quad F' > 0, F'' < 0. \tag{8.7}$$

The capital stock is treated as constant in the short-run and has been omitted from the production function to simplify the exposition. The money wage rate is predetermined,

$$w = w_0. \tag{8.8}$$

Goods markets are atomistic and assuming profit maximization, the money wage equals the expected value of the marginal product,

$$w_0 = p^e F'(L). \tag{8.9}$$

For given values of the expected price and the money wage, Equations (8.7) and (8.9) determine the level of output without any influence from the demand side:

$$Y = F\left(F'^{-1}\left(\frac{w_0}{p^e}\right)\right) = \psi(p^e; w_0); \quad \psi_1 > 0. \tag{8.10}$$

The demand side – Equations (8.1)–(8.6) – enters via its influence on the market clearing price, which may differ from the expected price in the ultra-short run. Figure 8.3 illustrates the determination of prices in ultra-short-run equilibrium. The intersection between the IS and LM curves generates excess demand in the goods market when price is below the equilibrium level and, as prices rise, the LM curve shifts so that it intersects with the IS curve at the predetermined level of output (Equation (8.10)). Formally, the price level in ultra-short-run equilibrium can be written as:

$$p = \tilde{\phi}(Y, i^*(Y), M) = \phi(Y, M); \quad \phi_1 < 0, \phi_2 > 0. \tag{8.11}$$

Intuitively, the IS relations (8.1)–(8.4) for the goods market determine the market-clearing level of the interest rate, $i^*(Y)$. This combination of output and interest rate must be consistent with financial market equilibrium, and Equations (8.5) and (8.6) define the price level as an implicit function of Y, i, and M. An increase in Y requires a reduction in the interest rate to preserve goods market equilibrium and stay on the IS curve; with a rise in output and a decline in interest rates, the LM Equations (8.5) and (8.6) now imply that with a given supply of money, the price level p must fall in order to shift the LM curve to the right. Analogously, a rise in prices is required in order to keep the LM curve unchanged following a rise in the money supply.

Price expectations are being met in a short-run equilibrium, and the model can be extended to examine a Marshallian process of adjustment toward this short-run equilibrium. The market clearing price exceeds the expected price when demand is higher than expected, and firms respond to this discrepancy by increasing their price expectations and raising output. Using a simple adaptive formulation of these dynamic feedback effects of deviations of p from p^e, suppose that

$$\dot{p}^e = \lambda(p - p^e).$$

Using Equations (8.10) and (8.11), we get

$$\dot{p}^e = \lambda[\phi(Y, M) - p^e] = \lambda[\phi(\psi(p^e, w_0), M) - p^e].$$

If the money supply M and the nominal wage rate w_0 are constant, this differential equation has a unique, stable stationary point: The economy converges to a Marshallian short-run equilibrium in which price expectations are being met and firms are on their short-run supply curves.

Figure 8.4 illustrates the analysis using an AD–AS diagram.[6] The AD curve depicts the inverse relation between Y and p in Equation (8.11); the AS curve shows the positive relation between p^e and Y in Equation (8.10). The economy is always on the AD curve, but output rises if actual price (as determined by the AD curve) exceeds the expected price that induced the current level of output (the AS curve).

In the *General Theory* Keynes focused on short-run equilibria in which expectations are being met.[7] Hicks and most subsequent versions of the IS–LM model have followed the *General Theory* in this respect. Short-circuiting the ultra-short run dynamics and combining the LM relations (8.5) and (8.6) with the production function (8.7), firms' first order condition (8.9), and the stationarity condition $p = p^e$, we have

$$M = M^d(pY, i) \tag{8.12}$$

$$p = \frac{w_0}{F'(F^{-1}(Y))}. \tag{8.13}$$

---

[6] The terminology is unfortunate from a pedagogical perspective. Rather than demand in a single market, the AD curve depicts combinations of p and Y that are consistent with market clearing in both goods and financial markets.

[7] Keynes (1937a) comments on the Swedish School and Bertil Ohlin in his notes on "Ex post and ex ante." The analysis in the *General Theory*, he argues, was "more classical than the Swedes, for I am still discussing the conditions of short run equilibrium" (Collected Writings, vol. XIV, p. 183).

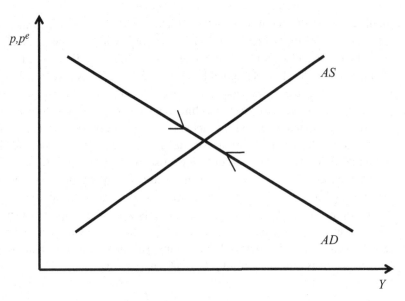

Figure 8.4 AD–AS representation of Keynesian model.

Equations (8.12) and (8.13) define i as an implicit function of Y, w_0 and M:

$$i = G(Y; w_0, M); \quad G_1 > 0, G_2 > 0, G_3 < 0. \tag{8.14}$$

Equation (8.14) describes the LM curve.

The downward-sloping IS curve is derived from Equations (8.1)–(8.4) in the standard way, and

$$Y = Y(i; G, T, Z_C, Z_I); \quad Y_1 < 0. \tag{8.15}$$

Conditional on the value of w_0 (and the other exogenous variables), the three equations (8.13)–(8.15) can be solved for $Y, i,$ and p. The price of output is endogenous, and the position of the LM curve is conditional on the money wage, w_0; a rise in money wage shifts the curve to the left. The graphical representation in Figure 8.5 shows LM curves for three different values of the money wage.

Discussion

The IS–LM model presented above may appear unconventional, both because prices are taken to be perfectly flexible in the short run and because of the explicit analysis of Marshallian ultra-short run dynamics.

The short-run flexibility of prices is consistent with the analysis in the *General Theory* as well as Hicks's original formalization. Many subsequent textbook expositions have taken the price level to be fixed, however, and the fix-price assumption has given rise to critiques of the IS–LM model and its close cousin, the AD–AS formulation, as being internally inconsistent. Barro (1994) and Colander (1995) have suggested that the model embodies mutually contradictory approaches to pricing and production: An

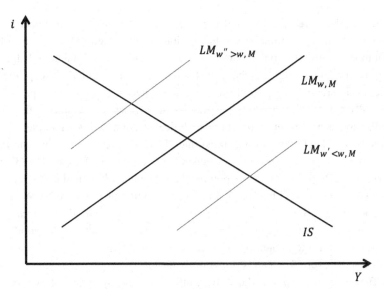

Figure 8.5 IS–LM representation of short-run equilibrium.

AD curve based on a goods market that clears with fixed prices and an AS curve based on profit maximization and diminishing returns to labor. The above version of the IS–LM argument circumvents these criticisms. The critique may apply to some textbook versions of the model, but the problems are not intrinsic to the approach and do not apply to Hicks's original formulation of the IS–LM model (Dutt and Skott 1996).[8]

At a more general level, IS–LM models and old Keynesian theory more broadly have been much maligned for their lack of microeconomic foundations and *ad hoc* character.[9] As argued in earlier chapters, the methodological alternative presented by contemporary macroeconomic theory is misguided. The IS–LM model is highly simplified, but as a general approach it is superior to 'micro founded models' that have perfectly optimizing representative agents at the core. In contrast with the latter theoretical structures, coordination problems are not assumed away, interactions across goods and financial markets are at the center of the analysis, and firms and households are treated as separate decisions makers.

It is not just Lucas and the New Classicals who have been critical of the IS–LM model. Many heterodox economists see it as an example of 'bastard Keynesianism,' a term used by Robinson (1974b) to describe the lumping together of "old and new orthodoxies" in the neoclassical synthesis, with post-Keynesian critics pointing to the

---

[8] Hicks (1980-81) himself became quite critical of the IS–LM model. When he criticized (on p. 145) the model for assuming fixed prices as well as fixed money wages, however, he must have forgotten that his own formulation did not impose fixed prices of output. In fact, he even allowed for distinct consumption and investment goods, each with its own flexible price.

[9] Lucas (1980) pronounced Keynesian economics dead, commenting that

at research seminars, people don't take Keynesian theorizing seriously anymore; the audience starts to whisper and giggle to one another.

mechanical nature of the model and the inadequate attention to uncertainty. To be sure, mathematical formalization has limitations that need to be recognized, and formal models must be supplemented by historical and institutional knowledge as well as empirical analysis. But 'mechanical' formalization is essential to keep track of complicated interactions, especially if one is interested in quantitative aspects, which we typically are. It is noteworthy that Keynes himself seemed to accept the IS–LM formalization as a representation of the analytical skeleton of his argument. Commenting on a draft of Hicks's paper, he stated that "I found it very interesting and really have next to nothing to say by way of criticism" (letter to Hicks, March 31, 1937; Collected Writings, XIV, p. 79). Hicks responded that "I had hardly hoped that you would be so much in agreement with it; but I am delighted to find that you are" (CW, XVI, p. 81).

The simple IS–LM model leaves out many insights of the *General Theory* but gives a reasonable account of the stylized interactions between the goods and financial markets in the context of an economy with a fixed money wage. Applied with 'fingerspitzengefühl' it can be immensely useful.[10]

Turning to the explicit Marshallian ultra-short run dynamics, it may be noted that this part of the analysis is at odds with common interpretations of the Keynesian revolution. Leijonhufvud (1968) viewed the reversal of Marshallian adjustment speeds as the central element of Keynes's analysis:

In the Keynesian macrosystem the Marshallian ranking of price and quantity adjustment speeds is reversed: In the shortest period flow quantities are freely variable, but one or more prices are given .... The "revolutionary" element in the *General Theory* can perhaps not be stated in simpler terms. (Leijonhufvud 1968, p. 52; italics in original)

Leijonhufvud's argument spurred a large literature on fix-price equilibria, including Barro and Grossman (1976) and Malinvaud (1977).[11] This literature, now largely forgotten, has very little to do with Keynes's analysis. The Marshallian interpretation, by contrast, finds support in Keynes's own work. In fact, the *Treatise on Money* (Keynes 1930b) describes an aggregate version of a Marshallian ultra-short run equilibrium in which rising prices and windfall profits clear the goods market with a predetermined level of output.

The IS–LM formulation in this section differs from the analysis in the *Treatise* by tracing out a sequence of ultra-short-run equilibria, with output adjusting to deviations of market clearing prices from expected prices. But there is also another difference. Following IS–LM tradition, the analysis in this section has ignored distributional effects on aggregate demand, relying instead on a fixed money supply and the effects

---

[10] Gordon (2009) and Krugman (2018a, 2018b) express similar views on the usefulness of the IS–LM apparatus.

[11] Leijonhufvud (1999) has subsequently changed his position:

In my 1968 book, I argued not only that Keynes dispensed with the auctioneer but also, to my frequent regret, that he 'reversed Marshall's ranking of the adjustment speeds' of price and output.

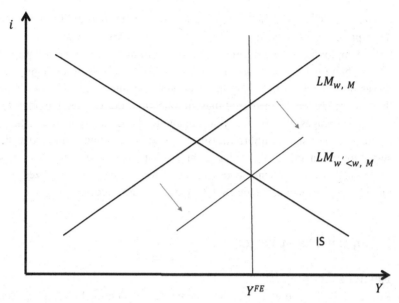

Figure 8.6 Misleading IS–LM dynamics.

of an increase in prices on interest rates and investment. By contrast, 'forced saving' – a negative impact of higher prices and windfall profits on consumption – plays an important role in the *Treatise*. Drawing on Chapters 3–4 above, this emphasis on income distribution and its effects on aggregate demand will reappear as a central element in the analysis of growth cycles in Chapters 9–10.

A Fundamental Flaw

Although the IS–LM model gives a reasonable account of the analytical skeleton of the fix-wage general equilibrium in Chapters 1–18 of the *General Theory*, problems arise from the way the model has been used to analyze the dynamic effects of changes in money wages.

Figure 8.5 describes static short-run equilibria for different levels of the money wage, and it is tempting to use the figure for a dynamic analysis along the following lines. Let Y^{FE} denote the level of output associated with full employment and assume that the initial position is one of involuntary unemployment, $Y < Y^{FE}$. A fall in w_0 shifts the LM curve to the right and – absent a liquidity trap or an inelastic (vertical) IS curve – there will be an increase in output and employment. If w_0 is reduced sufficiently, the economy reaches full employment (Figure 8.6). The market mechanisms work, it appears, and the pre-Keynesian conclusions do not depend on invalid, partial models but hold for Keynes's own analysis of the macroeconomic system as well. Involuntary unemployment would be eliminated quickly if only wages were flexible, a position that is shared by contemporary New Keynesian models.

Disregarding for the moment questions concerning the validity of this position as a description of real-world dynamics, it contradicts Keynes's own stated views. Involuntary unemployment, he insisted, would not be eliminated by increased wage flexibility. The problem is easy to locate. The IS–LM-based analysis of the adjustment process leaves out several destabilizing implications of falling nominal wages highlighted in the *General Theory*.[12] Insofar as these implications derive from the process of *changing* money wages, it is perfectly acceptable to leave them out of a static analysis of a short-run fix-wage equilibrium. But a diagram describing comparative statics is ill-suited for a dynamic analysis that includes changing money wages as a key element. The destabilizing mechanisms described by Keynes can be formalized, but dynamic models – rather than the static IS–LM analysis – are needed.

8.3   Changes in Money Wages

Keynes's Chapter 19

Keynes's fix-wage equilibrium in Chapters 1–18 identified three main determinants of output and employment: The propensity to consume (the consumption function), the marginal efficiency of capital (the investment function), and the interest rate (as determined by the equilibrium condition for the financial markets). A stability analysis therefore must ask

does a reduction in money-wages have a certain or probable tendency to affect employment in a particular direction through its certain or probable repercussions on these three factors? (*General Theory*, p. 260)

There is one clear benefit of a fall in money wages, Keynes argues: Lower nominal wages reduce the nominal interest rate (Equation (8.14)), thereby stimulating investment and output (Equation (8.15)). This interest rate effect (which has become known as the Keynes effect) is central to traditional IS–LM models, including the version presented in Section 8.2. But the same stimulus, Keynes comments, could be produced by increasing the money supply; the effect is therefore subject to the same limitations as monetary policy, including those stemming from an interest elastic demand for money and, in the limit, a liquidity trap with an infinite elasticity when interest rates become very low (p. 266 and 202–204). Putting it differently, if the interest rate is at or close to zero – as is likely to be the case in a deep recession – the Keynes effect no longer works.[13] Another stabilizing effect - the so-called Pigou effect, which was not included in Keynes's catalogue of effects – was proposed after the publication of the *General Theory* as a solution to the stability problem for an economy that finds itself in a liquidity trap. In principle, the increase in the real value of the stock of high powered

---

[12] As a more general weakness of IS–LM models, one may question the usefulness of a concept of short-run equilibrium as the building block for a dynamic theory. This issue, which will figure prominently in the analysis of medium and long run dynamics in Chapters 10–11, was highlighted by Hicks (1980–81).

[13] Another condition for the Keynes effect may also fail. The response of investment to changes in interest rates may be limited if aggregate demand is low and firms hold significant amounts of excess capacity.

money and other outside assets could raise demand if prices were to fall enough. This effect is recognized as being negligible in practice.

Both the Keynes and Pigou effects are stabilizing, but other forces work in the opposite direction. Two of these are particularly important:

- Reduced money wages and prices influence the distribution of wealth. Creditors gain and debtors lose; firms' balance sheets suffer, and heavily indebted firms may even become insolvent. Adverse balance sheet effects from falling prices, one may add, are not confined to firms, as evidenced by the housing crisis of 2007–2008 and its derived effects on households and financial institutions.
- A reduction in money wages stimulates demand if the reduction is expected to be temporary but if, more realistically, it leads to an expectation that further reductions will be coming in the future, then firms will have an incentive to postpone investment. Expected future deflation raises the real rate of interest, and an investment function that is written in terms of nominal rather than real interest rates will shift down. In Keynes's terminology, the expectation of future falls in money wages "will diminish the marginal efficiency of capital" (p. 263).

Induced changes in the distribution of income and wealth offer no hope for expansionary effects in a closed economy, Keynes argued, and it was mainly on the Keynes effect and the expectations effect that "we must base any hopes of favourable results to employment from a reduction in money-wages" (p. 265).[14] But the "actual practices and institutions," he continues, make is impossible to ensure a sudden reduction in money wages to a level compatible with full employment. Wage flexibility therefore implies that recessions will be accompanied by gradual downward movements in money wages, a process that will most likely generate destabilizing expectations of continued falls in money wages. Given the limitations of the Keynes effect, the net effects are unlikely to stimulate output.

Summarizing his argument with respect to money wage flexibility, Keynes concluded that

> if labor were to respond to conditions of gradually diminishing employment by offering its services at a gradually diminishing money-wage, this would not as a rule, have the effect of reducing real wages and might even have the effects of increasing them, through its adverse influence on the volume of output. The chief result of this policy would be to cause a great instability of prices, so violent perhaps as to make business calculations futile in an economic society functioning after the manner of that in which we live. To suppose that a flexible wage policy is a right and proper adjunct of a system which on the whole is one of laissez-faire, is the opposite of the truth ... the maintenance of a stable general level of money-wages is, on a balance of considerations, the most advisable policy (GT, pp. 269–270)

Tobin's Formalization

Keynes's analysis in Chapter 19 is sketchy and informal. Tobin (1975), however, introduced the destabilizing effects of gradually falling prices into a modified IS–LM

---

[14] An open economy may benefit from wage cuts because of improved international competitiveness. For the world economy, however, this beggar-thy-neighbor policy is not a solution.

model.[15] Following Tobin, let

$$\dot{Y} = A_Y(E - Y) \tag{8.16}$$

$$\dot{p} = p\left[A_p(Y - Y^*) + x\right] \tag{8.17}$$

$$\dot{x} = A_x(\hat{p} - x), \tag{8.18}$$

where, using Tobin's notation, E, Y, p, and x denote aggregate demand, output, the price level, and the expected inflation rate, respectively, and A_Y, A_p, and A_x are positive constants. Equation (8.16) describes adjustment toward goods market equilibrium: Output increases if aggregate demand exceeds current output. The accelerationist specification of the Phillips curve in Equation (8.17) presumes the existence of a well-defined natural rate of unemployment (or full employment in Keynes's terms). As argued in Chapters 5 and 6, this presumption is questionable. It is in line with Keynes's analysis in the General Theory, however, and harmless for present purposes. If prices are set as a constant markup on marginal cost and there is excess capital capacity and constant returns to labor, we have $\hat{w} = \hat{p}$. Thus, the parameter A_p in the Phillips curve measures the degree of flexibility of money wages. Equation (8.18) describes expectation formation as adaptive: Expected inflation increases if actual inflation exceeds expected inflation.

Aggregate demand in a closed economy is given by $E = C + I + G$, and we have

$$\begin{aligned} E &= C(Y - T, p) + I(Y, i - x) + G \\ &= C(Y - T, p) + I(Y, i(Y, p) - x) + G \\ &= E(Y, p, x); \quad 0 < E_1 < 1, \ E_2 < 0, E_3 > 0. \end{aligned}$$

The signs of the partial derivatives with respect to the price level and the level of output follow standard assumptions. An increase in income stimulates both consumption and investment, but the stability condition is taken to be satisfied: The marginal propensity to spend is positive but less than one ($0 < E_Y < 1$). The nominal interest rate is determined by the price level and the level of output (the LM relation), and the Keynes and Pigou effects imply that an increase in the price level reduces demand ($E_p < 0$). Real and nominal interest rates move together as long as the expected rate of inflation is given, but the distinction between the two rates becomes important if inflation expectations change endogenously: Investment depends on output and the real interest rate, $r = i - x$. Thus, expected inflation has a positive effect on aggregate demand ($E_x > 0$).

The stability conditions for a 3D system of differential equations are cumbersome, and a simplified 2D system is sufficient for present purposes (Tobin's 3D system is analyzed in Appendix A). The feedback effect from the level of output to the change

---

[15] Formalizations of Keynes's instability argument have also been presented by, among others, Flaschel and Franke (2000) and Chiarella and Flaschel (2000).

   Many 'old Keynesians' have fully recognized the stability problems (e.g., Hicks 1975, Hahn and Solow 1986, Tobin 1993). Post-Keynesians have also consistently stressed the destabilizing effects of falling nominal wages (e.g., Davidson 1972, Minsky 1975, Dutt 1986).

in output is negative, and for given values of p and x, Equation (8.16) describes a process of convergence toward a stationary point

$$Y = Y(p,x); \quad Y_1 < 0, Y_2 > 0,$$

where Y_1 and Y_2 are the partial derivatives of output with respect to the two state variables. Intuitively, an increase in prices reduces the equilibrium value of output because of the Pigou and Keynes effects; an increase in expected inflation reduces the real interest rate, which stimulates investment and raises the equilibrium value of output.

Assuming 'rapid' output adjustment ($A_Y \to \infty$ and $Y = Y(p,x)$), the dynamic system reduces to the following two equations:

$$\dot{p} = p \left[A_p (Y(p,x) - Y^*) + x \right] \tag{8.19}$$

$$\dot{x} = A_x(\hat{p} - x), \tag{8.20}$$

where $Y(p,x)$ is the short-run equilibrium value of output, given the values of the state variables p (the price level) and x (the expected rate of inflation).

The price level p must be positive for the system to be meaningful, and if $p > 0$, Equation (8.19) implies that $\hat{p}$ must be zero at a stationary point. From Equation (8.20) it follows that for $\dot{x}$ to be zero we must have $\hat{p} = x$, and substituting $\hat{p} = x = 0$ into Equation (8.19), we get $Y(p,0) = Y^*$. This equation determines a unique stationary value of the price p. Thus, the 2D system has a unique stationary point, $(p,x) = (p^*,0)$.

The local stability properties of the stationary point are determined by the Jacobian matrix of first partial derivatives (Chapter 4, Appendix A). This matrix, evaluated at the stationary point where $\dot{p} = \dot{x} = 0$, is given by

$$J(p,x) = \begin{pmatrix} pA_pY_1 & p\left(A_pY_2 + 1\right) \\ A_xA_pY_1 & A_xA_pY_2 \end{pmatrix}.$$

The system is locally stable if the determinant and trace of the Jacobian are positive and negative, respectively. The first of these conditions is satisfied: The partial derivative Y_1 is negative (output depends negatively on the price level) and the determinant is unambiguously positive,

$$det = -A_xA_ppY_1 > 0.$$

The sign of the trace, however, is ambiguous:

$$tr = A_p \left[pY_1 + A_xY_2 \right] \gtrless 0. \tag{8.21}$$

The trace will be positive if the destabilizing expectations effect (A_xY_2) dominates the stabilizing Keynes and Pigou effects (pY_1).

The trace condition (8.21) has two important implications. Rapid adjustments of expectations (high values of A_x) will tend to destabilize the system. Wage flexibility, second, cannot turn an unstable system into a stable system: The stability condition is independent of the adjustment speed for wages and prices (A_p). If the trace of the Jacobian is positive, a high value of the adjustment speeds A_p turns the stationary point

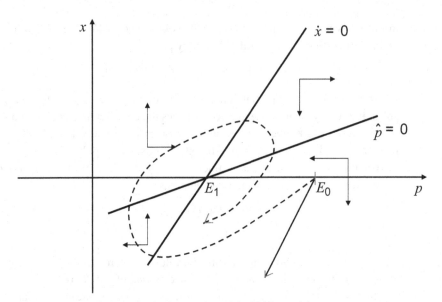

Figure 8.7 Phase diagram for the 2D version of the Tobin model.

into an unstable node (the discriminant $tr^2 - 4det$ becomes positive); with smaller values of A_p, the stationary point is a focus, and we get (locally) explosive cycles around the stationary point.

The phase diagram in Figure 8.7 illustrates the global dynamics. Both the $\dot{p} = 0$ and $\dot{x} = 0$ loci are upward sloping. An adverse shock to aggregate demand (a decline in animal spirits, for instance) shifts the two loci and the stationary point to the left: The new stationary point E_1 also has $x = 0$, but following the shock, a lower value of p (and thereby a lower interest rate) is needed to keep output at Y^*. The diagram indicates two possible trajectories, starting from the old stationary point E_0, one stable and the other unstable. The model demonstrates the potential instability, but it should be noted that by leaving out destabilizing distribution effects, the formalization fails to capture the full force of Keynes's argument. Thus, the model underestimates the risk of instability.

Instability may seem to be at odds with the evidence: An unstable stationary point and unbounded divergence offers a poor description of real-world economies. This objection is less compelling than it may appear. The introduction of nonlinearities can turn locally unstable movements into bounded fluctuations, and local instability can provide the starting point for a simple story of endogenous business cycles. The analysis of business cycles, however, must extend the time frame to the medium or long run, and in its present form the model is ill-suited for this task: Variables like the capital stock can no longer be taken as constant if the time frame is extended. Endogenous cycles will be discussed in Chapters 9–10.

Tobin highlights another possibility: Nonlinearities may imply that large shocks lead to divergence, even if the trace is negative and the stationary solution is locally stable. With corridor stability of this kind, the stabilizing market mechanisms work well in normal times but become insufficient if the economy is thrown into a deep recession; policy intervention will be needed if this happens in order to prevent a complete breakdown.

8.4   Kalecki

Staying as close as possible to the conventional theory of the time, Keynes assumed perfect competition in the goods market and diminishing returns to labor. He wanted to show that even with these assumptions, an economy may not converge to full employment. His assumptions imply, however, that real wages will be countercyclical and, as noted early on by Dunlop (1938) and Tarshis (1939), real wages do not, in fact, follow this pattern.

Independently of Keynes and at the same time, Kalecki developed a theory of aggregate demand and the failure of market mechanisms. Kalecki did not have a commensurate impact on the profession, but his analysis was in some ways clearer and more succinct; it was also immune to the Dunlop–Tarshis critique.

Unlike Keynes, Kalecki assumed imperfect competition. Firms typically hold some excess capital capacity, and if labor is the only variable input, movements in real wages depend on both the returns to labor (which need not be diminishing when competition is imperfect) and the cyclical patterns in the markup. In a benchmark case with constant marginal productivity of labor and a constant markup, the real wage is constant; deviations from this case readily produce procyclical or countercyclical real wages. Thus, Kalecki's version is compatible with a range of different cyclical patterns of real wages.

Like Keynes, Kalecki (1935) rejected the view that money wage reductions would be a solution to unemployment. His reasoning was also similar to that of Keynes:

what is to the advantage of a single entrepreneur does not necessarily benefit all entrepreneurs as a class. If one entrepreneur reduces wages he is able *ceteris paribus* to expand production; but once all entrepreneurs do the same thing the result will be entirely different. (Kalecki 1935, p. 26)

The fallacy of composition arises because firms are unlikely to respond to falling wages by immediately raising investment, and if they do not, their gains from falling wages will be "dissipated through price declines" (p. 28). Kalecki concludes that "a reduction of wages does not constitute a way out of depression." What is needed is a rise in aggregate demand: An "increase in investment *per se* unaccompanied by a wage reduction causes a rise in output" (p. 28).

Kalecki emphasized differences in the propensity to consume out of wage and capital income and saw the distribution of income as an importantdeterminant of aggregate demand. Unlike Keynes, however, he paid little attention to the possible effects of interest rates and the price level on aggregate demand. In this respect, his analysis represents a limiting case of the formalization in Section 8.3. Weak interest and price effects reduce the partial derivatives of E with respect to p and x. In the limiting case, both partials are zero, output is determined independently of p and x, and changes in money wages, prices and expected inflation have no effect on employment if the distribution of income remains unchanged.

8.5   Taylor Rules and the ZLB

A Modified Tobin Model

The treatment of the money supply as exogenously given in both the traditional IS–LM model and the Keynes–Tobin model has become outdated, even as a representation of prevailing views: The endogeneity of the money supply has become an integral part of contemporary macroeconomics. Central banks set 'the interest rate' in response to the state of the economy, and the money supply is allowed to adjust as needed.[16]

A benchmark version of a Taylor rule for interest rates can be written[17]

$$i = i(Y, x); \qquad i_1 \geq 0, \quad i_2 > 1. \tag{8.22}$$

The Tobin model can be modified to accommodate this rule for monetary policy, but the change in policy regime from an exogenous money supply to Taylor rules alters the stability properties of the system.

In the traditional IS–LM model, the equilibrium condition for the financial markets determines the nominal rate of interest as a function of output, the price level and an exogenously given money supply (cf. Equation (8.6)), with the real interest rate found by subtracting the expected inflation. In the modified model, the influence of output and expected inflation on the real rate follows directly from the Taylor rule. The level of prices does not influence the real interest rate, and the case for a significant Pigou effect, which is weak in the case with exogenous money, gets even weaker when the money supply is endogenous. Thus, we may assume that aggregate demand is determined by income and the real interest rate:

$$E = E(Y, i - x); \qquad E_1 > 0, E_2 < 0. \tag{8.23}$$

Unlike in the Tobin version, the nominal interest rate is determined by the Taylor rule in Equation (8.22), and the restrictions on the derivatives imply that the real interest rate will be an increasing function of Y and x:

---

[16] The endogeneity of the money supply was hinted at by both Keynes and Hicks. Keynes commented that the quantity of money could be "itself a function of the wage- and price-level" (GT, p. 266) and Hicks argued that

> Instead of assuming, as before, that the supply of money is given, we can assume that there is a given monetary system – that up to a point, but only up to a point, monetary authorities will prefer to create new money rather than allow interest rates to rise (Hicks 1937, p. 157).

As an empirical matter, the decline in the money supply 1929–1933 in the US was predominantly linked to bank failures and contractions, a fact that was passed over by Friedman and Schwartz (1963) in their economic analysis.

[17] Different specifications of the rule have been suggested. Some use actual inflation instead of expected inflation and some allow for inertia in the setting on interest rates. For present purposes these differences are of no importance. The policy rule takes its name from the analysis in Taylor (1993).

$$r = i - x = i(Y, x) - x = \phi(Y, x); \quad \phi_1 \geq 0, \ \phi_2 = i_2 - 1 > 0. \tag{8.24}$$

Now suppose, as in Section 8.3, that output adjustment is rapid and that $Y = E$. Using this equilibrium condition and Equation (8.23), we have

$$Y = Y(r); \quad Y' < 0. \tag{8.25}$$

Equations (8.24) and (8.25) define output as a decreasing function of the expected inflation rate[18]

$$Y = f(x); \quad f' < 0. \tag{8.26}$$

Retaining the Phillips curve (8.19) and adaptive inflation expectations, we get a 1D differential equation in x. Substituting Equation (8.26) into Equations (8.19) and (8.20) the change in inflation expectations is given by

$$\dot{x} = A_x A_p (f(x) - Y^*). \tag{8.27}$$

Since $f' < 0$, there is at most one stationary point, and if a stationary point exists, it will be stable and satisfy $x^* = Y^{-1}(Y^*)$. The Taylor rule has solved Keynes's instability problem.

Stabilization is the result of active policy. In a regime with an exogenous money supply, a passive monetary policy is one that keeps the money supply constant. Analogously, if the interest rate is the policy instrument, a passive policy maintains a constant interest rate; if stability requires adjustments in the interest rate, then stability – by definition – is contingent on active policy intervention. The Taylor rule in this sense represents an adoption of Keynes's recommendation (GT pp. 267–269) that monetary policy replace any reliance on adjustments in money wages. It can, he argued, "only be a foolish person who would prefer a flexible wage policy to a flexible money policy" (p. 268).

Active monetary policy is subject to limitations. The effects of changes in interest rates are subject to lags, and reducing interest rates may have limited effects in recessions when most firms have high levels of excess capacity (you cannot push on string, a phrase often attributed to Keynes but used by US congressman Alan Goldsborough during congressional hearings in 1935). Another limitation has received renewed attention in recent years: A liquidity trap – a perfectly elastic demand for money as nominal interest rates go to zero – may make it impossible for the monetary authorities to implement the Taylor rule in Equation (8.22). In fact, Equation (8.27) may not even have a stationary solution with an acceptable inflation rate: If a real interest rate r is needed and the nominal interest rate is subject to a zero lower bound, $i \geq 0$, the inflation rate would need to exceed $-r$, a value that can be positive and possibly

---

[18] Substituting Equations (8.24) in (8.25), we have

$$Y = Y(\phi(Y, x))$$

and, using the implicit function theorem,

$$\frac{dY}{dx} = \frac{Y'\phi_2}{1 - Y'\phi_1} < 0.$$

large for negative values of the required real rate.[19] If that happens, fiscal policy may become essential to prevent a meltdown, not just as a temporary policy in the short run, but on a long-term basis to avoid 'secular stagnation' (see Chapter 11 below). For now, however, I shall focus on stabilization policy, assuming that the equation has an acceptable stationary solution.

The ZLB

If nominal interest rates cannot be negative (or have a lower limit that is only slightly below zero)[20], the Taylor rule in Equation (8.24) no longer applies without modification. Taking into account the zero lower bound (ZLB), the real rate of interest will be given by

$$r = i - x = \max\{\phi(Y, x), -x\}; \qquad \phi_1 \geq 0, \phi_2 > 0. \tag{8.28}$$

The determination of output, consequently, has to be modified as well. Instead of Equation (8.26), we have

$$Y = Y(r) = \begin{cases} f(x); & f' < 0 \quad \text{if} \quad \phi(f(x), x) + x > 0 \\ g(x); & g' > 0 \quad \text{if} \quad \phi(f(x), x) + x < 0 \end{cases}.$$

For low values of the expected inflation rate, policymakers would like to boost output by setting a low real interest rate. The ZLB, however, will frustrate the policy and leave the real interest above the target value when x is below some threshold x_0. To see this, note that the expression $\phi(f(x), x) + x$ is increasing in x and goes to $\pm\infty$ for $x \to \pm\infty$. Intuitively, $\phi(f(x), x)$ – the real interest rate in the absence of a ZLB – is increasing in the inflation rate, and the nominal rate, $r + x$, therefore increases (decreases) without limit if x goes to infinity (to negative infinity).[21] Thus, there is a value x_0 such that $\phi(f(x), x) + x \gtrless 0$ for $x \gtrless x_0$, and the ZLB becomes a binding constraint when $x < x_0$.

When $\phi(f(x), x) + x > 0$, we have $Y = f(x)$, while $\phi(f(x), x) + x < 0$ implies that $i = 0$ and $Y = Y(-x) = g(x); g' > 0$. The resulting kink in the relation between

---

[19] Spending decisions will depend on risk-adjusted real rates of interest. Thus, the real policy rate of interest may be need to be negative, even if the required risk-adjusted rate remains positive.

[20] The lower limit derives from the presence of cash as an alternative asset. Abolishing cash or taxing cash holdings might not solve the basic problem, however: Reductions in the interest rate on money will not stimulate demand if it merely generates a portfolio shift toward other non-reproduced assets (Keynes 1936, Chapter 17; Palley 2019).

[21] $\phi(f(x), x)$ is the value of the real interest rate that would obtain in the absence of a zero lower bound. The real interest rate satisfies Equations (8.24) and (8.25), and we have

$$r = \phi(Y(r), x).$$

Using the implicit function theorem (taking total derivatives and rearranging), it follows that r is increasing in x:

$$\frac{dr}{dx} = \frac{\phi_2}{1 - \phi_1 Y'} > 0.$$

Thus, $r + x = \phi(f(x), x) + x$ goes to $\pm\infty$ for $x \to \pm\infty$.

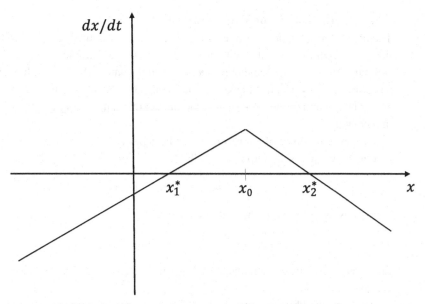

Figure 8.8 Multiple stationary solutions in the Tobin model with a Taylor rule and a ZLB.

output and expected inflation translates into a kink in the relation between $\dot{x}$ and x:

$$\dot{x} = \begin{cases} A_x A_p (f(x) - Y^*) & \text{if} \quad x > x_0 \\ A_x A_p (g(x) - Y^*) & \text{if} \quad x < x_0 \end{cases}.$$ (8.29)

The differential Equation (8.29) can have zero or two stationary points (or, as a fluke, a single stationary point). In the case with two stationary solutions (x_1^* and x_2^*, $x_1^* < x_0 < x_2^*$), the ZLB is binding at the low, unstable solution (see Figure 8.8). As long as the initial value of expected inflation is above this low solution (but below x_2^*), expected inflation will be increasing, the zero lower bound will cease to be binding at some point, and we get convergence to the high stationary solution with $i > 0$ and $Y = Y^*$. If the initial value of expected inflation is below the low stationary solution, however, the result is divergence: Both output and inflation fall, nominal interest rates will be stuck at the ZLB, and the contraction in output will continue unchecked.

The well-known and intuitive conclusion is that monetary policy loses its ability to prevent downward divergence once we hit the ZLB. Policymakers would like to reduce the interest rate but are unable to do so, and because output is below the natural level, inflation keeps falling.[22] Falling inflation corresponds to a rising real interest rate (since the nominal interest rate is stuck at zero), and a rising real interest rate implies a falling level of output (the IS relation).

---

[22] The problem is aggravated in recessions if the risk premium on corporate bonds and loans increases, which is typically the case.

Lags and the Effects of Wage Flexibility

The above formalization assumes a lot of simultaneity. Output is taken to be a function of the real interest rate (Equation (8.25)), with the real interest rate a function of contemporaneous output and expected inflation (Equation (8.28)). Both relations may be subject to lags. Central banks may not respond immediately to changes in output and inflation, and, more importantly, the impact of changes in interest rates is not felt immediately.

The gradual impact of interest rates can be captured in a simple way by introducing gradual adjustments an output. Formally, let

$$\dot{Y} = \lambda(\tilde{Y} - Y); \quad \lambda > 0, \tag{8.30}$$

where $\tilde{Y}$ is determined by the real rate of interest,

$$\tilde{Y} = \tilde{Y}(i - x). \tag{8.31}$$

Equation (8.31) takes the place of Equation (8.25), and output becomes a state variable.

Retaining the Phillips curve (8.19), the expectations equation (8.20), and the Taylor rule (8.28), we now get a 2D system:

$$\dot{Y} = \psi(Y,x); \quad \psi_1 < 0, \psi_2 \lessgtr 0 \text{ for } \phi(Y,x) + x \gtrless 0$$
$$\dot{x} = A_x A_p (Y - Y^*).$$

The phase diagram for this system is depicted in Figure 8.9. There are two stationary solutions, assuming that $\lim_{i-x\to-\infty} \tilde{Y}(i - x) > Y^*$ and $\lim_{i-x\to\infty} \tilde{Y}(i - x) < Y^*$.

The stationary solution at $E_2 = (Y^*, x_2^*)$ is locally stable, while the saddle point at $E_1 = (Y^*, x_1^*)$ is unstable.[23] These stability properties are independent of the parameters λ, A_p, A_x, but the independence does not make the adjustment parameters irrelevant for the global properties of the system: An increase in the parameters A_x and A_p will shrink the basin of stability for E_2; in this sense, high levels of wage and price flexibility are destabilizing. To see this, suppose the economy is initially at the locally stable equilibrium E_2 (at which the ZLB does not apply), and consider a negative shock to Y, that is, a horizontal, leftward displacement of (Y,x) from E_2. A high value of the adjustment speed for x (the product $A_x A_p$) will generate a rapid decline in expected inflation, potentially taking it below x_1^* before the level of output has recovered to Y^*, even if the shock is small. Thus, a high value of A_p implies that small shocks to output or expected inflation will be sufficient to produce instability. Rapid output adjustment, a high value of λ, by contrast, is stabilizing. At one extreme, as $A_x A_p/\lambda \to \infty$ any negative shock to output (starting from E_2) will lead to a collapse with $Y \to 0$. At the other extreme, as $A_x A_p/\lambda \to 0$ shocks to output (starting

---

[23] Macroeconomists have become used to thinking of saddle point *stability*. Unlike in models with rational expectations, however, neither Y not x is a jump variable that seeks out the stable saddle path. If initial values of Y and x are assigned randomly, the probability of hitting the stable saddle path is zero.

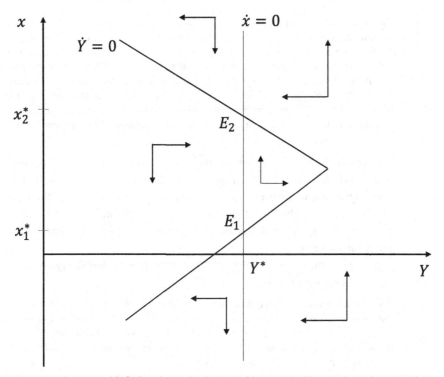

Figure 8.9 Output and inflation dynamics in the Tobin model with a Taylor rule and a ZLB.

from E_2) cannot produce instability, while shocks to inflation expectations only lead to instability, if they reduce inflation below x_1^*.

The extended 2D system abandons instantaneous interest rate effects on output in favor of a more realistic specification. As in the 1D system, the ZLB can lead to instability, but the 2D system reinforces and amplifies the case against wage flexibility: The condition for local stability may be independent of the degree of wage flexibility, but faster adjustment of wages and prices imply that even small shocks can activate the ZLB and lead to downward divergence.

Fortunately, as Keynes suggested – and as argued in Chapter 6 – there may be significant downward money-wage stickiness. Without it, the aftermath of the financial crisis of 2008 could have been much worse.

8.6   Conclusion

Involuntary unemployment in Keynes's sense denotes unemployment that exceeds the voluntary level (or 'full employment,' for short). Voluntary unemployment, however, was defined to include frictional unemployment as well as unemployment caused by legislation – high minimum wages, for instance – or by labor unions' demands for high wages. His definition emphatically was not based on an 'individual experiment,' as implied by Lucas (1981, p. 242):

The worker who loses a job in prosperous times does not *volunteer* to be in this situation: he has suffered a capital loss. Similarly, the firm which loses an experienced employee in depressed times suffers an undesired capital loss. Nevertheless, the unemployed worker at any time can always find *some* job at once, and a firm can always fill a vacancy instantaneously. That neither typically does so *by choice* is not difficult to understand given the quality of the jobs and the employees which are easiest to find. Thus there is an involuntary element in *all* unemployment in the sense that no one chooses bad luck over good; there is also a voluntary element in all unemployment, in the sense that however miserable one's current work options, one can always choose to accept them.

Lucas's observations are simply irrelevant. Keynes is not making an argument about the good or bad luck of individual workers. His argument is about the determination of the aggregate number of jobs, not about comparisons between the utility of those who do and those who do not have a job. Keynes's claim is that full employment may not be stable and that involuntary unemployment can be persistent in the absence of policy intervention.

Keynes, in the words of Tobin (1975, p. 195), made a double argument about money wages and unemployment:

One was that wage rates were very slow to decline in the face of excess supply. The other was that, even if they declined faster, employment would not – in depression circumstances – increase.... The real issue is not the existence of a long-run static equilibrium with unemployment, but the possibility of protracted unemployment which the natural adjustments of a market economy remedy very slowly if at all.

The analysis in Chapter 19 of the effects of changes in money wages was informal and sketchy. But the logic is sound: Stability is not guaranteed, and the likely scenario is one of instability. We may be better off with sticky money wages.

Neither Keynes's exposition nor formalizations like Tobin's employ a Walrasian auctioneer. But the primary conclusion – the likely instability of full employment – has a clear parallel in the work by Sonnenschein, Debreu, and Mantel in the 1970s on Walrasian general equilibrium. Microeconomic optimization imposes very few restrictions on the shape of aggregate excess demand functions (which makes it impossible, in general, to construct a representative agent, as discussed in Chapter 2), and without constraints on aggregate excess demand functions, the stability of a general equilibrium position cannot be established. In the simple example of aggregation problems in Section 2.3, the aggregate excess demand for good i was an increasing function of the relative price of good i. Hence, if prices adjust in the normal way to excess demand, the Walrasian equilibrium becomes unstable. The conditions for a general equilibrium to exist may be relatively weak, but uniqueness and stability of the equilibrium can only be established under highly restrictive assumptions.

For all its mathematical sophistication, most of contemporary macroeconomics has ignored this insight and remains stuck in a pre-Keynesian and pre-Debreu/Sonnenschein/Mantel time warp of presumed stability, one in which there would be no need for aggregate demand policy if only wages and prices were flexible.

Appendix A: Tobin's 3D System

Tobin's 'WKP' system is given by

$$\dot{Y} = A_Y(E - Y)$$
$$\dot{p} = p\left[A_p(Y - Y^*) + x\right]$$
$$\dot{x} = A_x(\hat{p} - x).$$

The Jacobian can be written

$$J(Y,p,x) = \begin{pmatrix} A_Y(E_1 - 1) & A_Y E_2 & A_Y E_3 \\ p A_p & 0 & p \\ A_x A_p & 0 & 0 \end{pmatrix}.$$

The stability conditions require (see Chapter 4, Appendix A) that

$$tr(J) = A_Y(E_1 - 1) < 0$$
$$\det(J) = A_X A_p A_Y E_2 p < 0$$
$$\det(J_1) + \det(J_2) + \det(J_3) = -A_p A_Y(pE_2 + A_x E_3) > 0$$
$$-tr(J)[\det(J_1) + \det(J_2) + \det(J_3)] + \det(J) = A_Y(E_1 - 1)A_p A_Y(pE_2 + A_x E_3)$$
$$+ A_X A_p A_Y E_2 p > 0.$$

The first two conditions are always satisfied. Tobin did not present and analyze the full set of stability conditions for the 3D system. Instead, he focused on the third condition, which is necessary but not sufficient; this third condition is also a necessary condition for stability in the 2D system. In the 3D system, however, the fourth condition need not hold, even if the first three are satisfied.

9   Growth and Cycles

9.1   Introduction

Shocks to aggregate demand have real effects on output and employment in the short run, but most of contemporary macroeconomics takes the view that the influence of demand – brought about by menu costs and sticky prices – disappears in the long run. Wages and prices become able to adjust as the time frame is extended, and it is presumed that in the absence of stochastic shocks the economy would converge to a growth path without Keynesian involuntary unemployment: Medium and long run outcomes are seen as determined by the supply side.

The short-run analysis in Chapter 8 challenged the faith in the stability of full employment. Broadening the analysis, the work of Harrod (1939) and Domar (1946) identified aggregate demand as an important determinant of the growth process. Harrod explicitly described his aim as one of extending the Keynesian revolution to the medium and long run. His analysis produced two startling conclusions: It suggested, first, that market economies may lack a reliable mechanism to permit sustained growth with full employment (the 'warranted growth rate' may deviate from the 'natural rate'), and, second, that the steady growth path (the warranted path) was likely to be unstable.

Many economies follow cyclical trajectories, but with fluctuations around a growth path with (near-) full employment. This observation may seem to contradict Harrod's conclusions, suggesting that his analysis can be safely dismissed – a view that is perhaps held by most economists. This and the following two chapters present a case against dismissal. Goods markets are likely to be (locally) unstable, and the reconciliation of warranted and natural growth rates in mainstream macroeconomics has serious weaknesses. Harrod identified problems that are intrinsic to capitalist economies and, recognizing these problems opens promising avenues for a very different theory of the dynamics of capitalist economies.

Section 9.2 outlines a streamlined version of Harrod's analysis, along with Solow's solution to Harrod's first problem. The Solow solution, the neoclassical production function and the Cambridge capital controversy are discussed in Section 9.3. Section 9.4 outlines an alternative solution that does not rely upon smooth substitution along a neoclassical production function. Section 9.5 turns to Harrod's second problem, discussing how local instability of the steady growth path can be converted to bounded fluctuations and produce endogenous growth cycles. Section 9.6 offers a few concluding remarks.

9.2 Harrod's Problems and the Solow Solution

9.2.1 A Harrodian Benchmark Model

Consider a closed, one-sector economy without a public sector and assume that the production function is Leontief with A and $\sigma^{\max}$ as the technical coefficients,

$$Y = \min\{AL, \sigma^{\max}K\}. \tag{9.1}$$

Employment, L, is measured in effective units (incorporating labor saving technical change), and both A and $\sigma^{\max}$ are constant. The utilization rate of capital exhibits substantial cyclical fluctuations. Firms, however, adjust their investment decisions decisions in response to persistent deviations of utilization rates from the rates that they consider optimal, and as a first approximation we may assume that in steady growth capital will be utilized at the desired rate. Formally,

$$\frac{Y}{K} = u^* \sigma^{\max} \tag{9.2}$$

$$\frac{Y}{L} = A, \tag{9.3}$$

where u^* is firms' desired rate of utilization of capital. The labor supply in effective units is denoted by N, and its growth rate – the 'natural rate of growth' – is taken to be exogenous,

$$\hat{N} = n. \tag{9.4}$$

A linear saving function, an equilibrium condition for the goods market and an accounting equation for the evolution of the capital stock complete this Harrodian benchmark model:

$$S = sY \tag{9.5}$$

$$I = S \tag{9.6}$$

$$\dot{K} = I - \delta K. \tag{9.7}$$

Equations (9.2)–(9.3) and (9.5)–(9.7) imply that

$$\hat{Y} = \hat{L} = \hat{K} = s\sigma^{\max}u^* - \delta = g_w. \tag{9.8}$$

This growth rate is the warranted rate of growth. It is warranted because of the consistency between expectations and outcomes: If firms invest at the rate $\hat{K} = g_w$ then, taking into account the multiplier effects of investment on output, they will achieve the desired rate of utilization of capital, u^*. Idiosyncratic, firm-level shocks imply that not all firms will be at their desired rates, but the investment decisions will turn out to have been warranted for the average firm.

This simple framework gives rise to two observations. If the natural rate of growth n and the values of $s, \sigma^{\max}$, and u^* are exogenously given, there is no reason to expect equality between the warranted and natural rates; only by a fluke will it be possible for a pure capitalist economy to follow a steady growth path with full employment. Second, the warranted growth path is likely to be unstable. The utilization rate u must satisfy the equilibrium condition (9.6), and if investment is predetermined at each moment, we have

$$u = \frac{\hat{K} + \delta}{s\sigma^{\max}}. \tag{9.9}$$

The right-hand side of Equation (9.9) is increasing in the accumulation rate. It follows that utilization will exceed the desired rate if for some reason $\hat{K} > g_w$. Faced with a shortage of capital, firms will tend to increase their investment, but a rise in $\hat{K}$ aggravates the problem: It causes the rate of utilization to increase further.

Simple formalizations of this instability argument relate changes in the accumulation rate to deviations of actual from desired utilization,

$$\frac{d\hat{K}}{dt} = \lambda_{\hat{K}}(u - u^*).$$

Using Equation (9.9) to substitute for u, the change in accumulation can be written

$$\frac{d\hat{K}}{dt} = \lambda_{\hat{K}}\left(\frac{\hat{K} + \delta}{s\sigma^{\max}} - u^*\right).$$

This differential equation has a unique stationary solution (the warranted growth rate) at $\hat{K}^* = s\sigma^{\max}u^* - \delta$. The solution is unstable, however.

9.2.2   The Solow Solution

Solow (1956) addressed Harrod's first problem, the reconciliation of warranted and natural growth rates. The equality between the two rates requires that

$$s\sigma u^* = n + \delta. \tag{9.10}$$

The five terms in Equation (9.10) cannot be set independently; at least one of them must be allowed to adjust to satisfy the equation.

Solow singled out Harrod's "crucial assumption that production takes place under conditions of fixed proportions" (Solow 1956, p. 65). Instead of imposing a fixed maximum output capital ratio, Equation (9.10) can be used to determine the value of the technical coefficient σ that is consistent with the equalization of natural and warranted growth rates. The existence of this growth path is ensured if the range of possible output capital ratios is sufficiently wide.

Merely solving for σ does not establish that the economy will converge to a steady growth path with a constant employment rate. Solow examined this dynamic issue, but the analysis is conducted under very restrictive conditions. Harrod had set out to examine whether a capitalist market economy would be likely to converge toward a steady growth path with full employment. Solow, by contrast, addressed a more limited question. He assumed that "full employment is perpetually maintained" (p. 67) and that there is also "full employment of the available stock of capital" (p. 68). He then went on to show that it was possible to construct a logically consistent story in which these assumptions were satisfied and that, if they are satisfied and the natural rate of growth is constant, then the economy may converge to a steady growth path, starting from arbitrary initial values of the labor supply and the stock of capital.

These results can be derived without any reference to markets and prices. If the production function, $Y = F(K,L)$, exhibits constant returns to scale and positive but diminishing marginal products, we have

$$y = F\left(\frac{K}{L}, 1\right) = f(k); \quad f' > 0, f'' < 0, \tag{9.11}$$

where $y = Y/L$ and $k = K/L$ denote output and capital per unit of effective labor, and f is the intensive form of the production function. The full-employment assumptions $(L = N)$ in combination with Equations (9.5)–(9.7), (9.4), and (9.11) imply the following dynamics for k

$$\dot{k} = k(\hat{K} - \hat{L}) = k\left(\frac{sY/L}{K/L} - \delta - n\right) = sf(k) - (n + \delta)k.$$

Because of the strict concavity of the f-function, this differential equation has at most one stationary solution with $0 < k < \infty$, and this solution k^*, if it exists, will be stable. The existence of the solution k^*, moreover, is guaranteed if the production function satisfies the Inada conditions: $\lim_{k \to 0} f'(k) = \infty, \lim_{k \to \infty} f'(k) = 0$. Under these conditions, starting from any positive values of N and K, the trajectory of k must converge to k^*.

It is worth noting that the Inada conditions are restrictive; they fail to be met, for instance, for all CES production functions, with the exception of the Cobb–Douglas case. The dynamics may imply $k \to 0$ if the elasticity of substitution is below 1, while in cases with high substitution elasticities and high saving rates, the system may become so productive and save so much that "perpetual full employment will increase the capital–labor ratio (and also output per head) beyond all limits" (p. 72). In the latter case an increase in the saving rate raises the long-run growth rate; the model produces endogenous growth.

As Solow points out, the irrelevance of factor prices for the derivation means that these growth paths "have no causal significance but simply indicate the course that capital accumulation and real output would have to take if neither unemployment nor excess capacity are to appear" (p. 78). Having determined the full employment trajectories for Y, K, and L, however, it is possible to derive the factor prices that must rule in order for the trajectories to be consistent with competitive markets.[1] By assumption, the supplies of capital and labor are completely inelastic, and if the production function is differentiable, profit maximizing firms hire factors of production up to the point where the value of the marginal product equals the price of the services of the factor. These first order conditions for profit maximization under perfect competition pin

---

[1] Solow puts it slightly differently, saying that "we can ask what kind of market behavior will cause the model economy to follow the path of equilibrium growth" (p. 78). This wording is inaccurate, however. The paper derives necessary conditions for the trajectories to be consistent with perfect competition, which is different from the much more demanding analysis of the kind of market behavior that would actually bring about the full employment trajectories. The latter question raises stability issues of the kind discussed in Chapters 2 and 8.

down the real wage and the rental price of capital: In a competitive market economy, full employment requires that the real wage rate and price of capital services satisfy the conditions $F_1(K, N) = r + \delta$ and $F_2(K, N) = w$.

The analysis leads Solow to conclude that "when production takes place under the usual neoclassical conditions of variable proportions and constant returns to scale, no simple opposition between natural and warranted rates of growth is possible" (p. 73). The warranted rate depends on the capital intensity σ, and Harrod's first problem may disappear when σ is variable. But Solow is also quite clear about the limitations of his analysis. It represents

the neoclassical side of the coin. Most especially it is full employment economics – in the dual aspect of equilibrium condition and frictionless, competitive, causal system. All the difficulties and rigidities which go into modern Keynesian income analysis have been shunted aside. It is not my contention that these problems don't exist, nor that they of no significance in the long run. My purpose was to examine what might be called the tightrope view of economic growth and to see where more flexible assumptions about production would lead a simple model. (p. 91)

He goes on to mention some Keynesian obstacles to full employment growth, including rigid wages and liquidity preference, and ends the paper by commenting on uncertainty (pp. 93–94):

No credible theory of investment can be built on the assumption of perfect foresight and arbitrage over time. There are only too many reasons why net investment should be at times insensitive to current changes in the real return to capital, at other times oversensitive. All these cobwebs and some others have been brushed aside throughout this essay. In the context, this is perhaps justifiable.

The profession has paid little or no attention to these qualifications. There has been virtually universal acceptance within mainstream economics that this neoclassical mechanism of adjustment provides a resolution of the issues raised by Harrod. Even if we disregard the Keynesian obstacles, however, the mechanism behind the adjustment of the warranted to the natural rate of growth invites other questions.

9.3   The Neoclassical Production Function

The neoclassical aggregate production function is ubiquitous in macroeconomic models. Solid microeconomic foundations, Robert Lucas argued, requires the specification of preferences and technological constraints, with the technology almost invariably taking the form of a neoclassical production function. But this production function is far from providing an incontestably solid foundation, empirically or analytically. The issues have been analyzed thoroughly in a voluminous literature and should be well known. Yet, they seem to have been forgotten or simply brushed under the rug; textbooks introduce the production function and the standard assumptions that go with it, but raise no questions about the justifications for this approach. The overview of the issues here is structured under three headings: The choice of technique, aggregation and the capital controversy, and empirical evidence.

9.3.1   The Choice of Technique and the Elasticity of Substitution

Capital intensity reflects firms' choice of technique, with factor prices playing a key role in the decisions of profit maximizing firms. Suppose that firms can choose from a range of blueprints when they make an investment decision but that *ex post* – once an investment has been made in particular plant and machinery – the substitutability becomes limited and complementarity becomes a useful first approximation. Thus, while capital intensity could be quite flexible in the long run, the capital stock and with it the technique embodied in this capital stock are largely predetermined in the short run.

Putting to one side the thorny aggregation problems, suppose that meaningful aggregate measures of capital, labor and output can be found and, for simplicity, that the *ex ante* production function is Cobb–Douglas,

$$Y = K^\alpha L^{1-\alpha}; \quad 0 < \alpha < 1.$$

Profit maximizing firms minimize cost. If we are interested in the long-run outcomes and confine attention to steady growth paths, the real rate of interest and relative input costs are constant. The minimization problem becomes static and can be written:

$$\min_{L,K} \frac{w}{p}L + (r + \delta)K$$

$$s.t. \quad (u^* K)^\alpha L^{1-\alpha} = Y,$$

where w, p, r, and δ denote the money wage rate, the price of capital goods, the cost of finance (the real rate of interest) and the rate of depreciation

Firms typically wish to maintain a certain amount of excess capacity on average, and the constraint in the minimization problem allows for the desired utilization rate of capital (u^*) to be less than one. The first order conditions imply that[2]

$$\frac{Y}{L} = \left(\frac{u^*}{r + \delta} \frac{\alpha}{1 - \alpha} \frac{w}{p} \right)^\alpha \tag{9.12}$$

$$\frac{Y}{u^* K} = \left(\frac{Y}{L} \right)^{-(1-\alpha)/\alpha} = \left(\frac{u^*}{r + \delta} \frac{\alpha}{1 - \alpha} \frac{w}{p} \right)^{-(1-\alpha)}. \tag{9.13}$$

The price of capital goods, p, is exogenous to the individual firm (and was treated as such in the minimization). In a one-good model, however, this price must be equal to the general price level. Assuming profit maximization, the pricing decision is based on marginal cost, and both the technical coefficients and the stock of capital are predetermined in the short run. Employment and output, by contrast, are taken to be variable. With excess capital capacity and constant labor productivity, this yields a markup on unit labor cost,

$$p = (1 + m)\frac{wL}{Y}, \tag{9.14}$$

---

[2] The derivation of Equations (9.12) and (9.13) is based on an *ex ante* Cobb–Douglas production function. The argument is quite general, however, and the general conclusion does not even depend on the existence of a smooth neoclassical production function. The choice of technique will depend on input prices.

where the markup (m) is determined by the perceived elasticity of demand, which is taken to be constant.

Combining Equations (9.12)–(9.14), we have

$$\frac{Y}{L} = \left(\frac{\alpha}{1-\alpha}\frac{u^*}{r+\delta}\frac{1}{1+m}\right)^{\alpha/(1-\alpha)}$$

$$\frac{Y}{u^*K} = \frac{1-\alpha}{\alpha}\frac{r+\delta}{u^*}(1+m).$$

Thus, the choice of technique is fully determined by the cost of finance, r. Intuitively, cost minimization produces one relation between labor productivity and the real wage (for given r); pricing decisions give another relation. In equilibrium these two relations – Equations (9.12) and (9.14) – must be mutually consistent. This consistency requirement pins down the real wage and the capital intensity (the cost-minimizing input coefficients) for any given interest rate. The real wage is endogenous but does not adjust to clear the labour market; movements in the money wage generate proportional movements in the price level.

The equalization of natural and warranted growth rates could in principle be accomplished through changes in the interest rate. But as argued in Chapter 8, it is not obvious that market forces will ensure the appropriate adjustment of the real interest rate. Monetary policy could perhaps do the trick, but discussing the effects of interest rates, Harrod suggests that "the rate of interest and the MARC [the minimum acceptable rate of return on capital] do not often have a big effect on the method chosen" and that an attempt to derive a rate of interest "which brought the warranted growth rate into equality with the natural growth rate ... really makes no sense" (Harrod 1973, pp. 172–3).

One can debate Harrod's empirical assessment that interest rates have small effects on the capital intensity of production (empirical estimates of aggregate production functions will be discussed below). The second part of his claim is straightforward, however: His qualitative conclusions do not depend on a knife-edge assumption of fixed coefficients. The strict Leontief assumption can be relaxed. There are smooth production functions for which the marginal product of capital becomes zero when k exceeds some threshold $k_{\max} < \infty$, while the marginal product of labor falls to zero when k is below a threshold $k_{min} < k_{max}$. The range of k–values with positive marginal products translates into a range of warranted growth rates. If the range is large, the neoclassical conclusion holds sway (the possibility that Solow highlighted, p. 76). If the range between k_{min} and k_{max} is narrow, conversely, a Leontief production function will provide a good approximation; in fact, Solow briefly notes this possibility.

The case for a narrow range of relevant k – values can be strengthened by observing that workers need to eat and that no investment will take place if the rate of return on capital falls too low. Thus, there are lower limits on the real wage and the rate of return, $w/p \geq (w/p)_{\min} > 0$ and $r \geq r_{\min} > 0$. These limits imply that all CES production functions with an elasticity of substitution below one produce a finite range of permissible k – values. If the elasticity of substitution is low and/or the lower limits $(w/p)_{\min}$ and $r_{\min}$ are high, then, as Harrod suggested, it "really makes no sense" to view the interest rate and the choice of technique as a mechanism to equalize the warranted and natural growth rates.

9.3.2   Aggregation and the Cambridge Capital Controversy

The aggregate capital stock K consists of a large bundle of buildings, machinery and other equipment.[3] This bundle cannot be seen as a random collection of capital goods: Production functions supposedly show the maximum level of output that can be produced from any given set of inputs. If more workers become available, the composition of the capital stock must be adjusted: The capital intensity and the efficient composition of the capital stock are jointly determined. The incentives to change techniques, moreover, come from changes in the prices of inputs and factors of production, and any such price changes affect the relative prices of all produced goods, including investment goods. These price effects complicate the construction of a measure of aggregate capital.

Theories simplify, and macroeconomic theory inevitably uses aggregates. Aggregation problems may impose limitations, however, on the uses that can be – or, at least, should be – made of the aggregates. The measurement of aggregate (real) output and aggregate employment also raises problems, but aggregation of capital is particularly thorny, both theoretically and in practice, and the Cambridge capital controversy focused on the use of aggregate capital as an argument in the production function.

Joan Robinson (1953–54) fired the opening shot of the controversy when she posed a simple question concerning the units in which real capital is measured.[4] Capital goods are heterogeneous, and buildings, desks, computers and industrial robots cannot be added in physical units. Aggregation requires that capital goods be measured in a common unit, and using prices as weights would seem the most obvious solution. But the dependence of prices on factor prices has implications for the relation between interest rates and capital intensity.

The neoclassical production function implies that the marginal product of capital (the slope of the intensive production function) gradually falls as the capital–labor ratio k increases and we move up the intensive production function; an increase in capital intensity is invariably associated with a decline in the real interest rate (the return on capital). In a world with heterogeneous capital goods, however, there can be no general presumption of an inverse relation between rates of return and capital intensity. In fact, the same technique may even be profit maximizing both at low and high rates of interest but not for intermediate interest rates. Eventually, this possibility – the 'reswitching of techniques' – was accepted by all participants, as indicated by

---

[3] In the contemporary world it also, to an increasing extent, contains agglomerations of legal claims in the form of intellectual property rights.

[4] See Harcourt (1972), Cohen and Harcourt (2003), and Felipe and Fisher (2003) for surveys of the capital controversy and aggregation in production functions. Some of the key contributions have been collected in Harcourt and Laing (1971). Avoiding aggregation, Kurz and Salvadori (1995) analyze long-period equilibria in economies with multiple goods and a linear technology.

Figure 9.1 Samuelson's champagne example.

the contributions in a symposium in the *Quarterly Journal of Economics* (November 1966).

In the symposium's last paper, appropriately entitled "A Summing Up," Samuelson (1966) presented a useful example that captures the intuition behind reswitching. In his example two different techniques can be used to produce champagne. Technique A requires 7 units of labor to make 1 unit of brandy in one period; the brandy then turns into champagne in one more period. Technique B requires the application of 2 units of labor to make 1 unit of grape juice in one period; the grape juice turns into wine when left by itself for another period, and at this time 6 units of labor are needed to turn the wine into champagne in one period. Figure 9.1 illustrates the two techniques with labor inputs below the time axis and champagne output above.

If the wage rate w and the interest rate i are constant, the costs of producing 1 unit of champagne using the two techniques are

$$c_A = 7w(1 + i)^2$$
$$c_B = 2w(1 + i)^3 + 6w(1 + i).$$

These cost equations imply that

$$c_A > c_B \text{ for } 0.5 < i < 1$$
$$c_A < c_B \text{ for } i < 0.5 \text{ or } i > 1.$$

It follows that a profit maximizing firm will choose technique B if the interest rate falls in the interval between 0.5 and 1, while technique A will be preferred at interest rates below 0.5 as well as for rates above 1. Thus, we have a case of reswitching of techniques.

To evaluate the dependence of capital intensity in value terms on the interest rate, consider a firm producing 1 unit of champagne every period. The firm will have wage costs of $7w$ and $8w$ per period if it uses technique A and B, respectively, and it will carry stocks of intermediate goods, brandy if it uses technique A and grape juice and wine if it uses technique B. The values of these stocks are $7w(1+i)$ and $2w[(1+i)+(1+i)^2]$ for A and B. For $i < 0.5$ or $i > 1$ the price of output is $7w(1 + i)^2$, and the capital output ratio is $7w(1+i)/[7w(1+i)^2] = 1/(1+i)$ which is monotonically decreasing in i.[5] Analogously, for $0.5 < i < 1$ the capital output ratio is $2w[(1+i)+(1+i)^2]/[2w(1+i)^3 + 6w(1 + i)] = (2 + i)/[3 + (1 + i)^2]$ which is also monotonically decreasing in

---

[5] The beauty of the example is its simplicity. Part of the simplicity comes from having inventories of intermediate goods as the only form of capital; neither of the techniques requires fixed capital with a

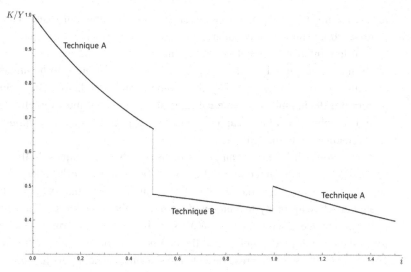

Figure 9.2 Capital output ratios in Samuelson's example.

i in the relevant range with $i > 0$. The techniques have the same costs and prices at the two switch points, where both techniques may be in use. Thus, at these points the capital output ratio in value terms can be anywhere between $(2 + i)/[3 + (1 + i)^2]$ and $1/(1 + i)$; these intervals are $\left(\frac{10}{21}, \frac{2}{3}\right)$ for $i = 0.5$ and $\left(\frac{3}{7}, \frac{1}{2}\right)$ for $i = 1$.

Putting it all together, Figure 9.2 shows the relation between the interest rate and the capital output ratio: As i increases, the capital output ratio declines continuously for $i < 0.5$; can take any value between $10/21$ and $2/3$ at $i = 0.5$; declines monotonically for $0.5 < i < 1$; can take any value between $3/7$ and $1/2$ at $i = 1$; declines again for $i > 1$. But capital intensity in value terms increases as i changes from just below $i = 1$ to just above: At $i = 1$ there is reverse capital deepening, in this case associated with reswitching of techniques. Reswitching must produce reverse capital deepening, but reverse deepening can also arise without the recurrence of the same technique at low and high interest rates.

The seemingly paradoxical possibility of reverse capital deepening derives from the fact that changes in the interest rate affect the relative prices of the different capital goods and output (in this example brandy, grape juice, wine and champagne). Samuelson's example is simple, but the main point is general: Measures of the capital output ratio that use relative prices as weights will be influenced by changes in these weights, which creates the possibility of reverse capital deepening.

Could it not be objected that price changes have no place in a production function, which is meant to describe a purely technical relationship between inputs and outputs? One might think that some other measure of aggregate capital could be constructed to

---

depreciation rate below 1. The reswitching result, however, carries over to the more general setting, as shown by Pasinetti (1966) and Morishima (1966) in the same QJE symposium.

restore the inverse relation between interest rates and capital intensity. The possibility of reswitching shows that this is not the case. In the example technique B is preferred to A at low interest rates but not at intermediate rates, and the candidate for a 'correctly measured capital intensity' of technique A would need to be higher than that of technique B in order to satisfy the standard inverse relation. But technique A is preferred to technique B for interest rates above 1, and it must therefore also be the case that technique A has a capital intensity that is below that of technique B. These requirements are mutually inconsistent.

Samuelson's illustrative example contains only two techniques. In the neoclassical production function, by contrast, there is a continuum of techniques which is what supposedly ensures the smoothness of the function. But the example also demonstrates that having many techniques does not imply smoothness: The capital output ratio can change discontinuously at all switch points. Furthermore, the heterogeneity of the capital goods implies that the composition of the optimal bundle of capital goods changes as the interest rate changes from just below to just above a switch point: "Two techniques may well be as near as one likes on the scale of variation of the rate of profit and yet the physical goods they require may be completely different" (Pasinetti 1969, p. 523). As a corollary, even if one were to accept a smooth production function, this function will depict the set of possible stationary positions. Moving from one point on the function to a point with a marginally higher capital intensity need not be a matter of investing a small amount, thereby incrementally adding some new capital goods to the existing capital stock: The marginally higher capital intensity may well be associated with an entirely different bundle of physical capital goods.

In a neoclassical production function, capital takes the form of what Joan Robinson called 'leets' (steel spelled backward):

leets, though all made of one physical substance, is endowed with the capacity to embody various techniques of production - different ratios of leets to labour - and a change of technique can be made simply by squeezing up or spreading out leets, instantaneously and without cost.... Nine spades are a lump of leets; when the tenth man turns up it is squeezed out to provide him with a share of equipment nine-tenths of what each man had before. (Robinson 1970, p. 312)

Everyone accepts that this story should not be taken literally. Charles Ferguson, a staunch defender of the neoclassical approach, concedes that

To be sure we live in a living present in which there are fixed proportions or very limited factor substitutability, discontinuous marginal product functions, and all sorts of price rigidities and market imperfections. (Ferguson 1971, p. 253)

He goes on, however, to express his faith that

In the long run I believe that the leets-labour-leets world of investment decisions made in light of known or expected factor prices is an adequate characterization of the economy. (Ferguson 1971, p. 254)

For Ferguson and most economists who have addressed the issues raised by the capital controversy, the ultimate theoretical response invokes Walrasian general equilibrium systems. These systems do not require any aggregation and are, it is argued, immune to the problems raised by the capital controversy.[6] But Walrasian general equilibrium systems provide a poor description of the dynamics of capitalist economies. Even proving the stability of a static Walrasian general equilibrium using fictional tatonnement processes comes up against difficulties (as discussed in Chapter 2 above).

A defense along these lines also comes up against what became Joan Robinson's main criticism: The real source of trouble in the neoclassical analysis of growth, she argued, "is the confusion between comparisons of equilibrium positions and the history of a process of accumulation" (Robinson 1974a, p. 9). References to general equilibrium simply evade the problem that "a change in demand ruptures the equilibrium, disappoints expectations – some for the better and some for the worse – and requires investment in one kind of stock and disinvestment in others" (Robinson 1978, p. 123). The production function is a 'pseudo production function,' and

Each point on a pseudo-production function is intended to represent a possible position of equilibrium. Time, so to say, is at right angles to the blackboard on which the curve is drawn. At each point an economy is conceived to be moving from the past into the future with the rate of profit and the technique of production shown at that point. (Robinson 1971, p. 255)

At the very least, an appeal to general equilibrium systems as a depiction of capitalist economies undergoing technical change and cyclical fluctuations would need to consider a sequence of temporary equilibria – not an easy task, and one that has not been seriously attempted.[7] Strong faith is needed for this belief in a non–existent theory of a sequence of temporary equilibria to serve as the justification of a macroeconomics centered on a neoclassical aggregate production function.

9.3.3   Pragmatic Defenses and Empirical Evidence

Samuelson concluded his "summing up" by saying that

---

[6] Bliss (1975) lays out the Walrasian response in detail.

[7] A fundamental reason was noted by Hicks (1965) in his analysis of the traverse from one steady state to another. The difficulties were immense, and he concluded that the

analysis which has emerged from our discussion of the Traverse could no doubt be carried further; but I shall not make any serious effort to carry it further in this book. It would evidently be necessary, if we were to elaborate it, to introduce some particular assumptions about investment policy: to assume that businesses, in carrying out their difficult task of adapting an inappropriate capital stock into something more appropriate, will go about that task in some particular way. But it is hard to see what particular assumption of this kind there can be that is especially deserving of study. Even in macroanalysis . . . there are no compelling principles for this function; there, however, it was possible to find some simple rules (capital stock adjustment and so on), the consequences of which it was at least of some interest to work out. Similar exercises could presumably be performed, even with a disaggregated model; but it would be blatantly obvious that they would be no more than exercises. Perhaps this is unduly pessimistic; all I ought to say is that I myself do not see any interesting way of taking this analysis further. (Hicks 1965, p. 201)

Some work on sequences of temporary equilibrium was done after Hicks's comments but very little, if any, after the late 1970s. In his survey of temporary general equilibrium theory, Grandmont (1977, p. 555) notes some progress with respect to pure exchange economies but also comments that the results for production economies are "far less impressive."

If all this causes headaches for those nostalgic for the old-time parables of neoclassical writing, we must remind ourselves that scholars are not born to live an easy existence. We must respect, and appraise, the facts of life. (p. 583)

Yet, today the old-time parables are unquestioned in mainstream macroeconomics.

Insofar as there is any awareness of its theoretical weaknesses, there appears to be a general perception that the neoclassical production function remains a useful tool, that it has empirical support, and that it is safe to ignore the anomalies brought up by the capital controversy. It may be impossible to justify the aggregate production function rigorously but, it is claimed, the production function represents a satisfactory approximation, with applied studies showing that the theory works well empirically. Solow (1966, pp. 1259–1260) expressed this pragmatic and instrumentalist defense explicitly when he explained that

I have never thought of the macroeconomic production function as a rigorously justifiable concept. In my mind it is either an illuminating parable, or else a mere device for handling data, to be used as long as it gives good empirical results, and to be abandoned as it doesn't, or as soon as something better comes along.

The Cobb–Douglas specification has been particularly popular. It is included as part of prominent DSGE models, and there is a widespread belief that it gives a good account of the data. The empirical support for a unit elasticity of substitution is weak, however. Antras (2004, p. 29), for instance, finds that "even for a country, the United States, with a relatively stable labor share, the evidence seems to reject a Cobb–Douglas specification of the aggregate production function."[8] But there is a more fundamental problem: Underlying accounting relations complicate the interpretation of estimated aggregate production functions.

Income (value added) can be split into wages and salaries (labor income) as one category and profits (nonlabor income) as another. If L and K are the chosen measures of employment and the capital stock, national income data on aggregate wage income imply associated measures of the average wage rate w and the average *ex post* gross rate of return on capital r. Thus, we have an accounting relation

$$Y = wL + rK. \tag{9.15}$$

Following Shaikh (1974), log differentiation of Equation (9.15) gives

$$\hat{Y} = \alpha(\hat{w} + \hat{L}) + (1 - \alpha)(\hat{r} + \hat{K})$$
$$= \eta + \alpha\hat{L} + (1 - \alpha)\hat{K},$$

where α is the share of wages in income and $\eta = [\alpha\hat{w} + (1-\alpha)\hat{r}]$ is a weighted average of the growth of the wage rate and the growth of the *ex post* profit rate. If both α and η are constant, this accounting relation implies, after integration, that

$$\log Y = c + \eta t + \alpha \log L + (1 - \alpha) \log K$$

---

[8] See also Sylos Labini (1995) and Felipe (2001). Canora et al. (2015) estimate an elasticity of substitution between capital and labour 0.15–0.18. They also find that using a production function with this low elasticity (instead of a standard Cobb–Douglas specification) leads to a marked improvement in the fit of their DSGE model.

or

$$Y = A_0 e^{\eta t} L^\alpha K^{1-\alpha}. \tag{9.16}$$

The Cobb–Douglas Equation (9.16) has been derived from accounting relations and two assumptions: The constancy of the wage share and the constancy of the weighted growth of the wage rate and the profit rate.

Now suppose that a researcher estimates the following loglinear 'production function'

$$\log Y_t = \beta_0 + \beta_1 t + \beta_2 \log L_t + \beta_3 \log K_t + \varepsilon_t. \tag{9.17}$$

If the constancy assumptions – neither of which has a direct and necessary relation to production functions or profit maximizing behavior – are satisfied, the regression equation includes the accounting equation as a special case, and the researcher will be able to report a perfect fit. The estimated equation, moreover, will show constant returns to scale, and the estimated coefficients on $\log L$ and $\log K$ will match the observed income shares. The researcher, seemingly, has found strong empirical evidence in favor of the neoclassical aggregate production function and the determination of factor prices by marginal productivity. But the accounting relation will always be satisfied, and the constancy assumptions could be satisfied for other reasons; a constant wage share, for instance, would be compatible with a Leontief production function and a constant markup on wage costs.

The accounting relation does not ensure that the regression equation will give a good fit if the constancy assumptions fail to be met.[9] In this case the regression results will depend on the correlations between income shares, weighted growth rates of factor prices, and factor inputs. Shaikh's analysis and the underlying accounting relation demonstrates, however, that estimated aggregate production functions must be interpreted with great care. Getting a good fit does not in itself prove that the equation has identified a technical production function. In fact, we know that it cannot have done so since there is no true aggregate production function. As Fisher (1971) put it, "the conditions under which the production possibilities of a technologically diverse economy can be represented by an aggregate production functions are far too stringent to be believable." If estimated production functions seem to give reasonable results, the explanation therefore must be different.

To examine this question, Fisher ran a number of simulations to explore the aggregation problem. The simulated economy contains a number of firms, each having its own Cobb–Douglas production function defined over labor and capital. Labor is homogeneous and mobile across firms, and all firms produce the same homogeneous output. Capital, by contrast, is firm specific, and the firm-level endowments of capital and their changes over time are exogenous, as are firm-level changes in productivity. Labor is allocated across firms so as to maximize total output. Feeding in parameters for the firm-level production functions as well as trajectories for firm-level capital

---

[9] But by replacing the linear time trend with a more flexible specification of the rate of technical change, Equation (9.17) can match data with variations in the weighted average θ.

stocks and productivity parameters, and adding random shocks, the economy can be simulated to generate paths of aggregate output. An index of aggregate capital is calculated as a weighted average of firm-level capital stocks, using the average rental rates over the period as weights.[10] Regressions are now run on the aggregate data. In general the fitted equations perform well, despite the fact that by construction no aggregate production function exists for this economy. These results lead to the conjectures that

> labor's share is not roughly constant because the diverse technical relationships of modern economies are truly representable by an aggregate Cobb-Douglas but rather that such relationships appear to be representable by an aggregate Cobb-Douglas *because* labor's share happens to be roughly constant. (Fisher 1971, p. 325; italics in original)[11]

The weakness of the empirical defense undermines the pragmatic case for a neoclassical aggregate production function. Thus, there are both theoretical and empirical reasons to reject this function as a core element in the foundation of macroeconomic models.

9.4 Reconciling Warranted and Natural Growth Rates without a Neoclassical Production Function

The aggregate neoclassical production function is asked to carry a very heavy load, given its flimsy foundations: Movements along this production function serve to maintain full employment during the transition to a stable steady growth path and, additionally, marginal products are used to determine factor incomes. One can produce logically consistent models that have these properties, but the assumptions are stringent, and Harrod's problems can be addressed in a different way.

All long-run macroeconomic models contain some kind of production function that links current investment to future capacity. But the Cambridge capital controversy and the literature on aggregation make it preferable to avoid models that rely heavily on movements along a smooth neoclassical production function. A Leontief

---

[10] The simulation experiment focuses on aggregation problems and leaves out some of the issues raised by the capital controversy discussed earlier. Each firm has a smooth production function in capital and labor, and firm-level capital takes the form of 'leets.' Exogenous trajectories of firms' capital endowments imply that several techniques are in use simultaneously and that the rates of return on capital differ among firms. If capital were produced and the production function were to describe the maximum output level for any given capital stock, only one of the techniques would be in use, except at switchpoints, where techniques are equally profitable.

[11] Fisher also comments that

> The development of the CES, for example, began with the observation that wages are an increasing function of output per man and that the function involved can be approximated by one linear in the logarithms. The present results suggest (but only suggest) that the explanation of that wage-output per-man-relationship may not be in the existence of an aggregate CES but rather that the apparent existence of an aggregate CES may be explained by that relationship (Fisher 1971, p. 325).

> The 1971 article does not consider CES production function. A subsequent study, Fisher et al. (1977), analyzes simulations in which the underlying firm-level production functions are CES. Fisher's 1971 conjecture for this case "is neither verified nor disproved" (Fisher et al. 1977, p. 307).

production function represents a simple alternative. It can be seen as a neutral starting point in much the same way that linear functions are often preferred as a benchmark specification if there are no good arguments for introducing nonlinearities.

Using fixed coefficients does not imply a claim that techniques never change, or that measured capital output ratios will fluctuate around a constant level. Exogeneity does not imply constancy; product and process innovation are obvious sources of changes in measured aggregate capital output ratios. Nor does the Leontief specification imply a claim that firms will never change techniques in response to changes in factor prices; the coefficients of the Leontief production may represent the choice of technique associated with some given 'normal interest rate' (cost of capital) around which interest rates fluctuate. The specification reflects our knowledge that capital goods are not leets, that changes in capital intensity typically require completely new physical goods, and that there is no guarantee that a rise in interest rates will lead to lower capital intensity. Exogenous technological change and induced changes in the choice of technique, with ambiguous effects on capital intensity, do not weaken the case for Leontief production functions as a benchmark assumption.

Returning to Harrod's first problem, it may be noted, first, that developing economies have small modern sectors and large reservoirs of underemployment in traditional and informal sectors. Harrod's first problem does not apply in these dual economies: The very process of economic development is characterized by a gradual reduction of underemployment and growth rates above the natural rate. But if capital intensity does not accommodate smoothly, as in the neoclassical model, then some other explanation is needed for the apparent reconciliation of natural and warranted growth in mature economies.

The rich OECD countries may not always have full employment, but employment rates fluctuate around fairly high levels, and these economies would come up against labor constraints if aggregate demand were to expand rapidly – at rates comparable to those achieved during the years of miracle growth in countries like Japan, Korea, and China – over periods lasting more than few years. Large-scale immigration could alleviate labor shortages but would almost certainly run into political constraints, and there are limits on how fast and to what extent these economies would be able to draw new groups into the domestic labor market, through changes in the retirement age, for instance, or increases in women's participation rate. On this reading of the empirical evidence, a full-employment path represents a good approximation to the long-run growth rate in mature economies, with Harrod's analysis seemingly overlooking essential aspects of the growth process.

If the production function has fixed coefficients, endogenous adjustments in the average saving rate become the obvious candidate for the reconciliation of natural and warranted growth in mature economies. DSGE models and the basic Ramsey model that they build upon typically include a smooth aggregate production function, but intertemporal optimization endogenizes the saving rate. Reacting to changes in the rate of return on capital, the optimizing representative household adjusts its saving rate, and the economy converges to full-employment growth, even if the production function has fixed coefficients (see Appendix A). This Ramsey solution is unconvincing

(Chapters 2–3), but there are other reasons for a dependence of the average saving rate upon income distribution (Chapters 3–4): The warranted rate may adjust to the natural rate if endogenous forces generate appropriate movements in the profit share.

9.4.1   A Kaldor–Solow Solution

Regarding steady growth at (near-) full employment as a reasonable approximation for most rich economies, Nicholas Kaldor presented his 'Keynesian' explanation of this stylized fact in Kaldor (1955).[12] Leaving problems of the trade cycle "outside the scope of this paper," he assumed that the natural growth rate "governs the growth rate over longer periods." With a Leontief production function (and the utilization of capital at the desired rate) the share of profits was, Kaldor argued, the accommodating variable behind the equalization of the warranted and natural rates. Formally, if ω denotes the share of wages in income and the saving propensities out of wages and profits are s_w and s_p, the share of wages (ω) must satisfy

$$[s_w\omega + s_p(1 - \omega)]\sigma = n + \delta$$

or

$$\omega = s_p - \frac{n + \delta}{(s_p - s_w)\sigma}.$$

Kaldor (1955) focused on the steady growth path without any discussion of firms' investment decisions and of how the accumulation rate came to be adjusted to the natural rate. The argument merely established that it was possible for the warranted rate to adjust, even if the output capital ratio is exogenously given. Kaldor was quite clear about this limitation, stating that his argument "does not mean that there will be an *inherent* tendency to a smooth rate of growth in a capitalist economy, only that the causes of cyclical movements lie elsewhere – not in the lack of an adjustment mechanism" (p. 232) to equalize natural and warranted rates. This important caveat is similar to Solow's explicit recognition that his model left out all Keynesian problems.

For the reasons brought up by the capital controversy, Kaldor explicitly rejected smooth neoclassical production functions and marginal productivity theory. But it is possible to embed Kaldor's argument in a Solow type framework, replete with marginal productivity theory and dynamic adjustments toward the steady growth path. Suppose, as in the Solow model, that factor prices are equal to marginal products; that labor and capital are supplied inelastically; that output is at the technical maximum (given available factor supplies), and that saving is automatically invested. With a Leontief production function, the marginal product of labor and the wage share are zero when labor is in excess supply, while the gross profit rate will be zero when capital is in excess supply. Thus, the average saving rate will be s_w if $AN < \sigma K$ and s_p if $AN > \sigma K$. It follows that

$$\hat{k} = \hat{K} - n = \begin{cases} s_w AN - (n + \delta) & \text{if} \quad AN < \sigma K \\ s_p\sigma - (n + \delta) & \text{if} \quad AN > \sigma K. \end{cases}$$

---

[12] Kaldor subsequently changed his views on this issue; see Kaldor (1966).

So long as $s_w\sigma < n + \delta < s_p\sigma$, the economy will converge to a steady growth path with full employment and $AN = \sigma K$, $k^* = \frac{A}{\sigma}$.

From this perspective, Kaldor's analysis (which can be extended to cases with a narrow range of feasible capital output ratios; cf. Section 9.3.1) has close affinities with that of Solow, but without a smooth production function and, unlike Solow, with an emphasis on the effects of changes in the distribution of income on aggregate demand.

9.4.2 A Marx–Goodwin Solution

His terminology was different, but Karl Marx discussed the relation between the warranted and natural growth rates in Chapter 25 of *Capital, Vol. 1*, entitled "The general law of capitalist accumulation." Rapid accumulation, he argued, reduces the size of the 'reserve army of labor'; a small reserve army strengthens workers and wages go up, but as the profit share decreases, accumulation falls, and low accumulation implies that the reserve army will be replenished. In Marx's words,

If the quantity of unpaid labour supplied by the working class, and accumulated by the capitalist class, increases so rapidly that its conversion into capital requires an extraordinary addition of paid labour, then wages rise, and, all other circumstances remaining equal, the unpaid labour diminishes in proportion. But as soon as this diminution touches the point at which the surplus labour that nourishes capital is no longer supplied in normal quantity, a reaction sets in: a smaller part of revenue is capitalised, accumulation lags, and the movement of rise in wages receives a check. The rise of wages therefore is confined within limits that not only leave intact the foundations of the capitalistic system, but also secure its reproduction on a progressive scale. (Marx 1867 [1906, p. 680])

The terminology may be unfamiliar, but the basic argument has two elements: Movements in the employment rate are determined by the accumulation of capital, while the employment rate affects income distribution and the rate of accumulation. These forces, Marx suggests, interact in a way that secures the reproduction of the capitalist system. Dynamic interactions can be tricky, however, making it useful to formalize the argument.[13]

A Version with Monotonic Convergence
Marx relates the accumulation rate to profitability, and to simplify the formalization we may assume that workers do not save, while capitalists save and invest a constant proportion of their profits,

$$I = S = s(1 - \omega)Y. \tag{9.18}$$

Now add a fixed coefficient production function with two inputs, labor and capital,

$$Y = \min\{AL, \sigma^{\max}K\}. \tag{9.19}$$

---

[13] Whatever Marx would have thought about the specific formalizations of his argument that have been proposed, he would almost certainly have welcomed the attempts to formalize. He devoted substantial time and effort to the exploration of mathematical techniques and their applications in economics; see Matthews (2021).

If there is no labor hoarding and capital is fully utilized, then

$$\frac{Y}{K} = \sigma^{\max} \tag{9.20}$$

$$L = \frac{1}{A}Y. \tag{9.21}$$

Measuring labor in effective units (so that A is constant), dividing through by K in Equation (9.18) and using Equation (9.20) and (9.21), we have

$$\hat{L} = \hat{Y} = \hat{K} = s(1 - \omega)\sigma^{\max}. \tag{9.22}$$

Wages, Marx argues, increase when high accumulation generates "an extraordinary addition of paid labor"; that is, when the reserve army of unemployed declines and workers' are strengthened in the battle over wages. The employment rate $e = L/N$ can be used as an inverse indicator of the size of the reserve army of labor, and Marx's analysis can be interpreted as positing a positive relation between the employment rate and the real wage per effective unit of labor or, equivalently, a positive relation between the wage share and the employment rate:

$$\omega = f(e); \quad f' > 0. \tag{9.23}$$

Combining Equations (9.22) and (9.23), the dynamics of the employment rate can be written

$$\hat{e} = \hat{L} - \hat{N} = \hat{K} - n = s(1 - f(e))\sigma^{\max} - n, \tag{9.24}$$

where $n = \hat{N}$ is the growth rate of the labor force in effective units. The differential Equation (9.24) has an interior stationary solution with $0 < e < 1$ if $s\sigma^{\max}(1 - f(0)) > n > s\sigma^{\max}(1 - f(1))$. These plausible conditions require that when workers' power is very weak ($e \to 0$), a low wage share ensures accumulation rates that exceed the natural rate of growth, while strong workers and low profitability ($e \to 1$) cause accumulation to fall below the natural rate. If the inequalities are satisfied, the employment rate converges to the interior stationary point,

$$e \to e^* = f^{-1}\left(1 - \frac{n}{s\sigma^{\max}}\right).$$

An endogenous distribution of income serves to align the warranted and natural rates. The convergence process is analogous to that in the Kaldor–Solow model but with a difference: The Marx version does not have an inelastic supply of labor, and marginal productivities do not determine factor prices. Instead, the wage share is determined by wage bargaining, or using Marxian terminology, by the balance of power in the class struggle between capital and labor.

A Version with Cycles

Monotonic convergence to steady growth is not a prediction usually associated with Karl Marx, and a minor modification of the model produces a very different outcome. Equation (9.23) stipulated a positive relation between the level of the employment rate and the level of the wage share. It may be more reasonable – and arguably also a more accurate interpretation of Marx's verbal argument – to view the level of employment as determining the growth rate of the wage share: Workers finding themselves in a relatively strong position will fight for and obtain *increases* in wages.

On this interpretation, Equation (9.23) must be replaced by a dynamic version,

$$\hat{\omega} = f(e); \quad f' > 0. \tag{9.25}$$

Goodwin (1967) used this specification in a formalization of Marx's general law of accumulation that has become the workhorse for numerous contributions in post-Keynesian and neo-Marxian macroeconomics.[14] Retaining all other equations and, following Goodwin, using a linear specification of the f–function ($f(e) = -\gamma + \rho e$), the model now yields a 2D system in the two state variables, e and ω:

$$\dot{e} = e[\sigma^{\max} s(1 - \omega) - n]$$
$$\dot{\omega} = \omega[-\gamma + \rho e].$$

If $\gamma < \rho$ and $n < s\sigma^{\max}$, the system has a unique nontrivial stationary solution with $1 > e > 0$ and $1 > \omega > 0$,

$$e^* = \frac{\gamma}{\rho}$$
$$\omega^* = 1 - \frac{n}{s\sigma^{\max}}.$$

Evaluated at the stationary point the Jacobian is given by

$$J(e,\omega) = \begin{pmatrix} 0 & -e^* \sigma^{\max} \\ \omega^* \rho & 0 \end{pmatrix}.$$

The determinant ($\det J = e^* \sigma^{\max} \omega^* \rho$) is unambiguously positive, which rules out saddle points. But the trace is zero, and a local stability analysis leaves the stability properties undetermined.[15] It can be shown, however, that this formalization of Marx's general law of accumulation yields endogenous growth cycles around the stationary point (e^*, ω^*): The system implies closed, counterclockwise loops in (e, ω) space as depicted in the phase diagram in Figure 9.3; see Appendix B for details. Starting from an initial position, the employment rate and the wage share exhibit perpetual fluctuations with a constant amplitude; an exogenous shock that shifts the initial position changes the amplitude of the fluctuations as the system moves to a new closed loop.

---

[14] Goodwin specified a real wage Phillips curve linking the growth rate of the real wage to the employment rate. This curve maps directly into a relation between employment and the growth rate of the wage share if labor productivity grows at a constant rate.

[15] A positive (negative) trace is sufficient for local instability (local stability) when the determinant is positive (Chapter 4, Appendix A). In a nonlinear system, however, a zero trace can be associated with local stability, instability or conservative fluctuations of constant amplitude. The intuition behind this indeterminateness when the trace is zero can be illustrated by a 1D system. Let $\dot{x} = g(x)$ and assume that this differential equation has a stationary point at x_0 ($g(x_0) = 0$). The derivative $g'(x_0)$ is the trace of the 1x1 Jacobian matrix for this 1D system, and it is readily seen that if $g'(x_0) = 0$, the stationary point can be locally stable ($g(x) = -(x - x_0)^3$, for example), unstable ($g(x) = (x - x_0)^3$, for example), or neutrally stable ($g(x) = 0$, for example).

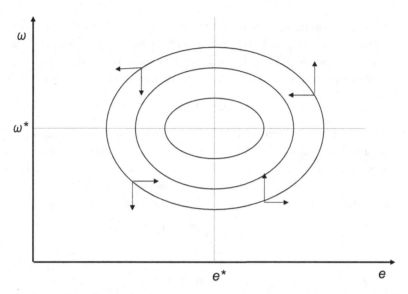

Figure 9.3 Phase diagram for the Goodwin model.

The stationary value of the employment rate is determined by the parameters of the distributive function (the exogenous elements of relative power), while the natural rate of growth and the parameters of the accumulation function (capitalists' saving rate and the output capital ratio) determine the wage share. Intuitively, if workers get stronger and more militant for any given employment rate, an increase in the reserve army will be needed to restore discipline in the labor market and prevent an ever-increasing wage share. Analogously, changes in the saving rate, the technical output-capital ratio or the growth rate of the labor force in effective units require adjustments in the wage share in order to maintain the equality between the rate of accumulation and the natural growth rates.

The Goodwin model depicts a capitalist economy that creates cyclical fluctuations endogenously, and in which homeostatic forces imply that the rise of wages "is confined within limits that not only leave intact the foundations of the capitalistic system, but also secure its reproduction on a progressive scale," in Marx's words. Elegant as it is, the model is not without shortcomings: It fails to capture essential features of the business cycle. Output is determined by capacity (as in the Solow model), and with fixed coefficients and unemployment, capital is the binding constraint: Capital is fully utilized at all times. This is not what we see in the data. Empirically, utilization rates exhibit large and systematic fluctuations over the cycle (Figure 9.4).

The source of these failures of the Goodwin model is the absence of Keynesian features. There is no separate investment function, full-capacity saving automatically gets invested, and aggregate demand problems never constrain output below full capacity. Related to this lack of attention to aggregate demand, the real wage is determined directly in the labor market. There is no discussion of firms' price setting; nor is there room for the issues that occupied Keynes in Chapter 19 of the *General Theory* and led him to reject self-correcting changes in real wages and employment. The Goodwin

Figure 9.4 Capacity utilization, US manufacturing (SIC). Data source: The Federal Reserve.

model essentially describes endogenous fluctuations in a Marxian version of a model with a time-varying natural rate of unemployment.[16]

9.5 Endogenous and Exogenous Growth Cycles

Business cycle theories can be categorized in different ways. One common distinction concerns the exogeneity or endogeneity of the cycles. In some theories, the fluctuations are caused by external shocks and the cycle, in this sense, is exogenous. The shocks constitute the impulse, and the cyclical pattern is produced by propagation mechanisms that spread out the effects of the impulse. The shocks can in principle be white noise without any persistence if the model contains strong internal propagation mechanisms. If the mechanisms are weak, however, autocorrelated shocks may be needed to produce cyclical patterns in observed variables.

According to the alternative, endogenous approach, external shocks may indeed hit the economy and affect movements in economic activity, but fluctuations would occur even in the absence of shocks. The fluctuations in this sense are created endogenously; the Goodwin cycle exemplifies this approach.

The time-paths of aggregate output and its main components exhibit significant fluctuations, as do other important variables, including employment, productivity, prices, wages and interest rates. The fluctuations are recurrent but not regular. In fact, the delineation of cycle from trend raises many issues, and cycles of different length

---

[16] The Goodwin model may be better suited for an analysis of medium or long run cycles rather than short-run business cycles. Atkinson (1969) included the Goodwin model in his analysis of the time frame of different models, suggesting that with plausible parameter values the model would generate a Kuznets cycle with a period length of about 16–22 years.

may coexist in the data: Short-run fluctuations may take place with reference to a long-run cycle, rather than around a constant exponential trend.

The irregularities of business cycles have been seen as an argument for the exogenous approach, which is the one that has been adopted by contemporary macroeconomics. Romer (2018, pp. 190–191) puts it as follows:

> Because output movements are not regular, the prevailing view is that the economy is perturbed by disturbances of various types and sizes at more or less random intervals, and that those disturbances then propagate through the economy. Where the major macroeconomic schools of thought differ is in their hypotheses concerning these shocks and propagation mechanisms.

This argument does not justify the plethora of shocks that are posited and the opaque nature of the identification assumptions in DSGE models. Nevertheless, the observed irregularities of business fluctuations could present difficulties for deterministic models of endogenous cycles which tend to generate cycles that are quite regular, at least asymptotically. Aside from this empirical inconsistency, regular deterministic cycles may also face theoretical hurdles: Both private agents and policymakers would, one might expect, be able to forecast (and take action to prevent) cycles that are regular and deterministic.[17]

These empirical and theoretical objections are not as powerful as they might seem. It may be noted, first, that deterministic, nonlinear dynamic models can produce 'chaotic' outcomes that are hard to distinguish from those of a stochastic model. Prediction in these models is virtually impossible, since even the smallest change in initial conditions has dramatic effects on the subsequent trajectories (e.g., Day 1994). Huge numbers of observations would be needed to identify whether a particular series is chaotic or asymptotically regular, and from a practical perspective the distinction may not matter much. But the possibility of chaos demonstrates that even hyper-sophisticated agents may be unable to predict outcomes in a deterministic model and, as argued in Chapter 4, most decision makers in the real world are far from hyper-sophisticated. They also typically face idiosyncratic shocks and uncertainties, whose effects on the outcome of their decisions dominate the effects of movements in aggregate activity. In such circumstances, they may simply ignore the possible influence of aggregate regularities altogether. This argument is reinforced if the economy is subject to perceived and/or actual structural change, which impedes any learning from past patterns.

Exogenous shocks clearly can and do affect economic trajectories. But proponents of endogenous cycles need not and do not deny the presence of shocks or the possibility of structural change. Agricultural output is subject to stochastic shocks; technological shocks can have a range of implications, including large sectoral shifts, workers who find themselves with obsolescent skills, and the creation of new financial instruments and markets; national economies are subjected to external shocks from the foreign sector, while COVID-19 represents an obvious recent global shock;

---

[17] This argument does not apply to models of endogenous cycles that assume perfect foresight and intertemporally optimizing agents (e.g., Grandmont 1985, Benhabib and Nishimura 1985). The real-world relevance of these models is questionable, however.

institutional changes and policy shocks can have powerful effects on economic outcomes as can the shocks to sentiments emphasized by Keynes (1936, 1937) and, more recently, Akerlof and Shiller (2009).

The presence or absence of shocks is orthogonal to claims about the cyclical properties of a hypothetical economy without shocks. The local instability of a steady growth path and the presence of endogenous cycles do not preclude exogenous shocks. Shocks remove the regularity but need not affect the underlying cyclical mechanism – if anything, the presence of shocks may exacerbate local instability and strengthen the mechanism behind endogenous cycles: They reinforce the behavioral argument concerning the inability of decision makers to anticipate macroeconomic fluctuations. Thus, the focus in this and the following chapter on deterministic models of endogenous cycles should not be seen as a denial of the empirical relevance of exogenous shocks. Endogenous cycles are relatively underexplored, however, and there are, I shall argue, theoretical reasons to expect local instability of the steady growth path as well as empirical evidence that supports this argument.

Suppose the variable x exhibits bounded fluctuations and that the dynamics of x are being examined using a linear ARMA specification. Local instability in a linear system implies unbounded divergence, and the estimation of linear models will therefore tend to give parameter estimates that imply stability: A linear specification of the regression model may preclude the identification of endogenous cyclical fluctuations in a system with nonlinearities and local instability of the stationary point. Beaudry et al. (2017) lay out this argument in detail and then consider several cyclical indicators of macroeconomic activity, including total hours worked per capita and the unemployment rate. When nonlinearities are allowed in the estimation of dynamic equations for these indicators, they "generally find that this significantly changes the local properties of the system; it often switches from being locally stable when the nonlinear terms are excluded to being locally unstable when they are included" (p. 480). Moreover, when the system is locally unstable, the non-stochastic dynamics have a unique stationary point and converge to a limit cycle. (p. 481).

Beaudry et al. (2020) expand the empirical analysis and suggest that complementaries in agent behavior are the likely source of local instability. They go on to estimate four different versions of a New Keynesian DSGE model, one of which allows for both complementaries and nonlinearities. Unlike the other versions, this version yields estimates that imply local instability and limit cycles if the shocks are removed. By contrast, a canonical version of the model without complementaries and nonlinearities yields parameter estimates that produce monotonic convergence; the internal propagation mechanisms are weak in this version, and the cycles in observed data are driven by persistent exogenous shocks.

The econometric results in Beaudry et al. (2017, 2020) highlight the importance of using empirical specifications that allow for the presence of local instability and nonlinearities. Their New Keynesian model, however, describes a fiction that seems pretty far removed from basic features of capitalist economies and behavioral evidence. It includes standard Euler equations and a New Keynesian Phillips curve, and to this they add a range of simplifying *ad hoc* assumptions. Labor is the only input in production, and firms therefore have no capital and do not invest. The focus instead is on households' investment in durable consumption goods. Households lease these durable goods to firms, and firms sell back the services of the durable consumption goods to households. Households are forced to borrow from banks because they have to pay for new investment in durable goods before they know whether they will find work. The lending is risky for banks because a fraction of households will end up unemployed and may default (despite owning assets in the form of durable consumption goods that have been leased to firms and that could, presumably be sold). It may be possible to fit this model to real-world data, and if that is the case, one could perhaps defend the estimation on instrumentalist grounds: The economy may seem to behave as if aggregate consumption were determined by Euler equations and inflation by the New Keynesian Phillips curve in an economy without fixed capital in production and no investment by firms. But it would seem difficult to make a strong case that this model has identified the main mechanisms operating in contemporary capitalist economies.

It should be noted before closing this section that the distinction between exogenous and endogenous cycles carries no direct implications for the desirability of economic policy. Most macroeconomists may favor an external-shock approach, and it may seem that the need for policy intervention must be greater if the cycles are endogenous. But policy intervention can be both feasible and desirable in models of exogenous cycles, including mainstream specifications as well as versions that deviate from the current orthodoxy. Conversely, endogenous cycles can be generated in models in which markets clear and outcomes are Pareto optimal, as well as in models characterized by important market failures. Whether the fluctuations are exogenous or endogenous, the feasibility and desirability of policy intervention depend on the precise structure of the theory and its cyclical mechanisms.

9.6   Conclusion

Keynes's analysis highlighted the potential failure of standard market adjustments to stabilize the economy at full employment. This instability can be analyzed, as in Chapter 8, using a short-run model with a predetermined capital stock.

The dynamics of the capital stock move center stage when the analysis is extended to the medium and long run, with Harrod's pioneering analysis suggesting that aggregate demand problems and instability may become even more pronounced as the time frame is extended: An unstable warranted growth path and the likely discrepancy between natural and warranted growth rates make full-employment growth seem almost impossible in a capitalist market economy. Yet, many economies achieve something approximating full employment growth, and the profession has largely dismissed and forgotten Harrod's analysis.

The favored solution to Harrod's first problem, which invokes movements along a neoclassical production, is unconvincing, while the second problem has been ignored. This state of affairs would have been understandable, had there been no other ways of reconciling the evidence with Harrod's analysis. But that is not the case. The reconciliation of warranted and natural growth rates does not require a neoclassical aggregate production and accommodating movements in the capital intensity of production. Local instability of the warranted growth path, moreover, does not disqualify Harrod's analysis. Instead, it provides a fruitful starting point for an analysis of endogenous business cycles, as argued in Chapter 10.

Appendix A: A Ramsey Model with Fixed Coefficients in Production

For simplicity, consider a version of the model in which the representative household owns capital and uses it directly to produce output. In this setting, the representative agent solves the optimization problem

$$\max \int_0^\infty e^{-\rho t} \frac{c^{1-\theta}}{1-\theta} e^{nt} \, dt$$

$$s.t.$$
$$\dot{k} = f(k) - c - (n + \delta)k$$
$$k \geq 0,$$

where c and k denote consumption and capital per worker; for simplicity, there is no technical change. The solution to this problem satisfies the equation of motion for k and the Euler equation

$$\hat{c} = \frac{1}{\theta}(f'(k) - \delta - \rho).$$

Assuming that $f'(0) > \delta + \rho > \lim_{k \to \infty} f'(k)$, the economy follows the stable saddle path to a steady growth path with $\hat{c} = \dot{k} = 0$ and $k = k^*, 0 < k^* < \infty$.

If the production function is CES, we have

$$Y = [(\sigma K)^\gamma + L^\gamma]^{1/\gamma}; \quad \gamma \leq 1$$
$$f(k) = \frac{Y}{L} = [(\sigma k)^\gamma + 1]^{1/\gamma}.$$

The CES function converges to a Leontief function for $\gamma \to -\infty$ (this well known property can be shown using L'Hôpital's rule); that is,

$$f(k) \quad \rightarrow \quad \begin{cases} \sigma k & \text{if } \sigma k < 1 \\ 1 & \text{if } \sigma k > 1 \end{cases}$$

$$f'(k) \quad \rightarrow \quad \begin{cases} \sigma & \text{if } \sigma k < 1 \\ 0 & \text{if } \sigma k > 1. \end{cases}$$

Assuming that $\sigma - \delta - \rho > 0 > -\delta - \rho$, it now follows that as $\gamma \to -\infty$, the stable stationary solution for k converges to $k^* = 1/\sigma$.

Appendix B: A Generalized Goodwin Model

The qualitative properties of Goodwin's model generalize to systems in which the functions describing the accumulation rate and the growth rate of the wage share are nonlinear. To see this, consider the dynamic system

$$\dot{x} = \phi_1(y)\chi_1(x); \qquad \phi_1' > 0, \chi_1 > 0$$
$$\dot{y} = \phi_2(x)\chi_2(y); \qquad \phi_2' < 0, \chi_2 > 0,$$

where ϕ_1, ϕ_2, χ_1, and χ_2 are continuously differentiable and where we assume that the system has a stationary solution x^*, y^*. This dynamic system includes the simple Goodwin model as a special case: Let $\phi_1(y) = -\gamma + \rho y$, $\phi_2(x) = s\sigma^{\max} - n - s\sigma^{\max}x$; specify $\chi_1(x) = x, \chi_2(y) = y$, and let x and y denote the wage share and the employment rate, respectively.

Now define p and q as

$$p = \theta_1(x) = \int_k^x \frac{1}{\chi_1(v)} dv$$
$$q = \theta_2(y) = \int_m^y \frac{1}{\chi_2(v)} du,$$

where m and k are arbitrarily chosen constants. Since χ_1 and χ_2 are both positive, the functions θ_1 and θ_2 are monotonically increasing. Furthermore,

$$\dot{p} = \frac{1}{\chi_1(x)}\dot{x} = \phi_1(y) = \phi_1(\theta_2^{-1}(q))$$

$$\dot{q} = \frac{1}{\chi_2(y)}\dot{y} = \phi_2(x) = \phi_2(\theta_1^{-1}(p)).$$

This transformed system takes the form

$$\dot{p} = f(q); \quad f' > 0 \tag{9.26}$$
$$\dot{q} = g(p); \quad g' < 0. \tag{9.27}$$

In order to show that the system (9.26) and (9.27) generates conservative fluctuations, we multiply the left-hand side of (9.26) by the right-hand side of (9.27) and the right-hand side of (9.26) with the left-hand side of (9.27) to get

$$g(p)\dot{p} = f(q)\dot{q}$$

or

$$f(q)\dot{q} - g(p)\dot{p} = 0. \tag{9.28}$$

The variables p and q (and their derivatives) are functions of t; integrating Equation (9.28) we get

$$\int f(q)\dot{q}dt - \int g(p)\dot{p}dt = \int f(q)dq - \int g(p)dp = C, \tag{9.29}$$

where C is an arbitrary constant. Now define

$$H(p(t), q(t)) = F(q) - G(p) = \int f(q)dq - \int g(p)dp. \tag{9.30}$$

Equation (9.29) implies that the function H is constant, $H(p,q) = C$; the value of the constant being determined by the initial conditions (i.e., by the initial values of p and q). Furthermore,

$$H_p = -G'(p) = -g(p); H_q = F'(q) = f(q) \qquad (9.31)$$

and

$$H_{pp} = -g' > 0, H_{qq} = f' > 0; H_{qp} = H_{pq} = 0. \qquad (9.32)$$

It follows that

- the function H is convex.
- at the stationary point $(p^*,q^*) = (\theta_1(x^*),\theta_2(y^*))$ we have $H_p = H_q = 0$.
- the H – function has a global minimum at (p^*,q^*).
- starting at some initial point (p_0,q_0) away from the stationary point, (p,q) will be cycling around the level curve corresponding to the constant C (which in turn is determined by the initial values p_0,q_0).

Conservative fluctuations of (p,q) around (p^*,q^*) imply conservative fluctuations of (x,y) around (x^*,y^*). Furthermore, suitable specifications of the functions ϕ_i and χ_i ensure that the equilibrium values x^* and y^* belong to the unit interval and that if the initial values x_0 and y_0 are in the unit interval, then all trajectories for (x,y) will remain inside the unit box; this boundedness can be achieved, for instance, if $\chi_1(x) = x(1 - x)$ and $\chi_2(y) = y(1 - y)$.

10 Endogenous Growth Cycles with or without Price Flexibility

10.1 Introduction

Distributional dynamics centered on the labor market create cycles in Goodwin's formalization of Marx's 'general law of capitalist accumulation.' Harrod also viewed the economy as being subject to endogenous cycles, but for him the source of the cycles was to be found in the goods market. The dynamic interactions in the goods market between multiplier and accelerator effects make the warranted growth path (locally) unstable, and the divergence becomes bounded because of "the limits of the region of centrifugal forces surrounding the warranted growth path" (Harrod 1973, p. 34).

Local instability can be turned into perpetual fluctuations rather than cumulative divergence by nonlinearities in one or more of the equations of the model. The imposition of ceilings and floors represents a simple example (gross investment may have a positive lower bound, for instance, and output cannot exceed a full-employment ceiling), but other, less crude nonlinearities can also keep the movements bounded and convert local instability into endogenous cyclical movements.[1]

The models in this chapter focus on interactions between goods and labor markets, with stabilizing feedback effects from the labor market averting cumulative divergence. The result may be local instability and limit cycles or, if the feedback is strong enough, the stationary solution may become locally stable. In the latter case, the convergence typically takes the form of damped oscillations; whether locally stable or locally unstable, the models contain strong cyclical tendencies.

Local instability implies that the economy will not converge to the warranted path, and by definition, demand expectations fail to be met, on average, when the economy is off the warranted growth path (Chapter 9). Thus, unlike the standard Keynesian analysis of the short run, these extensions of Keynesian theory to cover long-run developments and endogenous cycles take Keynesian disequilibrium as the normal state of affairs: Short-run expectations are not necessarily being met.

---

[1] The chapter draws on Skott (1989a, 2010, 2015) and Skott and Zipperer (2012). Kalecki (1937b), Samuelson (1939), Kaldor (1940), Hicks (1950) and Goodwin (1951) present early models in the multiplier-accelerator tradition. Later contributions to the Keynesian literature on endogenous cycles include Rose (1967), Torre (1977), Dutt (1992), Chiarella and Flaschel (2000), Barbosa and Taylor (2006), Ryoo (2010), Fazzari et al. (2013), von Arnim and Barrales (2015), Franke (2018) and Murakami (2018).

The capital stock is predetermined in the short run, and firms' decision problem with respect to employment and output would be static and independent of expectations if labor inputs and production could be adjusted instantaneously and costlessly in response to changes in demand. But the hiring process can be costly and time-consuming, especially for skilled labor, while even the simplest jobs require some amount of on-the-job training. Adjustments of hours for current employees provide some flexibility, but overtime pay and a drop-off in productivity as hours are extended add to costs and limit this option. Thus, although more flexible than capital, employment and labor input should not be treated as perfectly flexible in response to unanticipated movements in demand. Formally, both the capital stock and the level of employment can be modeled as state variables, with investment and the change in employment becoming the decision variables: Shifts in expected demand generate responses in the form of changes in the accumulation rate I/K and the growth rate of employment ($\hat{L}$).

Movements in inputs would be transmitted directly to output if the utilization rate of labor (and/or capital) were constant and production instantaneous. This is not the case. Production lags between changes in inputs and the appearance of final output on the shelves make output less flexible in the short run. The presence of excess capacity of both labor and capital (as evidenced by procyclical movements in both capital utilization and labor productivity), on the other hand, may allow adjustments in output, even without changes in employment and the capital stock.[2]

Sections 10.3–10.5 analyze models in which both output and employment are treated as state variables.[3] With output as a state variable, some other variables must do the adjusting when there is an unanticipated change in demand. The assumption in these sections is that prices adjust, an assumption that is at odds with new Keynesian models as well as with (almost all) post-Keynesian theory. Section 10.2 outlines the argument for price flexibility. Essentially, it reduces to an empirical assessment that – contrary to common claims – prices are quite flexible. The analysis in Sections 10.3–10.5 shows that a simple Keynesian model with flexible prices and profit margins can generate endogenous cycles, with simulations of the model matching stylized cyclical patterns in the United States. Section 10.6 extends the model by including a public sector and economic policy as well as cyclical variations in labor productivity (Okun's law) and gradual adjustments in investment.

The treatment of output as a state variable is questionable in some service industries. Retail workers, for instance, may work standard shifts, but their productivity (sales per hour) depends on the number of customers and, within limits, output responds instantaneously to changes in demand. Section 10.7 considers a model along

---

[2] Baily et al. (2001) describe the procyclicality of labor productivity at the plant level.

[3] Output may be a state variable because labor productivity is constant (or only grows in proportion to the growth in output). But predetermined levels of output could also be seen as a continuous-time approximation of the effects of production lags. In a discrete-time model, a production lag h implies that the firm's input decisions at time t determine output at time $t + h$. The firm sets the discrete-time growth rate $(Y_{t+h} - Y_t)/Y_t$, and the growth rate $\hat{Y}$ becomes the corresponding decision variable in a continuous-time setting.

these lines. Despite the quite different assumptions, this flex-output version of the model yields a reduced-form structure that is similar to the flex-price version. Section 8 offers a few concluding observations and comments.

10.2   Are Prices Flexible?

Consider a state of short-run Keynesian disequilibrium in which *ex ante* investment differs from *ex ante* saving. If output cannot adjust instantaneously, there are three possibilities: The *ex post* equality between investment and saving can be brought about by (i) direct rationing, (ii) unplanned changes in inventories, or (iii) changes in prices that eliminate excess demand.

Rationing occurs but does not seem empirically important. Flights and concerts can be sold out, and there may be a waiting list for a particularly popular new electronic gadget (like the PlayStation 5 when it was released in late 2020). But generalized rationing of this kind is not a feature of capitalist market economies in normal times. Households and firms rarely see their spending plans curtailed in this way.[4]

The second adjustment mechanism, a change in inventories, captures the immediate impact of a purchase: When a customer drives away with a new car, the inventory in the dealer's lot has been reduced by 1. Inventories are procyclical, however, and accommodating inventory adjustments do not act as a stabilizing buffer at the frequencies that are relevant for the business cycle: Inventories do not fall when demand grows rapidly during the upswing of a business cycle nor rise when demand declines in the downswing. On the contrary, movements in inventories amplify the business cycle. Thus, leaving out inventories will almost certainly bias the analysis in favor of stability and steady growth and against instability.[5]

Having excluded rationing and inventories as accommodating variables, we are left with the third possibility: Price changes. This adjustment mechanism runs counter to the widespread perception that prices are sticky and that nominal price rigidities are essential for Keynesian economics and the significance of aggregate demand. Romer's graduate text, for instance, explains, "For monetary disturbances to have real effects there must be some type of nominal rigidity or imperfection. Otherwise, even in a model that is highly non-Walrasian, a monetary change results only in proportional changes in all prices with no impact on real prices or quantities" (Romer 2018, p. 238). Nakamura and Steinsson (2013, p. 134), likewise, motivate their survey of microeconomic evidence on price rigidity by suggesting that Keynesian results require rigidities: "Consider a monetary shock. The efficient response to a doubling of the money supply is for all prices to double immediately and all real quantities to remain unchanged."

---

[4] More widespread rationing (as well as large price increases) appeared as a result of disruptions to supply chains associated with COVID-19 and the response to the pandemic.

[5] Chiarella et al. (2005) analyze models with inventory dynamics.

Tautologically, models that assume instantaneous and unbounded movements in prices in response to any deviation from market clearing cannot accommodate any outcome other than market clearing; aggregate demand problems and outcomes with Keynesian involuntary unemployment are precluded by assumption in such models. But, as argued by Keynes and discussed in Chapter 8, the market-clearing equilibrium may not be stable under plausible specifications of how prices adjust to disequilibrium. Fortunately, therefore, nominal wages show downward rigidity. Product prices, by contrast, were taken by Keynes to be perfectly flexible in the *General Theory* as well as in *A Treatise on Money* (Keynes 1930b).[6] In fact, changes in aggregate demand of the kind envisaged by Romer and Nakamura and Steinsson – exogenous shocks to the money supply and aggregate nominal demand – would seem to have their roots in the quantity theory and monetarist preoccupations with helicopter money, rather than in Keynesian concerns about the effects of shifts, whether endogenous or due to exogenous events, in consumer confidence or firms' animal spirits.

Claiming the need for price rigidities, new Keynesian theory finds a theoretical justification for rigidities by introducing menu costs of some kind. Undeniably, there are costs associated with changing prices (or with gathering and analyzing information to derive the optimal price).[7] But the notion that these menu costs exceed the costs of changing the levels of output and employment would seem to require a strong argument.[8] A more promising behavioral explanation of price stickiness could emphasize difficulties of understanding and processing price information and the perception that price change can be unfair (Kahneman et al. 1986, Rotemberg 2008). But while these behavioral arguments have merit, direct evidence suggests that, in fact, prices are much more flexible than commonly believed.

The general view in the 1990s was that prices changed about once a year on average (e.g., Kashyap 1995). In a survey of business managers, however, Blinder (1991) found that among twelve theories of price stickiness, the explanation that emphasized variations in delivery lags and service emerged with the largest support: Many firms react to low demand by shortening delivery lags or providing more auxiliary services. In other words, quality-adjusted prices may not be sticky after all.

As data improved in the 2000s, the estimated degree of stickiness decreased, and it now seemed that prices changed roughly every four months (Bils and Klenow 2004). This finding was based on monthly data. When weekly scanner data became increasingly available, the estimate was pushed down further, with Eichenbaum et al. (2011) reporting a median price duration of about three weeks. That may still be

---

[6] Unlike the *General Theory*, moreover, the *Treatise* considered positions of macroeconomic disequilibrium, using price changes and windfall profits as the adjustment mechanism consistent with a predetermined level of output.

[7] Levy et al. (1997) find that menu costs make up about 0.7 percent of total revenue and 35.2 percent of net profits in a sample of five supermarket chains. These proportions may seem large but say little about whether menu costs act as a substantial deterrent to price change. If menu costs were extremely high and prices therefore completely fixed, the shares would be zero. More relevant is the finding that in their weekly data about 15 percent of prices were changed in an average week.

[8] Bresnahan and Ramey (1994) discuss costs of output adjustment in the auto industry.

an underestimate. Using daily Japanese scanner data with three billion observations of prices and quantities from 1988 to 2005, Abe and Tonogi (2010) find that the mean frequency of price adjustment has been increasing and that in 2005 prices changed, on average, every three days in their sample of general merchandise stores, supermarkets, and food stores throughout Japan. Commenting on the results, they suggest that data frequency may be "the crucial factor creating these significant discrepancies" with other studies (p. 717).[9] They also note that temporary sales and discounts are important: A large share of the amount sold happens at bargain prices. The trend increase in the frequency of price changes in the Japanese data may have been reinforced since 2005 by the use of AI and dynamic pricing, especially in e-commerce; according to a McKinsey report, Amazon now reprices millions of items every few minutes (www.mckinsey.com/business-functions/growth-marketing-and-sales/our-insights/the-dos-and-donts-of-dynamic-pricing-in-retail).

Despite the downward revisions in estimated price duration, nominal rigidities are still seen as critical in the new Keynesian literature. The rigidities, it is suggested, "take the form of inertia in 'reference prices' and 'reference costs'," where the reference price (cost) is the "most often quoted price (cost) within a given time period, say a quarter" (Eichenbaum et al. 2011, p. 234). Many price changes are associated with temporary sales and discounts, after which the prices return to their reference levels. This feature of the evidence, which shows up strongly in high-frequency datasets, produces a dual challenge for new Keynesian theory: The theory has to explain the frequent temporary price changes but also develop reasons for why and how these price changes are compatible with the significant nominal rigidities that are seen as essential for the theory.

In their survey of price rigidity, Nakamura and Steinsson (2013) present three reasons "why temporary sales need to be treated separately in analyzing the responsiveness of the aggregate price level to various shocks":

First, sales are highly transitory, limiting their effect on the long-run aggregate price level, even if their timing is fully responsive to macroeconomic shocks. Second, retailers may have an incentive to stagger the timing of sales, reducing their impact on the aggregate price level. Finally, sales may be on autopilot (i.e., unresponsive to macroeconomic shocks). (pp. 144–145)

The first reason begs the question. It is not clear why firms would have to revert to the regular price after a sale, and if that is not required, the stickiness of the regular price is left unexplained. Moreover, even if prices have to go back to the 'regular price' after each sale, the average price can be adjusted – both in the short and the long run – by varying the frequency of sales or the size of the price reductions in response to market conditions.

With sufficient ingenuity, to be sure, one can explain temporary sales while also making sure to limit their effects. Kehoe and Midrigan (2015) provide two examples. They distinguish between temporary price changes that revert after one period and regular changes. In one version of their explanation, they simply extend the Calvo

---

[9] Weekly scanner data can also be misleading in other ways. Cavallo and Rigobon (2016) find that using weekly averages of prices creates many spurious small changes.

model by assuming that firms are assigned randomly to one of three categories in each period: A firm may be unable to change its price, have the option of changing it temporarily, or be allowed to change its regular price. Not surprisingly, appropriate probability assignments allow this specification to produce the desired conclusions. But the *ad hoc* nature of the 'explanation' is hard to miss – why are firms' pricing options restricted in this peculiar way?

Another version of their model introduces menu costs to provide a microeconomic justification of the temporary sales: They now assume that the costs of changes in regular prices are higher than the costs of temporary changes. It is not obvious why the costs of changing prices twice (as is implied by a temporary change) would be lower than the costs of changing prices once. But suitable calibrations of the menu costs and the pattern of transitory and permanent idiosyncratic shocks to demand can generate a combination of temporary and regular price changes that roughly matches observations, while retaining a large degree of stickiness. The menu cost assumptions have been chosen, however, so that the model can generate predictions that are consistent with observations, rather than because of any direct evidence to support them.

The analysis in Alvarez and Lippi (2020) provides a hint of the lack of robustness of the Kehoe–Midrigan result. Pursuing a variation on the same theme, Alvarez and Lippi assume that upon paying a menu cost, a firm can choose a 'price plan.' The plan has two prices, and the firm is free to change prices as often as it wishes within the plan; changes of the plan, however, require paying the fixed menu cost. This model also matches the patterns of temporary and regular price changes, but allowing for temporary changes of price substantially alters the real effect of a monetary shock in this setting.

One may be impressed by the technical skill and ingenuity on display in this literature, but even more striking to a disinterested reader may be the willingness to add pretty much any *ad hoc* assumption as long as the optimization problems that pass for microeconomic foundations are preserved.[10]

Nakamura and Steinsson's second reason is exemplified by Guimaraes and Sheedy (2011). Regular prices are adjusted at random intervals, as in the Calvo model. Temporary price changes – sales – are costless, however, and retailers have an incentive to hold temporary sales in their model: Consumers have different price elasticities, and temporary sales provide an imperfect route to price discrimination. But the model also implies that to serve this purpose, the sales should not be synchronized across firms. The implications are now clear: The sales produce frequent price changes, but the sales are asynchronous and the average price becomes largely orthogonal to macroeconomic conditions; average prices are rigid. Logically, the argument works. If prices

---

[10] The 'flexibility' of new Keynesian models is also illustrated by Uribe (2020). He notes that having many prices that do not change in a given quarter can be consistent with price indexation for some prices if one modifies the Calvo model "by allowing each period a fraction of randomly picked prices to change optimally, another fraction of randomly picked prices to change due to indexation, and the remaining prices to be constant." The result, again, is not surprising, but the justification for these modifications of the Calvo assumptions appears to be that they can 'explain' the empirical observation. The original Calvo assumptions are also hard to defend, but at least they had the virtue of simplicity.

can be changed costlessly, however, it is not clear why changes in regular prices have to follow a Calvo scheme of time-dependent adjustment.

The third reason is puzzling. Having sales on autopilot could perhaps be justified by bounded rationality, but bounded rationality fits badly in models that rely on hyper-rational, optimizing decision-makers. And even advocates of bounded rationality will hesitate to suggest that airlines adjust their fares without any consideration of how many seats have been filled already.

A simpler and more straightforward reading of the evidence may conclude that many prices are, in fact, very flexible. Clearly, not all price changes are motivated by changes in demand – firms may well use sales, coupons, and special offers as part of a general marketing strategy. But the use by some firms of these marketing strategies does not preclude an influence from market conditions on price setting, whether directly on 'regular' prices or on the timing and frequency of temporary sales and other incentives like cheap financing of consumer durables or upgrades of quality and service. Price flexibility, moreover, does not imply that average prices and profit margins must fluctuate violently. Nominal wages are sticky, and the amplitude of variations in prices and profit margins will depend, *inter alia*, on the speed with which output responds to changes in profit margins and on the amplitudes of the (endogenously or exogenously generated) fluctuations in demand.

Microeconomic evidence on the frequency and size of price adjustments also shows large differences across sectors and product categories. Klenow and Malin (2010) and Nakamura and Steinsson (2013) summarize some of the stylized facts, one of them being that service prices tend to be stickier than those of goods and that the prices of some services (like haircuts) seem to change very infrequently. This observation is consistent with the argument outlined briefly in the introduction and explored further in Section 10.7: Some service activities are characterized by output flexibility and variable labor utilization. Another stylized fact says that prices change more frequently for goods with highly cyclical demand, which is what one would expect if prices adjust in response to short-run disequilibrium.

Overall, the evidence shows that price adjustments are frequent and significant, and it strains credulity to suggest that these price adjustments are unrelated to the state of demand. Thus, the primary motivation for the flex-price model in the next section is empirical. Disregarding empirical issues, however, a model with flexible prices may be interesting from a theoretical perspective: With perfect price flexibility, unemployment and economic instability cannot be blamed on rigid prices.

10.3   A Model with Sticky Output and Flexible Prices

10.3.1   Output and Employment

Guided by an output adjustment principle, firms decide the growth rate of output in this model. They raise output if it falls below the level that would have been chosen, had the levels of output and employment been perfectly flexible, and reduce output if it falls below the full-flexibility level.

As a first step, it is useful to determine the full-flexibility level of output. Consider a case in which (i) the production function is Leontief, (ii) the firm has excess capital capacity, (iii) output and employment are perfectly flexible, (iv) the firm faces a labor supply that is perfectly elastic at the money wage w, and (v) the firm's perceived demand function takes the form

$$Y_i = B_i \left(\frac{p_i}{p}\right)^{-\gamma_i} ; \quad \gamma_i > 1, \tag{10.1}$$

where subscripts i indicate firm-specific variables and p is the average price. Under these conditions, a profit-maximizing firm's output and employment will be determined by the static maximization problem

$$\max p_i Y_i - w L_i$$
$$s.t.$$
$$Y_i = B_i \left(\frac{p_i}{p}\right)^{-\gamma_i}$$
$$Y_i = A_i L_i,$$

where A_i is the productivity of labor.

The solution to this problem yields a constant markup on unit labor cost and a constant profit share

$$p_i^* = \frac{\gamma_i}{\gamma_i - 1} \frac{w}{A_i} \tag{10.2}$$

$$\pi_i^* = \frac{1}{\gamma_i} \tag{10.3}$$

$$Y_i^* = B_i \left(\frac{\gamma_i}{\gamma_i - 1} \frac{w}{A_i p}\right)^{-\gamma_i}. \tag{10.4}$$

Equations (10.2)–(10.4) describe the outcome if output and employment had been perfectly flexible.

Adjustment costs – a simple way of introducing stickiness – prevent firms from moving instantaneously to this short-run equilibrium. An expansion of employment entails increased search and hiring costs, and it may be necessary to raise wages – or improve working conditions and benefits more generally – to attract workers.[11] Training costs also rise if rapid rates of expansion lead to the hiring of workers without the particular experience or skill that the jobs require. Contractions of employment, likewise, involve costs. Depending on labor market regulations and contracts, the firm may have to make redundancy payments. Layoffs, moreover, are likely to affect labor relations within the firm and cause declining morale and productivity.

Search and hiring costs increase in a tight labor market, while the negative effects of contractions may be less severe as quit rates increase.[12] This influence of the state

---

[11] The argument involves a kind of dynamic monopsony with labor costs depending on the rate of change of employment; Manning (2003) dsscribes a range of different sources of monopsony.

[12] According the BLS Job Openings and Labor Turnover Survey, the monthly quit rate for nonfarm workers in the United States doubled from 1.2 percent at the depth of the recession in 2009 to 2.4 percent at the pre-COVID peak in 2019.

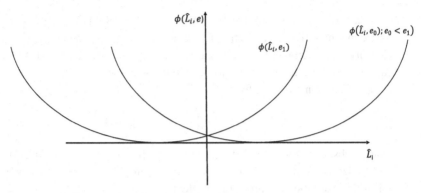

Figure 10.1 Adjustment cost function for employment.

of the labor market on adjustment costs can be captured by letting the position of the firm's adjustment cost function depend on the aggregate employment rate. Equation (10.5) defines an adjustment cost function with these properties:

$$c_i = L_i \phi(\hat{L}_i, e),$$ (10.5)

where

$$\phi_1 \gtrless 0 \text{ for } \hat{L}_i \gtrless \Phi(e), \ \Phi' < 0$$
$$\phi_2 \lessgtr 0 \text{ for } \hat{L}_i \gtrless \Phi(e), \ \Phi' < 0$$
$$\phi_{11} > 0.$$

This function, depicted in Figure 10.1, assumes that adjustment costs are convex as a function of the growth of employment and proportional to the level of employment, and that the growth rate that minimizes the firm's adjustment costs is a decreasing function of the aggregate employment rate e.

The firm chooses its rate of expansion by comparing the adjustment costs to the future benefits from a change in employment. If the current level of perfect-flexibility output is seen by the firm as an indicator of future demand, these benefits will depend positively on the ratio Y_i^*/Y_i. Prices are flexible and, by assumption, adjust to clear the goods market. Nominal wages are much less flexible, and the optimal perfect-flexibility level of output in Equation (10.4) exceeds the current level of output ($Y_i^* > Y_i$) if and only if the actual profit share exceeds the equilibrium profit share in Equation (10.3), that is, if $\pi_i > \pi_i^*$.[13]

The benefits of expanding employment are likely to depend not only on the profit share but also on the utilization rate of capital. Production requires capital as well as labor, and some firms may be at full capacity. Before any such absolute capital constraints become binding, firms will experience rising labor costs if the use of overtime or the introduction of additional shifts or weekend work are necessary to expand output. These cost increases blunt the incentive to expand output.

---

[13] Equations (10.2)–(10.4) imply that

$$\pi_i - \pi_i^* = \frac{\gamma_i - 1}{\gamma_i} \left[1 - \left(\frac{Y_i^*}{Y_i} \right)^{-1/\gamma_i} \right].$$

These considerations suggest that the benefits of changes in employment will be determined by the utilization rate and the deviation of the actual from full-flexibility profit share, while the costs of adjustment depend on the aggregate employment rate and the speed of adjustment. Hence, weighing costs and benefits, the firm sets the speed of expansion as a function of its profit share, its utilization rate, and the aggregate employment rate. By assumption the production function in Leontief, and to simplify notation, I shall use the output-capital ratio (σ) as an indicator of utilization in this chapter ($\sigma = u\sigma^{max}$, where σ^{max} and u are the technical coefficient and the utilization rate, respectively). Thus,

$$\hat{L}_i = h(\pi_i - \pi_i^*, \sigma_i, e); \qquad h_1 > 0, h_2 < 0, h_3 < 0.$$

For simplicity, labor productivity is taken to be constant, and we have $\hat{Y}_i = \hat{L}_i$. Thus, the aggregate growth rate of output is given by

$$\hat{Y} = \sum_i \frac{Y_i}{Y} \hat{Y}_i = \sum_i \frac{Y_i}{Y} \hat{L}_i = \sum_i \frac{Y_i}{Y} h(\pi_i - \pi_i^*, \sigma_i, e). \tag{10.6}$$

Both the full-flexibility profit shares (which reflect competitive conditions in the goods market) and the distribution of actual profit shares and utilization rates across firms may change over time, and strong assumptions would be needed to determine the joint distribution of the variables (Y_i/Y, $\pi_i - \pi_i^*$, σ_i and e) and the evolution of this distribution over time. As a first approximation, however, it seems reasonable to assume that the joint distribution can be parameterized by the aggregate values of π, π^*, σ, and e. Hence, if competitive conditions in the goods market are stable and π^* is constant, the growth rate of aggregate output becomes a function of the aggregate profit share, output-capital ratio, and employment rate:

$$\hat{Y} = h(\pi, \sigma, e); \qquad h_1 > 0, h_2 < 0, h_3 < 0. \tag{10.7}$$

The economic logic behind the aggregate 'output expansion function' (10.7) is straightforward. Firms adjust output in response to signals from both goods and labor markets. Favorable demand conditions (high profit shares) stimulate output growth in firms with excess capital capacity (utilization rates below an upper limit), while tight labor markets (high aggregate employment rates) make it harder and more costly to expand production. Employment effects on search and hiring costs may be reinforced by Marxian shifts in the balance of power between workers and capitalists: As the reserve army shrinks, firms may react to what they see as a general 'deterioration of the business climate' by reducing the rate of expansion.[14] The negative impact of the utilization rate derives from a rising share of firms facing capital constraints as the average utilization rate increases.

The output expansion function is likely to be highly nonlinear. The effects of variations in the utilization rate of capital or the employment rate will be quite minor if the levels are low, and there is abundant excess capital capacity and slack in the labor

---

[14] Skott (1989) develops a more formal derivation of the output expansion function but leaves out potential capital constraints and the associated impact of utilization rates on the growth rate of output.

market; the effects will become stronger as the levels increase. Thus, one will expect h to be strictly concave in σ ($h_{22} < 0$) and e ($h_{33} < 0$). The nonlinearity will be different with respect to the profit share π (the degree of short-run disequilibrium). Adjustment costs for output are likely to be convex as a function of $\hat{Y}$, and there may well be upper and lower limits on the rate of growth, $g^{\min} \leq \hat{Y} \leq g^{\max}$: In her classic study, Penrose (1959) argued that managerial resources "create a fundamental and inescapable limit to the amount of expansion a firm can undertake at any time" (p. 48). These limits would suggest a sigmoid-shaped relation between $\hat{Y}$ and π, with the growth rate being more sensitive to variations in the profit share for intermediate values of the profit share than for very high or very low shares.

10.3.2 Investment

Capital adjustment principles relate investment to the difference between the capital stock that the firm expects will be optimal (the target K^T) and the existing capital stock,

$$I = \lambda_K (K^T - K) + \delta K; \qquad \lambda_K > 0, \tag{10.8}$$

where δ is the depreciation rate and λ_K determines the speed of adjustment. In its general form, this principle is almost a truism. The determination of the target capital stock raises many questions, however.

A neoclassical production function allows capital to be fully utilized at all times, even if demand fluctuates. If the technology is Leontief, by contrast, firms typically want to maintain some excess capacity, and short-run fluctuations in demand produce variations in utilization rates. High firm-level volatility of demand will tend to increase the targeted average margin of excess capacity (reduce the target for average utilization); indivisibilities in plant size can also influence the determination of the average desired utilization rates, and firms may use excess capacity strategically in their competitive strategies as a deterrence to new entry (Dixit 1980). These and other structural features that influence the costs and benefits of maintaining excess capacity may change over time, and the desired utilization rate (like the technical coefficients in the Leontief production function) need not be constant. For present purposes, however, there is little loss in treating desired utilization as constant and the target capital stock as proportional to the expected level of demand.

Formally, let

$$K^T = \frac{1}{\sigma^d} Y^e.$$

The desired average output-capital ratio is the product of the maximum output-capital ratio (a parameter in the Leontief production function) and the desired average utilization rate; $\sigma^d = \sigma^{\max} u^d$; Y^e denotes the expected trend value of demand (disregarding expected, purely temporary movements in demand). Thus, the investment function can be written as

$$I = \lambda_K (K^T - K) + \delta K = K \lambda_K \left(\frac{Y^e}{\sigma^d K} - 1 \right) + \delta K. \tag{10.9}$$

The gradual adjustment of the capital stock toward a target level is often rationalized by introducing convex adjustment cost. This approach is analytically convenient, and I appealed to convex adjustment costs in the derivation of output adjustment. As pointed out by Nickell (1978), however, it is questionable whether capital adjustment costs are increasing at the margin. The rate of investment associated with a given increase in the capital stock is determined by the amount of new capacity that will be generated and the speed with which the investment program is carried out. While it may be reasonable to assume that costs are strictly convex in the speed of implementation (at least for rapid speeds of implementation), there is no reason to suppose that they will be convex as a function of the size of the program. On the contrary, one would expect firm-level investment patterns to be lumpy because of indivisibilities and increasing returns: (i) production plants often need to have some minimum scale to be efficient, (ii) the unit cost of new capacity is likely to be smaller for a completely new and purpose-built factory than for marginal additions and modifications to existing plant, (iii) there may be fixed costs associated with the installation of new machinery (e.g., halting ongoing plant activity), and (iv) information and learning by doing make the costs of installing two machines (or building two plants) less than double the costs of installing only one.

The lumpiness of investment is documented by firm-level evidence in Doms and Dunne (1998), and other studies confirm the failings of investment models with convex adjustment costs.[15] Thus, although one may feel unhappy about simply postulating an aggregate investment function like (10.9), little would be gained by a rigorous derivation based on the profit maximizing behavior of a representative firm with convex adjustment costs. The capital stock cannot be adjusted instantaneously, but inflexibility is not the same as convex adjustment costs.

In light of this evidence, the analysis in Appendix A follows a different approach. Investment is subject to indivisibilities and increasing returns that make it costly or impossible to adjust the capital stock continuously in response to changes in demand. Additional complications arise from irreversibility (the absence of second-hand markets for most investment goods) and the existence of a time lag between the investment decision and the appearance of new capacity. As a stylized version of these features, it is assumed that (i) investment projects have a minimum scale that is proportional to the size of the firm, (ii) the firm cannot undertake more than one investment project at the same time, and (iii) there is a gestation lag between investment and the appearance

---

[15] Cooper and Haltiwanger find that

a model with convex costs alone cannot produce the bursts of investment and inaction observed in the data. Thus, richer models of adjustment are needed. Both the non-convex and the irreversibility models are able to produce relationships between investment and fundamentals, which are much closer to the data.... *a combination of non-convex adjustment costs and irreversibility enables us to fit prominent features of observed investment behaviour at the plant level.* (2006, pp. 612–613; italics in original) of new capacity. Appendix A shows how these assumptions can make the aggregate accumulation rate an increasing function of the average utilization rate,[16]

$$\frac{I}{K} = f(\sigma); \quad f' > 0. \tag{10.10}$$

The analysis in the appendix also suggests that although the f-function may be quite flat for low values of the average utilization rate, it is likely to be highly sensitive to changes within a relevant range of normal utilization rates. It may be noted that although seemingly quite different from the one that was used in the formalization of Harrod's instability argument in Chapter 9, there is a close connection between the two formulations; see Appendix B.

The investment function (10.10), which is used in the baseline model in this section, is extended in Section 10.5 by adding more explanatory variables and dynamics.

10.3.3   Saving

The specification of aggregate saving draws on the analysis outlined in Chapters 3–4. Reproducing Equation (4.3), aggregate consumption is given by

$$C = c(1 - \pi)Y + v\Omega, \tag{10.11}$$

where Ω is household wealth.

Household wealth evolves endogenously, and the ratio of household wealth to capital (Tobin's q) need not be constant. Bubbles and financial instability, moreover, can be sources of fluctuations in employment and output, as evidenced by the financial crisis of 2008 and the prolonged recession that followed. This chapter, however, focuses on cycles that have their root in the goods market and, for simplicity, the ratio of household wealth to capital is taken to be constant. Setting the ratio equal to 1, Equation (10.11) implies that the aggregate saving rate can be written as

$$\frac{S}{K} = \frac{Y}{K} - \frac{C}{K} = \sigma - c(1 - \pi)\sigma - v$$
$$= g(\pi, \sigma); \qquad g_1 > 0, g_2 > 0. \tag{10.12}$$

10.3.4   A Baseline Model

The behavioral equations for the growth rate of output, the accumulation rate, and the aggregate saving rate – Equations (10.7), (10.10), and (10.12) – can be combined with two accounting relations and an equilibrium condition for the goods market:

---

[16] The analysis in Appendix A follows Skott (1989) with minor modifications. Caballero (1997) presents a related analysis of investment with nonconvex adjustment costs.

$$\hat{K} = \frac{I}{K} - \delta; \quad \delta > 0 \tag{10.13}$$

$$\hat{e} = \hat{Y} - n \tag{10.14}$$

$$I = S, \tag{10.15}$$

where δ and n are the depreciation rate and the natural rate of growth, respectively. Equation (10.13) relates the change in the capital stock to gross investment and depreciation. Equation (10.14), which links changes in the employment rate to the growth of output, follows from the fixed coefficient production function and the absence of labor hoarding. Unlike Equation (10.15), these two equations are quite standard.

Equation (10.15) is not a typical short-run Keynesian equilibrium condition. Short-term expectations are fulfilled in a Keynesian equilibrium: The equality between saving and investment is attained at prices and wages that give firms no incentive to change production and employment. The present model, by contrast, does not assume that short-term expectations are fulfilled. The level of output is predetermined at any moment, with Equation (10.15) defining an ultra-short-run Marshallian equilibrium in which prices and the distribution of income adjust to clear the market. The approach is similar to the one used in the Marshallian version of the IS-LM analysis in Chapter 8. The difference is that now both output and investment are predetermined, and adjustments in the distribution of income serve to align saving with investment (as opposed to the adjustment of investment to saving through changes in the interest rate in the Marshallian version of the IS-LM model).

Three conditions must be satisfied for the Marshallian mechanism to work in this setting. First, prices must be flexible and respond to excess demand. Second, distribution must be sensitive to price changes, a condition that is met if money wages are sticky: There is neither instantaneous feedback from output prices to money-wage rates nor perfect foresight about prices when wages are set. The real-wage rate and the share of profits in income, therefore, respond to movements in money prices. Third, aggregate demand needs to be sensitive to changes in distributive shares; in fact, aggregate demand must be inversely related to the share of profits. The inverse relation is required for stability reasons. Firms raise their prices, and the share of profits increases if there is excess demand. Unless the relation between demand and profits is inverse, this increase in profits exacerbates the initial disequilibrium, and the ultra-short-run equilibrium will be unstable. The stability condition clearly is met by the benchmark specifications in (10.10) and (10.12): Investment is independent of the current profit share, while an increase in the profit share raises aggregate saving.

10.4   Analysis

The overall working of the model is as follows. The employment rate, e, the rate of output, Y, the capital stock, K, and the utilization rate, σ, are all predetermined at any moment. For given values of these state variables, the equilibrium condition for the goods market determines a unique share of profits. Formally, Equations (10.10), (10.12), and (10.15) imply that

$$\frac{I}{K} = f(\sigma) = g(\pi,\sigma) = \frac{S}{K}$$

or, using the implicit function theorem,

$$\pi = \pi(\sigma); \quad \pi' = \frac{f' - g_2}{g_1}. \tag{10.16}$$

The sign of the derivative π' is ambiguous, positive if investment is more sensitive than saving to variations in output (if $f' > g_2$) but negative if it is less sensitive (if $f' < g_2$).

With the distribution of income determined by Equation (10.16), Equation (10.7) determines the rate of growth of output, and (10.14) links the rate of growth of the employment rate to output growth. The accumulation rate is determined by (10.10), and the dynamics of σ is determined by output growth and the accumulation rate. Thus, the complete time paths of σ and e are determined by the initial values of the same two variables.

Formally, Equations (10.7), (10.10), and (10.12)–(10.15) define a two-dimensional system of differential equations with the utilization rate σ and the employment rate e as state variables:

$$\hat{\sigma} = \hat{Y} - \hat{K} = h(\pi(\sigma),\sigma,e) - f(\sigma) + \delta$$
$$\hat{e} = h(\pi(\sigma),\sigma,e) - n$$

or

$$\dot{\sigma} = \sigma[h(\pi(\sigma),\sigma,e) - f(\sigma) + \delta] \tag{10.17}$$
$$\dot{e} = e[h(\pi(\sigma),\sigma,e) - n]. \tag{10.18}$$

Existence and uniqueness of a steady growth path.
The viability of a capitalist economy requires that accumulation and output grow at least as rapidly as the labor force in effective units when conditions are favorable, that is, when demand is strong and workers are weak. Formally, there must be economically meaningful values of σ and e such that $\hat{K} = f(\sigma) - \delta > n$ and $\hat{Y} = h(\pi(\sigma),\sigma,e) > n$. If this viability condition fails to be met, the employment rate will converge to zero.

From a purely mathematical point of view, the capitalist economy could also be 'too dynamic,' in the sense that $\hat{e}$ or $\hat{K} - n$ could be positive for all values of σ and e with $\sigma \in [0,\sigma^{\max}]$ and $e \in [0,1]$. This possibility can be discounted, however: The net accumulation rate must turn negative as $\sigma \to 0$ if the depreciation rate is positive, and output growth cannot exceed the natural growth rate if $e = 1$.

These viability and plausibility conditions are necessary but not sufficient for the existence of the nontrivial stationary solution.[17] To see this, note that setting $\dot{e} = \dot{\sigma} =$

---

[17] Equations (10.17)–(10.18) always have an additional, trivial stationary solution with $\sigma = e = 0$.

0, a nontrivial stationary solution with $e > 0$ and $\sigma > 0$ must satisfy

$$h(\pi(\sigma),\sigma,e) - f(\sigma) + \delta = 0 \tag{10.19}$$

$$h(\pi(\sigma),\sigma,e) - n = 0. \tag{10.20}$$

Substituting (10.18) into (10.17), we obtain

$$f(\sigma) - \delta = n. \tag{10.21}$$

The accumulation rate is strictly increasing in σ, and Equation (10.21) therefore has at most one solution, $\sigma = \sigma^*$; the existence of a solution with $0 < \sigma < 1$ follows from the viability and plausibility conditions which imply that $f(0) < n + \delta < f(\sigma^{\max})$. Substituting this solution for σ into the right-hand side of Equation (10.20) gives the stationarity condition

$$h(\pi(\sigma^*),\sigma^*,e) = n. \tag{10.22}$$

The partial derivative of h with respect to e is negative, and it follows that Equation (10.22) has at most one solution. The conditions of viability and plausibility do not, however, guarantee the existence of a solution. The viability conditions require that for some (σ,e), we have $h(\pi(\sigma),\sigma,e) > n$ and $f(\sigma) - \delta > n$, but these requirements do not imply that $h(\pi(\sigma^*),\sigma^*,e) \geq 0$ for some $e \in [0,1]$. Chapter 11 considers the implications of nonexistence of a steady growth path with a constant employment rate. For now, I assume the existence of a meaningful stationary solution (e^*,σ^*).

Local stability properties.
The local stability properties of the stationary solution are determined by the Jacobian of the system (10.17)–(10.18). At the stationary solution, the Jacobian is given by

$$J(\sigma,e) = \begin{pmatrix} \sigma^*(h_1\pi' + h_2 - f') & \sigma^*h_3 \\ e^*(h_1\pi' + h_2) & e^*h_3 \end{pmatrix}. \tag{10.23}$$

The determinant and trace are

$$\det = -\sigma^*e^*f'h_3 > 0$$
$$tr = \sigma^*(h_1\pi' + h_2 - f') + e^*h_3.$$

The determinant is unambiguously positive, which rules out a saddle point. The stationary solution will be a locally stable node or focus if the trace is negative and locally unstable if the trace is positive. The sign of the trace is ambiguous, and with three negative terms and only one positive term $(\sigma^*h_1\pi')$, stability might seem the most likely outcome.

A case can be made, however, for local instability. Short-run macroeconomic analysis examines variations in output that are rapid relative to any movements in the capital stock: The capital stock is taken to be constant, while the equilibrium level of output depends positively on the level of investment. This assumption in static short-run theory has a dynamic counterpart. Suppose that there is a rise in investment. If the level of output is predetermined, the immediate impact of the rise in investment is to reduce the ratio of output to investment below the short-run equilibrium level. Adjustments in output, however, restore the equilibrium relation, and during this adjustment process, $\hat{Y}$ must exceed $\hat{K}$. In fact, $\hat{Y}$ must be many times greater than $\hat{K}$ in order to justify the standard approach, which assumes that short-run equilibrium is established so quickly that the capital stock can be taken as fixed in short-run analysis. Formally, we must have

$$d\hat{Y} \gg d\hat{K}. \tag{10.24}$$

Suppose that the economy is initially in short-run equilibrium and consider the implications of a marginal increase in σ. With a given capital stock K, the increase in the output-capital ratio σ reflects a rise in Y:

$$dY = K d\sigma.$$

But the increase in utilization also affects both investment and the short-run equilibrium level of output:

$$dI = f'K d\sigma$$
$$dY^* = m dI = m f'K d\sigma,$$

where m and Y^* are the investment multiplier and the short-run equilibrium level of output, respectively. If it takes T periods (years) for the multiplier to work itself out, we have

$$d\hat{Y} \approx \frac{1}{T} d\left(\frac{Y^* - Y}{Y}\right) = \frac{1}{T}\frac{mf' - 1}{\sigma} d\sigma.$$

Now return to the model in Equations (10.17)–(10.18) and observe that the trace of the Jacobian can be written as[18]

$$tr = \sigma^*\left(\frac{d\hat{Y}}{d\sigma} - \frac{d\hat{K}}{d\sigma}\right) + e^*\frac{\partial\hat{Y}}{\partial e}$$

$$= \sigma^*\left(\frac{1}{T}\frac{mf' - 1}{\sigma} - f'\right) + e^*h_3. \tag{10.25}$$

Hence, with a multiplier well above 1 and a strong sensitivity of accumulation rates to changes in utilization in the neighborhood of the stationary point, a standard Keynesian assumption of rapid convergence to short-run equilibrium (a small value of T) is destabilizing: The first term on the right-hand side of Equation (10.25) will be positive, and local stability requires a strong negative effect from employment to the growth rate of output. Thus, in what follows, I shall focus mainly on the case of a locally unstable stationary solution.

Global boundedness and limit cycles.
Consider the phase diagram in Figure 10.2. The existence and uniqueness of the stationary solution imply that the $\dot{e} = 0$ and $\dot{\sigma} = 0$ curves intersect once in the positive

---

[18] The notation $d\hat{Y}/d\sigma$ is used here to indicate the 'partial total derivative': $d\hat{Y}/d\sigma = h_1\pi' + h_2$.

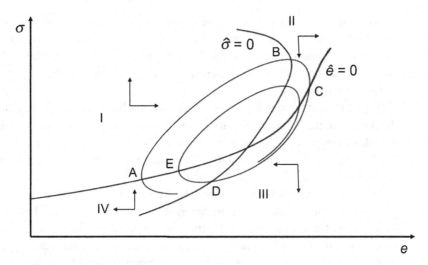

Figure 10.2 Phase diagram for the baseline model.

quadrant. If the stationary point is locally unstable, both curves must be positively sloped, and the $\dot\sigma = 0$ locus must be steeper than the $\dot e = 0$ locus at the intersection.[19]

The Leontief specification of the production technology provides an upper limit on the output-capital ratio ($\sigma \leq \sigma^{max}$), and the $\dot\sigma = 0$ locus, therefore, must bend back and become downward sloping for high values of σ. Analogously, the upper limit on employment ($e \leq e^{max} = 1$) implies that the $\dot e = 0$ curve rises sharply and has a vertical asymptote as the employment rate approaches 1 (cf. the discussion of nonlinearities in Section 10.3). Intuitively, an increase in the employment rate from 0.8 to 0.81 will have only minor effects on labor market conditions; the effects are large, however, if the rate increases from 0.98 to 0.99. These nonlinearities preclude cumulative upward divergence.

The system (10.17)–(10.18) also contains stabilizing forces that are strengthened when employment and utilization fall. Gross investment cannot turn negative, while nonlinearities in the output expansion function are likely to dampen feedback effects from market conditions to the growth rate of output at high and low levels of growth. Furthermore, the saving rate – which influences the market-clearing profit share and thereby the growth rate of output – is related to the inverse of the output-capital ratio, which strengthens the stabilizing forces at low levels of the output-capital ratio. As is

---

[19] The slopes are given by

$$\dot\sigma = 0: \quad \frac{d\sigma}{de} = -\frac{\partial\dot\sigma/\partial e}{\partial\dot\sigma/\partial\sigma} = \frac{-h_3}{h_1\pi' + h_2 - f'}$$

$$\dot e = 0: \quad \frac{d\sigma}{de} = -\frac{\partial\dot e/\partial e}{\partial\dot\sigma/\partial\sigma} = \frac{-h_3}{h_1\pi' + h_2}.$$

The $\dot e = 0$ locus is unambiguously positively sloped. The positive slope of the $\dot\sigma = 0$ locus follows from local instability, which requires that $\partial\dot\sigma/\partial\sigma > 0$ (otherwise, the trace of the Jacobian would be negative and the determinant positive). The denominator of the expression for the slope of the $\dot\sigma = 0$ locus is positive but smaller than the denominator of the expression for the $\dot e = 0$ locus, which establishes the relative steepness.

typically the case, however, it is difficult to establish a definite floor under the downturn. In the absence of additional assumptions about functional forms and parameter values, the possibility of collapse cannot be excluded: Some (or all) initial values away from the stationary solution may generate trajectories that have the employment rate go to zero asymptotically.

Assuming that the stabilizing forces are sufficiently strong to provide a floor under the downturn, the Poincaré–Bendixson theorem ensures the presence of endogenous, bounded fluctuations: The local instability of the unique, nontrivial stationary point implies that any trajectory that starts away from the stationary point must converge to a closed orbit, that is, to a locally stable limit cycle.[20]

Figure 10.2 illustrates this outcome. The low output-capital ratio (utilization rate) at point A depresses the rate of accumulation of capital below the natural rate of growth. Low accumulation rates reduce profitability, but the low output-capital ratio corresponds to a high wealth income ratio, which reduces the saving rate and raises the profit share. Output growth gets an additional boost from high unemployment rates, which reduce search cost and dampen workers' demands. The net effect of these different forces is for output and employment to grow at a rate that matches the rate of increase in the labor supply in effective units; with $\hat{K}$ below the natural growth rate, the output-capital ratio is rising. As the utilization rate increases, the economy moves into the area marked I. The rise in utilization stimulates investment, and product market equilibrium is maintained by increases in the profit share. The rise in profitability in turn stimulates the rate of growth of output, and both the output-capital ratio and the rate of employment are increasing.

The gradual increase in employment leads to a strengthening of worker power, increasing search cost, and downward pressure on the growth rate of output and employment. The rate of accumulation, on the other hand, is rising, and at point B, accumulation has caught up with output growth; the output-capital ratio attains its cyclical maximum. Employment is still expanding at B, but a tightening labor market generates declining growth rates of output as the economy moves beyond B. The output-capital ratio begins to fall. The decline in utilization rates discourages investment, and profitability suffers further as prices adjust to maintain product market equilibrium; falling profit shares now speed up the decline in the growth rate of output.

At C, the rate of growth of employment has become equal to the growth rate of the labor supply, and the employment rate has reached its cyclical peak. The share of profits and the output-capital ratio are still fairly high, but a tight labor market depresses the growth rate of output and employment. The movement that took the economy from A to C is now repeated in reverse: The decline in utilization comes

---

[20] The possibility that $e \to 0$ is excluded if there is a positive employment rate, $\bar{e} > 0$, with the property that $\hat{\sigma} > 0$ for all (e, u) for which $\hat{e} < 0$ and $e < \bar{e}$ (Skott 1989a, 1989b). The specification of the dynamic system in Skott (1989a, 1989b) is slightly different from the one here but also reduces to a two-dimensional system in utilization and employment, and the same proof of the existence of a compact, positively invariant subset of the strictly positive quadrant applies in the present context. The Poincaré–Bendixson theorem implies that any trajectory starting within this compact subset must either be stationary (have the stationary solution as its initial position) or converge to a closed orbit around the stationary point (e.g., Hale 1969).

to a halt at D, and the gradual recovery of utilization rates and profit shares from their nadir initiates from the stimulus to output growth arising from further falls in employment. After this first stimulus, the accelerator effects of investment produce the upward movement back toward the $\hat{e} = 0$ locus at E.

This baseline model treats output as a state variable, assuming that output growth depends on the degree of disequilibrium in the goods market and treating prices as perfectly flexible. It should be emphasized, however, that the presence of endogenous cycles does not depend on whether disappointed short-run expectations show up as price movements or rationing. *If* there is perfect price flexibility, the profit share can serve as an indicator of goods market disequilibrium, with the growth of output becoming a function of the profit share (an indicator of disequilibrium in the goods market), the utilization rate (an indicator of the proportion of firms facing capital constraints), and the employment rate (an indicator of the state of the labor market), as outlined in Equation (10.7). This specification, however, is contingent on prices being perfectly flexible, an assumption that was motivated by empirical evidence

If the flex-price assumption is dropped and disequilibrium leads to direct rationing, the output expansion function must be modified. Appendix C analyzes an intermediate case with finite adjustment speeds for prices. Firms still adjust output in response to disequilibrium in the goods market, but disequilibrium now manifests in a combination of (i) a profit share that deviates from what firms would have chosen had output been perfectly flexible and (ii) direct rationing of household consumption. The flex-price model emerges at one extreme (as the adjustment speed for price goes to infinity) and the fix-price model at the other (as the adjustment speed goes to zero). The local stability conditions are independent of whether disequilibrium takes the form of rationing or price changes, and the model generates endogenous business cycles.

10.5   Empirical Evidence and the Baseline Model

The endogenous cycles in the baseline model exhibit clockwise movements in the (e, σ) space, as indicated by the phase diagram in Figure 10.2. Cyclical fluctuations in the output-capital ratio reflect fluctuations in utilization rates (since, by assumption the production function is Leontief), and the clockwise cycles in (e, σ) translate into clockwise cycles in (e, u) with u denoting utilization. This implication of the model is consistent with empirical observations for the United States. But clearly, getting the orientation of these cycles right does not constitute strong support. There are many other patterns in the US data.

Zipperer and Skott (2011) examine data for the employment rate, the profit share, and the utilization rate. The US data for 1948–2008 show strong evidence of clockwise short-term cycles in three bivariate spaces: (e, π), (e, u), and (u, π).[21] Clockwise short-run cycles exist for $(e, \hat{Y}), (\pi, \hat{Y})$, and $(u, \hat{Y})$ as well, while the orientations of the

---

[21] The cycles are relative to long-term trends of the variables as measured by Hodrick–Prescott filters. The trends exhibit modest long-term variation. The percentage point difference between the maximum and minimum values of the HP trend is 2.7, 4.4, and 5.7 for employment, the profit share, and the utilization rate, respectively.

cycles in the $(e, \hat{K}), (\pi, \hat{K})$, and $(u, \hat{K})$ spaces are less consistent. The short-term cycles are synchronized with the standard NBER dating of business cycles, and the cyclical patterns appear to be quite robust to changes in the precise definition and measurement of the variables.[22]

As one would expect, the cyclical patterns in other countries are not as clean and regular as those in the US data: Small open economies are unlikely to exhibit the regular cyclical patterns that may arise from the private-sector interaction between accumulation, output, and pricing decisions in a closed capitalist economy without a public sector. Economic fluctuations in Luxembourg, to take an extreme example, are largely determined by what happens outside the country. In developing economies with large informal sectors and underemployment, moreover, changes in the employment rate may have little effect on the modern sector. The United States is as close as one gets to a closed economy, its public sector is relatively modest, and unlike Japan and many European economies, it has not had large sectors of traditional, family-based agriculture for a good part of the post-World-War II period.

Simulations can be used to get an idea of the consistency of the observed US patterns with the predictions of the baseline model. Specific functional forms and parameters are needed, however, and I use the following specifications:

$$\hat{Y} = \frac{0.3}{1 + \exp(-20(\pi - 0.3 + 0.02(0.1^{-0.5} - (1 - e)^{-0.5})) + 0.01((0.1^{-0.5} - (0.6 - \sigma)^{-0.5})))} - 0.12 \tag{10.26}$$

$$\hat{K} = \max\{-0.07, 0.03 + 1.0(\sigma - 0.5)\} \tag{10.27}$$

$$\frac{S}{K} = \pi\sigma - 0.05. \tag{10.28}$$

The sigmoid-shaped functional form of the output expansion function, which is consistent with the analysis in Section 10.3.1, constrains the growth rate of e to the interval between -0.15 and $+0.15$ if the natural growth rate is 0.03. The exponential term in the denominator is linear in the profit share but nonlinear in employment and utilization: Variations in e and σ have a much larger impact when the economy approaches full employment and full capacity than in periods with high unemployment and low utilization rates. The parameters are chosen to give partial derivatives at the stationary state of about 1.5 for the profit share, -0.5 for the employment rate and -0.25 for the output-capital ratio. These values are consistent with empirical estimates of the output expansion function in Skott and Zipperer (2012).

The nonnegativity of gross investment sets a lower limit on the growth rate of the capital stock: The depreciation rate is set to 0.07, and $\hat{K}$ is given as the maximum of this lower limit and a linear function of the output-capital ratio σ.[23] If the stationary solution for the output-capital ratio corresponds to a utilization rate of about 80 percent (roughly the average value of the utilization rate in the US data) and the output-capital

---

[22] See also Barrales-Ruiz et al. (2021) for a recent survey of evidence on distributive cycles.

[23] Induced scrapping at low rates of utilization could make the depreciation rate endogenous. Simulations without the lower bound on net accumulation produce qualitatively similar results.

ratio at normal utilization is 0.5, the specification and parameters in Equation (10.27) imply an increase in the accumulation rate of 5/8 percentage points following a 1 percentage point increase in utilization. This sensitivity of investment to changes in utilization is consistent with – but at the lower end of – the estimated long-run impact of utilization on investment in Skott and Zipperer (2012). The natural rate of growth is set to $n = 0.03$, and the functional form of the saving function follows the specification in Equation (10.12), with $c = 1$, $v = 0.05$. The unique, nontrivial stationary solution has $\sigma^* = 0.5$, $e^* = 0.9$, $\pi^* = 0.3$, $\hat{K}^* = \hat{Y}^* = 0.03$. The stationary solution is locally unstable; the system produces a limit cycle.

The simulation in Figure 10.3, which uses $\sigma = 0.52, e = 0.92$ as the initial values, reproduces the observed clockwise patterns in the bivariate $(e, \sigma), (e, \pi), (e, \hat{Y}), (\pi, \hat{Y})$, and $(\sigma, \hat{Y})$ spaces. The model cannot, however, generate cycles in (σ, π) space: Both σ and π fluctuate, but the profit share is determined as a function of the utilization rate, which precludes cycles in this space. The employment rate fluctuates with an amplitude of about 4.5 percentage points in the limit cycle, which is fairly close to the average for US business cycles. The amplitude for the profit share – about 2.6 percentage points – is also not too far off US average rates, but in contrast to the simulations, the amplitude in the fluctuations of utilization in the US data is significantly higher than those for employment and the profit share.[24]

Overall, the fit of the model is surprisingly good, given the parsimonious specification. But there are important caveats. The simulations, first, are sensitive to changes in parameter values and functional forms. Although the functional forms and parameters are, I would argue, behaviorally and empirically plausible, other, equally plausible parameters and functional forms can produce very different results.

The fragility of the results can be illustrated by changing the parameter in the investment function (the specification of this function may be especially shaky). If the coefficient on σ is reduced slightly from 1 to 0.985, the limit cycle disappears and the stationary solution becomes locally stable; increasing the coefficient above 1.075, on the other hand, generates unbounded cyclical fluctuations and, eventually, a complete collapse as the employment rate converges to zero. The window of cycles is not quite as narrow as these qualitative results suggest: For practical purposes, it makes little difference whether the system produces slow oscillatory convergence to the stationary solution or convergence to a closed orbit. But the point remains: The simulation results are fragile, and I deliberately chose a sensitivity of investment to changes in utilization at the low end of the empirical estimates in order to illustrate the possibility of limit cycles in the baseline model.

The specification of investment, second, may have more significant problems than the choice of parameters. There are lags between changes in demand and investment decisions as well as between investment decisions and the implementation of investment; these lags can be substantial for some types of investment, including the

---

[24] The parameter values used in the simulation imply that the predicted amplitude of about 0.02 in the fluctuations of the output-capital ratio translates into an amplitude of about 3.2 percentage points for the utilization rate.

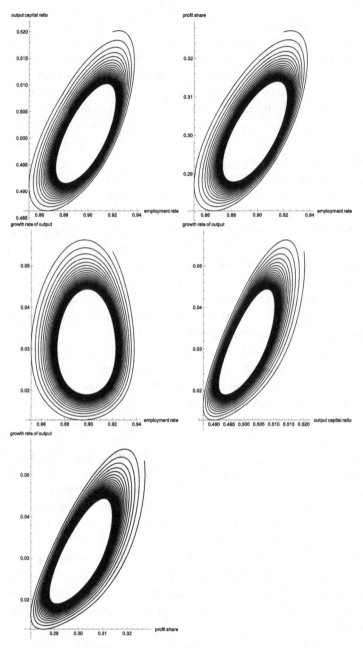

Figure 10.3 Baseline model.

construction of major new plants. The treatment of output as a state variable implies that shocks to demand have their initial impact on prices and profit shares, only gradually influencing the levels of output and utilization. But this indirect introduction of a delay between changes in demand and investment still fails to capture the lags that we observe in the data.

To approximate these lags in a continuous-time setting, a distinction can be made between actual and target investment, with actual accumulation rates adjusting toward the target rate. This gradual adjustment of investment is analogous to the capital adjustment principle but now applied to investment levels rather than capital stocks. If Equation (10.10) is used to describe target investment, a modified version of investment behavior in the baseline model is now represented by two equations:

$$\hat{K}^T = f(\sigma) - \delta; \quad f' > 0 \tag{10.29}$$

$$\frac{d}{dt}(\hat{K}) = \lambda_{\hat{K}}(\hat{K}^T - \hat{K}); \quad \lambda_{\hat{K}} > 0, \tag{10.30}$$

where $\hat{K}^T$ denotes the target rate of net accumulation.

Figure 10.4 depicts simulations of the modified baseline model. The functional forms and parameters are the same as in Equations (10.26)–(10.28), but Equation (10.27) now describes targeted accumulation. The adjustment speed of accumulation in Equation (10.30) is set to 1 ($\lambda_{\hat{K}} = 1$), and the initial values are $\sigma = 0.52, e = 0.91$, and $\hat{K} = 0.03$. The introduction of investment dynamics is destabilizing, and the trajectory spirals out, ultimately leading to economic collapse ($e \to 0$).[25] The orientation of cycles in the bivariate (e, σ), (e, π), $(e, \hat{Y})$, $(\pi, \hat{Y})$, and $(\sigma, \hat{Y})$ spaces are still correct. The modified model also produces cycles in the $\sigma - \pi$ space, but contrary to the observed US patterns, the movements are counterclockwise in this space. The amplitude of the fluctuations in utilization is still too low relative to the amplitudes for employment and the profit share.

10.6 An Extended Model: Economic Policy, Investment Dynamics, Credit Constraints, and Okun's Law

The baseline model leaves out a number of factors that clearly play a role in the US economy. It is not surprising, therefore, that there are discrepancies between the simulation of the baseline model and the observed patterns.

The evidence, first, shows output-capital ratios fluctuating more strongly than the employment rate. The failure of the model to capture this empirical regularity may be due to the assumption of a constant labor productivity. Okun's law implies procyclical productivity, and, intuitively, an increase in the volatility of output (relative to that of employment) may be expected to amplify the volatility of the output-capital ratio (relative to that of the employment rate).

A second missing factor is more fundamental: The public sector and economic policy influence macroeconomic dynamics. The public sector in the United States is smaller than that in many European countries, but taxes and transfers still generate automatic stabilizers. The relative stability of public spending on goods and services

---

[25] Limit cycles appear for values of the coefficient on σ in (10.27) that are below 0.95. As in the baseline model without investment adjustments, limit cycles give way to damped oscillations when the coefficient is reduced further.

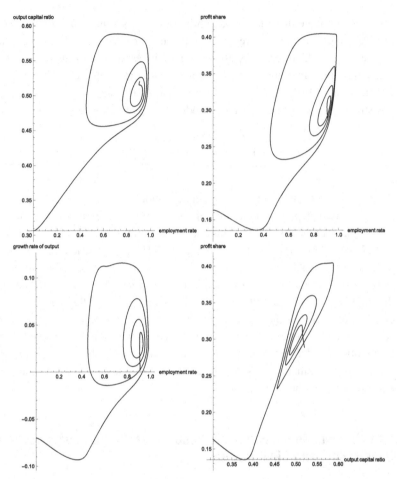

Figure 10.4 Baseline model with gradual adjustment of investment.

also contributes to stabilization, while serious downturns tend to induce discretionary fiscal measures – as evidenced in the United States by the stimulus bill in 2009 and the various packages in response to the COVID-19 pandemic and its economic fall-out. On the monetary side, interest rate adjustments are used routinely to stabilize the economy.[26]

Third, the equation describing target investment has left out the potential effects of credit constraints, the influence of labor market conditions on animal spirits, and endogenous changes in the expected trend rate of growth. The specification of investment could be amended to allow for these factors.

Fourth, the trajectories of output and employment are influenced, sometimes very powerfully, by foreign trade as well as by interactions of the real sectors with financial markets, including housing and stock market bubbles. To take an obvious example, the Great Recession of 2008–2009 cannot be understood without the previous housing

---

[26] Franke (2018) analyzes the stabilizing effect of Taylor rules; Ryoo and Skott (2017) consider fiscal and monetary policy rules in an economy with Harrodian instability.

bubble and the financial forces behind the bubble.[27] But while important, the influences from international trade and asset market bubbles are less regular and not closely tied to the business cycle mechanisms that emanate from the domestic goods and labor markets. Thus, the extensions of the model in this section will focus on the first three elements: Okun's law, economic policy, and the specification of the investment function. The ambition is not to capture all aspects of the three factors but, more modestly, to incorporate some systematic effects in simple and tractable ways.

Okun's Law

Okun's law indicates that a 1 percentage point increase in the growth rate of output above trend will raise the growth rate of employment by less than 1 percentage point – about one-third of a point in Okun's original estimates but closer to half a point in more recent data. Using a coefficient of 0.5, the law implies that the growth rate of e will be given by

$$\hat{e} = 0.5(\hat{Y} - 0.03). \tag{10.31}$$

This equation replaces (10.14) in the baseline model.

Taxes, Transfers, and Public Spending

The presence of a public sector changes the equilibrium condition for the goods market, which now requires that

$$Y = C + I + G. \tag{10.32}$$

The relative stability of government spending on goods and services can be captured by linking it to potential output. There are two natural indicators of potential output: The level of output associated with normal utilization of the capital stock ($\sigma^* K$) and the level of output associated with having employment and the productivity of labor at their normal values ($\bar{A}e^* N$). Thus, let[28]

$$G = \gamma_1 \sigma^* K + \gamma_2 e^* \bar{A}N. \tag{10.33}$$

Okun's law implies that labor productivity varies over the cycle, and $\bar{A}N$ denotes the labor supply in effective units along a steady growth path with $e = e^*$ and $\sigma = \sigma^*$.

Tax revenues may be determined largely by current income, but many transfers depend on the employment rate; unemployment benefits represent a prime example. As a simple specification, let

$$T = t_1 Y - t_2(e^* - e)\bar{A}N. \tag{10.34}$$

Private consumption is affected by taxes, and I assume that the specification in Equation (10.11) still applies, but with disposable wage income taking the place of wage

---

[27] The financial and housing bubbles of the 1990s and 2000s in turn may be symptomatic of long-term aggregate demand problems – a topic that will be addressed in Chapter 11.

[28] This specification is similar to one used by Thompson (2018). Fazzari et al. (2013) also emphasize the stabilizing effects of government spending in a related model.

income and private-sector wealth given by the sum of the capital stock (K) and public debt (B), that is, $\Omega = K + B$. If employment-dependent transfers are treated like wage income, the modified consumption function is given by

$$C = c[(1 - t_1)(1 - \pi)Y + t_2(e^* - e)\bar{A}N] + v(K + B). \tag{10.35}$$

Equations (10.32)–(10.35) can be combined to determine the market-clearing profit share:

$$\pi = \frac{1}{c(1 - t_1)} \left[\frac{\hat{K} + \delta + \gamma_1 \sigma^* + v(1 + b)}{\sigma} + (ct_2 + \gamma_2)\frac{e^*\bar{A}}{eA} - ct_2\frac{\bar{A}}{A} \right] - [1 - c(1 - t_1)]. \tag{10.36}$$

The dynamics of government debt follows the standard equation

$$\dot{B} = G - T + rB.$$

Deficits (surpluses) will appear in recessions (booms), leading to fluctuations in public debt, and because of asymmetries between expansions and downturns, the average level of debt over the cycle may deviate from zero. The tax, transfer, and spending parameters will be calibrated, however, to ensure that a balanced government budget and zero debt become consistent with steady growth. Chapter 11 considers fiscal policy and the role of public debt in the long run.

Credit Constraints, Animal Spirits, and Investment Dynamics

The baseline model of investment ignored the potential effect of credit constraints. An inability to obtain external finance (or, more generally, an inability to obtain it on reasonable terms) implies that firms' cash flow becomes important; the profit share may have a direct influence on investment (e.g., Fazzari et al. 1988).

There may also be feedback effects from the labor market to accumulation: The size of the reserve army of the unemployed may influence the business climate (animal spirits) and the willingness of firms to invest. The effects of monetary policy reinforce this argument. High wage demands when labor markets are tight tend to raise inflation, and even inflation-targeting central banks that pay little or no attention to real output and employment will raise real interest rates in the boom and reduce them in recessions. Thus, the negative effects on investment of a rise in employment can represent a direct Marxian influence on the business climate as well as the effects of employment-induced movements in real interest rates. As in the case of employment effects on output growth, the effects are likely to be highly nonlinear and stronger at high rates of employment.

Adding the profit share and the employment rate as determinants of the target rate of accumulation still leaves a question of dynamics. The derivation of the investment function in Appendix A assumed that firms expect to experience short-run shocks to the growth rate of demand, but their expected long-run growth rate was taken to be constant. If firms were identical and the economy fluctuated around a steady growth path, this assumption would be reasonable: The representative firm's long-run growth expectations could become anchored to the long-run steady growth rate – in this case, the exogenously given natural rate of growth. But firms differ. Some firms experience high growth rates, while others stagnate or decline. Hence, even if aggregate output fluctuates around a steady growth path with a constant employment rate, the growth expectations of individual firms will not be anchored to the natural rate.

Innovations or structural shifts in demand patterns can generate persistent shifts in the growth of demand for individual goods and services. Each firm will have to form an estimate of its own long-run prospects: When observing an increase in demand, it has to disentangle the role of temporary shifts (which can be firm specific or related to aggregate demand) from sustained, firm-specific shifts. In these circumstances, the firm is likely to interpret the increase in demand as a reflection of both temporary and permanent elements, and adjust expectations accordingly. The basic argument here is analogous to that in Phelps (1969) and Lucas (1972), in which each household-producer observes its own price but has no direct information about the aggregate price level. The producer, therefore, does not know whether a price increase reflects a change in its relative price and consumption real wage. Unlike in Phelps and Lucas, there is no presumption here of rational expectations, and the focus is on firms and their assessment of whether demand shifts are permanent or temporary, rather than on households' labor supply and their assessment of whether a price increase reflects a rise in the consumption real wage. But the qualitative argument is similar: A temporary increase in the growth rate of aggregate demand will have some, probably weak, effect on the average value of the expected future growth rate demand. Formally, let

$$\hat{K}^T = \gamma + f(\sigma, \pi, e); \qquad f_1 > 0, f_2 > 0, f_3 < 0 \tag{10.37}$$

$$\dot{\gamma} = \lambda_\gamma(\hat{Y} - \gamma). \tag{10.38}$$

Simulations

The simulations in Figure 10.5 are based on a specification that retains the output expansion function (10.26) as well as the parameter values $\delta = 0.07, n = 0.03, c = 1$, and $v = 0.05$. The government consumption parameters in (10.33) are $\gamma_1 = \gamma_2 = 0.1$; these values give equal weight to capital and labor capacity and make the average share of government consumption in income equal to 0.2. The tax and transfer parameters in (10.34) are $t_1 = 0.2$ and $t_2 = 0.125$[29]; as a stylized version of monetary policy, the real rate of interest on public debt is specified as $r = 0.5(e - 0.9)$. The adjustment parameter in (10.38) is set to 0.03, and the target investment function (10.37) is given by

$$\hat{K}^T = \gamma + 1.2(\sigma - 0.5) + 0.15(\pi - 0.375) + 0.03\left((1 - e^*)^{-0.5} - (1 - e)^{-0.5}\right).$$

The coefficient on σ in the baseline simulations was on the low side, and it has been raised from 1 to 1.2. Most firms do not face binding credit constraints, and the positive effect of the profit share is taken to be relatively small. The employment effect is nonlinear but, evaluated at the stationary solution, a 1 percentage point increase in employment reduces target accumulation by about 0.45 percentage points, a value

---

[29] These values of $t_1, t_2, \gamma_1, \gamma_2$ imply that the government budget is balanced along the steady growth path if there is no initial debt.

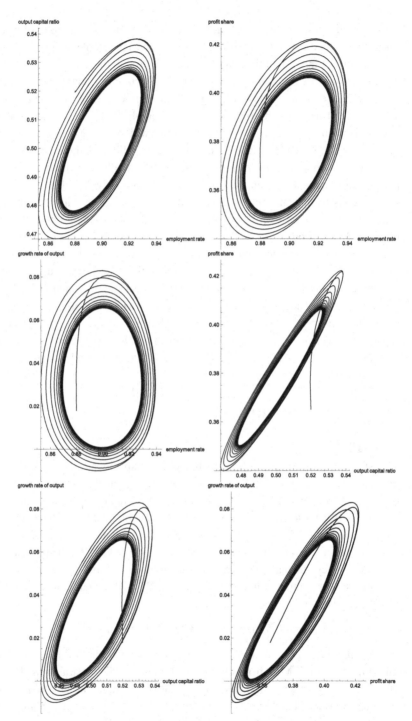

Figure 10.5 Extended version with a public sector, economic policy, Okun's law, and investment dynamics.

that reflects both the reduced-form interest effect from monetary policy and the direct effect of the state of the labor market on animal spirits.

The simulations show convergence to a stable limit cycle. All bivariate cycles now have the correct orientation, and the amplitude of the fluctuations in the utilization rate exceeds those for employment and the profit share.[30] More importantly, the qualitative outcomes are much more robust than was the case for the baseline model: Stable limit cycles around the stationary point continue to exist even if the investment coefficient on σ is raised as high as 10, far above the plausible range. The amplitude of the fluctuations increase as the coefficient is raised, with the shapes of the cycles also taking increasingly strange and complicated forms as the coefficient rises above 2 (which is still implausibly high). But the economy does not collapse and employment does not go to zero asymptotically. Reductions in the coefficient below 1.2 reduce the amplitude of the limit cycle, and the limit cycle gives way to damped oscillatory movements if the coefficient falls below 1.12.

Other simulations (not shown here) indicate that Okun's law, the positive effect of the profit share on accumulation, and the Harrodian expectation dynamics act to destabilize the stationary solution. The public sector and economic policy, by contrast, exert a powerful, stabilizing influence and serve to reduce the sensitivity of the limit cycle to changes in parameters.

Adding a public sector has another, arguably more significant implication: Economic policy responds to the state of the economy. If a destabilizing shift in behavioral parameters for the private sector occurs, the ensuing changes in economic performance will spark adjustments in policy. I shall return to this issue in the conclusion.

10.7 A Model with Flexible Output

The treatment of output as a predetermined state variable is reasonable if the model describes goods that cannot be produced instantaneously and for which production can be clearly separated from the delivery of the output to the customer. The services produced by a hairdresser – haircuts – cannot be separated from the delivery of these services to the consumer, however.

Not all service sector activities are like haircuts – scheduled buses and flights run even if few people board a particular departure – and many service industries may have elements of both flex price and flex output, with airlines as an example that may come closer to the flex-price model.[31] Even services like haircuts, moreover, are not without predetermined inputs. Cooks, hairdressers, and retail workers have to be hired, and they need kitchens, hair salons, and shops to work in. Neither capital nor labor can

---

[30] A range of about 0.05 for the output-capital ratio implies into a range of about 8 percentage points for the utilization rate if $\sigma = 0.5$ corresponds to a utilization rate of 80 percent.

[31] According to an article in the *New York Times*, travel providers, including airlines, increasingly use 'hyperdynamic pricing,' with the average price of domestic US flights changing 17 times in two days while "prices on high-traffic routes like New York to London can change up to 70 times over two days" (Weed 2020).

be adjusted instantaneously.[32] Output may be flexible, but employment and the stock of capital are predetermined at any moment, with the level of demand determining the utilization rates of labor and capital.

Consider a simple 'flex-output economy' along these lines.[33] There is excess capacity of both labor and capital, and output adjusts instantaneously to the level of demand (within the limits imposed by labor and capital capacity). Retaining a Leontief production function, the capacity constraints are given by

$$Y \leq \min\{AL, \sigma^{\max} K\}.$$

Short-run demand expectations are only being met if the utilization rate of labor is at the desired rate, but movements in output and utilization can absorb unanticipated demand shocks and make possible the equalization of saving and investment without direct rationing or adjustments in prices and profit shares. For simplicity suppose that there is no technical change and that both prices and wages are fixed, with $\omega = w/p$ denoting the real wage.

In this flex-output model, employment takes the place of output as a state variable, while the utilization rate of labor (the output labor ratio), rather than the profit share, becomes the fast moving indicator of short-run disequilibrium. The same behavioral reasoning that led to the output expansion function in the baseline model now yields an 'employment expansion function': Employment changes in response to demand signals from the output market (the utilization rate of labor), the employment capital ratio and the state of the labor market (the employment rate):

$$\hat{L} = h(y, l, e); \qquad h_1 > 0, h_2 < 0, h_3 < 0, \tag{10.39}$$

where $y = Y/L$ is a measure of labor utilization and $l = L/K$ denotes the employment capital ratio.

The investment function also needs modification compared to the baseline formulation. Capital adjusts more sluggishly than labor, and the accumulation rate now depends on the labor-capital ratio, rather than the output-capital ratio:

$$\frac{I}{K} = f(l); \qquad f' > 0. \tag{10.40}$$

Here again, the behavioral argument for the specification is analogous to the baseline case with flexible prices. Equations (10.39)–(10.40) and Equations (10.7) and (10.10) can be derived from the same basic behavioral assumptions; the differences arise because of changes in the assumptions about technologies and the nature of the output.

Retaining the saving function (10.12), the output labor ratio is determined by the condition

$$\frac{S}{K} = g(\pi, \sigma) = g(\pi, yl) = f(l) = \frac{I}{K}. \tag{10.41}$$

---

[32] There is an important qualifier for some segments of the workforce: The gig economy and an increasingly 'flexible' labor market in which workers are called in 'as needed' shift the costs of volatile demand and underutilization from firms towards workers.

[33] This section draws heavily on Skott (2015). The analysis has similarities with Diallo et al. (2011).

Shocks to demand affect labor productivity (labor utilization), and a constant real wage, therefore, does not imply constancy of the profit share; the profit share becomes an increasing function of labor utilization:

$$\pi = 1 - \frac{\omega}{y}. \tag{10.42}$$

Combining (10.41) and (10.42) and using the implicit function theorem, labor utilization can be written as a function of the labor-capital ratio:

$$y = y(l). \tag{10.43}$$

If the labor force grows at a constant rate, n, we obtain a two-dimensional system in the state variables e and l:

$$\dot{l} = l[h(y(l), l, e) - f(l) + \delta] \tag{10.44}$$

$$\dot{e} = e[h(y(l), l, e) - n]. \tag{10.45}$$

The employment rate is still a state variable. The new variable y has replaced π as the fast-moving variable, however, and l has taken the place of σ as the second state variable. The resulting dynamic system has the same mathematical structure as the system (10.17)–(10.18) for the baseline model with flexible prices. This similarity of the two systems comes out clearly in a simulation of the flex-output model.

The simulation in Figure 10.6 retains the saving function (10.28), and the investment function (10.27) is unchanged, except for the use of the employment capital ratio instead of the output-capital ratio as the determinant of accumulation. Labor productivity at the stationary solution is normalized to 1, which equalizes the steady-growth values of the labor-capital and output-capital ratios in the flex-price model; without this normalization, the coefficient on l would have to be adjusted to maintain the same sensitivity of accumulation to changes in the labor-capital ratio in the two models. The IS equation now determines output and labor productivity (with derived effects on the profit share), with Equation (10.39) relating employment growth to labor productivity. The simulation uses the same functional form as Equation (10.26), and, in order to compare the two models, they should be calibrated to have the same sensitivity of employment growth to disequilibrium. The normalization of labor productivity implies that this, too, is achieved with unchanged parameters.[34] Aside from the substitution of labor productivity for the profit share and of the employment capital ratio for the output-capital ratio, the labor expansion function, therefore, is identical to the output expansion function (10.26). The real wage is set to make the steady-growth value of the profit share equal to its steady-growth value in the flex-price model.

---

[34] A positive shock to $\hat{K}$ raises output and labor productivity in the flex-output model; the growth of employment reacts to this change in labor utilization, with the deviation of labor productivity from its steady-growth value entering the labor expansion function instead of the deviation of the profit share from its steady-growth value. Evaluated at the steady growth path, however, the normalization of labor productivity at the steady growth path and the functional forms of the saving and investment equations imply that the sensitivity of labor productivity to an increase in $\hat{K}$ in the flex-output model is equal to the sensitivity of the profit share to an increase in $\hat{K}$ in the flex-price model.

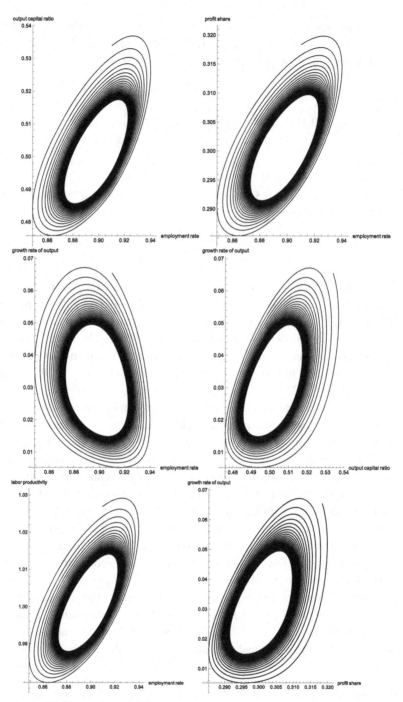

Figure 10.6 Flex-output model.

The patterns in Figure 10.6 are strikingly similar to those for the flex-price model in Figure 10.3. The stationary solution is locally unstable, and there is a stable limit cycle with clockwise movements in (e, σ), (e, π), $(e, \hat{Y})$, $(\sigma, \hat{Y})$, and $(\pi, \hat{Y})$ spaces.

The profit share can also be mapped against the capital utilization rate, but both $\sigma = ly(l)$ and $\pi = \pi(y(l))$ can be written as functions of l, and the calibrated model implies that, as in the baseline model, there are no cycles in the (σ, π) space. The shapes of the cycles are slightly different in some of the spaces, but overall the differences with respect to these cyclical patterns are quite minor. The one obvious difference is that, unlike the baseline model with flexible prices, the flex-output model produces clockwise cycles in labor productivity. These cycles mirror the movements in the profit share, which only changes in this model because of the movements in labor productivity.

The flex-output model can be extended in the same way as the baseline model, but flexible output also adds a degree of freedom to the determination of the functional distribution of income: The assumption of fixed real wages can be relaxed. At its simplest, this relaxation could involve making the real wage a function of labor utilization and the employment rate:

$$\omega = \psi(y, e). \tag{10.46}$$

Dynamic elements in the determination of the real wage can also be added, however. As an example, the real wage could be given by

$$\omega = \psi(a, y, e); \quad \psi_1 > 0 \tag{10.47}$$
$$\dot{a} = \lambda_a(l, e, \omega). \tag{10.48}$$

The state variable a in Equations (10.47) and (10.48) introduces gradual effects of labor utilization and employment on distribution. This determination of wages includes a simple Goodwin specification as a special case; if $\omega = \psi(a, y, e) = a$ and $\dot{a} = \lambda_a(l, e, \omega) = -\gamma + \rho e$, the system reduces to Goodwin's real-wage Phillips curve. As a further extension, the reduced-form specification of movements in the real wage can be replaced by separate equations for the formation of money wages and prices.[35] This extension would then also determine inflation, and explicit links between inflation and economic policy could be introduced (see Skott 2023).

10.8   Conclusion

The identification of destabilizing multiplier–accelerator dynamics dates back to the early days of the Keynesian revolution, with nonlinear models also demonstrating how local instability of the equilibrium could be the foundation for theories of endogenous cycles. This endogenous-cycle approach has been out of favor since the 1970s, however. Old Keynesian theories were rejected, and the monetarist, new classical, and new Keynesian models that took their place in mainstream macroeconomics have viewed the full-employment growth path as stable.[36] Fluctuations arise only as a result of stochastic shocks.

---

[35] Oh (2018) examines this case; see also Flaschel and Krolzig (2006) and Diallo et al. (2011).

[36] Consistent with Keynes's definition of full employment in the *General Theory*, the term is used as a shorthand for what came to be known as the natural rate of employment.

The analysis in this chapter has followed an old Keynesian tradition but deviates from early models of the business cycle in many ways, including greater attention to microeconomic behavior and the coupling of Keynesian–Harrodian goods market mechanisms with explicit feedback effects from the labor market to firms' output and investment decisions. The baseline model also differs from most other formulations by following a Marshall–Keynes–Kaldor tradition: Output is treated as a state variable, while prices and profit shares are flexible and adjust to clear the goods market. As outlined in Section 10.2, the motivation for the flex-price assumption is empirical. Prices, on my reading of the evidence, are much more flexible than commonly believed, and the model shows that flexible prices are perfectly compatible with Keynesian business cycles.

The local instability of the warranted growth path and the presence of endogenous cycles do not depend on price flexibility. Appendix C presents a model that combines rationing with price adjustment, while another variant of the baseline model flips the adjustment speeds completely, taking output (but not employment) as perfectly flexible and assuming a fixed real wage (Section 10.7). Surprisingly, perhaps, this flex-output version of the model generates reduced-form relations and dynamic patterns that are virtually identical to those of the baseline model with flexible prices. Capitalist economies contain sectors that are best approximated by the flex-price assumption as well as sectors for which the flex-output assumption may be more appropriate. The similarity in the properties of the two models suggests that the reduced-form equations of the baseline model may be a good starting point for analyzing business cycles in the aggregate economy. And, in fact, the baseline model can produce endogenous cycles with dynamic patterns that are broadly consistent with the US data. The qualitative properties of the baseline model are quite sensitive to the choice of functional forms and parameter values, however.

Straightforward extensions of the model improve the fit with the US data and increase the robustness of the results. Some of these extensions are destabilizing, but the introduction of a public sector and stylized fiscal and monetary policy rules has stabilizing effects, as one would expect. Importantly, while the baseline model generated cumulative divergence and eventual economic collapse for many plausible parameter values, the extended model shows much greater robustness: The stationary point (the steady growth path) may well be locally unstable, but this instability leads to limit cycles (rather than complete collapse) even when large, destabilizing changes are made to the parameters describing the private sector.

The simulations of the extended model have used policy parameters that seem empirically reasonable, but the behavior of central banks and governments is endogenous. Central banks may follow something like a Taylor rule, but the persistence of this rule and the chosen parameters are sustained by the experience that the policy seems to work reasonably well. If the behavior of the private sector changes and particular policy rules cease to bring about outcomes that seem acceptable, policymakers will modify their policy rules or add new policies. Central banks reacted to the financial crisis and a binding zero lower bound by adding quantitative and qualitative easing to their toolbox. Fiscal authorities likewise adjust their policies in light of economic outcomes – Japanese policymakers, for instance, have allowed public debt to rise to record levels because a stagnating economy needed persistent stimulus.

Lerner (1943) emphasized how the mere promise of Keynesian intervention in recessions would affect private investment and exert a stabilizing influence (exemplifying what is now commonly referred to as the Lucas critique, cf. Chapter 2), but causation runs both ways. Policy rules and the degree and form of stabilization by way of economic policy react to changes in the destabilizing forces. Putting it differently, arguments suggesting that the model could lead to complete economic collapse for some parameter values in the behavioral equations become much less powerful as a critique of the model if economic policy tends to react endogenously to changes in economic performance.

This general point emphatically does not imply that policymakers will pick optimal policies (assuming that such policies can be defined) in response to poor economic performance. Saying that policymakers will experiment with new tools or new ways to use old tools is very different from claiming that the new policies will work or even that there will always be improvements over previous policies. Policymakers, like everyone else, face profound uncertainty and may be guided by poor theories. Performance criteria and notions of optimal policy, moreover, are intrinsically contentious, as emphasized by Kalecki (1943). In a technical sense, Kalecki argued, governments may possess the ability to control aggregate demand at (near-)full employment, but the maintenance of full employment can generate cumulative changes in the balance of power between workers and capitalists. If that happens, he argued, increased worker militancy and associated inflationary pressures quickly bring together a powerful block of business leaders and rentiers, and – supported by economists who "declare that the situation is manifestly unsound" – the government will allow unemployment to rise. The result, Kalecki suggested, is a political business cycle. Although applied by Kalecki to short cycles, the argument is arguably better suited to deal with longer-term fluctuations. The rise in worker militancy in the late 1960s may be explained, at least in part, by the fact that by then the collective memory of mass unemployment in the 1930s had faded; the political and economic challenges to the economic system in the 1960s and 1970s, in turn, produced a combination of contractionary macroeconomic policy to rein in inflation and attempts to 'reform' labor markets and roll back the welfare state.

A Kalecki-1943 interpretation of the turn to neoliberal policy and the rise in unemployment in the 1970s and 1980s points to the historical contingency of economic models, and historical contingencies also lie behind Minsky's 'financial instability hypothesis' (e.g., Minsky 1993). Suppose that, having recovered from past turbulence, the economy now appears to be approaching a smooth equilibrium path. Along this path, expectations are largely being met and, using Minsky's terminology, there is 'financial tranquility': Borrowers are able to meet their financial commitments. This very state of tranquility will induce changes in the risk assessments of both lenders and borrowers, while – at the same time and induced by the same observations of "financial tranquility" – financial regulators and policymakers may loosen the regulatory standards. Risk premiums fall; lenders start giving loans they would have previously rejected, and borrowers increasingly finance their projects in speculative and risky ways. These behavioral changes relax the financial constraints on spending, and a boom ensues. Gradually, the 'fragility' of the financial system increases until a financial crisis causes a rapid rise in interest rates and a contraction of credit and investment. A return to cautious financial practices now follows.

The process repeats after a period of tranquility, but the precise financial instruments and institutions may be new and different. In the United States, the saving and loan crisis in the 1980s, the stock market bubble in the 1990s, and the housing bust and financial crisis of the 2000s may be manifestations of Minskian processes. But the lessons from earlier crises had no straightforward implications for how to handle the relaxation of lending standards during the housing boom. Instead, institutional changes and the creation of new financial instruments in the period leading up to the financial crisis led most observers, including the chair of the Federal Reserve, to perceive "a far more flexible, efficient, and hence resilient financial system than the one that existed just a quarter-century ago" (Greenspan 2005).[37]

Financial crises may be recurrent, as argued by Minsky, but the forms they take and the concrete mechanisms behind them change from one crisis to the next. The Minskian process of instability also tends to be less regular and to operate on a timescale that is longer than the typical business cycle. Thus, there has been no attempt to integrate Minskian financial instability into the formal models in this chapter: The focus has been on goods and labor markets. But the exclusion of financial instability makes it obvious that the models should not be seen as complete explanations of real-world business cycles. The aim is much more modest: The models formalize some systematic forces that may exert a powerful influence on the dynamics of a capitalist economy.

The broad consistency of the models and simulations with the stylized cyclical patterns in the US data is encouraging, but the key message of the chapter is unrelated to the precise magnitudes of parameters and amplitudes of the simulation exercise. What the simulation results indicate is that Keynesian–Harrodian mechanisms supplemented by feedback effects from the state of the labor market to production, investment, consumption, and economic policy tend to produce oscillations and that the qualitative patterns of these oscillations fit observed patterns quite well. These findings, to my mind, makes the general approach a much more promising foundation for understanding real-world business cycles than new-consensus models that have to rely on a slew of autocorrelated stochastic shocks to generate cyclical fluctuations.

Appendix A: Investment with Indivisibilities and Gestation Lags

Assume that (i) investment projects have a minimum scale that is proportional to the size of the firm, (ii) the firm cannot undertake more than one investment project at the

---

[37] Minsky's theories, not surprisingly, have received a great deal of attention after the financial crisis of 2007, and a number of formalizations have been developed; an example is Ryoo (2010) whose model produces short business cycles around a Minskian long wave.

same time, and (iii) there is a gestation lag between investment and the appearance of new capacity. The gestation lag makes it convenient to set out the basic argument using a discrete-time framework.[38]

A firm can estimate the current value of the term B_{it} in the perceived demand function (10.1) by substituting observed prices and production into the perceived demand function,

$$B_{it} = Y_{it} \left(\frac{p_{it}}{p_t} \right)^{\gamma}. \tag{10.49}$$

What matters for investment decisions at time t, however, is the trend in demand and the position of the demand curve when the new capacity becomes operational, that is, the values of B_{it+1} and p_{it+1}/w_{t+1}. Suppose (the firm believes that) the logarithm of the constant term B_{it} in the perceived demand function follows a random walk with drift, that is,

$$\log B_{it+1} = \log B_{it} + \alpha + \varepsilon_{it+1}; \quad \varepsilon_{it} \sim NID(0, \sigma_\varepsilon^2)$$

or

$$B_{it+k} = B_{it} \exp\left(\alpha k + \sum_{j=1}^{k} \varepsilon_{it+j} \right); \quad k \geq 1. \tag{10.50}$$

Using (10.4), (10.49), and (10.50), the perfect-flexibility level of output at time $t + k$ is

$$Y_{it+k}^* = \exp(\alpha k) \left[Y_{it} \left(\frac{p_{it}}{p_t} \right)^{\gamma} \right] \left\{ \left(\exp \sum_{j=1}^{k} \varepsilon_{it+j} \right) \left(\frac{p_{it+k}^*}{p_{t+k}} \right)^{-\gamma} \right\}.$$

The average price levels are independent of the firm's own decisions, and the (perceived) stationarity of the random shocks ε_{it} makes it reasonable to suppose that the firm will view the stochastic terms in curly brackets as having a stationary distribution with a constant expected value. If that is the case, the firm's expected value of Y_{it+k}^* will be an increasing function of $Y_{it} \left(\frac{p_{it}}{p_t} \right)^{\gamma}$.

The indivisibility and irreversibility of investment in combination with the proportionality between the minimum scale of investment and the size of the firm now suggest a simple threshold rule: Invest if $Y_{it} \left(\frac{p_{it}}{p_t} \right)^{\gamma} / K_{it}$ exceeds a threshold value. Firms may differ in their attitudes to risk as well as in their assessments of the precise distribution of $\left(\exp \sum_{j=1}^{k} \varepsilon_{it+j} \right) \left(p_{it+k}^*/p_{it+k} \right)^{-\gamma}$, and as a generalization, we may suppose that the probability of a firm investing is an increasing function of $Y_{it} \left(\frac{p_{it}}{p_t} \right)^{\gamma} / K_{it}$.

---

[38] Skott (1989b, Appendix 6.2) considers a continuous-time version for a slightly more complicated model.

Formally, if current capital is used to indicate scale, the expected value of firm i's investment (conditional on current output, capital and prices) is

$$E\left(I_{it} \mid Y_{it}, K_{it}, \frac{p_{it}}{p_t}\right) = \psi\left(\frac{Y_{it}}{K_{it}}\left(\frac{p_{it}}{p_t}\right)^{\gamma}\right) \beta K_{it},$$

where $\psi\left(Y_{it}\left(\frac{p_{it}}{p_t}\right)^{\gamma} / K_{it}\right)$ denotes the probability that the firm invests and βK_{it} is the minimum scale of investment.

To get an aggregate investment function, assume that (i) the ψ-function describing the investment probability is linear ($\psi(x) = -a + bx$ with $a > 0, b > 0$), (ii) the relative price p_{it}/p_t is independent of Y_{it}/K_t, (iii) $\left(\frac{p_{it}}{p_t}\right)^{\gamma}$ has a stationary distribution with mean θ, and (iv) there is a large number of firms, and $I_{it} - E\left(I_{it} \mid Y_{it}, K_{it}, \frac{p_{it}}{p_t}\right)$ and $I_{jt} - E\left(I_{jt} \mid Y_{jt}, K_{jt}, \frac{p_{jt}}{p_t}\right)$ are independent for all i, j. These aggregation conditions are clearly restrictive. In fact, the first of them cannot hold everywhere, as stated: Probabilities are constrained to the unit interval. The linear form of ψ may hold approximately within the relevant range, however. Turning to the second and third conditions, if actual firm-level shocks to log-demand (like the perceived shocks to $\log B$) are independent of the levels of current output and capital and follow a stationary distribution, then one would expect that a good approximation can be obtained by treating Y_{it} and $\left(\frac{p_{it}}{p_t}\right)^{\gamma}$ as independent and $\left(\frac{p_{it}}{p_t}\right)^{\gamma}$ as following a stationary distribution.

If the conditions are met, we have

$$\frac{I_t}{K_t} = \frac{1}{K_t} \sum_i \left[E\left(I_{it} \mid Y_{it}, K_{it}, \frac{p_{it}}{p_t}\right) + I_{it} - E\left(I_{it} \mid Y_{it}, K_{it}, \frac{p_{it}}{p_t}\right) \right]$$

$$\approx \frac{1}{K_t} \sum_i E\left(I_{it} \mid Y_{it}, K_{it}, \frac{p_{it}}{p_t}\right)$$

$$= \sum_i \left(\left(-a + b\left(\frac{Y_{it}}{K_{it}}\left(\frac{p_{it}}{p_t}\right)^{\gamma}\right)\right)\beta\frac{K_{it}}{K_t}\right)$$

$$= \sum_i -a\beta\frac{K_{it}}{K_t} + b\beta \sum_i \frac{Y_{it}}{K_t}\left(\frac{p_{it}}{p_t}\right)^{\gamma} \tag{10.51}$$

$$\approx -a\beta + b\beta\theta\frac{Y_t}{K_t}. \tag{10.52}$$

Hence, as a first approximation, the aggregate accumulation rate will be an increasing function of the aggregate output-capital ratio:

$$\frac{I_t}{K_t} = f(\sigma_t); \quad f' > 0. \tag{10.53}$$

The analysis also suggests that the elasticity of the accumulation function f will be greater than 1 for utilization rates above some lower bound. This property is clearly satisfied for the linear specification in Equation (10.52). It also holds for smooth versions of the function that satisfy the nonnegativity constraint on gross investment and approximate the linear specification in (10.52) for high values of σ. Intuitively, at low ratios of expected demand to current capital the incentives to invest are insensitive to marginal changes in expected demand. The sensitivity increases, however, as the ratio of expected demand to capital approaches and exceeds the target rate of utilization.

Appendix B: The Baseline Model and Harrodian Instability

The simple version of Harrod's argument in Chapter 9 took the desired utilization rate to be exogenous. The accumulation rate was predetermined in the short run but changed over time in response to deviations of actual from desired utilization. Using the output-capital ratio as a measure of utilization,

$$d\hat{K}/dt = \lambda_{\hat{K}} \left(\sigma - \sigma^d \right). \tag{10.54}$$

These assumptions make the long-run accumulation function perfectly elastic at σ^d: The accumulation rate would grow without limit if the output-capital ratio were kept at a level above σ^d.

Harrodian instability does not require this extreme assumption. Suppose instead that a high accumulation rate can only be sustained if the output-capital ratio is high; that is, there is a positive relation between the desired utilization rate and accumulation rate:

$$\sigma^d = \phi(\hat{K}). \tag{10.55}$$

With a constant saving rate ($S = sY$), the short-run multiplier relation between the gross accumulation rate and the output-capital ratio implies that

$$\sigma = \frac{\hat{K} + \delta}{s}. \tag{10.56}$$

Equations (10.54)–(10.56) now yield the following differential equation:

$$d\hat{K}/dt = \lambda_{\hat{K}} \left(\frac{\hat{K} + \delta}{s} - \phi(\hat{K}) \right). \tag{10.57}$$

Equation (10.57) has a unique, unstable stationary solution (the warranted growth rate) if $\phi' < 1/s$. Equivalently, the warranted path is unstable in this extended version of the Harrodian model if the long-run investment function ($\hat{K}^* = \phi^{-1}(\sigma)$) is steeper than the saving function, that is, if

$$d\hat{K}^*/d\sigma = 1/\phi' > s = d(S/K)/d\sigma. \tag{10.58}$$

The same condition – an investment function that is more sensitive than the saving function to variations in the output-capital ratio – is necessary for local instability in the baseline model in this chapter. Without this condition, the profit share becomes a decreasing function of the output capital (Equation (10.16)), and the stationary solution is locally stable: The trace of the Jacobian matrix (10.23) becomes unambiguously negative.

Appendix C: Combining Price Changes and Rationing

For simplicity, ignore inventories and assume that disequilibrium manifests in a combination of a profit share that deviates from what firms would have chosen, had output been perfectly flexible, and direct rationing of household consumption. Thus, if Δ is a measure of the degree of disequilibrium, we have

$$\Delta = \phi\left(\frac{I-S}{Y}, \pi\right), \qquad \phi_1 > 0, \phi_2 > 0, \tag{10.59}$$

where the desired saving rate S/Y depends on the profit share. The degree of direct rationing is given by $(I-S)/Y$, and π is the profit share. Investment plans are always realized, with actual saving determined as the difference between output and desired investment.

Retaining the investment and saving functions from the baseline model (Equations (10.10) and (10.12)), we have

$$\frac{I-S}{Y} = \frac{f(\sigma) - g(\pi, \sigma)}{\sigma}. \tag{10.60}$$

The profit share cannot be used as the indicator of disequilibrium in the goods market, and the output expansion function must be written as a function of Δ (rather than π):

$$\hat{Y} = H(\Delta, \sigma, e) = H\left(\phi\left(\frac{f(\sigma) - g(\pi, \sigma)}{\sigma}\right), \pi\right), \sigma, e\right). \tag{10.61}$$

The dynamics for utilization and employment are given by

$$\hat{\sigma} = \hat{Y} - \hat{K} = H\left(\phi\left(\frac{f(\sigma) - g(\pi, \sigma)}{\sigma}, \pi\right), \sigma, e\right) - f(\sigma) + \delta \tag{10.62}$$

$$\hat{e} = H\left(\phi\left(\frac{f(\sigma) - g(\pi, \sigma)}{\sigma}, \pi\right), \sigma, e\right) - n. \tag{10.63}$$

With finite adjustment speeds for prices, a dynamic equation for the profit share can now be added,

$$\dot{\pi} = \lambda_\pi \frac{I-S}{Y} = \lambda_\pi\left[\frac{f(\sigma) - g(\pi, \sigma)}{\sigma}\right]. \tag{10.64}$$

Equations (10.62)–(10.64) describe a 3D system of differential equations. The Jacobian of the system can be written as

$$J(\sigma, e, \pi) = \begin{pmatrix} \sigma\left[H_1\phi_1\left(\frac{f'-g_2}{\sigma} - \frac{f-g}{\sigma^2}\right) + H_2 - f'\right] & \sigma H_3 & \sigma\left[H_1\phi_2 - H_1\phi_1\frac{g_1}{\sigma}\right] \\ e\left[H_1\phi_1\left(\frac{f'-g_2}{\sigma} - \frac{f-g}{\sigma^2}\right) + H_2\right] & eH_3 & e\left[H_1\phi_2 - H_1\phi_1\frac{g_1}{\sigma}\right] \\ \lambda_\pi\left(\frac{f'-g_2}{\sigma} - \frac{f-g}{\sigma^2}\right) & 0 & -\lambda_\pi\frac{g_1}{\sigma} \end{pmatrix}. \tag{10.65}$$

The degree of disequilibrium – the deviation of actual demand curves from the demand curves that would have justified firms' current levels of output – does not depend on whether firms choose to respond to the disequilibrium by changing prices or by rationing. Thus, for a given output-capital ratio, an increase in the profit share may change the degree of quantity rationing but not the underlying disequilibrium. Using (10.59)–(10.60), this independence property implies that the disequilibrium indicator satisfies the condition

$$\frac{d\phi}{d\pi} = -\phi_1 \frac{g_1}{\sigma} + \phi_2 = 0, \qquad \text{for all } \pi, \sigma. \tag{10.66}$$

Using (10.66), the Jacobian matrix simplifies to

$$J(\sigma, e, \pi) = \begin{pmatrix} \sigma \left[H_1\phi_1 \left(\frac{f'-g_2}{\sigma} - \frac{f-g}{\sigma^2} \right) + H_2 - f' \right] & \sigma H_3 & 0 \\ e \left[H_1\phi_1 \left(\frac{f'-g_2}{\sigma} - \frac{f-g}{\sigma^2} \right) + H_2 \right] & e H_3 & 0 \\ \lambda_{\pi 1} \left(\frac{f'-g_2}{\sigma} - \frac{f-g}{\sigma^2} \right) & 0 & -\lambda_\pi \frac{g_1}{\sigma} \end{pmatrix}. \tag{10.67}$$

The 3D system (10.67) is separable, with self-contained 2D dynamics for (σ, e):

$$J(\sigma, e) = \begin{pmatrix} \sigma \left[H_1\phi_1 \left(\frac{f'-g_2}{\sigma} - \frac{f-g}{\sigma^2} \right) + H_2 - f' \right] & \sigma H_3 \\ e \left[H_1\phi_1 \left(\frac{f'-g_2}{\sigma} - \frac{f-g}{\sigma^2} \right) + H_2 \right] & e H_3 \end{pmatrix}. \tag{10.68}$$

The term $\phi_1(\frac{f'-g_2}{\sigma} - \frac{f-g}{\sigma^2})$ is the sensitivity of Δ to a rise in utilization, while the derivatives H_1, H_2, and H_3 describe the sensitivity of output growth to marginal deviations of the degree of disequilibrium (Δ), the utilization rate, and the employment rate from the stationary solution. None of these derivatives depends on whether the disequilibrium adjustment is via prices or rationing. The stability properties of the system, therefore, also become independent of whether disequilibrium shows up as rationing or price adjustments. What matters is the response of output growth to the degree of disequilibrium.

The flex-price version of the model represents the case when $\lambda_\pi \to \infty$. The dynamics for π are stable (for any given value of σ), and in this limiting case, we obtain

$$\frac{I-S}{Y} \to 0$$

$$\pi \to \pi(\sigma)$$

$$\Delta \to \phi(0, \pi(\sigma)), \tag{10.69}$$

where – as in Equation (10.16) – $\pi(\sigma)$ is given implicitly by the condition that $f(\sigma) - g(\pi, \sigma) = 0$ and

$$\pi' = \frac{f' - g_2}{g_1}. \tag{10.70}$$

Using (10.69)–(10.70) and (10.66), it now follows that

$$\frac{d\Delta}{d\sigma} = \phi_2 \pi'$$

$$H_1\phi_1 \left(\frac{f'-g_2}{\sigma} - \frac{f-g}{\sigma^2} \right) = H_1\phi_1 \frac{g_1}{\sigma}\pi' = H_1\phi_2\pi'$$

and the Jacobian can be written as

$$J(\sigma,e) = \begin{pmatrix} \sigma[H_1\phi_2\pi' + H_2 - f'] & \sigma H_e \\ e[H_1\phi_2\pi' + H_2] & eH_e \end{pmatrix}. \tag{10.71}$$

The specification of output growth in (10.7) in the flex-price model was based on a special case of (10.59) in which $I - S \equiv 0$ and $\Delta \equiv \phi(0,\pi)$. Thus, the partial h_1 in (10.7) can be written as $h_1 = \frac{\partial \hat{Y}}{\partial \Delta}\phi_2(0,\pi) = H_1\phi_2(0,\pi)$. Evaluated at the stationary point, we also have $h_2 = H_2$ and $h_3 = H_3$.

In short, as the adjustment speed for prices increases, the Jacobian converges to (10.71), which (with notational changes) is identical to the one in Equation (10.23); rapid but finite adjustment can be approximated by the perfect-flexibility system.

11 Secular Stagnation and Functional Finance

11.1 Introduction

Aggregate demand problems are commonly seen as short-run in nature. Temporary deviations from full employment occur, and temporary policy interventions may be needed to guide the economy back to full employment, but with no need for sustained aggregate demand stimulus. The analysis in Chapter 10 implicitly rejected this confinement of aggregate demand issues to the short run: Viability conditions had to be imposed to assure the existence of a steady growth path with a constant rate of employment.

This chapter examines the use of economic policy to maintain economic growth with full employment, assuming an exogenously given constant natural growth rate. Leaving out the issues discussed in Chapters 5–6, full-employment growth is used as a shorthand for a growth path with a constant, high rate of employment and a constant inflation rate. The stability issues addressed in Chapter 10 are also ignored: It is assumed that short-run stabilization policies keep the economy on, or fluctuating around, a steady growth path with a constant output-capital ratio and a constant profit share.

The analysis focuses on the potential for structural aggregate demand problems (secular stagnation): A low natural growth rate will put a damper on investment, thereby necessitating sustained fiscal stimulus to maintain full employment if there is a high private saving rate. Drawing on the functional finance literature, the analysis examines the implications of this full-employment policy for public debt in a closed economy with public debt denominated in a currency that is controlled by the central bank. A country whose debt is issued in its own sovereign currency cannot be forced to default on its debt obligations. The situation is fundamentally different for an open economy with debt denominated in foreign currency. The importance of this simple distinction, surprisingly, does not seem to be universally recognized. Collard et al. (2015) calculate sustainable public debt ratios using the same criteria for the United States and countries in the Eurozone; Reinhart and Rogoff (2010), likewise, make no distinctions among countries based on the currency denomination of the public debt; in the aftermath of the financial crisis, the popular press was full of references to Greece (a member of the Eurozone) as a cautionary tale for what could happen to the United States if public debt were not reined in.

The closed-economy and sovereign-currency assumptions mean that the analysis is not directly applicable to a country like Greece. But policy analysis should not focus narrowly on the options for Greece, treating the international environment in which it operates as given. An analysis of this kind indeed might show austerity in some form to have been the only viable option in the aftermath of the financial crisis, with the same conclusion following from an analysis of Portugal or Italy, each seen in isolation. But austerity policies cannot be justified in this way for the Eurozone as a whole. Small open-economy models are intrinsically 'partial' and, like other partial models, can be subject to a fallacy of composition. The Eurozone controls its own currency and, of less importance, most of the international trade of the Eurozone countries is with other countries within the zone. Models of a closed economy with debt in its own currency can provide essential tools for an analysis of what could and should have been done in the Eurozone as a whole.

Full employment constrains potential output in mature economies, such as the United States, Japan, and Germany, and (near-)full employment is a reasonable target in these economies. But most developing economies are dual economies with large amounts of underemployment in traditional and informal sectors of the economy. Dating back to Lewis (1954), stylized versions of dual economies contain two sectors, a modern/formal sector and a traditional/informal sector, with the supply of labor to the modern sector taken to be perfectly elastic. Thus, in a dual economy, the capital stock – rather than the labor supply – represents the binding supply-side constraint in the modern sector. This difference, when compared with mature economies, alters the policy problem fundamentally: Dual economies face structural transformation problems, not structural aggregate demand problems. It is the combination of a low natural rate of growth and high saving that generates a structural aggregate demand problem in mature economies. This problem does not arise in dual economies where, by assumption, there are no labor constraints. Rapid accumulation in the modern sector as well as public investment in education and infrastructure are desirable – the faster the accumulation rate the better – and high accumulation rates are associated with high shares of investment in income.[1]

Section 11.2 presents the formal framework for a mature economy. Section 11.3 outlines some mechanisms that could ensure the possibility of full-employment growth. Section 11.4 describes 'functional finance' and analyzes the dynamics of public debt under a functional finance regime: The long-run ratio of public debt to GDP does not increase without limit, converging instead to a level that depends (i) inversely on the rate of growth, (ii) inversely on government consumption, and (iii) directly on the degree of inequality. These implications of the analysis, its empirical relevance and the connections between functional finance and secular stagnation are considered

---

[1] The investment share has approached 50 percent in China, and the positive correlation between growth and the investment share is well established. Levine and Renelt (1992) identify this as a robust finding from the literature on 'growth regressions'; Girardi and Pariboni (2020) reach similar conclusions using a different approach. Building on Marx's schemes of reproduction, Fel'dman (1928) set up a formal model, demonstrating the need to shift resources to the sector producing investment goods in order to raise the long-run rate of growth.

in Section 11.5. The adaptation of functional finance to dual economies is discussed in Section 11.6. Rapid rates of economic development will be associated with high investment, and fiscal policy must make space for this investment. The structure of taxation also becomes important, however, to prevent inflationary pressures from building up and aborting the development process. Section 11.7 concludes the chapter.

11.2   Some Simple Algebra for a Mature Economy

The nature of the long-run demand issue can be illustrated by a few, simple equations. The first equation is the equilibrium condition for the goods market in a closed economy,

$$\frac{Y}{K} = \frac{C}{K} + \frac{I}{K} + \frac{G}{K}. \tag{11.1}$$

The familiar $Y = C + I + G$ equation has been divided through by the capital stock, which is a convenient normalization when dealing with long-run growth.

The ratio of government consumption to the capital stock is taken to be exogenous,

$$\frac{G}{K} = \gamma. \tag{11.2}$$

The choice of the government consumption ratio is contentious. How much should we spend on prisons, public education, or public health care, for instance? These are important questions, but the answers should not be based on the exigencies of demand management, and, for present purposes, debates about the appropriate size of the public sector are largely irrelevant. This chapter examines the need for aggregate demand policy in the long run, an issue that can be addressed independently of the determination of the desirable share of government consumption in total income.

The third equation represents straightforward accounting. In order to maintain full-employment growth and a constant output-capital ratio, the ratio of gross investment to the capital stock must be equal to the sum of the growth rate of the labor supply in effective units (n) and the rate of depreciation (δ):

$$\frac{I}{K} = n + \delta. \tag{11.3}$$

By definition, the output-capital ratio is constant in steady growth, but its steady-growth value may be endogenous. With capital and labor as the only inputs, the cost of finance and the wage rate determine the choice of technique. Under perfect competition, the zero profit condition pins down the real wage for any given cost of finance, while under imperfect competition, the real wage is determined by the markup and the cost of finance (Section 9.3.1). Thus, if we take the degree of competition as given, the output-capital ratio (σ) can be written as a function of the real interest rate (r):

$$\sigma = \frac{Y}{K} = f(r). \tag{11.4}$$

Equation (11.4) expresses the choice of technique along a hypothetical steady growth path with a constant interest rate and a constant markup. The capital controversy raised questions about the smoothness of the f-function and showed that even if the f-function is differentiable, we may have $f' < 0$, rather than $f' > 0$, while a Leontief production function without any choice of technique corresponds to the special case in which $f' \equiv 0$ (Section 9.3.2). The differences between the three cases can be critical for the adjustment process toward a steady growth path. As a characterization of steady growth paths, however, the general expression in (11.4) is consistent with all three cases, and for present purposes, there is no need to impose any restrictions of the range and functional form of $f(r)$. The analysis in this chapter neither requires nor excludes a neoclassical production function with smooth, well-behaved substitution, and $f' > 0$.

Combining Equations (11.1)–(11.4), the condition for steady growth with full employment can be written as

$$\sigma - \frac{C}{K} = f(r) - \frac{C}{K} = \gamma + n + \delta. \tag{11.5}$$

The variables on the right-hand side of (11.5) are exogenous, and any adjustment has to come through the output-capital ratio (the real rate of interest) or the consumption-capital ratio. The question is: Will these adjustments occur automatically or is there a need for active policy? If the adjustment occurs automatically via changes in interest rates and the output-capital ratio, one can ask whether these changes lead to a capital intensity that is 'socially optimal' in some sense. If the adjustment does not come via an endogenously determined choice of technique, the consumption ratio must do the adjusting, and we need to examine the determination of this ratio. In particular, is policy intervention needed to ensure the required consumption ratio and, if so, what kind of policy should be used?

11.3   Possible Answers

11.3.1   Dynamic Stochastic General Equilibrium

The traditional Solow model relies exclusively on variations in the output-capital ratio to ensure that the condition (11.5) will be satisfied. DSGE models include this mechanism but do not need it to achieve full-employment growth. In a Ramsey setting, the growth in per capita consumption satisfies the Euler condition

$$\hat{c} = \frac{1}{\theta}(r - \rho), \tag{11.6}$$

where ρ is the representative household's discount rate and θ is the intertemporal elasticity of substitution; r and c are the real rate of interest and per capita consumption, respectively a hat over a variable denotes a rate of growth ($\hat{x} = \dot{x}/x = (dx/dt)/x$). This determination of consumption obviates the necessity for adjustments in capital intensity to ensure full-employment growth: The saving rate becomes an endogenous variable, and if the output-capital ratio is exogenously given (the Leontief case), the saving rate (and thus C/K) will do all of the required adjustment to satisfy Equation (11.5); see Chapter 9, Appendix A.

The growth rate of per capita consumption is constant and equal to the rate of labor saving technical change in steady growth. Thus, Equation (11.6) has two important implications. The equation implies the existence, first, of a well-defined 'natural real rate of interest,'

$$r = \rho + \theta q, \tag{11.7}$$

where q is the rate of labor saving technical change. This natural rate of interest – determined by the parameters of the representative household's utility function and the rate of technical change – pins down the capital intensity (Equation (11.4)).

Second, despite its intrinsic biases (Chapter 2), the representative household's utility function is commonly used as a welfare criterion and, based on this criterion, the Ramsey model implies that the growth path and capital intensity will be optimal in the absence of externalities or other market imperfections. Specifically – and unlike in the Solow model with a fixed saving rate – there is no danger of 'dynamic inefficiency.' High saving rates will never take the capital intensity to a level above the 'golden rule.'

In short, DSGE models give a clear answer. They have a core based on Ramsey optimization by a set of household dynasties, and although short-run problems associated with nominal stickiness may call for active monetary policy, adjustments in real wages and interest rates in combination with the endogeneity of the saving rate serve to maintain full-employment growth and an optimal capital intensity in the medium and long runs.

The automatic adjustment is fortunate, since Ricardian equivalence makes fiscal policy ineffectual in this setting: Farsighted households adjust their saving in response to changes in taxes. The main concern of fiscal policy becomes to minimize tax distortions. If revenue cannot be raised exclusively through lump-sum taxes and the costs of distortion are convex, this objective translates into tax-smoothing (Barro 1979), and long-run fiscal policy should be geared toward attaining a target debt ratio (Schmitt-Grohe and Uribe 2007, Kirsanova et al. 2009).

11.3.2   Finite Lives and Overlapping Generations

The DSGE/Ramsey results have dominated mainstream thinking on aggregate demand policy. The optimality results of the models lack robustness, however, even if there is perfect optimization at the micro level and continuous full employment. If the models are relaxed by introducing finite lives, as in OLG models without intergenerational altruism, the optimality of the market outcome disappears. As an unambiguous example of suboptimality, OLG models – like the Solow model – can produce dynamic inefficiency: The capital intensity may be so high (and the return on capital so low) that all generations could be made better off by a reduction in saving.

As an empirical matter, the rate of return on capital typically exceeds the growth rate. This finding has been interpreted as evidence that actual economies are dynamically efficient (Abel et al. 1989). The interpretation, however, is based on an assumption of perfect competition. It does not apply without modification in more realistic cases with imperfect competition: High rates of profits may be due to monopoly rents rather than a high 'marginal product of capital.' This possibility can be seen most clearly if the production function is Leontief: Profit-maximizing firms that maintain some degree of excess capital capacity and set prices as a markup on marginal cost can show a positive rate of return, even though the marginal product is zero when there is excess capital capacity. The bias from using the rate of return as a measure of the marginal product of capital is not confined to the Leontief case, however. It can be substantial, even if one puts aside the problems raised by the capital controversy and assumes a smooth neoclassical production function (Skott and Ryoo 2014).

More generally, there can be no presumption that market solutions will be socially optimal in OLG models, even if dynamic inefficiency is avoided. The definition of social welfare raises a host of issues, but consider a simple case without any intragenerational inequality. Intergenerational distribution then becomes the only distributional issue, and the social discount rate will be central to the determination of a socially optimal trajectory. In the absence of discounting and technical change, and assuming a smooth neoclassical production function, the socially optimal trajectory requires equality between the marginal product of capital and the growth rate of the labor force (the golden rule); if, instead, the social welfare function calls for discounting future consumption, the steady-growth value of the capital intensity should be below the golden-rule level. Formally, let σ^* and r^* be the socially optimal capital intensity and the associated interest rate, respectively (conditional on the normative choice of a discount rate). Except by a fluke, the value of C/K (at $\sigma = \sigma^*, r = r^*$) will not clear the goods market at full employment:

$$\frac{C}{K} \gtreqless \sigma^* - \gamma - (n + \delta). \tag{11.8}$$

Thus, the socially optimal choice of technique will be inconsistent with market clearing. Intuitively, a single instrument – the real rate of interest – cannot simultaneously achieve two targets: Market clearing and a socially optimal capital intensity. Appendix A spells out the details for the neoclassical Diamond model as well as for a Keynesian version of the model.

The presence of finite horizons also brings a solution to the problem that it created: The ineffectiveness of fiscal policy disappears when households have finite horizons. Future taxes will be paid by different taxpayers, so that there is no Ricardian equivalence in the OLG model. Changes in current taxes influence current consumption, and fiscal policy can be used to maintain full employment with an optimal capital intensity. The flip side of these results is that fiscal policy affects the 'natural interest rate' and the choice of technique. Putting it differently, in contrast to models with Ramsey optimization, the natural rate of interest – the interest rate associated with full employment – cannot be defined independently of fiscal policy.

This result can be demonstrated for OLG models (Diamond 1965, Skott and Ryoo 2014, 2017) as well as for traditional Keynesian models. The qualitative results are the same, and, appealing as it may seem, the OLG structure has peculiar properties that find no support in data, even if we disregard farfetched assumptions of perfect optimization and foresight. It implies that the saving rate is inversely related to the profit share: Only the young save and the young get their income as wage income. Empirically, by contrast, saving rates are higher out of profits than wages. Thus, the saving assumptions that are at the center of the analysis in OLG models can be questioned and, in line with Chapters 3–4, the analysis in the next section will use a simple Keynesian specification.

Before closing this section, it should be noted that there is a close connection between the long-run questions in this chapter and the analysis in Chapter 10. One of the issues that came up in Chapter 10 was the need to introduce various conditions to guarantee the existence of a stationary solution of the dynamic system. The stationary solution for the output-capital ratio and the employment rate had to satisfy the following equations:

$$\frac{I}{K} = f(\sigma) = n + \delta \tag{11.9}$$

$$\frac{S}{K} = g(\pi, \sigma) = n + \delta \tag{11.10}$$

$$\hat{Y} = h(\pi, \sigma, e) = n. \tag{11.11}$$

Equation (11.9) pins down the output-capital ratio, $\sigma = \bar{\sigma}$, and if we consider a special case of Equation (11.11) in which $\hat{Y}$ is perfectly elastic at $\pi = \bar{\pi}$ – that is, in which $h_2 = h_3 = 0$ and $h_1 \to \infty$ at $\pi = \bar{\pi}$ – then both π and σ are now fixed. Turning to Equation (11.10), the saving-to-capital ratio is determined, and only by a fluke will it be equal to $n + \delta$. If it is not, however, there is no stationary solution. The situation is similar outside the special case if a target rate of employment ($\bar{e}$) is imposed. With $e = \bar{e}$ and $\sigma = \bar{\sigma}$ fixed, Equation (11.11) can be used to determine the value of π; $\pi = \pi(\bar{\sigma}, \bar{e}), \pi_1 > 0, \pi_2 > 0$. Again, there is no mechanism to equalize the ratio of saving to capital with $n + \delta$ and ensure equilibrium in the goods market.[2] Equation (11.8) describes this same problem expressed in terms of the ratio of consumption to capital.

11.4 Functional Finance

Twenty two years before, the Diamond model, Lerner (1943) had discussed the principle of 'functional finance.' Fiscal policy, he argued, is an essential instrument of Keynesian policy and should be used "with an eye only to the *results* of these actions on the economy and not to any established traditional doctrine about what is sound

---

[2] Dropping the employment target, as in Chapter 10, there is an extra degree of freedom, and a stationary solution will exist if $g(\pi(\bar{\sigma}, 0), \bar{\sigma}) < n + \delta < g(\pi(\bar{\sigma}, 1), \bar{\sigma})$. From a welfare and policy perspective, however, the interesting question concerns the existence of a stationary solution with near-full employment.

or unsound" (p. 39; italics in original). There is nothing virtuous about balancing the government budget over any particular period, he argued, and the public debt is of no importance in itself. Households may need to balance their budgets, but governments are under no such compulsion: Doctrines of 'sound finance' are based on a false analogy.[3]

Functional finance, Lerner explained,

prescribes, first, the adjustment of total spending (by everybody in the economy, including the government) in order to eliminate both unemployment and inflation. . .; second, the adjustment of public holdings of money and of government bonds, by government borrowing or debt repayment, in order to achieve the rate of interest which results in the most desirable level of investment; and, third, the printing, hoarding or destruction of money as needed for carrying out the first two parts of the program. (Lerner 1943, p. 41)

The "most desirable level of investment" is typically taken as given in the short run, and the extension of Lerner's argument to the analysis of long-run growth may need comment.

The change in the capital stock is equal to the difference between investment and depreciation, $\dot{K} = I - \delta K$. A trajectory of desirable levels of investment therefore defines a trajectory of desirable capital stocks, and if full employment is being maintained along this trajectory, we also have a trajectory for output. Hence, from a long-run perspective, Lerner's prescriptions for policies that produce full employment and desirable levels of investment can be stated alternatively as prescriptions for policies that produce a trajectory of full employment and desirable output-capital ratios. The output-capital ratio in steady growth is determined by the choice of technique, and we can use the simple framework in the previous section: Lerner's investment argument translates into the requirement that the steady-growth value of the interest rate satisfy the condition $r = f^{-1}(\sigma^*)$. This requirement pins down the steady-growth value of the real interest rate, and policymakers must turn to fiscal policy to adjust aggregate demand and maintain full employment.[4,5]

I have taken government consumption as exogenous (Equation (11.2)), but taxes and transfers can be used to influence consumption. Under functional finance, policymakers adjust taxes net of transfers to maintain aggregate demand at a level that ensures full-employment growth but prevents overheating and keeps inflation at a target rate. To simplify the presentation, let the target rate of inflation be zero, normalize the price level to 1, and assume that labor and capital income are taxed at the rates t

---

[3] A large Keynesian literature takes positions that are similar to functional finance (even if not always directly inspired by Lerner); examples include Schlicht (2006), Godley and Lavoie (2007), Arestis and Sawyer (2010), Davidson (2010), Palley (2010), and Nersisyan and Wray (2010).

[4] In a Leontief case without a choice of technique, the interest rate has no effect on the right-hand side of Equation (11.8), and it can be set to satisfy some other objective (to influence the share of income going to rentiers, for instance).

[5] The determination of the steady-growth value of the interest rate does not preclude short-run variations in the interest rate around its steady-growth value for stabilization purposes using some version of a Taylor rule; see Ryoo and Skott (2017), Franke (2018).

and τ, respectively. With these assumptions, tax revenue is given by

$$T = t(1 - \pi)Y + \tau(\pi Y + rB), \tag{11.12}$$

where B denotes the stock of public debt and T is taxes.[6]

The required adjustments in taxes depend on the precise specification of consumption. As argued in Chapter 3, a reasonable first approximation specifies consumption as a linear function of disposable labor income and wealth. Households do not own the capital stock directly in a corporate economy (Chapter 4), but to simplify the analysis, I shall take household wealth to be the sum of fixed capital and the stock of government bonds; Ryoo and Skott (2013) analyze the long-run implications of functional finance in a corporate economy in which household wealth consists of financial assets. Formally, let

$$C = c(1 - t)(1 - \pi)Y + v(K + B), \tag{11.13}$$

where the positive parameters c and v describe the propensities to consume out of current disposable labor income and wealth.

The consumption function (11.13) implies that the tax rate on capital income has no direct, short-run effect on consumption. Fiscal policy to ensure that aggregate demand is consistent with full employment pins down the tax rate on labor income as a function of the values of the stock variables K and B.

Formally, using Equations (11.5) and (11.13), the required tax rate on labor income is given by

$$t = 1 - \frac{\sigma^* - \gamma - (n + \delta) - v}{c(1 - \pi)\sigma^*} + \frac{v}{c(1 - \pi)\sigma^*}b, \tag{11.14}$$

where $b = B/K$ is the ratio of public debt to capital.

The dynamics of the public debt is described by the following equation:

$$\dot{B} = rB + G - T, \tag{11.15}$$

and – combining Equations (11.2), (11.4), (11.12), and (11.15) – we obtain a differential equation for the debt-to-capital ratio (see Appendix B for details):

$$\dot{b} = \frac{1}{c}[(1 - c)(\sigma^* - \gamma) + \sigma^*\pi c(1 - \tau) - v - (n + \delta)]$$
$$- [n + \frac{v}{c} - (1 - \tau)r]b. \tag{11.16}$$

This equation has a unique stationary solution,

$$b^* = \frac{(1 - c)(\sigma^* - \gamma) + \sigma^*\pi c(1 - \tau) - v - (n + \delta)}{v + c(n - (1 - \tau)r)}. \tag{11.17}$$

The stability properties depend on the sign of the coefficient on b: The stationary solution is stable if $cn + v - c(1 - \tau)r > 0$. Empirically, this condition is met. Estimates

---

[6] Employment-dependent transfers can be subsumed in proportional income taxes because, unlike in Chapter 10, the focus is on steady growth paths with a constant employment rate.

of v typically fall in the range between 0.02 and 0.05, and historically the growth rate has exceeded the after-tax interest rate on public debt, at least in the United States: The nominal after-tax interest rate on public debt averaged 3.8 percent between 1950 and 2018, while the growth rate of nominal GDP averaged 6.3 percent (Blanchard 2019). It should be noted also that high tax rates on capital income are stabilizing, relaxing the stability condition.[7,8]

The intuition behind stability is simple. An increase in public debt raises private wealth and stimulates consumption, with policymakers needing to raise taxes in order to prevent overheating and inflation. This stabilizing force is combined with the automatic erosion of the debt ratio B/K as the capital stock increases in a growing economy. These stabilizing forces could, in principle, be offset by the positive feedback effect from higher debt to increased interest payments, but the stabilizing forces dominate for plausible parameter values (and the destabilizing effect is tempered by taxation of capital income).[9]

The convergence result is at odds with dire warnings of unsustainability. Using an OLG model, Chalk (2000) assumes a constant primary deficit per worker. He finds that even if the economy is dynamically inefficient when public debt is zero (having a real rate of interest below the growth rate), a constant primary deficit may be unsustainable. Moreover, in those cases where a primary deficit is sustainable, convergence is to a steady growth path that is dynamically inefficient. Chalk's policy experiments make little sense, however. Why would a government want to pursue policies that maintain a constant primary deficit independently of the state of the economy? Economic analysis of monetary policy typically looks for 'optimal' policies or policy rules, given some welfare criterion and a model of how the economy operates. A functional finance

---

[7] The debt ratio is unconditionally stable if the consumption function is linear in aggregate disposable income and wealth,

$$C = c(Y - rB - T) + v(K + B).$$

With this specification, the value of the interest rate becomes irrelevant. Taxes must be adjusted at each moment to achieve a level of disposable income that is compatible with full employment. An increase in debt reduces the required level of disposable income; to achieve this reduction, taxes must be raised more than the rise in the interest payments rB, and the government deficit must fall (Skott 2015, 2016).

[8] If the debt ratio is explosive, a much more urgent inequality problem will have presented itself as the debt ratio rises: The tax rate on wage income is increasing in b, and the post tax income of workers without capital income will plummet. The solution, as with the stability issue, would be to raise taxes on capital income.

[9] Clearly, there are upper limits on the tax rates t and τ, and these limits constrain the share of the government consumption. An increase in the ratio of government consumption to capital must be offset by a decline in private consumption. This decline can be achieved by raising t (which has an immediate impact on disposable wage income and consumption) or τ (which generates a gradual fall in wealth and, thereby, in consumption).

Formally, Equations (11.14) and (11.17) define t as a function of γ and b, and b^* as a function of γ and τ. Combining the two equations, it can be shown that for plausible parameters, the steady-growth value of the tax rate t is decreasing in τ but increasing in γ,

$$t = \phi(\gamma, \tau); \phi_1 > 0, \phi_2 < 0.$$

If the tax rates have to meet the constraints $t \leq t^{\max}$ and $\tau \leq \tau^{\max}$, it follows that government consumption has an upper limit: $\gamma \leq \gamma^{\max}$, where $\gamma^{\max}$ satisfies $t^{\max} = \phi(\gamma^{\max}, \tau^{\max})$.

approach to economic policy is in a similar spirit, even if it introduces elements usually absent in the analysis of monetary policy. The primary deficit should not be kept at some arbitrary level.

11.5 Implications

11.5.1 . Public Debt and Economic Growth

Reinhart and Rogoff (2010, p. 575) (in)famously argued that countries with debt to GDP ratios above 90 percent have "mean levels of growth almost 4 percent lower." This finding was used repeatedly by policymakers as a justification for strict austerity policies. US House Budget Committee Chairman Paul Ryan declared that "[e]conomists who have studied sovereign debt tell us that letting total debt rise above 90 percent of GDP creates a drag on economic growth and intensifies the risk of a debt-fueled economic crisis." Meanwhile, on the other side of the Atlantic, European Commissioner Olli Rehn claimed that

it is widely acknowledged, based on serious research, that when public debt levels rise about 90% they tend to have a negative economic dynamism, which translates into low growth for many years. That is why consistent and carefully calibrated fiscal consolidation remains necessary in Europe. (quoted from Fernholz 2013).

The Reinhart and Rogoff numbers were wrong. When Thomas Herndon, a graduate student at the University of Massachusetts at the time, tried to replicate the study, he discovered simple spreadsheet errors and a peculiar weighting scheme (Herndon et al. 2014). The corrected figures still showed a negative correlation between economic growth and the debt ratio. But there was no cliff at 90 percent, which undermined the argument for austerity in the middle of a deep recession. If there is no cliff, the debt problem – if it is a problem – could be addressed when the economy had recovered, even if this postponement implied a temporary rise in debt.

More importantly, correlation does not imply causation. The policy argument against debt relies on the explicit or implicit assumption that high debt causes low growth. The causation could go the other way – or a third factor could explain both low growth and high debt, or the correlation could be completely spurious. Reinhart and Rogoff do not make strong claims about causality in their academic work, but interviews and comments on the results paint a different picture. In the words of O'Brien (2013), "R-R whisper 'correlation' to other economists, but say 'causation' to everyone else."[10]

---

[10] Coburn (2012, p. 30) describes an exchange at a meeting in 2011 between forty senators and Reinhart and Rogoff:

Johnny Isakson, a Republican from Georgia and always a gentleman, stood up to ask his question: "Do we need to act this year? Is it better to act quickly?".
"Absolutely," Rogoff said. "Not acting moves the risk closer," he explained, because every year of not acting adds another year of debt accumulation. "You have very few levers at this point," he warned us.

One may attempt to address the causation issue empirically. Irons and Bivens (2010), Basu (2013), and Ash et al. (2017) all find evidence that slow growth tends to precede the rise in debt. This result is not surprising: Tax revenues drop when growth falters, leading to rising debt. The more interesting question concerns the links between growth and debt in the long run, and a purely empirical analysis is unlikely to provide clear answers to this long-run question: Short- and medium-run Granger causality say little or nothing about long-run causal links between debt and growth.[11]

The analysis in Section 11.4 contributes a theoretical perspective. It follows from Equation (11.17) that fiscal policies that maintain full employment produce a long-run causal link from low growth rates to high debt ratios: The steady-growth value of the debt ratio depends inversely on the natural growth rate n.[12] The growth rate was taken to be exogenous so that, in this model, causality runs unambiguously from growth to debt. Intuitively, a higher growth rate implies that the share of investment in output must rise and that consumption must be squeezed. This squeeze is achieved by raising taxes, and higher taxes reduce the long-run debt ratio.

Causality could run both ways. The model in Section 11.4 identified a causal link from growth to debt, but this link from growth to debt does not preclude the existence of a reverse link from debt to growth. Several mechanisms have been suggested (see, e.g., the survey in Elmendorf and Mankiw 1999).

One set of arguments relies on increases in interest rates leading to the crowding out of investment. Figure 11.1 plots the real interest rate on three-month treasury bills against the debt-GDP ratio for the US, 1948–2019. The evidence fails to support the presence of crowding out. The United States has seen large variations in the debt ratio, but the correlation with interest rates is, if anything, negative. This lack of support for crowding out is confirmed in detailed studies. In the words of Engen and Hubbard (2005, p. 83), "some economists believe there is a significant, large, positive effect of government debt on interest rates, others interpret the evidence as suggesting that there is no effect on interest rates." Bohn (2010, p. 14) makes a similar statement about the difficulty of finding significant interest rate effects of debt. He goes on to suggest that a "leading explanation is Ricardian neutrality"; others, including Barro (1989) and Seater (1993), have reached the same conclusion. The analysis in Chapter 3 implies that this explanation is unconvincing; a more plausible alternative is the *de facto* pursuit by policymakers of an imperfect form of functional finance (see Section 11.5.6).

Clearly, expansionary fiscal policy and high debt can motivate central banks to increase interest rates to prevent overheating, and there are examples of this policy mix, the United States in the 1980s, for instance. But general claims that an increase

---

[11] The Goodwin model provides another illustration of the distinction between cyclical patterns and the determination of long-run average outcomes. The model implies that employment is profit-led in the short run: High profit shares are associated with rising employment. The stationary solution for the employment rate, however, is determined by the parameters of a real-wage Phillips curve.

[12] Qualitatively similar results about the long-run debt ratio and its determinants hold in OLG models (Skott and Ryoo 2014, 2017) as well as in stock-flow consistent models of a corporate economy in which household wealth takes the form of financial assets (Ryoo and Skott 2013).

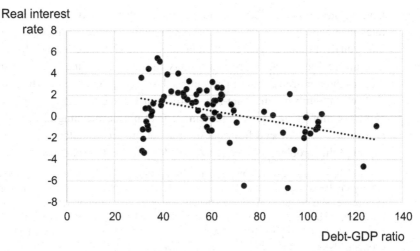

Figure 11.1 Real interest rate on three-month treasury bills and debt-GDP ratio; US 1948–2021. Data source: Federal Reserve and US Office of Management and Budget.

in the debt ratio of 1 percentage point will raise real interest rates by about 2–4 basis points – which seems to be a consensus estimate (Blanchard 2019, Rachel and Summers 2019) – make little sense. Aside from the fact that deficits and public debt often increase in response to weaknesses in aggregate demand, any estimation of reduced-form effects of debt on interest rates overlooks the importance of the structure of taxation and spending. The balanced-budget multiplier is not zero, and taxes on the rich do not have the same demand effects as taxes on the poor, just as corporate taxes differ in their effects from personal taxes. It would be surprising, therefore, if interest rates reacted in the same way to all increases in debt, independently of the sources of the increase.

Distortionary taxation represents another possible source of negative causal effects from debt to economic growth. The broad evidence is unkind to this hypothesis: The United States experienced its highest rates of sustained growth during the 'golden age' from 1950 to 1975, despite having top marginal tax rates on personal income above 70 percent throughout the period and above 90 percent from 1951 to 1963. Leaving aside doubts about the magnitude and relevance of incentive effects from distortionary taxation, the argument faces another problem: An increase in the debt ratio need not be associated with a rise in the tax rate. Both the long-run debt ratio and the long-run tax rate on labor income are endogenous variables and, as shown in Appendix C, the correlation between the tax rate and the debt ratio can be negative. Shifts in the consumption parameter v, for instance, will produce opposite movements in the long-run values of the debt ratio and the tax rates if $n > (1 - \tau)r$. Intuitively, an increase in the consumption rate out of wealth will raise consumption for any given debt ratio. Under a functional finance regime, the fiscal response is to raise the tax rate. The debt ratio now starts falling, and as it falls, consumption declines, which calls for a reduction in the tax rate. The net effect on the tax rate depends on the extent to which the debt ratio declines ($\partial b^*/\partial v$). Thus, if tax rates on labor income have negative growth effects, economies with high debt may experience higher growth rates than economies with low debt. Ambiguous reduced-form correlations between long-run debt ratios and tax rates on labor income also arise from shifts in some other parameters, but not all: A rise in the tax rate on capital income, τ, unambiguously reduces the long-run debt ratio as well as the long-run tax rate on labor income.

The ambiguity of the long-run correlation between tax rates and the debt ratio betrays a more fundamental problem: It may not be meaningful to look for a general answer to a reduced-form question about the growth effects of public debt. One aspect of this problem was recognized by Rogoff and Reinhart (2010, p. 6),

> ... war debts are arguably less problematic for future growth and inflation than large debts that are accumulated in peace time. Postwar growth tends to be high as war-time allocation of man-power and resources funnels to the civilian economy. Moreover, high war-time government spending, typically the cause of the debt buildup, comes to a natural close as peace returns. In contrast, a peacetime debt explosion often reflects unstable underlying political economy dynamics that can persist for very long periods.

As pointed out by Michl (2013, p. 127):

> To a Keynesian, the quote above would very sensibly read 'high recession-time government spending, typically the cause of the debt buildup, comes to a natural close as growth returns.' In fact, Keynes (1972, p. 144) once aptly described government borrowing as "nature's remedy" for preventing a recession from deteriorating into a total collapse in production. As for the rest of the quote, who would deny that 'unstable political dynamics' can be an obstacle to growth?

Fiscal expansions are neither good nor bad intrinsically. They can cause overheating, inflation, and macroeconomic instability in economies that are already at or above full employment, while austerity policies can aggravate negative demand shocks and send economies into deep recessions. Sensible fiscal policies are adjusted in light of prevailing economic circumstances. Policies are not always sensible, but even if they were, reduced-form correlations between debt and growth would depend on the underlying sources of the movements in the two variables.

11.5.2   Secular Stagnation and 'Equilibrium Interest Rates'

In his presentation at an IMF conference, Summers (2013) raised the prospect of secular stagnation as a relevant concern for advanced economies, including Japan, Europe, and the United States.[13] Summers' theoretical analysis was somewhat tentative, but the presentation caused a stir. Summers (2015a) elaborated on the argument, suggesting that because of the zero bound on nominal interest rates there is "no guarantee that the real rate will be low enough for full employment" (p. 61). Importantly, he argued, this state of affairs need not be short-lived since "equilibrium interest rates may be lower on a sustained basis" (p. 62). He concluded that "finding ways to increase the demand to spend, no matter how counterintuitive, is likely to be an important part

---

[13] The dangers of secular stagnation had been emphasized by (post-)Keynesians before Summers' intervention. Examples include Godley (1999), Wray (2000), Skott (2001), and Palley (2002).

of the way forward" (p. 65). Summers also accepted, however, that "fiscal policy may not be possible, given that the government cannot indefinitely expand its debt" (Summers 2015b).

Paul Krugman had been making similar points about the need for increased spending in his discussions of liquidity traps and the lessons from Japan (e.g., Krugman 1998, 2013). His insistence that the slump is not the time to reduce the debt is fully in line with functional finance. But, like Summers, he has seen high debt as a problem:

Yes, the United States has a long-run budget problem. Dealing with that problem is going to require, first of all, sharply bending the curve on Medicare costs; without that, nothing works. And second, it's going to require some combination of spending cuts and revenue increases, amounting to at least 3 percent of GDP and probably more, on a permanent basis. (Krugman 2010)

The nature of the long-run debt problem is not explained, and there appears to be no recognition that public debt need not expand indefinitely if fiscal policy is used to maintain full employment. The Summers and Krugman analysis presents a strong contrast to Reinhart–Rogoff claims about dramatic, negative effects of debt on growth. But the break is incomplete.

The reference to 'equilibrium interest rates' associated with full employment (also known as 'natural' or 'neutral' interest rates) raises a number of questions. The equilibrium interest rate may be well defined in DSGE models with Ramsey optimization and Ricardian equivalence. But secular stagnation finds no place in these models, and fiscal policy is ineffectual. Once we leave the DSGE setting, fiscal policy and the size of the public debt influence aggregate demand: The output-capital ratio that is required for steady growth with full employment – and thereby the interest rate that is required – will be contingent on the fiscal parameters. Putting it differently, assumptions must be made about fiscal policy and the debt ratio in order for statements about 'equilibrium interest rates' to be meaningful. Debt targets and austerity policies within the European Union have led to stagnation despite the best efforts of the European Central Bank, including negative interest rates on excess reserves. An expansionary fiscal policy would alleviate these problems and raise the 'equilibrium interest rate.'

Functional finance faces a similar question but approaches it differently: Interest rates are chosen to achieve the desirable capital intensity (possibly taking into account other criteria, including income distribution). Contingent on this choice, fiscal policy is adjusted to maintain full employment. The result will be an endogenously determined long-run debt ratio.

If there were strong reasons to prefer a particular debt ratio, one could start with a target for the debt ratio and let interest rates and the capital intensity do the adjusting: Assuming that the output-capital ratio depends strongly and reliably on the interest rate, monetary policy could target the interest rate that is consistent with full employment and the target debt ratio. This may have been Summers's implicit assumption in the 2013 and 2015 papers. But if it was, the target debt ratio should have been specified, and the choice of this target should have been justified. If the natural growth rate declines, for instance, why should adjustment fall entirely on the rate of interest and capital intensity? Assuming a well-behaved neoclassical production function, the capital intensity would need to rise. Should this be done, even if it were to lead to dynamic inefficiency? A high sensitivity of the choice of technique to changes in interest rates also becomes critical if one insists on maintaining a fixed target debt ratio. By contrast, policies based on functional finance operate equally well when the production function takes the Leontief form. Moreover, unlike functional finance, a reliance on adjustments in capital intensity to maintain growth with full employment must confront all the problems highlighted by the capital controversy.

The dependence of the 'natural' or 'neutral' interest rate on fiscal policy is recognized by Rachel and Summers (2019, p. 3): "Our main contribution of this paper is to recognize that the neutral real interest rate is not a deep structural feature of an economy but instead reflects both how it is embedded in the global economy and how fiscal policy is set."

Indeed! But it is mind-boggling to see this insight trumpeted as the main contribution in a 2019 paper by prominent economists who would – I expect – consider themselves Keynesian and who are certainly considered Keynesian by most of the profession. Even if the insight is not new, the accompanying analysis could potentially have made a valuable contribution: Rachel and Summers back up their argument with references to empirical evidence and a general equilibrium model to justify the claim theoretically. The evidence, however, is of the reduced-form character discussed above, in which interest rates are related to deficits and debt ratios, with no indication that both the context and the composition of fiscal policy are important.

The theoretical argument, like that of other similar recent contributions including Eggertsson et al. (2019), is based on an extended version of a household-driven, neoclassical OLG model. In the Rachel–Summers version, saving is determined by intertemporally optimizing households; households are identical at birth with the same utility preferences and no assets; all households go through two stages: Work and retirement; there are no aggregate risks, but working households face a constant probability of retiring in each period, while retired households have a constant probability of dying each period, as in Blanchard's (1985) OLG model of perpetual youth; capital markets are perfect, there is full employment, and investment is equal to full-employment saving; a Cobb–Douglas production function and perfect competition determine wages and interest rates. To this setting is added government policy in the form of exogenously given ratios of government consumption, debt, social security spending, and healthcare spending to output, leaving taxes to adjust to satisfy the government budget constraint.

The basic insight from the model is the same as that derived from a simple Diamond model with government consumption, transfers, and taxes. The extensions supposedly make it more realistic, and because workers live for many periods, the model can be calibrated to annual data. But are household-driven models with perfect intertemporal optimization and smooth movements along a Cobb–Douglas production function the most promising – and most 'realistic' – way to understand capitalist dynamics and, more specifically, the structural problems of aggregate demand and secular stagnation?[14]

To an outsider, the Summers-inspired literature can look like a slow and tortuous climb out of the big hole that mainstream macroeconomics finds itself in after forty years of the Lucas paradigm. The demand for explicit and perfect optimization as part of a 'micro-founded' model and a reliance on neoclassical production functions still rule and severely restrict the analysis. The recent developments are encouraging, but the counterrevolution remains incomplete. And as noted by Summers (2018, p. 227) in another paper, "if you get the paradigm right and the details wrong, it will not matter very much.... In contrast, if you operate within the wrong paradigm, you are prone to make enormously consequential and continuing errors."

11.5.3   Austerity

In the short run, austerity measures reduce output and may lead to recession. Reductions in output, in turn, raise the debt income ratio, and the short-run effect of austerity on the debt ratio can be positive (Leão 2013). The analysis in Section 11.4 extends this conclusion to the long run: The long-run debt ratio in Equation (11.17) depends inversely on government consumption γ if the propensity to consume out of wage income is less than 1. Thus, paradoxically austerity policies may also be counterproductive on their own terms in the long run, assuming that the aim is to reduce public debt and not just to squeeze the public sector.

Schlicht (2006) derives this result for a model that is closely related to the one in Section 11.4, and the result is quite robust. Ryoo and Skott (2013) show that it holds for a stock-flow consistent model of a corporate economy in which household wealth takes the form of bonds and stocks rather than direct ownership of fixed capital, and extended versions of the OLG models in Appendix A imply that reductions in social security or government consumption will also raise the required debt ratio (Skott and Ryoo 2017).[15]

Like the analysis in Section 11.4, the above papers take the employment trajectory associated with full employment to be independent of short-run movements in output. If severe recessions produce permanent (or very prolonged) negative effects

---

[14] It is striking that the authors single out one aspect of the model as unrealistic: Unlike in the model, "the timing of retirement is, for the most part, known." Without the constant probability of retirement, however, aggregation would be "problematic" (pp. 27–28). Their solution:

To deal with this unrealistic feature, we assume that there are perfect annuity markets for the retirees (neutralizing the influence of the risk of death on their behavior) and that workers' preferences have a certainty equivalence property (such that the *risk* of retirement does not affect workers' behavior in equilibrium). These two assumptions are both realistic and convenient (p. 28).

Stochastic retirement is not the feature that I would have singled out as being most in need of attention. And are perfect annuity markets realistic?

[15] Entitlement programs like social security or medicare have been prime targets of austerity programs. Aside from their long-term effects on public debt, cuts in these programs have obvious adverse intragenerational effects on distribution.

on the future employment trajectory, the paradoxical long-run effects of austerity on debt are magnified. Not surprisingly, the slow recovery after the financial crisis has renewed interest in the implications of employment hysteresis for economic policy (e.g., Blanchard 2018b, DeLong and Summers 2012, Blanchard 2018b).

11.5.4 Income Distribution and Saving

The rich, on average, have a higher rate of saving than the poor, and an increase in inequality tends to reduce the average rate of consumption (albeit with some caveats; cf. Chapters 3–4). A fall in consumption must be offset by fiscal expansion to prevent unemployment, and a rise in inequality therefore tends to raise the required debt ratio. As a corollary, a reduction in the tax rate on capital income raises the long-run debt ratio.[16]

These results, which follow directly from the expression for b^* in Equation (11.17), were anticipated by Lerner (1943, p. 49):

> if for any reason the government does not wish to see private property grow too much (whether in the form of government bonds or otherwise) it can check this by taxing the rich ... The rich will not reduce their spending significantly ... By this means the debt can be reduced to any desired level and kept there.

All else equal, an increase in the debt ratio unambiguously requires an increase in the tax rate on wage income (Equation (11.14)), and although the reduced-form relation between t and b^* can be negative, depending on the exogenous shock (Appendix C), a reduction in the tax rate on property income unambiguously raises b^* as well as the required tax rate t (Equations (11.14) and (11.17)). Thus, the distributional consequences of a reduction in taxes on capital income are amplified by the subsequent gradual increase in taxes on wage income.

These results are of particular interest because of the trend toward lower taxation of capital income in most OECD countries. The US tax reform that came into effect in 2018 is a well-known example, but the decline in corporate tax rates is widespread (OECD 2019a).[17] Aside from the intrinsic significance of the distribution of income, this switch in taxation away from capital income becomes troublesome if it is combined with political and institutional limits on the public deficits and debt: The rise in the debt ratio that is required for maintaining full-employment growth aggravates the negative effects of the fiscal constraints imposed by the European Union's (EU's) 'stability and growth pact.' The full-employment growth rate in the EU is low, and an ill-advised 60 percent constraint on the debt-GDP ratio becomes even more restrictive if the structure of taxation shifts away from capital income.

---

[16] As noted above, a reduction in the tax rate on property income also tightens the stability condition for the differential Equation (11.16): The stationary solution is stable if $n + \mu/c > (1 - \tau)r$.

[17] The picture is more mixed with respect to the taxation of household capital income (OECD 2019).

11.5.5 Negative Effects of Public Debt

Functional finance has traditionally prioritized employment and investment targets. A reduction in the debt ratio may be desirable, however, if it can be achieved without compromising these targets, since the debt ratio can influence other outcomes that we care about. Variations in interest rates around the long-run average, for example, can be an important instrument for short-run stabilization, but the effectiveness of monetary policy is influenced by the presence of public debt. A contractionary monetary policy – a rise in interest rates – generates an automatic fiscal expansion unless it is matched by an increase in tax rates. Thus, monetary policy is blunted when debt is high, and Taylor rules that are stabilizing for low debt ratios can become destabilizing if the debt ratio exceeds a certain threshold (Bell-Kelton and Ballinger 2006, Ryoo and Skott 2017).

Public debt also influences the distribution of income, with intragenerational effects that can be highly regressive if low-income households are taxed to pay interest on a large public debt held by rich households. These intragenerational effects on distribution can be significant and warrant attention. Distributional concerns, however, have focused mainly on intergenerational aspects. This is the case especially in popular debates, but the concern also appears in the academic literature. Having found that public debt has at most small effects on interest rates, Engen and Hubbard (2004, p. 132) go on to caution that public deficits and debt still matter because large levels of government debt "can represent a large transfer of wealth to finance current generations' consumption from future generations which must eventually pay down federal debt to a sustainable level."

This is a peculiar statement. Future generations can suffer if the current generation fails to invest in physical capital and education, if it fails to build and maintain well-functioning social and political institutions, or if it degrades the environmental resources that future generations rely on. But if interest rates do not rise and there is no crowding out, it is unclear how future generations can 'finance' the current generation's consumption. If future generations are taxed in order to pay interest on, or reduce, the public debt, then this will represent an intragenerational transfer from future tax payers to future holders of the government bonds.

Another peculiar fear also keeps showing up. Policymakers may, it is suggested, be unable to control the real rate of interest on public debt, and the government may even find itself in a situation where it is unable to meet its obligations. In other words, functional finance – which supposes that real interest rates can be controlled – is infeasible. Chalk (2000, p. 319) argues that some OECD countries "have seen an explosion in their indebtedness to such an extent that the solvency of the public sector is brought into question," while Collard et al. (2015, p. 382) "take it as the starting point for our analysis that maximum debt is determined by lenders: a country can only borrow as much as lenders are willing to provide."

It is clearly correct that countries with debt in foreign currency can face solvency problems and may be unable to control the interest rate on their debt. But there is no indication in these (and many other) papers that the argument is restricted to a subset of countries with debt in a currency they do not themselves control. Chalk discusses the US economy, and Collard et al. calculate their sustainable debt levels using the same criteria for the United States and Korea (with debt in their own currencies) as they do for Greece and Ireland (whose situation is closer to that of a city like Detroit that filed for bankruptcy in 2013). Sovereign states cannot become insolvent if their debt obligations are denominated in currencies that they can print at will. By the same token, high debt will not compel a country to pay high interest rates; Japan has a gross debt ratio that exceeds 200 percent – almost all of it in yen denominated obligations – and yet the interest rate on its ten-year bonds is below 0.5 percent. A country that controls its own currency always has the possibility of monetizing the debt. If the interest rate on long-term treasury bonds is deemed too high, the composition of public debt can be shifted toward short-term bonds; if the interest rate on short-term debt is too high, open market operations can be used to bring it down.[18]

A standard counterargument posits that the inflationary implications of monetization rule out this policy. Engen and Hubbard (2004) suggest that "federal government debt may also pose the temptation to monetize the debt, causing inflation." Inflation, however, is caused by excess demand pressures in goods markets and/or wage pressures in labor markets, and an overheating economy calls for contractionary policy. Functional finance implies a commitment to prevent overheating and rising inflation. Thus, the inflation fear essentially boils down to a concern that policy may not, in the future, be governed by the functional finance principle to "eliminate both unemployment and inflation" (Lerner 1943, p. 41). One may choose to postulate that future policymakers will pursue inflationary policies. But empirically, the correlation between federal debt and inflation has, in fact, been negative in post-War data for the United States (Engen and Hubbard (2004, p. 98). Reinhart and Rogoff (2010) also fail to find evidence for a link between debt and inflation in advanced economies.

To be persuasive, the inflation argument would need to show that high debt erodes the ability of policymakers to implement contractionary fiscal policies to counteract overheating. Otherwise, the inflation arguments, like the sustainability arguments, merely point to the possibility of unhappy consequences from bad policy (as argued above, Chalk and Collard et al. demonstrate that strange results may follow when arbitrary policies are combined with various *ad hoc* assumptions about, *inter alia*, growth prospects and default risks). Not exactly a surprising conclusion.

11.5.6 Empirical Relevance of Functional Finance

There is no question that excessive fiscal expansion and rising public debt can lead to high interest rates and crowd out investment. But policies of this kind do not represent functional finance. The link between debt and interest rates does not exist under functional finance: Debt is only allowed to increase if an increase is necessary to maintain

---

[18] Blanchard (2019) – in a paper that goes a long way to dispel the fear that high debt must always bring severe welfare costs – also gives serious attention to a potential, but unexplained, inability of the state to meet its obligations. Might there not, he asks, be a level of debt that is low enough to ensure that even if the state "cannot pay the stated rate, it can pay the safe rate"? If this is the case, "investors, if they are rational, should not and will not worry about risk" (p. 1226).

both full employment and the interest rate associated with the optimal capital intensity. By construction, the interest rate and the capital intensity of production are kept at levels that are deemed optimal.

In a stylized model of a perfectly operating regime of functional finance, the real interest rate is constant, and a plot of real interest rates against public debt will trace out a horizontal line. Fluctuations around the line arise if variations in interest rates are used for purposes of short-run stabilization and/or if there are variations in the value of the interest rate (the capital intensity) that is considered optimal.[19] 'Imperfect functional finance' – a regime in which fiscal policy does not follow the precise prescriptions of functional finance but tends to become more expansionary (contractionary) when unemployment is high (low) – will also produce deviations from the horizontal line, but again without a systematic long-run correlation. By contrast, if policy deviated fundamentally from functional finance and public debt evolved independently of the state of aggregate demand, one would expect to see evidence of crowding out: There should be a clear positive correlation between debt and interest rates. As indicated above, this is not the case in the United States (Figure 11.1).

Widespread austerity policies and recurrent obsessions with public debt, often politically driven, are reminders that sometimes fiscal policy deviates significantly from the principles of functional finance. Something close to functional finance, however, had substantial support within the profession during the heyday of Keynesian economics from the 1950s to the 1970s. Tobin (1986) commented that in "almost every recession prior to the most recent pair of 1979-82, fiscal stimulus, temporary or permanent, was deliberately applied to promote recovery" (p. 7). Criticizing the Reagan–Volcker policy mix, he noted that the tight-money-easy-budget combination "runs counter to long-run growth because it encourages present-oriented uses of GNP relative to future-oriented ones" (p. 12). The policy mix, in other words, created too little investment, thereby deviating from functional finance.

Macroeconomic theory swung away from Keynesian ideas in the late 1970s, but fiscal policy is still influenced by aggregate demand considerations. The stimulus package of 2009 is a prominent US example of discretionary, demand-motivated fiscal policy from this period, but the Bush tax cuts in 2001 and 2003 were also in part motivated (or at least presented as being motivated) by the weakness of aggregate demand at the time.[20] Outside the United States, it is no coincidence that, facing weak aggregate demand, policymakers in Japan have run deficits and, reluctantly, allowed public debt to increase dramatically since the early 1990s. The response to COVID-19 is harder to categorize. Deficits and debt have exploded in many countries, and there has clearly been a significant shift in attitudes to public debt. But, to a large extent, the COVID-19 response represented disaster relief following a large negative supply shock, as the pandemic forced widespread lockdowns as well as disruptions to supply chains.

---

[19] Central banks may use interest rates for short-term stabilization. As in most of this chapter, 'the interest rate' refers to the level around which actual rates fluctuate in the course of stabilization policy.

[20] Discussing the three US recessions between 1990 and 2019, Blanchard and Summers (2020, p. 129) find that, in addition to automatic stabilizers, "discretionary policy eventually came into play" in all three.

11.6   Functional Finance in Developing Economies

Structural aggregate demand problems – secular stagnation – can arise in mature economies in which the long-run growth rate is constrained by the growth rate of the labor force in effective units. Most developing countries, however, have dual economies with large amounts of hidden unemployment and underemployment.[21] They may experience shortages of some types of skilled workers, but underemployment, learning by doing, and the potential for technological catch-up imply that Chinese-style growth rates could be maintained for many years without a general labor shortage.

The supply-side constraints on the modern sector come from a combination of low stocks of private fixed capital, inadequate public infrastructure, and shortages of human capital. The precise form of these capital constraints differs across countries, and the details are crucial in the formulation of concrete development policies. For present purposes, however, the point is simply that current resources must be invested in order to expand the modern sector. In short, high saving rates may generate chronic aggregate demand deficiencies in mature economies, but this problem need not arise in dual economies: Rapid accumulation in the modern sector is desirable – the higher the accumulation rate the better – and high accumulation rates are associated with high shares of investment in income.

Dual economies face a *structural transformation problem*. With a small modern sector and large amounts of (open or hidden) unemployment, the policy targets must change. Capital constraints make it impossible to achieve full employment in a meaningful sense, and a development-oriented aggregate demand policy should aim for high utilization rates of the capital stock in the modern sector rather than full employment, and set targets for the growth rate of the modern sector. High saving rates do not cause structural aggregate demand problems in dual economies; they represent an opportunity to increase investment and the growth rate of the modern sector.

This perspective, which is in line with traditional development theory,[22] does not imply that there is no need for aggregate demand management. The private sector must have an incentive to invest, and macroeconomic policies should be used to stabilize the demand for the output of the modern sector. In open economies, additionally, balance of payments problems must be avoided, and the domestic modern sector must be internationally competitive. But successful development requires high saving, and a sensible aggregate demand policy will typically avoid persistent deficits and high public debt.

The one-sector model in Section 11.4 can be used to formalize this argument if the modern sector draws on an infinitely elastic labor supply from the traditional sector,

---

[21] The argument in this section, which is developed more fully in Skott (2021), has affinities with development theory, both new and old; for example, Razmi et al. (2012), Ros (2013), Bresser-Pereira et al. (2015), and Damill et al. (2016).

[22] As argued by Nurkse (1953, p. 1), for instance, the supply-side constraints in developing economies derive from a shortage of capital that is "at the centre of the problem of development."

but each sector is otherwise entirely self-contained. With these assumptions, the modern sector in a dual economy behaves like a mature economy without a natural rate of growth.

Traditional Lewis-type models (Lewis 1954) often identify the informal sector with a self-contained subsistence agriculture that neither sells output to the modern sector nor provides a market for the goods produced by the modern sector. This assumption fails to capture contemporary realities: Large parts of agriculture are now formal in many developing economies, while significant proportions of nonagricultural production belong to the informal sector. Workers in the informal sector consume both formal- and informal-sector goods, and incomes in the formal sector are spent on informal-as well as formal-sector goods. The sectors, consequently, are not self-contained.

The appropriate delineation of formal and informal sectors and the precise ways in which they interact depend on the particular application, but a stylized two-sector model can be used to illustrate some issues that cannot be addressed by a one-sector analysis.

11.6.1   A Two-Sector Model

The two-sector framework that was used in Section 6.5 to analyze inflation in dual economies requires modification. The focus now is on long-run development, and the analysis of functional finance requires that fiscal policy be included explicitly.

The utilization rate of capital in the formal (or modern) sector fluctuates but, as in the mature-economy model of functional finance, it is assumed that the fluctuations take place around average values that are approximately equal to the desired rates.[23] Formally,

$$M = \sigma K = AL_M,$$

where $M, K,$ and L_M denote output, capital, and employment in the formal sector, respectively. The output-capital ratio (σ) is constant, while labor productivity (A) may grow at a constant rate. The product real wage (w_M) in the modern sector is given by

$$w_M = A(1 - \pi), \tag{11.18}$$

where π is the profit share. The markup (and hence the profit share) is taken to be constant.

The capital stock and the productivity of labor are predetermined in the short run, which pins down employment in the modern sector,

$$L_M = \frac{\sigma K}{A}.$$

---

[23] The terms formal and modern sector will be used interchangeably.

The informal R-sector becomes the residual 'employer': Workers who fail to get a job in the modern sector move to this sector. Hence,

$$L_R = N - L_M = N\left(1 - \frac{L_M}{N}\right) = N\left(1 - \frac{\sigma K}{AN}\right), \tag{11.19}$$

where N is the total labor supply. The total labor supply in modern-sector effective units (AN) grows at a rate n,

$$\hat{N} + \hat{A} = n.$$

The informal sector produces the output R, using labor as the only input. If p_R denotes the relative price of informal goods, the sector's total real income in terms of formal-sector goods is $p_R R$, and the average income (w_R) becomes

$$w_R = \frac{p_R R}{L_R}.$$

Let

$$R = F(eL_R),$$

where e is the 'employment rate' in the informal sector, with unemployment typically taking the form of hidden underemployment.

Informal-sector workers may benefit from transfers and targeted public services, but pay no taxes.[24] Formal-sector wages and capital income are taxed at the rates t and τ, respectively; transfers to workers in the modern sector are included in the tax rate, which is net of transfers. Workers spend all transfers and after-tax wages on consumption.[25] The consumption by profit recipients in the modern sector is determined by their wealth. As in Section 11.4, wealth is taken to be the sum of the capital stock K and the government debt B, while government consumption is taken to be proportional to the capital stock, $G = \gamma K$; the ratio of government consumption to capital γ is exogenous. The transfer ζ to informal-sector workers – like the tax rates t and τ on wage and capital income – may be used as an instrument of fiscal policy.

Formally, consumption, investment, and government spending are given by

$$C = (w_R + \zeta)L_R + (1 - t)w_M L_M + v(K + B)$$
$$I = (g + \delta)K$$
$$G = \gamma K,$$

where C, G, I, and all prices and wages are measured in terms of formal-sector goods.

The specification of the composition of demand follows that in Section 6.5. It is assumed that both private consumption and government spending are split between the formal and informal sectors in the same, fixed proportions, with the proportion

---

[24]   The avoidance of taxes and regulations is sometimes seen as a defining characteristic of informality. If taxes are levied on informal-sector workers, the transfers should be interpreted as net of taxes.

[25]   Since workers do not save, it does not matter for present purposes whether transfers take the form of goods or cash: The demand effects are the same.

α going to the formal sector.[26] Investment goods, by contrast, tend to be relatively sophisticated (and often have to be imported in developing economies). Thus, as a first approximation, it seems reasonable to assume that investment is produced by the formal sector.

These assumptions about the composition of demand imply that the equilibrium condition for the informal R-sector can be written as

$$w_R L_R = p_R R = (1 - \alpha)(C + G) \tag{11.20}$$
$$= (1 - \alpha)\{(w_R + \zeta)L_R + (1 - t)w_M L_M + v(K + B) + \gamma K\}.$$

Solving for w_R and using Equation (11.19), we obtain

$$w_R = \frac{1 - \alpha}{\alpha} \frac{A}{\sigma}[(1 - t)(1 - \pi)\sigma + v(1 + b) + \gamma]\Theta + \frac{1 - \alpha}{\alpha}\zeta, \tag{11.21}$$

where Θ is the ratio of modern-sector employment to the labor force in the informal sector,

$$\Theta = \frac{L_M}{N - L_M} = \frac{\sigma K}{AN - \sigma K}.$$

The IS equation provides a second equilibrium condition,[27]

$$Y = M + p_R R = C + I + G$$
$$= (w_R + \zeta)L_R + (1 - t)(1 - \pi)\sigma K + v(K + B) + (g + \delta)K + \gamma K$$

or

$$\sigma K = \zeta L_R + (1 - t)(1 - \pi)\sigma K + v(1 + b)K + (g + \delta)K + \gamma K.$$

Dividing through by K, this equation can be solved for the accumulation rate g,

$$g + \delta = \sigma - \left[(1 - t)(1 - \pi)\sigma + v(1 + b) + \gamma + \zeta\frac{L_R}{K}\right]. \tag{11.22}$$

The ratio of government consumption to capital (γ) is kept constant by assumption, and the debt ratio b is predetermined at each moment. As in the case of the mature economy in Section 11.4, taxes on capital income affect the trajectory and long-run value of the public debt ratio (and thereby consumption), but a change in the tax rate on capital income (τ) has no immediate impact on consumption. Thus, Equation (11.22) implies that shocks to the growth rate must be accompanied by suitable adjustments in the tax and subsidy rates t and ζ in the short run.[28] Equation (11.22) also implies that

---

[26] Constant expenditure shares of consumption are consistent with a Cobb–Douglas utility function. Razmi et al. (2012) make a distinction between consumption out of wage income (which may go predominantly to the informal sector) and consumption out of profit income (which may go predominantly to the formal sector).

[27] The equilibrium condition for the formal good could have been used instead. The two conditions are equivalent in this two-sector model when the equilibrium condition for the informal sector is met.

[28] This property of the consumption function could be relaxed without affecting the main conclusions (Skott 2021).

if policymakers maintain a constant growth target, the tax and subsidy rates will need to be adjusted as the debt ratio evolves.

In this adaptation of functional finance to a dual economy, a growth target replaces the natural growth rate, but the differential equation for the debt ratio is similar, with a stationary solution for b given by

$$b^* = \frac{(1-\tau)\pi\sigma - (g + \delta + v)}{g + v - (1-\tau)r}.$$

Thus, the debt ratio depends inversely on the growth rate of the modern sector, again analogous to the one-sector model.[29] The intuition is straightforward. If the output-capital ratio is constant and investment goods are produced by the modern sector, an increase in accumulation must be offset by a reduction in the consumption of modern goods. This requires a rise in one or more tax rates, leading to a decline in the stationary solution for the debt ratio. Thus, rapid development tends to be associated with low deficits and low public debt ratios.

As argued in Chapter 6, developing economies face an inflation constraint, in addition to the consumption–investment tradeoff (11.22). The supply of labor to the formal sector will be highly elastic as long as the posttax wages in the modern sector exceed the average post-transfer incomes in the informal sector. But path-dependent pay norms, rather than the ability of the modern sector to hire workers, may be the effective constraint on relative wages. Even if workers receive a wage premium and willingly accept modern-sector jobs, unfair violations of the prevailing pay norms generate nominal wage pressures as well as adverse effects on morale and productivity.

Combining Equations (11.18)–(11.22), the posttax income ratio is[30]

$$\frac{w_R + \zeta}{(1-t)w_M} = \frac{1}{(1-t)(1-\pi)}\frac{1-\alpha}{\alpha}\frac{1}{\sigma}[\sigma - (g+\delta)]\Theta + \frac{\zeta}{(1-t)(1-\pi)A}. \tag{11.23}$$

Equation (11.23) determines the posttax wage ratio as a function of $t, \zeta, \pi, g,$ and Θ. The ratio depends positively on the employment composition $\Theta = L_M/(N - L_M)$, which changes during a process of successful development. As the formal sector expands, the average income in the informal sector rises for any given values of the growth rate, the profit share and the tax parameters (Equation (11.21)). This improvement for informal-sector workers carries over to the relative wage (Equation (11.23)); workers in the informal sector gradually catch up with workers in the modern sector as the economy develops and the modern sector expands.

A steady reduction in the pretax wage premium and associated, progressively increasing violations of any fixed norm for relative wages could be offset by adjustments in ζ and t to maintain the after-tax wage ratio. Wage norms are not fixed, however, and an expansion of the modern sector can go along with a gradual reduction

---

[29] A formal analysis of the debt dynamics can follow the same pattern as in Appendix B. Stability requires that $g + v - (1-\tau)r > 0$.

[30] The expression in Equation (11.23) becomes more complicated than Equation (6.56) in Chapter 6 because, unlike in Section 6.5, the model now includes taxes, transfers, government consumption, and consumption out of wealth.

in inequality. Large violations of the pay norm may generate explosive inflation but, as argued in Section 6.5, an erosion of inegalitarian pay norms can be achieved without sparking runaway inflation by allowing the relative wage premium to fall slightly below the norm. If μ is the prevailing norm for the ratio of after-tax modern-sector wages to average post-transfer incomes in the informal sector, this policy requires that $(1 - t)w_M = (1 - \varepsilon)\mu(1 + \zeta)w_R$ for some small $\varepsilon > 0$. Or, using (11.23),

$$\frac{1}{\sigma}\frac{(1 + \zeta)(1 - \alpha)}{(1 - t)(1 - \pi)\alpha}[\sigma - (g + \delta)]\Theta = \frac{1}{(1 - \varepsilon)\mu}. \tag{11.24}$$

Developmental macroeconomic policy has to consider both the consumption-investment tradeoff (11.22) and the inflation constraint (11.24).

11.6.2 Discussion

Some Implications

With a binding capital constraint in the modern sector, consumption must be squeezed to make space for additional investment. The inflation constraint highlights the importance of the way the squeeze is achieved. A reliance on taxes on formal-sector wages – raising t – leads to a violation of the inflation constraint, while cutting transfers to informal-sector workers relaxes the constraint and avoids this problem. A combination of increases in t and cuts to ζ could be used to satisfy both constraints with equality. This balanced squeeze on both formal- and informal-sector workers is distributionally regressive, however, and there are alternatives: The resources for investment could come from policies that curb luxury consumption by the rich. An increase in the tax parameter τ gradually reduces the debt ratio, bringing down wealth-related consumption and releasing resources for investment (Equation (11.22)) while leaving the wage premium and the inflation constraint unchanged. Since an increase in accumulation relaxes the inflation constraint (11.24), there may even be space for egalitarian increases in ζ if an increase in τ (and the associated declining debt ratio) is used to satisfy the consumption–investment tradeoff. In practice, of course, policies of this kind would need to overcome opposition from political and economic elites.

The detailed implications of the model are contingent on the precise assumptions, including the composition of demand and the specification of distributive conflict and wage inflation. These assumptions, which were deliberately kept simple, can be questioned. But the analysis has a robust, general message. A developing economy with large amounts of underemployment faces both consumption–investment tradeoffs (because of the capital constraints in the modern sector) and inflation constraints (because of distributional conflict). It is not enough to avoid persistent excess demand for modern-sector output. The choice of instruments in the management of aggregate demand to meet the consumption–investment tradeoff can be critical for the inflationary process and for the sustainability of a program of economic development, as well as for inequality.

The potential importance of the inflation constraint can be illustrated by returning to a stylized scenario mentioned briefly in Section 6.5. Suppose that a resource-rich open economy receives a windfall gain from rising commodity prices. This gain enables a rise in the import of modern goods without balance of payments problems; the consumption–investment tradeoff has been relaxed. Consumption by private owners of the resources and other direct beneficiaries of the rise in commodity prices increases, while a boost to resource taxes and royalties may give rise to increased government consumption, with derived effects on investment and private consumption. The relaxed consumption–investment tradeoff may be satisfied, and the government may balance its budget, but increased domestic consumption pushes up average incomes in the nontradable informal sector. In this situation, a significant violation of the prevailing relative wage norm generates strong inflationary pressures. An inflation-targeting central bank steps in by raising interest rates; this puts downward pressure on investment, and the real exchange rate appreciates (even more than may have already happened as a result of the commodity boom); the domestic modern sector becomes increasingly uncompetitive, both at home and abroad, and the initial expansion of the modern sector is now followed by declining utilization rates and low accumulation. In the presence of dynamic increasing returns, the negative impact of low accumulation on productivity growth in the modern sector may even send the economy into a development trap (Skott 2021).

The scenario, stylized as it is, captures the experience of many Latin American countries during and after the commodity boom that started around 2002: A Dutch disease was sparked by a violation of the inflation constraint and a misguided policy response. Fiscal instruments should have been adjusted differently in the early phases of the commodity boom; instead, a reliance on monetary policy to fight incipient inflation produced a contraction of the modern sector and set back the development process. Martins and Skott (2021) analyze an open economy model along these lines, relating the model directly to the Brazilian experience.

Limitations and Caveats

In a mature economy the full-employment target for economic policy is relatively uncontroversial and reasonably well defined, even if measurement problems and path dependencies complicate matters in practice. In the adaptation of functional finance to a dual economy, by contrast, the tradeoff between accumulation and current consumption implies that the choice of a target rate of growth will be contentious. In highly unequal dual economies, there are strong arguments in favor of a squeeze on the luxury consumption of the rich, but that does not settle the issue. The resources that were previously absorbed by luxury consumption could be used to increase accumulation or alleviate current poverty; decision-makers still face an intertemporal tradeoff.

If we disregard thorny questions about the appropriate weighting of current and future welfare, there is an additional issue: The nature of the tradeoff may not be well understood by policymakers and the population at large, and this lack of understanding can give rise to a short-termist bias. The benefits of investment come in the future, while low incomes in the informal sector can provide strong incentives for governments to engage in fiscal expansion and redistribution of income. If the accumulation rate – and thereby the growth rate of the formal sector – is adversely affected, future incomes will suffer, and underemployment will increase (or decline more slowly). But these losses will be less visible than immediate sacrifices associated with high accumulation and low current consumption.

The problems are aggravated by dynamic complications. The immediate impact of expansionary policies are positive, also in the modern sector. Indeed, any policy to raise accumulation and move the economy to a higher growth path needs to stimulate demand initially in order to raise the utilization rate and give firms the incentive to increase investment. But once accumulation rates start increasing, the demand stimulus must be reversed to make space for investment. This two-stage process creates obvious populist temptations to embrace the first stage but fail to follow through on the second. The temptation is likely to be especially strong for governments that lack the inclination or power to confront political and economic elites by imposing significant taxes on capital income and luxury consumption. Limited institutional capabilities of the fiscal authorities accentuate the dangers.

The tradeoff between current consumption and the rate of growth also calls for comment. Large parts of 'consumption' are mislabeled and should be considered investment. An obvious example is the misleading classification of public spending on education as public consumption. In addition to their immediate welfare benefits, spending on health care, food, and housing for low-income families also contain significant elements of investment: Healthier and better educated children can raise future labor productivity and improve the prospects for economic growth. Thus, prioritizing investment does not imply squeezing everything that is classified as consumption in the national income accounts.

Many essential investment projects, second, will not be carried out by the private sector. Public investment in infrastructure, education, and health is crucial for successful development, complementing and crowding in private investment.[31] This role for public investment introduces a caveat with respect to the inverse relation between public deficits and successful development. To the extent that successful development is associated with a large share of government investment in total investment, the implications for government deficits become ambiguous: Rapid growth need not be associated with low debt ratios.

Equation (11.5) and the formal analysis in this chapter, finally, have focused on stable growth paths. Macroeconomic instability deters long-term private investment, and aggregate demand policy in a dual economy should aim to secure a stable macroeconomic environment with appropriate levels and growth rates of demand for the output of the modern sector. Recessions should be countered by expansionary measures but, equally important, overheating of the economy should be avoided. The use of monetary policy to target inflation poses particular dangers in this respect: To the extent that the use of interest rates to control inflation is successful, it may owe its success in large part to its effects on the real exchange rate. Exchange rate appreciation puts a damper

---

[31] Not all modern-sector activities are equally conducive to long-term economic growth. Thus, going beyond the scope of traditional macroeconomic theory and demand management, industrial policy can play a decisive role in promoting structural transformation (e.g., Chang 2008).

on inflation, but overvalued exchange rates and balance of payments crises can cause great damage. Large fluctuations in real exchange rates, more generally, impede the long-run development of a modern tradable sector.

11.6.3   Japanese Growth and Stagnation

The distinction between mature and dual economies and the implied difference in policy can be illustrated by the case of Japan.

Japan experienced twenty-five years of miracle growth in the period after the World War II, with GDP per capita growing at an average annual rate of 8.2 percent between 1945 and 1970. The growth rate dropped to 3.6 percent between 1970 and 1990, and the Japanese economy has stagnated since then. Average per capita growth of only 0.8 percent between 1990 and 2020 has made Japan the poster case for secular stagnation, with policymakers appearing powerless. Interest rates have been at the zero lower bound, and public debt has climbed to more than 200 percent of GDP.

The Japanese economy had been characterized by large amounts of hidden unemployment and underemployment until the late 1960s. Throughout this period, the labor supply to the modern sector was highly elastic, and there was a large potential for technological catchup. As the experience of many developing economies demonstrates, these conditions do not ensure rapid growth: In the absence of decisive state intervention – improvements in infrastructure and education along with successful industrial strategies – the Japanese economy could have followed a very different, slow-growth trajectory. But the elastic labor supply and the catchup potential were important for the facilitation of rapid growth. High growth, in turn, was associated with high investment demand, which allowed the goods market to be in equilibrium, despite high saving rates.

Labor constraints began to appear around 1970, and by 1990, Japan had become the world leader in many industries, limiting the scope for further technological advance. The growth rates of the previous period exceeded the post-1990 'natural rate of growth,' and a decline in growth was inevitable. But a combination of high saving rates and slow growth produced a structural demand problem (Nakatani and Skott 2007).

With high saving rates, a low natural rate of growth, and reduced accumulation potential, Japan needed other sources of aggregate demand. The financial and real estate bubble of the 1980s alleviated the incipient demand problems for a while, but when the bubble burst, the public and foreign sectors would have had to pick up the slack to maintain full employment. International political constraints (primarily from the United States) excluded large and sustained trade surpluses, while domestic political constraints (supported by macroeconomic orthodoxy) restrained fiscal expansion. The result was limping growth with persistent underperformance, weak labor markets, and deflationary tendencies.

The structural problems have been loosened somewhat, partly as a result of the rise in government debt that has been allowed to take place. The fiscal stimulus may not have been as strong as it should have been, had the authorities followed a pure functional finance approach, but fiscal deficits and a large debt, nonetheless, have boosted demand and reduced private saving. Other factors have helped as well, with demographic changes and an aging population contributing to a fall in the saving rate. Overall, the household saving rate out of net disposable income has declined steeply from around 20 percent in the mid-1970s to about 2 percent after 2010 (until COVID-19).

Drawing on both demand- and supply-side elements, this broad story of the Japanese economy accounts for both the rapid growth and the subsequent stagnation within the same general framework. The fundamental change on the supply side was the transition from a dual to a mature economy. This transition and the associated decline in the share of investment in output led to structural problems of aggregate demand. Looking ahead, China and other rapidly growing developing economies will face a similar transition at some point and may have to tackle similar aggregate demand problems.

The supply side appears in most accounts of Japanese stagnation, but typically the story is told in a very different way. It is commonly argued that the Japanese economy needs fundamental reforms. The OECD Economic Surveys follow this line and persistently push for "bold structural reforms." In OECD (2015, p. 5), the "bold structural reforms" need to "improve the business climate" (by, *inter alia*, "promoting labor market flexibility" and "revitalising venture capital investment"), while on the fiscal side, the "top fiscal priority is reducing government debt." In OECD (2019b) "bold structural reforms" are still needed, and it is emphasized how "fiscal sustainability requires a detailed consolidation plan" (p. 15). A plan of this kind becomes especially important, it is argued, because the government will miss its previous target of a primary surplus by 2020. The failure to reach this target "strengthens the case for an independent fiscal institution" (p. 22). There appears to be little or no recognition in these reports that weak aggregate demand may lie behind the failure to meet the earlier target and that economic performance would have suffered had the original plans for fiscal consolidation been carried out. A disregard of aggregate demand is not confined to OECD. Rather than reflecting policy responses to weak demand, the Japanese case, according to Obstfeld (2013, p. 2), "illustrates how dangerous it can be to tolerate large public debt buildups."

11.7   Conclusion

Austerity policies have had devastating consequences for unemployment, poverty, and political instability, with some of the most dramatic examples coming from the Eurozone. The analysis in this chapter does not apply directly to individual countries in a currency union. It does apply to the Eurozone as a whole, however, and to the austerity measures that were imposed by Eurozone policy decisions. Less disastrously, but also with real and significant welfare costs, debt obsessions hampered economic policy and slowed the recovery in the United States after the financial crisis.

It is disturbing and deeply ironic that the main empirical justification for austerity policies and sound finance came from crude correlations between debt and growth.

It is disturbing because simple correlations leave open the question of causation. It is ironic because the advocacy came from a profession that had been preaching the Lucas critique and the impossibility of informed policy analysis based on mere statistical correlation. It is doubly ironic because the theoretical orthodoxy that emerged in the wake of the Lucas critique implies that, as a first approximation, public debt is a nonissue.

Another defense of sound finance has come from calculations that show the unsustainability of large, permanent primary deficits. These calculations are largely irrelevant: What purpose is being served by analyzing whether this or that arbitrary path of primary deficits is sustainable? Arbitrary policies generally do not produce good results, and no Keynesian economist advocates arbitrary primary deficits of this kind. The interesting question concerns the viability and sustainability of fiscal policies that are designed to achieve the policy objectives that we care about. The focus in this chapter has been on maintaining (noninflationary) full employment and generating a desirable balance between investment and consumption; other objectives could clearly be considered.

As argued in Chapters 5–6, capitalist economies may not have a well-defined state of full employment. A full-employment objective therefore loses precision, which complicates policymaking. These problems do not invalidate the main point, however: Fiscal deficits and public debt should be judged by their implications for employment, inflation, and investment, not by moralistic notions of sound finance and the intrinsic virtues of balanced budgets. There is no special virtue in balancing the budget "over a solar year or any other arbitrary period" (Lerner 1943, p. 41).[32]

Perhaps it is not the objectives of functional finance that are controversial, at least in academic circles. Economic analysis of monetary policy routinely uses a model of the economy and a welfare function that includes employment and inflation to look for 'optimal' policies (or policy rules). Lerner's approach, analogously, determines fiscal and monetary policies based on welfare criteria and economic theory. Thus, the core disagreements with respect to fiscal policy do not concern the general approach or the objectives of policy but the description and understanding of the economy in which the policies are meant to operate. Unlike the functional finance tradition, the DSGE models that have informed aggregate demand policy consider a world in which

---

[32] Functional finance is one of main inspirations behind Modern Monetary Theory (MMT), which has gained popularity and influence in recent years. In its most extreme versions, however, MMT violates basic principles of functional finance, suggesting that all socially desirable programs can be executed as a 'free lunch.' Kelton (2019), for instance, recommends, "[W]e simply invest in programs to benefit the non-rich (student-debt forgiveness, free child care and so on) without treating the rich as our piggy bank ...[since this option] ... is clearly better for both groups." In a similar vein, Tcherneva argues that the left can

render the wealthy obsolete – as in, we will stop pretending that we need them to pay for the good society. In a world with a sovereign currency and modern monetary and fiscal institutions, we never really did, and we sure don't now. And the public needs to know it. That's the MMT message (Tcherneva 2019).

Wray (2015) provides a primer on MMT; critical discussions of MMT include Epstein (2019), Palley (2020) and Aboobaker and Ugurlu (2023).

there can be no aggregate demand problem in the long run and in which market mechanisms automatically produce full employment and an optimal choice of technique. This setting represents a poor approximation to the world in which we live and results in dysfunctional policy recommendations.

Abandoning the infinitely lived representative agent and Ricardian equivalence, robust results from a range of models suggest that fiscal policy can be essential for the management of demand in the long run as well as in the short run. They show that *ceteris paribus* low growth in mature economies calls for a high public debt ratio. Moreover, the required debt ratio increases if government consumption is squeezed or if an increase in inequality raises the average saving rate.

The rediscovery of the possibility that economies can find themselves in situations of secular stagnation shows a growing recognition that aggregate demand problems need not be short-lived. It remains to be seen whether this recognition will lead macroeconomics to break with the Lucas-inspired research program. Although moving in the right direction, Summers and most other contributors to this literature seem reluctant to make that break. On a theoretical level, the rediscovery of secular stagnation has been associated with a move toward OLG models. The classic Diamond (1965) and Blanchard (1985) articles have been extended in various ways, but perfectly optimizing households remain center stage and drive the behavior of the private sector. The behavioral assumptions still misrepresent real-world decision-making, while structural and institutional factors receive little attention.

Macroeconomic policy must be tailored to the structural characteristics of the economy, and an adaptation of functional finance to dual economies brings up a range of different questions. Functional finance can overcome effective demand problems in mature economies and maintain (near-)full-employment growth. In dual economies, by contrast, the main problem is "the deficiency of productive capacity rather than the anomaly of its underutilisation" (Kalecki 1968, quoted from Kalecki 1976, p. 23).[33] The growth rate of developing countries is constrained by capital and a tradeoff between investment and current consumption of modern sector-goods, rather than by labor supplies. Development macroeconomics must recognize this supply-side constraint as well as inflation constraints that derive from relative wage norms and distributional conflict.

---

[33] 'Kaleckian models' often advocate pure demand-led growth, playing down all supply-side constraints (e.g., Hein 2014 and Lavoie 2014). Kalecki's position was quite different. He viewed economic policy as a way to maintain full employment in mature economies, with a full-employment objective implying the presence of a supply-side constraint in these economies. Developing economies do not face this constraint. Instead – and in line with the argument in Section 11.6 – Kalecki thought that the

crucial problem facing underdeveloped countries is thus to increase investment considerably, not for the sake of generating effective demand, as was the case in an underemployed developed economy, but for the sake of accelerating the expansion of productive capacity indispensable for the rapid growth of the national economy. (Kalecki 1968, quoted from Kalecki 1976, pp. 23–24)

Appendix A: Suboptimal Outcomes in Neoclassical and Keynesian OLG Models

A Neoclassical Version

Following Diamond (1965), assume that all agents live for two periods: They work in the first period and live off their savings in the second. The number of workers (N_t) grows at the constant rate $n \geq 0$,

$$N_{t+1} = (1 + n)N_t.$$

To keep the saving side simple, the utility function for a young agent in period t is taken to be logarithmic:

$$U = \log c_{1,t} + \frac{1}{1+\rho} \log c_{2,t+1},$$

where $c_{1,t}$ and $c_{2,t+1}$ are consumption when the agent is young and old, respectively. The labor supply is inelastic, and normalizing the supply of an individual worker to one, the budget constraint is given by

$$c_{1,t} + \frac{1}{1+r_{t+1}} c_{2,t+1} = w_{1,t},$$

where r_{t+1} is the rate of return on savings, and w_t is the real wage.

Utility maximization implies that

$$c_{1,t} = (1 - s)w_t,$$

where the young generation's saving rate s can be written as

$$s = \frac{1}{2+\rho}. \tag{11.25}$$

Households save in the form of fixed capital – saving decisions directly determine investment – and the total saving by the young determines the capital stock in the following period. Thus, full employment implies that the capital stock in period $t + 1$ will be given by

$$K_{t+1} = sw_t N_t. \tag{11.26}$$

Using (11.25) and (11.26), and dividing through by K_t, we have

$$\frac{K_{t+1}}{K_t} = s\frac{w_t N_t}{K_t} = \frac{1-\pi}{2+\rho}\frac{Y_t}{K_t}, \tag{11.27}$$

where π is the profit share. The output-capital ratio is constant in steady growth, and full-employment growth requires that $K_{t+1}/K_t = 1+n$. Thus, Equation (11.27) can be written as

$$\sigma(1 - \pi) = (1 + n)(2 + \rho), \tag{11.28}$$

where the parameters on the right-hand side are all exogenously given and $\sigma = Y/K$. If there is perfect competition and firms can move costlessly and instantaneously along a smooth production function, the profit share is equal to the elasticity of output with respect to capital (evaluated at full employment), and capital will always be fully utilized. Hence, π becomes a function of σ, and Equation (11.28) pins down the choice of technique. Only by a fluke will this equilibrium solution coincide with the capital intensity that is deemed socially optimal.

A Keynesian Twist

Instantaneous and costless adjustments along a smooth production function are implausible (Chapter 9), and investment decisions are made by firms, not households. As an alternative benchmark, consider a case in which the cost of finance is adjusted to achieve a socially optimal choice of technique ($\sigma = \sigma^*$). There is imperfect competition, prices are set as a constant markup on marginal cost ($\pi = \pi^*$), and firms decide the level of investment.

In this alternative setting, profit maximizing firms typically will want to maintain a certain level of excess capacity. They will not, however, maintain a constant rate of accumulation if their expectations are systematically wrong, and they find themselves with persistent, unwanted excess capacity (Chapter 9): Firms – on average – must achieve their desired utilization rate in steady growth (u^d). Thus, steady growth with full employment requires that $\sigma^* u^d (1 - \pi^*) = (1 + n)(2 + \rho)$. In this alternative case, the left-hand side of Equation (11.28) is determined independently of the exogenous right-hand side parameters.

Deviations of the utilization rate u from the desired rate could, in principle, ensure that (11.28) will be satisfied and make full-employment growth possible: If u can vary freely, full-employment growth can be achieved if $u = (1 + n)(2 + \rho)/[\sigma^*(1 - \pi)]$. Deviations of actual from desired utilization would affect investment, however: Profit maximizing firms would reduce investment, causing a decline in aggregate demand and the emergence of unemployment if the required utilization rate defined by Equation (11.28) falls below the desired rate u^d.

Using Harrod's terminology, Equation (11.27) can be used to determine the 'warranted growth rate,' $\hat{K}^*$, associated with the desired output-capital ratio, $Y/K = u^d \sigma^*$,

$$\hat{K}^* = \frac{K_{t+1}}{K_t} - 1 = \frac{1 - \pi}{2 + \rho} \frac{Y_t}{K_t} - 1 = \frac{1 - \pi}{2 + \rho} u^d \sigma^* - 1.$$

If the average saving rate $(1 - \pi)/(1 + \rho)$ is low and the warranted rate falls below the natural rate, $\hat{K}^* < n$, then accumulation will be insufficient to keep up with the growth in the labor force. More interesting for present purposes is the case of high saving rates and $\hat{K}^* > n$. In this situation, labor constraints imply that output cannot grow at the warranted rate. Excess capacity must emerge, with the dynamics depending on the full specification of investment behavior. The likely result is downward instability, but whatever the detailed dynamics, if $\hat{K}^* \neq n$, there is no steady growth path with full employment, equilibrium in the product market and $\sigma = \sigma^*$.

Appendix B: Stability of the Debt Ratio

The consumption-capital ratio is given by

$$\frac{C}{K} = c(1-t)(1-\pi)\sigma + v(1+b),$$

and in steady growth with full employment, we have

$$\frac{C}{K} = \sigma - \gamma - (n+\delta).$$

Putting these two equations together, the required tax rate can be written as

$$t = 1 - \frac{\sigma - \gamma - (n+\delta) - v}{c(1-\pi)\sigma} + \frac{v}{c(1-\pi)\sigma}b. \tag{11.29}$$

Using the expression for total taxes, we now have

$$\frac{T}{K} = t(1-\pi)\sigma + \tau(\pi\sigma + rb)$$

$$= (1-\pi)\sigma\left[1 - \frac{\sigma - \gamma - (n+\delta) - v}{c(1-\pi)\sigma}\right] + (1-\pi)\sigma\frac{v}{c(1-\pi)\sigma}b + \tau(\pi\sigma + rb)$$

$$= \frac{1}{c}[\gamma + (n+\delta) + v - \sigma(1 - c(1-\pi))] + \tau\pi\sigma + \left[\frac{v}{c} + \tau r\right]b.$$

Plugging this tax ratio into the dynamic equation for the debt ratio, we obtain

$$\dot{b} = b(\hat{B} - n)$$

$$= b\frac{rB + G - T}{B} - nb$$

$$= (r-n)b + \gamma - \frac{T}{K}$$

$$= (r-n)b + \gamma - \frac{1}{c}[\gamma + (n+\delta) + v - \sigma(1 - c(1-\pi))] - \tau\pi\sigma - \left[\frac{v}{c} + \tau r\right]b$$

$$= \frac{1}{c}[(1-c)(\sigma - \gamma) + \sigma\pi c(1-\tau) - v - (n+\delta)]$$

$$- \left(n + \frac{v}{c} - (1-\tau)r\right)b. \tag{11.30}$$

If the coefficient on b on the right-hand side of (11.30) is negative, it follows that

$$b \to b^* = \frac{(1-c)(\sigma - \gamma) + \sigma\pi c(1-\tau) - v - (n+\delta)}{cn + v - c(1-\tau)r}. \tag{11.31}$$

Appendix C: Correlation between the Long-Run Values of the Debt Ratio and the Tax Rate

The steady-growth values of the debt ratio b and the tax rate t are given by

$$b^* = \frac{(1-c)(\sigma - \gamma) + \sigma\pi c(1-\tau) - v - (n+\delta)}{cn + v - c(1-\tau)r}. \tag{11.32}$$

$$t^* = 1 - \frac{\sigma - \gamma - (n + \delta) - v}{c(1 - \pi)\sigma} + \frac{v}{c(1 - \pi)\sigma}b^*. \tag{11.33}$$

Both b^* and t^* are functions of $(c, v, \gamma, \sigma, n, \delta, \tau)$. Consider an increase in v. The debt ratio b^* unambiguously falls:

$$\frac{\partial b^*}{\partial v} = \frac{-1}{cn + v - c(1 - \tau)r} - b^* \frac{1}{cn + v - c(1 - \tau)r} = -\frac{1 + b^*}{cn + v - c(1 - \tau)r} < 0. \tag{11.34}$$

The effect on t^* is ambiguous, however. Total differentiation of (11.33) with respect to v gives

$$\frac{dt}{dv} = \frac{1}{c(1 - \pi)\sigma}(1 + b^*) + \frac{v}{c(1 - \pi)\sigma}\frac{\partial b^*}{\partial v}$$

$$= \frac{1}{c(1 - \pi)\sigma}(1 + b^*) + \frac{v}{c(1 - \pi)\sigma}\left[\frac{-1}{cn + v - c(1 - \tau)r}\right.$$

$$\left. -b^* \frac{1}{cn + v - c(1 - \tau)r}\right] \tag{11.35}$$

$$= \frac{1}{c(1 - \pi)\sigma}(1 + b^*)\left[1 - \frac{v}{cn + v - c(1 - \tau)r}\right]$$

$$= \frac{1}{c(1 - \pi)\sigma}(1 + b^*)c\left[\frac{n - (1 - \tau)r}{cn + v - c(1 - \tau)r}\right] \gtrless 0, \text{ for } n \gtrless (1 - \tau)r.$$

From Equations (11.34) and (11.35), it follows that an increase in v will generate a fall in the debt ratio but a rise in the tax rate if $n > (1 - \tau)r$.

The precise expressions are different, but shifts in other parameters can also produce ambiguous reduced-form correlations between the changes in the debt ratio and the tax rate on labor income. The tax rate on capital income is an exception: A rise in τ unambiguously reduces both the long-run debt ratio and the long-run tax rate on labor income.

12 Concluding Comments: Evidence-Based Macroeconomics and Economic Theory

The current orthodoxy in macroeconomic theory is based on the explicit or implicit claim that a direct derivation of macroeconomic relations from intertemporal optimization represents the only way to ensure a sound foundation for macroeconomics: Unlike any other, this methodological approach supposedly guards against the problems highlighted by the Lucas critique.

This book has argued the case for a structuralist and behavioral alternative. The Lucas critique is valid, and macroeconomists should pay close attention to microeconomic behavior. But the current orthodoxy has failed in this respect. Its core assumptions are primitive and misleading as depictions of real-world behavior, while a cavalier attitude to aggregation sidesteps the essential coordination problems that should be at the heart of macroeconomics. Methodologically, the orthodoxy has evolved into a sterile scholastic discipline, ignoring fundamental evidence about the complex macroeconomic reality and the way decisions are being made. It has, as noted by Caballero (2010, p. 85), become "so mesmerized by its own internal logic that it has begun to confuse the precision it has achieved about its own world with the precision is has about the real one."

The adoption of a common optimization procedure to describe all economic behavior has permitted the straightforward incorporation of elaborate analytical and mathematical techniques: On occasion, it is the very sophistication of the techniques themselves that appears to be the justification for the path pursued. Among many critics of this orthodoxy, as a result, there has been a tendency to be suspicious, or even to reject, formalized model building and sophisticated analytical procedures. This is not the path pursued here. On the contrary, formal mathematical methods are used in the development of the argument to elucidate the complex aspects of the logic employed and to act as a vehicle for verifying claims about the implications of particular assumptions. But the assumptions depict a world where the structural constraints cannot be reduced to production functions and in which decision-makers cannot be modeled as perfect optimizers with exogenous preferences of the traditional selfish kind.

The motivation for these departures from standard assumptions is grounded in empirical evidence. Thus, the reorientation of macroeconomic theory in this book is consistent with the call for economics to become more evidence based. The derivation of household consumption from infinite-horizon intertemporal optimization and rational expectations is rejected, ultimately, not because this approach involves conceptual errors or because of any claims that methodologies based on optimization are intrinsically wrong, but because the assumptions fly in the face of what we know about limitations on available real-world information as well as about the expectations and decision-making processes of economic actors. The objection to Modigliani–Miller assumptions about the irrelevance of corporate financial decisions, likewise, is empirically based, as is the emphasis on the role of fairness norms and power biases in wage formation. And the analysis of endogenous business cycles and functional finance would become uninteresting without the empirical plausibility of behaviors that easily lead to local instability and/or structural aggregate demand problems.

It is my hope that most of the empirical judgments that inform the models will be seen as reasonable, at least to an extent that justifies further investigation. Undoubtedly, readers will question some of the empirical assessments that motivate the formal exercises; indeed, some assessments may be proved wrong by evidence with which I am not familiar – my reading of the evidence, for instance, suggests far greater price flexibility than commonly assumed, but this empirical judgment may be wrong. Other assessments may be justified in some countries but misleading in others that have different structural characteristics.

I am confident, however, about the fundamental premises of this book – perfect optimization and rational expectations provide poor approximations to real-world behavior; interactions between decentralized decision-makers can generate instability and coordination failures; structural features of an economy cannot be reduced to the status of epiphenomena that facilitate the matching of outcomes to preexisting preferences, as Lucas would have it. The implications that follow from these premises depend on specific assumptions, however.

An empirical foundation implies that assumptions and models need modification as new evidence accumulates. The choice of assumptions also depends on the purpose of the model. Some models are purely heuristic, constructed with the sole aim of elucidating the operation and logic of particular causal mechanisms. But ultimately even purely heuristic exercises must be justified by the potential empirical relevance of the mechanism. The identification of a particular mechanism, moreover, should not be conflated with predictions of real-world outcomes: Other mechanisms may also be operating, and a heuristic model typically freezes potential interactions of the particular mechanism that is being investigated with the parts of the economy that were left out of the model.

The problem of moving from partial to general can be illustrated by a simple example. Suppose that an economy can be described by two dynamic equations

$$\dot{x} = f(x, y; z)$$
$$\dot{y} = g(x, y; z),$$

where z is a vector of exogenous variables. If we look at the dynamic equations for x and y separately – treating both y and z as given in the equation for $\dot{x}$ and both x and z as constant in the equation for $\dot{y}$ – we may find that both of these partial systems are stable. The stability of the one-dimensional systems, however, does not ensure that the full system will be stable. In order to determine the properties of the full system, we also need to know how the two subsystems interact: The system may be stable, but the interaction between x and y could also destabilize the system and produce a saddle point. Even if we examine the full two-dimensional system, the stability properties may depend on the particular values of the exogenous variables z: The system may exhibit stability for some values of z but instability for others. These properties of dynamic systems are well known, of course, and if the full system is two dimensional, there may be no great need to simplify by looking at the subsystems separately. But the dynamics that drive real-world economies are not one- or two dimensional. All models simplify, and the application of a model to predict or explain observed outcomes involves an explicit or implicit claim that other mechanisms and interactions are insignificant and can be safely ignored.

Similar issues afflict empirical work. Econometricians have been gaining access to more and better data, and significant progress has been made in the techniques and procedures that are used to extract information from the data. But even if the datasets have improved, they still do not speak for themselves. Econometricians try to identify exogenous shocks and estimate the effects of these shocks (using, for instance, difference-in-differences estimations); like the partial, heuristic models, these methods (attempt to) isolate a single exogenous change and derive the causal effects of this change (the 'identified moment,' using the terminology in Nakamura and Steinsson 2018), holding everything else constant.

Nakamura and Steinsson's (2014) estimation of regional fiscal multipliers exemplifies this approach and its limitations. The US military buildup in the 1980s generated spending increases that varied greatly across states in ways that could be seen as independent of the states' own economic conditions. These differences can be used to estimate regional multipliers to exogenous shocks. But further analysis is needed in order to decide whether the changes in other forms of government spending – or in nongovernment shocks to aggregate demand – would have similar effects and whether, or to what extent, the multipliers would be different in other time periods. Judgments about the external validity – the generalizability – of the findings have to rely on a broader understanding of why military spending increases output.

Our main interest, moreover, may concern the effects of changes in aggregate government spending on aggregate output, that is, we want to move from regional to aggregate multipliers. This step again requires assumptions. It may seem plausible (in light of our general understanding of how the economy works) to assume, for instance, that interstate trade tends to reduce the state-level multiplier, while, on the other hand, labor mobility could make real output respond more elastically to state-level demand shocks; one would also expect state-level multipliers to increase relative to aggregate multipliers insofar as central banks react to an increase in aggregate demand by raising interest rates. But the regional regressions say nothing about these propositions. Instead, theory must be brought in to evaluate the likely aggregate implications of the regional evidence.

Nakamura and Steinsson consider two versions of a DSGE model for an economy with two regions belonging to a monetary and fiscal union: A new Keynesian version in which prices are sticky and there is complementarity between consumption and labor in the representative household's utility function, and a neoclassical version without price stickiness. They go on to show that their "estimates are much more consistent with New Keynesian models in which 'aggregate demand' shocks – such as government spending shocks – have potentially large effects on output than they are with the plain-vanilla Neoclassical model." It is no surprise that neoclassical versions of the DSGE model have difficulty matching the empirical evidence. The choice of functional forms and the calibration of parameters offer great flexibility, however, allowing new Keynesian models to generate a large range of regional multipliers. Thus, while it may be worthwhile demonstrating the empirical superiority of the new Keynesian model and its ability to produce regional multipliers of about 1.5 for military spending in the US state data, this finding does not establish that new Keynesian models provide a good overall understanding of the economy. Do we have to choose between a neoclassical and a new Keynesian version of the DSGE model? Are there no other alternative theories? Do all theories that produce regional multipliers of 1.5 have the same aggregate implications?

A more recent paper by Hazell et al. (2022) uses panel data for the United States in a regression of state-level inflation rates for nontradable goods on state-level unemployment. Including time and state fixed effects, the coefficient on unemployment is small but statistically significant. Moreover, breaking the sample into two, Hazell et al. find that the coefficient displays greater stability than Phillips-curve estimates based on aggregate time series variation: The coefficient changes 'only' by a factor of 2 between 1978–1990 and 1991–2018.

These results are interesting but do not have any direct implications for the aggregate Phillips curve. In order to derive these implications Hazell et al. again set up a small new Keynesian model with two regions, assuming *inter alia* that there is no labor mobility between the regions and that prices are sticky with firms being permitted to change their prices only at random intervals (Calvo pricing). The model, they state, "clarifies that the slope of the aggregate Phillips curve is equal to the slope of the regional Phillips curve for nontradable goods" and shows that "when it comes to managing inflation, the elephant in the room is long-run inflation expectations" (p. 36). These are not statements of fact, however. The empirical evidence in the paper says nothing about the relation between regional and aggregate Phillips curves or about the importance of long-run inflation expectations. The claims are based on a particular interpretation of the regressions. The authors assume that the economy is well described by their simple new Keynesian model.

One of the key insights from the paper, the authors suggest, is that current inflation varies one-for-one with changes in the asymptotic value of the expected inflation rate for t going to infinity and that this correlation explains why econometric estimates based on aggregate time series estimates tend to exaggerate the changes in the slope of the Phillips curve. The authors may believe that there is this correlation between current inflation and the asymptotic value of expected inflation. They may even derive this result as an implication of a particular model. But that does not turn the belief into an evidence-based fact.[1] Indeed, the suggestion that wage and price settings should be influenced strongly by some well-defined notion of what the inflation rate will be in the remote future appears rather implausible in light of evidence showing that workers and firms do not even have a clear idea of the current and recent inflation rates (Coibion et al. 2018).

What we have here – and in much of the recent empirical literature – is a curious combination of sophisticated econometrics, dogmatic adherence to an untenable theoretical framework, and a willingness to engage in *ad hoc* handwaving when the framework is used to interpret real-world data. The stripped-down new Keynesian Phillips curve with rational expectations that form the basis of the analysis has been an abject empirical failure. Yet, it is used here to derive equations that are then assumed to apply more generally, even if, for instance, expectations are not rational. The observed decline in the estimated slope of the regional Phillips curve, moreover, is explained by changes in the frequency of price changes (p. 31). This explanation may fit well within a new Keynesian universe, but do we really want to disregard the possible effects of a host of other forces that could make the Phillips curve unstable and influence the sensitivity of inflation to changes in unemployment? Over the last forty years, the US economy has undergone substantial changes with respect to, *inter alia*, union density, labor market legislation and its enforcement, sectoral compositions of output, social norms of fairness, the structure of labor contracts, and the degree of monopoly in goods markets and monopsony in labor markets.

To avoid misunderstanding, let me emphasize that the econometric identification of causal effects – the regional multipliers associated with shocks to military spending, for instance – can provide valuable information. The papers by Nakamura and Steinsson and Hazell et al. make important contributions, even if the precise implications of their findings may not be entirely clear. The identification of causal effects may also help discriminate between rival theories that make different predictions about this particular effect. Thus, the imaginative use of new datasets and careful attempts to identify causal effects will indeed allow us to gain (more) "solid empirical knowledge about how the economy works at the macroeconomic level" (Nakamura and Steinsson 2018, p. 82). But these types of econometric studies – each one corresponding to the identification of the partial effects of a change in one of the variables in a dynamic equation $\dot{x} = f(x, y, z)$ – will not, as recognized by Nakamura and Steinsson (2018, p. 60),

---

[1] They provide an empirical illustration: If the asymptotic value of the expected unemployment rate is denoted by $E_t u_{t+\infty}$ ($E_t u_{t+\infty} = \lim_{k \to \infty} E_t u_{t+k}$), the illustration assumes (i) that the weighted sum $E_t \sum_{j=0}^{\infty} \beta^j (u_{t+j} - E_t u_{t+\infty})$ is determined by the value of $u_t - E_t u_{t+\infty}$, (ii) that $E_t u_{t+\infty}$ is equal to the Congressional Budget Office's estimate of the current natural rate of unemployment, and (iii) that the expected asymptotic inflation rate ($\lim_{k \to \infty} E_t \pi_{t+k}$) is equal to the ten-year inflation rate from the Survey of Professional Forecasters. These are heroic assumptions. If one wanted to relate the predictions of a new Keynesian Phillips curve to data, it would have seemed more reasonable to substitute survey evidence of one-period expectations for inflation into the standard equation, $\pi_t = \pi_{t+1}^e - \kappa(u_t - u_{nt})$, rather than solving this equation forward and impose strong assumptions on the determination of the expected asymptotic value of the unemployment rate and the cumulative sum of deviations of unemployment from the natural rate.

enable us to determine the properties of the interconnected economic system as a whole. Interpretations of empirical evidence will always be colored by our (explicit or implicit) theoretical presuppositions.

Our theoretical presuppositions also guide the selection of topics for detailed empirical investigation. An attempt to identify 'deep structural parameters' – the representative agent's intertemporal elasticity of the substitution or labor supply elasticity, for instance – becomes meaningless if there is no representative agent with exogenously given preferences. The analysis of the corporate economy in Chapter 4, meanwhile, suggests that corporate financial decisions can have significant effects on aggregate saving, an issue that, to my knowledge, has been largely ignored in the empirical literature. The same applies to questions of power bias raised in Chapter 7; to the role of interactions across sectors and relative wage norms as a source of inflation in developing economies (Chapter 6), and the relevance of destabilizing Harrodian forces for understanding cyclical fluctuations (Chapter 10). Many more examples could be added. It should be emphasized as well that presuppositions may color our perceptions of what constitutes valid evidence: Econometric studies are not the only source of empirical knowledge. Descriptive historical analysis as well as experimental and psychological studies can, and do, provide essential insights.

Any overall conception of the economy is comprised of numerous specific empirical observations and partial models. But it also embodies some vision of how these partial models fit together. We shall never have a 'complete model of the economy,' but without a general vision or framework, it becomes difficult or impossible to evaluate the significance and implications of empirical evidence. Unfortunately, progress in the field of macroeconomics is being held back by anchoring and interpreting data within a theoretical framework whose basic behavioral assumptions are at odds with real-world decision-making and in which structural constraints and the potential for coordination failures and endogenously created crises are played down (or excluded altogether in benchmark versions of the models).

I have no doubt that the current orthodoxy will be replaced by something else and that the Lucas-inspired research program will come to be seen by future historians of thought as a costly detour. Improved data and econometric techniques – as well as increased attention to findings from other social sciences and psychology – will contribute to the demise of this research program. Empirical evidence will also inform and help shape the new ideas that will emerge. But having witnessed the rapid ascent of monetarist ideas in the late 1970s and early 1980s, as well as their transformation into real business cycle theory, guards against optimistic beliefs in the inevitability of progress. My confidence about the demise of the current orthodoxy, therefore, does not extend to any firm beliefs about what will happen next.

Drawing on traditions that have been sidelined by contemporary fashion, my purpose in his book has been to present a critique of contemporary macroeconomic theory and offer a sketch of an alternative behavioral and structuralist approach.

References

Abe, N. and Tonogi, A. (2010). "Micro and Macro Price Dynamics in Daily Data." *Journal of Monetary Economics*, 57(6), pp. 716–728.

Abel, A.B. Mankiw, N.G. and Zeckhauser, R.J. (1989). "Assessing Dynamic Efficiency: Theory and Evidence." *Review of Economic Studies*, 56(1), pp. 1–20.

Abel, J. and Deitz, R. (2016). "Underemployment in the Early Careers of College Graduates Following the Grate Recession." NBER Working Paper 22654.

Aboobaker, A. and Ugurlu, E.N. (2023). "Weaknesses of MMT as a Guide to Development Policy." Forthcoming in *Cambridge Journal of Economics*, doi.org/10.1093/cje/bead009

Acemoglu, D. (2002). "Technical Change, Inequality, and the Labor Market." *Journal of Economic Literature*, 40(1), pp. 7–72.

Acemoglu, D. (2009). *Introduction to Modern Economic Growth*. Princeton: Princeton University Press.

Acemoglu, D. Aghion, P. and Violante, G.L. (2001). "Deunionization, Technical Change and Inequality." *Carnegie-Rochester Conference Series on Public Policy*, 55(1), pp. 229–264.

Acemoglu, D., He, A. and le Maire, D. (2022). "Eclipse of Rent-Sharing: The Effects of Managers' Business Education on Wages and the Labor Share in the US and Denmark." NBER Working Paper 29874.

Ackerman, F. and Heinzerling, L. (2005). *Priceless: On Knowing the Price of Everything and the Value of Nothing*. New York: The New Press.

Agarwal, S., Qian, W. and Zou, X. (2021). "Thy Neighbour's Misfortune: Peer Effects on Consumption." *American Economic Journal: Economic Policy*, 13(2), pp. 1–25.

Agell, J. and Lundborg, P. (1995). "Theories of Pay and Unemployment: Survey Evidence from Swedish Manufacturing Firms." *Scandinavian Journal of Economics*, 97(2), pp. 295–307.

Akerlof, G.A. (1991). "Procrastination and Obedience." *American Economic Review*, 81(2), pp. 1–19.

Akerlof, G.A. (2007). "The Missing Motivation in Macroeconomics." *American Economic Review*, 97(1), pp. 5–36.

Akerlof, G.A. (2019). "What Were They Thinking Then: The Consequences for Macroeconomics during the Past 60 Years." *Journal of Economic Perspectives*, 33(4), pp. 171–186.

Akerlof, G.A., Dickens, W.T. and Perry, G.L. (1996). "The Macroeconomics of Low Inflation." *Brookings Papers on Economic Activity*, 1(1996), pp. 1–75.

Akerlof, G.A., Dickens, W.T. and Perry, G.L. (2000). "Near-Rational Wage and Price Setting and the Long-Run Phillips Curve." *Brookings Papers on Economic Activity*, 1(2000), pp. 1–60.

Akerlof, G.A. and Shiller, R.J. (2009). *Animal Spirits How Human Psychology Drives the Economy, and Why It Matters for Global Capitalism*. Princeton: Princeton University Press.

Akerlof, G.A. and Yellen, J.L. (1990). "The Fair Wage-effort Hypothesis and Unemployment." *Quarterly Journal of Economics*, 105(2), pp. 255–283.

Albrecht, J. and Vroman, S. (2002). "A Matching Model with Endogenous Skill Requirements." *International Economic Review*, 43(1), pp. 283–305.

Alvaredo, F. and Saez, E. (2006). "Income and Wealth Concentration in Spain in a Historical and Fiscal Perspective." *Journal of the European Economic Association*, 7(5), pp. 1140–1167.

Alvarez, F. and Lippi, F. (2020). "Temporary Price Changes, Inflation Regimes, and the Propagation of Monetary Shocks." *American Economic Journal: Macroeconomics*, 12(1), pp. 104–152.

Alvarez-Cuadrado, F. and Long, N.V. (2011). "The Relative Income Hypothesis." *Journal of Economic Dynamics and Control*, 35(9), pp. 1489–1501.

An, C. and Bosworth, B. (2013). *Income Inequality in Korea: An Analysis of Trends, Causes, and Answers*. Cambridge, MA and London: Harvard University Asia Center.

Ando, A. and Modigliani, F. (1963). "The 'Life Cycle' Hypothesis of Saving: Aggregate Implications and Tests." *American Economic Review*, 53(1), Part 1, pp. 55–84.

Andreoni, J. (1989). "Giving with Impure Altruism: Applications to Charity and Ricardian Equivalence." *Journal of Political Economy*, 97(6), pp. 1447–1458.

Antràs, P. (2004). "Is the U.S. Aggregate Production Function Cobb-Douglas? New Estimates of the Elasticity of Substitution." *B.E. Journal of Macroeconomics*, 4(1), pp. 1–36.

Arestis, P. and Sawyer, M. (2010). "The Return of Fiscal Policy." *Journal of Post Keynesian Economics*, 32(3), pp. 327–346.

Ash, M. Basu, D. and Dube, A. (2017). "Public Debt and Growth: An Assessment of Key Findings on Causality and Thresholds." Working Paper 2017–10, University of Massachusetts Amherst.

Ashkenas, R.N., DeMonaco L.J. and Francis S.C. (1998). "Making the Deal Real: How GE Capital Integrates Acquisitions." *Harvard Business Review*, 76(1), pp. 165–178.

Atkinson, A.B. (1969). "The Timescale of Economic Models: How Long Is the Long Run?" *Review of Economic Studies*, 36(2), pp. 137–152.

Atkinson, A.B. (1999). *The Economic Consequences of Rolling Back the Welfare State*. Cambridge, MA: MIT Press.

Auerbach, P. (2016). *Socialist Optimism: An Alternative Political Economy for the Twenty-First Century*. London: Palgrave Macmillan.

Auerbach, P. and Skott, P. (2021). "Visions of the Future – A Socialist Departure from Gloom?" *PSL Quarterly Review*, 74(298), pp. 155–177.

Autor, D., Dorn, D., Katz, L.F., Patterson, C. and Van Reenen, J. (2020). "Fall of the Labor Share and the Rise of Superstar Firms." *Quarterly Journal of Economics*, 135(2), pp. 645–709.

Autor, D.H., Katz, L.F. and Kearney, M.S. (2008). "Trends in U.S. Wage Inequality: Revising the Revisionists." *Review of Economics and Statistics*, 90(2), pp. 300–323.

Autor, D., Manning, A. and Smith, C. (2016). "The Contribution of the Minimum Wage to US Wage Inequality Over Three Decades: A Reassessment." *American Economic Journal: Applied Economics*, 8(1), pp. 58–99.

Azar, J., Marinescu, I. and Steinbaum, M.I. (2017). "Labor Market Concentration." *Journal of Human Resources*, 57(S), pp. 167–199.

Baddeley, M. (2014). "Rethinking the Micro-Foundations of Macroeconomics: Insights from Behavioural Economics." *European Journal of Economics and Economic Policies: Intervention*, 11(1), pp. 99–112.

Backus, D. and Driffill, J. (1985). "Rational Expectations and Policy Credibility Following a Change in Regime." *Review of Economic Studies*, 52, pp. 211–222.

Baily, M.N., Bartelsman, E.J. and Haltiwanger, J. (2001). "Labor Productivity: Structural Change and Cyclical Dynamics." *Review of Economics and Statistics*, 83(3), pp. 420–433.

Bakija, J., Cole, A. and Heim, B. (2012). "Jobs and Income Growth of Top Earners and the Causes of Changing Income Inequality: Evidence from U.S. Tax Return Data." Working Paper, Williams College.

Ball, L. (1994). "What Determines the Sacrifice Ratio?." In N. Mankiw (ed.), *Monetary Policy*, National Bureau of Economic Research, University of Chicago Press, pp. 155–193.

Ball, L. (1996). "Disinflation and the NAIRU." NBER Working Papers 5520, National Bureau of Economic Research.

Ball, L. (1997). "Disinflation and the NAIRU." In Christina D. Romer and David H. Romer (eds.), *Reducing Inflation: Motivation and Strategy*, NBER, pp. 167–194.

Ball, L. (2014). "Long-Term Damage from the Great Recession in OECD Countries." *European Journal of Economics and Economic Policies: Intervention*, 11(2), pp. 149–160.

Ball, L., DeLong, B. and Summers, L. (2014). "Fiscal Policy and Full Employment." Center for Budget and Policy Priorities.

Ball, L. and Mazumbar, S. (2011). "Inflation Dynamics and the Great Recession." *Brookings Papers on Economic Activity*, 42(1), pp. 337–405.

Ball, L. and Mazumbar, S. (2015). "A Phillips Curve with Anchored Expectations and Short-Term Unemployment." IMF Working Paper No. 15/39.

Ball, L. and Moffitt, R. (2002). "Productivity Growth and the Phillips Curve." In A.B. Krueger and R.M. Solow (eds.), *The Roaring Nineties: Can Full Employment be Sustained?* New York: Russell Sage Foundation, pp. 61–90.

Barbosa-Filho, N.H. and Taylor, L. (2006). "Distributive and Demand Cycles in the US Economy – A Structuralist Goodwin Model." *Metroeconomica*, 57(3), pp. 389–411.

Barrales-Ruiz, J., Mendieta-Mũnoz, I., Rada, C., Tavani, D. and von Arnim, R. (2021). "The Distributive Cycle: Evidence and Recent Debates." *Journal of Economic Surveys*, 36(2), pp. 468–503.

Barro, R.J. (1979). "On the Determination of the Public Debt." *Journal of Political Economy*, 87(5), pp. 940–971.

Barro, R.J. (1989). "The Neoclassical Approach to Fiscal Policy." In Barro, R. (ed.), *Modern Business Cycle* Theory, Cambridge, MA: Harvard University Press, pp. 178–235.

Barro, R.J. (1994). "The Aggregate-Supply/Aggregate-Demand Model." *Eastern Economic Journal*, Winter, pp. 1–6.

Barro, R.J. (1995) "Inflation and Economic Growth." NBER Working Paper, w5326.

Barro, R.J. and Gordon, D. (1983). "A Positive Theory of Monetary Policy in a Natural Rate Model," *Journal of Political Economy*, 91, pp. 589–610.

Barro, R.J. and Grossman, H.I. (1976). *Money, Emnployment and Inflation*. Cambridge: Cambridge University Press.

Basu, D. (2013). "The Time Series of High Debt and Growth in Italy, Japan, and the United States." Next New Deal: The Blog of the Roosevelt Institute, April, 2012.

Baum, S. (2009). "Description, Prescription and the Choice Of Discount Rates," *Ecological Economics*, 69(1), 197–205.

Beaudry, P., Galizia, D. and Portier, F. (2017). "Is the Macroeconomy Locally Unstable and Why Should We Care?" In NBER Macroeconomics Annual, Vol. 31, M. Eichenbaum and J.A. Parker (eds.), Chicago: University of Chicago Press, pp. 479–530.

Beaudry, P., Galizia, D. and Portier, F. (2020). "Putting the Cycle Back into Business Cycle Analysis." *American Economic Review*, 110(1), pp. 1–47.

Bebchuk, L.A., Fried, J.M. and Walker, D.I. (2002). "Managerial Power and Rent Extraction in the Design of Executive Compensation." *The University of Chicago Law Review*, 69, pp. 751–846.

Bebczuk, R. and Cavallo, E. (2016). "Is Business Saving Really None of Our Business?" *Applied Economics*, 48(24), pp. 2266–2284.

Bell-Kelton, S. and Ballinger, R. (2006). "The Monetary Policy of Outcomes Curve: Can the Size and Structure of Public Debt Undermine Policy Objectives?." In P. Arestis, M. Baddeley and J. McCombie (eds.), *The New Monetary Policy: Implications and Relevance*, Cheltenham, UK: Edward Elgar Publishing, pp. 129–148.

Benhabib, J. and Nishimura, K. (1985). "Competitive Equilibrium Cycles." *Journal of Economic Theory*, 35(2), pp. 284–306.

Beniger, J.R. (1986). *The Control Revolution: Technological and Economic Origins of the Information Society*. Cambridge, MA: Harvard University Press.

Benmelech, E., Bergman, N. and Kim, H. (2022). "Strong Employers and Weak Employees: How Does Employer Concentration Affect Wages?" *Journal of Human Resources*, 57, pp. S200–S250.

Bernanke, B. (2010). "Monetary Policy Objectives and Tools in a Low-Inflation Environment." Speech at the Revisiting Monetary Policy in a Low-Inflation Environment Conference, Federal Reserve Bank of Boston, Boston, Massachusetts.

Bernanke, B., Gertler, M. and Gilchrist, S. (1999). "The Financial Accelerator in a Quantitative Business Cycle Framework." In J.B. Taylor and M. Woodford (eds.), *Handbook of Macroeconomics*, North-Holland Elsevier Science, New York.

Bernheim, B.D., Shleifer, A. and Summers, L.H. (1985). "The Strategic Bequest Motive." *Journal of Political Economy*, 93(6), pp. 1045–1458.

Bewley, T.F. (1998). "Why Not Cut Pay?" *European Economic Review*, 42, pp. 459–490.

Bewley, T.F. (1999). *Why Wages Don't Fall During a Recession*. Cambridge, MA: Harvard University Press.

Bhargava, S. and Loewenstein, G. (2015). "Behavioral Economics and Public Policy 102: Beyond Nudging." *American Economic Review: Papers & Proceedings*, 105(5), pp. 396–401.

Bhutta, N., Bricker, J., Chang, A.C., Dettling, L.J., Goodman, S., Hsu, J.W., Moore, K.B., Reber, S., Henriques Volz, A. and Windle, R.A. (2020). "Changes in U.S. Family Finances from 2016 to 2019: Evidence from the Survey of Consumer Finances." *Federal Reserve Bulletin*, September, 106, No. 5.

Bils, M. and Klenow, P.J. (2004). "Some Evidence on the Importance of Sticky Prices." *Journal of Political Economy*, 112(5), pp. 947–985.

Bivens, J., Mishel, L. and Schmitt, J. (2018). "It's Not Just Monopoly and Monopsony." Economic Policy Institute, epi.org/145564.

Black, S.E. and Lynch, L.M. (2001). "How to Compete: The Impact of Workplace Practices and Information Technology on Productivity." *Review of Economics and Statistics*, 83(3), pp. 434–445.

Blanchard, O.J. (1985). "Debt, Deficits, and Finite Horizons." *Journal of Political Economy*, 93(2), 223–247.

Blanchard, O.J. (2000). "What Do We Know about Macroeconomics that Fisher and Wicksell Did Not?" *Quarterly Journal of Economics*, 115, pp. 1375–1409.

Blanchard, O.J. (2008). "The State of Macro." *Annual Review of Economics, Annual Reviews*, 1(1), pp. 209–228.

Blanchard, O.J. (2016a). "Do DSGE Models Have a Future?" Policy Brief, Peterson Institute for International Economics, 11–16.

Blanchard, O.J. (2016b). "The Phillips Curve: Back to the '60s?" *American Economic Review*, 106(5), pp. 31–34.

Blanchard, O.J. (2018a). "On the Future of Macroeconomic Models." *Oxford Review of Economic Policy*, 34(1–2), pp. 43–54.

Blanchard, O.J. (2018b). "Should We Reject the Natural Rate Hypothesis?" *Journal of Economic Perspectives*, 32(1), pp. 97–120.

Blanchard, O.J. (2019). "Public Debt and Low Interest Rates." *American Economic Review*, 109(4), pp. 1197–1229.

Blanchard, O.J. (2021). *Macroeconomics*, 8th edition. Hoboken, NJ: Pearson.

Blanchard, O.J. and Summers, L. (1987). "Hysteresis in Unemployment." *European Economic Review*, 31(1–2), pp. 288–295.

Blanchard, O.J. and Summers, L.H. (2020). "Automatic Stabilizers in a Low-Rate Environment." *AEA Papers and Proceedings*, 110, pp. 125–130.

Blanchard, O.J., Rhee, C. and Summers, L. (1993). "The Stock Market, Profit, and Investment." *Quarterly Journal of Economics*, 108(1), pp. 115–136.

Blanchard, O.J. and Wolfers, J. (2000). "The Role of Shocks and Institutions in the Rise of European Unemployment: The Aggregate Evidence." *Economic Journal*, 110(March): C1–C33.

Blanchflower, D. and Oswald, A. (2004). "Well-Being Over Time in Britain and the USA." *Journal of Public Economics*, 88(7–8), pp. 1359–1386.06.

Bleaney, M. and Francisco, M. (2018). "Is the Phillips Curve Different in Poor Countries?" *Bulletin of Economic Research*, 70(1), pp. E17–E28.

Blecker, R.A. and Setterfield, M. (2019). *Heterodox Macroeconomics – Models of Demand, Distribution and Growth*. Cheltenham: Elgar.

Blinder, A.S. (1991). "Why Are Prices Sticky? Preliminary Results from an Interview Study." *American Economic Review*, 81(2), pp. 89–96.

Bliss, C.J. (1975). *Capital Theory and the Distribution of Income*. Amsterdam: North Holland.

Bohn, H. (2009). "Intergenerational Risk Sharing and Fiscal Policy." *Journal of Monetary Economics*, 56, pp. 805–816.

Boldrin, M. and Levine, D.K. (2008). *Against Intellectual Monopoly*. Cambridge: Cambridge University Press.

Bowles, S. (1989). "Social Institutions and Technical Choice." In M. DeMatteo, A. Vercelli and R. Goodwin (eds.), *Technological and Social Factors in Long Term Economic Fluctuations*, Berlin: Springer Verlag.

Bowles, S. (1998). "Endogenous Preferences: The Cultural Consequences of Markets and Other Economic Institutions." *Journal of Economic Literature*, 36(1), pp. 75–111.

Bowles, S. and Gintis, H. (1986). *Democracy and Capitalism: Property, Community, and the Contradictions of Modern Social Thought*. New York Basic Books.

Bowles, S. and Park, Y. (2005). "Emulation, Inequality, and Work Hours: Was Thorsten Veblen Right?" *Economic Journal*, 115(507), pp. F397–F412.

Boyer, R. (1990). *The Regulation School: A Critical Introduction*. New York: Columbia University Press.

Bresnahan, T.M. and Ramey, V.A. (1994). "Output Fluctuations at the Plant Level." *Quarterly Journal of Economics*, 109(3), pp. 593–624.

Bresser-Pereira, L.C. Oreiro, J.L. and Marconi, N. (2014). *Developmental Macroeconomics: New Developmentalism as a Growth Strategy*. Abingdon: Routledge.

Breza, E., Kaur, S. and Shamdasani, Y. (2018). "The Morale Effects of Pay Inequality." *Quarterly Journal of Economics*, 133(2), pp. 611–663.

Brock, W.A. and Hommes, C.H. (1998). "Heterogeneous Beliefs and Routes to Chaos in a Simple Asset Pricing Model." *Journal of Econonmic Dynamics and Control*, 22(8–9), pp. 1235–1274.

Bronfenbrenner, K. (2009). "No Holds Barred—The Intensification of Employer Opposition to Organizing." Briefing Paper 235, Economic Policy Institute.

Broome, J. (2012). *Climate Matters: Ethics in a Warming World*. New York: W. W. Norton & Company.

Browning, M., Deaton, A. and Irish, M. (1985). "A Profitable Approach to Labor Supply and Commodity Demands over the Life-Cycle." *Econometrica*, 53(3), pp. 503–543.

Bruno, M. and Easterly, W. (1998). "Inflation Crises and Long-Run Growth." *Journal of Monetary Economics*, 41(1), pp. 3–26.

Buiter, W. (2009). "The Unfortunate Uselessness of Most 'State of the Art' Academic Monetary Economics." blogs.ft.com/maverecon/2009/03/the-unfortunate-uselessness-of-most-state-of-the-art-academic-monetary-economics/.

Buiter, W.H. and Miller, M.H. (1983). "Changing the Rules: Economic Consequences of the Thatcher Regime." *Brookings Papers on Economic Activity*, 2, pp. 305–365.

Bulow, J. and Summers, L. (1986). "A Theory of Dual Labor Markets with Application to Industrial Policy, Discrimination, and Keynesian Unemployment." *Journal of Labor Economics*, 4(3), pp. 376–414.

Caballero, R.J. (1999). "Aggregate Investment." In Taylor, J.B. and Woodford, M. (eds.), *Handbook of Macroeconomics, 1, Part B*, pp. 813–862.

Caballero, R.J. (2010). "Macroeconomics after the Crisis: Time to Deal with the Pretense-of-Knowledge Syndrome." *Journal of Economic Perspectives*, 24(4), pp. 85–102.

Callaci, B. (2021). "What Do Franchisees Do? Vertical Restraints as Workplace Fissuring and Labor Discipline Devices." *Journal of Law and Political Economy*, pp. 397–444.

Calmfors, L. and Driffill, J. (1988). "Bargaining Structure, Corporatism and Macroeconomic Performance." *Economic Policy*, 6, pp. 14–47.

Calvo, G.A. (1983). "Staggered Prices in a Utility-Maximizing Framework." *Journal of Monetary Economics*, 12(3), pp. 383–398.

Camerer, C., Babcock, L., Loewenstein, G. and Thaler, R. (1997). "Labor Supply of New York City Cabdrivers: One Day at a Time." *Quarterly Journal of Economics*, 112(2), pp. 407–441.

Campbell, D.T. (1976). "Assessing the Impact of Planned Social Change." *Evaluation and Program Planning*, 2(1), pp. 67–90.

Campbell, C.M. and Kamlani, K.S. (1997). "The Reasons for Wage Rigidity: Evidence from a Survey of Firms." *Quarterly Journal of Economics*, 112(3), pp. 759–789.

Campbell, J. and Mankiw, N.G. (1989). "Consumption, Income, and Interest Rates: Reinterpreting the Time Series Evidence." *NBER Macroeconomics Annual*, 4, pp. 185–216.

Canzoneri, M.B., Cumby, R.E. and Diba, B.T. (2007). "Euler Equations and Money Market Interest Rates: A Challenge for Monetary Policy Models." *Journal of Monetary Economics*, 54, pp. 1863–1881.

Caplin, A.S. and Spulber, D.F. (1987). "Menu Costs and the Neutrality of Money." *Quarterly Journal of Economics*, 102(4), pp. 703–726.

Card, D., Kramarz, F. and Lemieux, T. (1999). "Changes in the Relative Structure of Wages and Employment: A Comparison of the United States, Canada and France." *Canadian Journal of Economics*, 32(4), pp. 843–877.

Card, D. and Krueger, A.B. (1995). *Myth and Measurement. The New Economics of the Minimum Wage*. Princeton, NJ: Princeton University Press.

Carr, M. and Jayadev, A. (2015). "Relative Income and Indebtedness: Evidence from Panel Data." *Review of Income and Wealth*, 61(4), pp. 759–772.

Cavallo, A. and Rigobon, R. (2016). "The Billion Prices Project: Using Online Prices for Measurement and Research." *Journal of Economic Perspectives*, 30(2), pp. 151–178.

Cengiz, D., Dube, A., Lindner, A. and Zipperer, B. (2019). "The Effect of Minimum Wages on Low-Wage Jobs: Evidence from the United States Using a Bunching Estimator." *Quarterly Journal of Economics*, 134(3), pp. 1405–1454.

Chalk, N.A. (2000). "The Sustainability of Bond-financed Deficits: And Overlapping Generations Approach." *Journal of Monetary Economics*, 45, pp. 293–328.

Chandler, A.D. Jr. (1977). *The Visible Hand: The Managerial Revolution in American Business*. Cambridge, MA: Harvard University Press.

Chang, H.J. (2002). *Kicking Away the Ladder: Development Strategy in Historical Perspective*. London: Anthem.

Chari, V.V. (2010). "Testimony before the Committee on Science and Technology, Subcommittee on Investigations and Oversight, U.S. House of Representatives." July 20, 2010. people.virginia.edu/~ey2d/Chari_Testimony.pdf.

Chari, V.V. and Kehoe, T. (2006). "Modern Macroeconomics in Practice: How Theory Is Shaping Policy." *Journal of Economic Perspectives*, 20(4), pp. 3–28.

Chetty, R., Friedman, J., Leth-Petersen, S., Nielsen, T. and Olsen, T. (2014). "Active vs. Passive Decisions and Crowd-Out in Retirement Savings Accounts: Evidence from Denmark." *Quarterly Journal of Economics*, 129(3), pp. 1141–1219.

Chiarella, C. and Flaschel, P. (2000). *The Dynamics of Keynesian Monetary Growth*. Cambridge: Cambridge University Press.

Chiarella, C., Flaschel, P. and Franke, R. (2005). *Foundations for a Disequilibrium Theory of the Business Cycle*. Cambridge: Cambridge University Press.

Cho, J. and Lee, K. (2007). Deregulation of Dismissal Law and Unjust Dismissal in Korea. *International Review of Law and Economics*, 27, 409–422.

Christiano, L.J., Eichenbaum, M. and Evans, C. (2005). "Nominal Rigidities and the Dynamic Effects of a Shock to Monetary Policy." *Journal of Political Economy*, 113(1), pp. 1–45.

Christiano, L.J., Eichenbaum, M.S. and Trabandt, M. (2017). "On DSGE Models." Mimeo, November 9, 2017.

Christiano, L.J., Eichenbaum, M.S. and Trabandt, M. (2018). "On DSGE Models." *Journal of Economic Perspectives*, 32(3), pp. 113–140.

Chun, H., Kim, J.W. and Morck, R. (2011). "Varying Heterogeneity among U.S. Firms: Facts and Implications." *Review of Economics and Statistics*, 93(3), pp. 1034–1052.

Coburn, T. (2012). *The Debt Bomb: A Bold Plan to Stop Washington from Bankrupting America*. Nashville: Thomas Nelson.

Cohen, A.J. and Harcourt, G.C. (2003). "Retrospectives: Whatever Happened to the Cambridge Capital Theory Controversies?" *Journal of Economic Perspectives*, 17(1), pp. 199–214.

Coibion, O. and Gorodnichenko, Y. (2015). "Is the Phillips Curve Alive and Well after All? Inflation Expectations and the Missing Disinflation." *American Economic Journal: Macroeconomics,* 7(1), pp. 197–232.

Coibion, O., Gorodnichenko, Y. and Kumar, S. (2018). "How Do Firms Form Their Expectations? New Survey Evidence." *American Economic Review*, 108(9), pp. 2671–2713.

Colander, D. (1995). "The Stories We Tell: A Reconsideration of AS/AD Analysis." *Journal of Economic Perspectives*, 9(3), pp. 169–188.

Collard, F., Habib, M. and Rochet, J.-C. (2015). "Sovereign Debt Sustainability in Advanced Economies." *Journal of the European Economic Association*, 13(3), pp. 381–420.

Comin, D. and Mulani, S. (2006). "Diverging Trends in Aggregate and Firm Volatility." *Review of Economics and Statistics*, 88(2), pp. 374–383.

Cooper, R.W. and Haltiwanger, J.C. (2006). "On the Nature of Capital Adjustment Costs." *Review of Economic Studies*, 73(3), pp. 611–633.

Corneo, G. (2018). "Time-poor, Working, Super-rich." *European Economic Review*, 101(January), pp. 1–19.

Crawford, V.P. and Meng, J. (2011). "New York City Cab Drivers' Labor Supply Revisited: Reference-Dependent Preferences with Rational-Expectations Targets for Hours and Income." *American Economic Review*, 101(5), pp. 1912–1932.

Cronqvist, H., Thaler, R.H. and Yu, F. (2018). "When Nudges are Forever: Inertia in the Swedish Premium Pension Plan." *American Economic Review Papers and Proceedings*, 108, pp. 153–158.

Cubitt, R.P. (1992). "Monetary Policy Games and Private Sector Precommitment." *Oxford Economic Papers*, 44(3), pp. 513–530.

Cukierman, A. and Lippi, F. (1999). "Central Bank Independence, Centralization of Wage Bargaining, Inflation and Unemployment: Theory and Some Evidence." *European Economic Review*, 43(7), pp. 1395–1434.

Curcuru, S., Heaton, J., Lucas, D. and Moore, D. (2005). Heterogeneity and Portfolio Choice: Theory and Evidence. In Y. Ait-Sahalia and L. Hansen (eds.), *Handbook of Financial Econometrics*, Amsterdam: North-Holland.

Cynamon, B.Z. and Fazzari, S.M. (2008). "Household Debt in the Consumer Age: Source of Growth – Risk of Collapse." *Capitalism and Society*, 3(2), Article 3.

Daly, M., Hobyn, B. and Lucking, B. (2012). "Why Has Wage Growth Stayed Strong?" Federal Reserve Bank of San Francisco, Economic Letter 2012–10 April 2, 2012.

Damill, M., Rapetti, M. and Rozenwurcel, G. (eds.), (2016). *Macroeconomics and Development: Roberto Frenkel and the Economics of Latin America*, New York: Columbia University Press.

Davidson, P. (1968). "Money, Portfolio Balance, Capital Accumulation and Economic Growth." *Econometrica*, 36(2), pp. 292–321.

Davidson, P. (2008). "Post World War II Politics and Keynes's Aborted Revolutionary Economic Theory." *Economia e Sociedade*, Campinas, 17, Número Especial, pp. 549–568.

Davidson, P. (2010). "Making Dollars and Sense of the U.S. Government Debt." *Journal of Post Keynesian Economics*, 32(4), pp. 661–665.

Davis, L. (2018). "Financialization and the Non-financial Corporation: An Investigation of Firm-level Investment Behavior." *Metroeconomica*, 69(1), pp. 270–307.

Davis, L. and Skott, P. (2012). "Positional Goods, Climate Change and the Social Returns to Investment." In Tom Michl, Armon Rezai and Lance Taylor (eds.), *Social Fairness and Economics: Economic Essays in the Spirit of Duncan Foley*, Routledge.

Day, R.H. (1994). "Complex Economic Dynamics – Vol. 1: An Introduction to Dynamical Systems and Market Mechanisms." Cambridge, MA: MIT Press.

Debreu, G. (1974). "Excess Demand Functions." *Journal of Mathematical Economics*, 1(1), pp. 15–21.

De Giorgi, G., Frederiksen, A. and Pistaferri, L. (2020). "Consumption Network Effects." *Review of Economic Studies*, 87(1), pp. 130–163.

De Grauwe, P. (2012). *Lectures on Behavioral Macroeconomics*. Princeton, NJ: Princeton University Press.

De Loecker, J. and Eeckhout, J. (2017). "The Rise of Market Power and the Macroeconomic Implications." *Quarterly Journal of Economics*, 135(2), pp. 561–644.

DeLong, B. (2009). "The Intellectual Decline Collapse of the Chicago School, Part XLIV." delong.typepad.com/sdj/2009/03/Employment-cost-index-since-2001.html.

DeLong, J.B. and Summers, L. (2012). "Fiscal Policy in a Depressed Economy." *Brookings Papers on Economic Activity*, Spring, pp. 233–274.

Diallo, M.B., Flaschel, P. Krolzig, H.-M. and Proano, C. (2011). "Reconsidering the Dynamic Interaction Between Real Wages and Macroeconomic Activity." *Research in World Economy*, 2(1), pp. 77–93.

Diamond, P.A. (1965). "National Debt in a Neoclassical Growth Model." *American Economic Review*, 55(5), pp. 1126–1150.

Domar, E.D. (1946). "Capital Expansion, Rate of Growth, and Employment." *Econometrica*, 14(2), pp. 137–147.

Doms, M. and Dunne, T. (1998). "Capital Adjustment Patterns in Manufacturing Plants." *Review of Economic Dynamics*, 1(2), pp. 409–429.

Dube, A. Giuliano, L. and Leonard, J. (2019). "Fairness and Frictions: The Impact of Unequal Raises on Quit Behavior." *American Economic Review*, 109(2), pp. 620–663.

Dube, A., Lester, T. and Reich, M. (2010). "Minimum Wage Effects Across State Borders: Estimates Using Contiguous Counties." *Review of Economics and Statistics*, 92(4), pp. 945–964.

Duesenberry, J. (1949). *Income, Saving and the Theory of Consumer Behavior*. Cambridge: Harvard University Press.

Dunlop, J.T. (1938). "The Movement of Real and Money Wage Rates." *Economic Journal*, 48(191), pp. 413–434.

Dutt, A.K. (1986). "Wage Rigidity and Unemployment: The Simple Diagrammatics of Two Views." *Journal of Post Keynesian Economics*, 9(2), pp. 279–290.

Dutt, A.K. (1992). "Conflict Inflation, Distribution, Cyclical Accumulation and Crises." *European Journal of Political Economy*, 8, pp. 579–597.

Dutt, A.K. (2003). "On Post Walrasian Economics, Macroeconomic Policy, and Heterodox Economics." *International Journal of Political Economy*, 33(2), pp. 47–67.

Dutt, A.K. (2009). "Happiness and the Relative Income Hypothesis." In A.K. Dutt and B. Radcliff, (eds.), *Happiness, Economics and Politics: Towards a Multi-Disciplinary Approach*. Elgar.

Dutt, A.K. and Skott, P. (1996). "Keynesian Theory and the Aggregate-Supply/Aggregate-Demand Framework: A Defense." *Eastern Economic Journal*, 22(3), Summer, pp. 313–333.

Dutt, A.K. and Skott, P. (2006). "Keynesian Theory and the AD-AS Framework: A Reconsideration." In C. Chiarella, P. Flaschel, R. Franke and W. Semmler (eds.), *Quantitative and Empirical Analysis of Nonlinear Dynamic Macromodels*. Amsterdam: Elsevier.

Dynan, K.E., Skinner, J. and Zeldes, S.P. (2004). "Do the Rich Save More?" *Journal of Political Economy*, 112 (2, April), pp. 397–444.

Easterlin, R. (1974)."Does Economic Growth Improve the Human Lot? Some Empirical Evidence." In R. David and M. Reder (eds.), *Nations and Households in Economic Growth: Essays in Honor of Moses Abramovitz*, New York: Academic Press. pp. 89–125.

Easterlin, R. (2001). "Income and Happiness, Towards a Unified Theory." *The Economic Journal*, 111(473), pp. 465–484.

Economic Policy Institute. (2018). "Policy Agenda." www.epi.org/policy/.

Economist. (2009). "What Went Wrong with Economics." 16 July, www.economist.com/leaders/2009/07/16/what-went-wrong-with-economics.

Economist. (2014). "Hail, the Swabian Housewife – Views on Economics, the Euro and Much else Draw on a Cultural Archetype." 1 March, www.economist.com/europe/2014/02/01/hail-the-swabian-housewife?.

Economist. (2018). "Labour Monitoring Technologies Raise Efficiency – and Hard Questions." 1 March, www.economist.com/finance-and-economics/2018/03/01/labour-monitoring-technologies-raise-efficiency-and-hard-questions.

Eggertsson, G.B., Mehrotra, N.R. and Robbins, J.A. (2019). "A Model of Secular Stagnation: Theory and Quantitative Evaluation." *American Economic Journal: Macroeconomics*, 11(1), pp. 1–48.

Eggertsson, G.B., Robbins J.A., and Wold, E.G. (2021). "Kaldor and Piketty's Facts: The Rise of Monopoly Power in the United States." *Journal of Monetary Economics*, 124, Supplement, pp. S19–S38.

Eichenbaum, M., Jaimovich, N. and Rebelo, S. (2011). "Reference Prices, Costs, and Nominal Rigidities." *American Economic Review*, 101(1), pp. 234–262.

Eidelson, J. (2019). "Instacart Doesn't Want 'No' for an Answer." *Bloomberg Businessweek*, 22 July, pp. 22–24.

Elmendorf, D. and Mankiw, N.G. (1999). "Government Debt." In J.B. Taylor and M. Woodford (eds.), *Handbook of Macroeconomics, Vol. 1C*, Amsterdam, North-Holland.

Elson, Charles M. and Ferrere, Craig K. (2012). "Executive Superstars, Peer Groups and Over-Compensation – Cause, Effect and Solution." Available at SSRN: ssrn.com/abstract=2125979 or dx.doi.org/10.2139/ssrn.2125979.

Engen, E.M. and Hubbard, R. Glenn (2004). "Federal Government Debts and Interest Rates." In Gertler, M. and Rogoff, K. (eds.), *NBER Macroeconomics Annual 2004*, 19, Cambridge and London: MIT Press.

Epstein, G. (2019). *What's Wrong with Modern Money Theory?: A Policy Critique.* London: Palgrave Macmillan.

Estevez-Abe, M., Iversen, T. and Soskice, D. (2001). "Social Protection and the Formation of Skills: A Reinterpretation of the Welfare State." In P.A. Hall and D. Soskice (eds.), *Varieties of Capitalism: The Institutional Foundations of Comparative Advantage*, Oxford: Oxford University Press.

Fafchamps, M. and Shilpi, F. (2008). "Subjective Welfare, Isolation, and Relative Consumption," *Journal of Development Economics*, 86(1), pp. 43–60.

Fairris, D. (1997). *Shopfloor Matters: Labor-Management Relations in Twentieth-Century American Manufacturing.* London: Routledge.

Farber, H.S. (2005). "Is Tomorrow Another Day? The Labor Supply of New York City Cabdrivers." *Journal of Political Economy*, 113(1), pp. 46–82.

Farber, H.S. (2008). "Reference-Dependent Preferences and Labor Supply: The Case of New York City Taxi Drivers." *American Economic Review*, 98(3), pp. 1069–1082.

Farber, H.S., Herbst, D., Kuziemko, I. and Naidu, S. (2021). "Unions and Inequality Over the Twentieth Century: New Evidence from Survey Data." *Quarterly Journal of Economics*, 136(3), pp. 1325–1385.

Fazzari, S.M., Hubbard, R.G. and Petersen, B.C. (1988). "Financing Constraints and Corporate Investment." *Brookings Papers on Economic Activity*, 1988(1), pp. 141–195.

Fazzari, S.M., Ferri, P.E., Greenberg, E.G. and Variato, A.M. (2013). "Aggregate Demand, Instability, and Growth." *Review of Keynesian Economics*, 1(1), pp. 1–21.

Feenstra, R.C. and Hanson, G.H. (1996). "Globalization, Outsourcing, and Wage Inequality." *American Economic Review*, 86(2), pp. 240–245.

Fehr, E. and Schmidt, K. (2003). "Theories of Fairness and Reciprocity – Evidence and Economic Applications." In M. Dewatripont, L. Hansen and St. Turnovsky (eds.), *Advances in Economics and Econometrics – 8th World Congress, Econometric Society Monographs*, Cambridge: Cambridge University Press.

Fehr, E., Goette, L. and Zehnder, C. (2009). "A Behavioral Account of the Labor Market: The Role of Fairness Concerns." *Annual Review of Economics*, 2009(1), pp. 355–384.

Fel'dman, G.A. (1928). "On the Theory of Growth Rates of National Income." Translated and Reprinted in Two Parts in N. Spulber (ed.), (1964). *Foundations of Soviet Strategy for Economic Growth*. Bloomington: Indiana University Press, pp. 174–199 and 304–331.

Felipe, J. (2001). "Endogenous Growth, Increasing Returns and Externalities: An Alternative Interpretation of the Evidence." *Metroeconomica*, 52(4), pp. 391–427.

Felipe, J. and Fisher, F.M. (2003). "Aggregation in Production Functions: What Applied Economists Should Know." *Metroeconomica*, 54(2–3), pp. 208–262.

Ferguson, C.E. (1971). "Capital Theory up to Date: A Comment on Mrs Robinson's Article." *Canadian Journal of Economics*, 4(2), pp. 250–254.

Fernholz, T. (2013). "How Influential Was the Rogoff-Reinhart Study Warning That High Debt Kills Growth?" *Quartz*, April 16, 2013, qz.com/75117/how-influential-was-the-study-warning-high-debt-kills-growth/.

Fershtman, C. and Segal, U. (2018). "Preferences and Social Influence." *American Economic Journal: Microeconomics*, 10(3), pp. 124–142.

Fisher, F.M. (1971). "Aggregate Production Functions and the Explanation of Wages: A Simulation Experiment." *Review of Economics and Statistics*, 53(4), pp. 305–25.

Fisher, F.M., Solow, R.M. and Kearl, J.M. (1977). "Aggregate Production Functions: Some CES Experiments." *Review of Economic Studies*, 44(2), pp. 305–320.

Flaschel, P. and Franke, R. (2000). "An Old-Keynesian Note on Destabilizing Price Flexibility." *Review of Political Economy*, 12(3), pp. 273–283.

Flaschel, P. and Krolzig, H.M. (2006). "Wage-Price Phillips Curves and Macroeconomic Stability: Basic Structural Form, Estimation and Analysis." In C. Chiarella, P. Flaschel, R. Franke and W. Semmler (eds.), *Quantitative and Empirical Analysis of Nonlinear Dynamic Macromodels, Elsevier*, Amsterdam, pp. 7–47.

Fogg, N. and Harrington, P. (2011). "Rising Mal-Employment and the Great Recession: The Growing Disconnection between Recent College Graduates and the College Labor Market." *Continuing Higer Education Review*, 75, pp. 51–65.

Foley, D.K., Michl, T.R. and Tavani, D. (2019). *Growth and Distribution*, 2nd ed. Cambridge: Harvard University Press.

Frank, R.H. (1985a). *Choosing the Right Pond*. New York: Oxford University Press.

Frank, R.H. (1985b). "The Demand for Unobservable and Other Nonpositional Goods." *American Economic Review*, 75(1), pp. 101–116.

Frank, R.H. (2005). "Positional Externalities Cause Large and Preventable Welfare Losses." *American Economic Review*, 95(2), pp. 137–141.

Frank, R.H. (2008). "Should Public Policy Respond to Positional Externalities?" *Journal of Public Economics*, 92(8–9), pp. 1777–1786.

Frank, R.H. (2012). "Why Do Americans Save So Little and Does It Matter?" In Joshua Yates and James Davison Hunter (eds.) *Thrift and Thriving in America: Capitalism and Moral Order from the Puritans to the Present*. Oxford Scholarship Online, pp. 417–436.

Franke, R. (2018). "Can Monetary Policy Tame Harrodian Instability?" *Metroeconomica*, 69(3), pp. 593–618.

Frederick, S., Loewenstein, G. and O'Donoghue, T. (2002). "Time Discounting and Time Preference: A Critical Review." *Journal of Economic Literature*, Vol. XL (June), pp. 351–401.

Freeman, C. (1995). The National System of Innovation in Historical Perspective. *Cambridge Journal of Economics*, 19(1), pp. 5–24.

Freeman, R.B. (2007). "The Great Doubling: The Challenge of the New Global Labor Market." In Edwards, J. Crain, M. and Kalleberg, A. (eds.) *Ending Poverty in America: How to Restore the American Dream*. New York: The New Press.

Freeman, R.B. and Medoff, J.L. (1984). *What Do Unions Do?* New York: Basic Books.

Frey, B. and Stutzer, A. (2002). "What Can Economists Learn from Happiness Research?" *Journal of Economic Literature*. 40(2), pp. 402–435.

Friedman, M. (1957). *A Theory of the Consumption Function*. Princeton: Princeton University Press.

Friedman, M. (1968). "The Role of Monetary Policy." *American Economic Review*, 58(1) (March), pp. 1–17.

Friedman, M. and Schwartz, A.J. (1963). *A Monetary History of the United States, 1867–1960*. Princeton: Princeton University Press.

Frydman, R. and Phelps, E.S. (eds) (1983). *Individual Forecasting and Aggregate Outcomes*. Cambridge: Cambridge University Press.

Gabaix, X. and Landier, A. (2008). "Why Has CEO Pay Increased So Much?" *The Quarterly Journal of Economics*, 123(1), pp. 49–100.

Gali, J. (2016). *Monetary Policy, Inflation and the Business Cycle*, 2nd edition. Princeton: Princeton University Press.

Gali, J. and Gertler, M. (1999). "Inflation Dynamics: A Structural Econometric Analysis." *Journal of Monetary Economics*, 44, pp. 195–222.

Gao, Z., Sockin, M. and Xiong, M. (2020). "Economic Consequences of Housing Speculation." *Review of Financial Studies*, 33, pp. 5248–5287.

Garicano, L. and Rossi-Hansberg, E. (2006). "Organization and Inequality in a Knowledge Economy." *Quarterly Journal of Economics*, 121(4), pp. 1383–1435.

Giglio, S., Maggiori, M. and Utkus, S. (2021). "Five Facts about Beliefs and Portfolios." *American Economic Review*, 111(5), pp. 1481–1522.

Girardi, D. and Pariboni, R. (2020). "Autonomous Demand and the Investment Share." *Review of Keynesian Economics*, 8(3), pp. 428–453.

Godley, W. (1999). "Seven Unsustainable Processes." Strategic Analysis, January, Levy Economics Institute. www.levyinstitute.org/publications/seven-unsustainable-processes.

Godley, W. and Lavoie, M. (2007). *Monetary Economics*. New York: Palgrave Macmillan.

Goldin, C. and Katz, L.F. (2008). *The Race Between Education and Technology*. Cambridge, MA: Harvard University Press.

Gomes, F., Haliassos, M. and Ramadorai, T. (2021). "Household Finance." *Journal of Economic Literature*, 59(3), pp. 919–1000.

Goodhart, C.A.E. (1975). "Problems of Monetary Management: The UK Experience." In *Papers in Monetary Economics, Vol I*, Reserve Bank of Australia. Reprinted in A.S. Courakis (ed.), *Inflation, Depression, and Economic Policy in the West*, Rowman & Littlefield, pp. 111–146.

Goodwin, R.M. (1951). "The Nonlinear Accelerator and the Persistence of Business Cycles." *Econometrica*, 19(1), 1–17.

Goodwin, R.M. (1967). "A Growth Cycle." In C.H. Feinstein (ed.), *Socialism, Capitalism and Economic Growth*. Cambridge: Cambridge University Press.

Goodwin, R.M. (1989). *Essays in Nonlinear Economic Dynamics*. Frankfurt am Main: Peter Lang.

Gordon, R.J. (1997). "The Time-Varying NAIRU and Its Implications for Economic Policy." *Journal of Economic Perspectives*, 11, pp. 11–32.

Gordon, R.J. (2009). "Is Modern Macro or 1978-era More Relevant to the Understanding of the Current Economic crisis?" Mimeo.

Grandmont, J.-M. (1985). "On Endogenous Competitive Business Cycles." *Econometrica*, 53(5), pp. 995–1045.

Green, F. (1981). "The Effect of Occupational Pension Schemes on Saving in the United Kingdom: A Test of the Life Cycle Hypothesis." *Economic Journal*, 91(361), pp. 136–144.

Green, F. (1988). "Technical Efficiency and Production Relations: An Expository Note." Mimeo.

Green, F. (1991). "Institutional and Other Unconventional Theories of Saving." *Journal of Economic Issues*, 25(1), pp. 93–113.

Green, F. (2004). "Why Has Work Effort Become More Intense?" *Industrial Relations*, 43(4), pp. 709–741.

Greenspan, A. (2005). "Economic Flexibility." Remarks by Chairman Alan Greenspan before the National Italian American Foundation, Washington, D.C. www.federalreserve.gov/boarddocs/speeches/2005/20051012/default.htm.

Gregg, P. and Manning, A. (1997). "Skill-Biassed Change, Unemployment and Wage Inequality." *European Economic Review*, 41(6), pp. 1173–1200.

Grissmer, D.W. (2000). The Continuing Use and Misuse of SAT Scores. *Psychology, Public Policy, and Law*, 6(1), 223–232.

Groot, W. and Maassen van den Brink, H. (2000). "Overeducation in the Labor Market: A Meta-analysis." *Economics of Education Review*, 19(2), pp. 149–158.

Gross, D.B. and Souleles, N.S. (2002). "Do Liquidity Constraints and Interest Rates Matter for Consumer Behavior? Evidence from Credit Card Data." *Quarterly Journal of Economics*, 117(1), pp. 149–185.

Grubb, D. (1986). "Topics in the OECD Phillips Curve." *Economic Journal*, 96(381), 55–79.

Guimaraes, B. and Sheedy, K.D. (2011). "Sales and Monetary Policy." *American Economic Review*, 101(2), pp. 844–76.

Gustman and Steinmeier (2002). "The Influence of Pensions on Behavior: How Much Do We Really Know?" TIAA-CREF Institute Working Paper No. RD71.

Guy, F. (2007). "Strategic Bundling: Information Products, Market Power, and the Future of Globalization." *Review of International Political Economy*, 14(1): 26–48.

Guy, F. and Skott, P. (2008). "Information and Communications Technologies, Coordination and Control, and the Distribution of Income." *Journal of Income Distribution*, 17(3–4), pp. 71–92.

Hahn, F.-H. (1973). "The Winter of Our Discontent." *Economica*, 40(159), pp. 322–330.

Hahn, F.H. and Solow R. (1986). *A Critical Essay on Modern Macroeconomic Theory*, Cambridge, MA: MIT Press.

Haldane, A.G. and Turrell, A.E. (2018). "An Interdisciplinary Model for Macroeconomics." *Oxford Review of Economic Policy*, 34(1–2), pp. 219–251.

Hale, J.K. (1969). Ordinary Differential Equations. New York: Wiley Interscience.

Hall, P.A. and Soskice, D. eds. (2001). *Varieties of Capitalism: The Institutional Foundations of Comparative Advantage*. Oxford: Oxford University Press.

Hamermesh, D.S. (1993). *Labor Demand*. Princeton: Princeton University Press.

Handel, M.J. (2003). "Skills Mismatch in the Labor Market." *Annual Review of Sociology*, 29, pp. 135–165.

Harcourt, G.C. (1972). *Some Cambridge Controversies in the Theory of Capital*. Cambridge: Cambridge University Press.

Harcourt, G.C. and Laing, N.F. (eds.), (1971). *Capital and Growth*. Harmondswirth: Penguin.

Hargreaves-Heap, S.P. (1980). "Choosing the Wrong Natural Rate: Accelerating Inflation or Decelerating Employment and Growth." *Economic Journal*, 90(359), pp. 611–620.

Hargreaves-Heap, S. and Varoufakis, Y. (2002). "Some Experimental Evidence on the Evolution of Discrimination, Co-operation and Perceptions of Fairness." *Economic Journal*, 112(481), 679–703.

Harrod, R. (1939). "An Essay in Dynamic Theory." *Economic Journal*, 49(193), 14–33.

Harrod, R. (1973). *Economic Dynamics*. London and Basingstoke: Macmillan.

Hazell, J., Herreño, J., Nakamura, E. and Steinsson, J. (2022). "The Slope of the Phillips Curve: Evidence from U.S. States." *Quarterly Journal of Economics*, 137(3), pp. 1299–1344.

Heckman, J.J. (2007). "Comments on Are Protective Labor Market Institutions at the Root of Unemployment? A Critical Review of the Evidence by David Howell, Dean Baker, Andrew Glyn, and John Schmitt." *Capitalism and Society*, 2(1), Article 5.

Hein, E. (2014). *Distribution and Growth after Keynes*. Cheltenham: Elgar.

Hendry, D.F. and Muellbauer, J.N.J. (2018). "The Future of Macroeconomics: Macro Theory and Models at the Bank of England." *Oxford Review of Economic Policy*, 34(1–2), pp. 287–328.

Herndon, T., Ash, M. and Pollin, R. (2014). "Does High Public Debt Consistently Stifle Economic Growth? A Critique of Reinhart and Rogoff." *Cambridge Journal of Economics*, 38(2), pp. 257–279.

Hicks, J.R. (1935). "Annual Survey of Economic Theory: The Theory of Monopoly." *Econometrica*, 3(1), pp. 1–20.

Hicks, J.R. (1937). "Mr. Keynes and the 'Classics'; A Suggested Interpretation." *Econometrica*, 5(2) (April), pp. 147–159.

Hicks, J.R. (1950). *A Contribution to the Theory of the Trade Cycle*. Oxford: Oxford University Press.

Hicks, J.R. (1965). *Capital and Growth*. Oxford: Oxford University Press.

Hicks, J. (1975). *The Crisis in Keynesian Economics*. Oxford: Blackwell.

Hicks, J. (1980–81). "'IS-LM': An Explanation." *Journal of Post Keynesian Economics*, 3(2) (Winter), pp. 139–154.

Hirsch, F. (1977). *Social Limits to Growth*, London: Routledge and Kegan Paul Ltd.

Hirschman, A.O. (1970). *Exit, Voice and Loyalty*. Cambridge, MA: Harvard University Press.

Hodgson, G. (1988). *Economics and Institutions: A Manifesto for a Modern Institutional Economics*. Philadelphia: University of Pennsylvania Press.

Hoel, M. and Sterner, T. (2007). "Discounting and Relative Prices." *Climatic Change*, 84(3–4), pp. 265–280.

Hoff, K. and Stiglitz, J. (2016). "Striving for Balance in Economics: Towards a Theory of the Social Determination of Behavior." *Journal of Economic Behavior and Organization*, 126, Part B, pp. 25–57.

Holt, R.P.F., Rosser, J.B. and Colander, D. (2011). "The Complexity Era in Economics." *Review of Political Economy*, 23(3), pp. 357–369.

Hoover, K.D. (1988). *The New Classical Macroeconomics: A Sceptical Inquiry*. Oxford: Blackwell.

Hoover, K.D. (2001). *The Methodology of Empirical Macroeconomics*. Cambridge: Cambridge University Press.

Howell, D.R., Baker, D., Glyn, A. and Schmitt, J. (2007). "Are Protective Labor Market Institutions at the Root of Unemployment? A Critical Review of the Evidence." *Capitalism and Society*, 2(1), Article 1.

Hubbard, R. and Palia, D. (1995). "Benefits of Control, Managerial Ownership, and the Stock Returns of Acquiring Firms." *RAND Journal of Economics*, 26(4), pp. 782–793.

Irons, J. and Bivens, J. (2010). "Government Debt and Economic Growth." EPI Briefing Paper #271. Economic Policy Institute.

Jensen, M.C. and Meckling, W.H. (1976). "Theory of the Firm: Managerial Behavior, Agency Costs and Ownership Structure." *Journal of Financial Economics*, 3, pp. 305–360.

Johansson-Stenman, O., Carlson, F. and Daruvala, D. (2002). "Measuring Future Grandparents' Preferences for Equality and Relative Standing." *Economic Journal*, 112(479), pp. 362–383.

Johnson, D.S., Parker, J.A. and Souleles, N.S. (2006). "Household Expenditure and the Income Tax Rebates of 2001." *American Economic Review*, 96(5), pp. 1589–1610.

Johnston, K. (2019). "What Makes You Work Harder? Strap on a Censor and Find Out." *The Boston Globe*, July 16.

Jones, C.I. and Klenow, P.J. (2016). "Beyond GDP? Welfare across Countries and Time." *American Economic Review*, 106(9), pp. 2426–2457.

Jonscher, C. (1994). "An Economic Study of the Information Technology Revolution." In T. J. Allen and M.S. Scott Morton. (eds.), *Information Technology and the Corporation of the 1990s: Research Studies*, New York: Oxford University Press.

Jonsson, T. and Österholm, P. (2012). "The Properties of Survey-based Inflation Expectations in Sweden." *Empirical Economics*, 42, pp. 79–94.

Kahn, S. (1997). "Evidence of Nominal Wage Stickiness from Microdata." *American Economic Review*, 87(5), pp. 993–1008.

Kahneman, D. (1994). "New Challenges to the Rationality Assumption." *Journal of Institutional and Theoretical Economics*, 150(1), pp. 18–36.

Kahneman, D., Knetsch, J.L. and Thaler, R. (1986). "Fairness as a Constraint on Profit Seeking: Entitlements in the Market." *American Economic Review*, 76(4), 728–741.

Kahneman, D., Knetsch, J.L. and Thaler, R. (1991). "The Endowment Effect, Loss Aversion and Status quo Bias." *Journal of Economic Perspectives*, 5(1), 193–206.

Kaldor, N. (1940). "A Model of the Trade Cycle." *Economic Journal*, 50(197), pp. 78–92.

Kaldor, N. (1955). "Alternative Theories of Distribution." *Review of Economic Studies*, 23(2), pp. 83–100.

Kaldor, N. (1966). "Marginal Productivity and the Macro-economic Theories of Distribution: Comment on Samuelson and Modigliani." *The Review of Economic Studies*, 33(4), pp. 309–319.

Kaldor, N. (1980). "Monetarism and U.K. Monetary Policy." *Cambridge Journal of Economics*, 4(4), 293–318.

Kalecki, M. (1935 [1971]). "The Mechanism of the Business Upswing." Reprinted in M. Kalecki (1971) *Selected Essays on the Dynamics of the Capitalist Economy*, Cambridge University Press.

Kalecki, M. (1937a). "The Principle of Increasing Risk." *Economica*, 4(16), pp. 440–447.

Kalecki, M. (1937b). "A Theory of the Business Cycle." *Review of Economic Studies*, 4(2), pp. 77–97.

Kalecki, M. (1943 [1971]). "Political Aspects of Full Employment." *The Political Quarterly*, pp. 322–330. Reprinted in M. Kalecki (1971) *Selected Essays on the Dynamics of the Capitalist Economy 1933–1970*, Cambridge: Cambridge University Press.

Kalecki, M. (1976). *Essays on Developing Economies*. Hassocks: Harvester Press.

Kaplan, G., Moll, B. and Violante, G.L. (2018). "Monetary Policy According to HANK." *American Economic Review*, 108(3), 697–743.

Kaplan, G. and Violante, G.L. (2018). "Microeconomic Heterogeneity and Macroeconomic Shocks." *Journal of Economic Perspectives*, 32(3), pp. 167–194.

Karanassou, M., Sala, H. and Snower, D.J. (2005). "A Reappraisal of the Inflation–Unemployment Tradeoff." *European Journal of Political Economy*, 21(1), pp. 1–32.

Kashyap, A. (1995). "Sticky Prices: New Evidence from Retail Catalogs." *Quarterly Journal of Economics*, 110(1), pp. 245–274.

Katz, L.F. and Murphy, K.M. (1992). Changes in Relative Wages, 1963–1987: Supply and Demand Factors: *Quarterly Journal of Economics*, 107(1), pp. 35–78.

Kehoe, P. and Midrigan, V. (2015). "Prices Are Sticky after All." *Journal of Monetary Economics*, 75, pp. 35–53.

Kelton, S. (2019). "The Wealthy Are Victims of Their Own Propaganda." Bloomberg, February 1, 2019, (www.bloomberg.com/opinion/articles/2019-02-01/rich-must-embrace-deficits-to-escape-taxes#xj4y7vzkg).

Keynes, J.M. (1930a [1981]). "The Question of HighWages." *The Political Quarterly*. Reprinted in *The Collected Writings of John Maynard Keynes Vol. XX*, London and Basingstoke: Macmillan, 1981, pp. 3–16.

Keynes, J.M. (1930b). *A Treatise on Money* Macmillan, The Collected Works of John Maynard Keynes, Vol. V.

Keynes, J.M. (1936). *The General Theory of Employment, Interest and Money*, London and Basingstoke: Macmillan.

Keynes, J.M. (1937a). "Ex Ante and Ex Post." Reprinted in *The Collected Writings of John Maynard Keynes Vol. XIV*, London and Basingstoke: Macmillan, 1978.

Keynes, J.M. (1937b). "The General Theory of Employment." *Quarterly Journal of Economics*, 51(2), pp. 209–223.

Keynes, J.M. (1939). "Relative Movements of Real Wages and Output." *Economic Journal*, 49(193), pp. 34–51.

Kim, H.K. and Skott, P. (2016). "Labor Market Reforms and Wage Inequality in Korea." *Metroeconomica*, 67(2), pp. 313–333.

King, J. (2012). *The Microfoundations Delusion*. Cheltenham: Elgar.

King, R.G. (2000). "The New IS-LM Model: Language, Logic and Limits." *Economic Quarterly*, 86(3), pp. 45–103.

Kirman, A. (1989). "The Intrinsic Limits of Modern Economic Theory: The Emperor has No Clothes." *Economic Journal*, 99(395), pp. 126–39.

Kirman, A. (1992). "Who or What Does the Representative Individual Represent?" *The Journal of Economic Perspectives*, 6(2), pp. 117–136.

Kirsanova, T., Leith, C. and Wren-Lewis, S. (2009). "Monetary and Fiscal Policy Interaction: The Current Consensus Assignment in the Light of Recent Developments." *Economic Journal*, 119(541), pp. F482–F496.

Klenow, P.J. and Malin, B.A. (2010). "Microeconomic Evidence on Price-Setting." In Friedman, B.M. and Woodford, M. (eds.), *Handbook of Monetary Economics, 3*, Amsterdam: North Holland, pp. 231–284.

Kleven, H. Jacobsen. (2014). "How Can Scandinavians Tax So Much?" *Journal of Economic Perspectives*, 28(4), pp. 77–98.

Klump, R., McAdam, P. and Willman, A. (2007). "Factor Substitution and Factor-Augmenting Technical Progress in the United States: A Normalized Supply-Side System Approach." *Review of Economics and Statistics*, 89(1), pp. 183–92.

Koszegi, B. and Rabin, M. (2006). "A Model of Reference-Dependent Preferences." *Quarterly Journal of Economics*, 121(4), pp. 1133–1165.

Kotz, D., McDonough, T. and Reich, M. (1994). *Social Structures of Accumulation*. Cambridge: Cambridge University Press.

Krueger, A.B. (1999). Measuring Labor's Share, in *American Economic Review, Papers and Proceedings*, 89(2), 45–51.

Krugman, P. (1994). "Past and Prospective Causes of High Unemployment." *Economic Review*, Federal Reserve Bank of Kansas City.

Krugman, P. (1998). "It's Baaack: Japan's Slump and the Return of the Liquidity Trap." *Brookings Papers on Economic Activity*, 29(2), pp. 137–206.

Krugman, P. (2010). "Notes on Rogoff." *The New York Times*, krugman.blogs.nytimes.com/2010/07/21/notes-on-rogoff-wonkish/.

Krugman, P. (2013). "The Japan Story." *The New York Times*, krugman.blogs.nytimes.com/2013/02/05/the-japan-story/?_r=0.

Krugman, P. (2018a). "Good Enough for Government Work? Macroeconomics Since the Crisis." *Oxford Review of Economic Policy*, 34(1–2), pp. 156–168.

Krugman, P. (2018b). "What Do We Actually Know about the Economy?" *New York Times*, 16 September.

Kurz, H.D. and Salvadori, N. (1995) *Theory of Production: A Long-Period Analysis*. Cambridge: Cambridge University Press.

Kurzweil, R. (1992). *The Age of Intelligent Machines*. Cambridge, MA: MIT Press.

Kydland, F.E. and Prescott, E.C. (1977). "Rules Rather than Discretion: The Inconsistency of Optimal Plans." *Journal of Political Economy*, 85(3), pp. 473–492.

Kydland, F.E. and Prescott, E.C. (1982). "Time to Build and Aggregate Fluctuations." *Econometrica*, Econometric Society, 50(6, Nov.), pp. 1345–1370.

Lachowska, M. and Mych, M. (2018). "The Effect of Public Pension Wealth on Saving and Expenditure." *American Economic Journal: Economic Policy*, 10(3), pp. 284–308.

Laibson, D. and List, J.A. (2015). "Principles of (Behavioral) Economics." *American Economic Review: Papers and Proceedings*, 2015, 105(5), 385–390.

La Porta, R. and Shleifer, A. (2014). "Informality and Development." *Journal of Economic Perspectives*, 28(3), pp. 109–126.

Lavoie, M. (2014). *Post-Keynesian Economics*. Cheltenham: Edward Elgar.

Lawler, P. (2001). "Centralised Wage Setting, Inflation Contracts, and the Optimal Choice of Central Banker." *Economic Journal*, 110(463), pp. 559–575.

Layard, R. Nickell, S. and Jackman, R. (1991). *Unemployment: Macroeconomic Performance and the Labour Market*. Oxford: Oxford University Press.

Leão, P. (2013). "The Effect of Government Spending on the Debt-to-GDP Ratio: Some Keynesian Arithmetic." *Metroeconomica*, 64(3), pp. 448–465.

Lebergott, S. (1964). *Manpower in Economic Growth. The American Record since 1800*. New York: McGraw-Hill.

Leijonhufvud, A. (1968). *On Keynesian Economics and the Economics of Keynes*. Oxford: Oxford University Press.

Leijonhufvud, A. (1999). "Mr. Keynes and the Moderns." In Pasinetti, L. and Schefold, B. (eds.), *The Impact of Keynes on Economics in the Twentieth Century*, Cheltenham: Edward Elgar.

Lerner, A.P. (1943). "Functional Finance and the Federal Debt." *Social Research*, 10(1), pp. 38–51.

Levine, R. and Renelt, D. (1992). "A Sensitivity Analysis of Cross-Country Growth Regressions." *American Economic Review*, 82(4), pp. 942–963.

Levy, D., Bergen, M., Dutta, S. and Venable, R. (1997). "The Magnitude of Menu Costs: Direct Evidence from Large U.S. Supermarket Chains." *Quarterly Journal of Economics*, 112(3), pp. 791–825.

Lewis, M. (2017). *The Undoing Project*. New York: W. W. Norton & Company.

Lewis, W.A. (1954). "Economic Development with Unlimited Supplies of Labor." *The Manchester School*, 22(2), pp. 139–191.

Lindbeck, A. and Snower, D.J (1988). *The Insider-Outsider Theory of Employment and Unemployment*, Cambridge, MA: MIT Press.

Linde, J., Smets, F. and Wouters, R. (2016). "Challenges for Central Banks' Models." Sveriges Riksbank Research Paper Series, 147.

Lucas, R.E. (1972). "Expectations and the Neutrality of Money." *Journal of Economic Theory*, 4(2), pp. 103–124.

Lucas, R.E. (1975). "An Equilibrium Model of the Business Cycle." *Journal of Political Economy*, 83 (Dec.), pp. 1113–1144.

Lucas, R.E. Jr. (1976). "Econometric Policy Evaluation: A Critique." In K. Brunner and A. Meltzer (eds.), *The Phillips Curve and the Labor Markets*, Carnegie-Rochester Conference Series on Public Policy, 1, 19–46.

Lucas, R.E. Jr. (1980). "The Death of Keynesian Economics." *Issues and Ideas*, Winter, pp. 18–19.

Lucas, R.E. (1981). *Studies in Business-cycle Theory*. Oxford: Blackwell.

Lucas, R.E. (2003). "Macroeconomic Priorities." *American Economic Review*, 93(1), pp. 1–14.

Lucas, R.E. (2004). "The Industrial Revolution: Past and Future." Federal Reserve Bank of Minneapolis, 2003 Annual Report Essay.

Luo, M. (2010). "Overqualified? Yes, but Happy to Have a Job." *New York Times*, 28 March 2010.

Luttmer, E. (2005). "Neighbors as Negatives: Relative Earnings and Well-being." *The Quarterly Journal of Economics*. 120(3), pp. 963–1002.

McNicholas, C., Mokhiber, Z. and von Wilpert, M. (2018). "Janus and Fair Share Fees: The organizations Financing the Attack on Unions' Ability to Represent Workers." Economic Policy Institute.

Maka, A. and Barbosa, F. (2013). "Phillips Curves: An Encompassing Test." XLI Encontro Nacional de Economia (ANPEC).

Malinvaud, E. (1977). *The Theory of Unemployment Reconsidered*. Oxford: Blackwell.

Mankiw, G. (2001). "The Inexorable and Mysterious Tradeoff between Inflation and Unemployment." *Economic Journal*, 111(471), pp. 45–61.

Mankiw. N. G. and Reis, R. (2018). "Friedman's Presidential Address in the Evolution of Macroeconomic Thought." *Journal of Economic Perspectives*, 32(1), pp. 81–96.

Mankiw, N.G. Rotemberg, J.J. and Summers, L.H. (1985). "Intertemporal Substitution in Macroeconomics." *Quarterly Journal of Economics*, 100, pp. 225–251.

Manning, A. (2003). *Monopsony in Motion: Imperfect Competition in Labor Markets*. Princeton: Princeton University Press.

Mantel, R. (1976). "Homothetic Preferences and Community Excess Demand Functions." *Journal of Economic Theory*, 12(2), 197–201.

Marglin, S.A. (1984). *Growth, Distribution, and Prices*. Cambridge, MA: Harvard University Press.

Marshall, A. (1887). "A Fair Rate of Wages." In A.C. Pigou (Ed.), 1956. *Memorials of Alfred Marshall*. New York: Kelley & Millman, pp. 212–226.

Martinez, I.Z., Saez, E. and Siegenthaler, M. (2021). "Intertemporal Labor Supply Substitution? Evidence from the Swiss Tax Holidays." *American Economic Review*, 111(2), pp. 506–546.

Martins, G.K. and Skott, P. (2021). "Macroeconomic Policy, Inflation and Deindustrialization in a Dual Economy." *Industrial and Corporate Change*, 30(2), pp. 409–444.

Marx, K. (1852 [1978]). *The Eighteenth Brumaire of Louis Bonaparte*. Beijing: Foreign Languages Press.

Marx, K. (1867 [1906]). *Capital. A Critique of Political Economy, vol. 1*. The Modern Library, New York.

Mas-Colell, A., Michael D., Whinston and Jerry R. Green (1995). *Microeconomic Theory*. Oxford: Oxford University Press.

Mason, J.W. (2018). "Income Distribution, Household Debt, and Aggregate Demand: A Critical Assessment." Levy Economics Institute Working Paper 901.

Matthews, P.H. (2021). "The Dialectics of Differentiation: Marx's Mathematical Manuscripts and Their Relation to His Economics." *Review of Social Economy*, 79(1), pp. 25–50.

Mavroeidis, S., Plagborg-Møller, M. and Stock, J.H. (2014). "Empirical Evidence on Inflation Expectations in the New Keynesian Phillips Curve." *Journal of Economic Literature*, 52(1), 124–188.

Mian, A. and Sufi, A. (2009). "The Consequences of Mortgage Credit Expansion: Evidence from the U.S. Mortgage Default Crisis." *Quarterly Journal of Economics*, 124(4), pp. 1449–1496.

Mian, A. and Sufi, A. (2011). "House Prices, Home Equity-Based Borrowing, and the US Household Leverage Crisis." *American Economic Review*, 101(5), pp. 2132–2156.

Mian, A. and Sufi, A. (2018). "Finance and Business Cycles: The Credit-Driven Household Demand Channel." *Journal of Economic Perspectives*, 32(3), pp. 31–58.

Michl, T.R. (2013). "Public Debt, Growth, and Distribution." *Review of Keynesian Economics*, 1(1), 272–296.

Miller, M.H. and Modigliani, F. (1961). "Dividend Policy, Growth, and the Valuation of Shares." *Journal of Business*, 34(4), pp. 411–433.

Minford, P. (1980). "Memorandum by Professor A.P. Minford." In *Memoranda on Monetary Policy*, House of Commons Treasury and Civil Service Committee, sess. 1979–80, HMSO.

Minsky, Hyman P. (1975). *John Maynard Keynes*. New York: Columbia University Press.

Minsky, H. (1986). *Stabilizing an Unstable Economy*. New Haven: Yale University Press.

Minsky, H. (1993). "The Financial Instability Hypothesis." In Arestis, P. and Sawyer, M. (eds.), *The Elgar Companion to Radical Political Economy*, pp. 153–158, Aldershot: Elgar.

Mishel, L. and Kandra, J. (2021). "CEO Pay Has Skyrocketed 1,322% since 1978." EPI Report, epi.org/232540.

Modigliani, F. and Miller, M.H. (1958). "The Cost of Capital, Corporation Finance and the Theory of Investment." *The American Economic Review*, 48(3), pp. 261–297.

Moore, B.J. (1988). *Horizontalists and Verticalists: The Macroeconomics of Credit Money*, Cambridge: Cambridge University Press.

Moriguchi, Chiaki and Emmanuel Saez. (2007). "The Evolution of Income Concentration in Japan, 1886–2005: Evidence from Income Tax Statistics." *Review of Economics and Statistics*, 90(4), pp. 713–734.

Morishima, M. (1966). "Refutation of the Nonswitching Theorem." *Quarterly Journal of Economics*, 80(4), pp. 520–525.

Muellbauer, J. (2010). "Household Decisions, Credit Markets and the Macroeconomy: Implications for the Design of Central Bank Models." Bank for International Settlements, Working Paper 306.

Muellbauer, J. (2020). "Implications of Household-Level Evidence for Policy Models: The Case of Macro-financial Linkages." *Oxford Review of Economic Policy*, 36(3), pp. 510–555.

Muellbauer, J. and Murphy, A. (1997). "Booms and Busts in the UK Housing Market." *Economic Journal*, 107(445), pp. 1701–1727.

Munnell, A.H., Chen, A. and Siliciano, R.L. (2021). "The National Retirement Index: An Update from the 2019 SCF." Center for Retirement Research at Boston College, Briefs, January, 21(2).

Murakami, H. (2018). "A Two-sector Keynesian Model of Business Cycles." *Metroeconomica*, 69(2), pp. 444–472.

Murphy, K.J. and Zábojník, J. (2004). "CEO Pay and Appointments: A Market-based Explanation for Recent Trends." *American Economic Review*, 94(2), pp. 192–196.

Musgrave, A. (1981). "'Unreal Assumptions' in Economic Theory: The F-Twist Untwisted." *Kyklos*, 34(3), pp. 377–387.

Muth, J.F. (1961). "Rational Expectations and the Theory of Price Movements." *Econometrica*, 29(3), pp. 315–335.

Nakamura, E. and Steinsson, J. (2013). "Price Rigidity: Microeconomic Evidence and Macroeconomic Implications." *Annual Review of Economics*, 5, pp. 133–163.

Nakamura, E. and Steinsson, J. (2014). "Fiscal Stimulus in a Monetary Union: Evidence from US Regions." *American Economic Review*, 104(3), pp. 753–792.

Nakamura, E. and Steinsson, J. (2018). "Identification in Macroeconomics." *Journal of Economic Perspectives*, 32(3), pp. 59–86.

Nakatani, T. and Skott, P. (2007). "Japanese Growth and Stagnation: A Keynesian Perspective." *Structural Change and Economic Dynamics*, 18(3), pp. 306–332.

Nersisyan, Y. and Wray, L.R. (2010). "Deficit Hysteria Redux? Why We Should Stop Worrying about U.S. Government Deficits." Public Policy Brief, no. 111, Levy Economics Institute of Bard College.

Newell, A. and Symons, J.S.V. (1987). "Corporatism, Laissez Faire, and the Rise in Unemployment." *European Economic Review*, 31(3), 567–601.

Nickell, S. (1978). *The Investment Decisions of Firms*. Cambridge: Cambridge University Press.

Nickell, S. (1997). "Unemployment and Labour Market Rigidities: Europe Versus North America." *Journal of Economic Perspectives*, 11(3), pp. 55–74.

Nickell, S. (1998). "Unemployment: Questions and Some Answers." The *Economic Journal*, 108(448), pp. 802–816.

Nickell, S. (2003). "Labour Market Institutions and Unemployment in OECD Countries." CESifo DICE Report 2/2003.

Nordhaus, W.D. (1994). *Managing the Global Commons: The Economics of Climate Change*. Cambridge, MA: MIT Press.

Nordhaus, W.D. (2008). *A Question of Balance: Weighing the Options on Global Warming*, New Haven: Yale University Press.

Noyola, J.F. (1956). "Inflation in Chile: An Unorthodox Approach." *International Economic Papers*, 10, pp. 603–648.

Nurkse, R. (1953). *Problems of Capital Formation in Underdeveloped Countries*. Oxford: Oxford University Press.

O'Brien, M. (2013). "Forget Excel: This Was Reinhart and Rogoff's Biggest Mistake – Correlation Is Not Causation." *The Atlantic*, www.theatlantic.com/business/archive/2013/04/forget-excel-this-was-reinhart-and-rogoffs-biggest-mistake/275088/.

Obstfeld, M. (2013). "On Keeping Your Powder Dry: Fiscal Foundations of Financial and Price Stability." Working Paper 9563, CEPR.

O'Donoghue, T. and Rabin, M. (1999). "Doing It Now or Later." *American Economic Review*, 89(1), pp. 103–124.

O'Donoghue, T. and Rabin, M. (2015). "Present Bias: Lessons Learned and to Be Learned." *American Economic Review Papers and Proceedings*, 105(5), pp. 273–279.

OECD. (1994). *Jobs Study*. Paris: OECD.

OECD. (2000). *Employment Outlook*. Paris: OECD.

OECD. (2015). *Economic Surveys – Japan April 2015*. Paris: OECD.

OECD. (2019a). *Economic Surveys – Japan April 2019*. Paris: OECD.

OECD. (2019b). Tax Policy Reforms 2019: OECD and Selected Partner Economies, OECD Publishing, Paris, doi.org/10.1787/da56c295-en.

Oh, J-S. (2018). "Macroeconomic Stability in a Flexible Labor Market." *Metroeconomica*, 69(3), pp. 655–680.

Oswald, A. (1997). "Happiness and Economic Performance." *The Economic Journal*, 107 (November), pp. 1815–1831.

Palley, T. (2002). "Economic Contradictions Coming Home to Roost? Does the U.S. Economy Face a Long-Term Aggregate Demand Generation Problem?" *Journal of Post Keynesian Economics*, 25(1), pp. 9–32.

Palley, T. (2010). "The Simple Macroeconomics of Fiscal Austerity, Public Sector Debt and Deflation." IMK Working Paper, no.8/2010. Dusseldorf.

Palley, T. (2019). "The Fallacy of the Natural Rate of Interest and Zero Lower Bound Economics: Why Negative Interest Rates May Not Remedy Keynesian Unemployment." *Review of Keynesian Economics*, 7(2), pp. 151–170.

Palley, T. (2020). "What's Wrong with Modern Money Theory: Macro and Political Economic Restraints on Deficit-financed Fiscal Policy." *Review of Keynesian Economics*, 8(4), pp. 472–493.

Parker, J.A., Souleles, N.S., Johnson, D.S. and McClelland, R. (2013). "Consumer Spending and the Economic Stimulus Payments of 2008." *American Economic Review*, 103(6), pp. 2530–2553.

Pasinetti, L.L. (1962). "Rate· of Profit and Income Distribution in Relation to the Rate of Economic Growth." *Review of Economic Studies*, 29(4), pp. 267–279.

Pasinetti, L.L. (1966). "Paradoxes in Capital Theory: A Symposium: Changes in the Rate of Profit and Switches of Techniques." *Quarterly Journal of Economics*, 80(4), pp. 503–517.

Pasinetti, L.L. (1969). "Switches of Technique and the 'Rate of Return' in Capital Theory." *Economic Journal*, 79(315), pp. 508–531.

Pástor, L. and Veronesi, P. (2009). "Technological Revolutions and Stock Prices." *American Economic Review*, 99(4), pp. 1451–1483.

Pedersen, P. and Smith, N. (2002). "Unemployment Traps: Do Financial Disincentives Matter?" *European Sociological Review*, 18(3), pp. 271–288.

Penrose, E. (1959). *The Theory of the Growth of the Firm*. Oxford: Oxford University Press.

Persson, T. and Tabellini, G. (1990). *Macroeconomic Policy, Credibility and Politics*, Chur: Harwood Academic Publishers.

Phelps, Edmund S. (1967). "Phillips Curves, Expectations of Inflation, and Optimal Unemployment Over Time." *Economica*, 34(135), pp. 254–281.

Phelps, E.S. (1969). "The New Microeconomics in Inflation and Employment Theory." *American Economic Review Papers and Proceedings*, 59(2), pp. 147–160.

Phillips, A.W. (1958). "The Relationship between Unemployment and the Rate of Change of Money Wages in the United Kingdom 1861–1957." *Economica*. 25(100), pp. 283–299.

Piketty, T. (2020). *Capital and Ideology*. Cambridge, MA: Belknap Press of Harvard University Press.

Piketty, T. and Saez, E. (2003). Income Inequality in the United States, 1913–2002. *Quarterly Journal of Economics*, 118(1), pp. 1–39.

Piketty, T., Postel-Vinay, G. and Rosenthal, J-L. (2006). "Wealth Concentration in a Developing Economy: Paris and France, 1807–1994." *American Economic Review*, 96(1), pp. 236–256.

Pollin, R. and Zhu, A. (2006). "Inflation and Economic Growth: A Cross-country Nonlinear Analysis." *Journal of Post Keynesian Economics*, 28(4), pp. 593–614.

Poterba, J.M. (1987). "Tax Policy and Corporate Saving." *Brookings Papers on Economic Activity*, 2:1987, pp. 455–503.

Rabin, M. (1998). "Psychology and Economics." *Journal of Economic Literature* XXXVI (March), pp. 11–46.

Rabinovich, J. (2019). "The Financialization of the Non-financial Corporation. A Critique to the Financial Turn of Accumulation Hypothesis." *Metroeconomica*, 70(4), pp. 738–775.

Rachel, L. and Summers, L. (2019). "On Secular Stagnation in the Industrialized World." *Brookings Papers on Economic Activity*, 50(1), pp. 1–54.

Ramsey, F.P. (1928). "A Mathematical Theory of Saving." *Economic Journal*, 38(152), pp. 543–559.

Raymond, E. (1999). "The Cathedral and the Bazaar." *Knowledge, Technology and Policy,* 12, pp. 23–49.

Razmi, A., Rapetti, M. and Skott, P. (2012). "The Real Exchange Rate and Economic Development." *Structural Change and Economic Dynamics*, 23(2), pp. 151–169.

Read, D., Loewenstein, G. F. and Kalyanaraman, S. (1999). "Mixing Virtue and Vice: Combining the Immediacy Effect and the Diversification Heuristic." *Journal of Behavioral Decision Making*, 12, pp. 257–273.

Reinhart, C.M. and Rogoff, K.S. (2009). "The Aftermath of Financial Crises." *American Economic Review: Papers and Proceedings*, 99(2), pp. 466–472.

Reinhart, C.M. and Rogoff, K.S. (2010). "Growth in a Time of Debt." *American Economic Review Papers and Proceedings*, 100(2), pp. 573–578.

Reis, R. (2006). "Inattentive Producers." *Review of Economic Studies*, 73(3), pp. 793–821.

Robinson, J. (1953–54). "The Production Function and the Theory of Capital." *Review of Economic Studies*, 21(2), pp. 81–106.

Robinson, J. (1970). "Quantity Theories Old and New: A Comment." *Journal of Money, Credit and Banking*, 2(4), pp. 504–512.

Robinson, J. (1971). "Capital Theory up to Date: A Reply." *Canadian Journal of Economics*, 4(2), pp. 254–256.

Robinson, J. (1974a). "History versus Equilibrium." *Thames Papers in Political Economy*.

Robinson, J. (1974b). "What Has Become of the Keynesian Revolution?" *Challenge*, 16(6), pp. 6–11.

Robinson, J. (1978). *Contributions to Modern Economics*. Oxford: Blackwell.

Rogoff, K. (1985). "The Optimal Degree of Commitment to an Intermediate Monetary Target." *Quarterly Journal of Economics*, 100, pp. 1169–1190.

Roine, J. and Waldenström, D. (2006). The Evolution of Top Incomes in an Egalitarian Society: Sweden, 1903–2004. Helsinki: IEHC.

Romer, D. (2018). *Advanced Macroeconomics*, 5th Ed. New York: McGraw-Hill.

Romer, P. (2016). "The Trouble with Macroeconomics." paulromer.net/the-trouble-with-macro/WP-Trouble.pdf.

Roose, K. (2019). "When Tech Takes over Boss's Role." *New York Times*, 24 June.

Ros, J. (2013). *Rethinking Economic Development, Growth and Institutions*. Oxford: Oxford University Press.

Rose, H. (1967). "On the Non-Linear Theory of the Employment Cycle." *Review of Economic Studies*, 34(2), pp. 153–173.

Rowthorn, R. (1977). "Conflict, Inflation and Money." *Cambridge Journal of Economics*, 1(3), pp. 215–239.

Rowthorn, R. (1995). "Capital Formation and Unemployment." *Oxford Review of Economic Policy*, 11(1), pp. 26–39.

Rudd, J. and Whelan, K. (2005). "New Tests of the New-Keynesian Phillips Curve." *Journal of Monetary Economics*, 52(6), pp. 1167–1181.

Ryoo, S. (2010). Long Waves and Short Cycles in a Model of Endogenous Financial Fragility. *Journal of Economic Behavior and Organization*, 74, pp. 163–186.

Ryoo, S. (2016). "Household Debt and Housing Bubbles: A Minskian Approach to Boom-bust Cycles." *Journal of Evolutionary Economics*, 26(5), pp. 971–1006.

Ryoo, S. and Kim, Y.K. (2014). "Income Distribution, Consumer Debt and Keeping Up with the Joneses." *Metroeconomica*, 65(4), pp. 585–618.

Ryoo, S. and Skott, P. (2013). "Public Debt and Full Employment in a Stock-Flow Consistent Model of a Corporate Economy." *Journal of Post Keynesian Economics*, 35(4), pp. 511–527.

Ryoo, S. and Skott, P. (2017). "Fiscal and Monetary Policy Rules in an Unstable Economy." *Metroeconomica*, 68(3), pp. 500–548.

Samuelson. P.A. (1939). "Interactions between the Multiplier Analysis and the Principle of Acceleration." *Review of Economics and Statistics*, 21(2), pp. 75–78.

Samuelson, P.A. (1966). "A Summing Up." *Quarterly Journal of Economics*, 80(4), pp. 568–583.

Samuelson, P.A. and Modigliani, F. (1966). "The Pasinetti Paradox in Neoclassical and More General Models." *Review of Economic Studies*, 33(4), pp. 269–301.

Samuelson, P.A. and Solow, R.M. (1960). "Analytical Aspects of Anti-Inflation Policy." *American Economic Review*, 50(2), pp. 177–194.

Sarel, M. (1996). "Nonlinear Effects of Inflation on Economic Growth." *Internation Monetary Fund – Staff Papers*, 43(1), pp. 199–215.

Sattinger, M. (2006). "Overlapping Labor Markets." *Labour Economics*, 13, pp. 237–257.

Schlicht, E. (2006). "Public Debt as Private Wealth: Some Equilibrium Considerations." *Metroeconomica*, 57(4), pp. 494–520.

Schmitt-Grohe, S. and Uribe, M. (2007). "Optimal Simple and Implementable Monetary and Fiscal Rules." *Journal of Monetary Economics*, 54, pp. 1702–1725.

Schneider, D. and Harknett, K. (2019). "It's about Time: How Work Schdule Instability Matters for Workers, Families and Racial Inequality." Research Brief, October 2019, shift.hks.harvard.edu/files/2019/10/Its-About-Time-How-Work-Schedule-Instability-Matters-for-Workers-Families-and-Racial-Inequality.pdf.

Seater, J.J. (1993). "Ricardian Equivalence." *Journal of Economic Literature*, 31(1), pp. 142–190.

Seers, D. (1962). "A Theory of Inflation and Growth in Under-Developed Economies Based on the Experience of Latin America." *Oxford Economic Papers*, 14 (June), pp. 174–195.

Sell, S. and May, C. (2001). Moments in Law: Contestation and Settlement in the History of Intellectual Property. *Review of International Political Economy*, 8(3) pp. 467–500.

Sen, A. (1983). "Poor, Relatively Speaking." *Oxford Economic Papers*, 35(2), pp. 153–169.

Sen, A. (1992). *Inequality Reexamined*. Cambridge, MA: Harvard University Press.

Sen, A. (2000). "The Discipline of Cost-benefit Analysis." *The Journal of Legal Studies*, 29(S2), pp. 931–952.

Sethi, R. (1996). "Endogenous Regime Switching in Speculative Markets." *Structural Change and Econonmic Dynamics*, 7(1), pp. 99–118.

Setterfield, M. and Thirlwall, A. (2010). "Macrodynamics for a Better Society: The Economics of John Cornwall." *Review of Political Economy*, 22(4), pp. 481–498.

Shaikh, A. (1974). "Laws of Production and Laws of Algebra: The Humbug Production Function." *Review of Economics and Statistics*, 56(1), pp. 115–120.

Shafir, E. Diamond, P. and Tversky, A. (1997). "Money Illusion." *Quarterly Journal of Economics*, 112(2), pp. 341–374.

Shapiro, C. and Stiglitz, J. (1984). "Equilibrium Unemployment as a Worker Discipline Device." *American Economic Review*, 74(3), pp. 433–444.

Shea, J. (1995). "Union Contracts and the Life-cycle/Permanent Income Hypothesis." *American Economic Review*, 85 (March), pp. 186–200.

Shefrin, H.M. and Thaler, R.H. (1988). "The Behavioral Life-cycle Hypothesis." *Economic Inquiry*, 26(4), pp. 609–643.

Sheffrin, S.M. (1983). *Rational Expectations*. Cambridge: Cambridge University Press.

Sims, C.A. (2003). "Implications of Rational Inattention." *Journal of Monetary Economics*, 50, pp. 665–690.

Simon, H.A. (1957). *Models of Man*. New York: Wiley.

Skott, P. (1981). "On the Kaldorian Saving Function." *Kyklos*, 34(3), pp. 563–581.

Skott, P. (1988). "Finance, Saving and Accumulation." *Cambridge Journal of Economics*, 12(3), pp. 339–354.

Skott, P. (1989a). "Effective Demand, Class Struggle and Cyclical Growth." *International Economic Review*, 30(1), pp. 231–247.

Skott, P. (1989b). *Conflict and Effective Demand in Economic Growth*. Cambridge: Cambridge University Press.

Skott, P. (1991). "Efficiency Wages, Mark-up Pricing and Effective Demand." In Michie, J. (Ed.), *The Economics of Restructuring and Intervention*. Aldershot: Edward Elgar, pp. 138–151.

Skott, P. (1997). "Stagflationary Consequences of Prudent Monetary Policy in a Unionized Economy." *Oxford Economic Papers*, 49(4), pp. 609–622.

Skott, P. (1999). "Wage Formation and the (Non-) Existence of the NAIRU." *Economic Issues*, 4, pp. 77–92.

Skott, P. (2001). "Demand Policy in the Long Run." In P. Arestis, M. Desai and S. Dow (eds.), *Money Macroeconomics and Keynes*, Routledge, pp. 124–139.

Skott, P. (2005). "Fairness as a Source of Hysteresis in Employment and Relative Wages." *Journal of Economic Behavior and Organization*, 57, pp. 305–331.

Skott, P. (2006). "Wage Inequality and Overeducation in a Model with Efficiency Wages." *Canadian Journal of Economics*, 39(1), pp. 94–123.

Skott, P. (2010). "Growth, Instability and Cycles: Harrodian and Kaleckian Models of Accumulation and Income Distribution." In M. Setterfield (ed.), *Handbook of Alternative Theories of Economic Growth*, Edward Elgar, pp. 108–131.

Skott, P. (2013). "Increasing Inequality and Financial Instability." *Review of Radical Political Economics*, 45(4), pp. 474–482.

Skott, P. (2015). "Growth Cycles and Price Flexibility." *Review of Keynesian Economics*, 3(3), pp. 374–386.

Skott, P. (2016a). "Aggregate Demand, Functional Finance, and Secular Stagnation." *European Journal of Economics and Economic Policies: Intervention*, 13(2), pp. 172–188.

Skott, P. (2016b). "Public Debt, Secular Stagnation and Functional Finance." In M.O. Madsen and F. Olesen (eds.), *Macroeconomics after the Financial Crisis: A Post-Keynesian Perspective*, Routledge pp. 20–37.

Skott, P. (2021). "Fiscal Policy and Structural Transformation in Developing Economies." *Structural Change and Economic Dynamics*, 56, pp. 129–140.

Skott, P. (2023). "Endogenous Business Cycles and Economic Policy." *Journal of Economic Behavior and Organization*, 210, pp. 61–82.

Skott, P. and Davis, L. (2013). "Distributional Biases in the Evaluation of Climate Change." *Ecological Economics*, 85, pp. 188–197.

Skott, P. and Guy, F. (2007). "A Model of Power-Biased Technological Change." *Economics Letters*, 95, 124–131.

Skott, P. and Guy, F. (2008). "Power, Productivity, and Profits." In Braham, M. and Steffen, F. (eds.), *Power, Freedom and Voting*, Berlin: Springer Verlag, pp. 385–404.

Skott, P. and Ryoo, S. (2008). "Macroeconomic Implications of Financialization." *Cambridge Journal of Economics*, 32(6), pp. 827–862.

Skott, P. and Ryoo, S. (2014). "Public Debt in an OLG Model with Imperfect Competition: Long-Run Effects of Austerity Programs and Changes in the Growth Rate." *BE Press Journal of Macroeconomics*, 14(1), pp. 533–552.

Skott, P. and Ryoo, S. (2017). "Functional Finance and Intergenerational Distribution in a Keynesian OLG Model." *Review of Keynesian Economics*, 5(1), pp. 112–134.

Skott, P. and Zipperer, B. (2012). "An Empirical Evaluation of Three Post-Keynesian Models." *Intervention – European Journal of Economics and Economic Policies*, 9(2), pp. 277–308.

Slonimczyk, F. and Skott, P. (2012). "Employment and Distribution Effects of the Minimum Wage." *Journal of Economic Behavior and Organization*, 84(1), pp. 245–264.

Smets, F. and Wouters, R. (2003). "An Estimated Stochastic Dynamic General Equilibrium Model." *Journal of the European Economic Association*, 1(5), pp. 1123–1175.

Smets, F. and Wouters, R. (2007). "Shocks and Frictions in US Business Cycles: A Bayesian DSGE Approach." *American Economic Review*, 97(3), pp. 586–606.

Smith, A. (1776). *An Inquiry into the Nature and Causes of the Wealth of Nations*. London: Everyman edition.

Solow, R.M. (1956). "A Contribution to the Theory of Economic Growth." *Quarterly Journal of Economics*, 70(1), pp. 65–94.

Solow, R.M. (1986). "What Is a Nice Girl Like You Doing in a Place Like This? Macroeconomics after Fifty Years." *Eastern Economic Journal*, 12(3), pp. 191–198.

Solow, R.M. (1990). *The Labor Market as a Social Institution*. Oxford: Blackwell.

Solow, R.M. (1998). "What Is Labour-Market Flexibility? What Is It Good For?" Keynes Lecture, British Academy, www.britac.ac.uk/pubs/proc/files/97p189.pdf.

Solow, R.M. (2008). "The State of Macroeconomics." *Journal of Economic Perspectives,* 22(1), pp. 243–246.

Somville, V. and Vandewalle, L. (2018). "Saving by Default: Evidence from a Field Experiment in Rural India." *American Economic Journal: Applied Economics,* 10(3), pp. 39–66.

Sonnenschein, H. (1972). "Market Excess Demand Functions." *Econometrica,* 40(3), pp. 549–563.

Staiger, D., Stock, J.H. and Watson, M.W. (1997). "The NAIRU, Unemployment and Monetary Policy." *Journal of Economic Perspectives,* 11(1), pp. 33–49.

Stallman, R. (1985). The GNU manifesto.

Stanton, E. (2010). "Negishi Welfare Weights in Integrated Assessment Models: The Mathematics of Global Inequality." *Climatic Change,* 107(3), pp. 417–432.

Starr, E. (2019). "The Use, Abuse and Enforceability of Non-Compete and No-Poach Agreements." Economic Policy Institute.

Stedman, L.C. (2009). "The NAEP Long-Term Trend Assessment: A Re-View of Its Transformation, Use, and Findings." Mimeo.

Stern, N. (2006). *The Economics of Climate Change: The Stern Review.* Cambridge: Cambridge University Press. Online at www.hm-treasury.gov.uk/independent_ reviews/stern_review_climate_change/sternreview_index.cfm.

Stevens, P. (2004). "Diseases of Poverty and the 10/90 Gap." International Policy Network.

Stiglitz, J.E. (1969). "A Re-Examination of the Modigliani–Miller Theorem." *American Economic Review,* 59(5), pp. 784–793.

Stiglitz, J.E. (1997). "Reflections on the Natural Rate Hypothesis." *Journal of Economic Perspectives,* 11(1), pp. 3–10.

Stiglitz, J.E. (2018). "Where Modern Macroeconomics Went Wrong." *Oxford Review of Economic Policy,* 34(1–2), pp. 70–106.

Stiglitz, J.E. and Weiss, A. (1981). "Credit Rationing in Markets with Imperfect Information." *American Economic Review,* 71(3), pp. 393–410.

Sturgeon, T.J. (2002). "Modular Production Networks: A New American Model of Industrial Organization." *Industrial and Corporate Change,* 11(3), pp. 451–496.

Sugden, R. (1986). *The Economics of Rights, Welfare and Co-operation.* Oxford: Blackwell.

Summers, L.H. (2013). [Presentation at the] "IMF Fourteenth Annual Research Conference in Honor of Stanley Fischer." larrysummers.com/imf-fourteenth-annual-research-conference-in-honor-of-stanley-fischer/.

Summers, L.H. (2015a). "Demand Side Secular Stagnation." *American Economic Review: Papers and Proceedings,* 105(5), pp. 60–65.

Summers, L.H. (2015b). "On Secular Stagnation: A Response to Bernanke." larrysummers.com/2015/04/01/on-secular-stagnation-a-response-to-bernanke/.

Summers, L.H. (2018). "Secular Stagnation and Macroeconomic Policy." *IMF Economic Review,* 66, pp. 226–250.

Sunkel, O. (1958). "La inflacion chilena: un enfoque heterodoxo." *El Trimestre Economico*, 25, pp. 107–131.

Sylos Labini, P. (1995). "Why the Interpretation of the Cobb–Douglas Production Function Must be Radically Changed." *Structural Change and Economic Dynamics*, 6(4), pp. 485–504.

Tarshis, L. (1939). "Changes in Real and Money Wage Rates." *Economic Journal*, 49(193), pp. 150–154.

Taylor, J.B. (1993). "Discretion Versus Policy Rules in Practice." *Carnegie-Rochester Conference Series on Public Policy*, 39, pp. 195–214.

Tcherneva, P.R. (2019). "MMT Is Already Helping." *Jacobin*, 02/27/2019.

Thaler, R.H. and Benartzi, S. (2004). "Save More Tomorrow – Using Behavioral Economics to Increase Employee Saving." *Journal of Political Economy*, 112(1), pt. 2, pp. S164–S187.

Thompson, S. (2018). "Employment and Fiscal Policy in a Marxian Model." *Metroeconomica*, 69(4), pp. 820–846.

Tirole, J. (1986). "Hierarchies and Bureaucracies: On the Role of Collusion in Organizations." *Journal of Law, Economics, and Organization*, 2(2), pp. 181–214.

Tobin, J. (1969). "A General Equilibrium Approach to Monetary Theory." *Journal of Money, Credit and Banking*, 1(1), pp. 15–29.

Tobin, J. (1972). "Inflation and Unemployment." *American Economic Review*, 62(1/2), pp. 1–18.

Tobin, J. (1975). "Keynesian Model of Recession and Depression." *American Economic Review*, pp. 195–202.

Tobin, J. (1980). *Asset Accumulation and Economic Activity*. Chicago: Chicago University Press.

Tobin, J. (1986). "High Time to Restore the Employment Act of 1946." *Challenge*, 29(2), pp. 4–12.

Tobin, J. (1993). "Price Flexibility and Output Stability: An Old Keynesian View." *Journal of Economic Perspectives*, 7(1), pp. 45–65.

Toksvig, L. (2007). "Forsyningen af tømmer til flådens skibe i 1800-tallet. Historien om de nordsjællandske flådeege." *DST*, Årg. 92. Hft. 1–28.

Torre, V. (1977). "Existence of Limit Cycles and Control in Complete Keynesian System by Theory of Bifurcation." *Econometrica*, 45(6), pp. 1457–1466.

Tversky, A. and Kahneman, D. (1992). "Advances in Prospect Theory: Cumulative Representation of Uncertainty." *Journal of Risk and Uncertainty*, 5(4), pp. 297–323.

Twenge, J.M., Campbell, S.M., Hoffman, B.J. and Lance, C. E. (2010). "Generational Differences in Work Values: Leisure and Extrinsic Values Increasing, Social and Intrinsic Values Decreasing." *Journal of Management*, 36(5), pp. 1117–1142.

Twenge, J.M., Campbell, S.M. and Freeman, E.C. (2012). "Generational Differences in Young Adults' Life Goals, Concern for Others, and Civic Orientation, 1966–2009." *Journal of Personality and Social Psychology*, 102(5), pp. 1045–1062.

Uribe, M. (2000). "Staggered Price Indexation." NBER working Paper w27657.

Veblen, T. (1899). *The Theory of the Leisure Class: An Economic Study of Institutions*. New York: The Macmillan Company.

Vedder, R., Denhart, C. and Robe, J. (2013). "Why Are Recent College Graduates Underemployed?" Institute of Education Science.

Vogelstein, F. (2013). "And Then Steve Said, 'Let There Be an iPhone'." *New York Times* (www.nytimes.com/2013/10/06/magazine/and-then-steve-said-let-there-be-an-iphone.html?pagewanted=all):

von Arnim, R. and Barrales, J. (2015). "Demand-Driven Goodwin Cycles with Kaldorian and Kaleckian Features." *Review of Keynesian Economics*, 3(3), pp. 351–373.

von Braun, C-F. (1990). "The Acceleration Trap." *Sloan Management Review*, 32(1), pp. 49–58.

Wade, J.B., Porac, J.F. and Pollock, T.G. (1997). "Worth, Words, and the Justification of Executive Pay." *Journal of Organizational Behavior*, 18, pp. 641–657.

Weed, J. (2020). "Looking for the Cheapest Airfare? Good Luck With That|." *New York Time*, print edition January 28, p. B4 (online edition, January 27, www.nytimes.com/2020/01/27/business/cheap-airfare.html?searchResultPosition=1).

Weitzman, M.L. (2007). "A Review of The Stern Review on the Economics of Climate Change." *Journal of Economic Literature*, Vol. XLV (September), 703–724.

Wilhelm, M.O. (1996). "Bequest Behavior and the Effect of Heirs' Earnings: Testing the Altruistic Model of Bequests." *American Economic Review*, 86(4), pp. 874–892.

Wood, A. (1994). *North-South Trade, Employment and Inequality: Changing Fortunes in a Skill-Driven World*. Oxford: Oxford University Press.

Wood, A.J. and Burchell, B. (2018). Unemployment and Well-being. In A. Lewis (ed.), *The Cambridge Handbook of Psychology and Economic Behaviour*. Cambridge: Cambridge University Press.

Woodford, M. (1999). "Revolution and Evolution in Twentieth-Century Macroeconomics." Paper presented at the conference, Frontiers of the Mind in the Twenty-First Century, U.S. Library of Congress, Washington DC. URL www.columbia.edu/~mw2230/macro20C.pdf.

Woodford, M. (2003). *Interest and Prices: Foundations of a Theory of Monetary Policy*. Princeton: Princeton University Press.

Wray, R. (2000). "Can The Expansion Be Sustained? A Minskian View." Levy Institute Policy Note 2000/5.

Wray, R. (2015). *Modern Money Theory: A Primer on Macroeconomics for Sovereign Monetary Systems*. Houndmills, Basingstoke, Hampshire New York, NY: Palgrave Macmillan.

Wren-Lewis, S. (2007). "Are There Dangers in the Microfoundations Consensus?" In P. Arestis (ed.), *Is There a New Consensus in Macroeconomics?* Basingstoke: Palgrave Macmillan, pp. 43–60.

Wren-Lewis, S. (2018). "Ending the Microfoundations Hegemony." *Oxford Review of Economic Policy*, 34(1–2), pp. 55–69.

Yagan, D. (2018). "Employment Hysteresis from the Great Recession." UC Berkeley and NBER.

Yoo, G. and Kang, C. (2012). The Effect of Protection of Temporary Workers on Employment Levels: Evidence from the 2007 Reform of South Korea. *Industrial and Labor Relations Review*, 65(3), pp. 578–606.

Zeldes, S. (1989). "Consumption and Liquidity Constraints: An Empirical Investigation." *Journal of Political Economy*, 97(2), pp. 305–346.

Zipperer, B. and Skott, P. (2011). "Cyclical Patterns of Employment, Utilization and Profitability." *Journal of Post Keynesian Economics*, 44(1), pp. 25–58.

Author Index

Abe, N., 260
Abel, A.B., 304
Abel, J., 189fn
Aboobaker, A., 330fn
Acemoglu, D., 11fn, 23, 24, 28, 32, 175, 176, 197fn, 199
Ackerman, F., 33fn
Agarwal, S., 53
Agell, J., 142
Akerlof, G.A., 6, 10, 45, 47, 47fn, 63, 104fn, 131–132, 134, 136, 139fn, 142, 143, 144fn, 145, 147, 149, 167, 251
Albrecht, J., 189
Alvaredo, F., 175
Alvarez, F., 261
Alvarez-Cuadrado, F., 57
Ando, A., 59, 60, 64, 68
Andreoni, J., 26
Antràs, P., 240
Arestis, P., 306fn
Ash, M., 310
Ashkenas, R.N., 194
Atkinson, A.B., 115, 249fn
Auerbach, P., 61–62, 166fn, 200fn, 201fn
Autor, D.H., 175–176, 194fn, 199, 200
Azar, J., 176

Backus, D., 116fn
Baily, M.N., 257fn
Bakija, J., 193
Ball, L., 107, 110fn, 111, 152, 153fn, 155
Ballinger, R., 317
Barbosa, F., 155fn
Barbosa-Filho, N.H., 256fn
Barrales, J., 256fn
Barrales-Ruiz, J., 276fn
Barro, R., 9, 103, 116fn, 121, 123, 124, 127, 163, 210, 212, 303, 310
Basu, D., 310
Baum, S., 33fn
Beaudry, P., 13, 251
Bebchuk, L.A., 197
Bebczuk, R., 79

Bell-Kelton, S., 317
Benhabib, J., 250fn
Beniger, J.R., 178
Benmelech, E., 176
Bernanke, B., 71, 111
Bernheim, B.D., 26
Bewley, T.F., 132, 142, 155, 190
Bhargava, S., 46
Bhutta, N., 91
Bils, M., 259
Bivens, J., 176, 310
Black, S.E., 179
Blanchard, O., 4, 6, 7, 9, 14, 25fn, 28, 29, 53, 66, 70, 86, 105, 108, 111, 115, 134, 139fn, 165, 308, 311, 314, 316, 318fn, 319fn, 331
Blanchflower, D., 50
Bleaney, M., 155fn
Blecker, R.A., 15fn
Blinder, A.S., 108, 259
Bliss. C. J., 82, 84fn, 239
Bohn, H., 310
Boldrin, M., 195
Bosworth, B., 186
Bowles, S., 58, 63, 146fn, 182
Boyer, R., 12
Bresser-Pereira, C.L., 320fn
Breza, E., 132
Brock, W.A., 89fn
Bronfenbrenner, K., 187
Broome, J., 30fn
Browning, M., 49
Buiter, W., 7, 107
Bulow, J., 189
Burchell, B., 131

Caballero, R., 268fn, 336
Callaci, B., 187
Calmfors, L., 118fn
Calvo, G.A., 108
Camerer, C., 49
Campbell, C.M., 142
Campbell, D.T., 19
Campbell, J., 28

Canzoneri, M.B., 28
Caplin, A.S., 109
Card, D., 191fn
Carr, M., 58
Cavallo, A., 260fn
Cavallo, E., 79
Cengiz, D., 191fn
Chalk, N.A., 308, 317, 318
Chandler, A.D. Jr., 178
Chang, H-J., 327fn
Chari, V.V., 4, 36
Chetty, R., 48
Chiarella, C., 216fn, 256fn, 258fn
Cho, J., 187
Christiano, L.J., 6, 7fn, 36, 53fn, 65
Chun, H., 193
Coburn, T., 309fn
Cohen, A.J., 235fn
Coibion, O., 44, 110, 111, 340
Colander, D., 210
Collard, F., 299, 317, 318
Comin, D., 193
Cooper, R.W., 267fn
Corneo, G., 58
Cornwall, J., 12fn
Crawford, V. P., 49fn
Cronqvist, H., 75
Cubitt, R.P., 118fn
Cukierman, A., 118fn
Curcuru, S., 91
Cynamon, B.Z., 58

Daly, M., 142
Damill, M., 320fn
Davidson, P., 205, 207fn, 216fn, 306fn
Davis, L., 53fn, 71
Day, R.H., 250
De Giorgi, G., 53
De Grauwe, P., 6fn
De Loecker, J., 194fn
Debreu, G., 8, 20, 23, 205, 226
Deitz, R., 189fn
DeLong, B., 7, 155fn, 316
Diallo, M.B., 286fn
Diamond, P.A., 25, 305, 331, 332
Domar, E.D., 228
Doms, M., 267
Driffill, J., 116fn, 118fn
Dube, A., 132, 191fn
Duesenberry, J., 50fn, 53, 57
Dunlop, J.T., 219
Dunne, T., 267
Dutt, A.K., 7, 41, 50fn, 63, 211, 216fn, 256fn
Dynan, K.E., 54

Easterlin, R., 50
Eeckhout, J., 194fn

Eggertsson, G.B., 194fn, 314
Eichenbaum, M., 108, 259, 260
Eidelson, J., 187
Elmendorf, D., 310
Elson, C.M., 196, 197
Engen, E.M., 310, 317, 318
Epstein, G., 330fn
Estevez-Abe, M., 181

Fafchamps, M., 50
Fairris, D., 179
Farber, H.S., 49fn, 199
Fazzari, S.M., 58, 256fn, 281fn, 282
Feenstra, R.C., 175
Fehr, E., 51, 132
Fel'dman, G.A., 300fn
Felipe, J., 235fn, 240fn
Ferguson, C.E., 238
Fernholz, T., 309
Ferrere, C.K., 196, 197
Fershtman, C., 64fn
Fisher, F.M., 235fn, 241, 242, 242fn
Flaschel, P., 216fn, 256fn, 289fn
Fogg, N., 188fn
Foley, D.K., 61
Francisco, M., 155fn
Frank, R.H., 50fn, 51, 53fn, 58, 61
Franke, R., 216fn, 256fn, 280fn, 306fn
Frederick, S., 46
Freeman, C., 195
Freeman, R.B., 35, 179, 187
Frey, B., 50fn
Friedman, M., 1, 16, 17fn, 44, 58fn, 64, 102, 105, 220fn
Frydman, R., 45

Gabaix, X., 193
Gao, Z., 96fn
Garicano, L., 193
Gertler, M., 109fn, 110fn
Giglio, S., 90
Gintis, H., 63
Girardi, D., 300fn
Godley, W., 72fn, 306fn, 312fn
Goldin, C., 200
Gomes, F., 75fn, 90
Goodhart, C.A.E., 19
Goodwin, R.M., 247, 256fn, 289
Gordon, D., 9, 103, 116fn, 121, 123, 124, 127
Gordon, R.J., 105, 106fn, 123fn, 144fn, 212fn
Gorodnichenko, Y., 110, 111
Grandmont, J.-M., 239fn, 250fn
Green, F., 48, 182, 186
Greenspan, A., 292
Gregg, P., 114
Grissmer, D.W., 188fn
Groot, W., 188

Gross, D.B., 48
Grossman, H.I., 212
Grubb, D., 153fn
Guimaraes, B., 261
Gustman, A., 48
Guy, F., 178fn, 182, 195

Hahn, F.H., 11fn, 216fn
Haldane, A.G., 66fn
Hale, J.K., 274fn
Hall, P.A., 181
Haltiwanger, J., 267fn
Hamermesh, D.S., 191fn
Handel, M.J., 188fn
Hanson, G.H., 175
Harcourt, G.C., 235fn
Hargreaves-Heap, S.P., 146fn, 165
Harknett, K., 62fn
Harrington, P., 188fn
Harrod, R., 42, 228, 230, 234, 252, 256, 268, 295, 333
Hazell, J., 339, 340
Heckman, J.J., 116
Hein, E., 15fn, 17fn, 331fn
Heinzerling, L., 33fn
Hendry, D.F., 60
Herndon, T., 309
Hicks, J.R., 13fn, 108, 145, 195fn, 205, 207, 207fn, 209–212, 214fn, 216fn, 220fn, 239fn, 256fn
Hirsch, F., 50fn
Hirschman, A.O., 50
Hodgson, G., 11
Hoel, M., 53fn
Hoff, K., 63
Holt, R.P.F., 66fn
Hommes, C.H., 89fn
Hoover, K.D., 17
Howell, D.R., 114–116, 154
Hubbard, R.G., 195, 310, 317, 318

Irons, J., 310

Jayadev, A., 58
Jensen, M.C., 193
Johansson-Stenman, O., 51
Johnson, D.S, 47fn
Johnston, K., 181
Jones, C.I., 34
Jonscher, C., 180
Jonsson, T., 44

Kahn, S., 142
Kahneman, D., 49fn, 55, 133fn, 136, 146, 259
Kaldor, N., 73, 76, 81–82, 207fn, 244, 245, 256fn
Kalecki, M., 59fn, 180, 206, 219, 256fn, 291, 331, 331fn
Kamlani, K.S., 142

Kandra, J., 192
Kang, C., 187
Kaplan, G., 7fn, 65
Karanassou, M., 109
Kashyap, A., 259
Katz, L.F., 191fn, 200
Kehoe, T., 4, 260, 261
Kelton, S., 317, 330fn
Keynes, J.M., 2, 7, 13, 18, 64, 74fn, 102, 108, 141, 145, 203–205, 209, 212–216, 219, 220fn, 222fn, 226, 248, 251, 259, 289fn
Kim, H-K., 187fn
Kim, Y.K., 58
King, J., 11, 17fn
King, R.G., 109
Kirman, A., 8, 17, 20, 52
Kirsanova, T., 303
Klenow, P.J., 34, 259, 262
Kleven, H.J., 115
Klump, R., 185
Koszegi, B., 49fn
Kotz, D., 12fn
Krueger, A.B., 173fn, 191fn
Krugman, P., 6, 7, 113fn, 212fn, 313
Kurz, H.D., 235fn
Kurzweil, R., 194
Kydland, F.E., 17, 116fn

La Porta, R., 156
Lachowska, M., 48
Laibson, D., 41
Laing, N.F., 235fn
Landier, A., 193
Lavoie, M., 15fn, 17fn, 41, 72fn, 306fn, 331fn
Lawler, P., 118fn
Layard, R., 113fn
Leão, P., 315
Lebergott, S., 104
Leijonhufvud, A., 212, 212fn
Lerner, A.P., 18, 291, 305–306, 316, 318, 330
Levine, D.K., 195
Levine, R., 300fn
Levy, D., 259fn
Lewis, M., 146
Lewis, W.A., 156, 300, 321
Lindbeck, A., 165
Linde, J., 70, 71
Lippi, F., 118fn, 261
List, J.A., 41
Loewenstein, 46
Long, N.V., 57
Lucas, R.E., 3, 4, 10, 11, 17–19, 34, 211fn, 225, 232, 283, 337
Lundborg, P., 142
Luo, M., 188

Luttmer, E., 50
Lynch, L.M., 179

Maassen van den Brink, H., 188
Maka, A., 155fn
Malin, B.A., 262
Malinvaud, E., 212
Mankiw, N.G., 28, 44, 49fn, 108, 110,
    144fn, 310
Manning, A., 114, 191fn, 263fn
Mantel, R., 8, 20, 23, 226
Marglin, S.A., 63fn, 96
Marshall, A., 145, 146
Martinez, I.Z., 49fn
Martins, G.K., 159fn, 161fn, 163, 326
Marx, K., 11, 61, 81, 176, 245–248, 256,
    300fn
Mas-Colell, A., 20, 30, 32fn
Mason, J.W., 58
Matthews, P.H., 245fn
Mavroeidis, S., 110, 110fn
May, C., 195
Mazumbar, S., 110fn, 111
McNicholas, C., 187
Meckling, W.H., 193
Medoff, J.L., 179
Meng, J., 49fn
Mian, A., 47, 70, 88fn, 89
Michl, T.R., 312
Midrigan, V, 260, 261
Miller, M., 107
Miller, M.H., 74, 337
Minford, P., 107
Minsky, H.P., 59fn, 83, 216fn, 291–292
Mishel, L., 192
Modigliani, F., 59–60, 64, 68, 74, 78, 81, 337
Moffitt, R., 153fn
Moore, B.J., 207fn
Moriguchi, C., 173
Morishima, M., 237fn
Muellbauer, J.N.J., 47, 59, 60, 90
Mulani, S., 193
Munnell, A.H., 46fn
Murakami, H., 256fn
Murphy, A., 90
Murphy, K.J., 193
Murphy, K.M., 191fn
Musgrave, A., 67
Muth, J.F., 42
Mych, M., 48

Nakamura, E., 6, 108, 258–262, 338, 340
Nakatani, T., 328
Nersisyan, Y., 306fn
Newell, A., 153fn
Nickell, S., 113fn, 114, 115, 267
Nishimura, K., 250fn

Nordhaus, W.D., 29, 30
Noyola, J.F., 156
Nurkse, R., 320fn

O'Brien, M., 309
O'Donoghue, T., 46, 47
Obstfeld, M., 329
Oh, J-S., 289fn
Österholm, P., 44
Oswald, A., 50, 131

Pástor, L., 193
Palia, D., 195
Palley, T., 222fn, 306fn, 312fn, 330fn
Pariboni, R., 300fn
Park, Y., 58
Parker, J.A., 28, 47fn
Pasinetti, L.L., 81, 82, 237fn, 238
Pedersen, P., 115
Penrose, E., 266
Persson, T., 116fn
Phelps, E.S., 45, 105, 283
Phillips, A.W., 104
Piketty, T., 173, 200fn
Pollin, R., 163
Poterba, J.M., 79
Prescott, E.C., 17, 116fn

Rabin, M., 46, 47, 49fn, 136
Rabinovich, J., 71
Rachel, L., 311, 314
Ramey, V.A., 259fn
Ramsey, F.P., 25fn
Raymond, E., 195
Razmi, A., 320fn, 323fn
Read, D., 47fn
Reinhart, C.M., 5, 89, 299, 309, 312, 313, 318
Reis, R., 43fn, 44
Renelt, D., 300fn
Robinson, J., 207fn, 211, 235, 238, 239
Rogoff, K., 5, 89, 116fn, 117fn, 299, 309, 312,
    313, 318
Roine, J., 175
Romer, D., 54, 55, 84–85, 107, 109, 250,
    258, 259
Romer, P., 7, 71
Roose, K., 181
Ros, J., 156, 320fn
Rose, H., 256fn
Rossi-Hansberg, E., 193
Rotemberg, J.J., 259
Rowthorn, R., 139, 141, 144fn, 154fn, 161–162,
    165, 166
Rudd, J., 109fn
Ryoo, S., 58, 72fn, 73fn, 76, 80fn, 91fn, 96fn,
    256fn, 280fn, 292fn, 304, 305, 306fn, 307,
    310fn, 315, 317

Saez, E., 173, 175
Salvadori, N., 235fn
Samuelson. P.A., 11, 81–82, 104, 236, 239, 256fn
Sarel, M., 163
Sattinger, M., 189
Sawyer, M., 306fn
Schlicht, E., 306fn, 315
Schmidt, K., 51
Schmitt-Grohe, S., 303
Schneider, D., 62fn
Schwartz, A.J., 220fn
Seater, J.J., 310
Seers, D., 156
Segal, U., 64fn
Sell, S., 195
Sen, A, 33fn, 50, 50fn
Sethi, R., 89fn
Setterfield, M., 12fn, 15fn
Shafir, E., 136, 137, 139, 141
Shaikh, A., 240
Shapiro, C., 136
Shea, J., 28
Sheedy, K.D., 261
Sheffrin, S.M., 44fn
Shefrin, H.M., 48
Shiller, R.J., 45, 251
Shilpi, F., 50
Shleifer, A., 156
Simon, H.A., 178fn
Sims, C.A., 43fn
Skott, P., 7, 53fn, 62fn, 72fn, 76, 80fn, 89fn, 118fn, 123, 146fn, 152fn, 159fn, 161fn, 163, 178, 182, 187fn, 188, 190, 191, 200fn, 211, 256fn, 265fn, 268fn, 274fn, 276, 277, 280fn, 286fn, 289, 293fn, 304, 305, 306fn, 307, 308fn, 310fn, 312fn, 315, 317, 320fn, 323fn, 326, 328
Slonimczyk, F., 178, 188, 190, 191fn
Smets, F., 53fn, 70
Smith, A., 50, 63
Smith, N., 115
Snower, D.J, 165
Solow, R.M., 6fn, 11, 13fn, 104, 131, 145, 146, 152, 216fn, 230–232, 234, 240, 245
Somville, V., 48, 62
Sonnenschein, H., 8, 20, 23, 226
Soskice, D., 181
Souleles, N.S., 48
Spulber, D.F., 109
Staiger, D., 106fn
Stallman, R., 195
Stanton, E., 33fn
Starr, E., 187
Steinmeier, T.L., 48
Steinsson, J., 6, 108, 258–262, 338, 340
Stern, N., 29, 30, 33fn
Sterner, T., 53fn
Stevens, P., 33fn

Stiglitz, J., 59fn, 63, 74fn, 136, 152fn
Sturgeon, T.J., 194
Stutzer, A., 50fn
Sufi, A., 47, 70, 88fn, 89
Sugden, R., 146fn
Summers, L., 6, 155fn, 165, 189, 311–316, 319fn, 331
Sunkel, O., 156
Sylos Labini, P., 240fn
Symons, J.S.V., 153fn

Tabellini, G., 116fn
Tarshis, L., 219
Tavani, D., 276fn
Taylor, J.B., 220fn
Taylor, L., 256fn
Tcherneva, P.R., 330fn
Thaler, R., 48, 62, 133, 136, 146
Thirlwall, A., 12fn
Thompson, S., 281fn
Tirole, J., 197fn
Tobin, J., 11, 13fn, 72fn, 143fn, 215, 218, 226, 319
Toksvig, L., 46
Tonogi, A., 260
Torre, V., 256fn
Turrell, A.E., 66fn
Tversky, A., 49fn, 55, 146
Twenge, J.M., 35fn

Ugurlu, E.N., 330fn
Uribe, M., 261fn, 303

Vandewalle, L., 48, 62
Varoufakis, Y., 146fn
Veblen, T., 50fn
Vedder, R., 189fn
Veronesi, P., 193
Violante, G.L., 65
Vogelstein, F, 196fn
von Arnim, R., 256fn
von Braun, C-F., 194
Vroman, S., 189

Wade, J.B., 197fn
Waldenström, D., 175
Weed, J., 285fn
Weiss, A., 59fn
Weitzman, M.L., 30
Whelan, K., 109fn
Wilhelm, M.O., 26
Wolfers, J., 115
Wood, A., 175
Wood, A.J., 131
Woodford, M., 4, 29, 110
Wouters, R., 53fn, 70
Wray, L.R., 306fn, 312fn, 330fn
Wren-Lewis, S., 35, 66

Yagan, D., 155fn
Yellen, J.L., 10, 131, 132, 134–135, 145–147, 149,
    167
Yoo, G., 187

Zábojník, J., 193
Zeldes, S.P., 47fn
Zhu, A., 163
Zipperer, B., 256fn, 276, 277

Subject Index

Accumulation rate. *See also* investment, 158, 229–231, 245–248, 257, 268, 270–272, 274, 277, 279, 282–283, 285–289, 294–295, 300, 320, 323–328, 333
AD–AS model, 209–210
Adjustment cost
  With respect to capital, 84–85
  With respect to employment and output, 263–264
  with respect to investment, 267, 279
Aggregation. *See also* Representative agent; Cambridge capital controversy
  Of capital, 235–241
  Of consumption, 68–69
  Of investment, 267, 292–294
  Of output growth, 265
Animal spirits, 45, 207, 218, 259, 280, 282, 285
Austerity policy, 5–6, 103, 309, 312, 319, 329
  And public debt, 309, 315–316
  In the EU, 300, 313, 329
Automatic stabilizers, 279–281

Barro–Gordon model, 116–117, 121–122
Business cycles. *See also* Growth cycles, 2, 13, 17, 48, 65, 218, 248–253, 258, 275–276

Calvo model, 108, 260–262, 339
Cambridge capital controversy, 13, 232, 235–240, 242, 244, 302, 304, 314
Capacity utilization
  And investment, 229–230, 266–268, 293–294
  And output adjustment, 264–266
  Cyclical pattern, 249, 276
  In growth cycle models, 273–274, 276, 283–285, 288–289
  In steady growth, 229, 270, 295
Capital controversy. *See* Cambridge capital controversy
Capital gains, 76, 80, 94–96, 101
Capital output ratio. *See also* Choice of technique; Utilization rate
  In Solow model, 230–232
CEO pay, 192–198

Choice of technique, 232–235, 304
Commodity boom, 163, 326
Consumption, aggregate. *See also* Saving rate, aggregate
  And differential saving rates, 73–74, 81–82, 243–245
  And economic welfare, 50–53, 61–64
  And Euler equations, 24–29, 35, 37, 56, 59–60, 65–67, 252–253, 303
  And income distribution, 57–59, 73–74, 91, 220, 316
  And neo-Pasinetti theorem, 76–80
  Hybrid consumption function, 59–61, 68–69, 268
  In Keynes's "General Theory," 64
  Life cycle hypothesis, 59–61
  Mislabeled, 61–62
  Relative income hypothesis, 53–59
  Wealth effects on, 87–90
Consumption, household, 46–57
Consumption norms, 62–64
Credit constraints
  Firms, 280, 282, 283
  Household, 47–48, 58–59, 65–66, 70, 74, 88–89, 96

Debt to GDP ratio
  And austerity policy, 315–316
  And economic growth, 309–312
  And income distribution, 317
  And inflation, 318
  And short-run stabilization, 317
  Sustainability, 307–308, 317–318, 329
Developing economies. *See* dual economies
Distribution of income. *See* Inequality; Profit share
Dividends, 73–77, 101
DSGE models. *See also* Representative agent, 3–9, 11, 13–14, 17, 60, 240, 243, 338–341
  And behavioral evidence, 41, 53
  And business cycles, 250–251
  And financial assets, 70–71
  And Leontief production function, 243, 254
  And Pasinetti theorem, 82

DSGE models (cont.)
   And secular stagnation, 302–303, 313
   HANK model, 65–66, 70, 82
   Methodological defense, 28–29, 35–36, 53, 66
   TANK model, 26, 66, 82–83
Dual economies
   Functional finance in, 320–328
   Inflation in, 155–165, 325–326
   Structural transformation problem, 300, 320
Dynamic inefficiency, 303–304, 314

Econometrics
   And economic theory, 338–341
Economic theory
   Behavioral assumptions, 8–10, 41–42, 336
   Core models, 6–8, 14, 35–36
Efficiency wage
   And labor mismatch, 189–190
   And power, 177, 182–186, 196–198
   Fairness based, 133–139, 196
Employment expansion function, 286–287
Equity, net issue of. *See* stock buybacks
Eurozone, 299–300, 318, 329
Excess capacity. *See* capacity utilization
Expectations
   Adaptive, 42–43, 89, 106–107, 140, 143, 147,
      149, 165, 209, 216
   And Lucas critique, 18–19
   And warranted growth, 42, 229
   Destabilizing, 215–218, 224
   Growth, 283
   Inflation, 44, 105–112, 117, 139–140, 149, 154,
      159, 165
   Rational, 3, 8–9, 14–15, 19, 42–46, 56, 59, 65,
      89, 107, 111–112, 117, 149, 165, 168,
      337–338, 340

Fallacy of composition, 73, 76, 204–219, 300
Fairness. *See* Wage norms
Finance, corporate. *See also* Neo-Pasinetti theorem
   Effects on aggregate saving, 79
   Feedback effects from household behavior,
      82–84
   Modigliani–Miller theorem, 74–76, 78, 337
   Net equity issues, 71–72
   Retention rates, 71–72
Financial instability, 89–91, 94–95, 291–292
Fiscal policy. *See also* Debt to GDP ratio;
      Functional finance; Public debt
   As stabilizer, 279–283, 285, 319
   Austerity, 5–6, 300, 309, 313, 315, 319, 329
   Multiplier, 7, 65, 229, 256, 272, 289, 295, 311,
      338–339
   Primary deficit, 308–309, 329, 330
Fix-price models, 211–212, 275, 296–298
Flex-price models, 108, 208–209, 211, 262–265,
      269–270
France, 115, 117, 175

Functional finance in dual economies, 300,
      320–328, 331
Functional finance in mature economies. *See also*
      Fiscal policy; Public debt, 300, 305–309,
      329–331

Goodhart's law, 18
Goodwin model, 247–249, 254–255
Great compression, 173–174, 179–180, 198–199
Great depression, 3, 16, 123, 141, 174, 203, 205
Great moderation, 4, 193
Great recession, 5–6, 70, 110–111, 155, 188, 263,
      268, 280, 309
Growth cycles. *See also* Goodwin model;
      Instability
   And economic policy, 279–285, 289–291
   In Harrodian model with fixed prices, 275,
      285–289
   In Harrodian model with price flexibility,
      269–275
   In Harrodian model with rationing, 275,
      296–298
   In New Keynesian model, 251–252

Harrodian instability, 42, 228–230, 253, 256, 268,
      271–272, 295
Hysteresis. *See also* Wage norms
   Employment, 10, 146–147, 152, 154–155, 161,
      165–166, 168
   Income distribution, 198

Inequality. *See also* CEO pay; Profit share; Power
      biased institutional change; Power biased
      technological change
   And consumption, 91–94, 316, 331
   And financial bubbles, 94–96
   And globalization, 35, 175
   And institutions, 173–175
   And SBTC, 175–176, 182, 186, 191, 198–200
   And social welfare, 29–34
   Trends in, 187, 192–193
Inflation aversion, 116, 118, 121–122, 128
Inflation. *See also* Monetary policy; Phillips curve
   Structuralist approach, 156–165
Informal sector. *See* Dual economy
Information and communication technology,
      178–181, 186, 193–194, 199
Instability. *See also* Goodwin model; Growth
      cycles; Harrodian instability
   Econometric evidence of, 13, 251
   Financial, 59, 83–84, 89–91, 94–95
   of full employment in Keynesian model, 141,
      204, 205, 214–225
   of Walrasian general equilibrium, 226–227
Institutions. *See also* Power biased institutional
      change; Power biased technological change
   And income distribution, 173–176, 186–188,
      190, 194–195, 199–200
   And technology, 178–180, 198–199

As epiphenomena, 10–11, 176, 199–200, 337
Interest rates. *See also* Choice of technique;
   Monetary policy
   And crowding out, 310–311, 317–319
   And functional finance, 306, 308–309, 313,
     317–318
   And stabilization, 221, 280, 317, 319
   Natural/neutral/equilibrium, 314
   Taylor rules, 150, 220–221, 290, 317
   Zero lower bound, 5, 70, 111, 222–225, 290, 328
Investment. *See also* Instability, Harrodian
   Aggregate, 18, 266–268, 279, 282–283,
     294–295
   Firm level, 267, 292–295
   Public, 300, 327
   q theory, 84–86
IS–LM model, 207–214

Japan, 144, 194, 243, 260, 276, 300, 312, 313, 318,
   319, 328–329

Keynesian unemployment. *See* Unemployment

Labor
   Intertemporal elasticity of supply, 48–49
   Skill mismatch, 177, 188–190
   Substitution between different types of, 184,
     185, 191–192
   Utilization rate of, 285–286
Labor unions, 113–124, 133, 154, 175–177,
   179–180, 187, 199–200, 225, 340
Learning, 44–45, 250
Loss aversion, 49, 55
Lucas critique, 3, 5, 8, 17–20, 34–36, 109, 291,
   330, 336

Mental accounts, 48, 75
Menu cost, 108–109, 228, 259, 261
Microeconomic foundations, 1–6, 11–12, 16–17,
   20, 28–29, 34–35, 108–110, 146, 232, 261,
   336
Minimum wage, 12, 35, 116, 153, 173–177,
   190–191, 199–200, 225
Mismatch in labor markets, 12, 177, 188–192, 200
Modigliani–Miller theorem, 74–76, 78, 337
Monetary policy. *See also* Interest rate; Taylor rule
   And functional finance, 306, 308, 310, 313,
     317–318
   And growth cycles, 280, 282–283, 290
   And hysteresis, 150–155
   In unionized economy, 118–124
   Inflation bias, 116–118
   UK experience 1979–1987, 107
Money illusion. *See also* Rowthorn model of
   inflation, 136–139
Monopoly power, 176, 194–196, 304, 340
Monopsony power, 176, 187, 190, 263fn, 340
Multiplier-accelerator, 256, 272, 289, 295

NAIRU. *See* natural rate of unemployment
Natural growth rate, 228–230, 232, 234–235,
   243–246, 248, 252–253, 328
   And growth expectations, 282–283
   And public debt ratio, 300, 310
   And secular stagnation, 299–300, 313–314
Natural rate of interest, 303–304, 313–314
Natural rate of underemployment, 157–161
Natural rate of unemployment, 9, 16, 102–103,
   105–107, 109–110, 112–116, 123–124, 134,
   144, 147, 150, 165–166, 216, 249, 340
Neo-Pasinetti theorem, 73, 76–82
Nudging, 62, 75

OECD, 6, 103, 112–115, 152, 155, 187, 188, 243,
   316–317, 329
Okun's law, 257, 279, 281, 285
OLG models, 14, 25, 37–38, 303–305, 308, 310,
   314–315, 331–333
Output expansion function, 265, 273, 275–276,
   283, 286–287, 296
Overeducation. *See* Mismatch in labor market

Pasinetti theorem, 81–82
Path dependency. *See* Hysteresis
Phillips curve. *See also* Expectations; Hysteresis;
   Natural rate of unemployment, 16–18,
   103–113, 122–124, 127
   And downward wage rigidity, 142–144
   Expectations augmented, 105–108, 216
   Germany, 112
   In Rowthorn model, 139–141, 161, 166
   New Keynesian, 108–110, 339–340
   Traditional, 16–17, 103, 106–107, 150, 152
   UK, 104, 106, 107, 141–142
   US, 104, 106–107, 110–111
Portfolio behavior, 27fn, 48, 60, 72–75, 78, 80,
   85–96, 100, 222
Power biased institutional change, 12, 177–178,
   186–187, 193
Power biased technological change, 12, 177–178,
   181–186, 193
Present bias, 46–47, 49, 60–61
Price flexibility. *See also* Profit share, cyclical
   fluctuations in; Profit share, in Kaldorian
   model
   In Keynes's analysis, 2, 108, 203–205, 210,
    212–214, 259
Price stickiness. *See also* Price flexibility
   Evidence on, 257, 259–260
   In New Keynesian theory, 13, 108–110, 258–262
Primary deficit, 308, 329–330
Production function, Leontief. *See also*
   Aggregation; Cambridge capital controversy
   And Cambridge capital controversy, 241–244
   And labor mismatch, 191–192
   As approximation, 234
   In functional finance, 304, 306, 314
   In Ramsey model, 243, 253

Production function, neoclassical, 231–234
Profit share
    And saving rate, 73–74, 77–79
    Cyclical patterns, 275
    In fix price growth cycle, 287–289
    In flex-price growth cycle, 264–266, 269–270,
        273–279, 282, 284
    In Goodwin model, 247–248
    In Kaldorian model, 244–245
    Trends in, 16, 173–174, 180
Public debt. See also Debt to GDP ratio; Fiscal
        policy; Functional finance in mature
        economies
    Dynamics, 282, 307–308
    Fiscal cliff, 309
    Interest rates and investment crowding out,
        310–312, 317–319

Ramsey model, 25, 36–38, 243, 253, 302–303, 313
Rational inattention, 43–44, 75
Representative agent
    As welfare criterion, 8, 29–33, 51–53
    Existence of, 8, 20–23
    Lucas critique of, 34–35
Retained earnings/ retention rate, 71–77, 79,
    83–84, 86, 95–96
Rowthorn model of inflation, 139–141, 161, 166

Saving, corporate. See Retained earnings/ retention
        rate
Saving, household, 46–57
Saving rate, aggregate
    And capital gains/ neo-Pasinetti theorem, 76–80,
        94–96
    And income distribution, 73–74, 79–82,
        244–248, 268
    And secular stagnation, 300, 316
    And social welfare, 302–304, 306
Secular stagnation, 222, 299–300, 312–315, 320,
    328, 331
Skill biased technological change, 113, 175–177,
    182, 186, 191, 198–201
Solow model. See also Cambridge capital
        controversy, 230–232, 234, 244, 245
Sonnenschein- Debreu-Mantel theorem, 20, 23–24,
    226–227
Stability. See also Instability
    In two and three dimensional systems of
        differential equations, 97–98
    Of Keynesian short-run equilibrium, 209
    Of ultrashort run equilibrium, 208, 269
Stock buybacks, 71–72, 79fn, 83, 86, 95, 200

Taxes
    And externalities, 51–52
    And functional finance, 306–312, 316, 319,
        334–335

And income distribution, 35, 200, 316–317
Automatic stabilizers, 279–283, 310
Distortions and incentives, 18, 25, 37–38, 74fn,
        103, 114–115, 117, 303, 305, 311, 314
In dual economies, 322–327
Taylor rule, 150, 207fn, 220–225, 280fn, 291,
        306fn, 317
Tobin's q, 76fn, 83–87, 268

UK
    Consumption function, 59, 60
    Phillips curve, 104, 106–107, 115, 141–142
    Price and wage flexibility, 205–206
    Work intensity, 186
Uncertainty, 8–9, 12fn, 15, 45, 55, 62–63, 75,
        198fn, 204, 212, 232, 291
Unemployment. See also Natural rate of
        unemployment; Phillips curve
    Impact on welfare, 131
    Keynesian involuntary, 2, 203–205, 213, 226,
        228, 259
US
    Business cycle patterns, 249, 275–279, 289, 290
    Economic growth, 4, 311
    Fiscal multipliers, 338–339
    Household consumption and portfolio behavior,
        47, 58, 60, 91
    Inequality, 35, 113, 173, 174, 177, 187, 192, 316
    Phillips curve, 103–104, 106, 111–112, 123,
        143–144, 339–340
    Price and wage flexibility, 205–206, 285fn
    Public debt and functional finance, 301,
        309–312, 316, 318–319

Valuation ratio. See Tobin's q
Volatility
    Firm-level, 193, 195, 198, 266
    Of shocks in DSGE models, 70–71

Wage distribution. See Inequality
Wage flexibility as source of instability, 204,
        214–219, 223–226
Wage norms See also Hysteresis; Wage stickiness
    Endogenous changes in, 145–146
    Exogenous shifts in, 152–153
    Real wage, 133–134
    Relative wage, 135–136
Wage stickiness See also Money illusion, 141–144,
        205
Warranted growth rate. See also Instability,
        Harrodian
    And choice of technique, 232, 234–235
    And profit share, 244
    And rational expectations, 42
    Definition and instability of, 228–230

Zero lower bound, 5, 70, 111, 225, 290, 312, 328

Printed in the United States
by Baker & Taylor Publisher Services

Printed in the United States
by Baker & Taylor Publisher Services